Introduction to Governmental and Not-for-Profit Accounting

FIFTH EDITION

Martin Ives
New York University

Joseph R. Razek
University of New Orleans

Gordon A. Hosch
University of New Orleans

Upper Saddle River, New Jersey 07458

Library of Congress Cataloging-in-Publication Data

Ives, Martin
    Introduction to governmental and not-for-profit accounting / Martin Ives, Joseph R. Razek,
Gordon A. Hosch.—5th ed.
      p. cm.
    Includes bibliographical references and index.
    ISBN 0-13-046414-7
    1. Fund accounting.   2. Finance, Public—Accounting.   3. Nonprofit
organizations—Accounting.   I. Razek, Joseph R.   II. Hosch, Gordon A.
III. Title.
HF5681.F84 R39   2003
657'.835—dc21
                    2002035457

Editor: Thomas Sigel
Executive Editor: Mac Mendelson
Editor-in-Chief: P. J. Boardman
Assistant Editor: Sam Goffinet
Senior Editorial Assistant: Linda Albelli
Senior Project Manager, Media: Nancy Welcher
Executive Marketing Manager: Beth Toland
Marketing Assistant: Christine Genneken
Managing Editor (Production): John Roberts
Production Editor: Kelly Warsak
Production Assistant: Joe DeProspero

Permissions Coordinator: Suzanne Grappi
Associate Director, Manufacturing: Vincent Scelta
Production Manager: Arnold Vila
Manufacturing Buyer: Michelle Klein
Cover Design: Bruce Kenselaar
Cover Photo: Getty Images, Inc.
Composition: BookMasters, Inc.
Full-Service Project Management: Jennifer Welsch,
  BookMasters, Inc.
Printer/Binder: R.R. Donnelley & Sons Company
Cover Printer: Phoenix Color Corp.

Credits and acknowledgments borrowed from other sources and reproduced, with permission, in this textbook appear on appropriate page within text.

FASB *Statement No. 117*, "Financial Statements of Not-for-Profit Organizations," is copyrighted by the Financial Accounting Standards Board, 401 Merritt 7, P.O. Box 5116, Norwalk, CT 06856-5116, U.S.A. Portions are reprinted with permission. Complete copies of this document are available from the FASB. The Codification of Governmental Accounting and Financial Reporting Standards (*Statement No. 34* Edition) is copyrighted by the Governmental Accounting Standards Board, 401 Merritt 7, P.O. Box 5116, Norwalk, CT 06856-5116, U.S.A. Portions are reprinted with permission. *AICPA Audit and Accounting Guide–Health Care Organizations* © 2002 The American Institute of Certified Public Accountants. ALL RIGHTS ARE RESERVED.

Pearson Education LTD.
Pearson Education Australia PTY, Limited
Pearson Education Singapore, Pte. Ltd.
Pearson Education North Asia Ltd.
Pearson Education, Canada, Ltd.
Pearson Educación de Mexico, S.A. de C.V.
Pearson Education–Japan
Pearson Education Malaysia, Pte. Ltd.

10 9 8 7 6 5 4 3
ISBN 0-13-046414-7

BRIEF CONTENTS

CONTENTS

PREFACE

This basic-level text on governmental and not-for-profit accounting has been updated to incorporate the recent changes in accounting standards. These new standards (such as GASB *Statement No. 34*) are presented in "plain English" and reinforced with illustrations drawn from financial statements issued by governments that have implemented the new standards earlier than required. To emphasize the practical, the application of "debits and credits" has been supplemented with a new chapter on financial statement analysis and with new examples in the feature called Financial Reporting in Practice.

This text is organized to permit its use by different types of readers. For example, people interested only in accounting for state and local governments can skip the chapters on the federal government, not-for-profit organizations, and health care entities. People interested only in not-for-profit hospitals can concentrate on the not-for-profit organization, health care entities, and financial statement analysis chapters. Public administration students who have not had a course in basic accounting should start with the chapter on the fundamentals of accounting and draw selectively on the governmental, not-for-profit, health care, and financial statement analysis chapters.

Consistent with its focus on flexibility, this text offers the opportunity to work questions and cases, exercises, and problems at the end of each chapter to students who want to emphasize the accumulation, reporting, and analysis of financial information. On the other hand, students interested in a more conceptual approach can avoid the presentation of detailed journal entries and financial statements by concentrating on the conceptual and analytical aspects of the text, questions, cases, exercises, and problems.

To make this text even more flexible, we divided most of the chapters into independent modules, which can be covered as separate units. Thus a section or two may be assigned for a particular class meeting, while an entire chapter may be assigned for another meeting.

Because of its built-in flexibility, this text can be used by the following groups:

1. Accounting majors who wish to learn the fundamentals of governmental and not-for-profit accounting in less than a full semester.
2. Accounting majors who desire a full semester course on governmental and not-for-profit accounting.
3. Nonaccounting majors (e.g., students in public administration programs) who desire a basic understanding of general, governmental, not-for-profit, and health care accounting, financial reporting, and financial statement analysis.
4. Persons employed by governmental and not-for-profit organizations, including the federal government, health care entities, colleges and universities, and voluntary health and welfare organizations.

5. Persons preparing for civil service examinations.
6. Persons preparing for the Uniform Certified Public Accountant (CPA) and the Certified Government Financial Manager (CGFM) examinations.
7. Persons who wish, on their own, to learn about the accounting and reporting practices of governmental and not-for-profit organizations.

NEW FEATURES OF THIS EDITION

Coverage of GASB *Statement No. 34*

GASB *Statement No. 34* (Basic Financial Statements—and Management's Discussion and Analysis—for State and Local Governments) was newly issued when the previous edition of this text was published. Because of its long implementation period—some aspects of GASB *Statement No. 34* are still in the implementation process—the previous edition emphasized earlier standards. This edition, however, contains significant changes to fully incorporate the requirements of GASB *Statement No. 34*.

To simplify presentation of the major changes brought about by GASB *Statement No. 34*, we deliberately separated accounting *within the funds* from financial reporting. We made this distinction because the current financial resources measurement focus and modified accrual basis of accounting continue to be used to account *within* the governmental-type funds and for *fund-level* financial reporting. As a result, the changes to Chapters 4 through 8 (which cover fund accounting) are limited to those concerned with the way accounting data is accumulated and reported at the fund level. The new fund types introduced in GASB *Statement No. 34* are discussed in Chapters 5 and 8.

Because the major changes brought about by GASB *Statement No. 34* concern financial reporting, this edition discusses financial reporting in two chapters. Chapter 9 covers financial reporting in general, fund-level financial reporting, and management's discussion and analysis. Chapter 10 covers the adjustments needed to present consolidated government-wide financial statements on the economic resources measurement focus and accrual basis of accounting, as well as actual government-wide financial statements. To illustrate the new financial reporting requirements, we made extensive use of financial statements prepared by the Village of Grafton, Wisconsin, an early implementer of GASB *Statement No. 34* and recipient of several awards for excellence in financial reporting.

Chapter on Financial Statement Analysis

Accounting and public administration students need to understand not only how accounting information is gathered and reported, but also how it is used. We introduced financial statement analysis in the previous edition and felt that the subject was sufficiently important to warrant a full chapter in this edition. Chapter 14 begins with a discussion of financial statement analysis indicators that are generally applicable to governmental, not-for-profit hospital, and other not-for-profit organizations. It then illustrates the calculation of the indicators for a not-for-profit hospital and a government. The governmental illustration uses the same financial statements shown in Chapters 9 and 10 for the Village of Grafton, Wisconsin, and contains excerpts from the report prepared by a bond-rating agency in connection with the long-term bonds issued by Grafton.

Continuous Problems

For those who like to reinforce the discussion of accounting principles with problems that carry throughout the text, we added two new "continuing problems." One problem, called Bacchus City, is designed to emphasize fund accounting. It starts at the end of Chapter 2, carries through budgeting in Chapter 3, and covers fund-level accounting and financial reporting in Chapters 5 through 8. The other, called CoCo City, is designed to emphasize the new financial reporting model. It is presented at the end of Chapters 9 and 10, and is developed so that portions of it can be assigned with Chapters 2, 4, 5, 6, 7, 9, and 10.

Other Features and Changes

All chapters of this text incorporate significant changes in accounting and financial reporting standards issued by the Governmental Accounting Standards Board, the Financial Accounting Standards Board, and the Federal Accounting Standards Advisory Board since preparation of the previous edition. In updating the text, we also considered the material in the relevant AICPA *Audit and Accounting Guides* and the GASB *Implementation Guides*.

In addition, we added current illustrations of accounting and financial reporting issues, simplified and clarified the material wherever possible, and updated the questions, exercises, and problems. Notice, for example, the coverage of the new fund types in Chapters 5 and 8; New York City's financial reporting on the 9/11 disaster in Chapter 9; social security reporting in Chapter 11; and the expanded discussion of investment accounting in Chapter 13.

The recent revelations of significant fraudulent financial reporting in the private sector should provoke discussion of ethical issues in governmental and not-for-profit financial reporting. We continue to present ethics cases at the end of several chapters, adding a new ethics case involving preparation of management's discussion and analysis required by GASB *Statement No. 34.* Many chapters also contain minicases that present the reader with issues requiring judgment and provide a vehicle for class discussion.

To provide room for the additional materials on governmental financial reporting, the new chapter on financial statement analysis, and the expansion of several other chapters, we now cover college and university accounting in an appendix to Chapter 12 (not-for-profit accounting), rather than in a separate chapter. Recent changes in accounting and reporting standards place college and university accounting in the realm of applications of not-for-profit and governmental accounting standards, rather than as an industry subject to special standards. Not-for-profit colleges and universities are required to apply the FASB's standards on not-for-profit accounting, covered in Chapter 12. GASB *Statement No. 35* (Basic Financial

Statements—and Management's Discussion and Analysis—Public Colleges and Universities) brings governmental colleges and universities within the scope of GASB *Statement No. 34.* Based on how they are financed, most governmental colleges and universities likely will use enterprise fund accounting (covered in Chapter 7), and others will use governmental fund accounting (covered in Chapters 4 through 6).

We left in the chapter on governmental budgeting. Balanced budgets are discussed and excerpts from the law of one state are included. Readers can follow a complete set of illustrations to prepare a budget and a control report for a governmental unit. The problems in this chapter form a case, permitting readers to prepare a complete budget using individual problem materials. They are set up as a computer project, with additional data and "what-ifs," which, along with a template, are available to adopters. The chapter on fundamentals of accounting also remains in this edition to make the text more readily adaptable for teaching public administration and other non-accounting majors.

Ancillary Package

To assist you in the classroom the following supplements accompany this text:

Instructor's Resource CD-ROM: This CD contains both the Solutions Manual and the Test Item File.

Companion Website: As a new feature with this edition, students and professors can access the Web site at *www.prenhall.com/ives.* The Test Item File and the Solutions Manual are password protected and available to faculty only. Contact your Prentice Hall representative to obtain a password. Student and faculty can view Author Updates, Selected Appendices, and Links to Pertinent Web sites.

ACKNOWLEDGMENTS

We sincerely appreciate the help of the many members of the professional community, students, and faculty in preparing this and previous editions of this text. In particular, we thank:

Those who reviewed and commented on drafts of chapters or helped us resolve matters requiring clarification include David Bean and Kenneth Schermann of the Governmental Accounting Standards Board and Wendy Comes of the Federal Accounting Standards Advisory Board.

Those who assisted us in obtaining the actual financial statements and other material that we used to make governmental and not-for-profit accounting and financial reporting come alive include Shirley Ritger, Village of Grafton, Wisconsin; Hugh Dorrian, City of Columbus, Ohio; Jerry Bridges, The Johns Hopkins University; Elizabeth B. Washington, City of Shreveport, Louisiana; Lynne Burkart, Postlethwaite & Netterville, Metairie, Louisiana; and Edward Roche, Moody's Investors Service. We made extensive use of the financial statements prepared by the Village of Grafton and particularly thank all those associated with the preparation and audit of its statements.

Other reviewers include John T. Rigsby, Mississippi State University; Robert S. Kravchuk, Indiana University; Barbara Chaney, North Carolina State University; Joann Noe Cross, University of Wisconsin–Oshkosh; and Thomas G. Amyot, College of St. Rose.

The people at Prentice Hall, especially our acquisitions editor, Thomas Sigel, who enthusiastically embraced this revision and helped coordinate the logistics; Kelly Warsak, our production editor, who skillfully handled the production process; and Beth Toland, our marketing manager, who let the world know that this new edition was forthcoming.

And most of all, our wives, Eunice Ives, Cordelia Razek, and Kathy Hosch, who kept our suppers warm and who graciously recognized that, when we stared at them blankly in response to something they said, we were thinking about this textbook.

MI

JRR

GAH

ABOUT THE AUTHORS

Martin Ives, MBA, CPA, CGFM, CIA, serves as the Distinguished Adjunct Professor of Public Administration at New York University's Wagner Graduate School of Public Service. Before entering the academic world, Ives was Vice Chair and Director of Research of the Governmental Accounting Standards Board, a member of the Federal Accounting Standards Advisory Board, First Deputy Comptroller of the City of New York, and Deputy Comptroller of the State of New York.

In addition to this text, Professor Ives has co-authored three books (*Program Control and Audit, Financial Condition Analysis and Management,* and *Government Performance Audit in Action*). He has also written chapters for audit and municipal finance handbooks, has authored more than 25 articles for *the Government Accountants Journal, the Journal of Accountancy, the Internal Auditor,* and other professional journals. In addition, he has spoken to numerous professional and civic organizations. He was founding president of the Albany chapter of the Institute of Internal Auditors and served on the governing boards of several other professional organizations.

Ives has received many honors and awards including the Public Service Award (Fund for the City of New York), the Governor Charles Evans Hughes Award (Capitol District chapter of the American Society for Public Administration), and the S. Kenneth Howard Award (Association for Budgeting and Financial Management). He has also been voted Adjunct of the Year by the students at NYU's Wagner Graduate School.

Joseph R. Razek, Ph.D., CPA (inactive), CGFM, is the Energy Accounting and Tax Conference Professor of Accounting at the University of New Orleans. A graduate of Ohio Wesleyan University, he received his master's of business administration from the University of Michigan and his doctorate from the University of Illinois. He is a certified public accountant and a certified government financial manager and has consulted for many governmental and not-for-profit organizations.

Dr. Razek has published articles in the *Accounting Review, Government Accountants Journal, Accounting Historians Journal, Nonprofit World* and other professional journals. He has also co-authored many chapters in governmental accounting handbooks, as well as a textbook on managerial accounting. Cited by his students as a dedicated and innovative teacher, Dr. Razek has received several teaching awards. He currently teaches courses in governmental and not-for-profit accounting and health care accounting at both the graduate and undergraduate level and is a member of the Louisiana Society of CPAs Health Care Task Force.

Gordon A. Hosch, Ph.D., CPA, CGFM, received his bachelor's degree from the University of New Orleans, a master's degree from the University of Arkansas, and his doctorate in accounting from Louisiana State University in Baton Rouge. He has served as chairman of the Department of Accountancy and is currently the KPMG Professor of Accounting and Graduate Programs Coordinator in Accounting at the University of New Orleans. He has public accounting experience with Peat, Marwick, Mitchell & Co. (now KPMG) and has served as a faculty intern with the Department of Agriculture's National Finance Center.

Dr. Hosch is a member of the Louisiana Society of CPAs Governmental Accounting and Auditing Committee. He has made presentations to various organizations including the American Society of Women Accountants, the American Software Users Group, the U.S. Navy, and the Internal Revenue Service. He received the Educator of the Year Award from the Louisiana Society of CPAs as well as numerous teaching awards, including the University of New Orleans College of Business Outstanding Alumnus Award. His publications have appeared in the *Governmental Accountants Journal* and other journals. In addition, he has co-authored numerous chapters in governmental accounting handbooks. He has also reviewed numerous textbooks and papers during his career.

Chapter 1

Governmental and Not-for-Profit Accounting Environment and Characteristics

After completing this chapter, you should be able to:

➤ *Describe the characteristics of governmental entities.*

➤ *Describe the characteristics of not-for-profit organizations.*

➤ *Describe the governmental and not-for-profit organization environment.*

➤ *Describe the users and uses of accounting information.*

➤ *Define the term* generally accepted accounting principles (GAAP).

➤ *Describe the jurisdictions of the accounting standards-setting bodies.*

➤ *Describe the objectives of governmental and not-for-profit entity financial reporting.*

➤ *Describe the major characteristics of governmental and not-for-profit organization accounting and financial reporting.*

A series of financial reporting scandals rocked the business world and the capital markets in recent years. Many large corporations overstated their profits by inflating revenues and understating expenses, overstated their financial positions by not reporting obligations, and wrote notes to financial statements that even sophisticated readers could not understand. These practices helped push the prices of their equity securities to levels not warranted by their underlying strength—only to collapse when the scandals erupted. Even within a growing body of "generally accepted accounting principles," some corporation managers were able to mislead investors by bending the accounting rules or by finding loopholes in them so as to avoid their intent.

This text, however, deals with governmental and not-for-profit organizations, which do not issue equity securities. Should the public nevertheless be concerned with the quality of financial reporting by these organizations? The answer, of course, is Yes. The implications of poor financial reporting by governmental and not-for-profit organizations do not differ significantly from for-profit entities. Taxpayers of governmental entities and bondholders of both governmental and not-for-profit organizations might well wonder whether poor financial reporting masks a weakening financial condition, leading ultimately to tax increases, service cutbacks, and defaults in the payment of debt service.

A variety of concerns led to significant changes in governmental and not-for-profit accounting and financial reporting in recent years. Because both sectors absorb a large part of the nation's gross domestic product, stakeholders (including taxpayers, donors, and service recipients) show a growing concern with the need for better accountability. The close brush with financial disaster experienced by several large governments during the last quarter of the twentieth century also focused increased attention on governmental accounting, financial reporting, and budgeting practices. As a result, the last decade saw new financial reporting models both for governmental and not-for-profit organizations. In addition, a new federal government accounting standards-setting board developed accounting standards, leading to the first set of audited federal financial statements for 1997.

GOVERNMENTAL AND NOT-FOR-PROFIT ORGANIZATIONS

It is not always easy to distinguish among governmental, not-for-profit, and for-profit organizations. The distinction does not lie in the functions these entities perform. Rather, the distinction lies in the details of how an entity is organized, governed, and financed. For example, hospitals may be for-profit, not-for-profit, or governmental organizations. A hospital is not necessarily a governmental one just because it was financed partly with tax-exempt debt issued by a governmental agency. An entity is not necessarily a not-for-profit one just because it was created under a state's not-for-profit corporation law.

Not-for-profit organizations exhibit certain basic characteristics that distinguish them from business enterprises. Not-for-profit entities (1) receive contributions of significant amounts of resources from resource providers who do not expect commensurate pecuniary return; (2) operate for purposes other than to provide goods and services at a profit; and (3) lack ownership interests like those of a business enterprise.[1] As a result, not-for-profit organizations may get contributions and grants not normally received by business enterprises. On the other hand, not-for-profit organizations do not engage in ownership-type transactions, such as issuing stock and paying dividends. Four broad categories of not-for-profit organizations are covered in this text: voluntary health and welfare organizations, health care organizations, colleges and universities, and other not-for-profit organizations.

Governmental entities include the following:

- Federal government
- General-purpose political subdivisions (such as states, counties, cities, and towns)

---

[1] *Statement of Financial Accounting Concepts No. 4*, "Objectives of Financial Reporting by Nonbusiness Organizations" (Stamford, CT: Financial Accounting Standards Board, 1980), para. 6.

- Special-purpose political subdivisions (such as school districts)
- Public corporations and bodies corporate and politic (such as state-operated toll roads and toll bridges)

Other organizations created by governments by statute or under not-for-profit corporation laws are governmental if they possess one or more of the following characteristics: (1) their officers are popularly elected or a *controlling* majority of their governing body is appointed or approved by governmental officials; (2) they possess the power to enact and enforce a tax levy; (3) they hold the power to *directly* issue debt whose interest is exempt from federal tax; or (4) they face the potential that a government might dissolve them unilaterally and assume their assets and liabilities.[2]

GOVERNMENTAL AND NOT-FOR-PROFIT ENTITY ENVIRONMENT

Governmental and not-for-profit organizations operate in a social, legal, and political environment different from the environment of commercial enterprises. As a result, some of their information needs, as well as many of their accounting and financial reporting practices, differ. Important aspects of their operating environment are discussed in this section.

Inability to Measure Efficiency and Effectiveness by Measuring Income

Commercial enterprises exist to enhance their owners' wealth. When they do engage in social-type activities, their intent ultimately lies in maximizing their income. Because income is quantifiable and can be measured in monetary terms, it is a useful means of evaluating the efficiency and effectiveness of commercial organizations. Potential stockholders look to a corporation's earnings per share, among other things, to help them decide whether to invest in it.

Governmental and not-for-profit entities exist to provide services to their constituents. From a financial perspective, some of them may strive to maintain a small excess of revenues over expenses to cushion against economic downturns or to provide for future needs, but they do not operate to maximize profits. Indeed, if a school district were to accumulate large operating surpluses, many taxpayers—depending on their perspective—would complain that the district was either overtaxing the citizens or failing to spend the amounts it was authorized to spend. For these organizations, an excess of revenues over expenditures does not necessarily mean that they accomplished their programs either efficiently or effectively.

Governmental entities are beginning to explore other ways to help taxpayers assess accountability. Many are developing measures of outputs (including cost per unit of service) and outcomes (program results) to supplement their financial reports.

---

[2] For further discussion, see American Institute of Certified Public Accountants, *AICPA Audit and Accounting Guide, Health Care Organizations* (New York: AICPA, 2001), p. 1; and Martin Ives, "What Is a Government," *The Government Accountants Journal* (Spring 1994), pp. 25–33.

Many Operational Decisions Governed by Legal Compliance

Commercial organizations are free to provide only those goods and services they feel will enhance their profits. They cannot usually be required to provide goods and services against their will, and if they cannot cope with the legal or social environment, they are free to leave the market.

Resources obtained by commercial enterprises, most of which come from the sale of products and services, can generally be spent as the enterprise sees fit. Their spending decisions may or may not be subject to budgets, but if they are, the budgetary amendment process is relatively simple. Commercial organizations can also borrow money when convenient, subject only to requirements of lenders and investors.

Governmental entities are required by law (constitution, charter, statute, and so on) to provide certain services. For example, most city charters provide for police and fire protection. Managers cannot refuse to provide these services because of cost or because they feel that residents do not deserve such services.

Most of the resources obtained by governmental entities come from taxes, higher-level government grants, and borrowing. Spending decisions made by the federal government, states, cities, and other general-purpose governments are based on budgets that have the force of law. These budgets, submitted by the executive branch and approved by the legislative branch, often cannot be exceeded without specific legislative approval.

Generally, resources provided by higher-level governments must be used only for the specific purposes designated by the higher-level government. Most governmental borrowings are constrained by law as to purpose, quantity, and timing. How much they borrow may be subject to specific limits, such as value of real property in the jurisdiction. New bond issues may require approval by the electorate or by a higher-level government.

Not-for-profit organizations derive most of their resources from providing services, donor contributions, and borrowings. Donor contributions may be subject to restrictions either as to what they can be used for or when they can be used. Recipient organizations are legally bound to adhere to these donor restrictions.

Because of these factors, internal accounting for governmental and not-for-profit organizations generally focuses on the controls needed to ensure legal compliance. Such accounting tends to be conservative in nature, designed to make sure that spending amounts authorized by the legally adopted budget are not exceeded, and that expenditures meet the purpose limitations of a bond issue or the spending restrictions imposed by grantors and donors. Although recent changes in external financial reporting emphasize entity-wide reporting, reporting standards continue to require that accounting distinguish between unrestricted and restricted resources.

Lack of Harmony of Purpose

If a commercial organization is to survive, its managers must share one overall goal: to make a profit. Without profits, a commercial organization cannot survive. Even though managers of an organization may disagree on the means of making a profit, they seldom disagree on the importance of the profit itself.

Though unconcerned with "profits," governments provide many types of services to their constituents. The relative importance of each service and the goals to be achieved tend to vary both among the constituency and their representatives in government. As a result, the level of resources devoted to each governmental activity is a function of the political process, and conflict is often present within the government, particularly when different political parties lead the executive and legislative branches.

The processes of government become more complicated as a result of a general lack of continuity of leadership. New administrations may make a "clean sweep" of top appointed officials and institute new policies. To demonstrate accomplishment, new administrations may focus on short-term strategies, rather than on longer-term needs.

USERS AND USES OF ACCOUNTING INFORMATION

Persons both internal and external to organizations use accounting information. In establishing financial reporting standards, those who set accounting standards emphasize the needs of external users (those not directly involved in the operations of the reporting entity) because they do not have ready access to the entity's information.

Resource providers, oversight bodies, and service recipients are the major external users of governmental and not-for-profit entity financial reports. Resource providers include taxpayers; donors and potential donors; investors, potential investors, and bond-rating agencies (which provide data to investors); and grant-providing organizations, such as higher-level governments. External oversight bodies include higher-level governments and regulatory agencies. Service recipients include citizen advocate groups. Internal oversight bodies, such as boards of trustees, are also major users of financial data.

Users of financial reporting might seek answers to the following types of questions:

- What is the likelihood of the repayment of short-term and long-term debt?
- What is the entity's ability to continue to provide a particular level of services?
- Does the entity have sufficient funds to provide a cushion against revenue shortfalls caused by economic downturns?
- Does the entity use its resources to the extent appropriated for specific purposes as well as comply with restrictions on the use of resources?
- Is the entity efficient and effective in using resources?
- Is the entity's ability to use its available resources restricted in any way?

ACCOUNTING PRINCIPLES AND STANDARDS

Rules guiding accounting and financial reporting are referred to as *generally accepted accounting principles (GAAP)*. The American Institute of Certified Public Accountants defines this term as follows:

[T]he consensus at a particular time as to which economic resources and obligations should be recorded as assets and liabilities by financial accounting, which changes in assets and liabilities should be recorded, when these changes should be recorded, how the assets and liabilities and changes in them should be measured, what information should be disclosed and how it should be disclosed, and which financial statements should be prepared.

Generally accepted accounting principles encompass the conventions, rules, and procedures necessary to define accepted accounting practice at a particular time. The standard of "generally accepted accounting principles" includes not only broad guidelines of general application, but also detailed practices and procedures.[3]

Establishing Generally Accepted Accounting Principles

The origins of GAAP can be traced back to the period just after the 1929 stock market crash, when attempts were made to formulate accounting principles. Many criticized the earliest statement of principles as being little more than a codification of then current accounting practices. Continued concerns with the way in which accounting principles were being established led to the formulation of the Financial Accounting Standards Board (FASB) in 1973 and then to the Governmental Accounting Standards Board (GASB) in 1984. Seven members are appointed to each of these bodies by the Financial Accounting Foundation (FAF), an entity whose members are appointed by certain professional accounting and financial organizations. Advisory councils to both the FASB and the GASB are comprised of individuals representing organizations concerned with the activities of the standards-setting bodies. The GASB-FASB structure is shown in Exhibit 1-1.

The FASB and the GASB are charged with establishing and improving standards of accounting and financial reporting within their respective areas of jurisdiction. The GASB's jurisdiction includes all state and local governmental entities, including government-sponsored colleges and universities, health care providers,

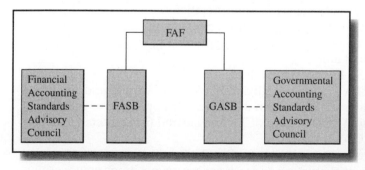

Exhibit 1-1
Relationship Between the FASB, the GASB, and the FAF

---

[3] *Statement No. 4,* "Basic Concepts and Accounting Principles Underlying Financial Statements of Business Enterprises" (New York: AICPA, 1970), paras. 137 and 138.

and utilities. The FASB establishes standards for all other entities, including not-for-profit colleges and universities and health care providers. Under this arrangement, it is possible for the two boards to establish different accounting and reporting standards for similar transactions of similar entities, such as hospitals. Although this situation occurs sometimes, the two boards cooperate with each other to keep differences to a minimum.

The Federal Accounting Standards Advisory Board (FASAB) was established in 1990 to consider and propose accounting principles for the federal government. Its nine members are appointed by heads of the agencies primarily responsible for federal accounting and financial management: the U.S. Comptroller General, the Director of the Office of Management and Budget, and the Secretary of the Treasury. FASAB proposals become standards unless a sponsor objects.

Standards promulgated by the three boards are GAAP by virtue of the due process used by the boards in developing them and the authority accorded them by the American Institute of Certified Public Accountants (AICPA). The due process used in developing the standards includes using task forces, holding public hearings, issuing "exposure drafts" of proposals for comment by interested parties, and carefully considering those comments before issuing the standards. AICPA rules provide that auditors may not express unqualified opinions on financial statements that are in violation of standards issued by the applicable board.

Hierarchy of Accounting Principles

Because the standards-setting bodies deal with large workloads and because they may choose not to address a host of less significant issues that might otherwise come before them, the AICPA has adopted a *hierarchy* of accounting principles. The hierarchy allows a practitioner to look to less authoritative guidance issued by the board with jurisdiction (or its staff) and to guidance given by other bodies in the event the board with jurisdiction has not issued guidance on a particular matter. To illustrate, the following hierarchy, ranked from most authoritative to least authoritative, applies to state and local governments:

Level I: GASB Statements and Interpretations
            AICPA and FASB pronouncements that GASB Statements or
            Interpretations have made applicable to state and local govern-
            mental units
Level II: GASB Technical Bulletins
            AICPA Industry Audit and Accounting Guides and AICPA
            Statements of Position that are made applicable to govern-
            mental units by the AICPA and cleared (not objected to) by
            the GASB
Level III: Consensus positions of a GASB-organized group of accoun-
            tants that attempts to reach consensus positions on govern-
            mental accounting issues
            AICPA AcSEC Practice Bulletins made applicable to govern-
            mental units by the AICPA and cleared by the GASB

Level IV: GASB Staff Implementation Guides
Current practices widely used by governmental units
Level V: Other accounting literature,
including GASB Concepts Statements and AICPA and FASB
pronouncements that are not made specifically applicable to
governmental entities

OBJECTIVES OF FINANCIAL REPORTING

All three standards-setting bodies issue *concepts statements* on the objectives of financial reporting in their areas of jurisdiction. (Concepts statements are not standards, but they help readers understand the framework within which the boards are developing standards.) The three statements on objectives of financial reporting show both similarities and differences, which reflect the somewhat different environments of the entities to which the standards apply. The governmental accounting standards-setting bodies, in particular, emphasize the need for data to help report users assess accountability.

State and Local Government Financial Reporting

The GASB statement of reporting objectives for state and local governments calls for financial reporting to assist in fulfilling government's duty to be publicly accountable and to help users assess that accountability. To meet those objectives, financial reporting needs to provide data to show whether current-year revenues were sufficient to pay for current-year services, to demonstrate whether resources were obtained and used in accordance with the legally adopted budget, and to help users assess the entity's service efforts, costs, and accomplishments.

In addition to helping users evaluate the entity's operating results for the year and assess the level of services that can be provided by the entity, financial reporting that follows GASB objectives also reveals an entity's ability to meet its obligations as they come due. Financial reporting should accomplish the latter objective by providing information about financial position and condition and about physical and other nonfinancial resources with useful lives that extend beyond the current year, and by disclosing restrictions on resources and risk of potential loss of resources.

Federal Government Financial Reporting

FASAB objectives for federal financial reporting cover budgetary integrity, operating performance, stewardship, and systems and controls. The objectives state that financial reporting should assist in fulfilling the government's duty to be publicly accountable for monies raised through taxes and other means and for their expenditure in accordance with the government's budget. Financial reporting should also assist report users in: (1) evaluating the entity's service efforts, costs, and accomplishments and its management of assets and liabilities; (2) assessing the impact on the nation of the government's operations and investments and how, as a result, the nation's financial condition has changed and may change in the future; and (3) understanding whether financial management systems and internal accounting and administrative controls are adequate.

Not-for-Profit Organization Financial Reporting

The FASB's financial reporting objectives for not-for-profit organizations focus on information useful to present and potential resource providers, as well as other users, in making rational decisions about allocating resources to those organizations. Such information helps in assessing (1) the services provided by the entity and its ability to continue to provide them, (2) how the entity's managers discharged their stewardship responsibilities, and (3) the entity's performance, including its service efforts and accomplishments. Information should be provided about the entity's economic resources, obligations, net resources, restrictions on the use of resources, and liquidity.

MAJOR ACCOUNTING AND FINANCIAL REPORTING CHARACTERISTICS

Several characteristics are unique to governmental and not-for-profit organization accounting and financial reporting. These characteristics flow primarily from the environmental factors discussed earlier. The characteristics are discussed briefly here and described in greater detail in other chapters of this text.

Use of Fund Accounting

Fund accounting is perhaps the most distinctive feature of governmental and not-for-profit organization accounting. For many years, fund accounting provided the foundation both for internal accounting control purposes and for external financial reporting by these entities. In response to concerns expressed by financial report users about the complexity of fund-based financial reporting, however, the reporting emphasis shifted away from funds and to the entity as a whole. Nevertheless, general-purpose government organizations and many special-purpose government organizations continue to use fund accounting, and the GASB requires both entity-wide and fund-level reporting. The FASB does not require not-for-profit organizations to use fund-based reporting, but does not preclude it provided the entity complies with the FASB requirements for entity-wide reporting.

What Is a Fund?

Fund accounting segregates an entity's assets, liabilities, and net assets into separate accounting entities based on legal restrictions, donor-imposed restrictions, or special regulations. It acts as a convenient control mechanism to help ensure that resources are spent for the intended purposes—like using separate cookie jars for food, rent, clothing, and so on.

The governmental accounting literature defines a fund as

> a fiscal and accounting entity with a self-balancing set of accounts recording cash and other financial resources, together with all related liabilities and residual equities or balances, and changes therein, which are segregated for the purpose of carrying on specific activities or attaining certain objectives in accordance with special regulations, restrictions, or limitations.[4]

In this definition, the term *fiscal entity* refers to the separate budgetary nature of a fund that has only spendable financial resources, and the term *accounting entity* refers to a separate financial unit that is treated as an entity for accounting purposes. (As discussed later, some types of funds also have nonspendable resources, such as capital assets.) Some governments use just a small number of funds, but others have many of them.

Because each fund is a separate accounting entity, each must have a set of *self-balancing accounts;* that is, the total of the assets of a particular fund must equal the total of its liabilities and fund balance (or net assets). Thus, the accounting records of a particular fund must be designed to identify the resources of that fund and the claims to those resources, as distinguished from all other funds.

Types of Funds Used

Both similarities and differences characterize the various types of funds used by state and local governments and not-for-profit organizations.

- Entities that use fund accounting generally maintain a fund called a General Fund or an Unrestricted Current Fund. Resources in these funds can be used for any purpose designated by the governing body.
- Virtually all entities that use fund accounting maintain separate funds for resources whose use is restricted by law, regulation, or donor requirement to specific purposes or to a specific period of time.
- State and local governments also distinguish among funds based on whether they have only financial resources and focus on measuring *spending* or whether they have both financial and nonfinancial resources and focus on measuring *capital maintenance.*

Incorporation of Budgets into Fund Accounting

A unique feature in governmental fund accounting (applicable not only to state and local governments, but to the federal government as well) incorporates budgetary accounting into the accounting system for certain types of funds. In federal government accounting, two accounting tracks operate side-by-side. State and local governments incorporate budgetary accounting to a somewhat lesser extent, but it is

---

[4] *GASB Codification of Governmental Accounting and Financial Reporting Standards* (GASB Cod.) as of June 30, 2001, Sect. 1300, "Statement of Principle—Fund Accounting Systems" (Norwalk, CT: GASB, 2001).

nevertheless pervasive. The requirement for incorporating budgetary accounting into governmental fund accounting systems demonstrates the importance of ensuring that legally adopted budgets are not exceeded.

Measurement Focus and Basis of Accounting

The term *measurement focus* refers to what an entity expresses or measures in its financial report, and the term *basis of accounting* refers to the timing of recognition (recording) of assets, liabilities, revenues, and expenditures or expenses. A particular basis of accounting helps to achieve the measurement focus. Thus, if an entity wants to measure net profit, it uses the full accrual basis of accounting, because full accrual accounting provides the most accurate measure of net profit.

Not-for-profit organizations use the full accrual basis of accounting both in their funds and when measuring the results of their operations. State and local governments also use full accrual accounting, but not for all purposes. They use full accrual accounting in the funds that account for their business-type activities, when they report on those activities, and when they report on a government-wide basis. Within their so-called governmental-type funds, however (the General Fund and certain other funds through which most governmental functions typically are financed), state and local governments use a hybrid-type basis of accounting called the *modified accrual basis of accounting.*

The modified accrual basis of accounting is a compromise between the full accrual basis of accounting and the cash basis. Capital assets, for example, are recorded as expenditures when acquired and are not depreciated under the modified accrual basis of accounting. Further, transactions and events creating obligations that will not be paid until well in the future, such as vacation leave, are not recognized as expenditures or as fund liabilities.

Funds using the modified accrual basis of accounting measure financial position and operating results under what the GASB calls a *current financial resources* measurement focus. (This is distinguished from funds that use the full accrual basis to measure position and results using the *economic resources* measurement focus.) Most state and local government budgets operate on a cash or a near-cash basis, and the modified accrual basis of accounting indicates the influence of budgeting on governmental accounting. These concepts will be discussed more completely in Chapters 2 through 6.

Entity-Wide and Fund-Level Reporting

Does the pervasive use of funds in governmental and not-for-profit internal accounting spill over into external financial reporting? For many years, the answer to that question was Yes. Recently, however, the financial reporting focus turned toward the entity as a whole. The change in emphasis came about for practical reasons. Entities with many types of funds and reporting on a fund basis often issue financial statements that may look complex and may not be readily comprehensible because of the number of details included. State and local governments issued financial statements with 10 or more columns, and many not-for-profit organizations issued statements showing each group of funds layered one atop another in a "pancake-type" format.

To make financial reporting more comprehensible and useful, those who set accounting standards stress the need for financial reporting on the entity as a whole. Specifically, they address the following aspects:

- Not-for-profit organization financial statements are required to "focus on the organization as a whole." Within those statements, they need to report on three classes of net assets: those that are unrestricted and those that are either temporarily restricted or permanently restricted by donors.
- State and local governments are now required to report on two levels: a government-wide level that distinguishes only between "governmental" and "business-type" activities, and a fund-level that reports on the major funds. Although the fund-level financial statements are prepared on the same basis of accounting used within the funds, the government-wide financial statements are prepared using the full accrual basis of accounting.

REVIEW QUESTIONS

Q1-1 Describe the characteristics that distinguish not-for-profit organizations from business enterprises.

Q1-2 Identify the various types of entities that constitute governmental organizations, and describe the characteristics of other organizations that, when created by governments, are also considered to be governmental entities.

Q1-3 Identify and briefly explain three major environmental characteristics of governmental and not-for-profit organizations.

Q1-4 Illustrate the kinds of restrictions placed by laws on the ability of governments to use resources, and by donors on the ability of not-for-profit entities to use resources.

Q1-5 Who are the users of governmental and not-for-profit entity accounting information and for what purposes might they use that information?

Q1-6 What are the jurisdictions of the accounting standards-setting bodies: GASB, FASAB, and FASB?

Q1-7 Why is a hierarchy of generally accepted accounting principles needed?

Q1-8 List the three ways identified by the GASB in which financial reporting can assist users to assess governmental accountability.

Q1-9 List three objectives of not-for-profit organization financial reporting.

Q1-10 Define a *fund*.

Q1-11 Describe one distinction between the full accrual basis of accounting and the modified accrual basis of accounting.

CASES

C1-1 Croton Hospital was a not-for-profit entity. Because it experienced financial difficulties, the county in which the hospital was located assumed control of Croton's assets and liabilities. The county executive appointed all five members of the hospital's new board of trustees. The hospital's chief accountant, who was not replaced, continued to use the same accounting principles and financial reporting used before the county takeover. Explain the position the county comptroller should take regarding Croton's accounting and financial reporting.

C1-2   State law provides that all cash not immediately needed by school districts to finance current operations be forwarded to the counties in which the school districts are located. The law also requires that county treasurers place these resources in a separate fund and invest them on behalf of the school districts. Because Contra County is experiencing some financial problems and to provide some badly needed funds to the county, the county treasurer tells the county administrator that he plans to invest the school district funds in "junk bonds" yielding 9 percent interest. He will credit the "normal" rate of return (5 percent) to school districts and the remaining 4 percent to the county itself. Explain the position the county administrator should take on the treasurer's proposal.

EXERCISES

E1-1   (Characteristics of not-for-profit and governmental entities)
The mayor of a large city approaches a group of citizens and suggests that they form an organization to provide social, educational, and recreational programs for local youth. The group agrees and forms an entity called the Community Youth Organization (CYO). The group also chooses a board of directors, and the board hires an executive director and several staff members. CYO's activities are financed entirely by grants from the city and many of CYO's programs are held after-hours in the local high school. Is the CYO a not-for-profit organization or a government? Why? What changes in characteristics would be needed to change it from one type of entity to the other?

E1-2   (Accounting standards-setting bodies)
Three accountants started talking about hospitals. One said he was treated at a not-for-profit hospital, another said she was treated at a county hospital, and the third said he had just returned from the hospital run by the U.S. Veterans Administration. They wondered why three different bodies established accounting standards for hospitals. Give reasons for and against the existence of three accounting standards-setting bodies.

E1-3   (Accounting standards-setting procedures)
Several not-for-profit organizations use television campaigns to obtain pledges to contribute cash. Some people think that not-for-profit entities should recognize pledges as revenues when the cash is actually received. Others would recognize revenues when the pledges are made, subject to a provision for amounts not likely to be collected. Based on that scenario, discuss (a) the need for an accounting standards-setting body, (b) the qualifications members of that body should possess, and (c) the procedures that body should adopt in establishing accounting standards.

E1-4   (Objectives of financial reporting)
FASB Concepts Statement No. 1, *Objectives of Financial Reporting by Business Enterprises,* says that the primary focus of business enterprise financial reporting is "information about an enterprise's performance provided by measures of earnings and its components." Contrast the notion of "performance" in business enterprises with that of not-for-profit and governmental organizations, and discuss how the difference might affect the nature of financial reporting among the various types of entities.

E1-5   (Objectives of financial reporting)
The FASAB said that financial reporting should assist users in understanding whether financial management systems and internal accounting and administrative controls are adequate. (See subsection on federal government reporting on page 9.) Why do you think the FASAB established this objective? How might this objective be implemented in financial reporting?

Chapter

2

The Use of Funds in Governmental Accounting

After completing this chapter, you should be able to:

➤ *Identify the major fund categories currently used in governmental accounting.*

➤ *Identify the fund types used within each of the major fund categories, describe the function of each fund type, and give examples of when each fund type is used.*

➤ *Compare and contrast the main features of the current financial resources measurement focus and modified accrual basis of accounting versus the economic resources measurement focus and accrual basis of accounting, as used by governmental units.*

➤ *Understand the measurement focus and basis of accounting used by each fund in a governmental accounting system.*

➤ *Identify the financial statements used by each fund in a governmental accounting system.*

OVERVIEW

Before reading financial statements, one must be aware of the measurement focus of the statements, the basis of accounting used to prepare them, and scope of the entity covered by them.

- *Measurement focus* refers to what is being expressed and which resources are being measured in reporting an organization's financial performance and position.

- *Basis of accounting* is a *timing* concept. It relates to *when* the assets, liabilities, revenues, and expenses (or expenditures) are recognized in the financial statements. Measurement focus and basis of accounting go together, because timing of recognition helps achieve what one is trying to measure. For example, to measure net profit, you would focus on all of the organization's economic resources and use the accrual basis of accounting.
- *Entity* is a scope concept. It defines the boundaries of a particular reporting unit by describing *whose* assets, liabilities, revenues, expenses, and equities are included in its financial report.

Knowing and understanding the implications of measurement focus of the statements, the basis of accounting used, and the scope of the entity covered are particularly important when reading financial statements prepared by state and local governments. Several types of measurement focus and basis of accounting are used in governmental financial reporting. In addition, several aspects to the notion of entity in governmental accounting affect financial statements.

Measurement Focus and Basis of Accounting   To account for its business-type activities, governments measure operating income, account for the consumption of the economic resources used by those activities, and use the accrual basis of accounting, just like private enterprise. To account for its basic day-to-day services, however, governments use a unique measurement focus and basis of accounting, known as the *current financial resources measurement focus* and the *modified accrual basis of accounting*. Using the current financial resources measurement focus and the modified accrual basis of accounting creates measurements that are a hybrid of the cash and the accrual bases of accounting. As will be explained shortly, governments report on these activities using both the modified accrual and the accrual bases of accounting. The concepts of current financial resources measurement focus and modified accrual basis of accounting will be introduced in this chapter and discussed in more detail in Chapters 4, 5, and 6.

The Reporting Entity and Fund Accounting   In business enterprise accounting, a "reporting entity" is described in terms of legally separate, but affiliated organizations. If a parent company, such as General Motors, exercises control over its legally separate subsidiaries, the financial activities of all the units are consolidated for financial reporting purposes. In governmental accounting and financial reporting, however, the entity concept has two aspects. One pertains to the treatment of legally separate but nevertheless affiliated organizations. The other relates to certain accounting subdivisions (known as funds) within the parent organization itself. For example, a legally separate organization, the New York City Health and Hospitals Corporation, is a part of the New York City financial reporting entity because of the nature of their relationships. At the same time, the financial activities of New York City itself are accounted for in various accounting subdivisions, called funds. There are three categories of funds, each containing various types of funds within each category.

The individual fund is the basic building block of governmental accounting and financial reporting because all transactions are initially recorded in funds. Within the funds used to account for their day-to-day activities, governments use the current financial resources measurement focus and the modified accrual basis of accounting. Within the funds used to account for their business-type activities, governments record transactions and events using the economic resources measurement focus and the accrual basis of accounting. The activities and balances of the individual funds can be displayed in separate fund financial statements. This chapter and Chapters 4 through 8 are devoted to a discussion of accounting within and reporting on the individual funds.

Reporting on Funds and Aggregating to Report on the Entity   Reporting on individual funds is useful for some purposes, but users of financial statements also need information on the entity as a whole. Aggregating the individual funds creates several problems, the most significant of which comes from using different measurement focuses and bases of accounting for the various fund categories.

Governmental financial reporting is covered in GASB *Statement No. 34*, "Basic Financial Statements—and Management Discussion and Analysis—for State and Local Governments" (June 1999). GASB *Statement No. 34* requires two sets of financial statements, one called *fund financial statements* and the other called *government-wide financial statements*. The fund financial statements report on the individual funds, using the same measurement focus and basis of accounting as that used to account within the funds. To prepare government-wide statements, adjustments are made to the fund financial statements that account for the day-to-day activities, so that all activities use the same measurement focus (economic resources) and basis of accounting (accrual). Also, funds that do not finance governmental activities are removed when preparing government-wide statements, and financial data for affiliated but legally separate organizations are included. Therefore, when you read Chapters 4, 5, and 6, keep in mind that certain adjustments will be needed for reporting purposes so that the government-wide financial statements can be prepared using the economic resources measurement focus and the accrual basis of accounting. The preparation of these financial statements is discussed in Chapters 9 and 10, but reference will be made to them throughout the text.

FUND CATEGORIES AND BASIS OF ACCOUNTING

Chapter 1 defined a fund as

> . . . a fiscal and accounting entity with a self-balancing set of accounts recording cash and other financial resources, together with all related liabilities and residual equities or balances, and changes therein, which are segregated for the purpose of carrying on specific activities or attaining certain objectives in accordance with special regulations, restrictions, or limitations.[1]

---

[1]   GASB Cod. Sec. 1300, Statement of Principle, Fund Accounting Systems.

As stated, the individual fund—a separate fiscal and accounting entity—provides the basic building block of state and local government accounting and financial reporting. Funds provide the means for establishing controls to ensure compliance with legal restrictions on the use of governmental resources. If the legislature, for example, wants to segregate gasoline taxes from all other revenues to ensure a steady flow of resources to repair roads, it may establish a special fund. If the citizens vote to approve a bond issue for a new firehouse, segregating the proceeds in a fund helps to ensure that the proceeds are used for no other purpose. The financial statements of these funds provide information about their resource inflows, outflows, and balances.

State and local governments perform a variety of functions. The day-to-day operating activities, such as police and fire suppression functions, are financed primarily by taxes. Other governmental activities, such as the operation of municipal electric and bus systems, are financed primarily with user fees or charges kept separate from the tax collections. Some governments accumulate resources, also kept separate from other governmental resources, to pay pension benefits to their employees. To account for activities that have somewhat different characteristics, state and local governments use three major categories of funds: governmental, proprietary, and fiduciary. Within each of these categories are various types of funds. A general relationship, though not a precise one, exists between the functions governments perform and the types of funds they use to account for those functions. This chapter introduces the three fund categories, the fund types within each category, and the basic accounting and fund-level financial reporting principles for each fund category. The effect of governmental budgeting on accounting within the governmental funds category will also be discussed.

Governmental Funds Category

State and local governments account for their basic services in the governmental funds category. Governmental-type funds are used to account for the accumulation and expenditure of resources to provide day-to-day operating services, such as education, police, fire, sanitation, parks, and highway maintenance. Governmental-type funds are used also to account for resources legally earmarked for a particular governmental purpose, and for the acquisition or construction of general governmental capital assets, such as roadways, maintenance depots, police stations, and firehouses.

Expenditures from governmental-type funds are driven generally by budgets proposed by the executive branch of government and legally adopted by the legislative branch. Indeed, the most significant governmental-type fund is the General Fund, the fund you are likely to read about at budget time because its proposed expenditures influence property tax rates and other tax rates. The way governments prepare budgets and the legal status accorded them profoundly affects both accounting *within* governmental-type funds and financial reporting *for* those funds.

Although well-run governments do long-range planning, their operating budgets for day-to-day operations are short-run in nature. They generally cover activities for 1 year. The budget process is one of estimating the yield from taxes and other financing sources and authorizing the expenditure of those resources. Although most state laws require state and local governments to have "balanced" budgets, they do not specify that "balance" needs to be achieved in an accrual accounting sense. Historically, the inflow and outflow aspects of budgeting are cash-oriented, rather than accrual-oriented.

The revenue aspect of budgeting generally is conservative in nature; it focuses on revenues that are available for spending. When budgets provide authority to spend, they are concerned with items requiring the current outflow of resources. For example, if a government wants to finance the purchase of some fire trucks, budgetary questions are raised: How should the trucks be financed and, if financed by incurring debt, how should the debt be paid off? From a budgeting perspective, buying a fire truck does not entail the expense of depreciation. Similarly, when budgeting for vacation pay that an employee may accumulate until retirement, the concern of most governments relates to the amount required to be paid out to the current year's retirees, not to the amount earned by current employees that will paid out for those employees, say, 20 years from now.

Measurement Focus and Basis of Accounting

Accounting within and financial reporting on governmental-type funds has historically tended to support the budgetary process. Although accounting standards setters prescribe a certain degree of accrual accounting when reporting on governmental-type funds, the accruals are short-run in nature. The accruals do not, for example, cover obligations resulting from current-year transactions and events that will not be paid until many years in the future. These issues create several significant departures from the accrual basis of accounting. As a result of these departures, fund-level financial statements for governmental-type funds are presented using a current financial resources (or spending) measurement focus and the modified accrual basis of accounting—a hybrid type of measure lying somewhere between the cash basis and the accrual basis of accounting.

Under the modified accrual basis of accounting, as prescribed by the GASB, revenues are recognized (and reported in the fund-level financial statements) in the period in which they are measurable and available. *Measurable* refers to the ability to state the amount of revenues in terms of dollars. *Available* means collectible within the current period or soon enough thereafter to be used to pay the bills of the current period. In the case of property taxes, for example, "soon enough thereafter" to pay current-period bills is interpreted to mean 60 days after the end of the accounting period.

Expenditures under the modified accrual basis of accounting generally are recognized in the period in which services and goods (such as salaries, professional services, supplies, and utilities) are received and a liability is incurred. This treatment, of course, is similar to the way such items would be recorded using the accrual basis of accounting. Specific exceptions to the general rule, however, could result in different measurements under the modified accrual basis as compared with the accrual basis of accounting. The exceptions relate to such items as compensated absences, claims and judgments, special termination benefits, pensions, and debt service. Expenditures and liabilities for compensated absences, for example, are recognized when liabilities mature (come due for payment when employees resign or retire), rather than when earned by the employees.

Because these concepts are likely to be new to you, let's consider them further and contrast them with the cash and accrual bases of accounting. Notice the key term *current financial resources measurement focus*. We can contrast that term with the *economic resources measurement focus*. First, the word *current* in *current financial resources* refers to cash and near-cash items and does not include long-term assets and liabilities, such as long-term debt. Second, the term *financial resources* means that capital assets (such as buildings and equipment) are not included within the accounting measurements. This measurement focus contrasts with the economic resources measurement focus, which includes not only all financial resources (regardless of when receivable or payable), but also capital resources.

How does the basis of accounting used to implement the measurement focus affect the revenue measurements? To answer this question, assume a government levies a property tax of $100,000 for a calendar year. It collects $80,000 within the year, and expects to collect $15,000 in the first 60 days of the next year and the remaining $5,000 later in the year. Under the cash basis of accounting, $80,000 would be recognized as revenues. Under accrual accounting, $100,000 would be recognized. Under modified accrual accounting (used by governmental-type funds in fund accounting and fund-level financial reporting), $95,000 would be recognized.

How does the basis of accounting affect expenditure measurements? To answer this question, assume a government is not insured against claims resulting from damages caused by its vehicle operators. It pays $50,000 on claims settled during the year, will pay $8,000 early in the next year on settled claims, and expects to pay $25,000 in a future year on claims that were filed during the year, but remain difficult to settle. Under the cash basis of accounting, $50,000 would be recognized as an expenditure; under accrual accounting, $83,000 would be recognized as an expense; and under modified accrual accounting, only $58,000 would be recognized as an expenditure. (Note that modified accrual accounting uses the term *expenditure*, rather than the accrual notion of *expense*.)

Finally, how does the measurement focus affect the accounting measurements? The answer is that the effect is profound. Using the current financial resources measurement focus causes governmental-type funds to recognize an expenditure made for capital assets not as an asset, but rather as an expenditure—an outflow of financial resources. It also causes the issuance of long-term debt to be recognized not as a liability, but rather as an inflow of financial resources.

Proprietary Funds Category

Proprietary-type funds are used by governmental activities that operate in a manner similar to that of private sector businesses in that they charge fees for their services. Although many of these activities are self-supporting because their fees are sufficient to cover their costs, others receive subsidies from the parent government and some provide net revenues for the government.

Examples of governmental activities that use proprietary fund accounting are central motor pools, hospitals, electric utilities, mass transit facilities, and lotteries. Some activities that use proprietary fund accounting are part of the legally constituted government. Governments sometimes create separate legal entities, often referred to as public benefit corporations or public authorities, to perform these functions.

Measurement Focus and Basis of Accounting

Proprietary funds focus on determining operating income (or recovering costs), changes in net assets, cash flows, and financial position. To measure operating income (or the extent to which costs are recovered) and financial position, proprietary funds use the economic resources (sometimes referred to as capital maintenance) measurement focus and the accrual basis of accounting.

As contrasted with recognition under the current financial resources measurement focus and modified accrual basis of accounting, proprietary funds treat expenditures for capital assets as assets (rather than expenditures) and depreciate them (to record the expense of consuming the asset over time). Revenues are recognized in the period in which they are earned, rather than when they are "measurable and available." Expenses are recognized when resources are consumed or liabilities are incurred, without the exceptions created by the modified accrual basis of accounting, which focuses on current liabilities resulting from when liabilities mature and become due and payable.

Fiduciary Funds Category

Fiduciary-type funds are used to account for resources held by the government in a trustee or agency capacity for *others* and therefore cannot be used to support the government's own programs. "Others" might be individuals, other governments, or private organizations. Examples of situations in which a government might be acting in a trust or agency capacity include assets held on behalf of employees participating in governmental pension plans; investment pools operated by a sponsoring government on behalf of itself and other governments; and sales taxes collected by a state government on behalf of county and city governments.

Measurement Focus and Basis of Accounting

Fiduciary-type funds use the economic resources measurement focus and the accrual basis of accounting, except for certain pension-related liabilities that will be discussed in a later chapter.

Tables 2-1 and 2-2 summarize the measurement focus, basis of accounting, and broad categories of activities embraced within the three fund categories. Several types of funds fall within each fund category. Table 2-3 lists the specific fund types within each category and shows the measurement focus and basis of accounting applicable to each fund type. An overview of these funds and several examples of individual fund financial statements are presented in the remainder of this chapter.

Table 2-1
Fund Categories

	GOVERNMENTAL-TYPE FUNDS	PROPRIETARY-TYPE FUNDS	FIDUCIARY-TYPE FUNDS
Focus	Current financial resources	Economic resources	Economic resources
Activity	General government activities	Activities financed by user fees	Resources held for others
	Legally dedicated resources		

Table 2-2
Cash, Accrual, and Modified Accrual Bases of Accounting

	CASH BASIS	ACCRUAL BASIS	MODIFIED ACCRUAL BASIS
Record revenue:	When cash is received	When revenue is earned	When measurable and available
Record expenses (expenditures):	When cash is paid	When expense is incurred	Generally when expenditure is incurred (with specific exceptions)
Applicable fund category:		Proprietary, Fiduciary	Governmental

Table 2-3
Summary of Accounting Procedures Within Funds

FUND TYPE	CATEGORY	MEASUREMENT FOCUS	BASIS OF ACCOUNTING
General	Governmental	Current financial resources	Modified accrual
Special Revenue	Governmental	Current financial resources	Modified accrual
Debt Service	Governmental	Current financial resources	Modified accrual
Capital Projects	Governmental	Current financial resources	Modified accrual
Permanent	Governmental	Current financial resources	Modified accrual
Enterprise	Proprietary	Economic resources	Accrual
Internal Service	Proprietary	Economic resources	Accrual
Pension Trust	Fiduciary	Economic resources	Accrual
Investment Trust	Fiduciary	Economic resources	Accrual
Private-Purpose Trust	Fiduciary	Economic resources	Accrual
Agency	Fiduciary	Economic resources	Accrual

Source: Adapted from GASB *Statement No. 34*, "Basic Financial Statements—and Management Discussion and Analysis—for State and Local Governments" (Norwalk, CT: GASB, 1999), Table B-2, p. 151.

GOVERNMENTAL-TYPE FUNDS

As previously mentioned, governmental-type funds are those funds used to account for basic day-to-day operating services provided by the governmental unit, and for resources earmarked for particular governmental functions. These funds use a current financial resources measurement focus and the modified accrual basis of accounting. Specifically, the governmental-type funds are the General Fund, Special Revenue Funds, Debt Service Funds, Capital Projects Funds, and Permanent Funds. Table 2-4 summarizes the purposes of each fund type and gives examples of their use. Fund-level financial statements prepared for governmental-type funds are the balance sheet and the statement of revenues, expenditures, and changes in fund balances.

The General Fund

Although the specific number and type of funds used by a governmental unit are determined by the particular operations of that unit, every governmental body must at least have a *General Fund*. Technically, this fund is a residual fund—it is used to account for all governmental operations not accounted for in some other fund. In reality, however, the General Fund encompasses the basic day-to-day operations of a governmental unit. Unless some legal, contractual, or managerial reason can be given for separately accounting for an activity, it is recorded in the General Fund.

Table 2-4
Purposes of Governmental-Type Funds

FUND TYPE	TO ACCOUNT FOR:
General	General operations of government; any activity not accounted for in another fund
	Examples: Police department, fire department
Special Revenue	Resources legally designated for specific purposes and separately reported
	Examples: A dedicated hotel-motel tax, a dedicated motor vehicle tax
Debt Service	Resources dedicated to pay principal and interest on general obligation debt
	Examples: Sales tax or revenue transfer to service general obligation bonds
Capital Projects	Resources dedicated to acquiring or constructing major capital facilities
	Examples: Construction of a new city hall or bridge
Permanent	Resources legally restricted so only earnings (and not principal) may be used to support governmental programs
	Examples: Public cemetery perpetual-care fund; public library endowment fund

Included in the General Fund records are such activities as police, fire, and sanitation services and the administrative operations of the government. The transactions recorded in the General Fund represent the collection of various sources of revenues (primarily taxes) and the spending of those resources for supplies, services, and so forth.

Assets found in the General Fund are primarily current financial resources, and usually include cash, investments, receivables (such as unpaid property taxes), and receivables from other funds. In governmental accounting terminology, the receivables from other funds are referred to as *due from other funds.* If these receivables are not currently due, they are referred to as *advances to other funds.* Liabilities found in the General Fund are also primarily currently due to be paid. They typically include claims of various suppliers and payables to other funds. The latter items are referred to as *due to other funds.* As in the case of receivables, if these liabilities are not currently due they are referred to as *advances from other funds.* (Notice that the inclusion of long-term loans between funds is an exception to the general rule regarding current financial resources. The special treatment required in this case is discussed in Chapter 5.)

Fund balance (equity) represents the excess of assets over liabilities. Fund balance is separated into two components: unreserved and reserved. The *unreserved* portion is the net amount of resources available for spending. Net assets (or individual assets) not available for current spending are reported as being *reserved.*

The accounting equation for governmental-type funds is similar to that used in commercial accounting. The only difference is that the equity section is referred to as *fund balance* rather than owners' equity. This equation is stated as follows:

$$\text{Assets} = \text{Liabilities} + \text{Fund Balance}$$

Balance Sheet for the General Fund Compared with Business Organization Balance Sheet

As mentioned at the beginning of this chapter, governments are required to prepare fund financial statements and government-wide financial statements. A simplified fund-level balance sheet for the General Fund is presented in Table 2-5. Carefully study this table and notice how the accounting equation is presented in the financial statement. Notice also that the balance sheet of a business organization is included in Table 2-5.

The most significant difference between fund-level financial reporting for governmental-type funds and commercial financial reporting results from the current financial resources measurement focus used by governmental-type funds. As previously stated, when fund-level balance sheets are prepared, governmental-type fund assets consist primarily of current financial assets (spendable resources). Business organizations, on the other hand, report other long-term assets as well, such as property, plant, equipment, and intangibles, on their balance sheets. Governmental-type fund-level balance sheets report only current liabilities, whereas business organization balance sheets also report long-term liabilities, such as bonds payable.

Another major difference between fund-level financial reporting for governmental-type funds and commercial organizations is that the latter use classified financial statements. The elements of the commercial financial statements usually

Table 2-5

General Fund—Balance Sheet Compared with Corporate Balance Sheet

The City of Angusville General Fund Balance Sheet December 31, 2004		Cool Wheels Co., Inc. Balance Sheet December 31, 2004	
Assets		**Assets**	
Cash and investments	$576,000	Current assets:	
Receivables (net of allowances for uncollectible accounts, $3,000)	89,000	Cash and investments	$ 50,000
Due from other funds	50,000	Accounts receivable (net of allowance for uncollectible accounts, $3,000)	135,000
Total assets	$715,000	Inventory	145,000
		Prepaid expenses	34,000
Liabilities		Total current assets	364,000
Accounts payable	$123,000	Property, plant, and equipment:	
Due to other funds	75,000	Land	100,000
Accrued liabilities	100,000	Buildings (net of accumulated depreciation, $55,000)	150,000
Total liabilities	298,000	Equipment (net of accumulated depreciation, $14,000)	45,000
Fund balance		Total property, plant, and equipment	295,000
Reserved	—	Intangibles:	
Unreserved	417,000	Patents	30,000
Total fund balance	417,000	Total assets	$689,000
Total liabilities and fund balance	$715,000		
		Liabilities	
		Current liabilities:	
		Accounts payable	$ 35,000
		Accrued expenses payable	55,000
		Dividends payable	10,000
		Total current liabilities	100,000
		Long-term liabilities:	
		Bonds payable	300,000
		Total liabilities	400,000
		Owners' Equity	
		Contributed capital	150,000
		Retained earnings	139,000
		Total owners' equity	289,000
		Total liabilities and owners' equity	$689,000

are reported in subgroups that distinguish the current from the noncurrent assets and liabilities.

The third major difference between governmental-type fund-level financial reporting and commercial reporting lies in the equity section of the balance sheet. In governmental-type funds, equity is reported as the fund balance and separated between reserved and unreserved. In business organizations, equity is reported as contributed capital and retained earnings because of limits that most states place on the distribution of dividends.

Income Statement for the General Fund Compared with Business Organization Income Statement

The fund-level income statement for a governmental-type fund is called a *statement of revenues, expenditures, and changes in fund balance.* Because governmental units do not usually operate to make a profit, the concept of income is not important. Throughout this text we will use the term *operating statement* to refer to the statement of revenues, expenditures, and changes in fund balance. Governmental fund operating statements are presented in the following format, with details shown for each caption, as appropriate. The net change in fund balance is added to or subtracted from the beginning-of-period fund balance to arrive at the end-of-period balance.

> Revenues
> − Expenditures
> = Excess (deficiency) of revenues over expenditures
> ± Other financing sources and uses, including transfers
> ± Special and extraordinary items
> = Net change in fund balance
> + Fund balance at beginning of period
> = Fund balance at end of period[2]

Revenues usually available for use by the General Fund include taxes, licenses and permits, and fines and forfeitures. Expenditures are generally associated with the services and supplies used in the various operating departments and are reported on the operating statement by function. Examples of these functions include general government, public safety, and recreation and parks.

An example of an operating statement of a governmental General Fund and the income statement of a business is shown in Table 2-6. Notice that the General Fund operating statement includes other financing sources (uses). These increases and decreases in fund balance are not revenues or expenditures. In governmental-type funds, they consist mainly of transfers (transfers of resources between funds). Transfers in are transfers received by a fund from other funds, whereas transfers out are transfers from a fund to other funds. A discussion of the technical aspects of transfers is included in a later chapter. At this point it is only necessary to understand that fragmenting resources into funds often results in resource transfers from one fund to another.

The major difference between the fund-level operating statement for the General Fund and a business organization results from the difference in measurement focus

---

[2] GASB Cod. (2001) Sec. 2200.156 (adapted).

Table 2-6

General Fund—Statement of Revenues, Expenditures,
and Changes in Fund Balance Compared with Corporate Income Statement

THE CITY OF ANGUSVILLE
GENERAL FUND
STATEMENT OF REVENUES, EXPENDITURES,
AND CHANGES IN FUND BALANCE
FOR THE YEAR ENDED DECEMBER 31, 2004

Revenues	
Income taxes	$ 990,000
Property taxes	900,000
Licenses and permits	550,000
Fines and forfeits	250,000
Miscellaneous	92,000
Total revenues	2,782,000
Expenditures	
Current:	
General government	550,000
Public safety	990,000
Human services	780,000
Health	300,000
Recreation and parks	50,000
Capital outlay	100,000
Total expenditures	2,770,000
Excess of revenues over expenditures	12,000
Other Financing Sources (Uses)	
Transfers in	50,000
Transfers out	(40,000)
Total other financing sources	10,000
Net change in fund balance	22,000
Fund balance at beginning of year	395,000
Fund balance at end of year	$ 417,000

COOL WHEELS CO., INC.
INCOME STATEMENT
FOR THE YEAR ENDED DECEMBER 31, 2004

Revenues	
Net sales	$988,000
Other revenue	10,000
Total revenues	998,000
Expenses	
Cost of goods sold	450,000
Salaries expense	280,000
Depreciation expense	175,000
Interest expense	25,000
Other expenses	20,000
Total expenses	950,000
Net income	$ 48,000

and basis of accounting. Notice, for example, that the Cool Wheels operating statement, which is prepared using the economic resources measurement focus and the accrual basis of accounting, shows depreciation expense, but no capital outlay expenditures. By contrast, the City of Angusville operating statement, which is prepared using the current financial resources measurement focus and the modified accrual basis of accounting, shows no depreciation, but does show capital outlay expenditures. This point will be explained in greater detail in a later chapter.

A second difference between the operating statement of a governmental-type fund and the income statement of a business organization is the presence of transfers from other funds. Transfers affect the operating results and changes in net assets of the individual governmental-type funds. Although transfers among related companies occur in commercial enterprise, they would be eliminated in the preparation of consolidated financial statements, because they do not affect the enterprise as a whole. (When governmental organizations prepare government-wide financial statements, the interfund transfers offset each other as discussed in Chapter 10.)

A third difference between business reporting of operations and that of governmental-type funds is the treatment of equity. Ending fund balance is reconciled with beginning fund balance on the operating statements of governmental-type funds. Although some commercial organizations use this form of reporting, the majority reconcile beginning and ending retained earnings on a separate statement—either a retained earnings statement or a statement of changes in owners' equity.

Finally, commercial operating statements often are prepared under what is called the single-step approach; that is, total revenues less total expenses. The operating statements for governmental units contain several levels of aggregation. They are similar to multiple-step income statements sometimes used by business organizations.

Special Revenue Funds

Special Revenue Funds are used to account for the proceeds of specific revenue sources (other than trusts for individuals, private organizations, or other governments, or those used for major capital projects) that are legally restricted to be spent for a particular purpose. The accounting treatment of these funds is identical to that of the General Fund. The primary difference between the two types of funds lies in the breadth of activities recorded in each.

As a general rule, Special Revenue Funds should be used only when legally mandated, such as by law or city charter. The main purpose of separating these types of activities from those of the General Fund is to maintain control over the collection and use of specific sources of revenue. For example, assume that a tax on gasoline is specifically dedicated to highway maintenance. Generally, the law establishing the tax requires establishment of a Special Revenue Fund. This separation makes it easier for a governmental unit to account for the dollars collected from the gasoline tax, as well as the expenditures for highway maintenance. If these funds were commingled with other revenues and expenditures, it would be more difficult to demonstrate accountability for the money collected and its use. Other examples of Special Revenue Funds include special income tax funds and hotel-motel tax funds earmarked for specific purposes, parks admission fees to support parks maintenance, and higher-level government grants for community development.

A governmental unit can have several Special Revenue Funds. Usually the law requires that separate records be maintained for the activity of a Special Revenue Fund. Each of these funds is treated as a separate accounting entity for record-keeping purposes.

The types of assets usually found in Special Revenue Funds include cash, investments, receivables (often taxes), and amounts due from other funds. Liabilities common to these funds include the claims of various suppliers and payables to other funds. Because the accounting for Special Revenue Funds is identical to that of the General Fund, the comments made regarding the fund balance in the discussion of the General Fund are also relevant here. The balance sheet and the statement of revenues, expenditures, and changes in fund balance for Special Revenue Funds are similar to that shown for the General Fund in Tables 2-5 and 2-6.

Generally, the sources of revenue for Special Revenue Funds are taxes, rents and royalties, fees, and intergovernmental items (grants, shared revenues, and so forth). Expenditures from these funds are usually for services and supplies specifically identified by the law establishing the particular fund. The current financial resources measurement focus and modified accrual basis of accounting are used for each Special Revenue Fund.

Debt Service Funds

Debt Service Funds are used to account for the accumulation of resources that will be used to make payments of principal and interest on general long-term debt. This type of fund can also be used for payments of long-term liabilities resulting from debt-like commitments, such as installment purchase contracts and lease-purchase agreements. Debt to be serviced by proprietary fund revenues is not general long-term debt, so resources accumulated for that purpose should be reported in the appropriate proprietary fund rather than in a Debt Service Fund.

Debt Service Funds should be used when legally mandated or when financial resources are being accumulated for principal and interest that comes due in future years. In the absence of those situations, debt service payments may be made directly from general revenues on an annual basis, and accounted for in the General Fund. A single Debt Service Fund should be used for all general long-term debt whenever possible. In many instances, however, each debt issue may require the establishment of a separate Debt Service Fund.

Debt Service Fund resources come most often from transfers from the General Fund (or other funds), income from the investment of resources held by the fund, and taxes assessed specifically to service the debt. Debt Service Fund expenditures generally result from payment of principal and interest on the debt. Debt Service Funds follow the modified accrual basis of accounting.

As a result of these types of transactions, the assets of Debt Service Funds usually consist of cash, investments, and sometimes receivables. The liabilities are generally for matured interest and principal that have not yet been paid. The long-term liability for principal not currently due is not reported in the Debt Service Fund balance sheet. The fund balance therefore represents the resources available to service (pay principal and interest on) the debt. Debt Service Fund balance sheets and statements of revenues, expenditures, and changes in fund balance are similar to those presented for the General Fund in Tables 2-5 and 2-6, except for the differences in the nature of the specific assets, liabilities, revenues, and expenditures.

Capital Projects Funds

Capital Projects Funds account for receipt and disbursement of resources used to acquire major capital facilities through purchase or construction. A Capital Projects Fund should be used to account for capital outlays financed from general obligation bond proceeds, and must be used whenever legally required. A Capital Projects Fund is not used to account for such assets acquired by an Enterprise Fund, an Internal Service Fund, or trust funds for individuals, private organizations, or other governments. A Capital Projects Fund is also not used for capital assets purchased directly with current revenues of the General Fund or a Special Revenue Fund.

Generally, a separate Capital Projects Fund is used for each project. When a bond issue is involved in the financing, a separate fund is used for each bond issue. Using a separate fund provides better control over individual projects and the proceeds of a bond issue.

Projects usually accounted for in these funds include construction of bridges, a new city hall, and acquisition of assets that involve long-term financing. Examples of the types of acquisitions that usually do not require the use of a Capital Projects Fund are purchases of automobiles, furniture, and minor equipment.

The balance sheet of a Capital Projects Fund is similar to that presented for the General Fund in Table 2-5. Assets normally found on the balance sheet of a Capital Projects Fund include cash, investments, receivables, and amounts due from other funds or governments. Liabilities include accounts payable and amounts due to other funds or governments for services and materials associated with the construction projects (or to construction companies if the projects are completed by outside contractors). Because Capital Projects Funds use a current financial resources measurement focus, neither the capital assets acquired with Capital Projects Fund resources nor long-term debt used to finance those resources are shown on the balance sheet of a Capital Projects Fund.

The statement of revenues, expenditures, and changes in fund balance for a Capital Projects Fund is similar in format to the General Fund operating statement shown in Table 2-6. Often, however, the amounts shown as other financing sources will be greater than the amounts shown as revenues in a Capital Projects Fund. The normal sources of revenue for these funds are federal and state grants and earnings on investments, while the normal other financing sources are proceeds from issuing debt securities and transfers from other funds. Expenditures are usually limited to amounts related to the capital projects and include construction and engineering costs. Because Capital Projects Funds are governmental-type funds, they follow the modified accrual basis of accounting.

Where are the capital assets acquired with Capital Projects Fund resources shown? Where is the long-term debt used to finance those assets reported? Until recently, capital assets and general long-term debt were required to be reported in accounting entities known as *account groups*. As discussed in Chapters 9 and 10, however, GASB *Statement No. 34* eliminated the requirement for reporting account groups. Because governmental-type funds use a current financial resources measurement focus, capital assets and long-term liabilities are not shown in fund-level financial statements. They are instead reported in the government-wide financial statements, which are prepared using the economic resources measurement focus and the accrual basis of accounting. To accumulate these data for government-wide reporting, this text (Chapter 10) suggests use of a Capital Investment Account Group.

Permanent Funds

Permanent Funds are used to report resources that are legally restricted so that only the earnings generated by the principal, and not the principal itself, may be used to support programs that benefit the government or its citizens. Permanent Funds do not include private-purpose trust funds, which are fiduciary-type funds discussed later in this chapter.

An example of a Permanent Fund is a perpetual-care public cemetery fund, whose resources generate revenues to maintain the cemetery. Another example is an endowment made to a public library, where the endowment must be maintained in perpetuity, and the income generated by the endowment must be used to purchase library books.

Financial statements prepared for Permanent Funds are similar to those shown in Tables 2-5 and 2-6. Assets of Permanent Funds generally include cash and investments. Liabilities might include amounts due to other funds. Permanent Fund revenues generally include investment income (interest, dividends, and net increase or decrease in the fair value of investments). Distributions of revenues to the fund designated as the beneficiary of Permanent Fund revenues—usually a Special Revenue Fund—are reported as transfers out.

GOVERNMENTAL FINANCIAL REPORTING IN PRACTICE
Fund Financial Statements vs. Government-Wide Financial Statements

As previously mentioned, GASB *Statement No. 34* requires two levels of financial reporting, fund financial statements and government-wide financial statements. Financial reporting is discussed in detail in Chapters 9 and 10. For now, the important thing to remember is that, with regard to governmental-type funds, the current financial resources measurement focus and modified accrual basis of accounting is used both for accounting within the funds and for preparing fund financial statements. After the fund financial statements are prepared, adjustments are made to convert the financial data to the economic resources measurement focus and accrual basis of accounting for the government-wide statements.

The differences between the two measurement focuses and bases of accounting become evident when you see a reconciliation between the fund-level statement of revenues, expenditures, and changes in fund

(continued)

GOVERNMENTAL FINANCIAL REPORTING IN PRACTICE
Fund Financial Statements vs. Government-Wide Financial Statements

(*continued*)

balances and the government-wide operating statement, which is called a statement of activities. For example, there was a net difference of $249.2 million between the modified accrual basis fund-level operating statement and the accrual basis government-wide operating statement prepared by New York City in its fiscal year 2001 financial report. The following factors accounted for the difference (numbers are in thousands of dollars):

Governmental funds report capital outlays as expenditures. However, in the government-wide statement of activities, the cost of those assets is allocated over their estimated useful lives and reported as depreciation expense. The amount by which capital outlays exceeded depreciation in the current period is:

Purchases of fixed assets	$3,366,818	
Depreciation expense	(1,243,000)	$2,123,818

The net effect of various miscellaneous transactions involving capital assets and other (i.e., sales, trade-ins, and donations) is to decrease net assets — (179,048)

The issuance of long-term debt (e.g., bonds, leases) provides current financial resources to governmental funds, while the repayment of principal of long-term debt consumes the current financial resources of governmental funds. Neither transaction, however, has any effect on net assets in the government-wide statements. The net effect of these differences in treating long-term debt and related items is:

Proceeds from sales of bonds	(2,844,665)	
Principal payments of bonds	1,777,037	
Other	(31,217)	(1,098,845)

Some expenses reported in the government-wide operating statement do not require use of current financial resources and, therefore, are not reported as expenditures in governmental funds. — (718,735)

Revenues in the government-wide operating statement that do not provide current financial resources are not reported as resources in the funds — 122,010

Difference between net change in fund balances for governmental-type funds reported in fund statements and change in net assets for governmental activities reported in government-wide statements — $ (249,200)

Source: Adapted from Comprehensive Annual Financial Report, the City of New York, New York, for the fiscal year ended June 30, 2001.

PROPRIETARY-TYPE FUNDS

Proprietary-type funds are used when a governmental unit handles its financial operations in a manner generally similar to that of business enterprises. Activities that use proprietary fund accounting and reporting charge user fees for their services and focus on determining operating income and changes in net assets (or cost recovery). Examples of such activities include the operation of electric utilities, airports, mass transit facilities, golf courses, and central motor pools. Although sometimes subsidized by transfers (often from the General Fund), these activities are financed by user charges that at least partially cover operating and capital costs. As a result, accounting principles followed by proprietary-type funds are similar to those followed by commercial organizations; that is, they use an economic resources measurement focus and the accrual basis of accounting. This approach provides governmental units with accurate measures of revenues and expenses to help in developing user charges, as well as cash flow information to help determine any subsidy needed to run an activity.

The two types of proprietary funds are Enterprise Funds and Internal Service Funds. Table 2-7 summarizes the purposes of these funds and gives examples of their use. Financial statements prepared for proprietary funds include a statement of net assets or balance sheet; a statement of revenues, expenses, and changes in fund net assets or fund equity; and a statement of cash flows.

Enterprise Funds

Enterprise Funds may be used to account for any activity whose products or services are sold for a fee to external users, such as the general public. Enterprise funds *must* be used if any one of the following criteria is met:

- The activity is financed with debt that is secured solely by a pledge of the net revenues from the activity's fees and charges.
- Laws or regulations require that the costs of providing services, including capital costs (such as depreciation or debt service) be recovered through fees and charges, rather than with taxes.
- The activity's pricing policies set fees and charges that are designed to recover its costs, including capital costs (such as depreciation or debt service).

Table 2-7
Purposes of Proprietary-Type Funds

FUND TYPE	TO ACCOUNT FOR:
Enterprise	Resources used to supply goods and services, for a fee, to users external to the governmental unit
	Examples: Municipal airport, municipal electric utility
Internal Service	Resources used to supply goods or services, based on cost reimbursement, within the governmental unit
	Examples: Central motor pool, central purchasing function

Operations normally accounted for in Enterprise Funds include municipally owned utilities, mass transit facilities, toll roads and toll bridges, airports, swimming pools, and golf courses. Generally a separate fund is established for each type of activity.

Enterprise Fund financial statements are prepared using the economic resources measurement focus and the accrual basis of accounting, at both fund level and government-wide level of financial reporting. The reason for using full accrual accounting is to account for the total cost of the goods or services provided. This information is used to develop user charges in a fashion similar to that followed by commercial enterprises.

The balance sheet of an Enterprise Fund is shown in Table 2-8. Several major features of this financial statement should be noted. First, notice that the balance sheet is prepared in classified form. A *classified balance sheet* presents the assets and liabilities so as to distinguish between those that are current and those that are noncurrent (or long-term). *Current assets* include cash and items that will be converted to cash or used up in operations within 1 year. *Noncurrent assets* generally include land, buildings, and equipment. *Current liabilities* are debts that are due to be paid within 1 year. *Noncurrent liabilities* are debts that will be paid later than 1 year in the future.

The second major point that should be noted is the presence of *restricted assets*. These assets represent resources set aside for some particular use that results from a contractual (such as a debt covenant), legal, or regulatory restriction. They are labeled "Restricted assets" on the balance sheet. Showing certain assets as restricted (such as cash held in a separate account to pay debt principal and interest, pursuant to a debt covenant) lets the reader know that the resources are not available to pay other current liabilities. Depending on the circumstances, the restricted assets may be offset by liabilities that will be satisfied either from those resources or by net assets. In Table 2-8, the related liabilities are labeled "Liabilities payable from restricted assets."

Other asset categories used on the balance sheet include Advances to other funds and Other assets. The Advances to other funds section is used to report long-term receivables from other funds. The Other assets section is used as a catchall category. Any asset that does not fit into one of the specific categories is reported in the "other" category.

Finally, notice that the balance sheet shown in Table 2-8 is presented in the traditional balance sheet format, where assets equal liabilities plus net assets. Proprietary fund balance sheets may also be shown in a net assets format, where assets minus liabilities equal net assets (called a statement of net assets). Net assets should be displayed in three major components, where applicable: invested in capital assets, net of related debt; restricted; and unrestricted. The components of net assets are discussed in Chapter 7.

The balance sheet shown here is in a form that is typical of commercial business, with current assets and liabilities preceding noncurrent. For utility enterprises, however, it is not uncommon to find plant and long-term debt displayed before current assets and liabilities. This is because of the much larger percentage of total assets or net assets these items represent for utilities, relative to other forms of businesses.

The operating statement for Enterprise Funds is presented in multistep format, with a separate caption for operating income (or loss) and a reconciliation between

Table 2-8

Enterprise Fund—Balance Sheet

THE CITY OF ANGUSVILLE
ENTERPRISE FUND
SEWERAGE AND WATER FUND
BALANCE SHEET
DECEMBER 31, 2004

Assets

Current assets:

Cash	$ 650,000	
Receivables (net of allowance for uncollectibles of $8,000)	547,000	
Due from other funds	75,000	
Inventory of parts and supplies	155,000	
Total current assets		$ 1,427,000

Restricted assets:

Customer deposits	879,000	
Current debt service account	500,000	
Total restricted assets		1,379,000

Noncurrent assets:

Advances to other funds	300,000	
Property, plant, and equipment (net of accumulated depreciation, $2,400,000)	8,500,000	
Total noncurrent assets		8,800,000
Total assets		$11,606,000

Liabilities

Current liabilities:

Accounts payable	$ 235,000	
Due to other funds	100,000	
Accrued liabilities	77,000	
Accrued vacation and sick leave	90,000	
Total current liabilities		$ 502,000

Liabilities payable from restricted assets:

Customer deposits	879,000	
Accrued interest	500,000	
Total liabilities payable from restricted assets		1,379,000

Noncurrent liabilities:

Bonds payable		7,890,000
Total liabilities		9,771,000

Net Assets

Invested in capital assets, net of related debt	610,000	
Unrestricted	1,225,000	
Total net assets		1,835,000
Total liabilities and net assets		$11,606,000

beginning and end-of-period net assets or fund equity. The general format for this statement (with details shown, as appropriate) is as follows:

Operating revenues
– Operating expenses
= Operating income (or loss)
± Nonoperating revenues and expenses
= Income before other revenues, expenses, gains, losses, and transfers
+ Capital contributions
± Special and extraordinary items
± Transfers
= Increase (decrease) in net assets
+ Net assets at beginning of period
= Net assets at end of period[3]

Operating revenues earned by Enterprise Funds usually result primarily from user charges. Enterprise fund operating expenses depend on the type of operations but usually include the cost of services, supplies used, utilities, depreciation, and so forth. Notice particularly the charge for depreciation. Because Enterprise Funds use the economic resources measurement focus and accrual basis of accounting, depreciation must be included as an expense. Nonoperating revenues and expenses might include investment revenue and interest expense. Capital contributions might include grants from higher-level governments to acquire capital assets and contributions from developers. *Extraordinary items* are transactions and events that are unusual in nature and occur infrequently, such as a loss from a flood. *Special items* refer to transactions and events within the control of management that are either unusual in nature or occur infrequently, such as a large one-time revenue from the sale of capital assets. Transfers include subsidies received from another fund. A statement of revenues, expenses, and changes in fund net assets is illustrated in Table 2-9.

Because operations of Enterprise Funds are essentially the same as those of profit-oriented businesses, an additional statement must be prepared. This statement, illustrated in Table 2-10, is a statement of cash flows. The purpose of this statement is to provide information regarding the sources and uses of cash by the fund for operating, investing, noncapital financing, and capital and related financing activities. Discussion of the preparation of cash flow statements is beyond the scope of this text, and Table 2-10 is included for illustrative purposes only.

Internal Service Funds

Internal Service Funds are used to account for providing goods or services within the governmental unit, or to other governmental units, on a user-charge, cost-reimbursement basis. The main reasons for establishing this type of activity include (1) reduction in the cost of obtaining goods or services, and (2) improvement in the distribution of goods or services within the governmental unit. Typical Internal Service Funds are those that account for supplies distribution, motor pool operations, and data processing.

---

[3] GASB Cod. (2001) Sec. 2200.167 (adapted).

Table 2-9

Enterprise Fund—Statement of Revenues, Expenses, and Changes in Fund Net Assets

THE CITY OF ANGUSVILLE
ENTERPRISE FUND
SEWERAGE AND WATER FUND
STATEMENT OF REVENUES, EXPENSES, AND CHANGES IN FUND NET ASSETS
FOR THE YEAR ENDED DECEMBER 31, 2004

Operating revenues		
Charges for services		$2,400,000
Operating expenses:		
Personal services	$980,000	
Contractual services	370,000	
Depreciation	620,000	
Materials and supplies	176,000	
Other	101,000	
Total operating expenses		2,247,000
Operating income		153,000
Nonoperating expenses:		
Interest expense		125,000
Income before capital contributions		28,000
Capital contributions *(Residual Equity Transfer) (one-time shot) Non-recurring*		100,000
Increase in net assets		128,000
Net assets at beginning of year		1,707,000
Net assets at end of year		$1,835,000

Because Internal Service Funds are classified as proprietary-type funds, the accounting system used for these funds is designed to accumulate the total cost of the goods or services provided. Therefore, similar to Enterprise Funds, the economic resources measurement focus and full accrual basis of accounting are used. Using full accrual accounting enables compilation of the total cost of goods or services provided, leading to the calculation of user charges based on cost per unit of product or service or total cost for a specific job.

The Internal Service Fund bills the funds receiving the goods or services (often, the General Fund), and this amount is treated as a revenue of the Internal Service Fund and as an expenditure (expense) of the other funds. A separate fund is used for each identifiable unit because the accumulation of costs of goods or services provided must be specifically associated with revenues earned from providing the goods or services.

The balance sheet for an Internal Service Fund is similar to that of a business organization. Several major points regarding this financial statement should be noted. First, the assets shown include not only financial resources but also capital resources, such as land and buildings. Second, the capital assets are reported net of accumulated depreciation. Because expenses are being measured, depreciation is calculated and

Table 2-10

Enterprise Fund—Statement of Cash Flows

THE CITY OF ANGUSVILLE
ENTERPRISE FUND
SEWERAGE AND WATER FUND
STATEMENT OF CASH FLOWS
FOR THE YEAR ENDED DECEMBER 31, 2004

Increase (Decrease) in Cash		
Cash flows from operating activities:		
Cash received from vehicle rentals to departments	$2,390,000	
Cash paid to suppliers for goods and services	(560,000)	
Cash paid to employees	(980,000)	
Net cash provided by operating activities		$850,000
Cash flows from capital and related financing activities:		
Purchase of equipment	(720,000)	
Interest paid on capital debt	(125,000)	
Capital contributions	100,000	
Net cash used from capital and related financing activities		(745,000)
Net increase in cash		105,000
Cash at beginning of year		545,000
Cash at end of year		$650,000
Reconciliation of operating income to net cash provided by operating activities:		
Operating income		$153,000
Adjustments to reconcile operating income to net cash provided by operating activities		
Depreciation	$620,000	
Decrease in accounts receivable	262,000	
Increase in due from other funds	(50,000)	
Increase in inventory of parts and supplies	(40,000)	
Decrease in accounts payable	(50,000)	
Decrease in accrued liabilities	(30,000)	
Decrease in accrued vacation and sick leave	(15,000)	
Total adjustments		697,000
Net cash provided by operating activities		$850,000

deducted from revenues. Third, the assets and liabilities are presented in a classified format, distinguishing between current and noncurrent. Finally, the difference between assets and liabilities may be characterized either as net assets or fund equity.

Assets usually found in these types of funds include cash, amounts due from other funds, inventory (where applicable), and property, plant, and equipment. Liabilities generally include payables arising from operations of the fund and, possibly, advances from the General Fund or other funds. A balance sheet for a typical Internal Service Fund is similar to that presented for Enterprise Funds in Table 2-8.

Chapter 2   The Use of Funds in Governmental Accounting

The operating statement (statement of revenues, expenses, and changes in fund net assets or fund equity) of an Internal Service Fund is prepared in the same way as the operating statement of the Enterprise Fund shown in Table 2-9. Operating revenues earned by an Internal Service Fund usually result from user charges. Operating expenses associated with the operations of the fund depend on the type of operations but usually include the cost of services, supplies used, and depreciation. The excess of operating revenues over operating expenses is called operating income, which is followed by nonoperating revenues and expenses, capital contributions, transfers, and so on. The exact items of revenue and expense depend on the particular types of services performed. Generally accepted accounting principles for Internal Service Funds also require a statement of cash flows, similar to that presented in Table 2-10.

FIDUCIARY-TYPE FUNDS

Fiduciary-type funds are used to account for assets held by a government in a trust or agency capacity for others (individuals, other governments, or private organizations). Because they are held for others, these resources cannot be used to support the government's own programs. The fiduciary fund category includes Pension (and other employee benefit) Trust Funds, Investment Trust Funds, Private-Purpose Trust Funds, and Agency Funds. Trust funds are distinguished from Agency Funds generally by the existence of a trust agreement that affects the degree of management involvement and the length of time the resources are held. Table 2-11 presents a summary of the fiduciary-type funds, showing the purpose and examples of each.

Pension (and Other Employee Benefit) Trust Funds

The most widely used and often most significant trust funds are *Pension (and other employee benefit) Trust Funds.* These funds are used to account for resources required to be held in trust for members and beneficiaries of public employee defined benefit and defined contribution pension plans, health care and other postemployment benefit plans, and other employee benefit plans. (*Defined benefit pension plans* guarantee specific benefits on retirement. *Defined contribution plans* do not guarantee specific benefits; instead, benefits are based on periodic contributions to the plans and the earnings on them.)

Investment Trust Funds

Some governments sponsor investment pools, wherein they invest and manage resources belonging both to the sponsoring government (the *internal* portion of the pool) and to governments that are external to the sponsoring government (the *external* portion of the pool). The internal portion of these investment pools is reported as assets of the funds for which the investments were made. The external portions, however, are reported in *Investment Trust Funds,* another type of fiduciary fund.

Private-Purpose Trust Funds

Private-Purpose Trust Funds are used to report all other trust arrangements under which the principal and income are held for the benefit of individuals, other

Table 2-11
Purposes of Fiduciary-Type Funds

FUND TYPE	TO ACCOUNT FOR:
Pension Trust	Resources held in trust for employee retirement plans and other employee benefit plans
	Examples: Defined benefit pension plan, postemployment health benefit plan
Investment Trust	Resources of an external investment pool managed by a sponsoring government
	Examples: Financial reporting of the portion of an external investment pool that belongs to other governments
Private-Purpose Trust	Resources of all other trust arrangements maintained for benefit of individuals, other governments, and private organizations
	Examples: Unclaimed (escheat) property, such as bank accounts, investment accounts, and other property held pending claim by rightful owners
Agency	Resources held in a custodial capacity that must be disbursed according to law or contractual agreement
	Examples: Sales or property taxes collected by a government on behalf of another government, social security taxes withheld from employees and kept in a separate fund pending distribution to the federal government

governments, and private organizations. An example of a Private-Purpose Trust Fund is an escheat property fund. *Escheat property* is private property that reverts to a governmental entity in the absence of legal claimants or heirs. Many governments have laws that enable a rightful owner or heir to reclaim such property into perpetuity if the claimant can establish a right to it.

Agency Funds

Agency Funds are used to account for resources held by governmental units in a purely custodial capacity. They generally involve only the receipt and subsequent transmittal, after a short period of time, of resources held for individuals, private organizations, or other governments. Agency Funds may be used also to account for resources belonging both to other governments and the custodial government. For financial reporting purposes, however, only the resources belonging to other governments are reported in an Agency Fund. Assets held for the reporting government, pending distribution within the reporting government, should be reported in the appropriate governmental or proprietary fund.

An example of an Agency Fund is a *Tax Agency Fund,* wherein the reporting government collects taxes (such as sales taxes or property taxes) both for itself and as agent for other governments. The resources are held for a short period of time in an Agency Fund, which serves as a clearing account, pending distribution to the appropriate government. Agency funds are also used to account for deposits made by contractors when submitting bids on construction contracts.

It is possible to use one Agency Fund to account for several different agency relationships, provided there are no legal restrictions. However, due to the legal problems that exist in situations involving trusts, a separate fund generally is used for each individual trust.

Reporting on Fiduciary-Type Funds

For the Trust Funds, governmental entities are required to prepare a statement of fiduciary net assets and a statement of changes in fiduciary net assets. These funds should be reported using the economic resources measurement focus and the full accrual basis of accounting, except for certain liabilities of defined benefit pension plans and postemployment health care plans. Agency Funds have no "net assets." Instead, all resources held are equal to the liabilities to be paid from the resources in the Agency Fund statement of fiduciary net assets. A statement of changes in fiduciary net assets is not prepared for Agency Funds.

A statement of fiduciary net assets for a Pension Trust Fund is shown in Table 2-12. Assets usually found in a Pension Trust Fund statement of fiduciary net assets

Table 2-12
Pension Trust Fund—Statement of Fiduciary Net Assets

THE CITY OF ANGUSVILLE
PENSION TRUST FUND
CITY EMPLOYEES' RETIREMENT FUND
STATEMENT OF FIDUCIARY NET ASSETS
DECEMBER 31, 2004

Assets		
Cash		$ 5,000
Receivables		50,000
Accrued income		25,000
Investments, at fair value:		
Bonds	$18,000,000	
Common stock	6,000,000	
Total investments		24,000,000
Office equipment and furniture (net of accumulated depreciation of $10,000)		75,000
Total assets		24,155,000
Liabilities		
Accounts payable	20,000	
Accrued expenses	35,000	
Total liabilities		55,000
Net assets		
Held in trust for pension benefits		$24,100,000

include cash, investments, and receivables (including interest receivable). Liabilities usually include accounts and refunds payable. The net assets of that Trust Fund represent the amount held in trust for pension payments to retirees, current employees, and their beneficiaries.

Table 2-13 shows the statement of changes in fiduciary net assets for a Pension Trust Fund. Notice that this statement is called a Statement of Changes in Fiduciary Net Assets, thus linking it with the Statement of Net Assets. Typical additions to plan net assets are contributions and investment earnings, which include interest, dividends, and net increase (or decrease) in the fair value of investments. Typical deductions are benefits paid to retirees, refunds of contributions, and administrative expenses.

Table 2-13

Pension Trust Fund—Statement of Changes in Fiduciary Net Assets

THE CITY OF ANGUSVILLE
PENSION TRUST FUND
CITY EMPLOYEES' RETIREMENT FUND
STATEMENT OF CHANGES IN FIDUCIARY NET ASSETS
FOR THE YEAR ENDED DECEMBER 31, 2004

Additions		
Contributions:		
Member contributions	$2,500,000	
Employer contributions	2,500,000	
Total contributions		$ 5,000,000
Investment income:		
Net appreciation in fair value of investments	875,000	
Interest	550,000	
Dividends	450,000	
Total investment income		1,875,000
Total additions		6,875,000
Deductions		
Benefits paid	4,375,000	
Administrative expenses	200,000	
Total deductions		4,575,000
Change in net assets		2,300,000
Net assets available for benefits:		
Beginning of year		21,800,000
End of year		$24,100,000

Q2-1 Define *fund* as the term is used in governmental accounting.

Q2-2 How has governmental budgeting influenced the measurement focus and basis of accounting used in the governmental funds category?

Q2-3 How does the measurement focus and basis of accounting of governmental-type funds differ from that of proprietary-type funds?

Q2-4 Describe the difference between the current financial resources measurement focus and the economic resources measurement focus.

Q2-5 Compare the timing of revenue and expense or expenditure recognition in the full accrual basis with that in the modified accrual basis of accounting.

Q2-6 Which funds use the modified accrual basis of accounting?

Q2-7 Which funds use the full accrual basis of accounting?

Q2-8 List the governmental-type funds and briefly describe the use of each.

Q2-9 The controller for the City of Walla Walla recently made the following comment: "As a minimum, we could run city government with the use of only one fund." Do you agree with this statement? Why or why not?

Q2-10 Special Revenue Funds and the General Fund are identical in accounting treatment. When are Special Revenue Funds used instead of the General Fund, and what purpose do they serve?

Q2-11 Why are there no capital assets in governmental-type funds?

Q2-12 List the proprietary-type funds and briefly describe the use of each.

Q2-13 Why do Enterprise Funds and Internal Service Funds use full accrual accounting?

Q2-14 What are restricted assets?

Q2-15 What is the difference between an Enterprise Fund and an Internal Service Fund?

Q2-16 List the fiduciary-type funds and briefly describe the use of each.

Q2-17 Do Agency Funds have a fund balance? Why or why not?

CASES

C2-1 Rollin N. Money wishes to establish a fund that will provide a college education for children of police and fire personnel killed on the job. Mr. Money contacted you as a government employee and asked you to provide information about how he might achieve his goal. He is concerned with security over the initial gift and control over the use of any income from the gift. He wants the gift to be a permanent one and the income to be spent for the purpose identified previously. A friend of Mr. Money's suggested that he require the establishment of a Special Revenue Fund because the gift and its income would be maintained separately from the other governmental resources. How would you advise Mr. Money?

C2-2 The newly elected mayor of Angusville recently received a copy of the city's annual report. After reviewing the many pages of this report, she feels that the city would be in a better financial position if it privatized its motor pool operations. In this situation, privatization means hiring a private firm to operate the motor pool, which includes a city garage and city-owned vehicles. The main concern of the mayor is that the Motor Pool Fund realized a loss last year of $54,500, resulting in the need for a city subsidy. How would you advise the mayor of Angusville?

ETHICS CASES

EC2-1 The mayor of Vaudeville wants to complete a pet project that involves providing extra lighting in the neighborhoods where his friends live. After the budget for the General Fund was fully appropriated, one of the mayor's friends called to ask for the additional lighting. The major has decided to "borrow" some money from the Parks Fund, a Special Revenue Fund established by the city council. As the city's bookkeeper, the mayor instructed you to transfer some Parks Fund cash into the General Fund—Miscellaneous account. You responded by questioning the action, but the mayor said: "No one reads a government financial report, and if someone does read it, he or she does not understand all of the funds and their uses." How should you respond?

EC2-2 During a heated campaign for mayor of Morganville, an unsuccessful candidate boasted that he would "do away with all the special interests in government. I will abolish all of the Special Revenue Funds and merge that money with the general operating resources of the city." You are the successful candidate in that race and now the local press is pressuring you to respond to the campaign promise of that other candidate. How would you respond to the press?

EXERCISES

E2-1 (Compare cash and accrual basis of accounting)
Without making journal entries, describe the different treatment an organization would give the following transactions under (a) the cash basis of accounting and (b) the accrual basis.
1. Provided services on credit.
2. Incurred cost of materials used to provide the services in part (1).
3. Received payment for services rendered in part (1).
4. Paid for materials used in part (2).

E2-2 (Compare current financial resources measurement focus and modified accrual basis of accounting with economic resources measurement focus and accrual basis of accounting)
Without making journal entries, describe the different treatment a governmental entity would give the following transactions under (a) the current financial resources measurement focus and modified accrual basis of accounting and (b) the economic resources measurement focus and accrual basis of accounting.
1. Constructed a new firehouse.
2. Sent property tax bills to taxpayers and, based on past experience, expected to collect 80 percent of the amount billed during the year and 20 percent late in the following year.

3. Salaries for the last week of the year will not be paid until the first week of the next year.
4. Experienced several lawsuits during the year. Although no settlements were reached on the claims, city attorneys anticipated that they would be settled ultimately at a cost to the city of $200,000.

E2-3 (Matching—general terminology)

Match the terms on the left with the descriptions on the right by placing the appropriate letter in the space provided (use each letter only once).

_____ 1. Governmental fund type
_____ 2. Fund categories
_____ 3. Definition of a fund
_____ 4. Economic resources
_____ 5. Basis of accounting
_____ 6. Recognition of revenue when resources are available and measurable
_____ 7. Available
_____ 8. Expenditure
_____ 9. Current financial resources
_____ 10. To evaluate operating results

a. Cash payment or incurrence of liability for services in a modified accrual accounting system
b. Collectible within the current period or soon enough thereafter (within 60 days) to be used to pay the liabilities of the current period
c. Modified accrual
d. Measurement focus for governmental-type funds
e. Refers to the timing of the recognition of assets, liabilities, revenues, and expenses or expenditures
f. Governmental, proprietary, fiduciary
g. A fiscal and accounting entity with a self-balancing set of accounts
h. An objective of accounting for governmental units
i. Type of fund that accounts for general governmental operations
j. Measurement focus for proprietary-type funds and fiduciary-type funds

E2-4 (Fill in the blanks—general terminology)

1. A _____ is a fiscal and accounting entity with a self-balancing set of accounts.
2. The current financial resources measurement focus is used for _____ funds.
3. The basis of accounting refers to the _____ of the recognition of revenues and expenses (expenditures).
4. In 2005 Water City collected revenue that was earned in 2004. Using accrual accounting, the entry to record the collection would include a credit to _____.

5. In 2004 Review City recorded an expenditure that was incurred but would be paid in cash in early 2005. The entry to record the expenditure in 2004 would include a credit to _____.

E2-5   (Fund definitions through examples)
For each of the following situations, indicate which fund would be used to report the transaction.
1. The city made payments to a contractor on a major bridge project that requires separate accounting.
2. The Department of Streets purchased materials to be used to repair roads.
3. The city paid salaries to employees of the Department of Safety.
4. The General Fund acquired a mainframe computer.
5. The city collected a special tax dedicated to maintaining parks and playgrounds.
6. The General Fund made its annual contribution to a bond retirement fund.
7. The city acquired land for bridge approaches as part of the project mentioned in part (1).

E2-6   (Use of funds)
The mayor of New West Wall wanted to simplify the accounting system used by the town. He approached you with the following task: reduce the number of individual funds used in our governmental-type funds. How might you achieve this purpose?

E2-7   (Fill in the blanks—general terminology)
1. A governmental unit may have _____ (one or more than one) General Fund.
2. Accounting for a _____ Fund is the same as that of the General Fund.
3. _____ Funds are used to account for the receipt and disbursement of resources used to acquire major capital facilities.
4. Payments of principal and interest on general obligation governmental debt are generally recorded in a _____ Fund.

E2-8   (Use of funds)
The city council asked you to explain why the accounting records for proprietary-type funds use a different basis of accounting than those of governmental-type funds. Write the explanation that you would provide to the council.

E2-9   (Fill in the blanks—general terminology)
1. Three fund financial statements required for proprietary-type funds are _____, _____, and _____.
2. The two funds included in the proprietary-type funds are _____ and _____.
3. The basis of accounting used for proprietary-type funds is _____.
4. Assets that are limited in use for a specific purpose are generally referred to as _____.
5. Transactions and events within the control of management that are either unusual in nature or occur infrequently are referred to as _____.

E2-10　(Matching—use of funds)

Using the following codes, indicate which description best fits the funds listed by placing the code in the space provided.

GF　　　General Fund
SRF　　Special Revenue Fund
CPF　　Capital Projects Fund
DSF　　Debt Service Fund
EF　　　Enterprise Fund
ISF　　Internal Service Fund

_____ 1. Services are provided to the general public and the costs of providing the services are financed by user charges.

_____ 2. Resources are accumulated to pay principal and interest on general long-term debt.

_____ 3. Accounting for the police department activities.

_____ 4. Goods or services are furnished to other segments of the governmental unit on a user charge basis.

_____ 5. Acquisition and use of resources provided by the U.S. government for a particular purpose.

_____ 6. Expenditures are made by the city's streets department.

_____ 7. An "operating income" figure is computed.

E2-11　(Fund definitions through examples)

For each of the following situations, indicate which fund would be used to report the transaction.

1. A city-owned electric utility sent bills to the city and a separate school board.
2. The General Fund made a periodic payment to a city-owned electric utility as a subsidy of its rates.
3. The city issued property tax bills. These are expected to be collected within the accounting year.
4. The city purchased new police cars.
5. The city paid the principal and interest on a bond issue from resources that were accumulated for the purpose of making the payment.
6. A centralized purchasing facility billed the general city operations for part of the cost of the purchasing operations.
7. The city levied a special hotel tax dedicated to paying principal and interest on outstanding debt.

E2-12　(Use of funds)

For each of the following independent situations, write a short paragraph describing a specific set of circumstances that would require use of the funds listed.

1. A Permanent Fund and a Special Revenue Fund
2. An Agency Fund
3. A Special Revenue Fund
4. A Capital Projects Fund
5. An Internal Service Fund
6. An Enterprise Fund

E2-13 (Fund definitions through examples)

For each of the following situations, indicate which fund or funds would be used to report the transaction.

1. A city-owned airport sent bills to various airlines and the mayor's office.
2. The city made an annual payment to the Motor Pool Fund to subsidize its operations.
3. The city issued property tax bills that are expected to be collected within the accounting year.
4. The city acquired a new computer for its accounting system. Assume the accounting function is included in the General Fund.
5. The city levied a gasoline tax for the purpose of maintaining streets. Assume the tax requires a separate accounting.
6. The city paid the principal and interest on a bond issue from resources that were accumulated for that purpose.

E2-14 (Reporting for fiduciary-type funds)

Several types of fiduciary funds and several financial statement classifications used in those funds are listed here. Match the fund type (or types) with the financial statement classifications that would probably be found on the statements for that fund type.

Pension Trust Fund	PTF
Investment Trust Fund	ITF
Private-Purpose Trust Fund	PPTF
Agency Fund	AF

_____ 1. Net assets held in trust for benefits
_____ 2. Amounts owed to contractors in a Bid Deposits Fund
_____ 3. Assets held for rightful owners
_____ 4. Investments (at fair value)
_____ 5. Benefits paid
_____ 6. Due to local governments
_____ 7. Employer contributions

E2-15 (Summary of general reporting)

Following is a listing of codes for several types of funds. Indicate next to each fund financial statement the code of the fund for which the financial statement must be prepared.

GF	General Fund
EF	Enterprise Fund
PTF	Pension Trust Fund
CPF	Capital Projects Fund
ISF	Internal Service Fund
AF	Agency Fund

_____ 1. Balance sheet (or statement of net assets)
_____ 2. Statement of revenues, expenditures, and changes in fund balance
_____ 3. Statement of cash flows

_____ 4. Statement of fiduciary net assets
_____ 5. Statement of revenues, expenses, and changes in fund net assets
_____ 6. Statement of changes in fiduciary net assets

PROBLEMS

P2-1   (Conceptual section review)
Answer each of the following questions.
1. Why is the accrual basis of accounting preferable to the cash basis of accounting?
2. What is generally required for recognition of revenues under the modified accrual basis of accounting? How is that different from the accrual basis of accounting?
3. What is generally required for recognition of expenditures under the modified accrual basis of accounting? How is that different from the recognition of expenses under the accrual basis of accounting?
4. Based on the material in this chapter, discuss the advantages and disadvantages of using the current financial resources measurement focus and modified accrual basis of accounting for reporting on revenues and expenditures in governmental-type funds.

P2-2   (Identification of fund categories)
Identify and differentiate among the three fund categories used in governmental accounting. For each category, include in your discussion such matters as the specific fund types, the uses of the category, the measurement focus, and the basis of accounting.

P2-3   (Differentiation between modified accrual and accrual basis accounting)
Explain what _basis of accounting_ means and identify at least two differences between the modified accrual basis of accounting and the accrual basis of accounting.

P2-4   (Journal entries—modified accrual versus accrual basis of accounting)
Prepare journal entries to record the following information, first under the accrual basis of accounting, and then under the modified accrual basis of accounting. (If no entry is needed, state that in your answer.)
1. At the beginning of the year, Dodge City sends property tax bills in the amount of $300,000 to taxpayers.
2. During the year, Dodge City collects $275,000 in cash against the tax bills.
3. At the end of the year, the Dodge City finance director concludes that the remaining $25,000 will be collected from the taxpayers, but not for about 10 more months.

P2-5   (Conceptual section review)
Answer each of the following questions.
1. Explain how the fund balance of a governmental-type fund represents available spendable resources.

2. Special Revenue Funds, Capital Projects Funds, and Debt Service Funds are similar in nature. Explain this similarity.
3. Why do governmental units use Special Revenue Funds, Capital Projects Funds, and Debt Service Funds?

P2-6   (Identification of activities recorded in governmental-type funds)
Using only the governmental-type funds, indicate which would be used to record each of the following events.

GF   General Fund
SRF   Special Revenue Fund
DSF   Debt Service Fund
CPF   Capital Projects Fund
PF   Permanent Fund

_____ 1. General governmental revenues were transferred to the fund used to accumulate resources to pay bond principal and interest.
_____ 2. The city received its share of a state sales tax that is legally required to be used to improve library facilities.
_____ 3. General property taxes are levied by the city.
_____ 4. The city purchased five fire engines.
_____ 5. The city received a grant from the state to build an addition to the city hall.
_____ 6. The city issued general obligation bonds to finance the construction of new police stations.
_____ 7. The mayor was paid his monthly salary.
_____ 8. Expenses for the operation of the police department were recorded.
_____ 9. A new bridge across the Red River was constructed.
_____ 10. Tax monies were collected. These amounts were legally required to be used to maintain the city park system.
_____ 11. General governmental revenues were transferred to the City Hall Construction Fund.
_____ 12. A contractor received partial payment for the work done on the new city hall.
_____ 13. The city workers were paid their weekly salaries.
_____ 14. Outstanding bonds were retired, using monies accumulated for that purpose.
_____ 15. A federal grant was received to help pay for the cost of constructing the new city hall.
_____ 16. The city received a donation from a taxpayer, with the stipulation it be invested and kept in perpetuity, so that the income from the investments could be used to buy library books.
_____ 17. The city received income from the investments made in part (16).

P2-7   (Statement preparation—General Fund)
Using the following data, prepare a statement of revenues, expenditures, and changes in fund balance for the General Fund of Jummonville for the year ended December 31, 2004.

Miscellaneous revenues	$ 180,000
Licenses and permits revenues	2,000,000
Expenditures for education	3,000,000
Expenditures for corrections	2,000,000
Transfers to other funds	1,500,000
Tax revenues	7,000,000
Expenditures for welfare	2,100,000
Federal grants	4,000,000
Expenditures for public safety	750,000
Expenditures for highways	900,000
Transfers from other funds	700,000
Fund balance at beginning of year	1,500,000

P2-8 (Comparison of financial statements)
Review the balance sheet and the operating statement for the General Fund (Tables 2-5 and 2-6) and the balance sheet and the operating statement for the Sewerage and Water Fund (Tables 2-8 and 2-9). Identify the major similarities and differences between each type of statement and the types of activities in which each fund is involved.

P2-9 (Conceptual section review)
Answer each of the following questions.
1. If you were setting up the accounting system for a governmental unit, what type of fund would you use for a municipal clinic? Why?
2. If you were setting up the accounting system for a governmental unit, what type of fund would you use for a centralized computing system? Why?
3. Several small governmental units decided to pool their resources and build a regional airport. What type of fund would you recommend for the airport? Why?
4. How are the assets of the Plainville township Electric Utility Fund likely to have been financed? Explain your answer.

P2-10 (Identification of activities recorded in governmental- and proprietary-type funds)
Using the governmental- and proprietary-type funds, indicate which would be used to record each of the following events.
GF   General Fund
SRF   Special Revenue Fund
DSF   Debt Service Fund
CPF   Capital Projects Fund
PF   Permanent Fund
EF   Enterprise Fund
ISF   Internal Service Fund
____ 1. Revenue bonds were issued by the Electric Utility Fund to build a new plant.
____ 2. The Motor Pool Fund loaned $50,000 to the Central Purchasing Fund.
____ 3. The Electric Utility Fund billed the General Fund for its share of the electricity cost.

_____ 4. The city charter required all hotel taxes to be accounted for in a separate fund. The collections for the period totaled $500,000.

_____ 5. The mayor was paid her salary.

_____ 6. Electric utility revenue bonds were retired.

_____ 7. General obligation city debt was retired, using resources previously accumulated for that purpose.

_____ 8. The General Fund made its annual contribution to the fund that pays principal and interest on outstanding debt.

_____ 9. The city acquired land as part of a city hall expansion program. The resources used to acquire the land were provided by a general obligation bond issue.

_____ 10. The Motor Pool Fund billed each department in the city for use of vehicles (assume all departments billed were accounted for in the General Fund).

_____ 11. A wealthy taxpayer donated securities to the city, with the request that the donation be kept in perpetuity, so that the resulting investment income could be used to help support the activities of the city museum.

_____ 12. The police department salaries were paid.

_____ 13. Income from the Cemetery Permanent Fund investments was transferred to the fund used to maintain the city cemetery.

P2-11 (Correcting a trial balance)
The bookkeeper of Clearview City recently quit. The clerks working in the records department prepared the trial balance, based on the following information in the accounts.

Clearview City
Enterprise Fund
Waldon Swimming Pool Fund
Trial Balance
June 30, 2004

Cash	$210,000	
Prepaid expenses	1,400	
Accounts receivable	303,164	
Supplies inventory	6,000	
Due from other funds	-0-	
Property, plant, and equipment	8,189,655	
Accumulated depreciation		$2,500,000
Accounts payable		681,786
Due to other funds		74,000
Revenue bonds payable		396,000
Net assets		5,121,048
Revenue		1,147,705
Operating expenses	748,120	
Administrative expenses	257,400	
Maintenance expenses	204,800	
	$9,920,539	$9,920,539

Your review of the financial records revealed the following:
1. Accounts payable included the following:
   Due to other funds $10,000
2. Accounts receivable includes $100 that is actually a receivable from other governmental funds.
3. Supplies of $300 purchased on credit and received on June 27, 2004, were not recorded in the accounting records.
4. Depreciation was not recorded for 2004. The proper amount was $100,000. Assume that the city treats depreciation as an operating expense.
5. The General Fund owes the Enterprise Fund $500 for services rendered in 2004. The previous bookkeeper recorded revenue from the General Fund only when cash was received; therefore, the $500 has not been recorded.

Required: Prepare adjusting journal entries and an adjusted trial balance for the Waldon Swimming Pool Fund.

P2-12 (Comparison of financial statements)
Review the balance sheet and the operating statement for the General Fund (Tables 2-5 and 2-6) and the statements of fiduciary net assets and changes in fiduciary net assets (Tables 2-12 and 2-13). Identify the major similarities and differences between each type of statement and the types of activities in which each fund is involved.

P2-13 (Transactions involving all funds)
Indicate which fund(s) would be used to record each of the following events, by the city, county, or state referred to in the transaction. Use the following codes:

GF   General Fund
SRF   Special Revenue Fund
DSF   Debt Service Fund
CPF   Capital Projects Fund
PF   Permanent Fund
EF   Enterprise Fund
ISF   Internal Service Fund
PTF   Pension Trust Fund
ITF   Investment Trust Fund
PPTF   Private-Purpose Trust Fund
AF   Agency Fund

1. The city made a contribution to the employees' retirement fund.
2. Taxes that are dedicated to street repairs were collected. The ordinance establishing the tax requires a separate accounting for these monies.
3. The contractors who were building a bridge were paid.
4. General governmental revenues were transferred to the fund that accumulates money to retire general long-term debt.
5. The salary of the chief of police was paid.
6. The central purchasing fund sent out bills for purchases to the police and fire departments and to the city airport.

SRE PF 7. The city received a gift from a citizen to be held in perpetuity. The investment income must be used to provide free concerts in city parks.

CPF 8. Bonds were issued to finance the construction of a new library.

GF 9. The police department purchased 10 police cars.

GF 10. Sales taxes were collected.

GF 11. The city sold some of its excess office equipment. The proceeds from the sale were to be used for general city operations.

DSF 12. General obligation bonds were retired, using monies accumulated in a fund dedicated for that purpose.

EPF 13. The city-owned airport is accounted for as a separate fund. This fund issues bonds to finance airport improvements.

ISF 14. The city uses a separate fund to account for its central purchasing function. Supplies were purchased by this fund.

PF 15. A wealthy citizen donated securities to the city. The principal amount donated must remain intact, and the income must be spent to provide free food to the elderly at the city-operated senior citizen centers.

AF-GF 16. The state tax department collected sales taxes, half of which were to be remitted to other governments that also levied sales taxes.

ITF 17. The county treasurer distributed to school districts in the county the school districts' shares of the earnings from investments made by the county-operated investment pool.

P2-14 (Multiple choice)
1. Which of the following fund types of a governmental unit has (have) current financial resources as a measurement focus?

Focus Spending / *Focus*

	General Fund	Enterprise Fund
a.	Yes	Yes
b.	Yes	No
c.	No	No
d.	No	Yes

2. In which fund should the proceeds of a federal grant made to assist in financing the future construction of an adult training center be recorded?
a. General Fund
b. Special Revenue Fund
c. Capital Projects Fund
d. Permanent Fund

3. In which fund should the receipts from a special tax levy to retire and pay interest on general obligation bonds issued to finance the construction of a new city hall be recorded?
a. Debt Service Fund
b. Capital Projects Fund
c. Enterprise Fund
d. Special Revenue Fund

4. Several years ago, a city provided for the establishment of a fund to retire general obligation bonds issued for the purpose of constructing a new police station. This year the city made a $50,000 contribution to that fund from its general revenues. The fund also realized $15,000 in revenue from its investments. The bonds due this year were retired. This year's transactions require accounting recognition in which fund(s)?
   a. General Fund
   b. Debt Service Fund and Special Revenue Fund
   c. Debt Service Fund and General Fund
   d. Capital Projects Fund and Debt Service Fund

5. Which fund should be used to account for the activities of a central motor pool that provides and services vehicles for the use of municipal employees on official business?
   a. Agency Fund
   b. General Fund
   c. Internal Service Fund
   d. Special Revenue Fund

6. Which fund would recognize a transaction in which a municipal electric utility paid $150,000 for new equipment out of its earnings?
   a. Enterprise Fund
   b. General Fund
   c. Capital Projects Fund
   d. Permanent Fund

7. Which of the following funds of a governmental unit records the acquisition of a fixed asset as an expenditure rather than as an asset?
   a. Internal Service Fund
   b. Pension Trust Fund
   c. Enterprise Fund
   d. General Fund

8. Which of the following funds of a governmental unit use the modified accrual basis of accounting?
   a. Internal Service Fund
   b. Enterprise Fund
   c. Pension Trust Fund
   d. Debt Service Fund

9. Under the modified accrual basis of accounting for a governmental unit, revenues should be recognized in the accounting period in which they _____.
   a. Become available and earned
   b. Become available and measurable
   c. Are earned and become measurable
   d. Are collected

10. Which fund would account for fixed assets in a manner similar to a for-profit organization?
    a. Enterprise Fund
    b. Capital Projects Fund
    c. Permanent Fund
    d. General Fund

(AICPA adapted)

P2-15 (Multiple choice)
1. In which fund should the fixed assets of a central purchasing and stores department organized to serve all municipal departments be recorded?
    a. Enterprise Fund
    b. Internal Service Fund
    c. General Fund
    d. Capital Projects Fund
    e. Debt Service Fund

2. Which fund would a city use if it had a separate fund to hold and then remit to an insurance company the lump sum of hospital-surgical insurance premiums collected as payroll deductions from employees?
    a. General Fund
    b. Agency Fund
    c. Special Revenue Fund
    d. Internal Service Fund
    e. Private-Purpose Trust Fund

3. Which fund would be used to account for the activities of a municipal employee retirement plan that is financed by equal employer and employee contributions?
    a. Agency Fund
    b. Internal Service Fund
    c. Permanent Fund
    d. Pension Trust Fund
    e. Private-Purpose Trust Fund

4. A transaction in which a municipal electric utility issues bonds (to be repaid from its own operations) requires accounting recognition in which fund?
    a. General Fund
    b. Debt Service Fund
    c. Capital Projects Fund
    d. Enterprise Fund
    e. Internal Service Fund

5. Which fund should be used to account for the operations of a public library receiving most of its support from property taxes levied for that purpose?
    a. General Fund
    b. Special Revenue Fund
    c. Enterprise Fund

d. Internal Service Fund

e. None of the above

6. In which fund should the liability for general obligation bonds issued for constructing a new city hall and serviced from tax revenues be recorded?

Tracked in GLTOAG

a. Enterprise Fund

b. General Fund

c. Capital Projects Fund

d. Special Revenue Fund

e. None of the above

7. To provide for the retirement of general obligation bonds, a city invests a portion of its general revenue receipts in marketable securities. In which fund should the city account for this investment activity?

Debt Service Fund

a. Trust Fund

b. Enterprise Fund

c. Capital Projects Fund

d. Special Revenue Fund

e. None of the above

8. Which fund should be used to account for the operations of a municipal swimming pool receiving the majority of its support from charges to users?

a. Special Revenue Fund

b. General Fund

c. Internal Service Fund

d. Enterprise Fund

e. None of the above

9. A city collects property taxes for the benefit of the local sanitary, park, and school districts (all of which are legally separate governmental units) and periodically remits collections to these units. Which fund is used to account for this activity?

a. Agency Fund

b. General Fund

c. Internal Service Fund

d. Private-Purpose Trust Fund

e. None of the above

10. Bay Creek's municipal motor pool maintains all city-owned vehicles and charges the various departments for the cost of rendering those services. In which of the following funds should Bay Creek account for the cost of such maintenance?

a. General Fund

b. Internal Service Fund

c. Special Revenue Fund

d. Enterprise Fund

e. None of the above

(AICPA adapted)

P2-16 (Financial statements used in governmental accounting)
Indicate which of the following fund financial statements generally would be used by each of the funds listed.

BS   Balance sheet (or statement of net assets)
SRECFB   Statement of revenues, expenditures, and changes in fund balance
SRECFNA   Statement of revenues, expenses, and changes in fund net assets
SCF   Statement of cash flows
SFNA   Statement of fiduciary net assets
SCFNA   Statement of changes in fiduciary net assets

SRECFB-BS   1. General Fund
SRECFB-BS   2. Special Revenue Funds
    "   "   3. Debt Service Funds
   "   "   4. Capital Projects Funds
   "   "   5. Permanent Funds
SRECFNA SCF -BS   6. Enterprise Funds
SRECFNA SCF -BS   7. Internal Service Funds
   SCFNA - SFNA   8. Pension Trust Funds
    "   "   9. Investment Trust Funds
    "   "   10. Private-Purpose Trust Funds
   SFNA   11. Agency Funds

CONTINUOUS PROBLEM

Note: Some of the chapters contain one or more problems as part of a continuing problem. This part of the problem concerns the funds used by Bacchus City to account for its activities. Chapter 3 contains a comprehensive problem on the Bacchus City budget. Problems related to each of the Bacchus City activities are in Chapters 5 through 8.)

Bacchus City is a small city in the southeastern part of the United States. Because of its colorful history and fine restaurants, it is a major tourist destination. It is located on a major river and is vulnerable to flooding in the spring. As a result, it is surrounded by a system of levies. In addition to many fine, old homes, it has a number of parkways connecting various parts of the city. Bacchus City uses separate funds to account for the following activities:

1. The city's day-to-day operating activities
2. Sources of funds and expenditures related to the construction of a new court house
3. Payment of debt service on long-term bonds issued to build the court house
4. A central activity that acquires supplies and sells them to the various city agencies
5. A city-owned utility that buys and sells electricity to its residents

6. A fund that accumulates resources to pay pensions to city employees
7. An activity that invests funds on behalf of two small neighboring cities
8. Administration of a private gift that provides scholarships for underprivileged children residing in the city
9. Disposition of sales taxes collected by the city on behalf of the county where it is located

Required: For each of the activities listed, state (1) the type of fund that Bacchus City will use, (2) the measurement focus and basis of accounting of each fund, and (3) the fund-level financial statements required for each fund.

Chapter 3

The Budgetary Process

After completing this chapter, you should be able to:

➤ *Discuss three types of budgets used by governmental units.*

➤ *Explain why budgets of governmental units are legal documents and describe the contents of a typical budget law.*

➤ *List the steps involved in preparing a budget.*

➤ *Prepare a revenue forecast.*

➤ *Use a trend analysis to project future revenues.*

➤ *Prepare an operating budget for a small governmental unit.*

➤ *Discuss the contents of a budget document.*

➤ *Calculate the millage rate used by a governmental unit.*

➤ *Explain how budgets are used to control operations of governmental units.*

*C*hapter 1 pointed out that commercial organizations are driven by one overriding goal, maximization of profits, whereas governmental units have many goals, all of which are considered important by their supporters and all of which compete for scarce resources. For example, a governmental unit may support police protection at the expense of street maintenance. Or it may determine that it will use available monies to support public housing, even though it needs to fund a program of economic development.

It also pointed out that, whereas commercial organizations are governed by boards of directors and managers who generally hold similar views as to what and how activities should be conducted, governmental units are governed by elected bodies representing diverse constituencies. Thus, by their very nature governmental units are faced ith competing goals and a high level of politicization in the u. f resources. Chaos and allocation of resources by means of poin. power are prevented by the budgetary process.

A *budget* is a formal estimate of the resources that an organization plans to expend for a given purpose over a given period, and the proposed means of acquiring these resources. It informs the reader what activities the organization plans to undertake and how the organization expects to finance these activities; and thus acts as a standard against which efficiency and effectiveness can be measured. It also acts as a representation of public policy in that its adoption implies certain objectives, as well as the means of accomplishing these objectives, as determined by the legislative body. In addition to serving as a framework for operations, the budget often acts as a legal document for certain types of organizations, principally governmental units, as it forms the basis for the appropriations made by the legislative bodies of these organizations.

Even if not required by law, the use of a budget is strongly recommended. The GASB, for example, expresses the need for budgets in the following principles:

a. An annual budget(s) should be adopted by every governmental unit.
b. The accounting system should provide the basis for appropriate budgetary control.
c. Budgetary comparisons should be presented as required supplementary information for the general fund and for each major special revenue fund that has a legally adopted annual budget.[1]

In this chapter we will discuss budget laws, some types of budgets, and the process of preparing a budget.

BUDGET LAWS

States usually have laws governing budgetary activities of local governmental units located within their borders. These laws deal with types of budgets to be prepared, funds required to have budgets, definition of a "balanced" budget, public input into the budgetary process, and means of putting the budget into effect. Table 3-1 contains excerpts from the budget law of the state of Louisiana.

To encourage fiscal responsibility, the Louisiana Local Government Budget Act, like budget laws of nearly all states, requires a balanced budget. In most states a budget is considered to be balanced if proposed expenditures do not exceed estimated monies available for the budget year. This latter amount is the sum of fund balances at the beginning of the year and estimated revenues. A few states take a more conservative approach to balanced budgets and define them as ones in which estimated revenues of the budget year equal or exceed the proposed expenditures of that year.

---

[1] GASB Cod. Sec. 1100.111.

Table 3-1

Excerpts from Louisiana Local Government Budget Act

---

§ 1301 SHORT TITLE

This Chapter may be cited as the "Louisiana Local Government Budget Act."

§ 1304 BUDGET PREPARATION

A. Each political subdivision shall cause to be prepared a comprehensive budget presenting a complete financial plan for the ensuing fiscal year for the general fund and each special revenue fund.

B. The chief executive or administrative officer of the political subdivision or, in the absence of such positions, the equivalent thereof shall prepare the proposed budget.

C. The budget document setting forth the proposed financial plan for the general fund and each special revenue fund shall include the following:

   (1) A budget message signed by the budget preparer which shall include a summary description of the proposed financial plan, policies, and objectives, assumptions, budgetary basis, and a discussion of the most important features.

   (2) A consolidated statement for the general fund, each special revenue fund and any other fund, showing estimated fund balances at the beginning of the year; estimates of all receipts and revenues to be received; revenues itemized by source; recommended expenditures itemized by agency, department, function, and character; and the estimated fund balance at the end of the fiscal year. . . .

D. A budget proposed for consideration by the governing authority shall be accompanied by a proposed budget adoption instrument. . . . The budget adoption instrument for any municipality, parish, school board, or special district shall be an appropriate ordinance, adoption resolution, or other legal instrument necessary to adopt and implement the budget document.

E. The total of proposed expenditures shall not exceed the total of estimated funds available for the ensuing fiscal year.

§ 1306 PUBLIC PARTICIPATION

A. Political subdivisions with total proposed expenditures of two hundred fifty thousand dollars or more from the general fund or any special revenue funds shall afford the public an opportunity to participate in the budgetary process prior to adoption of the budget.

B. Upon completion of the proposed budget and, if applicable, its submission to the governing authority, the political subdivision shall cause to be published a notice stating that the proposed budget is available for public inspection. The notice shall state that a public hearing on the proposed budget shall be held with the date, time, and place of the hearing specified in the notice.

§ 1308 ADOPTION

A. All action necessary to adopt and otherwise finalize and implement the budget for an ensuing fiscal year shall be taken in open meeting and completed prior to the end of the fiscal year in progress. . . .

B. The adopted budget shall be balanced with approved expenditures not exceeding the total of estimated funds available.

C. The adopted budget shall contain the same information as that required for the proposed budget. . . .

(continued)

Table 3-1

Continued

---

§ 1310 BUDGETARY AUTHORITY AND CONTROL

A. . . . The chief executive or administrative officer shall advise the governing authority or independently elected official in writing when:

(1) Revenue collection plus projected revenue collection for the remainder of the year, within a fund, are failing to meet estimated annual budgeted revenues by five percent or more.

(2) Actual expenditures plus projected expenditures for the remainder of the year, within a fund, are exceeding estimated budgeted expenditures by five percent or more.

(3) Actual beginning fund balance, within a fund, fails to meet estimated beginning fund balance by five percent or more and fund balance is being used to fund current year expenditures.

Source: Louisiana Local Government Budget Act R.S. 39:1304, as amended.

Despite these laws, many people believe that balanced budgets are more myth than fact. For example, in some states the chief executive may be required to submit a balanced budget, but the legislative body is not required to adopt a balanced budget. In addition, under many balanced budget laws true "balance" can be avoided by not budgeting for certain expenditures that are attributable to the current period but not required to be paid in cash until subsequent years, such as pensions and post-employment health care benefits.

TYPES OF BUDGETS

Nonbusiness organizations use many different types of budgets. They use short- and long-term operating budgets, capital budgets, and, in many cases, they prepare cash forecasts.

Operating Budgets

Operating budgets (also known as current budgets) are general-purpose budgets used by organizations to formalize their activities of a given period, usually a fiscal year. They include estimates of the resources expected to be available during the year and projections of how these resources will be expended.

For many organizations, the use of an operating budget is required by law. Many cities and states also require that by the beginning of each fiscal year, a balanced budget be approved by their legislative bodies (e.g., city councils, boards of trustees). Even if not required by law, however, every organization should adopt an annual operating budget to control its expenditures.

Operating budgets are generally prepared for each fund used, as well as for the organization as a whole. Revenues are broken down by source, and expenditures are broken down by type and by department, program, or other operating unit. Actual revenues and expenditures are generally shown for 1–2 years prior and, if possible, the current year. In addition, the estimated revenues and proposed expenditures of the budget year are shown.

A budget can provide information on the specific purpose of and services performed by each operating unit. It can also provide information on (1) personnel and salaries, (2) proposed bond issues, (3) proposed methods of reducing costs, and (4) the cost of operating specific facilities and providing specific services. Because the budget is often a widely read legal document, great care should go into its preparation. The organization should use it, along with an annual report, as a means of presenting its "story" to the public, as well as for control purposes.

Capital Budgets

Capital budgets (also known as capital programs) articulate the plans of expenditures, and the means of financing these expected expenditures for long-lived or "capital" assets, such as land, buildings, and equipment. They usually cover a 4- to 6-year period. Many organizations maintain a "running" or "continuous" capital budget, adding a future year and dropping the past year when annual revisions are made. Such budgets are especially helpful when an organization needs to determine when and if it will be necessary to incur debt.

Cash Forecasts

Cash forecasts are plans of the actual monies expected to be received and expended during a particular period. Most governmental units use the modified accrual basis of accounting, so their operating budgets often do not reflect the actual inflows and outflows of cash. In addition, most governmental units receive a large percentage of their revenues in an uneven manner during the year. Because their expenditures are generally spread out evenly over the year, cash shortages often result. Organizations that use cash forecasts can anticipate cash shortages and surpluses before they occur. As a result, these organizations are able to obtain more favorable interest rates than organizations that borrow or invest on a crisis basis. A cash forecast is shown in Table 3-2.

APPROACHES TO BUDGETING

Uses of budgets are many and varied. Budgets can serve as contracts (legal documents), control mechanisms, means of communication, planning tools, and bases for the creation of short- and long-term policies. Depending on their intended usage, they can be prepared under one of several approaches: object-of-expenditure, performance, program and planning-programming budgeting, or zero-based budgeting. Budgets prepared under each approach differ as to what type of information they present and as to how expenditures are aggregated. Today, most departments or agencies within governmental units use the object-of-expenditure approach.

Table 3-2

Sample Cash Forecast

	WOLVERINE CITY GENERAL FUND CASH FORECAST SECOND QUARTER, 2005			
	APRIL	MAY	JUNE	QUARTER
Beginning cash balance	$ 12,000	$ 10,500	$ 16,350	$ 12,000
Cash receipts:				
Property taxes	$ 13,000	$ 28,000	$ 230,500	$ 271,500
Sales taxes	95,000	97,000	96,000	288,000
Fixed asset sales	500	1,000	3,000	4,500
Fines and penalties	15,000	15,000	18,000	48,000
License fees	5,500	3,000	1,600	10,100
Total cash receipts	$ 129,000	$ 144,000	$ 349,100	$ 622,100
Cash available[a]	$ 141,000	$ 154,500	$ 365,450	$ 634,100
Cash disbursements:				
Personal services	$ 56,000	$ 58,000	$ 57,500	$ 171,500
Travel	2,500	4,000	11,000	17,500
Operating expenses	32,000	36,000	35,500	103,500
Equipment	10,000	30,000	25,000	65,000
Transfers to Capital Projects Funds	130,000	—	82,000	212,000
Transfers to Debt Service Funds	—	—	50,000	50,000
Total disbursements	$ 230,500	$ 128,000	$ 261,000	$ 619,500
Minimum cash balance	10,000	10,000	10,000	$ 10,000
Total cash required	$ 240,500	$ 138,000	$ 271,000	$ 629,500
Excess (deficiency) of cash available over cash required	$(99,500)	$ 16,500	$ 94,450	$ 4,600
Financing:				
Tax anticipation notes	$ 100,000	—	—	$ 100,000
Repayment of notes	—	$(10,000)	$ (90,000)	(100,000)
Interest	—	(150)	(800)	(950)
Net financing	$ 100,000	$(10,150)	$(90,800)	$ (950)
Ending cash balance	$ 10,500	$ 16,350	$ 13,650	$ 13,650

[a]Before financing.

The Object-of-Expenditure Approach

Under the *object-of-expenditure approach* (also known as the traditional or line-item approach), budgets are prepared to show, as line items, every category of expenditure to be made during the year. For example, the budget of a state-run university might show each faculty and administrative position by salary, by title, and, in many cases, by the name of the person holding that position, as a line item. Supplies used by a particular department, however, would be shown in their entirety, even though several purchases (and expenditures) might be made during the year.

After review and revision by the chief executive officer (CEO) of the organization, the budget is submitted to the organization's legislative body (e.g., city council, state legislature, board of trustees, and so forth). This body reviews and sometimes revises the budget. After it approves the budget, the legislative body makes line-item appropriations, which are incorporated into the organization's accounts.

Performance or program data may be included with an object-of-expenditure-type budget. Such data, however, are used only to support or supplement the various requests for funding. A portion of an object-of-expenditure budget is shown in Table 3-3.

Among the advantages of the object-of-expenditure approach to budgeting are the following:

1. The budgets are uncomplicated and can easily be prepared.
2. Not only the preparers but also the users can understand the budgets.
3. Information presented in this type of budget can easily be incorporated into the accounting system.
4. Detailed comparisons between budgeted and actual revenues and expenditures can easily be made.

Critics of this approach, however, cite the following points:

1. It provides data useful primarily in the short run. As a result, the long-run goals of the organization may be jeopardized.
2. It is oriented more toward providing a framework for sets of financial records that comply with legal requirements than with providing useful management-type information.
3. It encourages, rather than discourages, spending. Managers are led to believe that an important objective is to spend exactly the amount budgeted and that if this amount is not spent, the following year's appropriation will be cut. As a result, it offers little incentive for them to economize.
4. Legislative bodies are given more detail than they can handle. Therefore, they tend to focus on individual items (such as the amount of supplies needed) rather than on the overall goals and programs of the organization.

Even though it is subject to these deficiencies, the object-of-expenditure approach to budgeting is the one most commonly used by nonbusiness organizations. Because of its popularity, it will be the focus of the remainder of this chapter.

PREPARING A BUDGET

The preparation of a budget, although difficult at first, becomes easier with practice. After a while, it just becomes a matter of "doing it." It can, however, be time-consuming.

The budgetary process can best be thought of as a continuous cycle, wherein evaluation of this year's performance significantly influences next year's budget.

Table 3-3
Sample Object-of-Expenditure Budget

ORLEANS LEVEE BOARD
FY 20X5 BUDGET PRESENTATION
AIRPORT SAFETY

ACCT. #	ACCOUNT NAME	PREVIOUS ACTUAL FY 20X3	APPROVED BUDGET FY 20X4	PROPOSED FY 20X5
5410	Office supplies	$ 345	$ 1,572	$ 500
5411	Copier supplies	0	0	0
5412	Computer supplies	0	0	0
5431	Janitorial supplies	130	562	262
5432	Medical supplies	0	750	50
5433	Safety apparel and supplies	5,158	0	5,295
5434	Clothing supplies	8,129	10,875	10,000
5435	Police supplies	1,227	5,050	2,000
5436	Fire-fighting supplies	4,507	9,980	6,000
5437	Sodding/herbicides/fertilizer	0	0	0
5440	Improvements—other than buildings	0	0	0
5441	Hardware supplies	210	1,044	300
5442	Mounted patrol	0	0	0
5443	Dive team supplies	0	0	0
5451	Boat/motor/trailer—GOS	0	0	0
5452	Autos/trucks—GOS	8,447	7,706	9,000
5453	Tractors and grass cutters	120	0	0
5461	Buildings	36	0	0
5471	Airfield/runways/taxiway	0	0	0
5472	Bridges/floodgate/floodwall	0	0	0
5473	Grounds	0	0	0
5474	Levees	0	0	0
5475	Emergency supplies	0	0	0
5476	Fountain and pool supplies	0	0	0
5477	Piers, catwalks, bulkheads	0	0	0
5481	Miscellaneous equipment	0	0	0
5482	Autos (parts)	1,809	1,808	1,900
5483	Boats, motors, trailers	49	0	0
5484	Heavy construction equipment	0	0	0
5485	Office equipment—furniture	0	0	0
5486	Police	0	0	0
5487	Radio communications	194	0	0
5488	Recreational	0	0	0
5489	Tractors and grass cutters	0	0	0
5490	Trucks and trailers	0	0	0
5491	Hand tools and minor equipment	273	0	0
	Total material and supplies	$30,634	$39,347	$35,307

Source: A recent budget of the Orleans Levee Board.

The process itself can be broken down into the following steps, the order of which may vary among organizations:

1. Prepare budgetary policy guidelines.
2. Prepare a budget calendar.
3. Prepare and distribute budget instructions.
4. Prepare revenue estimates.
5. Prepare departmental (or program) expenditure requests:
   a. Personal services work sheet
   b. Travel work sheet
   c. Operating expense work sheet
   d. Equipment work sheet
6. Prepare nondepartmental expenditure and interfund transfer requests.
7. Prepare a capital outlay request summary (if appropriate).
8. Consolidate departmental expenditure requests, nondepartmental expenditure and interfund transfer requests, capital outlay requests and revenue estimates. Submit to the CEO for review and revision.
9. Prepare the budget document.
10. Present the budget document to the legislative body.
11. Record the approved budget in the accounts.
12. Determine the property tax (millage) rate.

Budgetary Policy Guidelines

Before considering the various segments involved in the budgetary process, the CEO, the budget officer, or both should discuss, with members of the legislative body, what policies will be followed when preparing the budget. During these discussions, fiscal conditions of the current year should be reviewed, along with the prospects for the following year. In addition, the following points need to be considered:

1. The level of revenues collected, to date, during the current year, and the level of revenues likely to be collected during the remainder of the year
2. Possible increases or decreases in current taxes and fees, and ideas for new taxes and fees
3. Current and future economic conditions, as well as any possible developments that might affect the revenues or expenditures of the following year (e.g., a plant closing or the loss of federal funds)
4. Items that fall due the following fiscal year and might require an unusually large expenditure, such as the repayment of a bond issue
5. The status of the current year's expenditures and the possibility of a surplus (or deficit)

An analysis of these issues will provide insight into the financial problems an organization is likely to face during the following year. From the discussions of these issues, budgetary policies satisfactory to the legislative body, the CEO, and other affected parties should emerge. These policies should cover, at a minimum, the following:

1. Permissible merit salary increases
2. Permissible cost-of-living adjustments
3. Inflationary adjustments to be used
4. Permissible increases or decreases in taxes and fees
5. Changes in capital spending
6. Types of programs and services to be emphasized and deemphasized

The budgetary policies should be disseminated, in the form of *budgetary policy guidelines,* to all persons responsible for preparing and reviewing the various segments of the budget.

Budget Calendar

In order for the budgetary process to proceed in an organized manner, certain deadlines must be met. If each person involved in this process is aware of when his or her part is due and if the time allotted to each task is reasonable, the process should take place smoothly with misunderstandings kept to a minimum. One way to ensure that each person knows when his or her (and everyone else's) part of the budgetary process is due is to prepare a budget calendar.

A budget calendar formalizes all key dates in the budgetary process. The calendar itself can be a simple listing of dates or it can be in the form of a complex flow chart. At a minimum, it should list the steps of the budgetary process and the dates on which each of the various steps should be finished. More elaborate calendars often list who is responsible for each step and what data must be provided by whom and to whom. A sample budget calendar is shown in Table 3-4.

Budget Instructions

To disseminate the budgetary policy guidelines and to assist the various subunits in the preparation of their expenditure requests, a set of budget instructions should be prepared and sent to each person responsible for a segment of the budget. These instructions should be distributed early enough to provide these persons sufficient time to prepare their budget requests in a thoughtful, orderly manner.

In addition to copies of the forms and work sheets to be used, the budget instructions should contain the following:

1. A budget calendar
2. A copy of the budgetary policy guidelines
3. A statement summarizing the organization's anticipated fiscal condition for the following year
4. A statement of specific policies to be followed when preparing expenditure requests

Table 3-4

Typical Budget Calendar

July 6	Departments receive instructions for the preparation of the budget.
August 15	Departmental expenditure requests are returned to the budget officer.
September 6–21	Departmental hearings are held with the mayor.
October 1–8	Review and preliminary presentation is made to the city council.
October 9–31	Budget is reviewed and finalized by the mayor.
November 5–18	Budget printing and production take place.
November 20	Mayor formally presents the budget to the city council.
November 21–December 15	City council conducts public hearings.
December 18	City council formally votes on the budget.
December 20–30	Budgetary information is entered into the computer.
January 1	New fiscal year begins.

5. A set of inflationary guidelines to be used in estimating the future costs of equipment, supplies, and so on
6. Specific instructions on how each form and work sheet should be completed
7. Instructions on where to seek help and clarification of any ambiguities that might arise

Revenue Estimates

A key part of the budgetary process is determining how much money the organization will have available for spending the next year. This amount consists of (1) the surplus or deficit (fund balance) carried forward into the budget year, and (2) the revenues expected to be collected during the budget year.

The process of determining how much money the organization will have available for spending the next year consists of the following steps:

1. Determine current-year revenues and the probable balance in each fund at the end of the current year.
2. Project revenues expected to be collected during the budget year:
   a. Determine revenues or revenue bases for several prior years and the current year.
   b. Apply a trend analysis to these data to obtain a preliminary estimate of revenues or revenue bases of budget year.
   c. Adjust preliminary estimates of revenues or revenue bases for factors likely to affect them, such as condition of the local economy, special events, changes in tax rates, and changes in level of support from outside sources.

d. If working with revenue bases, multiply by appropriate tax rates, license fees, and so on.

   e. Determine transfers expected from other funds.

3. Prepare a statement of actual and estimated revenues (and transfers-in), such as the one illustrated in Table 3-5.

Current-Year Revenues and Surpluses (Deficits)

A surplus can reduce the amount of revenue that must be raised to finance a given level of expenditures. A deficit, however, is likely to increase the amount of revenue that must be raised, because most state and local governmental units and not-for-profit organizations are either reluctant or unable to carry deficits forward from year to year.

To determine the amount of surplus or deficit to be carried forward, a projection must be made of the total revenues and expenditures that will be incurred during the current year. A separate projection should be made for each fund used (e.g., General Fund, Special Revenue Fund, and so on).

Current-year revenues are projected by

1. Comparing collections to date with budgeted and prior-year collections
2. Determining the causes of any significant differences found in step 1
3. Determining any factors that might affect the revenues of the remainder of the year (e.g., the effect that closing a major department store will have on sales tax collections during the year)
4. Projecting the revenue collections for the remainder of the year on the basis of information gathered in the preceding steps (by means of a combination of trend analysis, economic projections, and intuition)

Projecting current-year revenues becomes easier as the year passes. As a result, many organizations delay this process as long as possible. Such delays, however, increase the difficulty of realistically budgeting the following year's expenditures, because the persons preparing such estimates have no solid information on how much money will be available.

One solution to this problem is the preparation of tentative revenue estimates early in the budgetary process, deliberately erring on the side of conservatism. As better information becomes available, the current-year revenue estimates can be updated. Another approach is to use three levels of estimates—optimistic, probable, and pessimistic—and to ask the subunits to prepare three levels of expenditure requests. This approach, though providing flexibility, requires significantly more effort on the part of all concerned and can lead to misunderstandings and credibility gaps.

The methods used to project revenues vary from source to source. Property taxes are generally easy to project for the remainder of the year because they have already been levied and are secured by the property being taxed. In addition, most governmental units set up an allowance for uncollectibles early in the year, and patterns of collection usually remain constant from year to year. Unless some major event takes place (or is expected to), property tax collections can be assumed to follow prior-year patterns of activity.

Collections of other taxes, license fees, fines, and fees for services are more difficult to project. The best approach to predicting these sources of revenue is to apply a trend analysis to the prior-year collections and to temper the result with knowledge

Table 3-5

Statement of Actual and Estimated Revenues (and Transfers-In)

FUND: General

DATE: September 15, 2004

PREPARED BY: PNW

APPROVED BY: LVT

ACCT. #	SOURCE	2003 ACTUAL	JAN.–AUG. 2004 ACTUAL	SEPT.–DEC. 2004 EST. ACT.	TOTAL 2004 EST. ACT.	2004 BUDGET	2005 BUDGET	REMARKS
1110	Property tax	$3,246,575	$1,384,300	$1,940,700	$3,325,000	$3,325,000	$3,550,000	Reassessment of property
1112	Liquor tax	355,240	235,650	124,350	360,000	354,000	480,000	International Exposition
1114	Sales tax	1,864,680	1,252,840	857,160	2,110,000	2,200,000	2,650,000	Same as above
1116	Royalty payments	385,000	245,000	120,000	365,000	375,000	300,000	Decline in gas production
1119	Fines and penalties	84,610	63,450	30,000	93,450	92,000	100,000	International Exposition
1121	Rental charges	8,500	6,500	3,500	10,000	9,500	11,000	Same as above
	Subtotal	$5,944,605	$3,187,740	$3,075,710	$6,263,450	$6,355,500	$7,091,000	
2010	Transfer from Enterprise Fund	122,000	—	145,000	145,000	145,000	150,000	Major sporting events
	Total	$6,066,605	$3,187,740	$3,220,710	$6,408,450	$6,500,500	$7,241,000	

of current and future events (such as closing a large factory, a change in tax rates, or an increase in the legal drinking age).

The best way to project total current-year expenditures is to determine, on an item-by-item basis, whether the expenditures incurred to date are above or below the budgeted level and at what rate the various subunits will continue to spend. Because budgets usually show only annual dollar amounts, it is often necessary to assume a constant rate of spending and to project the year-to-date expenditures forward at this rate. The budget officer should also discuss the current year's spending with the director or manager of each subunit to determine the existence of any factors that might increase or decrease the rate of spending for the remainder of the year. This task can be simplified if each subunit produces periodic reports comparing budgeted and actual expenditures, such as the ones described at the end of this chapter.

The process of projecting annual expenditures is simplified in organizations that have rules against, or operate in jurisdictions that have laws against, overspending their budgets. In these organizations, the budget officer can usually assume that the amount budgeted is the amount that will be spent.

Central budget offices (those directly responsible to the mayor, governor, or county executive, for example) tend to maintain close control over the spending rate of individual departments or agencies. These controls help them to react promptly to revenue shortfalls or unforeseen budgetary demands. Expenditure control practices include the following:

- The use of quarterly allotments so that amounts appropriated are not fully spent early in the year (See Chapter 5 for a discussion of allotments.)
- Requiring agencies to seek approval to fill personnel vacancies
- Monitoring the placement of purchase orders all year so that purchases can be curtailed toward the end of the year, if necessary

After the current year's projected revenues and expenditures have been determined, the surplus or deficit to be carried to the next year can be calculated as follows:

> Prior-year surplus (deficit)
> Plus: Estimated current-year revenues
> Less: Estimated current-year expenditures

To illustrate, assume that at the end of the prior year the General Fund of a city had a surplus of $500,000. The budget officer of this city determines that the total revenues of the current year, recorded in this fund, will amount to $8 million and that the total expenditures will amount to $8.2 million. The projected surplus in this fund for the current year is calculated as follows:

	Prior-year surplus	$ 500,000
Plus:	Projected revenues	8,000,000
Less:	Projected expenditures	(8,200,000)
	Projected surplus	$ 300,000

The handling of surpluses varies among governmental units. Some governmental units try to build up and maintain a reasonable surplus to act as a "budgetary cushion" against future revenue shortfalls or emergency expenditure needs, and to improve their credit rating in anticipation of borrowing to finance capital needs. Others feel free (or are required by law) to spend their surpluses the following year. The policy to be followed in the treatment of surpluses should be made clear by law or by the legislative body of the organization.

Budget-Year Revenue Projections

When projecting the revenues of the budget year, each source should be considered separately. Revenue sources consist of two components:

1. A *revenue base:* The underlying source on which the revenues are based (e.g., property values, retail sales, number of parking tickets, number of admissions to municipal swimming pool, number of memberships, and so on)
2. A *revenue rate:* The percentage of the value of the revenue base that, by law or prior agreement, is transferred to the organization or the revenue per unit of service (e.g., New Orleans has a 4 percent city sales tax; therefore, an amount equivalent to 4 percent of the retail sales that take place there will eventually be transmitted to the city)

The amount of revenue collected is the product of the revenue base and the revenue rate:

$$\text{Revenues Collected} = \text{Revenue Base} \times \text{Revenue Rate}$$

To illustrate: Assume that the budget officer of a city estimates that the retail sales of the following year will amount to $10 million and that the city taxes retail sales at the rate of 3 percent. The estimated revenues from sales taxes will be

$$\$10,000,000 \times .03 = \$300,000$$

This analysis should be performed on all taxes, fees, and other revenues. For some types of revenues, the analysis can be fairly simple. For example, the tax assessor can generally supply information on the assessed value of all real property in the jurisdiction. The estimated property taxes can then be determined by multiplying the valuation provided by the tax assessor by the estimated millage (tax) rate.

Other revenues are more difficult to predict, because they are controlled by such factors as the national economy and the fortunes of a local industry. For example, a source of revenue for one tourist-oriented city is a hotel occupancy tax. Many of the people who visit this city are from the Midwest, a region whose economy is heavily dependent on the automotive and steel industries. A downturn in the level of activity of these industries results in fewer people visiting the city, fewer hotel bookings, and lower revenues from the hotel occupancy tax (as well as from the sales and amusement taxes). Thus, when forecasting revenues from "tourist-oriented" sources, the budget officer of this city must consider the condition of the economies of the various regions (and nations) from which visitors are drawn. The following factors must also be considered when projecting revenues:

1. *Local economic conditions* can be influenced by the projected activity of local industries as well as national and, in many cases, worldwide economic conditions. Measures of these conditions are found in the various business and commodity price indices and in locally generated statistics, such as housing starts,

school enrollments, sales tax collections, population trends, and trends in building permits.

2. *Special events* take place in a particular year; for example, a city might host an international exhibition. Such an event would attract an unusually large number of tourists, which would significantly increase revenues from various tourist-oriented sources.

3. *Legal factors* include changes in tax rates, the addition or deletion of fees and taxes, possible reassessments of real property, and changes in taxes and fees mandated by the courts or higher governmental units.

4. *Internal or administrative factors* are numerous, including examples such as opening a self-financing facility or the receipt of federal funds, the amount of which is based on the level of a particular activity.

When gathering information, outside sources should be used extensively but not exclusively. Groups such as the League of Women Voters and the Chamber of Commerce devote a great deal of time and effort to gathering information relevant to the operation of governmental and other not-for-profit organizations. This information can prove especially useful. It should be remembered, however, that the preparers of this information are often lobbying organizations. Persons using this information should therefore be alert for possible biases.

Certain types of revenues, such as fines and sales taxes, may be projected by using past trends. A tool commonly used to make such projections is *trend analysis*. Trend analysis can be used to estimate future revenues from any source that increases (or decreases) at a reasonably steady pace. To perform a trend analysis, data for the past 5 years or longer should be assembled, along with an estimate for the current year. The revenue base rather than the level of collections should be measured, because tax rates, the levels of fines, and so forth, tend to rise over a period of time, adding an extra variable. Determining the following year's revenue base and multiplying by the expected rates provides more accurate projections.

After the data are assembled, a trend analysis involves the following steps:

1. Determine year-to-year changes in the revenue base for each of the prior years.
2. Determine the average rate of change over the period.
3. Multiply the average rate of change (plus 100 percent) by the estimated revenue base of the current year to obtain the unadjusted projected revenue base.
4. Adjust the unadjusted projected revenue base for known factors that may cause a deviation from past patterns of behavior to obtain the adjusted projected revenue base.
5. Multiply the adjusted projected revenue base by the appropriate tax rate, license fee, level of average fine, and so on to obtain the projected revenues.

To illustrate, assume that a city wishes to project revenues from a tax on hotel occupancy. The tax rate for the budget year 2005 is expected to be 5 percent of the price paid for each room. The number of people visiting the city has been growing at a fairly steady rate, as have the room rates. Hotel occupancy rates have averaged about 80 percent. In the budget year, however, the city will host an international exposition. The local Chamber of Commerce estimates that hotel occupancy rates will average 96 percent that year. Due to the construction of several new hotels, the number of rooms available will rise by 10 percent, all of which will be available at the beginning of the year. Room rates, however, will rise at only about the same rate that they have in the past, due to the increased competition brought about by the new hotels.

Room occupancy revenues reported by the hotels in this city over the past 5 years are as follows (in millions of dollars):

1999	$1.2
2000	1.4
2001	1.7
2002	2.1
2003	2.5
2004	3.0 (est.)

To project the revenues from the hotel occupancy tax for the budget year, the following steps are performed:

1. Determine year-to-year changes in the revenue base for each of the prior years:

$$2000/1999 = 1.4/1.2 = 1.167 - 1.000 = \underline{\underline{16.7\%}}$$
$$2001/2000 = 1.7/1.4 = 1.214 - 1.000 = \underline{\underline{21.4\%}}$$
$$2002/2001 = 2.1/1.7 = 1.235 - 1.000 = \underline{\underline{23.5\%}}$$
$$2003/2002 = 2.5/2.1 = 1.190 - 1.000 = \underline{\underline{19.0\%}}$$
$$2004/2003 = 3.0/2.5 = 1.200 - 1.000 = \underline{\underline{20.0\%}}$$

2. Determine the average rate of change over the period. Because we are working with estimates, a simple arithmetic average will suffice:

```
  16.7%
  21.4
  23.5
  19.0
  20.0
100.6%/5 = 20.1%
```
= Average Rate of Change over Period

3. Multiply the average rate of change (plus 100 percent) by the estimated revenue base of the current year:

$$120.1\% \times \$3.0 = \underline{\$3,603,000}$$

= *Unadjusted* Projected 2005 Revenue Base

4. Adjust the unadjusted projected revenue base for known factors that may cause a deviation from past patterns of behavior. In this problem, the occupancy rate is expected to rise from 80 percent to 96 percent during the budget year because of the international exposition. In addition, the number of available hotel rooms is expected to increase by 10 percent, all of which will be available at the beginning of the year:

a. Percentage increase in occupancy rate = $96\%/80\% = 1.20 - 1.00 = 20\%$

b. Percentage increase in hotel rooms = 10%

$$\$3,603,000 \times 120\% \times 110\% = \underline{\$4,755,960}$$
$$= \textit{Adjusted} \text{ Projected 2005 Revenue Base}$$

Do not try to multiply the unadjusted projected 2005 revenue base by 130 percent, because each of the preceding factors is independent of the other. For example, even if no new rooms were added, the base would rise by 20 percent due to the increase in the occupancy rate. If the occupancy rate were to remain constant, the base would rise by 10 percent because of the new rooms.

5. Multiply the adjusted projected 2005 revenue base by the projected tax rate (5%):

$$\$4,755,960 \times 5\% = \underline{\$237,800} \text{ (rounded)} = \text{projected 2005 revenue}$$

Thus, the revenue from the hotel occupancy tax for 2005 can be budgeted at $237,800.

When dealing with estimates it is best to use simple, rounded figures to avoid falling into the garbage in–garbage out (GIGO) trap. This problem occurs when rough estimates are multiplied by various factors and odd numbers result. Regrettably, many people tend to assume that if a number is carried out to pennies or to several decimal places it must be correct, regardless of its source.

Revenues from grants and other financial assistance must be handled separately. These revenues are usually received from other governmental units and are known collectively as *intergovernmental revenues.* According to the Governmental Accounting Standards Board (GASB), grants and other financial assistance are "transactions in which one governmental entity transfers cash or other items of value to (or incurs a liability for) another governmental entity, an individual, or an organization as a means of sharing program costs, subsidizing other governments or entities, or otherwise reallocating resources to the recipients."[2]

The difficulty of projecting intergovernmental revenues varies by type of revenue. Revenues based on formula distributions of state revenues, such as sales taxes, are fairly easy to predict. Federal grants can usually be predicted for the current year with a degree of certainty because the federal fiscal year starts October 1, before completion of state and local budgetary processes. Budgeting for state grants, however, may cause problems for local governmental units because of budgetary timing problems. Potential cutbacks in grants from higher-level governmental units can also cause problems.

After the projected revenues have been determined, they should be recorded on a statement of actual and estimated revenues (and transfers-in). This statement is also known as a revenue summary. It is used to present the estimated revenues of the budget year and to compare these estimated revenues with the actual revenues of prior years and, as far as possible, the current year. It can also be used to present transfers expected to be received from other funds. When preparing a statement of actual and estimated revenues (and transfers-in), it is advisable to include an explanation of the assumptions made and the methods used to derive the estimates shown. Such a statement is shown in Table 3-5 (page 75). This particular summary is

---

[2] GASB, Cod., Sec. N50.504.

a simplified one and is applicable to a small city. The statements of large organizations, however, are similar. They just contain more detailed information.

Departmental Expenditure Requests

Expenditure requests should be prepared by each department, program, or other subunit of the organization. These documents show the expenditures of the prior year, the total estimated expenditures of the current year, and the proposed level of expenditures of the budget year. Detailed supporting statements for each major object of expenditure should accompany these requests. Such work sheets can be used to answer questions that may be raised by the budget officer, the CEO, or the legislative body. They can also be used to justify both new and continuing expenditures.

Expenditure requests serve a number of purposes. First, they enable the CEO and the legislative body to evaluate the performance of each subunit. (This same function, of course, can also be performed by quarterly or monthly budget comparisons, which will be discussed later.) They also enable persons making budgetary decisions to determine the propriety of each request in terms of the goals of the entire organization, as opposed to the individual subunits; and when resources are limited, they enable these persons to allocate resources to those activities of each subunit that best serve the organization as a whole.

Finally, expenditure requests force department heads and other managers, at least once a year, to take a close look at the objectives and the current levels of activity of their subunits and to determine whether more efficient methods can be developed to meet these objectives. If these persons wish to expand the scope of the activities of their subunits, they must be able to justify the additional expenditures necessary and to disclose the impact on the organization, as a whole, of disallowing the additional expenditures.

The following series of steps should be applied to each expenditure when preparing departmental expenditure requests:

1. Determine the level of the expenditure for the past year and project the level of the expenditure for the current year.
2. Apply inflation and cost-of-living factors and other allowances for "uncontrollable" factors to each current-year expenditure. This will result in a "stand-still" expenditure request.
3. Determine what activities should be expanded, contracted, or discontinued. Identify any new activities that, if funded, will commence the following year.
4. Adjust each proposed expenditure for the changes in the type and level of activities determined and identified in step 3.
5. Prepare a justification for each new activity or each increase in the level of an existing activity. Include in this justification the effect that not adopting, or increasing the level of, the activity will have on the organization.
6. Prepare a *budgetary work sheet* for each type of expenditure. The formats of the work sheets will vary with the type of expenditure being projected, although each work sheet should show the prior-year, current-year, and projected budget-year level of expenditures for each line item (object-of-expenditure).
7. Summarize the information from each work sheet on the expenditure request.

Departmental or program expenditures are generally broken into three categories: personal services, operating expenses, and equipment.

Personal Services

The heart of a personal services budget is the *position classification plan*. This document lists all the position titles and their corresponding salaries. From it, past and current personnel costs can be identified. The positions expected to be occupied during the budget year should be recorded on the budgetary work sheet, along with the past, current, and projected rate or salary attached to each position.

Employee (fringe) benefits should be treated as a separate item, although they can be combined with salaries and wages on the budgetary work sheet. The best approach to handling this item of cost is to determine the total expenditures for the prior year or the current year to date, and to divide this amount by the total payroll, to obtain the *employee benefit cost per payroll dollar*. This ratio can then be used when determining the full cost of new positions or existing positions at new salary levels.

Employee benefits (Social Security, vacation pay, sick pay, and so on) are generally a function of salaries, so this method usually provides accurate data. However, the cost of certain benefits, such as paid dental insurance, may be fixed; that is, it may be the same for all employees regardless of salary level. Generally speaking, however, the cost of such benefits is a relatively small part of the total employee benefit cost. In addition, it tends to average out, and because the budget is based on estimates, the cost of "fixed" benefits does not usually create any serious problems.

One final note: When budgeting employee benefits, be sure to apply the budget year's rates. Unemployment insurance and FICA (Social Security) rates, in particular, tend to change frequently.

Other personal service costs that must be considered are overtime, shift differentials, and requests for temporary help. For example, on certain holidays it is sometimes necessary to ask police officers to work overtime to handle the crowds of parade watchers. In addition, some cities hire students to perform special tasks, such as street repairs, during the summer. These costs are usually known well in advance and can easily be determined by multiplying projected hours by appropriate pay and fringe benefit rates.

Compensation for members of the legislative body must also be included in the personal services section of the budget request. These people are paid either a fixed salary per year or a certain stipend for each meeting attended. In the latter case, their compensation can be estimated by multiplying the number of meetings expected to be held (a number often set by law) by a fixed rate per meeting.

In many organizations, a *salary-vacancy factor (SVF)* is used to fine-tune the expected cost of personal services. A SVF represents the portion of the budgeted salaries that is not expected to be spent because of a delay in hiring personnel or because vacancies will be filled at lower-than-budgeted salaries. This factor can be estimated by looking at past experience and future hiring policies. If a hiring freeze is expected to be in effect during the budget year, the SVF can be significant.

A personal services (budgetary) work sheet is shown in Table 3-6. Notice that it includes prior- and current-year data, as well as adjustments for cost-of-living and changes in fringe benefit rates. Note also that it gives a brief justification for the

Table 3-6
Personal Services Work Sheet

Fund: General
Function: Public Safety
Department: Police

CODE	POSITION TITLE	PRIOR-YEAR ACTUAL			CURRENT-YEAR EST. ACTUAL			BUDGET REQUEST[b]			REMARKS
		No.	Rate[a]	Amount	No.	Rate[a]	Amount	No.	Rate[a]	Amount	
101	Chief	1	$51,300	$ 51,300	1	$54,000	$ 54,000	1	$59,474	$ 59,474	
102	Captain	2	44,888	89,775	2	47,250	94,500	2	52,324	104,648	
104	Lieutenant	4	38,475	153,900	4	40,500	162,000	4	42,903	171,612	
105	Detective	2	32,063	64,125	2	33,750	67,500	2	35,753	71,506	
106	Sergeant	5	29,925	149,625	5	31,500	157,500	5	33,369	166,845	
108	Police Officer	12	25,650	307,800	12	27,000	324,000	14	28,602	400,428	Two new positions[c]
	Total	26		$816,525	26		$859,500	28		$974,513	

[a]Includes employee benefits, which are budgeted at 13.5% of salaries and wages. This rate is 1% higher than the current rate because of an expected increase in the FICA rate (6%) and the state unemployment rate (.4%). The prior-year rate is 11.1% of salaries and wages. Actual salaries for the current year are expected to equal the amount budgeted.

[b]Includes a cost-of-living factor of 5.0% plus an additional merit increase of $2,000 each for the chief and captains.

[c]*Justification for new positions:* In the latter part of the current year, an area of 4 square miles was annexed. To provide an adequate level of protection in this area and the original parts of the city, an additional patrol unit is necessary. If this additional unit is denied, the annexed area containing 562 residents will receive inadequate police protection or the entire city will receive a lower level of protection due to the overextending of available personnel and equipment. In either case the level of crime can be expected to rise significantly if the additional unit is not approved.

expansion of the level of service. The total of the personal services expenditures is transferred to the departmental expenditure request (shown in Table 3-11, page 88). To assist in the preparation of their personal services work sheets, many governmental units prepare a salary work sheet, one of which is shown in Table 3-7.

Operating Expenditures

Operating expenditures are those outlays necessary in carrying out the organization's routine operations. Examples of such expenditures are postage, office supplies, utilities, printing, reproduction, professional services, employee travel, fuel, and vehicle maintenance. If the scope of the organization's operations does not change, the level of these expenditures can be estimated by using the current year's level plus an inflation factor.

When budgeting operating expenditures, each item should be questioned in order to determine whether it is necessary and, if so, whether its usage can be reduced. For example, can fuel be saved by replacing the existing police cruisers with more fuel-efficient models?

In the budgetary work sheet, the prior- and current-year outlays should be listed for each object of expenditure, along with the budget request. As with personal services, the inflation factor used should be shown. In addition, a justification should be made for any new items or any item whose usage is expected to increase significantly.

Travel

All employee travel should be shown on a separate work sheet that lists the name of the person traveling and the date, destination, purpose, and estimated cost of each trip. Many organizations also show employee travel as a separate item on their departmental expenditure requests. A sample operating expenditure worksheet is shown in Table 3-8. A sample travel work sheet is shown in Table 3-9.

Table 3-7

Salary Work Sheet

Fund: General					Prepared by ___PW___		
Function: Public Safety					Approved by ___PRT___		
Department: Police					Date: September 10, 2004		

CODE	POSITION TITLE	2004 BASE	COST-OF-LIVING ADJ.[a]	MERIT	2005 BASE	FRINGE BENEFITS[b]	BUDGET REQUEST
101	Chief	$48,000	$2,400	$2,000	$52,400	$7,074	$59,474
102	Captain	42,000	2,100	2,000	46,100	6,224	52,324
104	Lieutenant	36,000	1,800	—	37,800	5,103	42,903
105	Detective	30,000	1,500	—	31,500	4,253	35,753
106	Sergeant	28,000	1,400	—	29,400	3,969	33,369
108	Police Officer	24,000	1,200	—	25,200	3,402	28,602

[a]Cost of living adjustment is 5.0% of 2004 base.
[b]Fringe benefits are expected to average 13.5% of wages and salaries in 2005.

Table 3-8

Operating Expenditure Work Sheet[a]

Fund:	General				Prepared by	WPE
Function:	Public Safety				Approved by	PRT
Department: Police					Date: September 15, 2004	

CODE	OBJECT	PRIOR-YEAR ACTUAL	CURRENT-YEAR BUDGET	CURRENT-YEAR EST. ACTUAL	BUDGET REQUEST[b]	REMARKS
	Contractual Services					
301	Advertising	$ 110	$ 100	$ 85	$ 100	
310	Printing	1,500	1,600	1,650	1,800	
320	Vehicle maintenance	7,500	8,000	8,000	8,400	Improved radio system
330	Communication	6,000	5,600	6,000	6,200	
350	Dues and subscriptions	180	200	200	200	
360	Postage	280	300	325	350	
370	Telephone	580	600	750	600	Staff training, medical
380	Professional services	425	400	450	500	
	Subtotal	$16,575	$16,800	$17,460	$18,150	
	Supplies and Materials					
401	Office supplies	$ 1,200	$ 1,100	$ 1,150	$ 1,200	
410	Building maintenance	4,500	4,700	4,800	5,000	
420	Fuel	10,135	10,500	10,250	12,000	Extra patrol unit
430	Ground maintenance	975	1,000	950	1,000	
440	Reproduction	1,250	1,400	1,420	1,500	
450	Uniform allowances	175	400	250	800	New personnel
460	Security supplies	1,010	1,200	1,235	1,300	New personnel
490	Miscellaneous	450	400	350	500	
	Grand total	$60,500	$61,600	$61,450	$62,350	

[a]Employee travel is reported separately.
[b]An inflation factor of 4.5% is used where applicable

Equipment

The *equipment* category includes items that normally last more than 1 year and cost more than a predetermined dollar amount (e.g., $100). Items not meeting both criteria should be classified as operating expenditures. Typical items of equipment are furniture, typewriters, police cruisers, and lawn mowers.

Many organizations include purchases of equipment in their capital budget. Other organizations use their capital budgets to record only construction of buildings, streets, bridges, and so forth.

The work sheet used when budgeting expenditures for equipment should contain a description of each item of equipment requested and should state whether

Table 3-9

Travel Work Sheet

Fund:	General			Prepared by ____BNE____
Function:	Public Safety			Approved by ____PRT____
Department: Police				Date: September 15, 2004

NAME AND/OR POSITION	DATES OF TRAVEL	DESTINATION	PURPOSE OF TRAVEL	BUDGET REQUEST[a]
T. Ryan, Chief	3/1–3/3	Gulfport	Supervisory training	$ 500
L. Paradise, Detective	4/11–4/12	Las Vegas	Technical training	1,200
W. Pike, Captain	7/22	Local	Sensitivity training	100
L. Paradise, Detective	8/15	Local	Report-writing training	50
E. Johnson, Lieutenant	9/18	Seattle	Technical training	1,100
T. Ryan, Chief	11/15–11/18	Orlando	Professional meetings	800
W. Pike, Captain	11/15–11/18	Orlando	Professional meetings	800
R. Mankin, Lieutenant	11/15–11/18	Orlando	Professional meetings	800
Total requested				$5,350

[a]Includes conference fees or tuition, airfare, lodging, and a per diem allowance at locally authorized rates.

each item is an addition or a replacement for an existing item. The work sheet should also indicate the number of items of each type requested and cost per item. Finally, the work sheet should contain a justification for all additional items of equipment requested. An equipment work sheet is shown in Table 3-10.

Capital Outlays

The term *capital outlays* is used to describe the cost of major building and renovation projects undertaken by the organization. These activities include new construction as well as major repairs, alterations to and expansion of various facilities, such as buildings, roads, parks, bridges, airports, and levees. Capital projects can be performed by outside contractors or by organizational personnel. In many cases these projects are partially funded by state and federal grants. They can also be funded by the proceeds of bond issues.

Many organizations prepare capital budgets, which are approved separately from their operating budgets. Other organizations include capital projects in their operating budgets, treating their capital outlays in the same manner as other expenditures. In this text we will assume the former approach and will discuss capital outlay requests in Chapter 6.

One question that often arises is whether costly items, such as fire engines and paving machinery, should be placed in the capital budget or in the operating budget. The authors of this text believe that items of a routine nature, such as police cruisers, should be included in the operating budget, regardless of cost, and that the capital budget should be used exclusively for nonroutine items, such as buildings, bridges, and the initial paving of streets. This view is not, however, unanimously held. For

Table 3-10
Equipment Work Sheet

Fund: General
Function: Public Safety
Department: Police

Prepared by _____ TE
Approved by _____ PRT
Date: September 15, 2004

CODE	ITEM	ADDITION OR REPLACEMENT	NUMBER REQUESTED	NET COST PER UNIT[a]	BUDGET REQUEST	REMARKS
504	Motor scooter	R	1	$ 3,000	$ 3,000	
505	Police cruiser	R	2	24,000	48,000	
505	Police cruiser	A	1	25,000	25,000	Necessary because of annexation of 4 square miles of outlying area
506	.38-caliber pistol	A	3	250	750	Same as above
510	Computer	R	1	1,600	1,600	
515	Desk	R	2	350	700	
518	File cabinet	A	3	150	450	Necessary because of increased number of records that must be maintained due to federal grant
522	Radio transmitter (used)	A	1	7,600	7,600	Necessary to improve communication between police patrol and dispatcher
	Total				$87,100	

[a]Cost of new item less trade-in or resale value of item being replaced.

example, one large governmental unit treats the purchase of police cars as an operational expenditure because local procedures stipulate that items treated as capital outlays must have a life of at least 5 years and a cost of at least $25,000. Under these same rules, garbage trucks and fire engines are debt-financed capital projects.

Departmental Expenditure Request Document

When the work sheets for personal services, travel, operating expenditures, and equipment are finished, certain information is transferred from these forms to the *departmental expenditure request document.* This schedule contains, at a minimum, the title of each object-of-expenditure, the level of prior- and current-year expenditures, and the requested level of expenditures for the budget year. It can also contain a column in which the amount actually appropriated by the legislative body is recorded.

Some organizations summarize the requested level of expenditures by activity (e.g., vice squad, juvenile control, traffic control, and so on) and include this summary in a supplementary schedule. Such information can help the CEO and the members of the legislative body make judgments on the costs and benefits of specific activities. A departmental expenditure request is shown in Table 3-11.

Nondepartmental Expenditure and Interfund Transfer Requests

Nondepartmental expenditures are expenditures that do not relate to any one specific department or activity. Instead, they benefit the organization as a whole. Examples of nondepartmental expenditures include utility and maintenance costs of buildings

Table 3-11
Departmental Expenditure Request

Fund: General				Prepared by BER
Function: Public Safety				Approved by PRT
Department: Police				Date: September 15, 2004

Code	Object	Prior-Year Actual	Current-Year Budget	Current-Year Est. Actual	Budget Request
100	Personal services	$816,525	$859,500	$859,500	$ 974,513
200	Travel	4,600	4,800	4,800	5,350
3-600	Operating	60,500	61,600	61,450	62,350
700	Equipment	62,470	66,500	65,800	87,100
	Total	$944,095	$992,400	$991,550	$1,129,313

Narrative: The police department maintains law and order in the community. Major departmental expenditures are for personnel, operating, and equipment. Because of the increased area of the city, the department must add two police officers and an additional police cruiser. In addition, it must replace three police cruisers that have reached the end of their useful lives. Finally, the department must upgrade its communication system because of a recently passed law requiring that police departments throughout the state maintain comprehensive networks that are integrated into the state system.

used by different departments or programs (such as a city hall), certain pension costs, and liability insurance premiums for city-owned vehicles. In addition, many organizations set up a reserve to cover possible revenue shortfalls, emergencies, or contingencies (such as cleaning up after a flood). Interfund transfers are transfers of resources made between funds. Typical interfund transfers include ones for debt service, contributions toward the cost of capital projects, and operating subsidies to proprietary funds.

The work sheet used to budget nondepartmental expenditures and interfund transfers is similar to the one used to budget departmental operating expenditures. However, because nondepartmental expenditures and interfund transfers are often of a fixed nature (e.g., liability insurance), and because their planned level is usually determined by the budget officer or the CEO, the work sheet used to budget them is prepared by the budget officer. A nondepartmental expenditure and interfund transfer request is shown in Table 3-12.

Service Efforts and Accomplishments

Many organizations supplement their budget requests with data showing what they expect to accomplish during the year. These kinds of data are consistent with the current trend toward managing for results and service efforts and accomplishments (SEA) reporting. The following data are typically provided for each of the major functions performed by a department:

1. Description of the function
2. Inputs (service efforts)—numbers of personnel (and dollar amounts) and amounts of materials, supplies, and equipment needed to accomplish the function
3. Outputs—quantities of services expected to be performed (e.g., number of lane miles expected to be maintained during the budget year)
4. Outcomes—the results expected to be achieved during the budget year (e.g., 85 percent of the lane miles of road will be rated as "very good" or better as a result of efforts made during the budget year)

Information presented on service efforts and accomplishments should, at a minimum, cover the past year, current year, and budget year. The performance measures (i.e., anticipated outputs and outcomes) should be used by departmental managers and the chief executive of the governmental unit to monitor performance during the year and to report to the public at year-end.

Budgetary Review

The departmental expenditure request documents are submitted to the budget officer, along with the work sheets, work programs (if any), and any other supporting materials. The budget officer, or a member of his or her staff, determines whether each expenditure request document has been properly prepared and whether each requested item is justified and realistic, as well as appropriate. If the budget officer believes that the expenditure request documents have been properly prepared and

Table 3-12
Nondepartmental Expenditure and Interfund Transfer Request

Fund: General

Date: September 15, 2004

Prepared by ____CCW____

Approved by ____LVT____

CODE	OBJECT	PRIOR-YEAR ACTUAL	CURRENT-YEAR BUDGET	CURRENT-YEAR EST. ACTUAL	BUDGET REQUEST	REMARKS
730	City Dues	$ 1,500	$ 1,500	$ 1,500	$ 1,500	
810	Repairs	—	—	3,000	20,000	Damage to City Hall from dust storm
850	Legal settlements	150,000	120,000	210,000	200,000	Uninsured portion of damage claims
925	Audit fees	12,000	15,000	15,500	18,000	Inflation
930	Legal services	35,000	35,000	40,000	40,000	Inflation
950	Advertising	2,000	2,500	2,450	8,000	Promote international exposition
970	Res. for contingencies	205,000	180,000	180,000	165,000	
980	Transfer to Debt Service Fund	500,000	500,000	500,000	1,300,000	Bond issue
	Total	$905,500	$854,000	$952,450	$1,752,500	

that each item is justified, realistic, and appropriate, he or she summarizes the information received and transmits it, along with backup materials and revenue estimates, to the CEO. The CEO reviews the information and prepares recommendations for the legislative body. A budget summary is shown in Table 3-13.

Determining whether expenditure request documents have been properly prepared is a relatively simple procedure. It consists primarily of ascertaining that all requested information has been provided, that the arithmetic on each form is correct, and that no errors have been made when transferring information from one form to another.

Determining whether each requested item is justified, realistic, and appropriate is more difficult. The budget officer must determine the need for each activity and level of service, the validity of the assumptions underlying each budgetary calculation, and whether each requested item falls within the budgetary guidelines. If a requested item exceeds these guidelines, the budget officer must determine why, and whether the additional request is justified.

For example, in the personal services work sheet in Table 3-6 two additional police officers are requested, along with additional equipment, because of the annexation of an unincorporated area into the city. If the budgetary guidelines specify no new positions or if the revenue picture is not optimistic, the budget officer must determine whether the same level of services can be delivered with existing resources or whether a lower level of services will suffice.

If the CEO and the legislative body are to make informed decisions, supplementary data must be included with the expenditure requests. This information can come from the following sources:

1. *Performance reports:* Work plans, personnel reports, productivity studies, service efforts and accomplishments (SEA) reports, and so on
2. *Independent research:* Cost-benefit analyses, program audits, feasibility studies, and so on
3. *Reports and studies from outside sources:* Press releases, program status reports prepared for funding agencies, reports prepared by citizens' groups, and so on

At all times, the budget officer should be in close contact with department heads, program directors, and other persons responsible for preparing expenditure requests. A budget officer who feels that a request is questionable should meet with the person who prepared the request to resolve the matter. If the matter cannot be resolved at this level, the person preparing the request should have the right to appeal to the CEO.

The budget officer is also responsible, in most organizations, for ensuring that the total proposed expenditures do not exceed the estimated revenues plus any surplus likely to be on hand at the end of the current year. Because the total expenditure requests of most organizations usually exceed the projected revenues of those organizations, even after the screening process discussed previously, and because most organizations are required, by law or charter, to operate within a balanced budget, the budget director is usually forced to decide which requests should be included in the budget document and which requests should be reduced or eliminated.

Table 3-13
Budget Summary

	FUN CITY GENERAL FUND BUDGET SUMMARY FISCAL YEAR 2005		
Estimated Revenues			
Property tax		$ 3,550,000	
Liquor tax		480,000	
Sales tax		2,650,000	
Royalty payments		300,000	
Fines and penalties		100,000	
Rental charges		11,000	$7,091,000
Appropriations			
Administration:			
Personal services	$435,000		
Travel	22,400		
Operating expenditures	85,800		
Equipment	24,600	$ 567,800	
Fire:			
Personal services	$665,104		
Travel	12,500		
Operating expenditures	235,000		
Equipment	146,250	1,058,854	
Parks:			
Personal services	$215,573		
Travel	1,850		
Operating expenditures	82,350		
Equipment	72,300	372,073	
Police:			
Personal services	$974,513		
Travel	5,350		
Operating expenditures	62,350		
Equipment	87,100	1,129,313	
Streets:			
Personal services	$314,646		
Travel	1,150		
Operating expenditures	103,360		
Equipment	146,000	565,156	

Table 3-13
Continued

Nondepartmental:			
City dues	$ 1,500		
Repairs	20,000		
Legal settlements	200,000		
Audit fees	18,000		
Legal services	40,000		
Advertising	8,000		
Reserve for contingencies	165,000	452,500	4,145,696
Excess of revenues over appropriations			$2,945,304
Other Financing Sources (Uses)			
Transfer from Enterprise Fund		$ 150,000	
Transfer to Debt Service Fund		(1,300,000)	(1,150,000)
Excess of revenues and other sources over expenditures and other uses			$1,795,304
Estimated fund balance—January 1, 2005			1,000,000
Estimated fund balance—December 31, 2005			$2,795,304

When balancing the budget, the budget officer should first determine whether a perceived need for more resources can be met by shifting existing resources from another area. For example, the budget officer may agree with the need for an additional police officer position. Upon reviewing the budget of another department, the budget officer might discover that that department employs a security guard. In this case the budget officer might arrange a meeting between the police chief and the head of that department to determine whether the job performed by the security guard can be performed by extending the police patrols to include that department's facility. If the outcome of this meeting is positive, a transfer can be made from the budget of the department employing the security guard to the police department's budget at little cost to the organization. (The authors realize that not all trade-offs are this easy.)

The budget officer must also determine whether each activity should expand or reduce the level of its objectives and whether the objectives of each activity can be achieved just as effectively with fewer resources. To assist the budget officer in making such decisions (and to defend their subunits from the consequences of such decisions), persons preparing expenditure requests should include sound justifications and detailed backup data with each request.

The final review of the expenditure requests is made by the CEO. The data from the various subunits should be presented to this executive in summary form, with backup information readily available. Both subunit and organization-wide requests should be presented.

The purposes of the final review are (1) to obtain the input of the CEO into the budgetary process, (2) to act as a court of last resort for disputes between the budget officer and the persons preparing the expenditure requests, and (3) to enable the CEO to prepare specific budget recommendations before submitting them to the legislative body.

The best approach to the final review is to have each person responsible for preparing expenditure requests brief the CEO on those requests and provide supporting data or evidence that the CEO can use when presenting the budget to the legislative body. If the CEO has been involved in the budgetary process from its inception, and if all differences between the budget officer and the persons responsible for preparing the expenditure requests have been resolved, this final review can be a positive experience.

The Budget Document

After completion of the final review, the budget officer assembles the budget requests, the revenue projections, and the CEO's recommendations into a comprehensive *budget document*, which is presented to the legislative body. The magnitude of a budget document can range from one to several volumes, depending on the organization's size and complexity. At a minimum, a budget document should contain the following elements:

1. *A budget message*, which, in general terms, discusses the following:
   a. The fiscal experience of the current year
   b. The present financial position of the organization
   c. Major financial issues faced during the past year and ones expected during the budget year
   d. Assumptions used when preparing budget requests (e.g., expected rate of inflation)
   e. Significant revenue and expenditure changes from the current year's budget
   f. New program initiatives and anticipated accomplishments during the year
   g. Significant budgetary changes resulting from the proposed new program initiatives, such as increased numbers of personnel and new debt issues
   h. The future economic outlook of the organization
2. *A budget summary*, which lists the total budgeted revenues by source, and lists the total budgeted expenditures by program or department and for the organization as a whole. This part of the budget document can be enhanced by including comparisons between the budgeted revenues and expenditures and the actual revenues and expenditures of the current and past year. It can also be made more effective by highlighting significant changes in the levels of specific sources of revenue and specific expenditures.
3. *Detailed supporting schedules*, among which should be the following schedules:
   a. Estimated revenues by source
   b. Departmental and nondepartmental expenditure requests
   c. Budgeted fixed charges such as the repayment of debt
4. *A capital projects schedule*
5. *Detailed justifications of the budgetary recommendations*

6. *Supplementary information,* such as
   a. Departmental budget request work sheets
   b. Departmental work programs
   c. Pro forma balance sheets for each fund, as of the beginning and the end of the budget year
   d. A cash budget
   e. A schedule of interest payments, sinking fund contributions, and bond issues and retirements
7. *Drafts of appropriation and tax levy ordinances or acts*

Legislative Consideration and Adoption of the Budget

The completed budget document is sent to the legislative body, which reviews, modifies, approves, and adopts it. Before approving the budget document, the legislative body usually conducts both formal and informal administrative hearings, as well as formal public hearings. In some cases the budget document is turned over to a legislative finance or ways-and-means committee for recommendations. Such recommendations, however, are just that, recommendations. They are not binding on the entire legislative body.

Administrative hearings can be in the form of informal briefings, such as workshop sessions conducted by the CEO, the budget officer, or the persons responsible for preparing budgetary requests. They can also take the form of lists of questions to be answered in writing by officials of the organization, and of meetings between individual legislators and the CEO or budget officer. During these hearings, items of concern to the members of the legislative body can be discussed, as can the impact of programs in which the legislators are particularly interested. As a result, many issues and questions can be resolved by the time the budget is formally presented.

At a designated meeting, the CEO formally presents the budget document to the legislative body. This presentation should include a general overview of the contents of the budget document, a discussion of the assumptions made when preparing the budget document, and a discussion of the major financial difficulties that the organization will face during the budget year. The revenue estimates and budget requests should also be reviewed, as should the justification for each new or nonroutine request.

Many organizations are required by law (or political expediency) to hold public hearings on the budget. Citizen input to budgetary decisions is obtained by allowing interested parties to comment to the legislative body on their own concerns. The process of budgetary approval is expedited if copies of the budget document (or a summary) are disseminated to the members of the legislative body and to the public in advance of public hearings and the formal presentation. If the users of the budget document are allowed a reasonable amount of time to "digest" its contents, issues of concern can more readily be identified and the public hearings and deliberations of the legislative body will proceed more smoothly.

When the budget hearings are finished, the legislative body completes its deliberations, makes any modifications to the budget document it feels are necessary, and enacts a final *appropriation ordinance* or, in the case of a state, *appropriation act.* The purpose of this ordinance or act is to establish a spending ceiling for the budget year and to authorize the organization to make the expenditures listed in the budget.

After the appropriation ordinance or act has been passed, the budget document is returned to the organization, where the budgeted amounts are entered into the accounts. Most governmental units also publish their approved budget.

Property Tax Levy

After approval of the budget, the legislative body must take action to raise revenues necessary to finance the budgeted expenditures. The collection of many types of revenue does not require frequent action on the part of the legislative body. These revenues are usually the result of past actions (e.g., license fees, sales taxes, income from investments, and so on). Other revenue measures, however, require legal action more frequently, the most common example being property taxes.

Two different approaches can be used to determine the taxes to be assessed on each piece of property. Under the first approach the assessed value of the property (less any exemptions) is multiplied by a flat rate, which is "permanently" fixed by law. Under the second, and more common, approach the property taxes are treated as a residual source of revenue.

Before an organization using the second approach can send tax bills to the property owners, it must determine a tax (millage) rate that, when applied to the assessed valuation of the property, will provide the desired amount of revenue. This amount is usually shown as part of the revenue estimates in the budget. Although simple in concept, the second approach can become complicated because of (1) uncollectible or delinquent taxes and (2) property exempt from taxation (such as land belonging to religious organizations) and exemptions due to the military service, age, physical condition, and economic status of the owner, and the use of the property as a homestead. This last exemption can be particularly costly to taxing organizations. In Louisiana, for example, the homestead exemption is applied to the first $75,000 of the current market value of any piece of property used as the principal residence of its owner.

Using the residual approach, the tax (millage) rate is computed as follows:

Amount to be collected	$ 100,000	
Allowance for uncollectible property taxes	4%	
Required tax levy	$ 104,166 ($100,000/.96)	
Total assessed value of property	$10,000,000	
Less: Property not taxable	(2,000,000)	$8,000,000
Less: Exemptions:		
Homestead	$ 1,000,000	
Veterans	500,000	
Old age, blindness, etc.	900,000	2,400,000
Net assessed value of property		$5,600,000

$$\text{Tax (Millage) Rate} = \frac{\text{Required Tax Levy}}{\text{Net Assessed Value of Property}}$$

$$= \frac{104{,}166}{5{,}600{,}000} = \underline{.0186}$$

In this example, the property tax will be levied at the rate of $1.86 per $100 of net assessed valuation. If the tax rate is expressed in mills (thousandths of a dollar), it will be 18.60 mills. Thus, the owner of a piece of property with a net (after exemptions) assessed value of $200,000 will be required to pay property taxes of $3,720 ($200,000 × .0186).

USING BUDGETARY INFORMATION

One purpose of budgets is to provide a measure or "standard" against which actual results can be measured. If the actual expenditures are equal to the budget, the activity is *under control.* If the actual expenditures are greater than or less than the budget, the activity is *out of control.* Thus, by comparing actual expenditures with budgeted expenditures, managers, legislators, and other decision makers can judge the organization's performance and can take corrective action when necessary.

A good budget, however, is more than a statement of anticipated revenues and expenditures. It is also a statement of anticipated accomplishments and priorities. Therefore, as suggested previously, the budget should also be used to control *program performance.*

Budgetary comparisons can take several forms. For example, the Governmental Accounting Standards Board (GASB) requires budgetary comparison schedules for the General Fund and each major special revenue fund with a legally adopted budget. These schedules should show (1) the original adopted budget, (2) the final appropriated budget, and (3) actual inflows and outflows on the budgetary basis of accounting.[3]

Some organizations also produce monthly statements that detail budgeted and actual expenditures, by object, and the amount of remaining budget for each item. This latter piece of information is particularly important to organizations that are subject to *antideficiency laws* (laws that make the overspending of one's budget an act subject to civil and/or criminal penalties), as well as to those managers and program directors whose performance is judged, in some measure, by whether they meet their budgets. In addition, knowledge of this amount is helpful to organizational personnel when they plan the activities of their work unit for the remainder of the fiscal year. If the amount of the remaining budget is lower than originally planned, their unit must curtail its activities or ask for more money from the legislative body. If the amount of remaining budget is higher than originally planned, their unit can expand its activities.

A well-designed *budgetary control report* (budget comparison) is illustrated in Table 3-14. In addition to showing the budget for the current month and the year to

---

[3] GASB Cod. Sec. 1100.111.

Table 3-14
Budgetary Control Report

Fund: General
Function: Public Safety
Department: Police

Prepared by: RGS
Date: September 30, 2004

	Year to Date				Code	Object-of-Expenditure	Current Month				Available for Spending
	Budget	Actual	Variance	% Budget			Budget	Actual	Variance	% Budget	
						Contractual Services					
	$ 75	$ 60	$ 15(F)	20	301	Advertising	$ 8	$ 10	$ 2(U)	25	$ 40
	1,200	1,300	100(U)	8	310	Printing	133	120	13(F)	10	300
	6,000	6,200	200(U)	3	320	Vehicle maintenance	667	645	22(F)	3	1,800
	4,200	3,900	300(F)	7	330	Communication	467	378	89(F)	19	1,700
	150	180	30(U)	20	350	Dues and subscriptions	17	21	4(U)	24	20
	225	200	25(F)	11	360	Postage	25	30	5(U)	20	100
	450	550	100(U)	22	370	Telephone	50	35	15(F)	30	50
	300	300	—	—	380	Professional services	33	0	33(F)	100	100
	$ 12,600	$ 12,690	$ 90(U)	1		Subtotal	$ 1,400	$ 1,239	$ 161(F)	12	$ 4,110
						Supplies and Materials					
	$ 825	$850	$ 25(U)	3	401	Office supplies	$ 92	$ 97	$ 5(U)	5	$ 250
	3,525	3,595	70(U)	2	410	Building maintenance	392	370	22(F)	6	1,105
	7,875	7,750	125(F)	2	420	Fuel	875	825	50(F)	6	2,750
	$546,375	$563,430	$17,055(U)	3		Grand total	$60,708	$63,386	$2,678(U)	4	$165,070

date, it shows (1) actual expenditures incurred for these periods; (2) differences between budgeted and actual expenditures (called *variances*), in both absolute numbers and as a percentage of budget; and (3) amounts that can be spent for the remainder of the year without exceeding the budget. If the amount spent is less than the amount budgeted, a *favorable* (F) variance is shown. If the amount spent is more than the amount budgeted, an *unfavorable* (U) variance is shown.

The budgetary control report in Table 3-14 is presented in one of several possible formats and is based on the 2004 (current-year) budget. For example, some organizations show amounts that have been encumbered, as well as spent. Other organizations include the following month's budget in this report. Regardless of the format used, the report should meet the organization's needs; all the users should be able to understand the report; and the report's use should be strongly encouraged by the upper levels of management and the legislative body of the organization.

To control program performance, budgetary control reports should be supplemented with budgetary performance reports. Anticipated performance set forth in the submitted budget should be used to develop measures of actual performance. When this is done, anticipated performance (expressed in terms of expected quantities of outputs and outcomes) becomes a benchmark for measuring what actually happens during the year. The resulting reports (usually prepared monthly, but no less frequently than quarterly) help department managers and the chief executive to manage for results. When also used to report to the public, budgetary performance reports help governmental managers demonstrate accountability.

GOVERNMENTAL BUDGETING IN PRACTICE
Clark County, Nevada, Public Defender

In addition to serving as a financial plan, the budget can serve as an operations guide and a communication medium. Clark County, Nevada (the region surrounding Las Vegas), includes a mission statement and statements of goals, objectives and performance measurements, and major achievements of the past year for each operational unit. It also publishes a separate budget fact book, which contains summary budgets, statistical information, and graphical presentations of revenue sources and types of expenditures.

Shown following are the mission statement and certain program information of Clark County's public defender, and summary budgets and graphical presentations from that county's fact book.

MISSION STATEMENT

The mission of the Clark County Public Defender's Office is to provide effective criminal defense representation of indigent persons charged with crimes, as mandated by United States and Nevada Constitutions, statutes and case law.

(continued)

GOVERNMENTAL BUDGETING IN PRACTICE
Clark County, Nevada, Public Defender

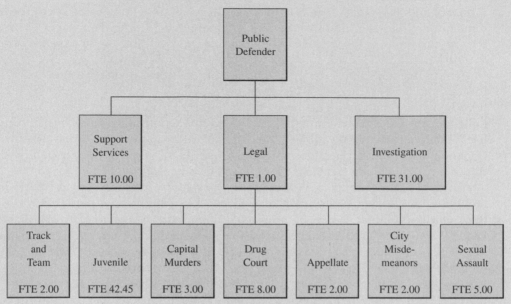

Total FTE 107.45

The office of the Public Defender is responsible for the representation of indigent defendants charged with a criminal offense in all the courts of Clark County. This responsibility includes providing defense representation to juveniles whose parents cannot afford to retain private counsel and to the City of Las Vegas on a contractual basis (per Nevada Revised Statues 171.188) for indigent persons charged with criminal misdemeanor offenses.

In FY 20X3–X4 payment for these services in the amount of $545,468 was received from the City of Las Vegas and deposited in the General Fund.

If the presiding judge determines a defendant is able to pay for part of his/her defense, the defendant is assessed an amount to reimburse the County for providing representation. In FY 20X3–X4, the total assessment fee collected was $23,012.

Expenditures

EXPENDITURES BY CATEGORY	20X2–X3 ACTUAL	20X3–X4 ESTIMATE	20X4–X5 BUDGET
Salaries and wages	$5,487,420	$6,380,918	$7,323,699
Employee benefits	1,637,785	1,857,144	2,089,036
Services and supplies	531,757	601,548	647,209
Capital outlay	0	0	0
Total	$7,656,962	$8,839,610	$10,059,944
Full-time equivalents	93.71	103.58	107.45

Note: The Clark County General Fund is reimbursed by the City of Las Vegas for salaries, wages, and benefits for five attorneys and three clerical positions.

GOVERNMENTAL BUDGETING IN PRACTICE
Clark County, Nevada, Public Defender

GOALS, OBJECTIVES AND PERFORMANCE MEASUREMENTS

Goal

Ensure that all adults and juveniles represented by the Public Defender's Office receive the highest quality representation guaranteed by law. (Supports countywide strategic plan goals A, B, C, and D)

Objectives

- Ensure quality representation, investigation, and support for each case.
- Continue and enhance existing partnerships to expand Drug Court programs.
- Create a sexual assault unit.

PERFORMANCE/WORKLOAD MEASUREMENTS	20X2–X3 ACTUAL	20X3–X4 ESTIMATE	20X4–X5 BUDGET
Quality representation, investigation, and support for each case	100%	100%	100%

Goal

Integrate computer network improvements for statistical reporting, case management, accounting system, imaging, and videoteleconferencing with criminal justice system agencies. (Supports countywide strategic plan goals A, B, and C)

Objectives

- Acquire, install, and replace personal computers for word processing, statistical reporting, tracking, and monitoring cases for any new positions approved in the budget process.

- Acquire multimedia computer hardware and software to give its office greater access to in-custody clients by enabling attorneys and investigators to conduct jail interviews and review case details electronically, thus allowing more time for staff to handle other defense issues and to partner with the Clark County Detention Center, thereby saving corrections officers time by not having to move inmates to and from attorney visits.

- Explore imaging as a solution to space limitations, cost reduction in supplies, and record retention.

PERFORMANCE/WORKLOAD MEASUREMENTS	20X2–X3 ACTUAL	20X3–X4 ESTIMATE	20X4–X5 BUDGET
Computer installation completed	100%	100%	100%
Videoteleconferencing project completed	n/a	5%	50%
Imaging solution completed	n/a	n/a	10%

Goal

Improve quality and quantity of communication/access between the Public Defender's Office and its attorneys and Public Defender clients. (Supports countywide strategic plan goals A and C)

Objectives

- Create and make available for distribution to clients a summary of information about the general nature of criminal charges and how such charges are processed within the criminal justice system.

- Explore/install a videoteleconferencing system between the jail and the Public Defender's Office.

(continued)

PERFORMANCE/WORKLOAD MEASUREMENTS	20X2–X3 ACTUAL	20X3–X4 ESTIMATE	20X4–X5 BUDGET
Summary of information completed	n/a	n/a	25%
Videoteleconferencing project completed	n/a	5%	50%

PRIOR-YEAR ACHIEVEMENTS (FY 20X3–X4)

OBJECTIVES	ACHIEVEMENT RESULTS
• Acquire personal computers for the remainder of the office staff to include all attorneys and investigators for word processing, statistical reporting, and tracking and monitoring cases.	*Achieved* All Public Defender employees have personal computers.
• Acquire multimedia computer hardware and software to give the office greater access to its in-custody clients by enabling our attorneys and investigators to conduct jail interviews and review case details electronically, thus allowing more time for staff to handle other defense issues.	*Partially achieved* Five percent completed. This is a joint project between this department and several other County departments.
• Complete plans and obtain funding for remodeling the existing office space.	*Achieved* The plans have been completed and the funding approved. Estimated completion date is in March.

NOTEWORTHY HIGHLIGHTS (FY 20X3–X4)

- Installed new server and 55 additional computers.

- Transferred existing systems and data from the County super server to the server in the Third Street Building.

- Made available to all employees the computerized application developed specifically for the automation of the Public Defender's Office.

GOVERNMENTAL BUDGETING IN PRACTICE
Clark County, Nevada

General Fund Summary

REVENUES	20X2–X3 ACTUAL	20X3–X4 ESTIMATE	20X4–X5 BUDGET
Taxes (ad valorem)	$ 86,755,498	$ 94,011,835	$105,076,299
Licenses and permits	66,408,199	70,821,875	74,159,841
Fines and forfeits	7,721,768	8,139,876	8,392,852
Charges for services	43,174,553	39,540,062	41,303,252
Intergovernmental			
Sales tax	118,142,476	129,557,402	138,467,971
Other	24,901,405	25,142,211	26,479,047
Miscellaneous	18,212,137	16,182,017	13,162,409
Total revenues	$365,316,036	$383,395,278	$407,041,671

FY 20X4–X5 Revenues

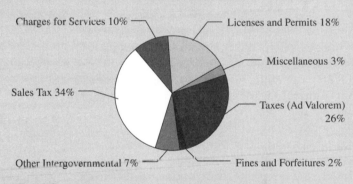

General Fund Summary

EXPENDITURES BY FUNCTION	20X2–X3 ACTUAL	20X3–X4 ESTIMATE	20X4–X5 BUDGET
General Government	$106,680,842	$111,101,179	$121,500,530
Judicial	50,092,622	56,385,343	61,076,892
Public Safety	78,283,452	86,368,495	93,799,449
Public Works	15,475,925	16,953,142	18,182,168
Health	11,673,435	13,417,936	13,779,964
Welfare	21,252,516	28,146,730	31,931,843
Culture and Recreation	12,719,528	14,335,576	15,796,957
Total Expenditures	$296,178,320	$326,708,401	$356,067,803

(continued)

GOVERNMENTAL BUDGETING IN PRACTICE
Clark County, Nevada

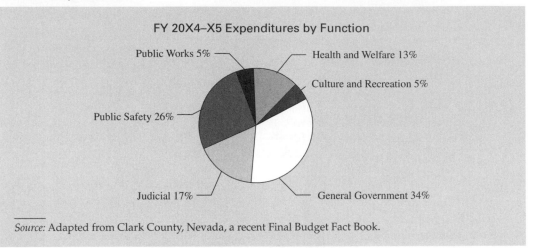

FY 20X4–X5 Expenditures by Function

Public Works 5%

Health and Welfare 13%

Culture and Recreation 5%

Public Safety 26%

Judicial 17%

General Government 34%

Source: Adapted from Clark County, Nevada, a recent Final Budget Fact Book.

REVIEW QUESTIONS

Q3-1 What is a budget? What purpose(s) does it serve?

Q3-2 List the steps involved in preparing a budget.

Q3-3 Why should revenue estimates be prepared before expenditure requests? What steps are taken when preparing revenue estimates?

Q3-4 What information should be contained in a set of budgetary instructions?

Q3-5 What is the purpose of a budget calendar?

Q3-6 How can the current year's surplus or deficit be calculated?

Q3-7 What factors should be considered when projecting (a) sales taxes, (b) property taxes, and (c) hotel occupancy taxes?

Q3-8 What are the three categories of departmental, or program, expenditures?

Q3-9 What are fringe benefits? How should they be handled in the budget?

Q3-10 What is a salary-vacancy factor? How can it be estimated?

Q3-11 What is a capital program? Why should it be prepared for several years beyond the budget year?

Q3-12 Name three sources of supplementary information that should be included with budget requests.

Q3-13 What is the purpose of a budgetary review? By whom should it be performed?

Q3-14 What is a millage rate? How is it determined?

Q3-15 What is the purpose of a cash budget? How can it assist in the smooth functioning of an organization?

Q3-16 Does your state have a budget law? Does it require a balanced budget? How is *balanced budget* defined in your state?

CASES

C3-1   The City of Toth produces monthly budgetary control reports. The amount shown in the budget column is one-twelfth of the annual budget. Over lunch, two department heads were discussing this report. The first manager said, "I like the idea of using one-twelfth of my annual budget each month. My costs are constant throughout the year. I can usually find small savings and show favorable variances each month." The second manager disagreed. "I don't like it. Most of my costs are incurred during Carnival and around Christmas. As a result, I always have unfavorable variances in March and December regardless of what I do. It is especially upsetting because employee performance appraisals are made in April and the council looks especially hard at our March results."

What is the problem with the way these control reports are prepared? What do you think should be done to make the reports more reflective of actual performance of the departments?

C3-2   You have just been elected to your state legislature. One piece of proposed legislation on your desk is a new law requiring all governmental units in the state to prepare balanced budgets. In this bill, balanced budgets are defined as ones in which expected resources available at the beginning of a fiscal year (beginning fund balance plus estimated revenues) must equal or exceed that year's appropriations. A conservative legislator from a rural county attached a rider to the bill deleting this definition of balanced budgets and substituting one in which budgets are balanced only if estimated revenues equal appropriations. Would you vote for this rider? State your reasons. Why might feelings vary on this issue between legislators from large cities and those from rural counties?

ETHICS CASE

EC3-1 During lunch, the director of Streets and Parkways of Thor City made the following comment: "For the past 10 years, I deliberately overstated my labor and equipment needs by 20 percent when preparing my budget request. I figure that the City Council will cut it by 10 percent and I can use the other 10 percent as slack. If there is money left over, I can always find a way to spend it." Do you consider this behavior to be ethical? If not, what steps might you, as budget director, take to cut down on this "padding"?

EXERCISES

E3-1   (Discussion of uses of budgeting)
Rex, a budget officer, conducted a class for nonaccounting managers and program directors on the subject of budgets. Rex began the class discussion by

asking, "What are some of the uses of a budget?" One manager replied, "Planning." Another said, "Evaluating performance." Still another suggested, "Coordinating activities." "What about implementing plans?" inquired another. "Or communicating them?" added still another. "Don't forget motivation," one manager warned from the rear of the room. "I'm on the school board," commented another, "and we use it to authorize actions." Finally, one manager asked, "Can budgets do all that?" "Yes," Rex responded, "all that and more."

Required: 1. Define the term *budget*.
2. Select any four of the uses suggested by the managers and explain how a budget might accomplish each of the four uses selected.

(IIA adapted)

E3-2 (Budgeting cash disbursements)
The City of Argus is preparing its cash budget for the month of July. The following information is available with respect to its proposed disbursements.

Items vouchered in July	$650,000
Estimated payments in July for items vouchered in July	50%
Items vouchered in June	$400,000
Estimated payments in July for all items vouchered in June	70%
Estimated payments in July for items vouchered prior to June	$ 50,000
Items purchased and vouchered in June but returned in July before payment was made	$ 20,000

Required: What are the estimated cash disbursements for July?

E3-3 (Budgeting cash receipts)
The City of Comus is preparing a cash budget for the month of May. The following information is available with respect to its sales tax collections.

Sales tax rate	5%
Estimated retail sales in May	$2,000,000
Actual retail sales in April	$1,500,000
Estimated payments by merchants to city in May of sales taxes collected in May	20%
Estimated payments by merchants to city in May of sales taxes collected in April	70%
Estimated payments by merchants to city in May of sales taxes collected prior to April	$10,000

Required: Compute the estimated cash receipts from sales tax collections in May.

E3-4 (Determination of property tax rate)
The legislative body of Pandorra County just approved the 2004–2005 fiscal year budget. Revenues from property taxes are budgeted at $800,000. According to the county assessor, the assessed valuation of all of the property in the county is $50 million. Of this amount, however, property worth $10 mil-

lion belongs to either the federal government or to religious organizations and, therefore, is not subject to property taxes. In addition, certificates for the following exemptions have been filed:

Homestead	$2,500,000
Veterans	1,000,000
Old age, blindness, etc.	500,000

In the past, uncollectible property taxes averaged about 2 percent of the levy. This rate is not expected to change in the foreseeable future.

Required: 1. Determine the property tax rate that must be used to collect the desired revenue from property taxes.
2. How much would the levy be on a piece of property that was assessed for $100,000 (after exemptions)?

E3-5 (Estimating the fund balance at the end of the year)
At the end of the preceding year, the General Fund of the Atlas Township School Board had a fund balance of $800,000. Revenues and expenditures of the current year are expected to be as follows:

	Year-to-Date Actual	Remainder of Year Estimated
Revenues		
Property taxes	$1,250,000	$500,000
Out-of-township tuition	50,000	20,000
Share of lottery receipts	100,000	50,000
State grants	500,000	—
Expenditures		
Salaries	$ 875,000	$450,000
Fringe benefits	90,000	40,000
Operating expenses	588,000	240,000
Equipment	110,000	50,000
Transportation	15,000	10,000
Repayment of debt	100,000	100,000

Required: Determine the projected year-end fund balance for this fund.

E3-6 (Trend analysis)
The City of Endymion levies a tax of 5 percent on all retail sales throughout the city. Retail sales for the current year and the past 5 years are as follows (rounded and in millions):

1999	$12.1
2000	15.4
2001	17.3
2002	20.8
2003	23.4
2004 (est.)	27.3

In 2005 a new retail complex will be opened that should attract shoppers from nearby cities. As a result, retail sales are expected to be 10 percent higher than if the complex had not been opened.

Required: Determine how much the city should budget for revenue from sales taxes in 2005.

E3-7   (Multiple-choice)
1. What is a key difference between budgets prepared by governmental units and by commercial organizations?
   a. Budgets prepared by commercial organizations must be approved by a governing body, whereas those prepared by governmental units need no approvals.
   b. Budgets prepared by governmental units are legal documents, whereas those prepared by commercial organizations are not.
   c. Operating, capital, and cash budgets are prepared by governmental units, but only operating budgets are prepared by commercial organizations.
   d. Budgets prepared by commercial organizations are formally recorded in the organizations' operating accounts, whereas those prepared by governmental units are not.

2. Which of the following is not included in a cash budget?
   a. Personal services
   b. Redemption of bonds
   c. Utilities
   d. Depreciation

3. Who prepares a nondepartmental expenditures request?
   a. The department heads as a group
   b. The auditor
   c. The city council
   d. The CEO or the budget director

4. Which of the following is an objection to the object-of-expenditure approach to budgeting?
   a. Budgets prepared under this approach are complicated and difficult to prepare.
   b. Information presented in this type of budget is difficult to incorporate into the accounting system.
   c. Legislative bodies are given more detail than they can handle; therefore, they tend to focus on individual items rather than on the overall goals and programs of the organization.
   d. Detailed comparisons between budgeted and actual revenues and expenditures are difficult to make.

5. What tool is commonly used to project certain types of revenues?
   a. Trend analysis
   b. PERT

c. Queuing theory

d. Cost-volume—profit analysis

6. Which of the following is *not* a basic rule to follow when using budgets?
   a. The budget must be presented in a positive manner.
   b. The budget must have the support of top management.
   c. Managers must only be held responsible for revenues and costs over which they have a degree of control.
   d. The budget must be prepared by top management.

7. A continuous budget
   a. Is used only by commercial organizations.
   b. Covers a specific period but is continuously updated.
   c. Is also known as a line-item budget.
   d. Is valid over a range of activity, rather than just one level.

8. What approach to budgeting is most commonly used by governmental units?
   a. Zero-based budgeting approach
   b. Planning-programming—budgeting approach
   c. Flexible budgeting approach
   d. Object-of-expenditure approach

E3-8   (Behavioral aspects of budgeting)
The operating budget is a common instrument used by many organizations. Although it usually is thought to be an important and necessary tool for management, some managers and researchers studying organization and human behavior criticize its use.

Required: 1. Describe and discuss some benefits of budgeting from the behavioral point of view.
2. Describe and discuss some criticisms leveled at the budgetary process from the behavioral point of view.
3. What solutions do you recommend to overcome the criticisms described in part (2)?

(CMA adapted)

E3-9   (Budget laws)
Every state has a law or laws regulating its own budgetary practices and those of its local governmental units. Check the law(s) of your state to determine the following:

1. Are budgets legally required by local governmental units, such as cities and counties, in your state?
2. For what funds must budgets be prepared?
3. Must governmental budgets prepared in your state be "balanced"? If so, what does your state law consider to be a "balanced" budget?
4. What legal provisions are made for public input into the budgetary process in your state?

P3-1 (Budgeting revenues)
The following information relates to the prior- and current-year revenues of the General Fund of Bacchus City.

	2003 Actual	Jan.–Sept. 2004 Actual	Oct.–Dec. 2004 Est. Act.	2004 Budget
Property taxes	$5,436,720	$4,084,000	$1,400,000	$5,504,000
Interest and penalties	38,486	22,800	15,000	38,000
Sales taxes	872,680	454,500	445,000	900,000
Fines and penalties	64,842	39,240	30,000	70,000
Share of lottery receipts	—	54,250	175,750	225,000
License fees	9,650	7,540	2,460	10,000

Additional information:

1. Because of a reassessment of commercial property, property taxes are expected to increase by $400,000 in 2005.
2. Interest and penalties and license fees are expected to remain constant over the next several years.
3. Because of an increase in the sales tax from 4 percent to 5 percent and the expectation of several large conventions in 2005, sales tax revenues are expected to increase by 20 percent.
4. Because of the conventions mentioned in part (3), fines and penalties should rise by 10 percent in 2005.
5. Because of the lottery's success in its first few months of operation, city officials expect the board's share of the lottery receipts to double in 2005.

Required: Prepare a statement of actual and estimated revenues for 2005. Assume that you are preparing it on October 15, 2004, and that the changes given above are with respect to the 2004 budget.

P3-2 (Personal services and travel work sheets)
The director of the Streets and Parkways Department of Bacchus City prepared the following position classification plan.

Code	Position	2003 No.	2003 Rate	2004 No.	2004 Rate
101	Director	1	$56,000	1	$60,000
102	Assistant director	1	48,000	1	52,000
104	Supervisor	4	35,000	4	38,000
110	Equipment operator II	8	28,500	7	32,000
112	Equipment operator I	12	24,000	13	28,000
115	Laborer, utility	30	18,000	26	20,000
120	Secretary	1	19,000	1	21,000

Additional information:

1. Fringe benefits are not included in these rates. In 2003 they averaged 12.2 percent of wages and salaries. In 2004 they are averaging 12.8 percent. In 2005 they are expected to average 13.6 percent.
2. Permission has been obtained from the City Council to budget an 8 percent cost-of-living increase for 2005. In addition, the mayor of Bacchus City has recommended that the director and the assistant director each be given a $1,000 merit increase, in addition to their cost-of-living increases.
3. Due to the building of several miles of new streets in 2004, the mayor believes that an additional maintenance crew, consisting of one supervisor, one equipment operator II, and two laborers should be hired.
4. From March 3 to March 7, the director of the Streets and Parkways Department plans to attend a professional conference in Milwaukee at a cost of $750. In addition, the director and the assistant director plan to attend a technical workshop in Tampa from April 21 through April 25, at a cost of $500 each. Finally, the five supervisors are expected to attend a team-building workshop, given at a nearby city on August 18. The cost of this travel for all five supervisors is expected to be $100. In 2003, travel costs amounted to $1,425. In 2004 they were budgeted at $1,500. A total of $1,600 is expected to be spent this year.
5. Assume that in 2004 budgeted salaries are the same as actual salaries. Assume also that the Streets and Parkways Department's activities are recorded in the General Fund and that this department's function falls under the heading of Public Works.

Required: For fiscal year 2005 prepare the following:

1. A personal services work sheet and a budget year salary work sheet
2. A travel work sheet

P3-3 (Equipment work sheet)
During 2005 the Streets and Parkways Department of Bacchus City plans to make the following purchases of equipment. Because these items each cost more than $400, they are budgeted under the category of Equipment. The items are the following:

1. Two three-quarter-ton pickup trucks. These trucks will be replacements for existing trucks and will have a net cost (after trade-in) of $9,500 each.
2. One two-ton flatbed truck. This truck is a new item that will be necessary because of the new work crew expected to be hired and the additional streets to be maintained. Estimated cost of the truck is $38,500.
3. Other new items to be purchased for use of the new work crew:
   a. One asphalt machine $5,000
   b. Two small cement mixers   1,400 each
   c. Two jackhammers   1,200 each
   d. One asphalt sealer   500
   e. One 5' × 8' trailer (used)   1,000

4. Other items, which are replacements for existing items, to be purchased:
   a. Three 22" lawn mowers $ 500 each
   b. Two grass trimmers   3,600 each
   c. One welding machine (used)   3,000

In 2003, the Streets and Parkways Department spent $48,250 on equipment. For 2004, $56,000 has been budgeted, but only $42,360 of this amount has been spent to date. The director of this department estimates that by the end of fiscal year 2004, another $12,000 will be spent for equipment.

Required: Prepare an equipment work sheet for the Streets and Parkways Department.

P3-4   (Operating expense work sheet)
From the following data, prepared as of August 30, 2004, prepare an operating expense work sheet to be used in the fiscal year 2005 budget of the Streets and Parkways Department of Bacchus City.

Code	Object of Expenditure	Prior-Year Actual	Current-Year Budget	Year-to-Date Actual	Rest of Year Est. Act.
	Contractual Services				
320	Vehicle and equipment maintenance	$18,450	$20,000	$15,000	$6,000
330	Communication	1,200	1,200	800	400
340	Rentals	648	800	600	200
365	Utilities	1,146	1,200	952	300
370	Telephone	240	240	180	80
380	Professional services	300	500	350	—
	Supplies and Materials				
410	Office supplies	214	200	158	42
415	Auto and truck	286	300	200	100
418	Equipment supplies	1,614	1,500	1,250	400
420	Asphalt	3,847	4,000	3,000	1,500
425	Fuel	1,206	1,200	860	300
430	Emergency supplies	152	200	50	100
440	Tools	876	1,000	800	200
450	Miscellaneous	136	100	75	—

Additional information:

1. Because of the crew expected to be added in 2005, the budgeted vehicle and equipment maintenance, equipment supplies, tools, and fuel expenditures are to be increased by 15 percent in 2005.
2. The budget for professional services is to be decreased by 20 percent.
3. The budgets for communications and miscellaneous supplies and materials should remain at their present levels.

4. An inflation factor of 8 percent should be applied to the fiscal year 2004 budget for the remaining items.
5. For this department, professional services consist largely of tree surgery and medical expenses for minor injuries of work crews.

P3-5   (Departmental expenditure request)
A description of the activities of the Streets and Parkways Department is as follows.

The function of the department is to assist in preserving the city's infrastructure by maintaining the streets, parkways, bridges, and levees in Bacchus City. These tasks consist primarily of caring for the grass and trees on the levees and parkways, filling potholes, inspecting and making minor repairs to the bridges, and replacing damaged traffic lights. Because of the growth of the city, new streets have been built in outlying areas and certain levees have been raised. The care of these new streets and levees puts a severe strain on the existing work crews' ability to maintain all of the city's infrastructure adequately.

Required: Using the information given in Problems 3-2 through 3-4 and the preceding information, prepare a departmental expenditure request for the Streets and Parkways Department of Bacchus City.

P3-6   (Budgeting nondepartmental expenditures and interfund transfers)
From the following data, prepare a nondepartmental expenditure and interfund transfer request for Bacchus City for fiscal year 2005.

Code	Object of Expenditure	Prior-Year Actual	Current-Year Budget	Jan.–Sept. Actual	Oct.–Dec. Est. Act.
710	Liability insurance	$ 15,435	$ 16,500	$ 12,285	$ 4,000
815	Advertising	550	600	454	100
830	Legal services	10,000	10,000	8,500	1,000
840	Audit fees	9,000	10,000	—	9,600
910	Transfer to Debt Service Fund	715,000	900,000	450,000	450,000
915	Transfer to Venus Park Fund	52,000	60,000	30,000	30,000

Additional information:

1. Because of the new streets, the City is increasing the amount of its insurance coverage. The 2005 premium is expected to amount to $20,000.
2. The cost of advertising, legal services, and the annual audit are expected to be 10 percent higher than the amount budgeted for 2004. The 2005 budget should be adjusted accordingly.
3. In 2005, the General Fund will make a transfer of $1 million to a Debt Service Fund, and $50,000 to the Venus Park Fund.

P3-7 (Budget summary)

Using the information given in P3-1 through P3-6 and the following information, prepare a budget summary for the General Fund of Bacchus City for fiscal year 2005. Assume that fund balance at the beginning of 2005 is $2,607,241.

1. Bacchus City has three departments: Streets and Parkways, Public Safety, and Administration.
2. Budgeted data pertaining to the Public Safety and Administration departments for fiscal year 2005 are as follows:

	Public Safety	Administration
Personal services	$1,115,000	$1,450,000
Travel	10,000	20,000
Equipment	650,000	100,000
Operating expenses	85,000	60,000

P3-8 (Control report)

Refer to P3-4. Prepare a control report, like the one shown in Table 3-14, for operating expenses of the Streets and Parkways Department for the month of August 2004. Assume that August is the eighth month of the fiscal year and that the year-to-date budget is two-thirds of the entire 2004 budget. Assume also that the budget for August is one-twelfth of the entire 2004 budget. Year-to-date actual results are given in P3-4. Actual results for the month of August are as follows:

Contractual services:	
Vehicle and equipment maintenance	$1,567
Communication	75
Rentals	89
Utilities	110
Telephone	15
Professional services	50
Supplies and materials:	
Office supplies	$15
Auto and truck	30
Equipment supplies	110
Asphalt	300
Fuel	120
Emergency supplies	25
Tools	75
Miscellaneous	5

Chapter

The Governmental Fund Accounting Cycle

An Introduction to General and Special Revenue Funds

After completing this chapter, you should be able to:

➤ *Compare the objectives of fund accounting with those of commercial accounting.*

➤ *Contrast the accounting cycle of a governmental unit with that of a commercial organization.*

➤ *Explain why separate budgetary entries are used.*

➤ *Prepare operating entries in the funds of a governmental unit.*

➤ *Prepare closing entries in the funds of a governmental unit.*

➤ *Explain why revenues from property taxes are recorded when these taxes are levied, rather than when they are collected.*

➤ *Describe how control and subsidiary accounts are used.*

➤ *Explain the use of encumbrances and how they should be recorded in the accounts.*

➤ *Discuss the need for and accounting treatment of short-term borrowings.*

*T*he most basic funds used by nonbusiness organizations are the General Fund and Special Revenue Funds. The *General Fund* is used to record the overall operations of the organization and provides a catchall for revenues and expenditures not recorded in other funds. Activities accounted for in this fund include police and fire protection and other day-to-day operations of the governmental unit.

Special Revenue Funds are used to account for the proceeds of specific revenue sources (other than trusts for individuals, private organizations, or other governmental units, or those used for major capital projects) that must be spent for particular purposes. Examples of Special Revenue Funds may include funds used to account for the activities of libraries and parks and for federal and state grants. From an accounting standpoint, General Funds and Special Revenue Funds are similar.

Because General Funds are the most commonly used funds and the accounting for most other funds is based on that of General Funds and Special Revenue Funds, these funds are discussed first. If you understand the entries used by these funds, you can easily learn those unique to the other funds.

As in commercial accounting, the objective of fund accounting is to convey to the reader of financial statements a picture of what happened in the past. From this information, the reader can make financially related decisions. Fund accounting, however, is also concerned with the future and with certain legal considerations. As a result, the fund accounting cycle is somewhat more complicated than the commercial accounting cycle—even though the end products are essentially the same. The two cycles are contrasted in Table 4-1.

Table 4-1

Fund Accounting versus Commercial Accounting

FUND ACCOUNTING OBJECTIVES[a]	COMMERCIAL ACCOUNTING OBJECTIVES
• To show the financial position of the organization's funds • To show the results of operations of the organization's funds • To show changes in the financial position of the organization's funds • To show compliance with legal restrictions	• To show the financial position of the firm • To show the results of operations of the firm • To show changes in the financial position of the firm
ACCOUNTING CYCLE	ACCOUNTING CYCLE

• Record the budget in the accounting records
 • Record transactions for the period
 • Prepare closing entries
 • Prepare fund financial statements and schedules
   Balance sheet
   Statement of revenues, expenditures, and changes in fund balance (or net assets)
   Statement of cash flows (only for proprietary-type funds)
   Schedule comparing budgeted and actual revenues and expenditures (of certain governmental-type funds)
 • Prepare government-wide financial statements
	• Record transactions for the period
	 • Prepare closing entries
	 • Prepare financial statements
	   Balance sheet
	   Income statement and statement of changes in retained earnings
	   Statement of cash flows

[a]For a more detailed listing of fund accounting objectives, see Chapter 9.

A BASIC FUND ACCOUNTING SYSTEM

The steps in the fund accounting cycle are also shown in Table 4-1. Notice that the cycle begins with the budget and that, unlike commercial accounting, the budget is formally recorded in the accounts.

The Budget

In fund accounting, the *budget* is usually a legal document. It is an estimate of the expenditures of a fiscal year and the means proposed to finance them. It is also the end product of a series of requests and proposals that originate with department heads and other managers and, after being screened and adjusted by the budget officer, are put into budgetary form. A typical budget is shown in Table 4-2.

Table 4-2
Budget of Orleans Levee Board

ORLEANS LEVEE BOARD
GENERAL FUND
ESTIMATED REVENUES, APPROPRIATIONS, AND OTHER SOURCES (USES)
FISCAL YEAR JULY 1, 20X4, TO JUNE 30, 20X5

Estimated Revenues		
Ad valorem taxes	$6,720,232	
Royalties	1,000,000	
State revenue sharing	600,000	
New Orleans Lakefront Airport	1,086,361	
Orleans Marina	1,004,000	
Lake Vista Community Center	132,759	
Other locations	330,105	
Lakefront camps	15,450	
Interest on investments	785,000	
Miscellaneous	5,700	
Total estimated revenues		$11,679,607
Appropriations		
Personal services	$6,305,764	
Travel	40,000	
Contractual services	2,670,040	
Materials and supplies	1,061,792	
Professional services	497,905	
Other charges	34,806	
Equipment	609,897	
Total appropriations		11,220,204
Excess of estimated revenues over appropriations		$ 459,403
Other Financing Sources (Uses)		
Transfer from Special Levee Improvement Project Fund	$821,640	
Transfer to General Improvement Project Fund	(862,500)	
Transfer to Debt Service Fund	(70,878)	
Orleans Marina transfer to South Shore Harbor	(1,004,000)	
Contingent transfer from South Harbor to Board	384,657	
Designations:		
Contingency—unemployment compensation payments	(9,500)	
Contingency—materials and supplies purchases	(5,000)	
Contingency—equipment purchases	(3,000)	
Contingency—A/C replacements	(25,000)	
Major heavy equipment replacement	(105,000)	
Amount provided for Capital Projects from prior-year project allocations	425,000	
Total other sources (uses)		(453,581)
Excess of estimated revenues and other financing sources over appropriations and other financing uses		$ 5,822

Source: Adapted from an *Annual Approved Budget* of the Orleans Levee Board.

The principal items in this budget are Estimated revenues, Appropriations, and Other financing sources (uses). *Estimated revenues* are resources available to or expected to be available to the organization. They include taxes, fines and penalties, and service charges. One such resource, unique to governmental units, is the right to levy taxes on real and personal property. In this budget, Estimated revenues are broken down into those obtained from ad valorem (property) taxes and from other sources of income such as royalties, revenue sharing, and interest on investments.

Appropriations are allocations of resources that will be used to carry out the activities of the organization (proposed expenditures). They represent the authority to spend money in accordance with the approved budget, which is not to imply, of course, that the money must be spent. Appropriations are made with the expectation of providing a certain level of services. If such services should happen to be provided at less cost, the monies saved can be used to increase the fund balance or to provide additional services.

Appropriations are broken down by category or object and, in some cases, by department or function as well (e.g., police salaries). In most of this text, however, we will assume that appropriations are budgeted by object. This simplification makes it appear that each organization has only one department. In reality, of course, most organizations have many departments (or functions), with each department using its own set of operating accounts. Nevertheless, the entries illustrated in this chapter and Chapter 5 are applicable to nearly all nonbusiness organizations, the only difference being the level of detail involved.

Other financing sources are receipts of resources that are not revenues. Examples include the proceeds of an issue of bonds and certain types of transfers from other funds, such as those from a Permanent Fund to a Library (Special Revenue) Fund.

Other financing uses are disbursements of resources that are not expenditures. Examples include payments made by the General Fund to a Capital Projects Fund for the General Fund's share of the cost of constructing new facilities, and payments made by Special Revenue Funds to Debt Service Funds for the retirement of debt. Other financing sources (uses) are broken down by type of transfer to and from the budgetary unit.

Opening Entries

At the beginning of the fiscal year, the approved budget is recorded in the accounts. Debits are made to estimated revenue accounts and credits are made to appropriation accounts. Any difference between Estimated revenues and Appropriations is debited or credited to Budgetary fund balance. The dollar amounts shown in these entries, which are known as *budgetary entries,* correspond to the ones shown in the budget. Because budgetary accounting should be kept separate from nonbudgetary accounting, entries to budgetary and nonbudgetary accounts should always be recorded separately. They should never appear in the same journal entry.

The use of separate budgetary accounts requires the use of two fund balance accounts. The first, *Budgetary Fund Balance* is the difference between Estimated revenues and Appropriations. It represents the anticipated change in fund balance as a result of the budget. Like other budgetary accounts, it is "temporary" in nature and is closed out at the end of the period.

The second fund balance account, the nonbudgetary or "actual" fund balance, is a residual account whose balance is the difference between the assets and the liabilities of the fund. At the end of the fiscal year, revenues and expenditures are closed out to this account. The account itself is "permanent" in nature, and its balance is carried forward into future periods. It is usually called *Unreserved Fund Balance*. The term *unreserved* indicates that this part of the fund balance has not been set aside or reserved for any special purpose. Reserves will be discussed in Chapter 5.

To illustrate the fund accounting cycle, assume that the city council of Simple City just approved the budget shown in Table 4-3. At the beginning of the fiscal year, the following budgetary entry is made:

Estimated revenues	1,000,000	
Appropriations		990,000
Budgetary fund balance		10,000
To record estimated revenues and appropriations for FY 2004.		

After this entry is posted, the general ledger appears as follows:

Estimated revenues = Appropriations + Budgetary fund balance
$1,000,000 = $990,000 + $10,000

Estimated revenues and Appropriations are budgetary accounts. *Budgetary accounts,* by definition, are accounts used to enter the formally adopted annual budget into the general ledger. At the end of the period, all budgetary accounts are closed out (their balances are reduced to zero). Many nonbudgetary accounts, by contrast, are "permanent" in nature (e.g., Unreserved fund balance); their balances carry forward to the next accounting period.

Table 4-3
Illustrative Budget

SIMPLE CITY GENERAL FUND BUDGET FISCAL YEAR 2004		
Estimated Revenues		
Property taxes	$900,000	
Fines, licenses, etc.	100,000	$1,000,000
Appropriations		
Salaries	$700,000	
Materials	200,000	
Other	90,000	990,000
Projected Increase in Fund Balance		$ 10,000

Recording Revenues and Expenditures

Revenue and expenditure accounting provides information for several purposes:

1. To determine whether all revenues have been received. Revenue accounting is the process of recording the amount of taxes, fees, and other revenues that have been received, as well as those still outstanding. Although the organization has the right to tax, it does not necessarily follow that the taxes have actually been collected.
2. To determine whether expenditures were made in accordance with the budget. Expenditure accounting is the process of recording the actual monies spent, on an item-by-item basis. It provides information on the relationship between budgeted and actual expenditures, as to both their nature and their size.
3. To prepare fund-level financial statements. Revenue and expenditure accounting provide information for fund balance sheets and for fund statements of revenues, expenditures, and changes in fund balance (or net assets). Adjustments are then needed for the preparation of government-wide financial statements.
4. To assist in the preparation of future budgets. Actual revenues collected are often used as a base in determining the size and composition of future tax levies and service charges. Actual expenditures determine the cost of services rendered. Both provide inputs into decisions as to what services should be made available in the future.

Revenue and expenditure accounts, like their commercial counterparts, are nominal accounts. They are not permanent in nature, as are assets and liabilities. Instead they are closed out (reduced to zero) at the end of each period.

Entries to record revenues are similar to those found in commercial accounting—debits to Cash or receivable accounts and credits to revenue accounts. To continue with the previous example, if all revenues are collected at once and in cash, the entry is

Cash	1,000,000	
Revenues		1,000,000
To record collection of FY 2004 revenues.		

Entries to record expenditures are also similar to those used in commercial accounting: debits to expenditure accounts and credits to Cash or payable accounts. If all monies appropriated for the period are spent (expended), the entry is

Expenditures	990,000	
Cash		990,000
To record incurrence of FY 2004 expenditures.		

Closing Entries

The *closing process* usually takes place at year-end. Its purpose is to close (reduce to zero) the nominal (revenue and expenditure) and budgetary (estimated revenue and appropriation) accounts and, if necessary, to adjust Unreserved fund balance to its "correct" amount.

In commercial accounting, revenues and expenses are matched, and any difference is added to or deducted from retained earnings. In governmental accounting, a similar process is followed. The nonbudgetary revenue and expenditure accounts are matched, and the difference is added to or deducted from Unreserved fund balance. Unlike commercial accounting, however, the budgetary accounts are also closed. This latter "closing" is different in that Budgetary fund balance is reduced to zero, along with the other budgetary accounts. The closing procedure can usually be accomplished by simply reversing out the opening budgetary entry.

Continuing with the illustration, assume that revenues of $1,000,000 are collected and that $990,000 is expended (paid out) during the year. The closing entries are

1. Appropriations   990,000
     Budgetary fund balance   10,000
          Estimated revenues   1,000,000
     To close budgetary accounts for FY 2004.

2. Revenues   1,000,000
          Expenditures   990,000
          Unreserved fund balance   10,000
     To close nonbudgetary accounts for FY 2004.

Each of the five accounts closed out now shows a zero balance. Because actual revenues were not equal to actual expenditures, it was necessary to adjust Unreserved fund balance at the end of the year.

An Alternative Approach

Some accountants prefer to only use a nonbudgetary fund balance account. When the budget is recorded, the difference between Estimated revenues and Appropriations is credited (or debited) to Unreserved fund balance. At the end of the period, Estimated revenues are closed to Revenues, and Appropriations are closed to Expenditures. Any differences between Estimated revenues and Revenues and between Appropriations and Expenditures are debited or credited to Unreserved fund balance.

Under this approach the opening, or budgetary, entry in the preceding illustration would be:

Estimated revenues   1,000,000
     Appropriations   990,000
     Unreserved fund balance   10,000
     To record estimated revenues and appropriations for FY 2004.

The operating entries would be

1. Cash   1,000,000
          Revenues   1,000,000
     To record FY 2004 revenues.

2. Expenditures   990,000
          Cash   990,000
     To record FY 2004 expenditures.

The closing entries would be

1. Revenues   1,000,000

       Estimated revenues   1,000,000

     To close revenue and estimated revenue accounts for FY 2004.

2. Appropriations   990,000

       Expenditures   990,000

     To close appropriation and expenditure accounts for FY 2004.

      The net effect of these entries is the same as that of the entries previously illustrated, that is, zero balances in the Revenue, Estimated revenue, Expenditure, and Appropriations accounts and a $10,000 balance in Unreserved fund balance. Although this approach is used by many organizations, the authors of this text do not recommend it. Its use of only one fund balance account violates the principal of separation of budgetary and nonbudgetary accounting, creates the appearance of fund balance before it actually exists, and can be confusing to unsophisticated preparers and users of the resulting reports. This text will follow the first approach, which is conceptually sound and easier to understand.

      After the closing entries are posted, a postclosing trial balance is prepared, followed by financial statements. The postclosing trial balance for Simple City is shown in Table 4-4. The resulting financial statements are shown in Table 4-5.[1]

      Table 4-5 is simplified and not very realistic. Nevertheless, all the elements of the fund accounting cycle are present. If you understand the example, you will readily master the refinements that are present in real-world problems.

      The example used in this section is summarized in Table 4-6. Before continuing, be certain that you understand why each entry was made and its effect on the accounting equation. The budget from which the opening entries are derived is on page 120. The statements are on page 124.

Table 4-4
Postclosing Trial Balance

SIMPLE CITY
GENERAL FUND
POSTCLOSING TRIAL BALANCE
DECEMBER 31, 2004

	DEBITS	CREDITS
Cash	$10,000	
Unreserved fund balance		$10,000
	$10,000	$10,000

---

[1] For the sake of brevity, it is assumed that the reader is able to make entries to the ledger. The mechanics of posting are discussed in Chapter 15.

Table 4-5
Illustrative Financial Statements

SIMPLE CITY
GENERAL FUND
BALANCE SHEET
DECEMBER 31, 2004

ASSETS		LIABILITIES AND FUND BALANCE	
Cash	$10,000	Unreserved fund balance	$10,000

SIMPLE CITY
GENERAL FUND
STATEMENT OF REVENUES, EXPENDITURES, AND
CHANGES IN FUND BALANCES
FISCAL YEAR 2004

Revenues	$1,000,000
Expenditures	990,000
Excess of revenues over expenditures and net changes in fund balances	$ 10,000
Fund balance, 1/1/04	-0-
Fund balance, 12/31/04	$ 10,000

Table 4-6
Summary of Accounting Cycle of General Fund of Simple City for FY 2004

The *opening* or budgetary entry is		
Estimated revenues	1,000,000	
Appropriations		990,000
Budgetary fund balance		10,000
To record estimated revenues and appropriations for FY 2004.		
The *operating* entries are		
Cash	1,000,000	
Revenues		1,000,000
To record FY 2004 revenues.		
Expenditures	990,000	
Cash		990,000
To record FY 2004 expenditures.		
The *closing* entries are		
Appropriations	990,000	
Budgetary fund balance	10,000	
Estimated revenues		1,000,000
To close budgetary accounts for FY 2004.		
Revenues	1,000,000	
Expenditures		990,000
Unreserved fund balance		10,000
To close nonbudgetary accounts for FY 2004.		

A More Refined System

The example in the preceding section, although theoretically correct, is oversimplified. Revenues are actually collected, and expenditures are actually incurred, in uneven amounts throughout the year. As a result, revenues and expenditures seldom equal Estimated revenues and Appropriations. In addition, many different revenue and expenditure accounts are used by governmental units, resources are set aside (encumbered) when certain goods or services are ordered, and governmental units must often borrow money for short periods of time. Finally, events that require unplanned expenditures sometimes occur, necessitating the transfer of appropriations from other activities. In this section, several refinements will be made to the basic system previously illustrated: receivables, subsidiary accounts, encumbrances, short-term borrowings, and budgetary interchanges.

Receivables

After the approved budget of a governmental unit is recorded in the accounts, property taxes are levied. The governmental unit now has a claim against each taxpayer for his or her share of the property taxes due. To recognize this *receivable,* a debit is made to Property taxes receivable and a credit to a revenue account. When the taxes are collected, Cash is debited and Property taxes receivable is credited. The legal claim against the taxpayer or taxpayers has now been satisfied.

This procedure differs from the one discussed in the preceding section in that revenues from property taxes are recorded when they are levied, rather than when they are collected. Under the modified accrual basis of accounting, which is used by governmental-type funds, such a procedure is required. This approach is used because the amounts received from property taxes, unlike those received from other sources, are available and measurable, with a reasonable degree of accuracy, when the property taxes are levied.

In addition, the collection of revenues from property taxes is, in theory, fairly certain because the organization has a claim against specific tangible property. In the event of nonpayment of taxes, the governmental unit has the legal right to force the sale of the property and to deduct the taxes due from the proceeds.

To illustrate, assume that property taxes of $900,000 are levied by Refined City. The entry to recognize (record) the receivable is

Property taxes receivable	900,000	
Revenues—property taxes		900,000
To set up receivable for FY 2004 property taxes.		

When the property taxes are collected, the entry is

Cash	900,000	
Property taxes receivable		900,000
To record the collection of property taxes.		

This entry assumes, for illustrative purposes, that all taxes are collected at once. In reality, smaller amounts are collected each day. As a result, a series of entries, similar to the one shown, is made, with the collections totaling $900,000.

Receivable accounts are generally used to record the assessment of property taxes, because property taxes are levied against a given base (the assessed value of the property within the governmental unit). When the millage (tax rate) has been determined (usually when the budget is approved), the amount that should be received is known with a reasonable degree of certainty.

Income taxes, fees, fines, and other sources of revenue, however, are influenced by such variables as the level of employment, housing starts, and number of tourists. These revenues cannot be determined with certainty. At the fund level, they are generally recognized through a debit to Cash and a credit to a revenue account when the cash is collected.

To illustrate, assume that the monies actually collected from "other" sources of revenue are $100,000 and that they all are received at once. The entry to recognize these revenues is

Cash	100,000	
Revenues—other		100,000
To record revenues from sources other than property taxes, FY 2004.		

Control and Subsidiary Accounts

In the preceding examples all revenues were combined into one account, as were all expenditures. This approach is not realistic or practical. Nonbusiness organizations, like their commercial counterparts, use control and subsidiary accounts. A *control account* is a summary account whose balance is equal to the total of the individual balances of its *subsidiary accounts*. The balances in the control accounts are changed when, and by the same amount that, changes are made in the subsidiary accounts. Examples of control accounts include Property taxes receivable (which are backed up by accounts for each taxpayer), Estimated revenues, Appropriations, and Expenditures (see Table 4-7).

An alternative to subsidiary and control accounts is the use of a large number of specialized accounts, similar in nature but different in detail. Many organizations use this approach on several levels. For example, appropriation and expenditure accounts are sometimes broken down by function or department (public safety, welfare, etc.) and then by object or category (salaries, supplies, etc.). Thus the account used to record the salaries of police officers would be Expenditures—Police Department—salaries. An account used to record revenues from licenses issued to owners of tour buses would be Revenues—license fees—tour buses.

Except for the following illustration, in which control and subsidiary accounts are used to record the collection of property taxes, a one-step breakdown is used throughout this text and control and subsidiary accounts are combined. This method keeps the illustrative problems to a manageable size. Expanding the illustrations to include a two- or three-level breakdown or to include separate subsidiary and control accounts is fairly simple.

Table 4-7

Examples of Control and Subsidiary Accounts

CONTROL	SUBSIDIARY	DETAIL
Revenues	—Taxes	Property taxes Sales tax Penalties and interest on delinquent taxes
	—Licenses and permits	Business licenses and permits Nonbusiness licenses and permits
	—Intergovernmental revenue	Federal grants State grants
	—Charges for services	General government Public safety Highways and streets Sanitation
	—Fines and forfeitures	Fines Forfeitures
Expenditures	—General government	Salaries Supplies Capital outlays Other services
	—Public safety	Salaries Supplies Capital outlays Other services
	—Highways and streets	Salaries Supplies Capital outlays Other services
	—Sanitation and health	Salaries Supplies Capital outlays Other services
	—Education	Salaries Supplies Capital outlays Other services
Receivables	—Property taxes receivable	J. Bach F. Chopin W. Mozart J. Strauss A. Sullivan

To illustrate the use of control and subsidiary accounts, as well as a number of different revenue and expenditure accounts, assume that Refined City has the following budgeted sources of revenue:

Property taxes	$ 900,000
License fees	50,000
Fines	40,000
Service charges	10,000
Total	$1,000,000

Assume also that the city has five property owners, whose property taxes are levied as follows:

J. Brill	$500,000
R. Jewett	300,000
G. Kuhlman	45,000
A. Niles	30,000
P. Thomas	25,000
Total	$900,000

Finally, assume that the city has one department whose appropriations are as follows:

Salaries	$700,000
Supplies	200,000
Other	90,000
Total	$990,000

The opening, or budgetary, entry is

Estimated revenues—property taxes	900,000	
Estimated revenues—license fees	50,000	
Estimated revenues—fines	40,000	
Estimated revenues—service charges	10,000	
Appropriations—salaries		700,000
Appropriations—supplies		200,000
Appropriations—other		90,000
Budgetary fund balance		10,000

  To record estimated revenues and appropriations for FY 2004.

If subsidiary and control accounts are used for property taxes, the entry to set up the receivable is

Property taxes receivable—control	900,000	
Revenues—property taxes		900,000
To set up receivable for FY 2004 property taxes.		

Property Taxes Receivable—Subsidiary Ledger	
Debit	
J. Brill	$500,000
R. Jewett	300,000
G. Kuhlman	45,000
A. Niles	30,000
P. Thomas	25,000
	$900,000

If these taxpayers pay their property tax bills in full during the period, the entry to record the payments is

Cash	900,000	
Property taxes receivable—control		900,000
To record collection of FY 2004 property taxes.		

Property Taxes Receivable—Subsidiary Ledger	
Credit	
J. Brill	$500,000
R. Jewett	300,000
G. Kuhlman	45,000
A. Niles	30,000
P. Thomas	25,000
	$900,000

Other revenues are recorded when collected or, in the case of self-assessed taxes like those on income and sales, when available and measurable.[2] The entry to record these revenues (amounts assumed) is

Cash	96,000	
Revenues—license fees		47,000
Revenues—fines		38,000
Revenues—service charges		11,000
To record receipt of nonproperty tax revenues, FY 2004.		

---

[2] Self-assessed taxes and the meaning of the term *available and measurable* are discussed in Chapter 5.

Entries to record expenditures and their subsequent payment (amounts assumed) are

Expenditures—salaries	700,000	
Expenditures—supplies	195,000	
Expenditures—other	89,000	
Cash		700,000
Vouchers payable		284,000
To record FY 2004 expenditures.		

Vouchers payable	284,000	
Cash		284,000
To record payment of outstanding FY 2004 vouchers.		

Finally, the closing entries are

Appropriations—salaries	700,000	
Appropriations—supplies	200,000	
Appropriations—other	90,000	
Budgetary fund balance	10,000	
Estimated revenues—property taxes		900,000
Estimated revenues—license fees		50,000
Estimated revenues—fines		40,000
Estimated revenues—service charges		10,000
To close budgetary accounts for FY 2004.		

Revenues—property taxes	900,000	
Revenues—license fees	47,000	
Revenues—fines	38,000	
Revenues—service charges	11,000	
Expenditures—salaries		700,000
Expenditures—supplies		195,000
Expenditures—other		89,000
Unreserved fund balance		12,000
To close nonbudgetary accounts for FY 2004.		

Notice that these entries are similar to those found in earlier illustrations. The only differences are that specific revenues and expenditures are now recorded in the accounts and that estimated revenues and appropriations do not exactly match actual revenues and expenditures. Notice also that budgetary accounts are kept separate from nonbudgetary accounts.

Vouchers

In the preceding example, the account Vouchers payable was used. A *voucher* is a written document that provides evidence that a transaction is proper. It also indicates the accounts in which the transaction is recorded.

The term *vouchers payable* is used in fund accounting in the same manner that the term *accounts payable* is used in business accounting—to represent the recording of a liability. The use of a voucher, however, indicates that payment has been approved by the appropriate authority and will definitely be made at a particular time. It also serves as a basis for classifying expenditures (i.e., putting them into various accounts).

Most governmental units use a voucher system for all payments, including salaries. However in this text, to avoid creating excessive debits and credits for liabilities that are either paid immediately or are previously established, we will use vouchers only where indicated.

Expenditure Control—Encumbrances

Before a nonbusiness organization makes an expenditure for materials or services, a *requisition* (a formal written order or request) is prepared. After this document has been approved, a *purchase order* is sent to the vendor. The organization now takes on an obligation to make sufficient funds available to pay the vendor within a reasonable length of time after the arrival of the materials or the performance of services.

To meet this obligation, an *encumbrance* is recorded. The recording of the encumbrance signifies that resources are now set aside for a specific use and are no longer available for other expenditures. Because the materials or services are not yet received, however, the organization bears no legal financial obligation to the vendor. No liability (in the accounting sense) has been incurred, assets have not been increased, and the total fund balance has not been changed.

An encumbrance is recorded by means of a budgetary entry. Recording the encumbrance causes a portion of the appropriation to be set aside, or encumbered, until the materials are received or the services are performed. After the materials are received or the services performed, the encumbrance is reversed out and a liability and an expenditure are recorded.

To determine the amount available for spending at any given point in time, both expenditures and encumbrances must be deducted from the appropriation or appropriations. To illustrate:

FY 2004 appropriation	$990,000
Expenditures to date	500,000
Unexpended balance	$490,000
Outstanding encumbrances	200,000
Unencumbered (free) balance (available for spending)	$290,000

This information tells us that the organization is authorized to spend up to $990,000 during the current fiscal year, of which $500,000 has already been spent and $200,000 is committed to specific purchases. Therefore, the organization has $290,000 to spend for the remainder of the fiscal year.

When an encumbrance is recorded, a debit is made to an encumbrance account (e.g., Encumbrances—supplies) and a credit is made to an offsetting account called *Budgetary fund balance reserved for encumbrances*. This text uses these account titles because they are in general usage. The entry might be better understood, however, if the debit were to an account called "Appropriations encumbered" and the credit were to "Appropriations reserved for encumbrances." Such an entry would make it more evident that the effect of the entry was to set aside a portion of the governmental unit's spending authority for specific purposes.

Like other reserves, the reserve for encumbrances is used to identify resources committed, but not expended, so that the unencumbered balance will reflect only resources that can still be spent. It also indicates that even though goods and services have not yet been received, an outstanding commitment exists for a given dollar amount. Finally, it provides information on outstanding purchase orders.

To illustrate, assume that an order is placed for supplies costing, at the time of the order, $200,000. When the order is placed, an encumbrance is set up by means of the following entry:

Encumbrances—supplies	200,000	
Budgetary fund balance reserved for encumbrances		200,000
To record the encumbering of Purchase Order No. 1426.		

Upon receipt of the supplies, the encumbrance is removed (reversed out) and an expenditure and a liability or a reduction of cash is recorded.

Budgetary fund balance reserved for encumbrances	200,000	
Encumbrances—supplies		200,000
To record receipt of supplies ordered under Purchase Order No. 1426.		
Expenditures—supplies	200,000	
Cash or Vouchers payable		200,000
To record expenditure for the supplies purchased under Purchase Order No. 1426.		

When an encumbrance is removed, the reversing entry is for the amount of the purchase order. The entry to record the expenditure, however, is for the amount of the invoice, the "actual" cost of the materials or services received. As long as these two dollar amounts are equal, no problems arise.

In many cases, however, the amount of the invoice differs from the amount of the purchase order. It is not unusual, for example, to have a price change between the time an order is placed and the time the materials or services ordered are received. In such a situation, the amount reversed out is still the amount of the purchase order.

For example, if the actual invoice cost in the preceding illustration had been $195,000, the entry removing the encumbrance would still have been for the amount shown in the purchase order, $200,000. The original amount is always used, because the purpose of the reversing entry is to remove the purchase order and encumbrance from an outstanding status, not to record the expenditure. The expenditure, of course, would have been for $195,000.

If there is a difference between the amount of the purchase order and the invoice amount, the unencumbered balance of the appropriation is automatically adjusted because the outstanding encumbrance is replaced by an expenditure for the actual amount of the purchase.

To illustrate, assume that a city's appropriation for materials is for $100,000 and that a purchase order is issued for materials costing $34,000 (see Table 4-8). The balance of the appropriation, at the time the order is placed, is shown on the left. The

Table 4-8

Effect of Different Invoice Amounts on an Unencumbered Balance

	WHEN PURCHASE ORDER IS SENT TO VENDOR	CASE 1 ACTUAL INVOICE IS $34,000	CASE 2 ACTUAL INVOICE IS $33,000	CASE 3 ACTUAL INVOICE IS $35,000
Appropriations—materials	$100,000	$100,000	$100,000	$100,000
Expenditures—materials	-0-	34,000	33,000	35,000
Unexpended balance	$100,000	$ 66,000	$ 67,000	$ 65,000
Amount encumbered for materials	34,000	-0-	-0-	-0-
Unencumbered ("free") balance—available for the purchase of additional materials	$ 66,000	$ 66,000	$ 67,000	$ 65,000

effect of three different "actual" invoice amounts is shown on the right. Notice the following:

1. Regardless of the size of the invoice, the encumbered amount (the amount of the purchase order) is reversed out when the purchased materials arrive or the services ordered are provided.
2. If the amount of the invoice equals the amount of the purchase order (Case 1), recording the expenditure does not alter the unencumbered balance.
3. If the amount of the invoice is smaller than the amount of the purchase order (Case 2), the unencumbered balance is increased by the amount of the difference.
4. If the amount of the invoice is greater than the amount of the purchase order (Case 3), the unencumbered balance is decreased by the amount of the difference.

Budgetary and actual data are accumulated, for control purposes, in an *appropriation/expenditure ledger*. To illustrate, assume that the legislative body of a city approves the purchase of four police cruisers for $100,000. On January 15, two cruisers are ordered. The vehicles are expected to cost a total of $46,000. On March 18 the two cruisers arrive, along with an invoice for $45,000. On May 8, two more police cruisers are ordered, at an estimated total cost of $54,000. On June 6, these cruisers arrive, along with an invoice for $55,000. Table 4-9 shows how this information would appear in an appropriation/expenditure ledger account.

Notice how both the budgetary information and the actual information in Table 4-9 are used to control expenditures.

1. The original budgetary appropriation is the absolute maximum that can legally be spent without further action by the legislative body.
2. The placement of each order reduces the available balance, because of the effect of the encumbrance procedure.

Table 4-9
Appropriation/Expenditure Ledger (Police Vehicles)

Date	Item	Appropriation CR	Encumbrances DR	Encumbrances CR	Expenditures DR	Available Balance CR
1/1	Budget	$100,000				$100,000
1/15	Order 2 vehicles		$46,000			54,000
3/18	2 vehicles arrive			$46,000		100,000
3/18	Record invoice				$45,000	55,000
5/8	Order 2 vehicles		54,000			1,000
6/6	2 vehicles arrive			54,000		55,000
6/6	Record invoice				55,000	-0-

3. The receipt of each order causes the available balance to be increased or decreased. In this illustration, the actual cost of the first order of police cruisers was less than the amount encumbered. Therefore, the available balance increased from $54,000 to $55,000. As a result, the city was able to order better-equipped vehicles on May 8. If the actual cost of the first order of vehicles had been greater than the amount encumbered, the available balance would have been reduced. As a result, it would have been necessary for the city to order either fewer vehicles or the same number of vehicles with less equipment.

Revenue Control

Revenues are controlled by means of a comparison of budgetary and actual data. This information is accumulated, by type of revenue, in a revenue ledger. An account from a revenue ledger is shown in Table 4-10.

Short-Term Borrowings

Governmental units sometimes make short-term (1 year or less) borrowings. These are generally in the form of notes, which are often issued to banks and other financial institutions. A note is a written promise to pay a given amount of money at a particular point(s) in time. It can be secured by collateral, as in the case of a note signed by the purchaser of an automobile, or it can be unsecured. The latter type is more common in governmental units. Loans to these organizations are generally not risky because these organizations (theoretically) have the power to raise taxes in the event of a need for more revenues.

Among the more commonly used types of notes are tax anticipation notes. They are used by governmental units to cover current financial obligations until the taxes are collected, which may occur later in the year. The taxes collected are then used to retire the debt. Notes are also issued in anticipation of receiving funds from a bond issue. When the bonds are sold (issued), the proceeds are used to repay the notes.

Table 4-10

Revenue Ledger (Parking Meter Receipts)

DATE	ITEM	ESTIMATED REVENUES DR	ACTUAL REVENUES CR	DIFFERENCE DR (CR)
1/1	Budget	$25,000		$25,000
1/31	Jan. collections		$2,000	23,000
2/28	Feb. collections		2,500	20,500

The entries used to account for the issuance and repayment of notes are similar to those used by commercial enterprises. To illustrate, assume that Refined City borrows $100,000 from a bank, to be repaid (during the same fiscal year) from future tax collections. The entry to record this transaction is

Cash	100,000	
Tax anticipation notes payable		100,000
To record issuance of tax anticipation notes.		

When the notes are repaid, this entry will be reversed. This will result in a reduction of Cash and a reduction of the outstanding liability.

Governmental units also make long-term (more than 1 year) borrowings. These borrowings are usually in the form of bonds. When bonds are issued, fund-level entries are made in the fund receiving the proceeds of the bond issue, usually a Capital Projects Fund. Long-term borrowings are discussed in Chapter 6.

Budgetary Interchanges

Sometimes events that were not anticipated when the budget was prepared occur, and they require unplanned expenditures. To provide the budgetary authorization for these expenditures, appropriations are sometimes transferred from other activities. To make this transfer, a portion of the unexpended appropriation of one or more activities is reduced and the appropriation of the activity making the unplanned expenditure is increased.

Assume, for example, that a fire engine belonging to Windy City is destroyed by a tornado and must be replaced immediately. Assume also that the vehicle has a replacement value of $150,000. The City Council notices that the Fire Department has a number of budgeted, but unfilled, positions and that it is unlikely to spend a portion of its appropriation for salaries. As a result, the City Council reduces that department's appropriation for salaries by $150,000 and increases its appropriation for capital equipment by the same amount. The entry to record this transfer is:

Appropriations—salaries	150,000	
Appropriations—capital equipment		150,000
To record revision to budget necessary because of tornado damage.		

The Fire Department now has the budgetary authority to purchase a new fire engine. It cannot, however, fill all of its vacant positions until it receives budgetary authority to do so.

SUMMARY PROBLEM

This problem brings together the illustrations in this chapter. If you have any questions as you review the problem, turn back to the appropriate sections and reread the material.

On December 31, 2003, the city council of Refined City approved the budget shown in Table 4-11. Refined City has five property owners, whose fiscal year (FY) 2004 property taxes are as follows:

J. Brill	$500,000
R. Jewett	300,000
G. Kuhlman	45,000
A. Niles	30,000
P. Thomas	25,000
Total	$900,000

Table 4-11
Annual Budget

REFINED CITY GENERAL FUND BUDGET FOR THE YEAR ENDED DECEMBER 31, 2004		
Estimated Revenues		
Property taxes	$900,000	
License fees	50,000	
Fines	40,000	
Service charges	10,000	$1,000,000
Appropriations		
Salaries	$700,000	
Supplies	200,000	
Other	90,000	990,000
Projected Increase in Fund Balance		$ 10,000

Among the accounting policies of Refined City are the following:

1. All purchases of supplies are encumbered.
2. Other expenditures do not require encumbrances.
3. Separate accounts (as opposed to control and subsidiary accounts) are maintained for each taxpayer.
4. Vouchers are used to record all purchases.

The opening, or budgetary, entry is

Estimated revenues—property taxes	900,000	
Estimated revenues—license fees	50,000	
Estimated revenues—fines	40,000	
Estimated revenues—service charges	10,000	
Appropriations—salaries		700,000
Appropriations—supplies		200,000
Appropriations—other		90,000
Budgetary fund balance		10,000
To record estimated revenues and appropriations for FY 2004.		

The operating entries are as follows:

Property taxes receivable—Brill	500,000	
Property taxes receivable—Jewett	300,000	
Property taxes receivable—Kuhlman	45,000	
Property taxes receivable—Niles	30,000	
Property taxes receivable—Thomas	25,000	
Revenues—property taxes		900,000
To set up receivable for FY 2004 property taxes.		
Encumbrances—supplies	200,000	
Budgetary fund balance reserved for encumbrances		200,000
To record encumbering of Purchase Order No. 1426.		
Cash	100,000	
Tax anticipation notes payable		100,000
To record issuance of tax anticipation notes.		
Cash	900,000	
Property taxes receivable—Brill		500,000
Property taxes receivable—Jewett		300,000
Property taxes receivable—Kuhlman		45,000
Property taxes receivable—Niles		30,000
Property taxes receivable—Thomas		25,000
To record collection of FY 2004 property taxes.		
Budgetary balance fund reserved for encumbrances	200,000	
Encumbrances—supplies		200,000
To record receipt of supplies ordered under Purchase Order No. 1426.		
Expenditures—supplies	195,000	
Vouchers payable		195,000
To record expenditure for supplies purchased under Purchase Order No. 1426.		

Cash	96,000	
Revenues—license fees		47,000
Revenues—fines		38,000
Revenues—service charges		11,000

To record collection of nonproperty tax revenues, FY 2004.

Vouchers payable	195,000	
Cash		195,000

To record payment for supplies purchased under Purchase Order No. 1426.

Expenditures—salaries	700,000	
Expenditures—other	89,000	
Cash		700,000
Vouchers payable		89,000

To record expenditures for salaries and other items during FY 2004.

Vouchers payable	89,000	
Cash		89,000

To record payment of outstanding FY 2004 vouchers.

Tax anticipation notes payable	100,000	
Cash		100,000

To record repayment of tax anticipation notes.

(*Note:* For the sake of simplicity, no provision is made in this entry to record the payment of interest on this borrowing.)

The closing entries are as follows:

Appropriations—salaries	700,000	
Appropriations—supplies	200,000	
Appropriations—other	90,000	
Budgetary fund balance	10,000	
Estimated revenues—property taxes		900,000
Estimated revenues—license fees		50,000
Estimated revenues—fines		40,000
Estimated revenues—service charges		10,000

To close budgetary accounts for FY 2004.

Revenues—property taxes	900,000	
Revenues—license fees	47,000	
Revenues—fines	38,000	
Revenues—service charges	11,000	
Expenditures—salaries		700,000
Expenditures—supplies		195,000
Expenditures—other		89,000
Unreserved fund balance		12,000

To close nonbudgetary accounts for FY 2004.

After closing entries have been posted, the postclosing trial balance will appear as shown in Table 4-12. The resulting fund financial statements are shown in Table 4-13.

Table 4-12
Postclosing Trial Balance

REFINED CITY
GENERAL FUND
POSTCLOSING TRIAL BALANCE
DECEMBER 31, 2004

	DEBITS	CREDITS
Cash	$12,000	
Unreserved fund balance		$12,000
	$12,000	$12,000

Table 4-13
Fund Financial Statements

REFINED CITY
GENERAL FUND
BALANCE SHEET
DECEMBER 31, 2004

ASSETS		LIABILITIES AND FUND BALANCE	
Cash	$12,000	Unreserved fund balance	$12,000

REFINED CITY
GENERAL FUND
STATEMENT OF REVENUES, EXPENDITURES, AND CHANGES IN FUND BALANCE
FOR THE FISCAL YEAR ENDED DECEMBER 31, 2004

Revenues		
Property taxes	$900,000	
License fees	47,000	
Fines	38,000	
Service charges	11,000	
Total revenues		$996,000
Expenditures		
Salaries	$700,000	
Supplies	195,000	
Other	89,000	
Total Expenditures		984,000
Excess of Revenues over Expenditures and Net Change in Fund Balance		$12,000
Fund balance, 1/1/04		-0-
Fund balance, 12/31/04		$12,000

REVIEW QUESTIONS

Q4-1 How does the accounting cycle of a governmental unit differ from that of a business firm?

Q4-2 Define the term *budget*. What principal items are contained in a budget of a governmental unit?

Q4-3 Distinguish between expenditures and expenses.

Q4-4 What is an appropriation? How does it differ from an expenditure?

Q4-5 Why is the budget used by governmental units a "legal" document?

Q4-6 What are budgetary entries? When are they made?

Q4-7 Does the unreserved fund balance account usually have a debit or a credit balance? What does the amount accumulated in the fund balance account represent?

Q4-8 Why can a governmental unit record property tax revenues in the accounts before these revenues are actually received in cash? Why are other types of revenues, such as income taxes and license fees, recorded in the accounts after cash is received?

Q4-9 What is a control account? A subsidiary account?

Q4-10 What is a voucher? What purpose does it serve?

Q4-11 What is a purchase order? A requisition? An invoice?

Q4-12 How is a levy of property taxes recorded in the accounting records? How is the collection of the taxes recorded?

Q4-13 What is an encumbrance? When is it used? Is it used for all expenditures of a governmental unit?

Q4-14 Why are city officials interested in the unencumbered balance of an appropriation?

Q4-15 What is the effect of encumbrances on the amount of an appropriation available for spending?

Q4-16 What is a budgetary interchange? When is it used?

CASES

C4-1 Because of lax tax collections, the City of Bliss has run out of money on several occasions. Upon reviewing this situation, the new finance director noticed that most purchases of goods and services are actually for less than amounts encumbered for these purchases. As a result, he requested that, when removing encumbrances, only the actual amount of the purchase be reversed out, not the entire amount encumbered. Using this method, he reasoned, will provide a "cushion" that can be used to make up any shortfall that might arise by the end of the year.

Do you think this accounting practice is sound?

ETHICS CASES

EC4-1 The newly elected mayor of Wherever noticed that in the recently enacted budget of that city's General Fund, revenues exceed expenditures by $15,000. Later that year, after a hurricane caused a large amount of damage, she ordered the city's finance officer to write a check for $15,000, on the General Fund, to an emergency relief fund. Because of the unexpected nature of the hurricane, no appropriation had been made to cover this transaction. When confronted by the press, she pointed out that the General Fund was only required under the balanced budget laws of the state to "break even" and that she could not, in good conscience, allow the city to retain idle monies when people needed help.

From an accounting standpoint, did the mayor do the right thing? From an ethical standpoint?

EC4-2 You are the finance director of Bloomfield City. Recently, the voters of your city approved a special property tax to finance the purchase of new books and software for the local library. The day the first receipts from this new tax arrived, you ate lunch with the mayor. After finishing his second piece of pie, the mayor suggested that you record the proceeds of this tax in the General Fund. "I know that this is a dedicated tax, but we need the money now to pay for the new computers and police cars we just purchased. This fall, when sales tax collections peak, we will buy some books and software for the library. If sales tax collections are down, the library patrons will just have to reread the old books." Assuming that the mayor is a reasonable person, how would you respond to his comments?

EXERCISES

E4-1 (Budgetary entries)
The city council of Alhambra approved the following budget:

Estimated Revenues		
Property taxes	$150,000	
Fines and fees	25,000	
Service charges	15,000	
Licenses	10,000	$200,000
Appropriations		
Salaries	$100,000	
Materials and supplies	60,000	
Equipment	30,000	190,000
Projected Increase in Fund Balance		$ 10,000

Required: Prepare the appropriate budgetary entry.

E4-2   (Budgetary entries)
The budget for the Perlita Park Fund is as follows:

Estimated Revenues
Property taxes	$2,400,000
Greens fees	600,000
Camping fees	400,000
Fines and permits	200,000

Appropriations
Wage and salaries	$1,600,000
Grass seed	200,000
Animal food	200,000
Operating supplies	400,000
Outside services	600,000
Repave driveways	200,000
Move locomotive	50,000
Construct shelters	300,000

Required: 1. Prepare the entry to record the approved budget at the beginning of the year.
2. If this year is the park's first year of operation, how much should the fund balance contain at the end of the year if actual revenues and expenditures are as planned?

E4-3   (Closing entries)
The ledger of the General Fund of the City of New Rachel shows the following balances at the end of the fiscal year:

Estimated revenues	$300,000
Appropriations	285,000
Budgetary fund balance	15,000
Revenues	300,000
Expenditures	285,000

Required: Prepare closing entries.

E4-4   (Closing entries)
At the end of FY 2004, the following balances were found in the ledger of the Castle Rock Park Library Fund:

Estimated revenues	$800,000
Appropriations	750,000
Budgetary fund balance	50,000
Revenues	775,000
Expenditures	760,000

Required: Prepare closing entries. What was the net effect on Unreserved fund balance?

E4-5   (Complete budgetary cycle)

The board of supervisors of Delaware County approved the following budget for FY 2004:

Estimated Revenues		
Property taxes	$66,000	
Traffic fines	40,000	$106,000
Appropriations		
Salaries	$80,000	
Supplies	12,000	
Other	8,000	100,000
Projected Increase in Fund Balance		$ 6,000

Transactions for FY 2004 were as follows:

1. Sent out property tax bills amounting to $66,000 at the beginning of the year.
2. Collected property taxes of $66,000 in cash during the year.
3. Purchased supplies for $12,000.
4. Paid salaries of $80,000.
5. Collected traffic fines of $40,000.
6. Purchased a membership in the Kenner Country Club for Sheriff Lee in recognition of his services to the county. The cost of the membership was $8,000.

Required: Prepare journal entries to set up the budgetary accounts, to record these transactions, and to close the budgetary and nonbudgetary accounts. Do not make entries to record encumbrances.

E4-6   (Complete budgetary cycle)

The city council of Avalon approved the following budget for FY 2004:

Estimated Revenues		
Property taxes	$150,000	
Fines and penalties	40,000	
Service charges	10,000	$200,000
Appropriations		
Salaries	$100,000	
Supplies	30,000	
Equipment	65,000	195,000
Projected Increase in Fund Balance		$ 5,000

In FY 2004, the following transactions took place:

1. Sent out property tax bills for $150,000 at the beginning of the year.
2. Collected property taxes of $150,000 during the year.
3. Purchased equipment for $60,000.
4. Purchased supplies for $34,000.
5. Collected fines and penalties of $38,000 and service charges of $7,000 in cash.
6. Paid salaries of $98,000.

Required: Prepare journal entries to set up budgetary accounts, to record these transactions, and to close the budgetary and nonbudgetary accounts. Do not make entries to record encumbrances.

E4-7 (Complete budgetary cycle)
The board of supervisors of Arabi Township approved the following budget for FY 2004:

Revenues		
Licenses	$10,000	
Fines	5,000	
Parking	3,000	
Parade permits	2,000	
Gas royalties	20,000	$40,000
Appropriations		
Salaries	$25,000	
Materials	10,000	
Equipment	3,000	38,000
Projected Increase in Fund Balance		$ 2,000
Actual Revenues		
Licenses	$11,000	
Fines	7,000	
Parking	3,000	
Parade permits	2,500	
Gas royalties	19,500	
Actual Expenditures		
Salaries	$24,000	
Materials	8,000	
Equipment	5,000	

The township does not use encumbrances. All expenditures are paid in cash. Assume that property tax bills totaling $150,000 were sent out at the beginning of the year.

Required: 1. Prepare opening entries.
2. Prepare operating entries.
3. Prepare closing entries.

E4-8 (Receivables)
The city council of Llanerch has budgeted property tax revenues of $10,000 for FY 2004. The city has four property owners, whose property tax levies are as follows:

Able	$4,000
Baker	3,000
Charles	2,000
Delta	1,000
	$10,000

During the year, each of these property owners paid his or her taxes in full and on time. The city uses a one-step breakdown when recording revenues (e.g., Property taxes receivable—Baker).

Required: Prepare journal entries to record setting up the receivable for property taxes due and the payment of the property taxes.

E4-9 (Encumbrances)

In February 2004, the City of Golders Green ordered a fire engine, for which the manufacturer quoted a price of $120,000. The machine arrived the following month, along with an invoice for $120,000.

Required:

1. Make the appropriate journal entries to record setting up the encumbrance, the removal of the encumbrance, and the expenditure and the liability to the vendor.
2. Assume that the actual cost of the fire engine was $125,000. Would your entries be the same as in the preceding question? Why?

E4-10 (Encumbrances)

On January 10, the City of Wynnewood issued a purchase order to its stationery supplier for $50,000. On March 20, the stationery arrived, along with an invoice for $50,000, which was immediately approved for payment. The invoice was paid on April 15.

Required: Prepare the entries necessary to record setting up the encumbrance, the arrival of the stationery and approval for payment of the invoice, and the payment of the invoice.

E4-11 (Encumbrances)

On April 25, the City of Bryn Mawr ordered supplies with a quoted price of $80,000. On May 15, one half of the supplies arrived, along with an invoice for $40,000. On June 6, the other half of the supplies arrived, accompanied by an invoice for $42,000. Both invoices were paid at the end of the month of arrival. Assume that there are sufficient resources in the appropriation to pay both invoices and that invoices are approved for payment upon receipt of the accompanying goods or services.

Required: 1. Prepare entries to record setting up the encumbrance, the arrival of the supplies in May and June and approval of the invoice, and the payment for the supplies.
2. What effect, if any, will the second invoice have on the balance of the appropriation?

E4-12 (Receivables)

The city council of Tabiona budgeted revenues of $100,000 from the following sources:

Property taxes	$ 60,000
Fines and penalties	30,000
Service charges	10,000
	$100,000

The city has three property owners, whose tax bills are as follows:

M. Sobel	$30,000
E. Johnson	20,000
J. Jordan	10,000
	$60,000

During the year, all property owners paid their taxes on time and in full. Collections from other sources of revenue were:

Fines and penalties	$30,000
Service charges	10,000
	$40,000

Assume that appropriations amount to $100,000.

Required: Using a one-step breakdown (e.g., Revenues—income taxes), prepare the following:
1. Budgetary entry
2. Entry to set up receivable accounts for property taxes
3. Entry or entries to record the collection of revenues
4. Entry to close out the revenue accounts

E4-13 (Receivables—subsidiary and control accounts)
The city council of New Nutley estimated that revenues of $95,000 would be collected for the General Fund. The sources and amounts would be as follows:

Property taxes	$80,000
Parking meters	10,000
Fines and penalties	5,000

The city has four taxpayers, whose shares of the tax levy are as follows:

T. Canyon	$40,000
M. Rose	30,000
C. Sark	6,000
S. Vasa	4,000

All of the taxpayers paid their property taxes on time and in full. Other collections throughout the year were as follows:

Parking meters	$6,000
Fines and penalties	8,000

Required: Prepare journal entries to record the following:
1. The entry of the budgeted revenues into the accounts
2. The setting up of the receivable, using a subsidiary account for each taxpayer
3. The collection of the taxes
4. The collection of the other revenues

E4-14 (Budgetary Interchanges)

Due to increased concern about security during a large sporting event, the city council of Carnival City authorized the Police Department to spend $50,000 to hire more officers. In order to provide resources for the additional protection, the city council directed you to transfer $50,000 from the appropriation for the purchase of new equipment to the appropriation for salaries.

Required: Prepare the entry necessary to record this budgetary interchange.

PROBLEMS

P4-1 (Discussion question on governmental accounting)

Governmental accounting gives substantial recognition to budgets, with those budgets being recorded in the accounts of the governmental unit.

Required: 1. What is the purpose of a governmental accounting system, and why is the budget recorded in the accounts of a governmental unit? Include in your discussion the purpose and significance of appropriations.

2. Describe when and how a governmental unit records its budget and closes it out.

(AICPA)

P4-2 (Complete set of entries and statements)

The following transactions apply to the FY 2004 operations of the Arctic City Levee Board, a recently formed organization:

a. Revenues were estimated at $150,000. Appropriations of $145,000 were made.

b. Property tax bills totaling $120,000 were sent out at the beginning of the year. During the year, the entire amount was collected. Fines and penalties amounted to $28,000.

c. Supplies worth $33,000 were purchased during the year. Salaries paid amounted to $100,000, and utilities for the year amounted to $9,000. The Board does not use encumbrances. All expenditures were paid in full and in cash during the year.

Required:

1. Prepare journal entries to record the transactions.
2. Post the entries made in part (1). (Use T-accounts.)
3. Prepare a preclosing trial balance.
4. Prepare closing entries.
5. Post the entries made in part (4).
6. Prepare a postclosing trial balance.
7. Prepare, in good form, a balance sheet and a statement of revenues, expenditures, and changes in fund balance for FY 2004. Assume that the fund balance at the beginning of the year was zero.

P4-3   (Beginning balances, complete set of statements)
        The December 31, 2004, postclosing trial balance of the General Fund of the
        City of Pompano was as follows:

	Debits	Credits
Cash	$500	
Accounts receivable	300	
Vouchers payable		$400
Unreserved fund balance		400
	$800	$800

a. The city council estimated revenues for FY 2004 to be $1,500 and expendi-
   tures to be $1,450.
b. The city's outstanding voucher payable, due to a contractor for remodel-
   ing city hall, was paid off in March.
c. Service charges of $800 were collected during the year.
d. The Provo Bread Company paid the city $300 it owed for repairs to a fire
   hydrant because of damage done by a runaway delivery truck.
e. Speeding tickets, which resulted in fines of $500, were issued to tourists en
   route to Fun City. The fines were paid in cash.
f. Salaries of $1,000 were paid to the mayor and the city clerk. Supplies cost-
   ing $125 were purchased for cash.
g. A used traffic light was purchased from the City of Clarkson for $150, to be
   paid the following year.

Required: 1. Prepare journal entries to record the listed transactions in the
                  General Fund.
               2. Post these journal entries to the ledger. (Use T-accounts.)
               3. Prepare a preclosing trial balance.
               4. Prepare closing entries and post to the ledger.
               5. Prepare a postclosing trial balance.
               6. Prepare, in good form, a balance sheet and a statement of reve-
                  nues, expenditures, and changes in fund balance.

P4-4   (Multiple choice)
        1. Which of the following revenues can be recorded when levied (when bills
           are sent out), rather than when actually received? Because its
                                                                Available &
           a. Fines   Measurable
           b. Property taxes
           c. Service charges
           d. Licenses and permits
        2. Which of the following events causes the Estimated revenues control
           account of a governmental unit to be debited?
           a. Budgetary accounts are closed at the end of the year.
           b. The budget is recorded.
           c. Actual revenues are recorded.
           d. Actual revenues are collected.

3. Which of the following accounts of a governmental unit is debited when a purchase order is approved?

Could be different from invoice

a. Encumbrances
b. Budgetary fund balance reserved for encumbrances
c. Vouchers payable
d. Appropriations

4. When a police car is received by a governmental unit, the entry on the books of the General Fund should include a debit to which of the following?

Spending in focus.

a. Appropriations—police cars
b. Expenditures—police cars
c. Encumbrances—police cars
d. Unreserved fund balance

5. Which of the following terms refers to an actual cost, rather than an estimate?

Budgetary accounts

a. Expenditure
b. Appropriation
c. Budget
d. Encumbrance

6. In approving the budget of the City of Troy, the city council appropriated an amount greater than expected revenues. What will be the result of this action?
a. A cash overdraft during the fiscal year
b. An increase in outstanding encumbrances by the end of the fiscal year
c. A debit to Budgetary fund balance
d. A necessity for compensatory offsetting action in the Debt Service Fund

7. Which of the following statements about the Budgetary fund balance reserved for encumbrances is not true?
a. It is used to set aside monies for specific purposes.
b. It is used to identify resources committed, but not expended.
c. It is used to identify liabilities resulting from the purchase of goods and services.
d. It provides information on outstanding purchase orders.

8. Which of the following is a budgetary account?
a. Expenditures—supplies
b. Appropriations
c. Revenues—property taxes
d. Vouchers payable

9. If estimated revenues exceed appropriations, closing the budgetary accounts must include which of the following entries?
a. A debit to Estimated revenues
b. A debit to Revenues—control
c. A debit to Budgetary fund balance
d. A credit to Budgetary fund balance

10. Entries similar to those for the General Fund may also appear on the books of a municipality's _____.
    a. Enterprise Fund
    b. Private Purpose Trust Fund
    c. Agency Fund
    d. Special Revenue Fund

11. What type of account is used to earmark a portion of the appropriation to liquidate the contingent obligation for goods ordered but not yet received?
    a. Appropriation
    b. Expenditure
    c. Obligation
    d. Budgetary fund balance reserved for encumbrances

12. Authority granted by a legislative body to make expenditures and to incur obligations during a fiscal year is the definition of _____.
    a. An appropriation
    b. An authorization
    c. An encumbrance
    d. Budgetary fund balance reserved for encumbrances

(AICPA adapted)

P4-5 (Complete set of entries; breakdown of revenue and expenditure accounts) The city council of Ongar approved the following budget for its General Fund on December 31, 2003:

Revenues	
Property taxes	$ 85,000
Service charges	35,000
Parking meters	15,000
Fines and penalties	10,000
Liquor licenses	5,000

Appropriations	
Salaries	$100,000
Supplies	20,000
Equipment	15,000
Motor scooters	10,000

The city has four property owners, whose tax assessments for FY 2004 are

J. Cook	$30,000
H. DeSoto	25,000
F. Drake	20,000
L. Ericson	10,000

FY 2004 is the first year of operation for this city. As a result, there are no balances in the accounts as of January 1, 2004. Assume that the city uses encumbrances and a voucher system to record all expenditures, except for salaries. During 2004, the following transactions took place:

a. FY 2004 tax bills were sent to the property owners.

b. Ordered supplies expected to cost $20,000.

c. The supplies arrived, along with an invoice for $19,000; the invoice was paid immediately.

d. Paid salaries of $97,000 for the year.

e. Ordered equipment costing $15,000.

f. Collected property taxes for the year, in full, from all property owners. Collections of service charges were $33,000.

g. Four motor scooters were ordered from a local dealer, who had submitted a bid for $10,000.

h. Parking meter revenues for the year were $18,000, and receipts from the issuance of liquor licenses amounted to $2,000.

i. Collections from fines and penalties were $9,000.

j. The equipment ordered arrived, along with an invoice for $15,000; the invoice was paid immediately. Track in GFAAG

k. The motor scooters arrived; because of an increase in their costs, the dealer asked the city to pay an additional $500 over the amount bid. Because of political considerations, the city agreed to this additional cost and promptly issued a check for $10,500 to the dealer for the motor scooters. Before issuing the check, the city made a budgetary revision—it increased the appropriation for motor scooters by $500 and reduced the appropriation for supplies by the same amount.

Required:
1. Prepare appropriate journal entries to record the budget and these transactions (including the budgetary revision).
2. Post the entries and prepare a preclosing trial balance.
3. Make closing entries and prepare a postclosing trial balance.
4. Prepare, in good form, a balance sheet and a statement of revenues, expenditures, and changes in fund balance.

P4-6 (Prior balances, encumbrances, complete cycle)

The city council of Watford approved the following budget for the General Fund for FY 2004.

Revenues		
Property taxes	$50,000	
License fees	10,000	
Fines and penalties	15,000	
Parking meters	5,000	
Federal grants	20,000	$100,000
Appropriations		
Salaries	$50,000	
Materials	20,000	
Motorcycles	24,000	
Interest	1,000	95,000
Projected Increase in Fund Balance		$ 5,000

The postclosing trial balance for the fund, as of December 31, 2003, was as follows:

	Debits	Credits
Cash	$ 5,000	
Due from federal government	10,000	
Vouchers payable		$8,000
Unreserved fund balance		7,000
	$15,000	$15,000

Transactions for FY 2004 include the following:
a. FY 2004 property tax bills were sent to the property owners, $50,000.
b. Ordered two new motorcycles at an estimated total cost of $24,000.
c. Received a check from the federal government to cover 2003 and 2004 federal grants, $30,000.
d. Borrowed $15,000 from the Canal Bank for 6 months in anticipation of tax receipts.
e. Ordered materials costing $20,000.
f. Paid vouchers outstanding at the end of 2003, $8,000.
g. License fees for 2004 were $9,500. Fines and penalties were $16,000.
h. The motorcycles arrived, along with an invoice for $23,400.
i. Parking meter revenues for 2004 were $6,500.
j. Repaid loan to bank, along with accrued interest of $900.
k. The materials arrived, accompanied by an invoice for $19,500.
l. Paid the outstanding voucher for $23,400 to the vendor who supplied the motorcycles.
m. Salaries for the year were $50,000.
n. Property taxes received during the year were $50,000.

Required: 1. Prepare journal entries to record the budget and these transactions.
2. Prepare a preclosing balance.
3. Prepare closing entries.
4. Prepare a postclosing trial balance.
5. Prepare a balance sheet and a statement of revenues, expenditures, and changes in fund balance for FY 2004.

P4-7 (Comprehensive problem on fund accounting cycle)
The general ledger of the Fairhill Park Fund shows the following balances as of December 31, 2003:

	Debits	Credits
Cash	$ 9,500	
Accounts receivable—White	500	
Property taxes receivable—Doris	1,500	
Due from General Fund	2,000	

Vouchers payable		$ 4,000
Tax anticipation notes payable		2,000
Due to Debt Service Fund		3,000
Unreserved fund balance		4,500
	$13,500	$13,500

The budget for FY 2004 is as follows:

Revenues and Transfers

Property taxes	$10,000
Rentals	4,000
Concession fees	2,000
Transfer from General Fund	4,000

Appropriations

Salaries	$ 8,000
Outside services	4,000
Materials	3,000
Equipment	2,000
Interest	1,000

The Fairhill Park Fund collects taxes directly from five property owners, whose land adjoins the park. The property owners and their FY 2004 property tax assessments are

G. Almstead	$5,000
L. Clarke	800
B. Doris	2,000
H. Lynch	1,000
T. Zimmerman	1,200

The Park Fund follows a policy of encumbering purchases of materials, equipment, and outside services. Because collections have never posed a problem, no provision is made for uncollectible accounts. Transactions for FY 2004 are as follows:

a. Bills for their FY 2004 taxes were sent to property owners.
b. G. Almstead and T. Zimmerman paid their taxes upon receipt of their tax bills.
c. L. Clarke paid one-half of her FY 2004 property tax bill.
d. The Park Fund paid the vouchers open (unpaid) as of the end of FY 2003.
e. The Park Fund issued notes of $10,000 on January 1. These notes bore interest at the rate of 6 percent per year. (Note: These notes are recorded only in the Fairhill Park Fund.)
f. B. Doris paid his taxes of $1,500 for FY 2003 and $2,000 for FY 2004.
g. Materials expected to cost $2,500 were ordered.
h. A contract was awarded to Morganics, Inc., to conduct a series of training programs for park personnel. The contract price was $4,000.

i. A check was received from the General Fund for $6,000 to cover its obligations from FY 2003 and for FY 2004. (*Hint:* Make a credit to Transfers in from General Fund for $4,000.)

j. A new lawn mower was ordered. The price quoted by the dealer was $2,000.

k. The tax anticipation notes outstanding at the end of FY 2003 were paid off, along with accrued interest of $100.

l. A check for $300 was received from the parents of Bob White, a local juvenile delinquent, who were paying for damage he did to the park in FY 2003.

m. Paid $3,000 (in cash) to the Debt Service Fund. This amount represented the final payment on a bond issue and was owed to the Debt Service Fund at the end of FY 2003.

n. The materials ordered in part (g) arrived, along with an invoice for $2,800, which the park commissioners agreed to eventually pay.

o. Received a check for $1,800 from the operator of the park's concessions to cover her fee for the year.

p. Received a check for $1,000 from H. Lynch for payment of his property taxes.

q. The lawn mower arrived in December, along with an invoice for $1,800.

r. Paid the vendor for the materials, $2,800.

s. Repaid the notes recorded in part (e), $10,000 plus accrued interest of $500.

t. Received rentals of $4,800 from people who camped in the park.

u. Morganics finished conducting the training programs and submitted a bill for $4,000, which was approved by the finance officer.

v. Paid salaries in cash, $7,500.

w. Paid voucher for payment of $4,000 to Morganics.

Required: 1. Prepare appropriate opening and operating entries.
2. Prepare a preclosing trial balance.
3. Prepare closing entries.
4. Prepare a postclosing trial balance.
5. Prepare appropriate financial statements.

P4-8   (Relationship between encumbrances and free balance; appropriation/expenditure ledger)

The city council made an appropriation to the police department of $100,000 for the purchase of supplies, equipment, and vehicles.

a. The department placed an order for 10 motorcycles, estimated to cost $5,000 each.

b. The department placed an order with Owen Supply Company for crime prevention supplies; the estimated cost of the order was $30,000.

c. The motorcycles arrived in good condition, along with an invoice for $50,000.

d. An order was placed for radio equipment; estimated cost was $10,000.

e. The supplies ordered in part (b) arrived, along with an invoice for $32,000.

f. The radio equipment was received in acceptable condition; actual cost was $9,000.

g. The department purchased a new firearm for $250 cash, on an "emergency" basis, directly from a local dealer; no order had been placed.

Required: 1. Prepare an appropriation/expenditure ledger. Use columns for Appropriations, Encumbrances (Dr. and Cr.), Expenditures, and Available balance.

2. What was the free balance at the end of the period?

Chapter

5

The Governmental Fund Accounting Cycle

General and Special Revenue Funds—Special Problems and Permanent Funds

After completing this chapter, you should be able to:

➤ *Show how to account for uncollectible property taxes.*

➤ *Explain the purpose of liens and how to account for them.*

➤ *Demonstrate how to account for encumbrances when partial orders are received.*

➤ *Explain how to account for encumbrances that are still outstanding at the end of the fiscal year.*

➤ Explain how accounting for grants differs from accounting for other inflows of resources.

➤ Explain the use of and accounting for allotments.

➤ Identify and account for four types of interfund transactions.

➤ Show how a budget revision is handled in the accounts.

➤ Explain the accounting for prepaid expenses.

➤ Demonstrate two methods of accounting for inventories.

➤ Prepare the closing entries necessary when a surplus or deficit occurs.

➤ Prepare financial statements for the General Fund, Special Revenue Funds, and Permanent Funds.

*U*p to this point we assumed that almost everything falls into place. For example, all property taxes assessed are collected, and all encumbrances are removed by the end of the fiscal year. Such assumptions, of course, are unrealistic. Taxpayers are sometimes unable or unwilling to pay their taxes or, if they do pay them, it is too late to treat them as revenues of the year in which they were assessed. In addition, certain encumbrances are removed on a piecemeal basis whereas others are still outstanding at the end of the fiscal year. Finally, many transactions take place between various funds of governmental units. The treatment of these and certain other problems are discussed in this chapter, along with Permanent Funds.

PROPERTY TAX ACCOUNTING

The major source of revenue for many governmental units is property taxes. When accounting for these taxes, a number of problems arise. For example, (1) property taxes might not be collected in a timely manner, (2) assessments on certain properties may be too low or too high and require adjustment after taxes have been levied, and (3) governmental units may elect to seize properties for nonpayment of taxes. These issues, along with tax discounts and deferred property taxes, are discussed in this section.

Uncollectible Property Taxes

As noted in Chapter 4, revenues from property taxes are recorded when those taxes are levied, rather than when they are collected. This approach is used because property taxes meet the "measurable" and "available" criteria at this point in time. Although governmental units can, and sometimes do, jail people or seize their property for nonpayment of taxes, such actions are not always expedient, especially in periods of high unemployment. Therefore, it is necessary to make some provision for uncollectible property taxes.

The most commonly used method of handling uncollectible property taxes is the *allowance method*. This procedure contains a built-in assumption that a certain portion of the taxes levied will not be collected. Using past experience and predictions of future economic conditions, finance officials can estimate what percentage of the total taxes will be uncollectible. This forecasting is possible even though, at the time of the levy, it is not known which particular accounts will not be collected.

When the taxes are levied, an *Allowance for uncollectibles* is recorded. This account carries a credit balance and is a *contra asset*. Recording the allowance effectively reduces the revenues of the period in which taxes are levied, rather than the period in which they are determined to be uncollectible, and provides a better measurement of revenues for each period. When it becomes known that a specific taxpayer's account is uncollectible, the Allowance for uncollectibles is debited (reduced) and the receivable in question is credited (also reduced).

To illustrate, assume that the property taxes levied in a given year amount to $1 million and that past experience shows 4 percent of the taxes levied are usually not collected. Therefore, an allowance of $40,000 is necessary. The entry to set up this allowance is

Property taxes receivable—Morgan	525,000	
Property taxes receivable—Lohmann	350,000	
Property taxes receivable—Parker	35,000	
Property taxes receivable—Davis	50,000	
Property taxes receivable—Gales	40,000	
Allowance for uncollectible property taxes		40,000
Revenues—property taxes		960,000

To set up receivable for FY 2004 property taxes, including an estimated
4 percent that is expected to remain uncollectible.

Assume further that in June it becomes apparent that Parker will be unable to pay his property taxes and it is not expedient to force a sale of his property. Thus, the account must be written off. The following entry makes this adjustment:

Allowance for uncollectible property taxes	35,000	
Property taxes receivable—Parker		35,000

To write off Parker account for FY 2004.

The entry to record the collection of the remaining property taxes is the same as the one previously illustrated:

Cash	965,000	
Property taxes receivable—Morgan		525,000
Property taxes receivable—Lohmann		350,000
Property taxes receivable—Davis		50,000
Property taxes receivable—Gales		40,000

To record collection of property taxes in FY 2004.

Notice that when the allowance method is used, writing off a bad debt does not affect revenues. The effect on revenues occurs when the allowance is set up, that is, when taxes are levied. Notice also that a bad debts expense account is not used, as in commercial accounting. The reason is that, under the current financial resources concept used in fund-level governmental accounting, noncash items such as depreciation and bad debts do not represent an outflow of resources and, as a result, are not reported. Because the focus of accounting by governmental-type funds is on spending, rather than on capital maintenance, it causes (theoretically) no distortion of operating results.

Adjustments to the Allowance for Uncollectible Property Taxes

Sometimes the estimate of uncollectible property taxes is either too high or too low. Then, an adjustment is required, either during or at the end of the year. If, for example, the allowance is too low and an upward adjustment is needed, the allowance account is credited (increased) and the revenue account is debited (decreased).

To illustrate, assume that in July city officials conclude that uncollectible property taxes will be $5,000 higher than anticipated. The adjusting entry is

Revenues—property taxes	5,000	
Allowance for uncollectible property taxes		5,000

   To adjust the revenue and allowance for uncollectible property tax accounts to
     reflect an increase in the estimate of uncollectible property taxes.

If, on the other hand, city officials conclude that uncollectible property taxes will be $5,000 lower than anticipated, the reverse of this entry is made:

Allowance for uncollectible property taxes	5,000	
Revenues—property taxes		5,000

   To adjust the revenue and allowance for uncollectible property tax accounts to
     reflect a decrease in the estimate of uncollectible property taxes.

At the end of the year, the balance in the Allowance for uncollectible property taxes account may not agree with taxes still outstanding. For example, the account may have a credit balance after all taxes have been collected or written off (the actual collections were higher than anticipated). In this case the remaining allowance must be reversed out, by reducing the allowance to zero and increasing property tax revenues accordingly. This entry is necessary because when the original entry to record the tax levy was made, the amount that would prove uncollectible was overestimated and revenues underestimated.

To continue with the illustration on page 159, assume that the original allowance is $40,000 and uncollectible accounts for the year amount to $35,000, leaving a credit balance of $5,000 in the Allowance for uncollectible property taxes account. The adjusting entry is

Allowance for uncollectible property taxes	5,000	
Revenues—property taxes		5,000

   To decrease the FY 2004 allowance for uncollectible property taxes to reflect
     actual collections.

If, on the other hand, the allowance turns out to be inadequate and no adjustment was made during the year (the Allowance for uncollectible property taxes account has a debit balance), an adjusting entry must be made to bring the balance in this account back to zero or to the remaining amount not expected to be collected. This adjustment is made by crediting the allowance account for the shortfall and debiting (reducing) property tax revenues for the same amount.

To illustrate, assume that the original Allowance for uncollectible property taxes for 2004 is $40,000, that FY 2004 taxes of $35,000 have been written off so far, and that another $15,000 of taxes is not likely to be collected, resulting in a total of $50,000 of uncollectible, or potentially uncollectible, property taxes. The adjusting entry is

Revenues—property taxes	10,000	
Allowance for uncollectible property taxes		10,000
To increase the FY 2004 allowance for uncollectible property taxes to reflect actual collections.		

Property Tax Refunds

Governmental units are often required to make refunds of property taxes. These refunds can be due to errors in tax assessments, or due to actions of the legislative body, like the refunding of property taxes to businesses that hire a certain number of people locally (tax abatements). In order to present a more realistic picture of the property taxes actually expected to be received during a fiscal year, governmental units are now required under GASB *Statement No. 33* to recognize revenue from property taxes, net of estimated refunds and estimated uncollectible amounts, in the period in which the taxes are levied.[1] The procedure used to record these estimated refunds is similar to the one just shown for recording estimated uncollectible property taxes—a debit is made to Revenues—property taxes and a credit is made to Allowance for property tax refunds (as shown in the following illustration). If only one entry is desired, the credit is made to the allowance and Revenues—property taxes is reduced by the same amount. The result is the same under either approach.

To illustrate, assume that the city estimates that it will be required, for various reasons, to refund 5 percent of the property taxes levied ($1,000,000). The entry to record this estimate is

Revenues—property taxes	50,000	
Allowance for property tax refunds		50,000
To record allowance for estimated property tax refunds.		

When a refund is made, the allowance account is debited and Cash or Property taxes receivable is credited, as will be illustrated in the next section.

Over- and Underassessed Property Taxes

Even the best of systems is prone to error. Those used by governmental units are no exception. One source of error lies in assessing taxes. Taxpayers often appeal their assessments and, as a result, their tax bills are adjusted. These adjustments, of course, increase or, more commonly, decrease the revenues of the governmental unit.

To adjust for an *overassessment*, the Allowance for property tax refunds is debited (decreased) and the receivable account is credited (also decreased). If the taxpayer already paid his or her entire tax bill, a cash refund is issued.

---

[1] GASB Cod. Sec. N50.115.

To illustrate, assume that the taxes originally levied on W. M. Lohmann's property are $350,000 and that when Lohmann appeals to his assessor, the taxes are lowered to $300,000. If Lohmann's tax reduction takes place before he pays his tax bill, the adjusting entry will be

Allowance for property tax refunds	50,000	
Property taxes receivable—current—Lohmann		50,000
To adjust for overassessment on the FY 2004 tax assessment of W. M. Lohmann.		

If, however, Lohmann pays the $350,000 when due and successfully appeals the assessment at a later date, the entry will be

Allowance for property tax refunds	50,000	
Vouchers payable		50,000
To adjust for an error on the FY 2004 tax assessment of W. M. Lohmann and to set up a liability for a refund.		

In the case of *underassessments,* the receivable (and revenue) accounts are increased to cover the additional assessments. Assume, for example, that Lohmann not only loses his appeal but is assessed an additional $75,000. The adjusting entry is

Property taxes receivable—current—Lohmann	75,000	
Revenues—property taxes		75,000
To adjust for an error on the FY 2004 tax assessment of W. M. Lohmann.		

Notice that the Allowance for estimated refunds is not affected by underassessments.

Tax Discounts

Sometimes governmental units allow cash discounts to encourage early payment of property taxes. Revenue losses from this practice are usually offset by reduced borrowings and a lessened need to carry over a sizable cash balance from the preceding year. If allowable, discounts should be treated as a reduction of revenue—in the same manner as uncollectible accounts. To illustrate, assume that a governmental unit levies property taxes of $600,000. To encourage the early payment of taxes, it offers a 2 percent discount for prompt payment. For purposes of this illustration assume that all taxpayers take the discount and that all taxes are received in a timely manner. When taxes are levied, the entry is

Property taxes receivable—current	600,000	
Estimated discounts on property taxes		12,000
Revenues—property taxes		588,000
To set up receivable for property taxes, together with an allowance for a 2 percent discount for prompt payment.		

When the taxes are collected, the entry is

Cash	588,000	
Estimated discounts on property taxes	12,000	
Property taxes receivable—current		600,000
To record collection of property taxes.		

If the governmental unit records estimated revenues of $600,000 in its budget, it is not possible for actual revenues to equal estimated revenues. To get around this problem, the governmental unit should budget the amount it actually expects to receive ($588,000), or treat the discounts as a reduction of revenue. If the latter approach is followed, the entries will be

Property taxes receivable—current	600,000	
Revenues—property taxes		600,000
To set up receivable for property taxes.		

Cash	588,000	
Revenues—property taxes	12,000	
Property taxes receivable—current		600,000
To record receipt of property taxes and reduction of property tax revenue because of discounts allowed for prompt payment.		

Delinquent Property Taxes

Often a governmental unit will not write off a property tax receivable until officials are certain that the tax is uncollectible. Sometimes this certainty comes several years after the tax was levied. Prudent management, however, necessitates keeping past due or delinquent taxes separate from those levied in the current year. To separate them, receivables are classified as current and delinquent. At some point in time (often the day they are due), outstanding current receivables are reclassified as delinquent. To illustrate, assume that on September 30, the due (delinquent) date, taxpayers Davis and Gales owe $50,000 and $40,000, respectively, some of which the city reasonably expects to collect in the future. The adjusting entry is

Property taxes receivable—delinquent—Davis	50,000	
Property taxes receivable—delinquent—Gales	40,000	
Property taxes receivable—current—Davis		50,000
Property taxes receivable—current—Gales		40,000
To reclassify FY 2004 property taxes not collected by due date as delinquent.		

In addition, the related Allowance for uncollectible property taxes must also be adjusted. Assume that this allowance is equal to $15,000, which is the amount of the FY 2004 property tax levy that city officials feel is unlikely to be collected. The entry to make this adjustment is

Allowance for uncollectible property taxes—current	15,000	
Allowance for uncollectible property taxes—delinquent		15,000
To adjust allowance for uncollectible property taxes—current for FY 2004 property taxes that are no longer current.		

Sometimes interest is charged on the delinquent taxes, or penalties are assessed against the taxpayer. When this happens, a debit is made to a receivable account in order to recognize this additional claim against the taxpayer. An offsetting credit to a revenue account is also made. If penalties totaling $900 are assessed against Davis and Gales, the entry is

Interest and penalties receivable—Davis	500	
Interest and penalties receivable—Gales	400	
Revenues—interest and penalties		900
To record assessment of late payment penalties.		

If the receivables are eventually determined to be uncollectible, the previous entry will be reversed.

Sometimes an Allowance for uncollectible interest and penalties account is used. In most cases, however, the balance in the Interest and penalties receivable account is not large enough to warrant the extra effort involved in setting up an off-setting allowance.

When back taxes are owed, a governmental unit will sometimes place a lien against a piece of property. A *lien* is the legal right to prevent the sale of a piece of property to satisfy a claim against its owner. Such property cannot be sold or transferred by its owner until the lien is removed.

In extreme cases a governmental unit will exercise its right to seize the property and sell it to the highest bidder. After the taxes, penalties, and expenses of the sale have been deducted, the proceeds will be remitted to the former owner or owners of the property.

When a lien is placed against a piece of property, existing receivable accounts are replaced by a new account called *Tax liens receivable*. To illustrate, assume that a lien is placed against the Davis property. At that time, delinquent taxes, interest, and penalties are also reclassified to reflect their new status.

Tax liens receivable—Davis	50,500	
Property taxes receivable—delinquent—Davis		50,000
Interest and penalties receivable—Davis		500
To reclassify property taxes, interest, and penalties receivable to reflect the lien on the Davis property.		

If it costs $300 to process and advertise the lien, this cost will be added to the new receivable:

Tax liens receivable—Davis	300	
Cash		300
To record the cost of processing and advertising the tax lien against the Davis property.		

If the Davis property is sold for $120,000 and an auctioneer is paid $1,500 to dispose of the property, the following entries are made to record the sale and the amounts due to the auctioneer and to R. Davis:

Cash	120,000	
Tax liens receivable—Davis		50,800
Vouchers payable—auctioneer		1,500
Vouchers payable—Davis		67,700
To record sale of Davis property, removal of lien, and expenses related to sale.		

Vouchers payable—auctioneer	1,500	
Vouchers payable—Davis	67,700	
Cash		69,200

To record payment of expenses of sale of Davis property and amount
due to R. Davis.

Deferred Property Taxes

Under the modified accrual basis of accounting, revenues are not "available" unless
they are "collected within the current period or expected to be collected soon enough
thereafter to be used to pay liabilities of the period."[2] The GASB specifies that, unless
a governmental unit justifies a longer period in the notes to its financial statements,
the period should not be more than 60 days.[3] Revenues expected to be collected after
this period should be reclassified and reported as deferred revenues.

To illustrate, assume that at the end of 2004 a governmental unit determines that
property tax revenues amounting to $250,000 will not be collected until the middle of
the following year. Because the expected time of collection is more than 60 days past
year-end, it must make the following entry:

Revenues—property taxes	250,000	
Deferred revenues—property taxes		250,000

To record deferral of property taxes expected to be collected in FY 2005.

At the beginning of 2005, this entry would be reversed, and the monies collected
would be treated as revenue of that year, rather than 2004.

Payments in Lieu of Property Taxes

Governmental units sometimes receive payments from other governmental units, or
from certain not-for-profit organizations, to reimburse them for revenues lost
because these organizations are not required to pay property taxes. Amounts
received are usually based on amounts the governmental units would have received
if the paying organizations had been required to pay these taxes.

Examples of payments in lieu of property taxes include impact payments made
by the federal government to school districts near military installations and
amounts contributed by certain religious organizations owning large amounts of
real estate. Payments in lieu of property taxes are treated in the same manner as
other tax revenues.

Escheats

In most states, net assets of persons who die intestate (without a valid will) and who
have no known relatives revert to the state, as do inactive bank accounts (after a certain period of time, often 7 years). Such reversions are known as *escheats.* Escheats are
initially recorded in a Private Purpose Trust Fund, pending claim by rightful owners.

---

[2] GASB Interpretation No. 5, *Property Tax Recognition in Governmental Funds.*
[3] GASB Cod. Sec P70.104.

If not claimed within a statutory period, the resources are transferred to the General Fund (if cash or securities) or are recorded as assets under government-wide reporting (if fixed assets). In either case, a liability is recorded at the same time for amounts reasonably expected to be claimed "to the extent that it is probable that escheat property will be reclaimed and paid to claimants."[4]

BUDGETARY ACCOUNTING

When dealing with the budget, some accounting-related issues arise. These issues include budget revisions, allotments, the receipt of partial orders, and encumbrances that are still open at year-end. These issues are discussed in the following sections.

Budget Revisions

Sometimes budgets are revised during the year. Conditions such as disasters or severe unemployment can cause serious shortages of actual revenues. If such events do happen and a balanced budget is to be maintained, appropriations must be reduced (many city charters and state constitutions require a balanced budget). Such adjustments are recorded by debiting Appropriation accounts, crediting Estimated revenue accounts, and reflecting any differences in Budgetary fund balance. Assume, for example, that a city begins FY 2004 with the following budget:

Estimated revenues	$1,000,000
Appropriations	990,000
Increase in Budgetary fund balance	$ 10,000

Several months after the beginning of the year, the city council concludes that revenues for the year will be $20,000 less than projected and votes to reduce appropriations by $15,000. The appropriate adjusting entry is

Appropriations	15,000	
Budgetary fund balance	5,000	
Estimated revenues		20,000
To reflect revisions to 2004 budget.		

Budget revisions should not be confused with budgetary interchanges (discussed in Chapter 4), in which resources budgeted for one purpose are later budgeted for another. When budgetary interchanges are made the overall amount budgeted does not change, as it does when budget revisions are made.

---

[4] GASB Cod. E70.103.

Allotments

To maintain closer control over their own expenditures, as well as those of organizations to which they award grants, governmental units sometimes divide their appropriations into *allotments*. These segments of the appropriation may be encumbered (obligated) or expended during the *allotment period*, which can be a month, a quarter year, or a half year.

When allotments are used, *Unallotted appropriations* replaces Appropriations. The budgetary entry is (amounts assumed)

Estimated revenues—various sources	1,000,000	
Unallotted appropriations		990,000
Budgetary fund balance		10,000
To record estimated revenues and unallotted appropriations for FY 2004.		

At the time formal allotments are made, Unallotted appropriations is reduced (debited) and an allotment account is set up by means of a credit to Allotments. If, in this illustration, the first period's allotment is $495,000, the following entry is appropriate:

Unallotted appropriations	495,000	
Allotments		495,000
To record allotment for first half of FY 2004.		

If $485,000 is actually expended during the allotment period, the following entry is appropriate:

Expenditures (various)	485,000	
Vouchers payable		485,000
To record expenditures incurred during first half of FY 2004.		

Under the more commonly used procedure, allotments are controlled by means of a three-column subsidiary ledger, which provides a running total of the balance available for spending.

To illustrate, assume that in FY 2004, of the $990,000 allotted to an organization, $978,000 is actually spent. Assume also that this organization receives its funding in semiannual allotments of $495,000 and that the subsidiary ledger illustrated in Table 5-1 is maintained by this organization.

At year-end, Revenues are closed out to Expenditures, with any difference between these account balances being added to or deducted from Unreserved fund balance. Estimated revenues are closed out to Allotments, with any difference between these account balances being added to or deducted from Budgetary fund balance.

January 1	Estimated revenues—various sources	1,000,000	
	Unallotted appropriations		990,000
	Budgetary fund balance		10,000
	To record estimated revenues, unallotted appropriations, and projected increases in fund balance for FY 2004.		

Table 5-1

Subsidiary Ledger for Allotments

DATE	ALLOTMENT	EXPENDITURES	REMAINING BALANCE
1/1	$495,000		$495,000
1/8		$ 75,000	420,000
3/15		200,000	220,000
5/17		150,000	70,000
6/25		60,000	10,000
7/1	495,000		505,000
7/15		200,000	305,000
9/26		75,000	230,000
11/15		100,000	130,000
12/18		30,000	100,000
12/29		88,000	12,000
	$990,000	$978,000	$ 12,000

January 1	Unallotted appropriations		495,000	
	Allotments			495,000
	To set up allotments for first half of FY 2004.			
January 1–	Cash		500,000	
June 30	Revenues—various sources			500,000
	To record revenues of first half of FY 2004.			
	Expenditures—various		485,000	
	Vouchers payable			485,000
	To record expenditures of first half of FY 2004.			
July 1	Unallotted appropriations		495,000	
	Allotments			495,000
	To set up allotment for second half of FY 2004.			
July 1–	Cash		500,000	
December 31	Revenues—various sources			500,000
	To record revenues of second half of FY 2004.			
	Expenditures—various		493,000	
	Vouchers payable			493,000
	To record expenditures of second half of FY 2004.			
December 31	Revenues—various sources		1,000,000	
	Expenditures—various			978,000
	Unreserved fund balance			22,000
	To close out revenue and expenditure accounts for FY 2004.			
	Allotments		990,000	
	Budgetary fund balance		10,000	
	Estimated revenues—various sources			1,000,000
	To close out allotment and estimated revenue accounts for FY 2004.			

Warrants

Before a check can be written and payment made, a warrant is usually prepared. A *warrant* is an order, drawn by the appropriate authority, requesting the treasurer (or someone designated by that person) to pay a specified sum of money to a particular person or organization. Its purpose is to assist in the prevention of unauthorized payments. No journal entries are necessary when warrants are prepared.

Partial Orders

In our previous discussion of encumbrances we emphasized that when an encumbrance is removed, the amount reversed out is the amount of the encumbrance. This procedure is used even if the actual purchase cost is different. The amount shown as an expenditure, of course, always equals the amount actually paid.

The example used to illustrate the previous points involves assuming that the entire order was received at one time. In many cases, however, orders of goods and services are received piecemeal throughout the year. A governmental unit will often place a *blanket order* for a quantity of goods or services, to be received gradually over a period of time (e.g., one-sixth of the order each month for 6 months). Payment for these goods or services is usually made shortly after the receipt of each shipment rather than at the end of the period covered by the order.

This situation creates the problem of knowing exactly when the encumbrance should be removed. Although some accountants advocate waiting until the last item is received, most realize that this approach causes a loss of control over expenditures and defeats the purpose of the encumbrance. In addition, before all goods or services are received, the order may be canceled by operating personnel without informing the accounting department. Then, monies that could be used elsewhere are tied up until year-end because accounting personnel are unaware that the funds will not be spent. As a result, they inadvertently turn down spending requests even though monies are actually available.

The alternative used by most organizations requires more paperwork but results in tighter control over expenditures. Under this approach, a portion of the encumbrance equivalent to the portion of the goods or services that have been received is removed when the voucher for payment is prepared. Thus, when one-fourth of an order arrives, one-fourth of the encumbrance is removed.

To illustrate, assume that one-fourth of the $200,000 of supplies ordered in the example in the previous chapter are received, along with an invoice for $45,000. One-fourth of the encumbrance, $50,000, is removed, and a voucher for the actual invoice amount is prepared:

Budgetary fund balance reserved for encumbrances	50,000	
Encumbrances—supplies		50,000
To record receipt of one-fourth of supplies ordered under Purchase Order No. 1426.		
Expenditures—supplies	45,000	
Vouchers payable		45,000
To record liability for payment of one-fourth of goods received under Purchase Order No. 1426.		

The first entry removes one-fourth of the original encumbrance. This entry reflects the fact that one-fourth of the goods were received. The second entry records the actual expenditure and liability.

This method gives managers a fairly accurate idea of how much of the order arrived. It also prevents tying up large amounts of money until year-end, by which time the appropriation may have expired, and allows managers to adjust the encumbrances to correspond with actual prices.

Open Encumbrances

Until now it has been assumed that all materials and services ordered during a given period are received in that period. In reality, however, it seldom happens that way. Deliveries are sometimes made after year-end. Materials ordered near the end of one year often arrive the following year. Finally, certain items require long lead times between order and delivery dates (e.g., fire engines). Because encumbrances are not removed until materials or services are received, a problem arises as to what to do with them at year-end.

Accounting for the open encumbrances depends on (1) whether the governmental unit requires its unexpended (but encumbered) appropriations to lapse or to remain open, and (2) its policy concerning reporting of open encumbrances.

Appropriations Lapse

Laws or regulations may require that all unexpended appropriations lapse at the end of the year, even if some of the appropriations are encumbered and the governmental unit is committed to eventually accepting the goods and services. The expenditures relating to the open encumbrances will be charged to the appropriations of the following year.

To illustrate the accounting for and reporting of open encumbrances, assume that a city has $50,000 of open encumbrances at year-end. If the city follows a policy of closing out open encumbrances and describing them in the notes to its financial statements, it will make the following entry:

Budgetary fund balance reserved for encumbrances	50,000	
Encumbrances		50,000
To close outstanding encumbrances for FY 2003.		

If the city reports the amount of its open encumbrances as a reservation of fund balance (a more common practice) it will first close out its open encumbrances, as in the preceding entry. Then, a reservation of Unreserved fund balance (rather than Budgetary fund balance) will be established by means of the following entry:

Unreserved fund balance	50,000	
Fund balance reserved for encumbrances		50,000
To record reservation of fund balance for open encumbrances.		

At the beginning of the following year (in this case, FY 2004), the entry establishing the Fund balance reserved for encumbrances will be reversed. Open encumbrances will then be reestablished by means of the same entry used to establish any other encumbrances, as shown here:

Fund balance reserved for encumbrances	50,000	
Unreserved fund balance		50,000
To remove reservation of fund balance for encumbrances open at end of FY 2004.		
Encumbrances	50,000	
Budgetary fund balance reserved for encumbrances		50,000
To reestablish encumbrances open at end of FY 2004.		

Appropriations Remain Open

For budgetary purposes, some governmental units allow the encumbered portion of their unexpended appropriations at year-end to remain open. This practice does not affect their financial reporting because the expenditures are reported as expenditures of the following year (FY 2004), whether or not the appropriations lapse for budgetary purposes. It does, however, affect the governmental unit's budgetary accounting.

For financial accounting purposes, two entries are required. First, a closing entry is made to reverse out the encumbrances. (Remember, encumbrances are budgetary accounts and all budgetary accounts must be closed at year-end.) Then, because the appropriation has not lapsed, an entry must be made to record the fund balance reserved for encumbrances. For the city in the illustration, the entries would be

Budgetary fund balance reserved for encumbrances	50,000	
Encumbrances		50,000
To close outstanding encumbrances for FY 2003.		
Unreserved fund balance	50,000	
Fund balance reserved for encumbrances		50,000
To record reservation of fund balance for open encumbrances.		

Notice that these same entries are made when appropriations lapse. The entries made at the beginning of the following year are also the same entries made when appropriations lapse. However, for budgetary purposes, the governmental unit will now carry 2 years of appropriations accounts: the old year (in this illustration, FY 2003) and the new year (FY 2004).

Reserves and Designations

According to governmental GAAP, "use of the term *reserve* should be limited to indicating that a portion of the fund balance is not appropriable for expenditure or is legally segregated for a specific future use."[5] An example of the first use of reserves (to indicate to the reader of the financial statements that a portion of the fund balance is not appropriable for future expenditures) is the Reserve for inventories, which is

---

[5] GASB Cod. 1800.139.

discussed later (on page 178). An example of the second use of reserves (to indicate to the reader of the financial statements that a portion of the fund balance is legally segregated for a specific future use) is the Reserve for encumbrances. This reserve reflects the purchase orders outstanding at the end of the fiscal year.

Sometimes a governmental unit will set aside or designate a portion of its fund balance to inform the readers of its financial statements of tentative or "informal" plans for the future use of financial resources, such as extra police protection for a special event or equipment replacement. These designations reflect managerial plans rather than any formal legal basis. As a result, they should be clearly distinguished from formal reserves of fund balance. Unlike fund balance reserves, they are subject to change at the discretion of the management, rather than the legislative body, of the governmental unit. For example, the mayor of a city might decide that resources designated for extra police protection during Mardi Gras parades should be used to provide security for the Superbowl. Such a decision does not usually require the approval of the city council.

INTERFUND ACTIVITY

Transactions between individual funds of a governmental unit are collectively referred to as *interfund activity*. Under GASB *Statement No. 34*, each of these transactions falls into one of four categories. Transactions that result from reciprocal interfund activity (the internal equivalent of exchange or exchange-like transactions) are categorized as interfund loans or interfund services provided and used. Transactions that result from nonreciprocal interfund activity (the internal equivalent of nonexchange transactions) are categorized as interfund reimbursements or interfund transfers.[6] Each of these transaction types is discussed in the following sections.

Interfund Loans

Interfund loans arise when one fund lends money to another fund. The recipient fund recognizes a liability to the paying fund, and the paying fund recognizes a receivable from the recipient fund. When recording short-term receivables and payables (those due within 1 year), the terms *Interfund loans receivable—current* and *Interfund loans payable—current* are used. When recording long-term receivables and payables (those due after 1 year), the terms *Interfund loans receivable—noncurrent* and *Interfund loans payable—noncurrent* are used. The amounts shown on the financial statements as Interfund loans receivable and Interfund loans payable, for the governmental unit as a whole, should be equal at all times. The entries to record interfund loans are (amounts assumed) as follows:

Entry in the books of the lending fund	Interfund loans receivable from XX Fund—current	5,000	
	Cash		5,000
	To record loan to XX Fund.		

---

6 GASB Cod. 1800.102.

Entry in the books of the borrowing fund	Cash	5,000	
	Interfund loans payable to YY Fund—current		5,000
	To record loan from YY Fund.		

To inform readers of the financial statements that current financial resources are not available for spending, noncurrent loans to other funds are generally accompanied by reservations of fund balance. The entry to record such a reservation is

Entry in the books of the lending fund	Unreserved fund balance	5,000	
	Reserve for loans to other funds		5,000
	To record reservation of fund balance for loan to XX Fund.		

Interfund Services Provided and Used

Interfund services provided and used refers to interfund transactions that result in the recognition of revenues and expenditures (or expenses) to the funds involved. These transactions are unique in that they are the only ones, not involving parties external to the governmental unit, in which revenues and expenditures (or expenses) are recognized.

Interfund services provided and used transactions occur when one fund sells goods to or performs services for another fund for a price approximating what it would receive from an outside party. Assume, for example, that a fund recognizes revenue when it provides services to an outside party. If, instead, it provides those same services to another fund, it is still appropriate for the fund to recognize revenue.

To continue with the analogy, if the fund receiving the services mentioned previously contracted with an outside party for the same services, it would incur an expenditure (or expense). The fact that the supplier of the services is another governmental unit will not change the recognition of the expenditure (or expense).

To illustrate, assume that an Enterprise Fund (Water Utility Fund) provides water and sewerage services to the governmental unit. The billing from the Water Utility Fund to the General Fund will be recorded as follows (amounts assumed):

Entry in the books of the Enterprise Fund	Due from General Fund	150,000	
	Sale of water and sewerage services		150,000
	To record billing to General Fund.		

Entry in the books of the General Fund	Expenditures—water and sewerage services	150,000	
	Due to Water Utility Fund		150,000
	To record billing from Water Utility Fund.		

Because these transactions involve the recognition of revenues and expenditures (or expenses), they are reported on the statement of revenues, expenditures (or expenses), and changes in fund balance (or fund net assets).

Interfund Reimbursements

In some instances expediency may require that an expenditure (or expense) be paid by a fund other than the one properly chargeable for the transaction. The repayment to the paying fund by the one properly chargeable for the transaction is an *interfund reimbursement*. For example, assume that the General Fund makes an expenditure of $25,000 for consulting services that benefit several different funds. If the General Fund initially pays the bill, with the allocation of the charges to be made at a later date, and if it is determined that the amount of the charge allocable to the Auditorium Fund, a Capital Projects Fund, is $5,000, the following entries are made:

Entry in the books of the General Fund	Expenditures—consulting services	25,000	
	Cash		25,000
	To record payment for consulting services that benefit several funds.		
Entry in the books of the Auditorium Fund	Expenditures—consulting services	5,000	
	Cash		5,000
	To record payment for consulting services.		
Entry in the books of the General Fund	Cash	5,000	
	Expenditures—consulting services		5,000
	To record reimbursement by Auditorium Fund for consulting services paid for by General Fund.		

These entries shift the expenditure from the books of the General Fund to the books of the Auditorium Fund. This ensures that the expenditure will not be recorded more than once and that the fund receiving the benefit will recognize the expenditure. The reimbursements themselves will not appear on the governmental unit's financial statements.

Interfund Transfers

Interfund transfers are used to record "flows of assets (such as cash or goods) without equivalent flows of assets in return and without a requirement for repayment."[7] They account for the largest part of the interfund activity of most governmental units. A typical interfund transfer is the annual debt service payment made by the General Fund to a Debt Service Fund. Other examples include (1) an operating subsidy from the General Fund to an Electric Utility Fund (Enterprise Fund), (2) a payment made by the General Fund for its share of the cost of constructing a civic auditorium, and (3) a transfer of the remaining fund balance of a Debt Service Fund to the General Fund, after the principal and interest have been paid.

Interfund transfers should not be treated as revenues or expenditures (or expenses) by either fund involved in the transaction. Instead they should be reported as other financing sources (uses) for governmental-type funds in the statement of revenues, expenditures, and changes in fund balance. Proprietary-type funds should report these transactions after nonoperating revenues and expenses in the statement

---

[7] GASB Cod. 1800.102.

of revenues, expenses, and changes in net assets.[8] Reporting of these transfers is illustrated in Chapters 2, 6 and 9.

A typical interfund transfer is one from the General Fund to a Capital Projects Fund. The following entries are used to record this transfer (amounts assumed):

Entry in the books of the General Fund	Transfer out to Capital Projects Fund	8,000	
	Cash		8,000
	To record transfer to Capital Projects Fund.		
Entry in the books of the Capital Projects Fund	Cash	8,000	
	Transfer in from General Fund		8,000
	To record transfer from General Fund.		

ACCOUNTING FOR GRANTS

Grants received by governmental units are frequently restricted for specific activities. To maximize control over these resources, restricted grants should be accounted for in Special Revenue Funds. Revenues from restricted grants, like those from other voluntary nonexchange transactions, are recognized in the period in which "all eligibility requirements have been met."[9] As a result, revenue from restricted grants is not usually recognized until the agreed-upon expenditures have taken place.

If a grant is received before its eligibility requirements are met, Cash is debited and an offsetting credit to Deferred revenue, a liability account, is made to indicate that no revenue was earned. When agreed-upon expenditures take place, revenues are recognized in the amount of the expenditures.

To illustrate, assume that a city receives a grant for $500,000, to be used to supplement salaries of police officers. When the grant is received, the following entry is made:

Cash	500,000	
Deferred revenues—grants		500,000
To record receipt of grant.		

During the year, $300,000 is spent in accordance with the terms of the grant. The entries to record the expenditures and to recognize revenue from the grant are:

Expenditures—salaries	300,000	
Cash		300,000
To record payment of supplemental pay to police officers.		
Deferred revenues—grants	300,000	
Revenues—grants		300,000
To record revenue from grant.		

The remainder of the revenue from the grant will be recognized the following year, when the appropriate expenditures are made.

---

[8] Ibid.
[9] GASB Cod. N50.901.

Governmental units often receive grants which they can spend on behalf of, or transfer to, a secondary recipient, but for which they have "administrative involvement." For example, a state might receive a grant for security enhancements from the federal government, which it divides among various cities. These grants are known as *pass-through grants*. They should be reported by the governmental unit as revenues when received and as expenditures when passed on.[10] In those instances when a governmental unit serves only as a "cash conduit" for a grant (that is, it maintains no administrative involvement) the grant should be reported in an Agency Fund.[11]

OTHER ISSUES

Other issues faced by governmental units include derived tax revenues, acquiring assets with lives of more than 1 year, depreciation on long-lived assets, inventories, prepaid items, and the special accounting treatment given to items like compensated absences, claims and judgements, special termination benefits, and landfill closure and postclosure costs.

Derived Tax Revenues (Taxpayer-Assessed Revenues)

Certain taxes are assessed by individual taxpayers, following legal guidelines set out by the governmental units. Examples include sales taxes and income taxes. Sales taxes collected from their customers are paid by merchants at a fixed percentage of the merchants' sales. Income taxes represent taxpayers' income, less certain deductions and credits. In both cases, the initial amount of taxes that must be paid is determined by the taxpayers, rather than the governmental units. Revenues from these taxes are known as *derived tax revenues.*

GASB *Statement No. 33* requires that derived tax revenues (formerly known as *taxpayer-assessed revenues*) be recognized in the accounting period in which the underlying exchange occurred and the resources are available.[12] As a result, an adjusting entry must be prepared at the end of each fiscal year to recognize derived tax revenues that will be received early enough in the following year (usually 60 days) to pay the bills of the period covered. Fortunately, tax collections tend to be predictable over time and it is generally possible to make reasonable estimates of the amount of each tax that will be collected and when it will be collected.

To illustrate, assume that at the end of FY 2004 it is estimated that outstanding income taxes for this year, less estimated refunds and uncollectible amounts, amount to $500,000 and will be collected early the following year. The adjusting entry to record these revenues is

Income taxes receivable	500,000	
Revenues—income taxes		500,000
To record FY 2004 income taxes expected to be collected early in FY 2005.		

---

[10] GASB Cod. N50.128.
[11] Ibid.
[12] GASB Cod. N50.127.

Assets with a Life of More Than 1 Year

Generally speaking, the purchase of assets with a life of more than 1 year (capital assets) is treated as an expenditure. That is, if a governmental unit acquires real estate or equipment, the entire outlay is charged against an appropriation of the year of purchase. This practice is different from commercial accounting, in which a building or a piece of equipment expected to last for more than 1 year is recorded as an asset and "written off," as an expense, over its useful life.

Capital assets purchased by governmental-type funds are not shown on the balance sheets of these funds. For the purpose of control, however, many governmental units record capital assets in a memorandum set of records called a Capital Investment Account Group (CIAG). The mechanics of this process are described in Chapter 10.

To illustrate the treatment of capital assets in governmental-type funds, assume that equipment costing $975,000 is purchased by the General Fund of a governmental unit. The entry to record this purchase would be

Expenditures—capital equipment	975,000	
Vouchers payable		975,000
To record purchase of equipment in General Fund and to recognize liability to vendor.		

Sometimes it is necessary to dispose of property or equipment, either because the asset is no longer needed by the governmental unit (surplus property) or because it has become obsolete or damaged. Such a transaction requires entries in the General Fund (or the fund that financed the purchase of the asset). Cash is debited and either a "special item" or a revenue account is credited. To illustrate, assume that a governmental unit disposes of a fire engine, which originally cost $75,000, for $15,000. The entry to record this sale is

Cash	15,000	
Revenues (or proceeds from)—sale of general fixed assets		15,000
To record sale of one fire engine.		

Government-wide financial reporting entries will be covered in Chapter 10.

Depreciation

Except for the Internal Service, Enterprise, and certain Trust Funds, no formal entries are made for depreciation at the fund level. Depreciation is not recorded in most fund-level statements for three reasons:

1. Governmental units are concerned with matching actual revenues and expenditures with estimated revenues and appropriations rather than determining net income. Because depreciation is a "noncash" expense, it does not require an appropriation; and because there is no appropriation for depreciation, there is no need to recognize an expenditure. When an asset is replaced, an appropriation is made for the entire cost of the new asset.

2. Governmental units do not pay income taxes. Therefore, accounting for the tax deduction that can be taken for depreciation is irrelevant.
3. No need exists for information on "return on investment," because governmental units are not expected to make a profit. Hence this measure of performance is superfluous at the fund level.

Depreciation on government-wide financial statements is discussed in Chapter 10.

Inventories

Governmental units normally record purchases of materials and supplies at the fund level as expenditures when those purchases take place, even though the items purchased might be inventoried and not used until a later fiscal year. Under this procedure, called the *purchases method,* inventories are treated in the same manner as fixed assets; that is, they are "expensed" when purchased. As a result, no record of their existence appears on the balance sheet.

When the purchases method is used, *spending* is defined as "the *acquisition* of assets." To meet the principle of full disclosure and to indicate that they are not "available spendable resources," the existence of material amounts of inventories is reported on the balance sheet by means of inventory accounts and a reserve account. To illustrate, assume that supplies costing $10,000 are still on hand at the end of a fiscal year and that this fact should be disclosed to readers of the financial statements. The appropriate entry is

Supplies on hand	10,000	
Fund balance reserved for supplies on hand		10,000
To record amount of supplies on hand at the end of FY 2004.		

At the end of the following year, the inventory accounts and the reserve account should be adjusted to reflect the balance on hand at that point in time. For example, if the cost of the supplies on hand at the end of the second year is $14,000, the balance in the inventory and in the reserve account should be adjusted to this amount, as follows:

Supplies on hand	4,000	
Fund balance reserved for supplies on hand		4,000
To adjust supplies and reserve accounts to reflect the amount of supplies on hand at the end of FY 2004.		

If the amount of supplies on hand had decreased rather than increased, the supplies account would have been credited and the reserve account would have been debited by the amount necessary to bring their balances down to the new level. Notice that only the reserve changes, not Unreserved fund balance, because no change in available spendable resources took place.

Many governmental units, especially those with a large number of proprietary-type funds, follow the same practice as commercial organizations when recording inventoriable items. They record these items as assets when purchased, and as expenditures when "consumed." This method is known as the *consumption method.*

The logic behind the consumption method is that "spending" occurs when an asset is used. Therefore, the acquisition of an inventoriable item merely represents the exchange of one asset for another. To illustrate, assume that during the year purchases of supplies amount to $8,000 and that supplies costing $6,500 are used. The entry to record the purchase of supplies is

Supplies on hand	8,000	
Vouchers payable		8,000
To record purchase of supplies in FY 2004.		

The entry to record the usage of supplies is

Expenditures—supplies	6,500	
Supplies on hand		6,500
To record usage of supplies in FY 2004.		

Because inventories are spendable assets, reserves are required only in those instances in which a certain minimum amount of inventory must be kept on hand and, therefore, is not considered to be a spendable asset.

Prepaid Items

Prepaid items (e.g., prepaid rent, prepaid insurance) are charged to expenditure accounts when the payment is made. At the fund level, such items are not usually reported on the balance sheet, as they are in commercial accounting. If the governmental unit does decide to report prepaid items on the balance sheet, the purchases method is generally used and, as discussed in the previous section on inventories, Fund balance reserved for prepayments should be credited.

More on Expenditures

Under modified accrual accounting, the general rule regarding expenditures is that, unless a specific requirement states to do otherwise, a fund liability and an expenditure should be accrued in the period in which a liability is incurred. Expenditures requiring accrual include liabilities that, once incurred, are normally paid in a timely manner and in full from current financial resources.[13]

The rule just stated however, is subject to a number of specific exceptions. Among them are compensated absences, claims and judgments, special termination benefits, and landfill closure and postclosure costs. These items should be recognized as fund liabilities and expenditures only to the extent that they are "normally expected to be liquidated with expendable available financial resources."[14] The GASB interpreted that phrase to mean that governmental units are normally expected to liquidate liabilities with expendable available financial resources to the extent the liabilities mature or come due for payment each period.[15]

To illustrate, assume that a governmental unit allows its employees to accumulate vacation pay and, on resignation or retirement, to receive cash for unused vacation time up to 30 days leave. Under modified accrual accounting, the amount

---

[13]   GASB Cod. 1600.119.
[14]   GASB Cod. 1500.108.
[15]   GASB Cod. 1600.122.

reported as accrued vacation pay at the end of an accounting period would be the amount that has matured and is due to be paid to specific employees who resigned or retired as of the end of the accounting period. That accrual would generally be significantly lower than the liability under full accrual accounting, which would cover all employees whether or not they had resigned or retired. Another exception to the general rule, pertaining to interest on long-term debt, is discussed in Chapter 6.

YEAR-END FINANCIAL STATEMENTS

Financial statements prepared at year-end for the General Fund and each Special Revenue Fund include a balance sheet and a statement of revenues, expenditures, and changes in fund balance. A budgetary comparison schedule is also prepared for the General Fund and each Special Revenue Fund. If desired, this schedule may be presented as a statement. GASB *Statement No. 34* requires that the original approved budget, as well as the budget in effect at the end of the fiscal year, be shown on the budgetary comparison schedule. For the sake of simplicity, however, we will assume that the original budget and final budget are identical. (Examples of year-end statements are found in Tables 5-8, 5-9, and 5-10 on pages 189, 190, and 191, respectively.)

When preparing a budgetary comparison schedule, a problem arises if the budget is recorded on one basis and actual data are recorded on another (e.g., the budget is recorded on the cash basis and actual data are recorded on the modified accrual basis). To make budget and actual comparisons meaningful, it is necessary to present actual data on the same basis as budgetary data. As a result, if the budget is prepared on a basis other than that provided by GAAP, actual data must be converted so that they follow the measurement rules used to develop the budget (e.g., from the modified accrual basis to the cash basis). This practice will often result in inconsistencies between this statement and the statement of revenues, expenditures, and changes in fund balance.

Even when the budget is prepared on the modified accrual basis, differences may appear between the statement of revenues, expenditures, and changes in fund balance and the budgetary comparison schedule. For example, in Table 5-9, expenditures for supplies are shown as $154,500, the amount actually spent. In Table 5-10, they are shown as $204,500. This difference is due to an outstanding encumbrance of $50,000, which was charged against departmental budgets but not spent by year-end. A reconciliation of differences between the two statements should be provided, either on the budgetary comparison schedule or in the notes to the financial statements.

PERMANENT FUNDS

Permanent Funds are used to account for resources that are legally restricted in a manner that (1) only earnings on the principle of these resources can be expended (spent), and (2) the earnings must be used to support programs that benefit the government or its citizens, as opposed to specific individuals, organizations, or other governmental units. Examples of Permanent Funds include perpetual care cemetery funds and endowments to public libraries, whose income must be used to purchase books. These funds, to a certain extent, replace the Nonexpendable Trust Funds used before GASB *Statement No. 34* went into effect.

Activities of Permanent Funds

Assets of Permanent Funds generally consist of cash and investments, while liabilities generally consist of amounts due to other funds. Revenues of Permanent Funds generally consist of interest and dividends, as well as increases (or decreases) in the fair market value of the funds' investments. Periodic transfers are made to funds designated as beneficiaries of Permanent Funds, usually Special Revenue Funds, and are reported as transfers out.

Permanent Funds should be established only when a legal trust agreement exists or when required by law. When legal or contractual agreements requiring the use of Permanent Funds are not present, the General Fund or a Special Revenue Fund should be used.

Control of Fund Activities

The operations of Permanent Funds are controlled through applicable state laws and provisions of individual trust agreements. Therefore, the accounting system must be designed to provide information and reports that permit a review of this stewardship role. Unless legally stipulated, formal integration of the budget into the accounting system is not usually required. Activities financed by Permanent Funds are budgeted in the funds receiving the Permanent Funds' earnings (usually Special Revenue Funds).

Recognition of revenues and expenditures is determined by the rules established for governmental-type funds—the current financial resources measurement focus. Like other governmental-type funds, Permanent Funds use the modified accrual basis of accounting for determining the timing of the recognition of revenues and expenditures.

Accounting for Fund Activities

Operating Entries

Assume that the estate of Dr. Jo Breaux makes a bequest to the City of Llanerch of $10,000,000. Under the terms of the bequest, the City is to purchase securities and to use the earnings on these securities to provide support for the municipal zoo. Because only the earnings on the securities can be expended and these expenditures must support programs that benefit the city, a Permanent Fund, the Breaux Bequest Fund, is used to account for the use of these resources.

Shortly after receiving the bequest the City purchases government securities for $10,000,000. The entries to record the bequest and the purchase of securities are

Cash	10,000,000	
Revenues—bequest		10,000,000
To record bequest from Breaux estate.		

Investments	10,000,000	
Cash		10,000,000
To record investment of fund resources.		

During the year, investment earnings of $500,000 are recorded. Of this amount, $400,000 is received in cash.

Cash	400,000	
Investment income receivable	100,000	
Revenues—investment income		500,000
To record investment income for year.		

A transfer of $350,000 is made to the Zoo Operating Fund, a Special Revenue fund.

Entry in the books of the Permanent Fund

Transfer out to Zoo Operating Fund	350,000	
Cash		350,000
To record transfer to Zoo Operating Fund.		

Entry in the books of the Special Revenue Fund

Cash	350,000	
Transfer in from Breaux Bequest Fund		350,000
To record transfer from Breaux Bequest Fund.		

During the year, the fund incurs the following operating costs:

Audit	$ 2,500
Investment fees	10,000
Total	$12,500

Assume that the investment fees have already been paid, but the audit item is still open (unpaid).

Expenditures—audit	2,500	
Expenditures—investment fees	10,000	
Vouchers payable		2,500
Cash		10,000
To record operating costs.		

By the end of the year, the marketable securities increased in value by $2,000,000. Because investments are generally reported at fair market value, an adjustment to record this increase in value must be made. The adjustment is

Investments	2,000,000	
Revenues—net appreciation in fair market value		2,000,000
To record increase in market value of investments.		

Note: This adjustment represents an increase in the principal of the fund. Unless specifically allowed by the trust agreement, these resources cannot be used to support the zoo.

Closing Entries

At the end of the fiscal year, the following entries would be made to close the books of this fund.

Revenues—bequests	10,000,000
Revenues—investment income	500,000
Revenues—net appreciation in fair market value	2,000,000
Transfer out to Zoo Operating Fund	350,000
Expenditures—audit	2,500
Expenditures—investment fees	10,000
Unreserved fund balance	12,137,500

To close revenue, expenditure, and transfer accounts to Unreserved
fund balance.

After closing entries are made, the postclosing trial balance appears as shown in Table 5-2. The resulting financial statements are shown in Tables 5-3 and 5-4.

Table 5-2
Permanent Fund—Postclosing Trial Balance for the City of Llanerch

CITY OF LLANERCH
PERMANENT FUND
BREAUX BEQUEST FUND
POSTCLOSING TRIAL BALANCE
DECEMBER 31, 2004

	DEBITS	CREDITS
Cash	$ 40,000	
Investment income receivable	100,000	
Investments	12,000,000	
Vouchers payable		$ 2,500
Unreserved fund balance		12,137,500
	$12,140,000	$12,140,000

Table 5-3
Permanent Fund—Balance Sheet for the City of Llanerch

CITY OF LLANERCH
PERMANENT FUND
BREAUX BEQUEST FUND
BALANCE SHEET
DECEMBER 31, 2004

Assets		
Cash		$ 40,000
Investment income receivable		100,000
Investments		12,000,000
Total		$12,140,000
Liabilities and Fund Balance		
Vouchers payable		$ 2,500
Unreserved fund balance		12,137,500
Total		$12,140,000

Table 5-4

Permanent Fund—Statement of Revenues, Expenditures and Changes
in Fund Balance for the City of Llanerch

CITY OF LLANERCH
PERMANENT FUND
BREAUX BEQUEST FUND
STATEMENT OF REVENUES, EXPENDITURES, AND CHANGES IN FUND BALANCE
FOR THE FISCAL YEAR ENDED DECEMBER 31, 2004

Revenues		
Bequests	$10,000,000	
Investment income	500,000	
Net appreciation in fair market value	2,000,000	$12,500,000
Expenditures		
Audit	$ 2,500	
Investment fees	10,000	12,500
Excess (Deficiency) of Revenues over Expenditures		$12,487,500
Other Financing Sources (Uses)		
Transfer out to Zoo Operating Fund		(350,000)
Net change in fund balance		$12,137,500
Fund Balance at Beginning of Year		-0-
Fund Balance at End of Year		$12,137,500

SUMMARY PROBLEM ON THE GENERAL FUND

The city council of Realistic City approved the budget shown in Table 5-5 for that municipality's General Fund on December 31, 2004.

Realistic City currently has five property owners, whose fiscal 2004 property taxes are as follows:

H. R. Morgan	$ 525,000
W. M. Lohmann	350,000
G. R. Parker	35,000
J. R. Davis	50,000
R. R. Gales	40,000
	$1,000,000

One former property owner, L. J. Ahrens, still owes $500 of FY 2003 property taxes. Past experience indicates that 4 percent of the property taxes levied are usually not collected.

Table 5-5
Budget of Realistic City

REALISTIC CITY
GENERAL FUND
BUDGET
FOR THE YEAR ENDED DECEMBER 31, 2004

Estimated Revenues and Proceeds		
of Issue of General Obligation Bonds		
Property taxes	$935,000	
License fees	70,000	
Interest and penalties	40,000	
Income taxes	55,000	
Proceeds from issue of bonds	820,000	$1,920,000
Appropriations and transfers		
Salaries	$585,000	
Supplies	220,000	
Capital equipment	975,000	
Transfer to Frazer Park Fund	20,000	
Transfer to Debt Service Fund	100,000	1,900,000
Projected Increase in Fund Balance		$ 20,000

Among the city's accounting principles are the following:

1. All purchases of supplies and capital equipment are encumbered.
2. Expenditures for salaries, interest, and transfers to other funds do not require encumbrances.
3. Encumbrances lapse at the end of the fiscal year; however, the Reserve for encumbrances is shown on the year-end balance sheet.
4. Separate accounts are maintained for each taxpayer.

The postclosing trial balance of the General Fund of Realistic City, as of December 31, 2003, is as follows:

	Debits	Credits
Cash	$51,850	
Property taxes receivable—delinquent—Ahrens	500	
Allowance for uncollectible property taxes—delinquent		$ 400
Interest and penalties receivable—Ahrens	50	
Vouchers payable		8,000
Due to Frazer Park Fund		9,000
Fund balance reserved for encumbrances		20,000
Unreserved fund balance		15,000
	$52,400	$52,400

During fiscal year 2004, the following transactions take place:

1. Purchase orders outstanding at the beginning of the year are encumbered. They are for supplies and amount to $20,000.
2. Individual accounts for Property taxes receivable are set up, along with an Allowance for uncollectible property taxes equal to 4 percent of the amount levied. An allowance of $25,000 for property tax refunds is also set up.
3. Property taxes are collected on time and in full from H. R. Morgan.
4. L. J. Ahrens is unable to pay her FY 2003 property taxes in full. She pays the $50 penalty and $100 of these taxes. The remainder of her account is written off.
5. The city council decides, in late August, that the Allowance for uncollectible property taxes is too low and orders the city's finance director to increase it by $10,000.
6. The amount due to the Frazer Park Fund and the vouchers that were outstanding at the end of FY 2003 are paid.
7. G. R. Parker is unable to pay his FY 2004 property taxes. The city decides to write off the account without foreclosing on this property because of Parker's adverse financial circumstances.
8. J. R. Davis and R. R. Gales fail to pay their property taxes by the due date (September 30). The taxes are reclassified as delinquent, along with the current balance in the Allowance for uncollectible property taxes, $15,000.
9. Penalties of $500 and $400, respectively, are levied against Davis and Gales.
10. A tax lien is placed against the Davis property.
11. Costs of processing and advertising the lien amount to $300. They are paid immediately.
12. In November, the Davis property is sold for $120,000. The auctioneer submits a bill for $1,500. Davis and the auctioneer are paid in full.
13. W. M. Lohmann protests his tax bill. As a result, it is lowered to $325,000. Lohmann then pays the tax bill in full.
14. Supplies and equipment ordered the previous year arrive. Actual cost is $19,500. Payment is made the following week.
15. A cash payment of $13,000, representing part of the FY 2004 contribution, is made to the Frazer Park Fund. Because of a shortfall in property tax collections, the General Fund will be unable to contribute the budgeted amount. A liability for the amount it expects to contribute by the end of the fiscal year or shortly thereafter, $5,000, is set up.
16. Supplies costing $200,000 are ordered on Purchase Order No. 1426.
17. New fire engines, expected to cost $975,000, are ordered on Purchase Order No. 1427.
18. One-fourth of the supplies ordered arrive, along with an invoice for $45,000. The invoice is paid the following week.
19. One-half of the supplies arrive, along with an invoice for $90,000. Payment will not be made until the following year.
20. Salaries for the year amount to $580,000. They are paid in cash.
21. General obligation bonds are issued in March. Proceeds from these bonds, $810,000, will be used by the General Fund to help pay for the fire engines ordered in number 17.

22. In December, a transfer of $100,000 to the Debt Service Fund is recorded. Actual payment will be made the following year.
23. At the end of the year, it is determined that the balance in the Allowance for uncollectible property taxes account is too low. The allowance is raised by $5,000.
24. The city disposes of an old fire engine for $10,000.
25. The new fire engines arrive, along with an invoice for $975,000. The invoice is paid immediately.
26. Revenues from other sources, which have been collected but not yet recorded, are as follows:

License fees	$75,000
Interest and penalties	38,000
Income taxes	47,000

Income taxes are considered to be derived taxes. The city's finance director estimates that, in addition to the amount shown above, another $5,000 of income taxes will be collected early in the following year.
27. Supplies costing $10,000 are still on hand at the end of the year. It is felt that this fact should be reported in the financial statements.

For FY 2004, complete the following accounting tasks:

1. Prepare appropriate budgetary and operating entries in the General Fund.
2. Prepare a preclosing trial balance (Table 5-6).
3. Prepare closing entries.
4. Prepare a postclosing trial balance (Table 5-7).
5. Prepare appropriate financial statements (Tables 5-8, 5-9, and 5-10).

The budgetary, or opening, entry is as follows:

Estimated revenues—property taxes	935,000	
Estimated revenues—license fees	70,000	
Estimated revenues—interest and penalties	40,000	
Estimated revenues—income taxes	55,000	
Estimated proceeds from issue of bonds	820,000	
Appropriations—salaries		585,000
Appropriations—supplies		220,000
Appropriations—capital equipment		975,000
Transfer to Frazer Park Fund		20,000
Transfer to Debt Service Fund		100,000
Budgetary fund balance		20,000

To record estimated revenues, estimated proceeds from issue of bonds, appropriations, and projected increase in fund balance for FY 2004.

The operating entries are as follows:

1a. Fund balance reserved for encumbrances	20,000	
Unreserved fund balance		20,000

To remove reservation of fund balance for encumbrances open at end of FY 2003.

Table 5-6

General Fund—Preclosing Trial Balance for Realistic City

REALISTIC CITY
GENERAL FUND
PRECLOSING TRIAL BALANCE
DECEMBER 31, 2004

	DEBITS	CREDITS
Cash	$ 283,000	
Property taxes receivable—delinquent—Gales	40,000	
Allowance for uncollectible property taxes—delinquent		$ 20,000
Interest and penalties receivable—Gales	400	
Income taxes receivable	5,000	
Supplies on hand	10,000	
Vouchers payable		90,000
Due to Frazer Park Fund		5,000
Due to Debt Service Fund		100,000
Encumbrances—supplies	50,000	
Fund balance reserved for supplies on hand		10,000
Unreserved fund balance		35,000
Budgetary fund balance reserved for encumbrances		50,000
Budgetary fund balance		20,000
Estimated revenues—property taxes	935,000	
Estimated revenues—license fees	70,000	
Estimated revenues—interest and penalties	40,000	
Estimated revenues—income taxes	55,000	
Estimated proceeds from issue of bonds	820,000	
Appropriations—salaries		585,000
Appropriations—supplies		220,000
Appropriations—capital equipment		975,000
Transfer to Frazer Park Fund		20,000
Transfer to Debt Service Fund		100,000
Revenues—property taxes		920,000
Revenues—license fees		75,000
Revenues—interest and penalties		38,900
Revenues—income taxes		52,000
Revenues—sale of general fixed assets		10,000
Proceeds from issue of bonds		810,000
Expenditures—salaries	580,000	
Expenditures—supplies	154,500	
Expenditures—capital equipment	975,000	
Transfer out to Frazer Park Fund	18,000	
Transfer out to Debt Service Fund	100,000	
	$4,135,900	$4,135,900

Table 5-7

General Fund—Postclosing Trial Balance for Realistic City

REALISTIC CITY
GENERAL FUND
POSTCLOSING TRIAL BALANCE
DECEMBER 31, 2004

	DEBITS	CREDITS
Cash	$283,000	
Property taxes receivable—delinquent—Gales	40,000	
Allowance for uncollectible property taxes—delinquent		$ 20,000
Interest and penalties receivable—Gales	400	
Income taxes receivable	5,000	
Supplies on hand	10,000	
Vouchers payable		90,000
Due to Frazer Park Fund		5,000
Due to Debt Service Fund		100,000
Fund balance reserved for supplies on hand		10,000
Fund balance reserved for encumbrances		50,000
Unreserved fund balance		63,400
	$338,400	$338,400

Table 5-8

General Fund—Fund-Level Balance Sheet for Realistic City

REALISTIC CITY
GENERAL FUND
BALANCE SHEET
DECEMBER 31, 2004

Assets		
Cash		$283,000
Property taxes receivable—delinquent	$40,000	
Less: Allowance for uncollectible property taxes	(20,000)	20,000
Interest and penalties receivable		400
Income taxes receivable		5,000
Supplies on hand		10,000
		$318,400
Liabilities and Fund Balance		
Vouchers payable		$ 90,000
Due to Frazer Park Fund		5,000
Due to Debt Service Fund		100,000
Fund balance reserved for supplies on hand		10,000
Fund balance reserved for encumbrances		50,000
Unreserved fund balance		63,400
		$318,400

Table 5-9

General Fund—Fund-Level Statement of Revenues, Expenditures, and Changes in Fund Balance for Realistic City

REALISTIC CITY
GENERAL FUND
STATEMENT OF REVENUES, EXPENDITURES,
AND CHANGES IN FUND BALANCE
YEAR ENDED DECEMBER 31, 2004

Revenues		
Property taxes	$920,000	
License fees	75,000	
Interest and penalties	38,900	
Income taxes	52,000	
Sale of general fixed assets[a]	10,000	$1,095,900
Expenditures		
Salaries	$580,000	
Supplies	154,500	
Capital equipment	975,000	1,709,500
Excess (Deficiency) of Revenues over Expenditures		$ (613,600)
Other Financing Sources (Uses)		
Proceeds from issue of bonds	$810,000	
Transfer to Frazer Park Fund	(18,000)	
Transfer to Debt Service Fund	(100,000)	692,000
Net Change in Fund Balances		$ 78,400
Reserves and (Unreserved) Fund Balance at Beginning of Year		35,000
		$ 113,400
Increase in Reserve for Supplies on Hand		10,000
Reserves and (Unreserved) Fund Balance at End of Year		$ 123,400

[a]The sale of general fixed assets should be classified as a special item when material.

1b. Encumbrances—supplies	20,000	
Budgetary fund balance reserved for encumbrances		20,000

To reestablish encumbrances for supplies ordered, but not received, in FY 2003.

2a. Property taxes receivable—current—Morgan	525,000	
Property taxes receivable—current—Lohmann	350,000	
Property taxes receivable—current—Parker	35,000	
Property taxes receivable—current—Davis	50,000	
Property taxes receivable—current—Gales	40,000	
Allowance for uncollectible property taxes—current		40,000
Revenues—property taxes		960,000

To set up receivable for FY 2004 property taxes, along with an allowance for uncollectible property taxes of 4 percent.

Table 5-10
General Fund—Fund-Level Budgetary Comparison Schedule for Realistic City

REALISTIC CITY
GENERAL FUND
BUDGETARY COMPARISON SCHEDULE
YEAR ENDED DECEMBER 31, 2004

	ORIGINAL AND FINAL BUDGET	ACTUAL	VARIANCE— FAVORABLE (UNFAVORABLE)
Revenues:			
Property taxes	$ 935,000	$ 920,000	$(15,000)
License fees	70,000	75,000	5,000
Interest and penalties	40,000	38,900	(1,100)
Income taxes	55,000	52,000	(3,000)
Sales of general fixed assets		10,000	10,000
Total revenues	$1,100,000	$1,095,900	$ (4,100)
Expenditures			
Salaries	$ 585,000	$ 580,000	$ 5,000
Supplies[a]	220,000	204,500	15,500
Capital equipment	975,000	975,000	—
Total expenditures	$1,780,000	$1,759,500	$ 20,500
Excess (Deficiency) of Revenues over Expenditures	$ (680,000)	$(663,600)	$ 16,400
Other Financing Sources (Uses)			
Proceeds from issue of bonds	$ 820,000	$ 810,000	$(10,000)
Transfer to Frazer Park Fund	(20,000)	(18,000)	2,000
Transfer to Debt Service Fund	(100,000)	(100,000)	—
Total other financing sources (uses)	$ 700,000	$ 692,000	$ (8,000)
Net change in fund balances	$ 20,000	$ 28,400	$ 8,400
Reserves and Unreserved Fund Balance at beginning of year	35,000	35,000	—
	$ 55,000	$ 63,400	$ 8,400
Increase in Reserve for supplies on hand	—	10,000	10,000
Reserves and Unreserved Fund Balance at end of year	$ 55,000	$ 73,400	$ 18,400

[a]Expenditures shown for supplies include the amount actually spent in FY 2004 ($154,500) plus outstanding encumbrances of $50,000, which will be honored the following year but are charged against the FY 2004 budget.

| 2b. Revenues—property taxes | 25,000 | |
| Allowance for property tax refunds | | 25,000 |

To set up an allowance for property tax refunds.

| 3. Cash | 525,000 | |
| Property taxes receivable—current—Morgan | | 525,000 |

To record payment of property taxes by H. R. Morgan.

4. Cash	150	
Allowance for uncollectible property taxes—delinquent	400	
Interest and penalties receivable—Ahrens		50
Property taxes receivable—delinquent—Ahrens		500

To record collection of penalties and part of FY 2003 property taxes levied on L. J. Ahrens and to write off remainder of account.

| 5. Revenues—property taxes | 10,000 | |
| Allowance for uncollectible property taxes—current | | 10,000 |

To increase FY 2004 allowance for uncollectible property taxes to reflect actual collections.

6. Due to Frazer Park Fund	9,000	
Vouchers payable	8,000	
Cash		17,000

To record payment of liabilities outstanding at end of 2003.

| 7. Allowance for uncollectible property taxes—current | 35,000 | |
| Property taxes receivable—current—Parker | | 35,000 |

To write off Parker account for FY 2004.

8a. Property taxes receivable—delinquent—Davis	50,000	
Property taxes receivable—delinquent—Gales	40,000	
Property taxes receivable—current—Davis		50,000
Property taxes receivable—current—Gales		40,000

To reclassify FY 2004 property taxes not collected by due date as delinquent.

| 8b. Allowance for uncollectible property taxes—current | 15,000 | |
| Allowance for uncollectible property taxes—delinquent | | 15,000 |

To adjust allowance for uncollectible property taxes—current for FY 2004 property taxes that are no longer current.

9. Interest and penalties receivable—Davis	500	
Interest and penalties receivable—Gales	400	
Revenues—interest and penalties		900

To record assessment of late payment penalties.

10. Tax liens receivable—Davis	50,500	
Property taxes receivable—delinquent—Davis		50,000
Interest and penalties receivable—Davis		500

To reclassify property taxes, interest, and penalties receivable to reflect lien on Davis property.

| 11. Tax liens receivable—Davis | 300 | |
| Cash | | 300 |

To record cost of processing and advertising tax lien against Davis property.

12a. Cash	120,000	
Tax liens receivable—Davis		50,800
Vouchers payable		69,200

To record sale of Davis property, removal of lien, and expenses related to sale ($1,500).

12b.	Vouchers payable	69,200	
	Cash		69,200
	To record payment to J. R. Davis and of expenses related to sale of Davis property ($1,500).		

13a.	Allowance for property tax refunds	25,000	
	Property taxes receivable—current—Lohmann		25,000
	To adjust for error in FY 2004 tax assessment of W. M. Lohmann.		

13b.	Cash	325,000	
	Property taxes receivable—current—Lohmann		325,000
	To record payment of W. M. Lohmann's FY 2004 property taxes.		

14a.	Budgetary fund balance reserved for encumbrances	20,000	
	Encumbrances—supplies		20,000
	To record receipt of supplies ordered in FY 2004.		

14b.	Expenditures—supplies	19,500	
	Vouchers payable		19,500
	To record liability for payment of supplies ordered in FY 2003.		

14c.	Vouchers payable	19,500	
	Cash		19,500
	To record payment of voucher.		

15.	Transfer out to Frazer Park Fund	18,000	
	Due to Frazer Park Fund		5,000
	Cash		13,000
	To record FY 2004 contribution to Frazer Park Fund.		

16.	Encumbrances—supplies	200,000	
	Budgetary fund balance reserved for encumbrances		200,000
	To record placement of order for FY 2004 supplies, Purchase Order No. 1426.		

17.	Encumbrances—capital equipment	975,000	
	Budgetary fund balance reserved for encumbrances		975,000
	To record placement of order for new fire engines, Purchase Order No. 1427.		

18a.	Budgetary fund balance reserved for encumbrances	50,000	
	Encumbrances—supplies		50,000
	To record receipt of one-fourth of supplies ordered under Purchase Order No. 1426.		

18b.	Expenditures—supplies	45,000	
	Vouchers payable		45,000
	To record liability for payment of one-fourth of supplies received under Purchase Order No. 1426.		

18c.	Vouchers payable	45,000	
	Cash		45,000
	To record payment of voucher.		

19a.	Budgetary fund balance reserved for encumbrances	100,000	
	Encumbrances—supplies		100,000
	To record receipt of one-half of supplies ordered under Purchase Order No. 1426.		

19b.	Expenditures—supplies	90,000	
	Vouchers payable		90,000
	To record liability for payment of one-half of supplies received under Purchase Order No. 1426.		

20. Expenditures—salaries   580,000
      Cash   580,000
    To record salaries paid during FY 2004.

21. Cash   810,000
      Proceeds from issue of bonds.   810,000
    To record issue of general obligation bonds.

22. Transfer out to Debt Service Fund   100,000
      Due to Debt Service Fund   100,000
    To record liability for FY 2004 contribution toward service
      of bond issue.

23. Revenues—property taxes   5,000
      Allowance for uncollectible property taxes—delinquent   5,000
    To adjust property tax revenues for expected uncollectible
      amounts in excess of adjusted FY 2004 allowance.
      (*Note:* Because FY 2004 property taxes outstanding are past
      due at this point, the "delinquent" allowance is increased.)

24. Cash   10,000
      Revenues—proceeds from sale of fixed assets   10,000
    To record sale of one surplus fire engine.

25a. Budgetary fund balance reserved for encumbrances   975,000
      Encumbrances—capital equipment   975,000
    To record receipt of fire engines ordered under Purchase Order
      No. 1427.

25b. Expenditures—capital equipment   975,000
      Vouchers payable   975,000
    To record liability for payment for fire engines received under
      Purchase Order No. 1427.

25c. Vouchers payable   975,000
      Cash   975,000
    To record payment of voucher.

26. Cash   160,000
    Income taxes receivable   5,000
      Revenues—license fees   75,000
      Revenues—interest and penalties   38,000
      Revenues—income taxes   52,000
    To record FY 2004 revenues from various sources.

27. Supplies on hand   10,000
      Fund balance reserved for supplies on hand   10,000
    To record amount of supplies on hand at end of FY 2004.

The closing entries are as follows:

Appropriations—salaries   585,000
Appropriations—supplies   220,000
Appropriations—capital equipment   975,000

Transfer to Frazer Park Fund	20,000	
Transfer to Debt Service Fund	100,000	
Budgetary fund balance	20,000	
Estimated revenues—property taxes		935,000
Estimated revenues—license fees		70,000
Estimated revenues—interest and penalties		40,000
Estimated revenues—income taxes		55,000
Estimated proceeds from issue of bonds		820,000
To close budgetary accounts for FY 2004.		
Revenues—property taxes	920,000	
Revenues—license fees	75,000	
Revenues—interest and penalties	38,900	
Revenues—income taxes	52,000	
Revenues—sale of general fixed assets	10,000	
Proceeds from issue of bonds	810,000	
Expenditures—salaries		580,000
Expenditures—supplies		154,500
Expenditures—capital equipment		975,000
Transfer out to Frazer Park Fund		18,000
Transfer out to Debt Service Fund		100,000
Unreserved fund balance		78,400
To close revenue and expenditure accounts for FY 2004.		
Budgetary fund balance reserved for encumbrances	50,000	
Encumbrances—supplies		50,000
To close outstanding encumbrances for FY 2004.		
Unreserved fund balance	50,000	
Fund balance reserved for encumbrances		50,000
To record reservation of fund balance for open encumbrances.		

GOVERNMENTAL ACCOUNTING IN PRACTICE
City of Shreveport, Louisiana

Shreveport (2001 population, 201,059) is a medium-sized city, located on the west bank of the Red River in Northwest Louisiana. Its economy is based on agriculture and manufacturing, but has a large service component.

The financial statements of the General Fund of Shreveport follow, including a balance sheet (Table 5-11); a statement of revenues, expenditures, and changes in fund balances—governmental funds (Table 5-12); a statement of revenues, expenditures, and changes in fund balance—actual and budget (Table 5-13), and selected notes to the financial statements (Table 5-14). Notice that the results prepared on the GAAP basis for the General Fund (Table 5-12) and the budgetary basis (Table 5-13) differ slightly. Table 5-11 is an extract of the General Fund from the city's fund-level statements.

Table 5-11

General Fund—Balance Sheet for Shreveport, Louisiana

CITY OF SHREVEPORT, LOUISIANA
BALANCE SHEET
GENERAL FUND
DECEMBER, 31, 20X4

ASSETS

Cash and cash equivalents	$ 9,412
Investments	—
Property taxes receivable, net	8,813,514
Franchise taxes receivable	1,439,510
Accounts receivable, net	2,875,463
Due from other governments	10,588,081
Due from other funds	—
Inventories, at cost	735,863
Notes receivable, net	—
Assets held for resale	—
Total assets	$24,461,843

LIABILITIES AND FUND BALANCE

Liabilities:

Accounts payable	$ 1,840,230
Accrued liabilities	325,861
Due to other governments	598,695
Due to other funds	7,740,915
Due to component unit	16,917
Deferred revenue	1,417,452
Deposits and deferred charges	348,361
Notes payable	—
Total liabilities	$12,342,431

Fund balance:

Reserved for:

Debt service	—
Encumbrances	$ 2,290,891
Assets held for resale	—
Inventories	735,863
Endowments	14,719

Unreserved, designated for:

Subsequent years' expenditures	—
Landfill closure	1,693,376
Unreserved, undesignated	7,384,563
Special revenue funds	—
Capital project funds	—

Unreserved, undesignated reported in nonmajor:

Special revenue funds	—
Total fund balance	12,119,412
Total liabilities and fund balance	$24,461,843

Source: Shreveport, Louisiana, annual report.

Table 5-12

Fund-Level Statement of Revenues, Expenditures, and Changes in Fund Balance for Shreveport, Louisiana

CITY OF SHREVEPORT, LOUISIANA
STATEMENT OF REVENUES, EXPENDITURES, AND CHANGES IN FUND BALANCES
GOVERNMENTAL FUNDS
FOR THE YEAR ENDED DECEMBER 31, 20X4

	GENERAL	COMMUNITY DEVELOPMENT	DEBT SERVICE	20X2A GENERAL OBLIGATION BONDS	OTHER GOVERNMENTAL FUNDS	TOTAL GOVERNMENTAL FUNDS
REVENUES						
Taxes:						
Property	$ 19,572,536	$ —	$ 28,656,516	$ —	$ —	$ 48,229,052
Sales	75,481,654	—	—	—	—	75,481,654
Franchise	7,086,954	—	—	—	—	7,086,954
Licenses and permits	6,590,052	—	—	—	—	6,590,052
Intergovernmental	8,066,389	12,639,210	—	—	2,066,411	22,772,010
Charges for services	15,286,721	21,347	—	—	—	15,308,068
Fines and forfeitures	3,051,065	—	—	—	—	3,051,065
Gaming	—	—	—	—	14,819,542	14,819,542
Investment earnings	151,096	189,599	1,054,020	4,351,853	3,848,859	9,595,427
Miscellaneous	644,528	675,003	1,495,690	—	1,563,057	4,378,278
Total revenues	$135,930,995	$13,525,159	$ 31,206,226	$ 4,351,853	$ 22,297,869	$207,312,102
EXPENDITURES						
Current:						
General government	$ 21,193,843	$ 2,182,949	—	—	—	$ 23,376,792
Public safety	61,812,341	—	—	—	$ 1,967,502	63,779,843
Public works	27,155,205	—	—	—	—	27,155,205
Culture and recreation	11,026,051	425,000	—	—	24,386	11,475,437

(continued)

197

Table 5-12

Continued

Health and welfare	—	493,450	—	—	—	493,450
Community development	—	8,883,571	—	—	—	8,883,571
Economic development	—	443,871	—	3,114,923	—	3,558,794
Economic opportunity	—	2,749,050	—	—	—	2,749,050
Payment to component units	3,469,751	—	—	—	—	3,469,751
Debt service:						
Principal	—	—	$ 26,360,111	—	—	26,360,111
Interest and other charges	—	—	16,755,523	—	—	16,755,523
Bond issuance costs	—	—	—	125,055	$ 11,305	136,360
Capital outlay	—	—	—	27,975,892	6,878,063	34,853,955
Total expenditures	$124,657,191	$15,177,891	$ 43,115,634	$ 33,207,758	$ 6,889,368	$223,047,842
Excess (deficiency) of revenues over (under) expenditures	$ 11,273,804	$ (1,652,732)	$(11,909,408)	$(10,909,889)	$(2,537,515)	$(15,735,740)
OTHER FINANCING SOURCES (USES)						
Transfers in	$ 2,000,000	$ 2,529,884	$ 16,914,569	$ 6,920,892	—	$ 28,365,345
Transfers out	(14,330,290)	(1,202,337)	—	(15,511,987)	—	(31,044,614)
Bond proceeds	—	—	—	33,000,000	—	33,000,000
Premium on bond proceeds	—	—	—	3,182	—	3,182
Capital lease	418,986	32,088	—	—	—	451,074
Total other financing sources and (uses)	$(11,911,304)	$ 1,359,635	$16,914,569	$ 24,412,087	—	$ 30,774,987
Net change in fund balances	(637,500)	(293,097)	5,005,161	13,502,198	(2,537,515)	15,039,247
Fund balances—beginning	12,756,912	3,060,556	28,977,467	78,740,296	85,900,049	209,435,280
Fund balances—ending	$12,119,412	$ 2,767,459	$33,982,628	$ 92,242,494	$83,362,534	$224,474,527

Source: Shreveport, Louisiana, annual report.

Table 5-13

General Fund—Statement of Revenues, Expenditures, and Changes in Fund Balance—
Budget and Actual for Shreveport, Louisiana

CITY OF SHREVEPORT, LOUISIANA
GENERAL FUND
STATEMENT OF REVENUES, EXPENDITURES, AND CHANGES IN FUND BALANCE
BUDGET AND ACTUAL ON BUDGETARY BASIS
FOR THE YEAR ENDED DECEMBER 31, 20X4

	BUDGETED AMOUNTS		ACTUAL AMOUNTS BUDGETARY BASIS	VARIANCE WITH FINAL BUDGET POSITIVE (NEGATIVE)
	ORIGINAL	FINAL		
REVENUES				
Taxes	$104,035,000	$105,673,700	$102,141,144	$(3,532,556)
Licenses and permits	6,838,800	6,838,800	6,590,052	(248,748)
Intergovernmental	1,681,000	4,221,400	4,379,718	158,318
Charges for services	12,701,400	16,605,000	15,286,721	(1,318,279)
Fines and forfeitures	2,945,000	3,305,000	3,051,065	(253,935)
Investment earnings	300,000	300,000	151,096	(148,904)
Miscellaneous	5,667,300	1,671,300	1,444,528	(226,772)
Total revenues	$134,168,500	$138,615,200	$133,044,324	$(5,570,876)
EXPENDITURES				
General government:				
Office of mayor:				
Salaries, wages and employee benefits	$ 2,076,828	$ 2,021,880	$ 1,990,133	$ 31,747
Materials and supplies	46,788	46,687	41,258	5,429
Contractual services	217,849	217,850	181,141	36,709
Other charges	20,050	15,708	8,948	6,760
Improvements and equipment	9,308	13,651	9,601	4,050
Total office of mayor	$ 2,370,823	$ 2,315,776	$ 2,231,081	$ 84,695
City council:				
Salaries, wages and employee benefits	$ 898,405	$ 730,405	$ 724,528	$ 5,877
Materials and supplies	15,950	15,950	12,478	3,472
Contractual services	259,683	256,683	194,498	62,185
Improvements and equipment	40,800	51,800	27,501	24,299
Total city council	$ 1,214,838	$ 1,054,838	$ 959,005	$ 95,833
Finance:				
Salaries, wages and employee benefits	$ 3,968,738	$ 3,813,739	$ 3,809,007	$ 4,732
Materials and supplies	291,670	353,759	295,412	58,347
Contractual services	1,244,126	1,194,673	1,184,965	9,708
Other charges	100	100	—	100
Improvements and equipment	529,705	458,204	438,195	20,009
Total finance	$ 6,034,339	$ 5,820,475	$ 5,727,579	$ 92,896

(continued)

Table 5-13
Continued

Other—unclassified:				
Salaries, wages and employee benefits	$ 2,060,115	$ 2,169,962	$ 2,029,289	$ 140,673
Materials and supplies	1,000	1,000	2,767	(1,767)
Contractual services	329,000	429,000	398,232	30,768
Interest and civic appropriations	2,405,240	2,510,240	2,787,262	(277,022)
Payments to component units	3,489,400	3,672,400	3,469,751	202,649
Claims	7,000,000	7,668,900	7,492,427	176,473
Total other—unclassified	$ 15,284,755	$ 16,451,502	$ 16,179,728	$ 271,774
Total general government	$ 24,904,755	$ 25,642,591	$ 25,097,393	$ 545,198
Public safety:				
Police:				
Salaries, wages and employee benefits	$ 28,167,760	$ 28,080,260	$ 27,580,912	$ 499,348
Materials and supplies	959,342	1,042,642	1,028,271	14,371
Contractual services	1,726,940	1,634,440	1,631,424	3,016
Other charges	76,300	62,400	54,248	8,152
Improvements and equipment	1,641,160	1,618,860	1,618,315	545
Total police	$ 32,571,502	$ 32,438,602	$ 31,913,170	$ 525,432
Fire:				
Salaries, wages and employee benefits	$ 27,931,762	$ 27,983,595	$ 28,116,324	$ (132,729)
Materials and supplies	878,537	1,028,538	1,001,207	27,331
Contractual services	762,787	1,445,588	1,395,344	50,244
Other charges	1,800	1,800	—	1,800
Improvements and equipment	1,429,885	1,429,885	1,177,296	252,589
Total fire	$ 31,004,771	$ 31,889,406	$ 31,690,171	$ 199,235
Total public safety	$ 63,576,273	$ 64,328,008	$ 63,603,341	$ 724,667
Public Works:				
Salaries, wages and employee benefits	$ 11,983,970	$ 11,828,970	$ 11,595,041	$ 233,929
Materials and supplies	1,748,928	1,933,314	1,585,013	348,301
Contractual services	12,547,262	13,620,942	13,405,405	215,537
Other charges	6,000	6,000	1,074	4,926
Improvements and equipment	4,611,566	4,692,694	4,584,817	107,877
Total public works	$ 30,897,726	$ 32,081,920	$ 31,171,350	$ 910,570

Table 5-13
Continued

Culture and recreation:				
Salaries, wages and employee benefits	$ 7,196,080	$ 7,034,500	$ 6,764,640	$ 269,860
Materials and supplies	966,844	1,001,679	985,030	16,649
Contractual services	2,522,673	2,922,544	2,808,655	113,889
Improvements and equipment	847,933	909,036	891,851	17,185
Total culture and recreation	$ 11,533,530	$ 11,867,759	$ 11,450,176	$ 417,583
Total expenditures	$130,912,284	$133,920,278	$131,322,260	$ 2,598,018
Excess of revenues over expenditures	$ 3,256,216	$ 4,694,922	$ 1,722,064	$(2,972,858)
OTHER FINANCING SOURCES (USES)				
Transfers in	$ 1,200,000	$ 1,200,000	$ 1,200,000	—
Transfers out	(6,670,400)	(5,581,800)	(5,850,455)	$ (268,655)
Total other financing sources and uses	$ (5,470,400)	$ (4,381,800)	$ (4,650,455)	$ (268,655)
Net change in fund balance	(2,214,184)	313,122	(2,928,391)	(3,241,513)
Fund balances—beginning	12,756,912	12,756,912	12,756,912	—
Fund balances—ending	$ 10,542,728	$ 13,070,034	$ 9,828,521	$(3,241,513)

Source: Shreveport, Louisiana, annual report.

Table 5-14
Notes to Financial Statements for Shreveport, Louisiana

CITY OF SHREVEPORT, LOUISIANA
NOTES TO FINANCIAL STATEMENTS
FOR THE YEAR ENDED DECEMBER 31, 20X4

I. *Summary of Significant Accounting Policies*

The accounting policies of the City of Shreveport conform to generally accepted accounting principles as applicable to governments. The following is a summary of the more significant accounting policies:

A. The Financial Reporting Entity

The City of Shreveport (the "City") was incorporated in 1839, under the provisions of Louisiana R.S. 67. In May of 1978, the present City Charter was adopted which established a mayor-council form of government. The City provides a full range of municipal services as authorized by the charter. These include police and fire protection, emergency medical services, public works (streets and waste collection), public improvements, water and sewer services, parks and recreation, planning and zoning, public transportation, social, cultural and general administrative services.

(continued)

Table 5-14
Continued

The basic criterion for determining whether another governmental organization should be included in a primary governmental unit's reporting entity for general purpose financial statements is financial accountability. Financial accountability includes the appointment of a voting majority of the organization's governing body and the ability of the primary government to impose its will on the organization, or if there is a financial benefit/burden relationship. In addition, an organization which is fiscally dependent on the primary government should be included in its reporting entity.

The financial statements present the City of Shreveport (the primary government) and its component units. The operations of the Shreveport Municipal and Regional Airports and the Shreveport Area Transit System are included as a part of the primary government. The discrete component units discussed below are included in the City's reporting entity because of the significance of their operational or financial relationships with the City. There are no blended component units in the City.

Discretely Presented Component Units

The component units columns in the government-wide financial statements include the financial data of the City's component units. They are reported in a separate column to emphasize that they are legally separate from the City.

B. **Government-wide and Fund Financial Statements**

The government-wide financial statements (i.e., the statement of net assets and the statement of activities) report information on all of the nonfiduciary activities of the primary government and its component units. For the most part, the effect of interfund activity has been removed from these statements. Governmental activities, which normally are supported by taxes, intergovernmental revenues, and other nonexchange transactions, are reported separately from business-type activities, which rely to a significant extent on fees and charges for support. Likewise, the primary government is reported separately from certain legally separate component units for which the primary government is financially accountable.

The statement of activities demonstrates the degree to which the direct expenses of a given function of governmental activities and different business-type activities are offset by program revenues. Direct expenses are those that are clearly identifiable with a specific function or program. Program revenues include (1) fees, fines, and charges to customers or applicants who purchase, use, or directly benefit from goods, services, or privileges provided by a given function or program and (2) grants and contributions that are restricted to meeting the operational or capital requirements of a particular function or program. Taxes and other items not properly included among program revenues are reported instead as general revenues.

Separate financial statements are provided for governmental funds, proprietary funds, and fiduciary funds, even though the latter are excluded from the government-wide financial statements. Major individual governmental funds and major individual enterprise funds are reported as separate columns in the fund financial statements.

C. **Measurement Focus, Basis of Accounting, and Financial Statement Presentation**

The government-wide financial statements are reported using the economic resources measurement focus and the accrual basis of accounting, as are the proprietary fund and fiduciary fund financial statements. Revenues are recorded when earned and expenses are recorded when a liability is incurred, regardless of the timing of related cash flows. Property taxes are recognized as revenues in the year for which they are levied. Grants and similar items are recognized as revenue as soon as all eligibility requirements imposed by the provider have been met.

Table 5-14
Continued

Governmental fund financial statements are reported using the current financial resources measurement focus and the modified accrual basis of accounting. Revenues are recognized as soon as they are both measurable and available. Revenues are considered to be available when they are collectible within the current period or soon enough thereafter to pay liabilities of the current period. For property taxes, the City considers revenues to be available if they are collected within 60 days of the end of the current fiscal period. For revenues other than property taxes, the City considers them to be available if they are collected within 90 days of the end of the current fiscal period. Expenditures generally are recorded when a liability is incurred, as under accrual accounting. However, debt service expenditures, as well as expenditures related to compensated absences are recorded only when payment is due.

Property taxes, sales taxes, franchise taxes, and interest associated with the current fiscal period are all considered to be susceptible to accrual and so have been recognized as revenues of the current fiscal period. All other revenue items except landfill fees are considered to be measurable and available only when cash is received by the government.

The City reports the following major governmental funds:

The General Fund is the City's primary operating fund. It accounts for all financial resources of the general government, except those required to be accounted for in another fund.

The Community Development Fund is responsible for programs to increase housing opportunities, assist in the creation of employment, develop business expansion and regulate codes enforcement.

The Debt Service Fund accounts for the resources accumulated and payments made for principal and interest on long-term general obligation debt of governmental funds.

The 20X2A General Obligation Bond Fund accounts for proceeds of bonds issued for construction of a new convention center and multicultural museum.

Source: Shreveport, Louisiana, annual report.

REVIEW QUESTIONS

Q5-1　What two methods are used to handle open encumbrances at year-end? What are the advantages and disadvantages of each method?

Q5-2　What is an allotment? Describe two methods of accounting for allotments. Describe the advantages of each.

Q5-3　Why is depreciation not always recorded by governmental units at the fund level?

Q5-4　What is the usual method of handling uncollectible receivables? What is the advantage of this method?

Q5-5　Why are inventories of governmental units usually not treated in the same manner as those of commercial enterprises? When it is necessary to record a change in the level of inventories at year-end, what entry is appropriate?

Q5-6 Why is a portion of an encumbrance removed from the accounting records when an order is only partially filled?

Q5-7 How are transfers between funds of the same organization recorded?

Q5-8 In the balance sheet of a commercial entity, assets are classified as short-term or long-term. Is this classification necessary for a governmental-type fund? Explain.

Q5-9 What does the term *lapse* mean when referring to encumbrances?

Q5-10 What events take place when a receivable becomes a lien and the property is subsequently seized and sold at auction? What are the appropriate entries?

Q5-11 An Allowance for uncollectible taxes account is often set up when uncollectible taxes are not expected to be few in number and/or relatively small in amount. What is the main advantage of this method?

Q5-12 What is interfund activity?

Q5-13 Which type or types of interfund activity result in the recognition of revenues and expenditures (expenses)?

Q5-14 Name two types of derived tax revenues. When are these revenues recognized? Is a year-end adjusting entry necessary in order to recognize some of these revenues?

Q5-15 When should the expenditures and liabilities related to landfill closure and postclosure costs be recognized?

Q5-16 When is a Permanent Fund used?

CASES

C5-1 When reviewing the financial statements of Crescent City, Councilwoman Peggy Doubleton noticed that the city uses an Allowance for uncollectible property taxes. This seemed odd to her because the city had recently sold several acres of land that had been seized for nonpayment of property taxes. At the next council meeting, Councilwoman Doubleton made a motion that the city no longer use an Allowance for uncollectible property taxes. She argued that the city had the right to seize property for nonpayment of taxes. As a result it could eventually recover any lost revenue and did not need to provide for uncollectible property taxes. Furthermore, by eliminating this allowance, revenues would be raised by a substantial amount and additional services could be provided without incurring a deficit. Would you vote for Councilwoman Doubleton's motion if you were a member of the city council? Why?

C5-2 The City of Khatt recently received a $500,000 grant from the federal government to operate a daycare center for 2 years. This grant was to be the only source of funding for the daycare center. Feeling pressure to maximize revenues, the city's accountant credited a revenue account for the entire $500,000 when the check arrived. He explained to you that because the entire amount was in the city's possession, it was "measurable and available" and, therefore, should be treated as revenue. Do you agree? Why?

C5-3   Joe Babitt, a former executive of T-Mart, just started a term as mayor of Saulk Center. For the past several days he has been looking for a way to keep his campaign promise to increase services without raising taxes or service charges. While lunching at the local country club with the treasurer of T-Mart, the subject of a recent sale and leaseback of one of T-Mart's stores came up. Following a common practice in retailing, T-Mart erected a building and sold it to an investor. It then signed a long-term lease on the building. Bingo!! That's it, thought Mayor Babitt. We can sell several of the city's buildings, as well as police cars, fire engines, and other vehicles, to investors and lease them back. That will give us the revenues we desperately need. In addition, we won't need to worry about depreciation or future capital outlays. Now I can concentrate on fighting crime. Do you agree with Mayor Babitt? If not, what are the flaws in his reasoning?

ETHICS CASES

EC5-1   River City requires not-for-profit organizations owning real property and personal property, like vehicles and construction equipment, to make payments in lieu of property taxes. Homes for People, a large, not-for-profit organization, owns several rental properties in the city's central business district and operates a large fleet of trucks and bulldozers. Sy Sutter, the city's assessor, is an active member of this organization. Recently, Sutter informed the director of Homes for People that that organization would no longer be required to make payments in lieu of property taxes because of the assistance it had provided the city in cleaning up after a recent hurricane, thus saving the city a large sum of money. Sutter did not notify the city council of this action, reasoning that, "in the end, it will all balance out." Was this action ethical? Why or why not? How could such an action be prevented in the future?

EC5-2   An accounting professor purchased residential property in a certain city for $72,000, the amount for which the property was assessed. Three years later, the professor received a notice from the local tax assessor that his property was now assessed for $150,000. The general opinion of several realtors, who were familiar with the professor's neighborhood, was that the property was worth no more than $120,000. With this information in hand the professor confronted the assessor, who was sympathetic and suggested that the professor appeal his assessment at a hearing that was to be held for that purpose. As the professor was leaving the assessor's office, a secretary stopped him and suggested that he not proceed with this matter because "the appeal process could go either way and the board of assessors could (and sometimes did) raise appealed assessments by as much as 50 percent." That evening, the professor was called by a "politically connected" neighbor, whose property was considerably more valuable than that of the professor, and told him not to appeal his assessment because it could "hurt the entire neighborhood." Being a state employee and a nonnative of the city, the professor decided not to pursue the matter. Several months later, when working on a research project, the professor gained access to the city's property tax rolls and discovered that the neighbor's property was assessed for $80,000. Were these actions an ethical way to treat taxpayers? What might the city do to prevent such abuses?

EXERCISES

E5-1   (Uncollectible accounts—allowance method)
The City of Chalmette levied property taxes of $150,000 in FY 2004. Prior experience shows that 10 percent of these taxes will not be collected.

Required:
1. What is the appropriate entry to set up the receivable for FY 2004 property taxes if the allowance method is used?
2. Taxpayer Holmes, whose tax levy is $2,000, is unable to pay her property taxes. The city decides to write off her account. Make the entry necessary to record this event.
3. If the Holmes account is not written off until FY 2005, what effect will this have on the FY 2005 revenues? Why?

E5-2   (Prior-year encumbrances that remain open)
The City of Eleanor follows a policy of allowing encumbrances to remain in force until the goods are delivered or the purchase orders are canceled. At the end of FY 2004, supplies costing $10,000 have not been delivered. In March 2005, the supplies arrive, accompanied by an invoice for $12,000.

Required: 1. What entry or entries should be made at the end of FY 2004?
2. What entry or entries should be made at the beginning of FY 2005?
3. What entry or entries should be made when the supplies arrive?

E5-3   (Grant not used up by year-end)
In July 2004, Crescent City received a federal grant of $100,000, to be used to purchase food for horses used by that city's mounted police. By year-end, hay and oats costing $70,000 had been purchased by the city and eaten by the horses. In 2005, the remainder of the grant was spent on more hay and oats.

Required: 1. What entry should be made when the grant is received?
2. What entry or entries should be made when the hay and oats are received? Assume that the city pays for these goods as soon as they are received.

E5-4   (Interfund transactions)
Identify four types of interfund transactions and briefly explain the purpose of each type.

E5-5   (Treatment of inventories—purchases method)

At the end of FY 2003, the City of Kensington has a balance of $6,000 in its Reserve for supplies account. An inventory, taken at the end of 2004 reveals that supplies valued at $7,000 are on hand. Kensington uses the purchases method to account for supplies.

Required: 1. What entry should be made at the end of 2004 to disclose this change in the amount of supplies on hand?

               2. Suppose the inventory shows that supplies valued at $4,000 are on hand. What entry should be made to disclose this fact?

E5-6   (Multiple choice—General and Special Revenue Funds)

1. The budget of Laxey County shows estimated revenues in excess of appropriations. When preparing budgetary entries at the beginning of the fiscal year, an increase will be recorded in which of the following accounts?
   a. Encumbrances
   b. Due from other funds
   c. Budgetary fund balance
   d. Reserve for encumbrances

2. What are reversions of property of persons not leaving a will, and with no known relatives, to a state called?
   a. Reversions
   b. Entitlements
   c. Escheats
   d. Contributions

3. Which of the following involves a routine transfer from the General Fund to a Debt Service Fund, to provide resources to pay interest and principal on a bond issue?
   a. An interfund reimbursement
   b. An interfund transfer
   c. An interfund loan
   d. An interfund service provided and used

4. At the end of FY 2004, Carson City has outstanding encumbrances of $15,000. Although the city follows a policy of allowing outstanding encumbrances to lapse, it plans to honor the related purchase orders in FY 2005. The management of the city wants users of its financial statements to be aware of these outstanding purchase orders. Therefore, at year-end, the city's accountant should take which of the following actions?
   a. Credit Fund balance reserved for encumbrances.
   b. Credit Appropriations.
   c. Credit Unreserved fund balance.
   d. Debit an expenditure account.

5. Which of the following revenues of the General Fund are usually recorded before they are actually received?
   a. Sales taxes
   b. Property taxes

c. Fines and penalties

d. Parking meter receipts

6. If the City of Castletown sells an ambulance, which had been purchased by its General Fund several years earlier, to a local rock group, the entry to record this sale on the books of the General Fund should include which of the following?

   a. A credit to Revenues—proceeds from sale of general fixed assets

   b. A debit to Unreserved fund balance

   c. A debit to Encumbrances—capital equipment

   d. A credit to a fixed asset account

7. The town council of Bayou Brilleaux adopted a budget for FY 2004 that indicated revenues of $750,000 and appropriations of $800,000. Which entry is used to record this budget into the accounts?

	DR	CR
a. Estimated revenues	750,000	
Reserve for deficits	50,000	
Appropriations		800,000
b. Appropriations	800,000	
Budgetary fund balance		50,000
Estimated revenues		750,000
c. Estimated revenues	750,000	
Budgetary fund balance	50,000	
Appropriations		800,000
d. Only a memorandum entry is necessary		

8. Which of the following will increase the fund balance of a governmental unit at the end of a fiscal year?

   a. Estimated revenues are less than expenditures and reserve for encumbrances.

   b. Appropriations are less than expenditures and encumbrances.

   c. Revenues are greater than expenditures and encumbrances.

   d. Appropriations are greater than estimated revenues.

9. What does a governmental unit record in its Fund balance reserved for encumbrances account?

   a. Current-year purchase orders that will be honored the following year

   b. Expenditures that were made in the current year for which payment will be made the following year

   c. Excess expenditures of the prior year that will be offset against the current-year budgeted amounts

   d. Unanticipated expenditures of the prior year that become evident in the current year

10. The budget of the General Fund of the City of Dhoon Glen shows an appropriation for capital equipment of $150,000. So far a fire engine,

costing $50,000, has been received and paid for. Another fire engine, expected to cost $60,000, has been ordered and an encumbrance for this amount is outstanding. How much can the city legally spend for a third fire engine this year?

a. $100,000
b. $90,000
c. $40,000
d. $0

11. Which of the following accounts of a governmental unit is (are) closed out at the end of the fiscal year?

	Estimated Revenues	Fund Balance
a.	No	No
b.	No	Yes
c.	Yes	Yes
d.	Yes	No

12. Which of the following is an appropriate basis of accounting for the General Fund of a governmental unit?

	Cash Basis	Modified Accrual Basis
a.	Yes	No
b.	Yes	Yes
c.	No	Yes
d.	No	No

13. Which of the following is not included among the financial reporting requirements of the General Fund of a city?

a. Balance sheet
b. Statement of revenues, expenditures, and changes in fund balance
c. Budgetary comparison schedule
d. Statement of cash flows

14. In 2004 Manx City received a capital grant from the federal government to purchase a fleet of horse-drawn streetcars for its Promenade line. It also received a grant from the state to cover certain operating costs of this line. Because of an unexpectedly short operating season, only 60 percent of the operating grant was spent by the end of 2004 and the city does not expect to spend the remainder until mid-2005. Because of an unexpected increase in the price of horse-drawn streetcars, however, the entire capital grant was spent by the end of the first half of 2004. With respect to these grants, what should Manx City record as revenues from grants on its FY 2004 financial statements?

	100% of Operating Grant	60% of Operating Grant	Capital Grant
a.	Yes	No	Yes
b.	No	Yes	Yes
c.	Yes	No	No
d.	No	Yes	No

E5-7   (Tax discounts and deferred property taxes)

The City of Snape allows taxpayers who pay their property taxes by the end of the fiscal year to take a 3 percent discount for prompt payment. The city budgets, as Estimated revenues, the amount it actually expects to receive. During FY 2004 the city sent bills to property owners totaling $150,000 (gross amount). Two-thirds of the amount billed (less discounts) was received by the end of the year. The remainder, $50,000, will not be collected until the middle of the following year.

Required: 1. Prepare an entry recording the collection of property taxes in FY 2004.

               2. Prepare a year-end adjusting entry recording FY 2004 property taxes expected to be collected in FY 2005.

E5-8   (Using the Internet in governmental accounting)

The Internet is a great source of information on governmental accounting. To acquaint yourself with what is available on the Internet, select a topic relating to governmental accounting, such as operating transfers, and locate five Web sites related to that topic. Prepare a description of each site and the links from that site to other related sites. The best place to start is a search engine such as Yahoo! or Google.

PROBLEMS

P5-1   (Theory problem on the basis of accounting)

The accounting system of the municipality of Kemp is organized and operated on a fund basis. Among the types of funds used are a General Fund, a Special Revenue Fund, and an Enterprise Fund.

Required: 1. Explain the basic differences in revenue recognition between the accrual basis of accounting and the modified accrual basis of accounting as it relates to governmental accounting.

               2. What basis of accounting should be used for each of the following funds? Why?
- General Fund
- Special Revenue Fund
- Enterprise Fund

3. How should an entity account for fixed assets and long-term liabilities related to the General Fund?

(AICPA adapted)

P5-2 (Preparation of financial statements)

The commissioners of the Regents Park Commission approved the following budget. Assume that the Unreserved fund balance at the beginning of the year was $10,000 and that no encumbrances were outstanding and no supplies were on hand at the beginning or the end of the year.

Estimated Revenues		
Property taxes	$300,000	
Concession rentals	100,000	
User charges	200,000	$600,000
Appropriations		
Wages and salaries	$200,000	
Capital equipment	300,000	
Supplies	50,000	550,000
Projected Increase in Fund Balance		$ 50,000

During the year, actual revenues were

Property taxes	$300,000
Concession rentals	120,000
User charges	185,000

Actual expenditures were

Wages and salaries	$205,000
Capital equipment	290,000
Supplies	40,000

Required:
1. Prepare a statement of revenues, expenditures, and changes in fund balance.
2. Prepare a budgetary comparison schedule. Assume that originally approved budget and final budget are identical.

P5-3 (Allowance for uncollectible property taxes—allowance method)

The City of Aldwich uses the allowance method of handling uncollectible property taxes. In FY 2004, the following transactions took place:

1. At the end of FY 2003, property taxes receivable were $10,000. The allowance for uncollectible property taxes was $3,000.
2. In FY 2004, collections of FY 2003 property taxes were $5,000 from J. Bond and $3,000 from J. Steed. J. Tebbe, who owed $2,000, was unable to pay his property taxes. The account was written off.

3. During FY 2004, property taxes of $50,000 were levied. An allowance for uncollectible property taxes of 6 percent was established for this particular tax levy. The property taxes were levied as follows:

J. Bond	$10,000
J. Steed	20,000
T. King	10,000
E. Peel	5,000
S. Templar	5,000
	$50,000

4. Bond and Steed paid their FY 2004 property taxes in full and on time.
5. King refused to pay his FY 2004 property taxes. As a result, a lien was placed against his property. Costs of processing the lien amounted to $200. Shortly thereafter, his property was seized and sold for $30,000. Costs of the sale were $2,000. After the appropriate deductions had been made, a check for the balance of the sale price of the property was sent to King.
6. E. Peel was unable to pay her taxes. Because her property was not salable, the account was written off without further legal action.
7. At the end of FY 2004, S. Templar had not paid his property taxes. The Templar account was reclassified as delinquent.
8. In FY 2005, the city established an allowance for uncollectible property taxes of $15,000 and an allowance for property tax refunds of $20,000. The FY 2005 property taxes were levied as follows:

J. Bond	$10,000
J. Steed	25,000
E. Peel	10,000
S. Templar	5,000
J. Bergerac	10,000
	$60,000

9. J. Steed appealed his tax assessment, and his levy was lowered to $20,000.
10. In FY 2005, S. Templar paid his FY 2004 property taxes. He was, however, unable to pay his FY 2005 property taxes. Therefore, the account was written off.
11. Other collections during FY 2005 were

J. Bond	$10,000
J. Steed	20,000
E. Peel	10,000

12. J. Bergerac was unable to pay his property taxes. The account was written off because of Bergerac's adverse situation.

　　The city identifies receivables by year and by taxpayer (e.g., Property taxes receivable—FY 2004—Bond, $10,000); and it identifies the allowance for uncollectible property taxes by year (e.g., Allowance for uncollectible property taxes—FY 2004).

Required: Prepare entries to record (in chronological order):

1. The setting up of the FY 2004 and the FY 2005 receivable (and allowances for uncollectible property taxes and for property tax refunds)

2. The collection of property taxes in each year
3. The writing off of uncollectible accounts and property tax refunds
4. The treatment of the prior-year allowance for uncollectible property taxes in FY 2004 and FY 2005
5. The lien against, seizure, and sale of the King property

P5-4 (Allotments)

The City of Picadilly divides its appropriations into allotments, which are expended during the allotment period. In this city, allotments are made at the beginning of each quarter. In FY 2004, estimated revenues are $500,000 and unallotted appropriations are $480,000. A $20,000 increase is projected for the fund balance. Actual revenues are $500,000. The allotments for the year are as follows:

1st quarter	$150,000
2nd quarter	100,000
3rd quarter	130,000
4th quarter	100,000

Expenditures for the year are as follows:

1/8	$20,000	7/28	$30,000
2/2	80,000	8/16	40,000
3/15	40,000	9/14	19,000
4/18	35,000	10/15	10,000
5/20	45,000	11/18	30,000
6/15	20,000	12/22	35,000
7/12	50,000	12/30	5,000

Required: 1. Prepare journal entries to record the allotments, expenditures, and unallotted appropriations for each period, including the year-end closing entries.
2. Prepare a subsidiary ledger for the allotments, using the following format:

Date   Allotments   Expenditures   Remaining Balance

P5-5 (Complete accounting cycle of a General Fund)

The Sherwood Park Commissioners approved the following budget for FY 2004 for that governmental unit's General Fund:

Estimated Revenues		
Property taxes	$85,000	
License fees	25,000	
Fines and penalties	35,000	
Sales taxes	25,000	
Federal grant	30,000	$200,000
Appropriations and Transfers		
Salaries	$80,000	
Supplies	40,000	
Capital equipment	40,000	
Transfers to other funds	20,000	180,000
Projected Increase in Fund Balance		$ 20,000

The park uses the allowance method of handling past-due accounts. An allowance equal to 15 percent of property taxes billed is recorded when the bills are sent. The park's accounting policies include the following:

1. All purchases of supplies and capital equipment are encumbered.
2. Expenditures for salaries and transfers to other funds do not require encumbrances.
3. Outstanding encumbrances lapse at the end of each fiscal year. Outstanding purchase orders that will be honored the following year, however, are reported on its financial statements.
4. Separate accounts are maintained for each taxpayer.
5. At the end of each fiscal year, all outstanding property tax receivables are reclassified as delinquent.
6. The park uses the purchases method to record the purchase and use of supplies. An inventory taken at the end of FY 2003 revealed that supplies costing $5,000 were still on hand.

The park has four property owners, whose taxes for FY 2004 are

R. Hood	$40,000
F. Tuck	10,000
M. Marian	20,000
A. Adale	30,000
	$100,000

Encumbrances still outstanding at the end of FY 2003 amounted to $10,000 and were for capital equipment.

The postclosing trial balance of the General Fund of Sherwood Park, as of December 31, 2003, was

	Debits	Credits
Cash	$20,000	
Property taxes receivable—L. John	3,000	
Property taxes receivable—A. Adale	8,000	
Allowance for uncollectible property taxes—current		$ 3,000
Supplies on hand	5,000	
Vouchers payable		8,000
Fund balance reserved for encumbrances		10,000
Fund balance reserved for supplies on hand		5,000
Unreserved fund balance		10,000
	$36,000	$36,000

During FY 2004, the following transactions occurred:

1. FY 2004 encumbrances for capital equipment were restored.
2. Tax bills amounting to $100,000 were sent to FY 2004 property taxpayers. Of the amount billed, $15,000 was not expected to be collected.
3. L. John left town suddenly. When he departed, his account was written off.

4. A. Adale paid his FY 2003 property taxes in full, along with a late payment penalty of $100.
5. R. Hood and M. Marian paid their property taxes on time and in full.
6. The capital equipment ordered in FY 2003 arrived, along with an invoice for $10,000. The invoice was paid immediately.
7. Supplies expected to cost $40,000 were ordered.
8. An operating transfer of $18,000 was made to the Hyde Park Fund. Of this amount, $10,000 was paid in cash. The remainder will be paid in the future.
9. All outstanding FY 2003 vouchers were paid.
10. The federal grant, $30,000, was received.
11. Salaries for the year were $80,000.
12. Five motorcycles, costing $8,000 each, were ordered.
13. One half of the supplies arrived in August, along with an invoice for $25,000. The invoice was paid in October.
14. Three of the motorcycles arrived. The actual cost of $28,000 was paid immediately.
15. F. Tuck was unable to pay his property taxes. The account was written off.
16. A. Adale paid $25,000 of his FY 2004 property taxes. He hopes to pay the remainder next year.
17. Other FY 2004 revenues were

| License fees | $25,000 |
| Fines and penalties | 40,000 |

Sales taxes amounting to $25,000 were collected during the year. The park's accountant estimates that another $5,000 will be collected in January 2005 and, therefore, is "available."

18. One-fourth of the supplies arrived, along with an invoice for $9,000.
19. By the end of 2004, only $20,000 of the federal grant had been spent. The remainder will be spent in the middle of 2005.

Required: 1. Prepare budgetary, operating, and closing entries for FY 2004 for the General Fund. Assume that outstanding purchase orders will be honored the following year and that supplies on hand at the end of FY 2004 amount to $8,000.
2. Prepare preclosing and postclosing trial balances for FY 2004.
3. Prepare a balance sheet and a statement of revenues, expenditures, and changes in fund balance for FY 2004.
4. Prepare a budgetary comparison schedule for FY 2004.

P5-6 (Journal entries and financial statement presentation—interfund transactions) Following are several transactions for the City of Cricklewood:

Enterprise Fund

1. The Water Purification Fund billed its customers for $124,000. Included in this amount were $12,000 to the General Fund (not encumbered by the General Fund) and $5,000 to the Electric Utility Fund. Both the Water Purification Fund and the Electric Utility Fund are Enterprise Funds.

2. A Special Revenue Fund lent a Capital Projects Fund $25,000, to be repaid in 9 months.
3. The General Fund made a permanent contribution of capital to the Civic Swimming Pool Fund, an Enterprise Fund. The amount of the contribution was $50,000.
4. The General Fund made its annual payment of $200,000 to a Debt Service Fund.
5. The General Fund paid $34,000 for consulting services. At the time the transaction was incurred, a debit for the entire amount was made to Expenditures—consulting services. Later a Capital Projects Fund paid the General Fund $9,000 for its share of the consulting costs.

Required: Prepare the journal entries necessary to record these transactions and to identify the fund or funds used.

 P5-7 (Errors in recording interfund transfers)
Recently, the General Fund of the City of Cats received monies from the following sources:

1. $10,000 from a Debt Service Fund when that fund was closed out after a bond issue was repaid
2. $25,000 from the Library Fund, representing that fund's share of the annual audit
3. $5,000 as a yearly contribution from the Royal Park Fund, to be used for general operations of the city
4. $15,000 from the Regional Transit Authority (an Enterprise Fund) to be used to pay salaries of police riding on its buses in high-crime areas
5. $50,000 from the federal government as a grant to fund a program for homeless accountants, of which the city already spent $35,000, with the remainder to be spent in the latter part of the following year
   Each of these receipts was recorded in the General Fund as a current revenue. Do you agree? If not, how should they be recorded?

P5-8 (Complete accounting cycle of a Permanent Fund)
In FY 2004, Henry Comstock made a gift to the City of Gold Hill. Under the terms of the gift, the City was to purchase securities and to use the earnings on these securities to purchase books on history for the local library. Only the earnings on the securities can be expended.
During FY 2004, the following transactions occurred:

1. The City received the gift from Mr. Comstock, a check for $2,500,000.
2. Shortly after receiving the gift, the City purchased government securities for $2,500,000.
3. Investment income of $100,000 was received in cash.
4. A transfer of $85,000, cash, was made to the Library Fund, a Special Revenue fund.
5. Salaries of $7,000 were paid in cash during the year.
6. A payment of $6,000 was made to the General Fund to cover the cost of supplies ($2,000) and office space ($4,000).

7. The fund received a bill for its annual audit, amounting to $3,000, from Yerington and Company, CPAs, which it will pay next year.
8. Investment income of $50,000 was received in cash.
9. A transfer of $40,000 was made to the Library Fund. Of this amount, $30,000 was paid in cash. The remainder will be paid to the Library Fund next year.
10. Investment income of $25,000 was accrued at the end of FY 2004.
11. By the end of FY 2004, the marketable securities had increased in value by $40,000.

Required: 1. Prepare the journal entries necessary to record these transactions on the books of the Permanent Fund.
2. Prepare a balance sheet and a statement of revenues, expenditures, and changes in fund balance for the Permanent Fund.

P5-9 (Preparing financial statements from a trial balance)
Following is the preclosing trial balance of Ocean City at the end of FY 2004. Assume that at the beginning of the year no encumbrances were outstanding, that the Reserve for supplies on hand amounted to $4,000, and that the Unreserved fund balance was $21,000.

Ocean City General Fund
Preclosing Trial Balance
December 31, 2004

	Debits	Credits
Cash	$ 22,450	
Marketable securities	50,000	
Property taxes receivable	35,525	
Allowance for uncollectible property taxes		$ 18,000
Sales taxes receivable	8,500	
Due from state government	16,000	
Supplies on hand	7,000	
Vouchers payable		12,275
Due to other funds		13,400
Interfund loans payable—noncurrent		35,000
Encumbrances—contractual services	10,000	
Fund balance reserved for supplies on hand		7,000
Unreserved fund balance		21,000
Budgetary fund balance reserved for encumbrances		10,000
Budgetary fund balance		21,500
Estimated revenues—property taxes	125,000	
Estimated revenues—sales taxes	73,000	
Estimated revenues—charges for services	14,000	
Estimated revenues—fines and forfeits	8,500	
Estimated revenues—federal grants	10,000	
Estimated transfer in from Enterprise Fund	30,000	

(*continued*)

Appropriations—salaries		107,000
Appropriations—contractual services		27,000
Appropriations—materials and supplies		15,000
Appropriations—capital equipment		70,000
Appropriations—transfer out to Debt Service Fund		20,000
Revenues—property taxes		117,500
Revenues—sales taxes		73,600
Revenues—charges for services		12,400
Revenues—fines and forfeits		8,900
Revenues—federal grants		10,000
Transfer in from Enterprise Fund		35,000
Expenditures—salaries	105,200	
Expenditures—contractual services	15,000	
Expenditures—materials and supplies	15,300	
Expenditures—capital equipment	69,100	
Transfer out to Debt Service Fund	20,000	
	$634,575	$634,575

Required: 1. Prepare closing entries for FY 2004.
2. Prepare a postclosing trial balance for FY 2004.
3. Prepare a balance sheet for FY 2004.
4. Prepare a statement of revenues, expenditures, and changes in fund balance for FY 2004.
5. Prepare a budgetary comparison schedule for FY 2004. Show outstanding encumbrances as expenditures, in order to provide a more meaningful comparison, and prepare a note to this effect on the statement (see Table 5-10). Assume that the originally approved budget and the final budget are identical.

P5-10 (CPA Examination question on activities of a General Fund)
The General Fund trial balance of the City of Solna at December 31, 2004, was as follows:

	Debits	Credits
Cash	$ 62,000	
Taxes receivable—delinquent	46,000	
Estimated uncollectible taxes—delinquent		$ 8,000
Stores inventory—program operations	18,000	
Vouchers payable		28,000
Fund balance reserved for stores inventory		18,000
Fund balance reserved for encumbrances		12,000
Unreserved, undesignated fund balance		60,000
	$126,000	$126,000

Collectible delinquent taxes are expected to be collected within 60 days after the end of the year. Solna uses the purchases method to account for stores inventory. The following data pertain to 2004 General Fund operations:

1. Budget adopted:

Revenues and Other Financing Sources

Taxes	$220,000	
Fines, forfeits, and penalties	80,000	
Miscellaneous revenues	100,000	
Share of bond issue proceeds	200,000	$600,000

Expenditures and Other Financing Uses

Program operations	$300,000	
General administration	120,000	
Stores—program operations	60,000	
Capital outlays	80,000	
Periodic transfer to special revenue fund	20,000	580,000
Projected Increase in Fund Balance		$ 20,000

2. Taxes were assessed at an amount that would result in revenues of $220,800, after deduction of 4 percent of the tax levy as uncollectible.

3. Orders placed:

Program operations	$176,000
General administration	80,000
Capital outlay	60,000
	$316,000

4. The city council designated $20,000 of the unreserved, undesignated fund balance for possible future appropriation for capital outlays.

5. Cash collections and transfer:

Delinquent taxes	$ 38,000
Current taxes	226,000
Refund of overpayment of invoice for purchase of equipment	4,000
Fines, forfeits, and penalties	88,000
Miscellaneous revenues	90,000
Share of bond issue proceeds	200,000
Transfer of remaining fund balance of a discontinued fund	18,000
	$664,000

6. Vouchers received against encumbrances:

	Estimated	Actual
Program operations	$156,000	$166,000
General administration	84,000	80,000
Capital outlay	62,000	62,000
	$302,000	$308,000

7. Vouchers processed on items not requiring encumbrances:

Program operations	$188,000
General administration	38,000
Capital outlays	18,000
Transfer to special revenue fund	20,000
	$264,000

8. Albert, a taxpayer, overpaid his 2004 taxes by $2,000. He applied for a $2,000 credit against his 2005 taxes. The city council granted his request.
9. Vouchers paid amounted to $580,000.
10. Stores inventory on December 31, 2004, amounted to $12,000.

Required: Prepare journal entries to record the effects of the foregoing data as well as closing entries. Omit explanations.

(AICPA adapted)

CONTINUOUS PROBLEM (COMPLETE ACCOUNTING CYCLE OF GENERAL FUND)

The City Council of Bacchus City approved the following budget for FY 2004 for that city's General Fund:

Estimated Revenues		
Property taxes	$5,504,000	
Interest and penalties	38,000	
Sales taxes	900,000	
Fines and penalties	70,000	
Lottery receipts	225,000	
License fees	10,000	$6,747,000
Appropriations and Transfers		
Salaries	$3,500,000	
Travel	31,500	
Equipment	600,000	
Contractual services	120,000	
Supplies and materials	40,000	
Liability insurance	16,500	
Advertising	600	
Legal services	10,000	
Audit fees	10,000	
Transfer to Debt Service Fund	900,000	
Transfer to Venus Park Fund	60,000	5,288,600
Projected Increase in Fund Balance		$1,458,400

The city's accounting policies include the following:

1. All purchases of supplies and materials and equipment are encumbered.
2. Expenditures for salaries, travel, services and transfers to other funds do not require encumbrances.
3. Expenditures for salaries include fringe benefits paid by the City.
4. Outstanding encumbrances lapse at the end of each fiscal year. Outstanding purchase orders that will be honored the following year, however, are reported on its financial statements.
5. At the end of each fiscal year, all outstanding property tax receivables are reclassified as delinquent.
6. What are shown as operating expenses in the budget in Chapter 3 are broken down into Contractual services and Supplies and materials accounts in this problem.
7. The City uses the purchases method to record the purchase and use of supplies and materials. An inventory taken at the end of FY 2003 revealed that supplies and materials costing $30,000 were still on hand.

Encumbrances still outstanding at the end of FY 2003 amounted to $25,000 and were for construction equipment ordered by the Streets and Parkways Department.

The postclosing trial balance of the General Fund of Bacchus City, as of December 31, 2003, follows.

	Debits	Credits
Cash	$300,000	
Investments	500,000	
Property taxes receivable—delinquent	50,000	
Supplies and materials on hand	30,000	
Vouchers payable		$ 20,000
Fund balance reserved for encumbrances		25,000
Fund balance reserved for supplies and materials on hand		30,000
Unreserved fund balance		805,000
	$880,000	$880,000

During FY 2004, the following transactions occurred:

1. FY 2003 encumbrances for construction equipment were restored.
2. Tax bills amounting to $5,504,000 were sent to FY 2004 property taxpayers. The entire amount billed is expected to be collected.
3. Property taxes outstanding at the end of FY 2003 were paid in full, along with a late payment penalty of $800.
4. Collections on FY 2004 property taxes during the year amounted to $5,200,000.
5. A property tax rebate of $20,000 was given to a property owner because of this company's effort to increase employment during the year. The city had previously made no provision for tax rebates. Assume that the property owner already paid its FY 2004 property taxes.

6. The equipment ordered in FY 2003 arrived, along with an invoice for $25,000. The invoice was paid immediately.
7. All outstanding FY 2003 vouchers were paid.
8. Travel costs of city personnel amounted to $31,000.
9. Supplies and materials expected to cost $40,000 were ordered.
10. Expenditures for contractual services amounted to $115,000. All were paid in cash upon completion of the services.
11. A transfer of $60,000 was made to the Venus Park Fund. Of this amount, $50,000 was paid in cash. The remainder will be paid in FY 2005.
12. Interest on investments amounting to $37,000, was received during the year.
13. Salaries for the year were $2,900,000. This amount includes $300,000 withheld from the employees' checks for their share of contributions to the Pension Fund. Another $300,000 was paid by the City as its share of the contribution to the Pension Fund. (*Hint:* treat the City's contribution as an additional salaries expenditure.) The amount due to the Pension Trust Fund was paid several days after the city workers were paid.
14. A computer network was ordered for the use of the Public Safety and Administration Departments. It was expected to cost $544,000.
15. A transfer of $900,000 was made, in cash, to the Debt Service Fund.
16. By late November, the computer system had been installed and the vendor presented the city with a bill for $545,000. The bill was paid immediately.
17. Construction equipment expected to cost $31,000 was ordered.
18. Some of the construction equipment arrived, along with an invoice for $17,360, which was paid immediately. The City had expected the equipment to cost $19,000.
19. One-half of the supplies and materials ordered in part (9) arrived, along with an invoice for $22,000. The invoice was paid immediately.
20. Other FY 2004 revenues were

Fines and penalties	$ 69,240
Lottery receipts	230,000
License fees	10,000

Sales taxes amounting to $850,000 were collected during the year. The city's accountant estimates that another $49,500 will be collected in January 2005 and, therefore, is "available."

21. The remainder of the construction equipment ordered in part (17) arrived, along with an invoice of $12,000. The invoice will be paid in FY 2005.
22. One-fourth of the materials and supplies arrived, along with an invoice for $8,000. The invoice was paid immediately.
23. During the year, the following amounts were paid, in cash, for nondepartmental expenditures.

Liability insurance	$16,285
Advertising	554
Legal services	9,500
Audit fees	9,600

24. Property taxes amounting to $304,000 not collected by the end of the year were reclassified as delinquent. The City expects to collect these taxes in FY 2005.

Required:

1. Prepare budgetary, operating, and closing entries for FY 2004 for the General Fund. Assume that outstanding purchase orders will be honored the following year and that supplies on hand at the end of FY 2004 amount to $18,000.
2. Prepare preclosing and postclosing trial balances for FY 2004.
3. Prepare a balance sheet and a statement of revenues, expenditures, and changes in fund balance for FY 2004.
4. Prepare a budgetary comparison schedule for FY 2004.

Chapter 6

The Governmental Fund Accounting Cycle

Debt Service Funds and Capital Projects Funds

After completing this chapter, you should be able to:

➤ *Explain why and how Debt Service Funds are used in governmental accounting.*

➤ *Prepare the journal entries normally used within the Debt Service Funds.*

➤ *Prepare fund financial statements for Debt Service Funds.*

➤ *Explain why and how Capital Projects Funds are used in governmental accounting.*

➤ *Prepare the journal entries normally used within the Capital Projects Funds.*

➤ *Prepare fund financial statements for Capital Projects Funds.*

*I*n Chapters 2, 4, and 5 we discussed the accounting procedures used within the General Fund, Special Revenue Funds, and Permanent Funds as well as the fund financial statements prepared for those funds. In this chapter we will review the accounting and reporting procedures used within the Debt Service Funds and Capital Project Funds, along with the fund financial statements prepared for those funds. In addition, we will discuss the accounting and reporting procedures for issuances of general obligation long-term debt and the acquisition and construction of long-lived assets. We begin with a review of what is measured in the accounting records (measurement focus) and when the items are recorded (basis of accounting).

IMPLICATIONS FOR DEBT SERVICE AND CAPITAL PROJECTS FUNDS OF THE MEASUREMENT FOCUS AND BASIS OF ACCOUNTING

Measurement focus refers to what is being measured. *Basis of accounting* refers to the timing of the recognition of the resources that are available for spending and the related expenditures (expenses). As discussed in previous chapters, governmental-type funds use the current financial resources measurement focus and the modified accrual basis of accounting. To understand the implications for debt service and capital projects funds of the current financial resources measurement focus, consider how the term *current financial resources* might apply to the issuance of long-term debt to finance the acquisition of capital assets.

On its face, long-term debt embraces a period much greater than that covered by the term *current.* Further, the term *financial resources* covers spendable assets like cash and taxes receivable that will become cash in a short period of time. It does not cover capital assets. On the liabilities side of the balance sheet, current financial resources covers short-term liabilities such as accounts payable and other amounts to be repaid in a short period of time. In other words, when funds measure inflows and outflows of current financial resources, they include neither capital assets nor long-term liabilities. These funds account only for increases and decreases of *financial* resources, and, within financial resources, only for current assets and liabilities as those terms are used in accounting for governmental-type funds.

Thus, in the discussion of Capital Projects Funds, the issuance of long-term debt creates a cash inflow to the fund (a financial resource). The offset to that cash inflow is not a long-term liability, but rather a source of financing that increases the net assets of the fund. Where is the long-term liability reported? Because the *long-term* liability cannot be reported in the fund financial statements, it is reported in a different set of statements—the government-wide statements mentioned in Chapter 2, which will be discussed in detail in Chapter 10. Also, when discussing Debt Service Funds, repayment of the long-term debts results, not in the reduction of a recorded liability, but rather a decrease in the net resources of the fund. As a result, it is recorded as an expenditure.

In addition, when Capital Projects Funds financial resources are expended to acquire a capital asset, the cash outflow simply decreases the net resources of the fund. It too is recorded as an expenditure. Because capital assets (*nonfinancial resources*) are not reported in fund financial statements, they also will be reported in the government-wide statements discussed in Chapter 10.

The implications of the modified accrual basis of accounting on these funds can be seen best in the Debt Service Fund. As previously mentioned, modified accrual accounting results in a number of exceptions to the rules for accrual accounting. One of the specific exceptions concerns interest on long-term debt. When long-term debt is issued, repayment terms generally provide for interest and part of the principal twice a year, for example, on April 1 and October 1. If financial statements were issued on December 31, a "stub" period of 3 months occurs between October 1 and December 31. If accrual accounting were used in governmental-type funds, there would be an accrual of interest for that period. Under modified accrual accounting, however, no accrual is required for reporting on the fund. As discussed in Chapter 10, an accrual will be made for this stub period for government-wide reporting.

DEBT SERVICE FUNDS

Definition of Fund

Almost every government issues *general obligation debt*. This debt is in the form of liabilities, usually bonds, that are secured by the "full faith and credit" of the governmental unit. The payment of principal and interest on a debt is called *servicing the debt*. Thus *Debt Service Funds* are used to accumulate resources that will be used to pay principal and interest on general obligation long-term debt. General obligation debt does not include debt that will be serviced from resources accumulated in Enterprise Funds or Internal Service Funds.[1]

In many instances debt that becomes due in installments, such as *serial bonds*, can be serviced directly by the General Fund. However, if a legal requirement dictates a separate Debt Service Fund, such a fund must be established. In addition, a separate Debt Service Fund must be established if the governmental unit is accumulating resources now for the future servicing of debt. Although this section will concentrate on bonds, it is important to remember that any form of long-term obligation, such as installment purchases or notes, may require the establishment of a Debt Service Fund.

Summary of Fund Activities

Although the exact events recorded in Debt Service Funds will vary according to the specific requirements of the bond indenture or the ordinance authorizing the bond issue, the following general summary of activity reflects the types of events that normally occur in Debt Service Fund operations. First, the resources are received by the fund. They are recorded as revenues or transfers from other funds, usually the General Fund. During the time period between receipt of the resources and payment of principal and interest, the governmental unit will invest the assets. These investments are made to accumulate additional resources that can be used to service the debt, thus reducing the direct drain on existing assets. The investing activities also are recorded in the Debt Service Fund. Finally, as the principal and interest come due, they are paid from the Debt Service Fund assets.

---

[1] Although it is possible to have general obligation debt that will be serviced by an Enterprise Fund, a discussion of such debt is beyond the scope of this section. It is also possible, but not likely, that Permanent Funds could contain long-term debt that is serviced in that fund. This discussion, too, is beyond the scope of this section.

Control of Fund Activities

The operations of Debt Service Funds generally are controlled through the provisions of bond indentures and budgetary authorizations. Many governmental units do not actually record a budget for these funds. For purposes of uniformity, however, we will assume that a budget is recorded and used for control purposes.

Encumbrance accounting is seldom found in Debt Service Funds because of the lack of purchase orders, contracts, and so forth. The expenditures of these funds primarily consist of payments of principal and interest. Because these types of expenditures are made according to the terms prescribed in the bond indenture, encumbrance accounting would not improve control over the use of these resources.

Measurement Focus and Basis of Accounting for Fund Activities at the Fund Level

As with all governmental-type funds, the measurement focus of Debt Service Funds is current financial resources, which means that the accounting system centers on the accumulation of resources and the expenditure of those resources. As a result, long-lived assets are not found in Debt Service Funds, nor do the accounts contain any long-term debt. The current financial resources criterion focuses on assets currently available and the claims due and payable against those assets.

The timing of the recognition of revenues and expenditures is the same for Debt Service Funds as for all other governmental-type funds—modified accrual. Therefore, the rules for recognition discussed at the beginning of this chapter are applicable to Debt Service Funds. In general, revenues are recorded when they are measurable and available, and expenditures are recorded when due and payable.

When accounting for the operations of Debt Service Funds, it is important to remember that as few individual funds as possible should be used. In other words, individual Debt Service Funds should be combined into a single Debt Service Fund whenever the law or the individual debt instruments do not prohibit such a combination.

Accounting for Fund Activities

Operating Entries—Within the Fund

For illustrative purposes, assume that the City of Angusville issues $10 million of serial bonds on March 1, 2004, for the construction of a sports complex. The bond indenture provides for semiannual interest payments of 5 percent on March 1 and September 1 (the annual interest rate is 10 percent on the outstanding debt), with $1 million of principal to be repaid on March 1, 2006, and every year thereafter until the bonds mature on March 1, 2015 (10 payments later). Further assume that the city desires to spread the taxpayers' burden of servicing the debt evenly throughout the life of the bonds. To meet this goal, the voters approved a special addition to the local property tax for servicing the bonds. This tax should provide $1.25 million of revenue in 2004. In addition, it is agreed that the General Fund will transfer $250,000 to the Debt Service Fund on July 1, 2004. (Entries involved in the actual issuance of the bonds are illustrated in the section "Capital Projects Funds.")

The entry to record the budget for the fund for the calendar year beginning in January 1, 2004, is as follows (amounts assumed):

Estimated revenues	1,250,000	
Estimated other financing sources	250,000	
Appropriations		505,000
Budgetary fund balance		995,000
To record the budget.		

The account *Estimated other financing sources* is the budgetary account used to record the anticipated transfer from the General Fund.

Appropriations for the year include one interest payment that will be made on September 1, 2004, $500,000, and a fee of $5,000 that will be paid to the fiscal agent, who will keep records of the sale of the bonds and will make semiannual interest payments and payments of principal as they come due. Usually a fiscal agent is a local bank or other financial institution. Notice that only one interest payment will be made in 2004; therefore, only that amount is included in the current year's annual budget.

Recording the tax levy requires the following entry:

Property taxes receivable—current	1,256,000	
Allowance for uncollectible property		
taxes—current		6,000
Revenues—property taxes		1,250,000
To record the tax levy.		

The preceding entry assumes that $6,000 of the taxes will be uncollectible. Therefore, the governmental unit will have to bill $1,256,000 to collect the needed $1,250,000.

Collection of $1,150,000 of the taxes results in the same entries as those illustrated for the General Fund and the Special Revenue Funds.

Cash	1,150,000	
Property taxes receivable—current		1,150,000
To record collection of current taxes.		

If $2,500 of uncollectible taxes are written off, the following entry is made:

Allowance for uncollectible property taxes—current	2,500	
Property taxes receivable—current		2,500
To write off uncollectible accounts.		

To generate resources in addition to those contributed by the taxpayers and the General Fund, the tax receipts are invested in marketable securities. If $1 million is invested, the following entry is made:

Investments	1,000,000	
Cash		1,000,000
To record the investment of excess cash.		

When some of the investments mature, the following entry is made:

Cash	470,000	
Investments		450,000
Revenues—interest earned on investments		20,000
To record investments liquidated and related income.		

The interest due to the city's bondholders on September 1, 2004, is recorded as follows:

Expenditures—interest	500,000	
Matured interest payable		500,000
To record matured interest.		

When cash is transferred to the fiscal agent for the September 1 interest payment, the following entry is made:

Cash with fiscal agent	500,000	
Cash		500,000
To record the payment of cash to the fiscal agent.		

Periodically the fiscal agent will report to the city regarding the amount of principal and interest paid. The entry to record this amount is as follows (amount assumed):

Matured interest payable	500,000	
Cash with fiscal agent		500,000
To record payment of interest made by fiscal agent.		

The transfer of $250,000 from the General Fund is classified as a transfer and recorded as follows:

Entry in the books of the General Fund

Transfer out to Debt Service Fund	250,000	
Cash		250,000
To record transfer out to Debt Service Fund.		

Entry in the books of the Debt Service Fund

Cash	250,000	
Transfer in from General Fund		250,000
To record transfer in from General Fund.		

When the fiscal agent submits a bill for $5,000 to the fund for servicing the debt, the following entry is made:

Expenditures—fiscal agent fees	5,000	
Cash		5,000
To record fiscal agent fees.		

The treatment of taxes receivable from the current stage through the delinquent and, finally, the lien stage in the Debt Service Fund is the same as in the General Fund. If you do not remember the sequence of entries, review Chapters 4 and 5.

One of the exceptions to the use of full accrual accounting, for expenditures in a modified accrual system, is interest on long-term debt. The general rule is that such interest is recorded as an expenditure in the period in which it becomes legally due (matures). The reason for this rule is that most governmental units provide only enough resources to service principal and interest due each period. If interest payments are accrued or principal payments are recorded before due, it is possible that a debit balance (a deficit) will occur in fund balance. The reason an accrual is not "made" is that the liability is not yet due to be paid, which means the resources are not required to be available. An accrual for interest will be made when the fund financial statements are converted to government-wide statements, as discussed in Chapter 10.

In those instances when resources are available for Debt Service Fund payments and those payments will be made within the first month of the next period, governmental units have the option, under GAAP, of recording the liability and the associated expenditure at the end of the year before the payments are due. The appropriate entry is the same as that used when the interest matures, except that an additional liability is established for the bond principal payable and the account titles do not include the word *matured*.

In contrast, an end-of-year entry is needed to record interest earned but not received on the investments:

Interest receivable on investments	55,000	
Revenues—interest earned on investments		55,000
To record the interest earned on investments.		

Investments generally are reported at fair market value.[2] Changes in the market value of most governmental investments are reported in the operating statement, along with interest and dividends received. Investments that are not reported at market value are those purchased with a maturity date of 1 year or less, for example, commercial paper and U.S. Treasury obligations. These investments are reported at amortized cost.

If the remaining $550,000 of marketable securities previously acquired, and still held at December 31, 2004, had a market value of $575,000, the following journal entry would be made to record the increase in value:

Investments	25,000	
Revenues—net increase in fair market value of investments		25,000
To record the increase in the fair market value of investments.		

A trial balance for the city at the end of the year is shown in Table 6-1.

Closing Entries

At the end of the accounting period, December 31, 2004, in our example, the following entries will be necessary to close the books:

Appropriations	505,000	
Budgetary fund balance	995,000	
Estimated revenues		1,250,000
Estimated other financing sources		250,000
To close the budgetary accounts for 2004.		

Revenues—property taxes	1,250,000	
Revenues—interest earned on investments	75,000	
Revenues—net increase in fair market value of investments	25,000	
Transfer in from General Fund	250,000	
Expenditures—interest		500,000
Expenditures—fiscal agent fees		5,000
Unreserved fund balance		1,095,000
To close the operating accounts for 2004.		

---

[2] GASB Cod. Sec. I50.

Table 6-1

Trial Balance—Debt Service Fund

THE CITY OF ANGUSVILLE
DEBT SERVICE FUND
SPORTS COMPLEX BOND FUND
TRIAL BALANCE
DECEMBER 31, 2004

	DEBITS	CREDITS
Cash	$ 365,000	
Property taxes receivable—current	103,500	
Allowance for uncollectible property taxes—current		$ 3,500
Investments	575,000	
Interest receivable	55,000	
Revenues—property taxes		1,250,000
Revenues—interest earned on investments		75,000
Revenues—net increase in fair market value of investments		25,000
Transfer in from General Fund		250,000
Expenditures—interest	500,000	
Expenditures—fiscal agent fees	5,000	
Estimated revenues	1,250,000	
Estimated other financing sources	250,000	
Appropriations		505,000
Budgetary fund balance		995,000
	$3,103,500	$3,103,500

Entry Necessary for Interest Payment in March 2005

As already mentioned, interest generally is not accrued at the end of the year under the current financial resources model. When the March interest payment is made in 2005, the following entries are necessary:

Expenditures—interest	500,000	
Matured interest payable		500,000
To record matured interest.		

Cash with fiscal agent	500,000	
Cash		500,000
To record transfer of cash to fiscal agent.		

The remainder of the entries for the payment of the interest are the same as those previously illustrated for the September 1 payment.

Selected Entries for Payment of Principal

When all or a portion of the principal of the bond issue is due to be paid, the liability must be recorded in the Debt Service Fund. The following entries are made for this purpose (assume we are recording the first principal payment in 2006):

Expenditures—bond principal	1,000,000	
Matured serial bonds payable		1,000,000
To record matured bond principal.		
Cash with fiscal agent	1,000,000	
Cash		1,000,000
To record transfer of cash to fiscal agent.		
Matured serial bonds payable	1,000,000	
Cash with fiscal agent		1,000,000
To record payment of matured principal.		

Financial Statements Illustration

The fund financial statements for the Debt Service Funds are a balance sheet and an operating statement. These are illustrated for 2004 in Tables 6-2 and 6-3. The overall reporting process is discussed in Chapters 9 and 10.

Table 6-2
Statement of Revenues, Expenditures, and Changes in Fund Balance

THE CITY OF ANGUSVILLE
DEBT SERVICE FUND
SPORTS COMPLEX BOND FUND
STATEMENT OF REVENUES, EXPENDITURES,
AND CHANGES IN FUND BALANCE
FOR THE YEAR ENDED DECEMBER 31, 2004

Revenues		
Property taxes	$1,250,000	
Interest earned on investments	75,000	
Net increase in fair market value of investments	25,000	
Total revenues		$1,350,000
Expenditures		
Interest	$ 500,000	
Fiscal agent fees	5,000	
Total expenditures		505,000
Excess of revenues over expenditures		845,000
Other Financing Sources		
Transfer in		250,000
Net change in fund balance		1,095,000
Fund balance at beginning of year		-0-
Fund balance at end of year		$1,095,000

Table 6-3
Balance Sheet—Debt Service Fund

THE CITY OF ANGUSVILLE
DEBT SERVICE FUND
SPORTS COMPLEX BOND FUND
BALANCE SHEET
DECEMBER 31, 2004

Assets	
Cash	$ 365,000
Property taxes receivable—current (net of allowance for uncollectibles of $3,500)	100,000
Interest receivable	55,000
Investments	575,000
Total assets	$1,095,000
Fund Balance	
Fund balance—reserved for debt service	$1,095,000

GOVERNMENTAL ACCOUNTING IN PRACTICE
The City of Columbus, Ohio

The City of Columbus maintains five Debt Service Funds:

1. *General Bond Retirement Fund.* This fund is required by the State of Ohio statutes and is used to account for all general obligation debt, except for Enterprise Fund general obligation debt of the city. As mentioned earlier in this chapter, this option provides an acceptable alternative to a separate fund for each bond issue if it does not violate any provisions of the bond indentures.

2. *Special Income Tax Fund.* This fund is used to account for 25 percent of income tax collections set aside for debt service and related expenses.

3. *Recreation Debt Service Fund.* This fund is used to account for revenues set aside to pay for debt service on bonds issued for the acquisition of and improvements to city golf courses and other recreation facilities.

4. *Tax Increment Financing Fund.* This fund contains resources intended for the payment of principal and interest on long-term debt that was issued to pay for certain public improvements, primarily infrastructure.

5. *Capitol South Debt Service Tax Fund.* This fund is used to account for resources that will be used to service general obligation long-term debt that was previously accounted for in a special revenue fund.

Tables 6-4 and 6-5 contain a balance sheet and operating statement for the General Bond Retirement Fund for the City of Columbus.

Notice that in Table 6-5 some of the expenditures from the General Bond Retirement Debt Service Fund were used for general government expenditures. The majority of the expenditures, however, were for servicing the debt.

Table 6-4

Balance Sheet—Debt Service Fund—City of Columbus, Ohio

CITY OF COLUMBUS, OHIO
DEBT SERVICE FUND
GENERAL BOND RETIREMENT FUND
BALANCE SHEET
DECEMBER 31, 20X4

Assets	
Cash and cash equivalents	
Cash and investments with treasurer	$ 3,958
Investments	3,271,158
Receivables (net of allowances for uncollectibles)	694,624
Total assets	$3,969,740
Liabilities	
Accounts payable	$ 1,773
Due to other funds	448,753
Deferred revenue and other	524,380
Matured bonds and interest payable	1,532,126
Total liabilities	2,507,032
Fund Balance	
Unreserved, undesignated	1,462,708
Total liabilities and fund balance	$3,969,740

Source: Adapted from a recent annual report of the City of Columbus, Ohio.

CAPITAL PROJECTS FUNDS

Definition of Fund

Acquisition or construction of major capital facilities, other than those financed by proprietary and trust funds, is accounted for in *Capital Projects Funds.* Capital Projects Funds must be used when they are legally required or when the projects are at least partially financed with restricted resources. Such projects generally include the construction of a new city hall, a new civic auditorium, or a bridge. The resources used to finance Capital Projects Funds usually come from general obligation debt, transfers from other funds, intergovernmental revenues, or private donations.

Acquisition of a capital asset of a relatively minor nature, such as a piece of furniture or an automobile, usually is financed through the General Fund or a Special Revenue Fund. For example, the purchase of a new police car or a desk for the mayor's office is recorded as an expenditure in the fund that made the acquisition (see Chapter 5).

Table 6-5

Statement of Revenues, Expenditures, and Changes in Fund Balance—Debt Service Fund—City of Columbus, Ohio

CITY OF COLUMBUS, OHIO
DEBT SERVICE FUND
GENERAL BOND RETIREMENT FUND
STATEMENT OF REVENUES, EXPENDITURES, AND CHANGES IN FUND BALANCE
YEAR ENDED DECEMBER 31, 20X4

Revenues	
Income taxes	$89,777,690
Investment earnings	136,155
Special assessments	161,423
Miscellaneous	35,145
Total revenues	$90,110,413
Expenditures	
Current	
General government	$ 245,627
Debt Service	
Principal retirement and payment of obligation under capital lease	59,991,053
Interest and fiscal charges	33,399,088
Total expenditures	93,635,768
Excess of expenditures over revenues	(3,525,355)
Other Financing Sources	
Transfers in	3,406,072
Net change in fund balance	(119,283)
Fund balance at beginning of year	1,581,991
Fund balance at end of year	$ 1,462,708

Source: Adapted from a recent annual report of the City of Columbus, Ohio.

Capital Budgets

A typical capital budget is illustrated in Table 6-6. Notice that a description of each project is given in addition to the amount requested and the source of funding. In the illustration, the city has been given a plantation house, which it intends to restore and turn into a museum. In addition, the city is planning to build a new police station, work on a stadium (a 3-year project), and repair several bridges.

Some organizations prepare narrative explanations of the various projects under construction. Such explanations usually contain detailed descriptions of the projects, as well as discussions of the cost of finishing the projects and maintaining them when they are complete. The narrative explanations can also contain information on sources of financing, completion dates, and justifications for the projects.

Many governmental units supplement their capital outlay request summaries with *long-run capital programs*. A long-run capital program presents information on

Table 6-6

Capital Budget

| Date: September 15, 2004 | | Prepared by _____ BER _____ |
PROJECT DESCRIPTION	BUDGET REQUEST	SOURCE OF FUNDING
Restore Ellett plantation house		
Purchase furniture	$ 200,000	Federal and state grants
Fire station—First and Magazine Streets		
Remodel	300,000	Bond proceeds
Repair bridges		
Short Bayou and Cutoff Bayou	700,000	Bond proceeds and federal grant
"Doc" Williams Stadium	300,000	Tax revenues
Total	$1,500,000	

the capital improvements desired over a long period of time (e.g., 5 years). It lists the projects planned, the estimated cost of each project, and the proposed source or sources of funding for each project. Generally it is prepared on a "continuous" basis, with a future year added, the past year dropped, and the other years "fine-tuned."

Although some people may regard long-run capital programs as "wish lists" and many projects may never be started, long-run capital programs are good organizing, planning, and communicating tools. They enable users to see at a glance what is needed, what is wanted, and what the organization can afford. Such information is particularly valuable to legislators who must balance the needs of one organization against the needs of others to allocate limited resources.

Summary of Fund Activities

Because GAAP requires that the number of funds used be held to a minimum, related projects should be combined into a single Capital Projects Fund whenever possible. However, careful attention must be paid to any bond indenture provisions or restrictions placed on the use of certain types of resources. In many instances such restrictions will prevent the combination of different projects into the same fund.

The nature and order of events involving capital projects vary according to local ordinances and procedures, the relative size of the project, and the type of financing involved. However, these projects usually begin in the capital budget of the governmental unit. After approval, financing arrangements are made and contracts are let, if applicable.

To obtain financing for projects, governmental units usually issue general obligation bonds, solicit federal or state grants, and so forth. These funds are not always spent immediately upon receipt. In such cases the Capital Projects Fund will contain some investment activity.

As the construction work progresses, investments are liquidated and payments are made to the contractor until the project is completed and finally accepted. At this time, any financial resources remaining in the fund are transferred to another fund or returned to the donors.

Control of Fund Activities

The operations of a Capital Projects Fund are generally controlled through provisions of bond indentures, restrictive provisions of grant agreements, and so forth. Therefore, formal budgetary integration into the accounts, as used in the General Fund and Special Revenue Funds, is not always necessary. For purposes of uniformity, however, we will assume that a budget is recorded and used for control purposes. Such accounting procedures are especially helpful if a single fund is being used to account for more than one project.

Encumbrance accounting is ordinarily used for these funds because of the extent of involvement with contracts and purchase orders and because of the need to control the related expenditures. Thus, in our example of a construction project, a regular encumbrance entry is made upon signing the contract. Expenditures on the contract are treated in the manner previously illustrated for encumbered purchase orders.

As with all governmental-type funds, the measurement focus of Capital Projects Funds is current financial resources. Thus the accounting system is designed to provide information regarding the receipt and disbursement of financial resources. As a result, long-lived assets are not found in these types of funds, nor do they contain any long-term debt. The "available spendable" criterion focuses on assets currently available and the current claims against those assets.

The modified accrual basis of accounting is used for Capital Projects Funds. Thus the timing of the recognition of revenues and expenditures is the same as that followed by the other governmental-type funds.

Accounting for Fund Activities

Operating Entries

For illustrative purposes, assume that the City of Angusville decides to build a sports complex and includes the project in its 2004 capital budget. This project was also described in the section on Debt Service Funds. Financing for the project consists of a general obligation bond issue for $10 million and an $8 million grant from the state. Because the state grant is considered as revenue to the Capital Projects Fund and the proceeds from the bond issue are considered to be an "other financing source," the following entry is made to record the budget:

Estimated revenues	8,000,000	
Estimated other financing sources	10,000,000	
Appropriations		18,000,000
To record the budget.		

If the bonds are sold at par (face) value, the following entry is made:

Cash	10,000,000	
Proceeds from bond issue		10,000,000
To record the issuance of bonds.		

The principal of the bonds is not recorded as a liability of a Capital Projects Fund for three reasons: (1) Capital Projects Funds follow a current financial resources measurement focus, therefore, long-term liabilities are not included in these funds; (2) Capital Projects Funds are used to account only for acquisition or construction activities; and (3) Debt Service Funds are used to account for debt service activities (payment of principal and interest).

In the Debt Service Fund, the issuance of bonds may be accompanied by recording the budget. The entry to record the budget is (see the section "Debt Service Funds"):

Entry in the Debt	Estimated revenues	1,250,000	
Service Fund	Estimated other financing sources	250,000	
	Appropriations		505,000
	Budgetary fund balance		995,000
	To record the budget.		

The entry to record the budgets of the Debt Service Fund and the Capital Projects Fund can be made at the beginning of the year or at a later time when the information is available.

Part of the cost of the sports complex is to be financed by a grant from the state. A grant is determined to be measurable and available based on its terms. Some are recognized as revenue immediately, while others are considered revenue only when the money is spent. Most grants for construction-type projects are considered to meet the measurable and available criteria as the monies are used to finance expenditures.

If cash is received from the grantor before costs are incurred, receipt of the cash is recorded as follows:

Cash	8,000,000	
Deferred revenues—construction grant		8,000,000
To record receipt of state grant.		

As the monies from the state grant are used to finance expenditures, revenue is recognized and the deferred revenue account is reduced.

After the financing is completed, the government will place the project in the hands of an architect. In this instance, assume the architectural firm agreed to work on it for $400,000. At this time the contract with the architect is encumbered as follows:

Encumbrances—capital project	400,000	
Budgetary fund balance reserved for		
encumbrances		400,000
To record encumbrance of architect's fee.		

(For purposes of simplicity, a single encumbrance control account will be used in the remainder of this text.)

The contract with the architect requires the city to pay 90 percent of the fee when the plans are completed. The architect agreed to act as the adviser to the city for the project, so the remainder of the fee will be paid upon completion of the sports complex. The following entries are made when the plans for the sports complex are accepted:

Budgetary fund balance reserved for encumbrances	360,000	
Encumbrances—capital project		360,000
To remove the part of the encumbrance earned by the architect.		

Expenditures—architect's fees	360,000	
Vouchers payable		360,000
To record the liability for architect's fees.		

Vouchers payable	360,000	
Cash		360,000
To record payment of vouchers payable.		

After soliciting bids for the project, the city accepts the low bid of PPK Construction Company of $17.6 million. Upon signing the contract, the following entry is made:

Encumbrances—capital project	17,600,000	
Budgetary fund balance reserved for encumbrances		17,600,000
To record encumbrance of construction contract.		

The funds on hand are not needed immediately, so the city invests $9 million in short-term securities:

Investments	9,000,000	
Cash		9,000,000
To record investment of idle cash.		

Several months later the contractor sends a progress billing report to the city requesting payment of $5.5 million on the project. The payment is approved, less the standard 10 percent retained percentage. The *retained percentage* will not be paid to the contractor until the project is accepted and the work determined to be satisfactory with no outstanding liens relative to the contract. The following entries are made for the billing:

Budgetary fund balance reserved for encumbrances	5,500,000	
Encumbrances—capital project		5,500,000
To record removal of part of the encumbrance for the construction contract.		

Expenditures—construction costs	5,500,000	
Retained percentage on construction contracts		550,000
Construction contracts payable		4,950,000
To record voucher for payment to contractor.		

Note the use of the Retained percentage on construction contracts account. Retaining a certain amount from each payment to a contractor enables the city to accumulate enough resources to ensure that the contractor will complete the job satisfactorily or provide the monies to pay another contractor to complete the project. Because this amount is owed to the contractor, it is reported as a liability on the balance sheet of the appropriate fund, in this instance the Capital Projects Fund. The following entry is made to record payment of the construction voucher:

Construction contracts payable	4,950,000	
Cash		4,950,000
To record payment of the voucher.		

Assuming the state agreed that the grant monies would be used before the bond proceeds, recording the $5,500,000 construction expenditure drives the recognition of construction grant revenue, so the following entry is needed:

Deferred revenues—construction grant	5,500,000	
Revenues—construction grant		5,500,000
To record revenues from state construction grant.		

Interest earned on the investments is $300,000. This amount is not received in cash but is accrued. Assume that the local laws permit Capital Projects Funds to use any interest earned through the investment of idle funds to enhance the project. The entry to record this interest is

Interest receivable on investments	300,000	
Revenues—investments		300,000
To record interest earned on investments.		

Notice that during the year, all costs incurred in the construction of the sports complex are charged (debited) to expenditures. At the end of the year, the Expenditures—construction costs account will be closed into Unreserved fund balance. As a result, no permanent record of the asset acquired will remain on the books of the Capital Projects Fund. This approach is consistent with the financial resources measurement focus used for governmental-type funds. As mentioned in Chapter 5, these types of assets are reported in the entity-wide financial statements. Financial reporting of these assets is explained in more detail at the end of this chapter and in Chapters 9 and 10.

At this time in excess of $3 million remains in the Cash account. Prudent management requires that at least $3 million be invested in short-term securities. The entry to record the investment is

Investments	3,000,000	
Cash		3,000,000
To record investment of excess cash.		

The same rules for measuring and reporting the fair value of investments that were discussed in the "Debt Service Funds" section are relevant here. However, because this project is short term, the investments are likely to be short term, like certificates of deposit or Treasury notes. As a result, the interest is the only entry needed in this year, unless an adjustment is needed for amortization of premium or discount.

All entries for the year have been recorded, so a trial balance can be prepared (see Table 6-7).

Table 6-7

Trial Balance—Capital Projects Fund

THE CITY OF ANGUSVILLE
CAPITAL PROJECTS FUND
SPORTS COMPLEX FUND
TRIAL BALANCE
DECEMBER 31, 2004

	DEBITS	CREDITS
Cash	$ 690,000	
Investments	12,000,000	
Interest receivable	300,000	
Retained percentage on construction contracts		$ 550,000
Deferred revenue—state construction grant		2,500,000
Revenues—state construction grant		5,500,000
Revenues—investment interest		300,000
Proceeds from bond issue		10,000,000
Expenditures—architect's fees	360,000	
Expenditures—construction costs	5,500,000	
Estimated revenues	8,000,000	
Estimated other financing sources	10,000,000	
Appropriations		18,000,000
Encumbrances—capital project	12,140,000	
Budgetary fund balance reserved for encumbrances		12,140,000
	$48,990,000	$48,990,000

Closing Entries, 2004

At the end of the accounting period, December 31, 2004, the following entries are necessary to close the books:

Appropriations	18,000,000	
Estimated revenues		8,000,000
Estimated other financing sources		10,000,000
To close the budgetary accounts.		
Revenues—state construction grant	5,500,000	
Revenues—investments	300,000	
Proceeds from bond issue	10,000,000	
Expenditures—architect's fees		360,000
Expenditures—construction costs		5,500,000
Unreserved fund balance		9,940,000
To close the operating accounts.		
Budgetary fund balance reserved for encumbrances	12,140,000	
Encumbrances—capital project		12,140,000
To close encumbrance accounts.		

Unreserved fund balance	12,140,000	
Fund balance reserved for encumbrances		12,140,000
To establish the fund balance reserved for encumbrances.		

Financial Statements Illustration

Individual financial statements used by Capital Projects Funds include an operating statement and a balance sheet. These statements for the Sports Complex Fund are illustrated in Tables 6-8 and 6-9 for the first year of the fund. The overall reporting process is discussed in Chapters 9 and 10.

The details regarding the composition of fund balance—such as reserves for encumbrances and so forth—are reported on the financial statements. In this example, Unreserved fund balance has a debit balance of $2,200,000 ($9,940,000 − $12,140,000) and Fund balance reserved for encumbrances has a credit balance of $12,140,000.

Continuation of the Project: The Following Year

Although most governmental units use the fiscal year as their accounting period, authorization and control of capital projects are related to the projects' entire lives. In our illustration, therefore, it is necessary to record the remainder of the original

Table 6-8
Statement of Revenues, Expenditures, and Changes in Fund Balance

THE CITY OF ANGUSVILLE
CAPITAL PROJECTS FUND
SPORTS COMPLEX FUND
STATEMENT OF REVENUES, EXPENDITURES, AND
CHANGES IN FUND BALANCE
FOR THE YEAR ENDED DECEMBER 31, 2004

Revenues		
State construction grant	$5,500,000	
Investments	300,000	
Total revenues		$ 5,800,000
Expenditures		
Construction costs	$5,500,000	
Architect's fees	360,000	
Total expenditures		5,860,000
Excess of expenditures over revenues		60,000
Other Financing Sources		
Proceeds from bond issue		10,000,000
Net change in fund balance		9,940,000
Fund balance at beginning of year		-0-
Fund balance at end of year		$ 9,940,000

Table 6-9
Balance Sheet—Capital Projects Fund

THE CITY OF ANGUSVILLE
CAPITAL PROJECTS FUND
SPORTS COMPLEX FUND
BALANCE SHEET
DECEMBER 31, 2004

Assets		
Cash		$ 690,000
Investments		12,000,000
Interest receivable		300,000
Total assets		$12,990,000
Liabilities		
Retained percentage on construction contracts		$ 550,000
Deferred revenue—State construction grant		2,500,000
Total liabilities		$ 3,050,000
Fund Balance		
Reserved for encumbrances	$12,140,000	
Unreserved	(2,200,000)	
Total fund balance		9,940,000
Total liabilities and fund balance		$12,990,000

budget, $12,140,000. This amount is the originally approved total ($18,000,000) less the expenditures in 2004 ($5,860,000). In addition, we must record the budgeted revenues from the investments in 2005 ($750,000) and the state grant ($2,500,000) and reestablish the budgetary accounts for encumbrances ($12,140,000) at the beginning of 2005. We will assume the project will be completed in 2005, and, therefore, the remainder of the state grant will be reported as a revenue item. The entries to record these items are as follows:

Fund balance reserved for encumbrances	12,140,000	
Unreserved fund balance		12,140,000
To close the fund balance reserved for encumbrances account.		
Encumbrances—capital project	12,140,000	
Budgetary fund balance reserved for encumbrances		12,140,000
To establish the encumbrances account.		
Estimated revenues	3,250,000	
Budgetary fund balance	8,890,000	
Appropriations		12,140,000
To record the remainder of the budget for the sports complex.		

Notice that the management of the City of Angusville does not budget changes in the fair market value of its investments in Capital Projects Funds, because the investments are generally short-term in nature and not marketable securities.

When the project is completed, the contractor will submit a final bill for the amount due, $12,100,000 (assume, for simplicity, that only one billing is made in 2005), and that the architect will submit a final bill for $40,000. Because the project has not yet been inspected and accepted, the city will withhold the 10 percent retained percentage from the payment to the contractor. The entries to record these events are the following:

Budgetary fund balance reserved for encumbrances	12,140,000	
Encumbrances—capital projects		12,140,000
To remove the encumbrances for the remaining cost of the contracts.		

Expenditures—architect's fees	40,000	
Vouchers payable		40,000
To record the amount owed the architect.		

Expenditures—construction costs	12,100,000	
Retained percentage on construction contracts		1,210,000
Construction contracts payable		10,890,000
To record the amount owed to the contractor.		

To be able to pay these amounts, the city will need to liquidate all the investments held by the Capital Projects Fund and record the related income. The entry to record these amounts, assuming $12,430,000 is received, is as follows:

Cash	12,430,000	
Interest receivable on investments		300,000
Revenues—investment interest		130,000
Investments		12,000,000
To record liquidation of investments and related revenues.		

Upon receipt of the proceeds of the sale of the investments, the contractor and the architect will be paid the amounts due:

Construction contracts payable	10,890,000	
Vouchers payable	40,000	
Cash		10,930,000
To record payment of vouchers to contractor and architect.		

At this time, the Retained percentage on construction contracts account will show a $1,760,000 balance. Assume that upon final inspection, the project manager finds several defects that need to be repaired before the project can be accepted. Because the construction company already removed its equipment and employees, its owner authorized the city to have the repairs made by another contractor. If these repairs cost $450,000, the following entry will be made:

Retained percentage on construction contracts	450,000	
Cash		450,000
To record payments to contractor to repair building defects.		

All of the expenditures related to the sports complex have been incurred, so we can recognize the remainder of the state grant as revenue as follows:

Deferred revenue—state construction grant	2,500,000	
Revenues—state construction grant		2,500,000
To record revenue from state construction grant.		

After the building has been accepted, the contractor will be paid the remaining amount under the contract, $1,310,000 ($1,760,000 – $450,000). This payment will be recorded as follows:

Retained percentage on construction contracts	1,310,000	
Cash		1,310,000
To record the final payment to the contractor on the sports complex.		

Closing Entries, 2005

Upon completion and acceptance of the project, the Sports Complex Fund must be closed. To close the fund, the following entries are made:

Appropriations	12,140,000	
Estimated revenues		3,250,000
Budgetary fund balance		8,890,000
To close the budgetary accounts for 2005.		

Revenues—investment interest	130,000	
Revenues—state construction grant	2,500,000	
Unreserved fund balance	9,510,000	
Expenditures—architect's fees		40,000
Expenditures—construction costs		12,100,000
To close the operating accounts.		

After completion of the project, the Capital Projects Fund for the sports complex has two account balances: Cash, $430,000, and Unreserved fund balance, $430,000. These monies are equal to the earnings of the investments. Use of these resources will depend on the provisions of the state grant and the bond issue. For illustrative purposes, assume these amounts must be used to retire the bonds, which will require the following entries:

Entry in the books of the Capital Projects Fund

Transfer out to Debt Service Fund	430,000	
Cash		430,000
To record the transfer to the Debt Service Fund.		

Entry in the books of the Capital Projects Fund

Unreserved fund balance	430,000	
Transfer out to Debt Service Fund		430,000
To close the transfer account.		

Entry in the books of the Debt Service Fund

Cash	430,000	
Transfer in from Capital Projects Fund		430,000
To record the transfer from the Capital Projects Fund.		

Issuance of Bonds at a Premium or Discount

The bonds issued for the construction of the sports complex were sold at face value. Often government bonds are sold at a price above or below face value because of the prevailing interest rates. When the bond price is different from par, the entries made in the fund that receives the bond proceeds must properly account for the issue price.

As an example, assume that the bonds issued by the City of Angusville had been sold for $11 million. Because the face value of these bonds is $10 million, the city must account for the extra $1 million. The treatment of the premium is dependent on the bond indenture. In some instances, a premium may be used for the purpose for which the bonds were issued. In other instances, a premium must be used to retire the debt. If we assume that this premium may be used for construction of the sports complex, the following entry is made in the Capital Projects Fund when the bonds are issued:

Cash	11,000,000	
Proceeds from bond issue		11,000,000
To record the issuance of bonds.		

If the premium must be used to retire the bonds, the following entries are made:

Entries in the books of the Capital Projects Fund

Cash	11,000,000	
Proceeds from bond issue		11,000,000
To record the issuance of bonds.		
Transfer out to Debt Service Fund	1,000,000	
Cash		1,000,000
To record transfer of bond premium to Debt Service Fund.		

Entry in the books of the Debt Service Fund

Cash	1,000,000	
Transfer in from Capital Projects Fund		1,000,000
To record transfer of bond premium from Capital Projects Fund.		

Although other methods of recording a premium are possible, this approach maintains the total proceeds upon issuance in the fund that received the monies and clearly develops an audit trail for the transfer.

If bonds are issued for less than face value, the total proceeds are recorded in the Capital Projects Fund, as indicated previously. This lower bond price may cause a problem, however, if the bonds do not provide enough resources to complete the project. At this point, the project manager must either scale down the project or seek additional funds.

Issuance of Bonds Between Interest Payment Dates

If bonds are issued between interest payment dates, the interest accrued to the date of sale must be paid by the buyer to the city. Because this amount will be used to pay interest on the next interest date, it is recorded directly in the Debt Service Fund. It is not recorded in the Capital Projects Fund.

Arbitrage

The Internal Revenue Code (the Code) has strict rules regarding tax-exempt interest paid by a governmental unit and investment interest earned. These rules provide that interest earned on the investment of tax-exempt debt proceeds cannot be greater than interest paid. If the interest earned is higher, then the governmental unit is subject to the arbitrage provisions of the Code. Excess interest earned by a governmental unit must be paid to the federal government or the governmental unit will be subject to either a 50 percent excise tax or revocation of the tax-exempt status of its debt. Revocation of the tax-exempt status of its debt would not harm the governmental unit immediately, but it would play an important role in the cost of future debt issues.

The arbitrage provisions of the Code are complex, and a complete discussion is beyond the scope of this text. Because of complex laws regulating the types of securities in which a governmental unit may invest and the arbitrage regulations, governmental units usually seek the aid of their accountants and attorneys whenever tax-exempt debt proceeds are invested.

GOVERNMENTAL ACCOUNTING IN PRACTICE
The City of Columbus, Ohio

The City of Columbus, Ohio, maintains 37 Capital Projects Funds. The purpose of each fund is to account for resources received and used for construction and development of specific projects. The balance sheet and statement of revenues, expenditures, and changes in fund balance illustrated in Tables 6-10 and 6-11 describe the Federal State Highway Engineering Fund. Columbus identifies its funds based on the primary sources of funding. Included in this fund are highway projects funded by grant revenue and other funding sources.

Notice that this fund contains the types of assets and liabilities described in this chapter as common to Capital Projects Funds. Other Capital Projects Funds used by the City of Columbus show similar assets and liabilities, although none have all of the items included on the balance sheet of the Federal State Highway Engineering Fund. Also notice that the net fund balance of the Federal State Highway Engineering Fund is zero.

LEASED ASSETS

Governmental units often lease assets rather than purchase them. Because governmental-type funds report only spendable resources, a lease presents problems beyond those found in commercial accounting. The illustration presented in this section is not intended to be all-inclusive with respect to leased assets. Complications like residual values and bargain purchase options are omitted in favor of a straightforward general lease model.

Table 6-10

Balance Sheet—Capital Projects Fund—City of Columbus, Ohio

CITY OF COLUMBUS, OHIO
CAPITAL PROJECTS FUND
FEDERAL STATE HIGHWAY ENGINEERING FUND
BALANCE SHEET
DECEMBER 31, 20X4

Assets

Cash and cash equivalents with treasurer	$1,454,002
Due from other governments	97,368
Total assets	$1,551,370

Liabilities

Accounts payable	$ 29,924
Due to other funds	4,440
Deferred revenue and other	1,517,006
Total liabilities	1,551,370

Fund Balance

Reserved for encumbrances	4,458,759
Unreserved, undesignated	(4,458,759)
Total fund balance	-0-
Total liabilities and fund balance	$1,551,370

Source: Adapted from a recent annual report of the City of Columbus, Ohio.

Table 6-11

Statement of Revenues, Expenditures, and Changes
in Fund Balance—Capital Projects Fund—City of
Columbus, Ohio

CITY OF COLUMBUS, OHIO
CAPITAL PROJECTS FUND
FEDERAL STATE HIGHWAY ENGINEERING FUND
STATEMENT OF REVENUES, EXPENDITURES, AND CHANGES IN FUND BALANCE
FOR THE YEAR ENDED DECEMBER 31, 20X4

Revenues

Grants and subsidiaries	$899,863

Expenditures

Capital outlay	899,863
Excess of revenues over expenditures	-0-
Beginning fund balance	-0-
Ending fund balance	$ -0-

Source: Adapted from a recent annual report of the City of Columbus, Ohio.

As in commercial accounting, governmental units enter into operating leases and capital leases in their everyday operations. A lease is classified as an *operating lease* if the lessee does not acquire any property rights through the contract. These leases are generally short-term and are recorded by a debit to an expenditure account and a credit to Cash when the rental payments are made.

A lease is classified as a *capital lease* for the lessee if the lessee acquires property rights through the contract, the lease is noncancelable, and it meets at least one of the following tests:

1. The lessee owns the property at the conclusion of the lease, through either a transfer of title or a bargain purchase option.
2. The life of the lease is 75 percent or more of the expected economic life of the asset.
3. The present value of the minimum lease payments is 90 percent or more of the fair market value of the leased asset.

Items 2 and 3 are not considered if the lease term is in the last 25 percent of the economic life of the asset.

For a capital lease, the lessee must record the leased asset as an expenditure and an other financing source. To illustrate, assume the City of Angusville leases a new computer from JCN, Inc., which has a fair market value of $862,426 and an economic life of 5 years. Assume further that the relevant interest rate is 8 percent. Based on this information, the government (lessee) must record the present value of the minimum lease payments as an expenditure. If these payments are $200,000 per year, payable on January 1 of each year, the present value of the rental payments is $862,426 ($200,000 × 4.31213). If the computer is to be used by a department in the General Fund, the following entry is required:

Expenditures—capital outlay	862,426	
Other financing sources—capital leases		862,426
To record a capital lease.		

Notice that the initial recording of the lease has no effect on the fund balance of the General Fund. The expenditure is offset by the other financing source.

Because the first lease payment is due at the time the lease is signed, the following entry would also be made in the General Fund:

Expenditures—capital lease principal	200,000	
Vouchers payable		200,000
To record lease payment due.		

Two additional points can be made regarding the two preceding transactions. First, no interest is paid initially because the first payment is made as soon as the lease is signed. Second, the obligation is financed through the General Fund. Often leases are financed without the use of a Debt Service Fund. It is possible, however, that a Debt Service Fund could be used.

The second payment on the lease obligation occurs one period after the lease is signed. As a result, accrued interest is due. Because the interest payment is not usually appropriated until the period in which it is due, no entry to accrue the interest is made. Instead, the following entries are made at the beginning of the second year of the lease:

Expenditures—capital lease principal	147,006	
Expenditures—interest on capital leases	52,994	
Vouchers payable		200,000
To record capital lease payment.		

Interest calculation:	
Initial debt	$862,426
Less: first payment	200,000
Book value of obligation during first year	$662,426
Interest rate	× .08
Interest due	$ 52,994

Governmental leases usually contain a fiscal funding clause. A fiscal funding clause is a provision in the lease that permits the government to cancel the lease if resources are not appropriated to make lease payments. If the possibility of actual cancelation is remote, a fiscal funding clause does not affect the noncancelable test. In other words, the lease is still capitalized.

CONCLUDING COMMENT

As previously indicated, GASB *Statement No. 34* does not require reporting capital assets and long-term debt in the fund-level financial statements. Depending on the size of the government, however, capital assets are required to be reported in the government-wide financial statements. In any event, all governments should keep detailed records of their capital assets and periodically verify their physical existence with these records.

Capital asset adjustments needed for preparing government-wide financial statements generally can be made simply by analyzing capital asset expenditures and sales during the year. However, not all transactions affecting capital assets flow through the financial accounting records; for example, assets may be written off because of expiration of useful life or theft. To improve internal controls over capital assets and to facilitate preparation of the government-wide financial statements, we suggest that governments establish a memorandum set of records. These records can be called the Capital Investment Account Group (CIAG). Chapter 10 contains a description of the workings of the CIAG.

REVIEW QUESTIONS

Q6-1 How are the activities of Debt Service Funds controlled?

Q6-2 Are budgets usually used for Debt Service Funds?

Q6-3 When is interest recorded as an expenditure in Debt Service Funds?

Q6-4 When is the principal of general long-term debt recorded in Debt Service Funds?

Q6-5 What information can a city oversight body obtain from a Debt Service Fund?

Q6-6 How are investments valued on governmental balance sheets?

Q6-7 When are Capital Projects Funds used?

Q6-8 How are Capital Projects Funds controlled?

Q6-9 Why is encumbrance accounting generally used for Capital Projects Funds?

Q6-10 Are closing entries necessary in the accounting records for a capital project that is not completed in the first year?

Q6-11 Are fixed assets recorded in Capital Projects Funds? Why or why not?

Q6-12 Bonds that finance capital projects are sometimes issued at a premium or a discount. What is the effect on the accounting records of the premium or discount?

Q6-13 Explain the relationship among Debt Service Funds and Capital Projects Funds.

CASES

C6-1 Julius I. Tornado is the chief operating officer of Green Valley. One day last week he came to your office to discuss the terms of a new bond issue the city plans to sell. The proceeds from these bonds will be used to construct a new city hall and courthouse building. The total estimated cost of the project is $100 million. Tornado feels that as chief finance officer, you should have some input into the terms included in the bond indenture. The bonds will be redeemed in a lump sum at the end of 25 years. The city is barely balancing its budget now, so Tornado is concerned that there will not be enough resources available to pay the interest for the next 25 years and redeem the principal when it comes due. What recommendations do you have for Tornado?

C6-2 Janet Figg, the chief financial officer for Pine City, is involved in the planning process for a new arena. The city is trying to attract a professional basketball team and to do so, it must have a first-class arena available. If you were Figg, what suggestions would you bring to the first committee meeting regarding financing and construction of the new arena?

ETHICS CASES

EC6-1 Assume you are the accounting supervisor for the City of Secret Valley, and you discover a violation the city made regarding its bond indentures. The city has four bond issues outstanding, and the bond indenture for each requires a separate accounting. In error, a new entry-level accounting clerk did not set up separate debt service funds for each bond issue. It is the end of the current year, and you are responsible for preparing the annual report. In desperation, you go to your superior, Janet Well, the chief financial officer of the city, and ask her for guidance. She suggests that you not worry about such a petty thing—"No one reads these reports anyway." What would you do?

EC6-2 Ramos Diablo, the mayor of the City of San Angeles, is trying to locate available resources in the governmental-type funds to help "bail out" the General Fund. The General Fund expenditures currently exceed budgetary amounts by $10 million, with 2 months remaining in the fiscal year. Diablo feels some unused resources in a Capital Projects Fund or a Debt Service Fund could be transferred to the General Fund to alleviate the impending budget deficit. Each of these funds has a fund balance of at least $50 million. If Diablo cannot locate the needed resources, he will have to borrow money using tax anticipation notes based on an emergency tax levy. This prospect is a major problem for him because the current year is an election year. Is Diablo's plan ethical? If you were the chief financial officer of San Angeles, how would you respond to Diablo? How could such a situation be prevented?

EXERCISES

E6-1 (Fill in the blanks—general terminology)
1. Payment of principal and interest on debt is referred to as ____ .
2. A periodic transfer of resources from the General Fund to a Debt Service Fund is reported as a(n) ____ on the operating statement of both funds.
3. Payment of principal is reported as a(n) ____ on the ____ of a Debt Service Fund.
4. A financial institution that makes principal and interest payments in the name of a governmental unit is called a ____ .
5. A debit balance in Fund balance is called a(n) ____ .

E6-2 (Use of a Debt Service Fund)
The City of Crestview has only one Debt Service Fund for all of its bond issues. Is the city in compliance with GAAP for governmental units? Explain.

E6-3 (Multiple choice)
1. Several years ago a city established a sinking fund to retire an issue of general obligation bonds. This year the city made a $50,000 contribution to the sinking fund from general revenues and realized $15,000 in revenue from securities in the sinking fund. The bonds due this year were retired. These transactions require accounting recognition in which of the following funds?
   a. General Fund
   b. Debt Service Fund
   c. Debt Service Fund and General Fund
   d. Capital Projects Fund, Debt Service Fund, and General Fund
   e. None of the above

   (AICPA adapted)

2. To provide for the retirement of general obligation bonds, a city invests a portion of its general revenue receipts in marketable securities. This investment activity should be accounted for in which of the following funds?
    a. Trust Fund
    b. Enterprise Fund
    c. Special Assessment Fund
    d. Special Revenue Fund
    e. None of the above

(AICPA adapted)

3. In preparing the General Fund budget of Brockton City for the forthcoming fiscal year, the city council appropriated a sum greater than expected revenues. What will be the result of the council's action?
    a. A cash overdraft during the fiscal year
    b. An increase in encumbrances by the end of the fiscal year
    c. A debit to Budgetary fund balance
    d. A necessity for compensatory offsetting action
    e. None of the above

(AICPA adapted)

4. Which of the following funds is used to account for the operations of a public library receiving the majority of its support from property taxes levied for that purpose?
    a. General Fund
    b. Special Revenue Fund
    c. Enterprise Fund
    d. Internal Service Fund
    e. None of the above

(AICPA adapted)

5. A special tax was levied by Downtown City to retire and pay interest on general obligation bonds that were issued to finance the construction of a new city hall. Where are the receipts from the tax recorded?
    a. Capital Projects Fund
    b. Special Revenue Fund
    c. Debt Service Fund
    d. General Fund
    e. None of the above

6. Which of the following funds uses modified accrual accounting?
    a. All governmental-type funds
    b. General Fund and Special Revenue Funds only
    c. Only the General Fund
    d. Only Debt Service Funds
    e. None of the above

7. To what does the term *current financial resources* measurement focus refer?
    a. The use of the modified accrual basis of accounting
    b. The measurement of resources available for spending
    c. The use of the full accrual basis of accounting

    d. The timing of the recognition of revenues and expenditures

    e. None of the above

E6-4   (Discussion of control in the General Fund and in Debt Service Funds)
Compare and contrast the method used to control expenditures in the
General Fund and in Debt Service Funds. Be sure to explain the reasons for
any differences.

E6-5   (Journal entries for long-term debt)
Green Valley issued $20 million of general obligation bonds to construct a multi-
purpose arena. These bonds will be serviced by a tax on the revenue from events
held in the arena and will mature in 2013. During 2004, Green Valley budgeted
$2,500,000 of tax revenues and expenditures related to maintenance of the arena
totaling $750,000. In addition, interest on the bonds for 2004 totaled $2 million.

Required: Prepare the journal entry (entries) necessary to record this information in the Debt Service Fund.

E6-6   (Fill in the blanks—general terminology)
1. Encumbrance accounting usually (is or is not) _____ used in Capital
Projects Funds.
2. The entry to record the budget of a Capital Projects Fund would include a
(debit or credit) _____ to Appropriations.
3. A contractor recently completed a bridge for the City of Paige. After the
contractor removed his workers and equipment, several deficiencies were
noticed. Another contractor was hired to repair these deficiencies. The cost
of the repairs should be charged to _____ .
4. Long-term bonds issued by a Capital Projects Fund (are or are not)
_____ reported as a liability of that fund.
5. During the year, a city acquired new furniture for the mayor's office, land
for a parking garage, and a new fire truck. The furniture was financed from
general city revenues; the land and the cost of the parking garage were
financed primarily from bond proceeds; and the fire truck was financed
from general tax revenues. Which of these projects would require the use
of a Capital Projects Fund?

E6-7   (Use of Capital Projects Funds)
The City of New Falls is planning to acquire furniture and fixtures for the
mayor's office and the council chambers. One of the council members,
Council Member Dunn, sent you a memo asking whether a Capital Projects
Fund is needed to record the acquisition of the furniture. Write a memo in
response to Council Member Dunn.

E6-8   (Multiple choice)
1. The resources used to finance Capital Projects Funds may come from
which of the following sources?
    a. Private donations
    b. General obligation debt
    c. Intergovernmental revenues
    d. All of the above

2. The issuance of bonds to provide resources to construct a new courthouse should be recorded in a Capital Projects Fund by crediting which of the following accounts?
   a. Bonds payable
   b. Revenues—bonds
   c. Fund balance
   d. Proceeds from bond issue

3. What special entry must be made at the beginning of the new period when encumbrance accounting is used for a construction project that continues beyond the end of an accounting period?
   a. A credit to Revenues
   b. A debit to Cash
   c. A debit to Expenditures
   d. A debit to Encumbrances

4. What is done with resources that remain in a Capital Projects Fund after the project is completed?
   a. Always transferred to a Debt Service Fund
   b. Always returned to the provider(s) of the funds
   c. Disbursed according to any restrictions in the agreement between the provider of the resources and the government
   d. Always transferred to the General Fund

5. What journal entry is made in the Capital Projects Fund when a contract is signed and encumbrance accounting is used?

   a. Encumbrances   xxxx
        Budgetary fund balance reserved for encumbrances   xxxx
   b. Vouchers payable   xxxx
        Reserve for encumbrances   xxxx
   c. Expenditures—construction costs   xxxx
        Vouchers payable   xxxx
   d. Reserve for encumbrances   xxxx
        Fund balance   xxxx

6. The principal amount of bonds issued to finance the cost of a new city hall would be recorded as a liability in which of the following funds?
   a. General Fund
   b. Special Revenue Fund
   c. Capital Projects Fund
   d. Debt Service Fund
   e. None of the above

7. Why is encumbrance accounting usually used in Capital Projects Funds?
   a. Long-term debt is not recorded in these funds.
   b. The budget must be recorded in these funds.
   c. It helps the government to control the expenditures.
   d. The modified accrual basis of accounting is used.

8. The City of New Easton constructed a new convention center. After completion of the project, the convention center should be recorded as an asset in which of the following funds?
   a. General Fund
   b. Capital Projects Fund
   c. Debt Service Fund
   d. Both b and c
   e. None of the above

E6-9 (Use of a Capital Projects Fund)
Tutorville recently hired a new bookkeeper, Pete Pencil, from "Accountants R Us." Pencil was preparing to record some expenditures on a new bridge over False Creek, a local tourist attraction. He noticed that other expenditures on the project were not recorded in the General Fund, which made him curious. He comes to you, the chief financial officer, for advice. Explain to Pencil why a separate fund is generally used to account for the construction and acquisition of major general fixed assets.

E6-10 (Closing journal entries)
The following are selected accounts from the trial balance of the Walker Tunnel Fund, a Capital Projects Fund, as of June 30, 2004 (the end of the fiscal year):

Appropriations	$4,711,000
Fund balance	78,000
Cash	245,000
Encumbrances	1,345,000
Revenues—grants	3,000,000
Estimated revenues	2,020,000
Expenditures—construction costs	3,000,000
Investments	75,000
Revenue—investments	19,000

Required: 1. Prepare the closing entry for June 30, 2004.
2. Assuming no revenues are budgeted for fiscal 2005, prepare the opening entries necessary for July 1, 2004.

E6-11 (Leases)
Plymouthville leased equipment with a fair market value of $905,863. The life of the noncancelable lease is 10 years and the economic life of the property is 10 years. Using an 8 percent interest rate, the present value of the minimum lease payments is $905,863. The first payment of $125,000 is due January 1 of the current year. Each additional payment is due on the first of January in the next 9 years. What is the amount of the asset to be recorded in Plymouthville's Capital Projects Fund? If no asset will be recorded, explain why.

PROBLEMS

P6-1 (Journal entries, financial statements, and closing entries for a Debt Service Fund)

The following are a trial balance and several transactions that relate to Napoleonville's Concert Hall Bond Fund:

	Napoleonville Debt Service Fund Concert Hall Bond Fund Trial Balance July 1, 2004	
Cash	$ 60,000	
Investments	40,000	
Unreserved fund balance		$100,000
	$100,000	$100,000

The following transactions took place between July 1, 2004, and June 30, 2005:

1. The city council of Napoleonville adopted the budget for the Concert Hall Bond Fund for the fiscal year. The estimated revenues totaled $100,000, the estimated other financing sources totaled $50,000, and the appropriations totaled $125,000.
2. The General Fund transferred $50,000 to the fund.
3. To provide additional resources to service the bond issue, a tax was levied upon the citizens. The total levy was $100,000, of which $95,000 was expected to be collected. Assume the allowance method is used.
4. Taxes of $60,000 were collected.
5. Income received in cash from the investments totaled $1,000.
6. Taxes of $30,000 were collected.
7. The liability of $37,500 for interest was recorded, and that amount of cash was transferred to the fiscal agent.
8. The fiscal agent reported that all the interest had been paid.
9. A fee of $500 was paid to the fiscal agent.
10. Investment income totaling $1,000 was received.
11. The liabilities for interest in the amount of $37,500 and principal in the amount of $50,000 were recorded and the total was transferred to the fiscal agent.
12. The fiscal agent reported that $45,000 of principal and $35,000 of interest were paid.
13. Investment revenue of $500 was accrued.

Required: 1. Prepare all the journal entries necessary to record the preceding transactions on the books of the Concert Hall Bond Fund.
2. Prepare a trial balance for the Concert Hall Bond Fund as of June 30, 2005.
3. Prepare a statement of revenues, expenditures, and changes in fund balance and a balance sheet for the Concert Hall Bond Fund.
4. Prepare closing entries for the Concert Hall Bond Fund.

P6-2 (Journal entries, financial statements, and closing entries for a Debt Service Fund)

Following is a trial balance for the City of Dolby and the transactions that relate to the Debt Service Fund:

City of Dolby
Debt Service Fund
Bridge Bonds Fund
Trial Balance
December 31, 2003

	Debit	Credit
Cash	$60,000	
Investments	30,000	
Unreserved fund balance		$90,000
	$90,000	$90,000

1. The city council of Dolby adopted the budget for the Debt Service Fund for 2004. The estimated revenues totaled $1 million, the estimated other financing sources totaled $500,000, and the appropriations totaled $202,000.
2. The receivable from the General Fund for $500,000 was recorded.
3. To provide additional resources to service the bond issue, a tax was levied upon the citizens. The total levy was $1 million, of which $975,000 was expected to be collected. (Assume the allowance method is used.)
4. Taxes of $780,000 were collected.
5. Receivables of $5,000 were written off.
6. Income received in cash from investments totaled $5,000.
7. Taxes of $150,000 were collected.
8. The liability of $50,000 for interest was recorded, and that amount of cash was transferred to the fiscal agent.
9. The fiscal agent reported that $45,000 of interest had been paid.
10. The fiscal agent was paid a fee of $1,000.
11. Investment income of $3,000 was received in cash.
12. The liabilities for interest in the amount of $50,000 and principal in the amount of $100,000 were recorded, and the total was transferred to the fiscal agent.
13. The fiscal agent reported that interest of $51,000 and principal of $95,000 had been paid.
14. Investment revenue of $1,000 was accrued.
15. The amount due was collected from the General Fund.
16. Investments totalling $1 million were purchased.

Required: 1. Prepare all the journal entries necessary to record these transactions on the books of the Debt Service Fund.
2. Prepare a trial balance for the Debt Service Fund as of December 31, 2004.

3. Prepare a statement of revenues, expenditures, and changes in fund balance for 2004 and a balance sheet as of December 31, 2004, for the Debt Service Fund.
4. Prepare closing entries for the Debt Service Fund.

P6-3 (Journal entries for several funds)
Following are several transactions that relate to Crestview for the fiscal year 2004 (assume a voucher system is not used):

1. The general operating budget was approved. It included estimated revenues of $1,200,000, estimated other financing sources of $300,000, appropriations of $1,150,000, and estimated other financing uses of $100,000.
2. The police department paid its salaries of $50,000.
3. The General Fund made its contribution to a Debt Service Fund of $100,000.
4. The office furniture previously ordered for $45,000 was received and the bill was paid. Old furniture that cost $23,000 was sold for $500. The proceeds could be used in any manner by the city.
5. The fire chief ordered $1,000 of supplies.
6. General obligation long-term debt principal matured, and the final interest payment became due. These amounts were $75,000 and $7,500, respectively. (Assume a Debt Service Fund and a fiscal agent are used.)
7. The appropriate amount of cash was sent to the fiscal agent to process the debt service payments described in part (6).
8. The supplies ordered in part (5) arrived along with an invoice for $1,025. The excess amount was approved and a check was sent to the supplier.
9. The fiscal agent for the bonds notified the government that $70,000 of principal and $7,000 of interest had been paid.
10. The property tax for the year was levied by the General Fund. The total amount of the tax was $500,000. City officials estimated that 99 percent would be collected.
11. Collections of property taxes during the year totaled $490,000.
12. The remaining property taxes were classified as delinquent after $2,000 was written off as uncollectible.
13. The General Fund received a $1,000 transfer from an Enterprise Fund (record only the General Fund portion).

Required: Prepare all the journal entries necessary to record these transactions in the appropriate governmental-type funds and identify the fund(s) used.

P6-4 (Journal entries for several funds and a trial balance for a Debt Service Fund)
Following are several transactions that relate to Irontown in 2004.

1. The general operating budget was approved. It included estimated revenues of $500,000, appropriations of $400,000, and estimated other financing uses of $90,000.
2. Encumbrances of $50,000 were recorded in the General Fund.
3. The budget for the Parks Special Revenue Fund was approved. It included estimated revenues of $60,000 and appropriations of $59,000.

4. The General Fund made its annual contribution of $100,000 to a Debt Service Fund.
5. The Debt Service Fund recorded the liability for principal and interest, $20,000 and $40,000, respectively.
6. The Debt Service Fund invested $10,000 of Debt Service Fund cash in securities.
7. The salaries of the general governmental administrative staff were paid, $15,000. Assume that salaries were not encumbered.
8. The fiscal agent who manages the investment activities of the Debt Service Fund was paid a fee of $1,000.
9. The tax used to partially service the bond issue was levied. The total levy was $30,000, of which $29,000 is expected to be collected.
10. A cash expenditure for office supplies for the mayor's office was made, $900. The encumbered amount was $1,000.
11. Debt Service Fund cash of $60,000 was paid to the fiscal agent to pay interest and principal.
12. The principal and interest previously recorded were paid by the fiscal agent.

Required: 1. Prepare all the journal entries necessary to record these transactions. In addition, identify the fund(s) in which each entry is recorded.
2. Prepare a trial balance for the Debt Service Fund as of December 31, 2004.

P6-5 (Journal entries for several funds)
Prepare journal entries for each of the following transactions. In addition, identify the fund in which each entry would be recorded.

1. The General Fund made its annual contribution of $1,500,000 to the fund that will pay $1 million principal and $500,000 interest on outstanding general obligation debt.
2. The city paid $1 million of principal and $500,000 of interest on outstanding general obligation bonds from resources previously accumulated.
3. A Debt Service Fund previously paid the total principal and interest on an outstanding bond issue. Currently the fund carries a balance of $300,000. These resources can be spent by the General Fund in any way the city manager feels is appropriate.
4. The police chief paid $300,000 for equipment. This equipment was ordered 3 months prior to delivery at an estimated cost of $295,000 (assume a voucher system is used and the excess expenditure is approved).
5. The fiscal agent for the city was paid its annual $10,000 fee from resources accumulated in the only Debt Service Fund used by the city.

P6-6 (Journal entries and financial statements—Capital Projects Fund)
The following transactions occurred during 2004:

1. The City of Watersville approved the construction of an enclosed concert arena for a total cost of $75 million to attract professional events. On

the same day, a contract with a 6 percent retainage clause was signed with B. P. Construction Company for the arena. The arena will be financed by a $75 million general obligation bond issue. Investment revenue of $4 million was also included in the budget. (Assume that the budget is recorded in the accounts and encumbrance accounting is used.)

2. The bonds were issued for $76 million. The amount received over $75 million was immediately transferred to the appropriate Debt Service Fund.
3. The city invested $74.9 million in securities.
4. The contract signed with B. P. stipulated that the contract price included the architect fees. On this date, the architects were paid their fee of $25,000 by Watersville. (Assume that a vouchers payable account was not used.)
5. The contractor submitted a progress billing of $3 million.
6. Investments that cost $3 million were redeemed for $3 million plus $50,000 interest.
7. B. P. was paid the amount billed less a 6 percent retained percentage.
8. Income totaling $3.7 million was received on the investments.
9. B. P. submitted another progress billing of $8 million.
10. Additional investments were redeemed to make the payment to B. P. The investments originally cost $7.8 million. The proceeds of $8.1 million included investment income of $300,000.
11. The contractor was paid, less the 6 percent retainage.
12. Investment income of $60,000 was accrued.
13. Investment income of $10,000 was received in cash.

Required:

1. Prepare the journal entries necessary to record these transactions in the Capital Projects Fund. Assume that the city operates on a calendar year.
2. Prepare a trial balance for the Capital Projects Fund at December 31, 2004, before closing.
3. Prepare any necessary closing entries at December 31, 2004.
4. Prepare a statement of revenues, expenditures, and changes in fund balance for 2004, and a balance sheet as of December 31, 2004.
5. Prepare the journal entries necessary to record the remainder of the budget and to reestablish the budgetary accounts for encumbrances at January 1, 2005.

P6-7 (Journal entries, financial statements, and closing entries for a Capital Projects Fund)

The following transactions occurred during the fiscal year July 1, 2004, to June 30, 2005:

1. The City of Red Ridge approved the construction of a city hall complex for a total cost of $120 million. A few days later, a contract with a 5 percent retainage clause was signed with Walker Construction for the complex. The buildings will be financed by a federal grant of $25 million and a general obligation bond issue of $100 million. During the current year, invest-

ment revenue of $4 million is budgeted. (Assume the budget is recorded in the accounts and encumbrance accounting is used.)

2. The bonds were issued for $90 million (the principal was $100 million). The difference between the actual cost of the project and the bonds and the grant was expected to be generated by investing the excess cash during the construction period.

3. The city collected the grant from the government.

4. The city invested $90 million.

5. The contract signed with Walker stipulated that the contract price included architect fees. On this date, the architects were paid their fee of $45,000 by Red Ridge. (Assume a vouchers payable account is used.)

6. Walker submitted a progress billing for $25 million. Assume that the city will use resources from the federal grant to make this payment.

7. Investments that cost $5 million were redeemed for a total of $5,020,000.

8. Investment income totaling $3,500,000 was received in cash.

9. The contractor was paid the amount billed in part (6), less a 5 percent retainage.

10. The contractor submitted another progress billing for $25 million.

11. Investments totaling $14,600,000 were redeemed, together with additional investment income of $1,400,000.

12. The contractor was paid the amount billed in part (10), less a 5 percent retainage.

13. Investment income of $250,000 was accrued.

14. Bond interest totaling $10 million was paid.

Required: 1. Prepare the journal entries necessary to record these transactions in a Capital Projects Fund for the City of Red Ridge. Assume the city operates on a fiscal year: July 1 to June 30.

2. Prepare a trial balance for the fund at June 30, 2005, before closing.

3. Prepare any necessary closing entries at June 30, 2005.

4. Prepare a statement of revenues, expenditures, and changes in fund balance for the year ended June 30, 2005, and a balance sheet as of June 30, 2005.

5. Prepare the journal entry (entries) necessary to record the remainder of the budget and to reestablish the budgetary accounts for encumbrances as of July 1, 2005. Assume investment revenues of $2 million are expected in the 2005 fiscal year.

P6-8 (Journal entries regarding a bond issue and accounting for a premium) The City of Lands-A-Lot authorized a bond issue for a parking garage. The estimated cost was $4 million. The garage would be financed through a $3 million bond issue and a $1 million contribution from the General Fund. The General Fund made its contribution and the bonds were sold for $3,200,000.

Required: 1. Prepare journal entries to record the budget for the parking garage, the payment and receipt of the General Fund's contribution, and the issuance of the bonds, assuming the premium remained in the Capital Projects Fund. Identify the fund(s) used to record the transactions.

2. Discuss alternate methods of dealing with the bond premium.

P6-9 (Journal entries for several funds and financial statements for a Capital Projects Fund)

Following is a trial balance for the Old York Marina Capital Projects Fund and the transactions that relate to the 2004–2005 fiscal year:

Old York		
Capital Projects Fund		
Boat Marina Fund		
Trial Balance		
July 1, 2004		
	Debits	Credits
Cash	$ 30,000	
Investments	500,000	
Retained percentage on construction contracts		$ 10,000
Fund balance reserved for encumbrances		500,000
Unreserved fund balance		20,000
	$530,000	$530,000

1. The budget for the marina project provided for a remaining appropriation of $500,000. Record the budget and reestablish the budgetary accounts for encumbrances. Assume $30,000 of investment income (dividends and interest) is budgeted.

2. The contractor, Sir Fixit, submitted a progress billing on the marina for $300,000. The retained percentage was 10 percent.

3. Investments were redeemed for $320,000. This amount included $20,000 of investment income.

4. Sir Fixit was paid the amount billed, less a 10 percent retainage.

5. Investment income of $15,000 was received in cash.

6. The final billing was received from Sir Fixit for $200,000.

7. All remaining investments were redeemed for $205,000. This amount included $5,000 of investment income.

8. Sir Fixit was paid the amount billed, less a 10 percent retainage.

9. Before the project was formally approved, one of the piers fell into the lake. Because Sir Fixit had already removed its workers and equipment, the city was authorized to have the repairs made by a local contractor at a cost not to exceed $40,000. The actual cost of the repairs totaled $32,000. The remainder of the retainage was sent to Sir Fixit.

10. After the repairs, the project was formally approved and the accounting records were closed. The remaining cash was transferred to the Debt

Service Fund. The funds for this project came from a general obligation bond issue.

Required: 1. Prepare all the journal entries necessary to record these transactions and close the Capital Projects Fund. In addition, identify the fund(s) used. A vouchers payable account is not used.
2. Prepare a statement of revenues, expenditures, and changes in fund balance for the Marina Capital Projects Fund for the 2004–2005 fiscal year.

P6-10 (Prepare a budget for a capital project and the related bond issue)
Dellville plans to build an auditorium. The plans were drawn by an architect for $100,000. The city accepted a bid from Cracks R Us contractors for $8 million for the entire project. The project should take 2 years to build. It will not be started until October 1, 2004, so the completion date is September 30, 2006. The town manager of Dellville, Phyllis Dell, plans to establish a Debt Service Fund for the bonds that will be issued to finance the project. These bonds will be serviced from tax revenues. During 2004, $100,000 of revenue is expected to be available. The bonds will pay interest on April 1 and October 1 of each year, beginning in 2005.

Required: Prepare the journal entries necessary to record the preceding budgetary information in the appropriate funds for 2004.

P6-11 (Journal entries for several funds)
The following transactions were incurred by East Minster Township.

1. The township paid cash for four new police cruisers. Each car cost $18,000. They were originally ordered at $20,000 each.
2. The township issued bonds for the purpose of constructing playgrounds in the city. The bonds had a face value of $20 million and were sold for $19,500,000.
3. JoJo Smith, the mayor of the township, signed a contract with the Dumas Office Furniture Company to buy new furniture for his office. The total cost of the furniture was $8,900. The furniture will be delivered next month.
4. Two additional police officers were hired to help patrol the new playgrounds.
5. The fire department sold several pieces of old equipment. They originally cost the township $20,000. The fire chief, Blaze More, negotiated a selling price of $3,000 for the used equipment.
6. The township made its annual payment of principal and interest on its outstanding debt. A total of $5 million was paid: $1 million of principal and $4 million of interest.
7. The township levied a property tax to service the outstanding debt. The total amount of the tax was $4 million, of which $3,900,000 was expected to be collected.
8. The city hall construction project was completed this year. Due to construction delays, it took 3 years to build the new office building. This year

$1,500,000 of costs were incurred. In previous years a total of $7,500,000 was incurred. Financing for the project came from a bond issue that was sold at the time the project was started.

9. The township's board of supervisors approved a budget amendment for the General Fund. An extra $300,000 appropriation was included in the budget for the current year.

10. The township made payments on outstanding leases totaling $300,000. This amount included $175,000 for interest. The leases are accounted for in the General Fund and encumbrance accounting is used.

Required: Record these transactions in journal form. Also indicate the fund in which each transaction is recorded.

P6-12 (Leased assets)

On January 1, 2004, the chief operating officer of New Innport signed a non-cancelable lease for street equipment. The lease was for 10 years, the economic life of the property. The fair market value of the equipment (and present value of the minimum rentals) is $72,469. The township's incremental borrowing rate is 8 percent and the rate implicit in the lease is 8 percent. The $10,000 annual lease payment is due on the first day of the year.

Required: Prepare all journal entries necessary to record the lease for 2004 and the payment made in 2005.

P6-13 (Journal entries for several funds)

The following transactions took place during 2005:

1. The city sold some of its street repair equipment. The equipment originally cost $50,000, but it was sold for $500.

2. A $2 million bond issue was sold at par. The bonds were general obligation debt issued to finance the cost of an addition to the local court system building.

3. Nondedicated property taxes totaling $100,000 were collected.

4. Construction of a bridge across the Mississippi River was completed at a total cost of $8 million. The bridge had been under construction since 2003. Costs incurred in previous years totaled $7 million. With respect to the Capital Projects Fund, prepare only the closing entry for the expenditure. The cost of construction was entirely financed by a federal grant.

5. A Debt Service Fund paid the interest on outstanding debt, $800,000.

6. A Debt Service Fund retired bonds with a face value of $3 million.

7. The General Fund made its annual payment of $6 million to a Debt Service Fund. Of this amount, $4 million was for retirement of principal.

8. Old office equipment in the mayor's office was discarded. The original cost of the equipment was $900.

9. A contract was signed with Legal, Inc., to construct an addition to the court building. The amount of the contract was $5 million.

10. The construction costs paid during the year on the court addition were $500,000. With respect to the Capital Projects Fund, record only the closing entry for the expenditure. Bonds were used to finance the project.
11. The fire department acquired a new fire engine. The vehicle was ordered earlier in the year. The order was encumbered for $140,000. The actual cost was $138,000.

Required: Record these transactions in journal form. Also indicate the fund in which each transaction is recorded.

P6-14 (Leased assets)
The police department of Titusville signed a noncancelable lease for computer equipment. The lease was for 5 years, the economic life of the property. The fair market value of the equipment (and present value of the minimum rentals) is $18,954. The city's incremental borrowing rate is 10 percent. The annual rentals are $5,000 and are due on the first day of the year, beginning January 1, 2004.

Required: Assuming the equipment is delivered when the lease is signed, prepare all journal entries necessary to record the lease for 2004 and the payment made in 2005.

P6-15 (Journal entries and correcting entries for several funds)
The Proteus City Levee Board recently hired an inexperienced bookkeeper. Accounting records prior to January 1, 2004, were maintained by the same individual who designed the accounting system and were audited each year. On January 2, 2005, the bookkeeper accepted a job in another state and a new bookkeeper was hired. Following is a selection of transactions that occurred during 2004 and a description of how each transaction was recorded.

1. The levee board adopted a budget for the General Fund for 2004 that included estimated revenues of $900,000, estimated other financing sources of $200,000, appropriations of $800,000, and estimated other financing uses of $150,000. The budget was not recorded in the books.
2. The levee board purchased a fire truck in February. The bookkeeper made the following entry in the General Fund:

Fire truck	125,000	
Vouchers payable		125,000

Payment of the voucher was not recorded.

3. A property tax levy was made in March. The total levy was $500,000. Approximately 3 percent was expected to be uncollectible. By the end of the year $390,000 had been collected and the remainder was delinquent. The only entries made during the year were for the collections as a debit to Cash and credit to Revenues—property taxes.
4. Bonds were retired in June. The township accumulated $505,000 in a Debt Service Fund by the end of 2003. Part of these resources ($500,000) were

used to retire the bonds. The remainder were available to be used by the township in any way it desired. The only entries recorded during the year were as follows (these entries were recorded in the General Fund, using Debt Service Fund resources):

Bonds payable	500,000	
Vouchers payable		500,000
Vouchers payable	500,000	
Cash		500,000

5. Some surplus equipment was sold in September for $20,000 (with no restrictions on the use of these resources). The equipment was originally purchased for $245,000 several years ago. The following entry was made in the General Fund:

Cash	20,000	
Loss on sale of equipment	225,000	
Equipment		245,000

6. The General Fund made its annual contribution to a Debt Service Fund. These resources will be used to pay interest. The only entry made was in the General Fund:

Bonds payable	100,000	
Cash		100,000

7. The interest paid during 2004 on the debt mentioned in part (6) was recorded in the General Fund as follows:

Interest expense	100,000	
Cash		100,000

Required: Record the adjusting or correcting entries required by these events. Also identify the fund(s) involved. Closing entries are not required. If no entry is required, write "None" next to the description number on your paper. The books for the current year, 2004, have not been closed.

CONTINUOUS PROBLEM

Bacchus City included in its capital budget a new courthouse. The city issued $25 million of 10 percent bonds on March 1, 2004. These bonds pay interest semi-annually on September 1 and March 1. The bonds were sold for $26 million. In addition, the city negotiated with the federal government for a $50 million construction grant. The bonds are to be serviced from an annual $1 million transfer from the General Fund and a 3 percent hotel-motel tax. The following is a listing of the events that took place during 2004.

1. The budget was recorded in the Capital Projects Fund and the Debt Service Fund as follows:

Capital Projects Fund
Estimated revenues—federal construction grant $25,000,000
Estimated other financing sources—bond issue 25,000,000
Other revenues—investment revenues 3,000,000
Appropriations—construction costs 50,000,000
Debt Service Fund
Estimated revenues—hotel-motel tax 2,000,000
Estimated other financing sources—transfer from
General Fund 900,000
Appropriations—bond servicing 1,250,000

2. The bonds were issued (sold) for $26 million. The entire proceeds were recorded in the Capital Projects Fund and the premium was transferred to the Debt Service Fund immediately.
3. Bacchus City received $25 million from the federal government as a construction grant.
4. $20 million was invested in interest-bearing securities.
5. A contract was signed with Thomas Brothers for the construction of the courthouse totaling $50 million.
6. The General Fund transferred $900,000 to the fund that will service the bonds.
7. The fund that will service the bonds collected $1,300,000 of hotel-motel taxes.
8. Thomas Brothers submitted a bill to Bacchus City for work done to date. The total amount of the bill was $3 million. The construction contract provided for a 5 percent retained percentage.
9. Investments in the Capital Projects Fund matured. The principal was $5 million. In addition, $250,000 of interest income was collected.
10. The progress billing in part (8) was paid.
11. An additional $750,000 of hotel-motel taxes were collected.
12. Interest on the construction debt was paid; $1,250,000 was paid to the fiscal agent who would distribute the money to the bondholders.
13. The fiscal agent reported that $1,200,000 of interest had been paid.
14. Thomas Brothers submitted another progress billing. The amount of the bill was $5 million.
15. The remainder of the September 1 interest was reported as paid by the fiscal agent.
16. Interest was accrued on the investments in the Capital Projects Fund in the amount of $580,000.
17. Based on the provisions of the federal grant, one-half of the construction expenditures incurred each year could be charged against the grant.

Required: 1. Prepare the journal entries necessary to record the preceding transactions and identify the fund(s) used.
2. Prepare a trial balance at December 31, 2004, for the Capital Projects Fund and the Debt Service Fund, before closing.
3. Prepare any necessary closing entries for the Capital Projects Fund and the Debt Service Fund.
4. Prepare a statement of revenues, expenditures, and changes in fund balance for the Capital Projects Fund and the Debt Service Fund for 2004.
5. Prepare a balance sheet as of December 31, 2004, for the Capital Projects Fund and the Debt Service Fund.

Chapter 7

The Governmental Fund Accounting Cycle
Proprietary-Type Funds

After completing this chapter, you should be able to:

➤ *Explain why and how Internal Service Funds are used in governmental accounting.*

➤ *Prepare the journal entries normally used in Internal Service Funds.*

➤ *Prepare fund financial statements for Internal Service Funds.*

➤ *Explain why and how Enterprise Funds are used in governmental accounting.*

➤ *Prepare the journal entries normally used in Enterprise Funds.*

➤ *Prepare fund financial statements for Enterprise Funds.*

*T*his chapter contains a discussion of fund-level financial accounting and reporting for proprietary funds: Internal Service Funds and Enterprise Funds. Entity-wide financial reporting of these funds is discussed in Chapters 9 and 10.

INTERNAL SERVICE FUNDS

Definition of Fund

Governmental units often find that certain goods or services can be supplied by departments or agencies to other departments or agencies at a lower cost than if the same functions were to be provided by outside organizations. It is also possible that an internal department or agency can supply these goods or services more conveniently or dependably than private contractors. To take advantage of these types of benefits, governmental units establish *Internal Service Funds* to account for business-type activities of supplying goods or services to departments or agencies, or to other governments on a cost-reimbursed basis. The key element is that the governmental unit is the predominant participant. Otherwise, such activities should be reported as an Enterprise Fund.[1]

Internal Service Funds are usually established to account for activities such as central data-processing services, motor pools, and inventory and supply functions.

---

[1]   GASB Cod. Sec. 1300.110.

The result is that a government establishes a business-type operation. The accounting and management procedures followed should be similar to those followed by business organizations outside the governmental unit. The amount of the charges for the goods or service generally should be at least enough to recover the costs incurred. Some Internal Service Funds price goods and services somewhat more than cost so that equipment can be replaced at higher prices to cover anticipated inflation. Therefore, it is necessary to measure the full cost of the goods or services. Because the purpose of this type of fund is to provide information for a businesslike evaluation of its operations, it is essential that each activity be accounted for by a separate fund.

In some governmental units the goods and services provided by Internal Service Funds and Enterprise Funds are deliberately underpriced and subsidized by General Fund revenues. By computing the activity's full cost of operations, and comparing these costs with the revenues earned, the extent of the subsidy needed can easily be determined.

Summary of Fund Activities

As previously mentioned, many different types of activities require the use of an Internal Service Fund. In this chapter we limit our discussion to a central motor pool. The operations of this type of service are typical for governmental units and are illustrative of the general operations of Internal Service Funds.

The first step is to acquire capital from the General Fund or some other fund. This money is used to acquire automobiles, trucks, and so forth. As the vehicles are being used, each department is billed based on the miles driven. Revenue from the billings is used to pay the operating costs of the vehicles and, possibly, for their replacement.

Control of Fund Activities

The operations of Internal Service Funds are controlled indirectly by the operating budgets of the funds using the goods or services and directly by means of flexible budgets. Because other funds must pay for the goods or services supplied, the approval of their budgets acts as an indirect control device for Internal Service Funds.

A *flexible budget* is a budget in which most of the budgeted expenses are related to the level of operations. Thus, in our example of a central motor pool, the allowable gasoline and oil costs will vary directly with the number of miles the vehicles are used. Governmental-type funds, by contrast, operate under a *fixed budget*. Thus, if a department head is given $4,000 for supplies for the year, that amount cannot be exceeded—regardless of the level of operations. In effect, the use of a fixed budget actually sets a limit on the level of operations of governmental-type funds.

The difference in budgeting practices between governmental-type funds and Internal Service Funds results because the revenue generated by the latter increases as the level of operations increases. Because of a general cause-and-effect relationship between the level of operations and revenues earned and expenses incurred, a flexible budget allows higher levels of expenses at higher levels of operating activity. As previously explained, no such relationship usually exists between revenues and expenditures of governmental-type funds. For example, a police department usually must request an additional budget allocation if it uses all of its appropriation; such an allocation does not result automatically.

When flexible operating budgets are used, we do not find the budget recorded in the accounts of Internal Service Funds, nor do we usually find the use of encumbrance accounting for these funds. Without an absolute spending limit, the use of encumbrance accounting serves no purpose. A few state or local governments are subject to laws that require the use of encumbrances for Internal Service Funds, but for our purposes here we will assume that encumbrance accounting is not used.

The operations of an Internal Service Fund are similar to those of a private business. The users of goods or services are charged a fee based on what is provided. Therefore, it is necessary to measure the full costs incurred in providing goods or services, which results in an economic resources measurement focus and the use of a full accrual basis of accounting.

Based on an *economic resources measurement focus,* all of the costs incurred in providing the goods or services are recorded. These costs include depreciation on fixed assets, an item not found in the governmental-type funds because they use a current financial resources measurement focus and a modified accrual basis of accounting. In addition, fixed assets are included on the balance sheet of an Internal Service Fund. Use of the *full accrual basis of accounting* for Internal Service Funds means revenues are reported when they are earned and expenses are reported when they are incurred in earning the revenues. Following the economic resources measurement focus, together with the full accrual basis of accounting, makes accounting and reporting for Internal Service Funds similar to the process used for commercial enterprises.

GASB *Statement No. 20,* "Accounting and Financial Reporting for Proprietary Funds and Other Governmental Entities That Use Proprietary Fund Accounting," defines the applicability of business-type pronouncements for governmental entities. In general, these funds must follow applicable FASB Statements and Interpretations, APB Opinions, and Committee on Accounting Procedure (CAP) Accounting Research Bulletins issued on or before November 30, 1989, unless they conflict with a GASB pronouncement. These funds *may* follow all FASB Statements and Interpretations issued after November 30, 1989, that do not conflict with a GASB pronouncement.[2]

Accounting for Fund Activities

Operating Entries

For illustrative purposes, let us continue with the example of a central motor pool. Assume that to start up the fund, the General Fund makes a transfer of $500,000 to the Motor Pool Fund. The entries to record this transfer are

Entry in the books of the General Fund	Transfer out to Motor Pool Fund	500,000	
	Cash		500,000
	To record transfer to Internal Service Fund for start-up purposes.		

---

[2] GASB Cod. Sec. P80.102.

Entry in the books of the Internal Service Fund	Cash	500,000	
	Transfer in from General Fund—capital contribution		500,000
	To record transfer from General Fund.		

If the Internal Service Fund acquires a fleet of vehicles for $400,000, the following entry is made:

Automobiles	300,000	
Trucks	100,000	
Cash		400,000
To record the acquisition of vehicles.		

Billings of $57,000 to the various departments for use of the vehicles are recorded as follows:

Entry in the books of the Internal Service Fund	Due from departments	57,000	
	Revenues—vehicle charges		57,000
	To record charges to departments for use of vehicles.		

Entry in the books of a governmental-type fund using the vehicles	Expenditures—vehicle usage	8,000	
	Due to Motor Pool Fund		8,000
	To record the use of vehicles during the period.		

Payments of $45,000 from the departments are recorded as follows:

Entry in the books of the Internal Service Fund	Cash	45,000	
	Due from departments		45,000
	To record payments received from departments using vehicles.		

Entry in the books of a governmental-type fund using the vehicles	Due to Motor Pool Fund	8,000	
	Cash		8,000
	To record payment to Motor Pool Fund.		

The preceding illustration shows how billings to the departments and collections are recorded. Notice that for illustrative purposes, the entries regarding the departmental usage are limited to a single department and that the "due to" and "due from" account titles are still used for intergovernmental receivables and payables.

During the year, gasoline, oil, and maintenance expenses totaling $14,000 are incurred, of which $10,000 are paid in cash. These expenses are recorded in the Internal Service Fund as follows:

Gasoline and oil expense	9,500	
Maintenance expense	4,500	
Cash		10,000
Accounts payable		4,000
To record the gasoline and oil and maintenance expense for the period.		

Chapter 7   The Governmental Fund Accounting Cycle

Payment of salaries of $10,000, ignoring withholdings and so forth, is recorded as follows:

Salaries expense	10,000	
Cash		10,000
To record salaries expense.		

If the motor pool rents warehouse space from the government for $2,000 per year, the entry to record the rental will be as follows:

Rent expense	2,000	
Cash		2,000
To record the rent for the year.		

The General Fund will record the receipt of the rent as follows:

Entry in the books of the General Fund

Cash	2,000	
Revenues—rental of warehouse space		2,000
To record the receipt of the rent from the motor pool.		

As previously indicated, depreciation is an expense that is recognized in Internal Service Funds. Assuming the amounts given, the entry to record depreciation for the year is

Depreciation expense—automobiles	20,000	
Depreciation expense—trucks	10,000	
Accumulated depreciation—automobiles		20,000
Accumulated depreciation—trucks		10,000
To record depreciation for the year.		

Although additional entries can be made, the preceding summary journal entries are sufficient to reflect the type of activities engaged in by Internal Service Funds and the recording of the related revenues and expenses.

A trial balance for the Motor Pool Fund at the end of the year is shown in Table 7-1.

Closing Entry

The closing process for Internal Service Funds is similar to the one used for commercial enterprises. Each of the revenue, expense, and other temporary accounts is closed and the change in assets recorded in the Net assets account. The following entry relates to the previous illustration.

Revenues—vehicle charges	57,000	
Transfer in from General Fund—capital contribution	500,000	
Gasoline and oil expense		9,500
Maintenance expense		4,500
Salaries expense		10,000
Rent expense		2,000
Depreciation expense—automobiles		20,000
Depreciation expense—trucks		10,000
Net assets		501,000
To close the revenue, expense, and transfer accounts for the period.		

Table 7-1

Trial Balance—Internal Service Fund

CITY OF ANGUSVILLE
INTERNAL SERVICE FUND
MOTOR POOL FUND
TRIAL BALANCE
DECEMBER 31, 2004

	DEBITS	CREDITS
Cash	$123,000	
Due from departments	12,000	
Automobiles	300,000	
Accumulated depreciation—automobiles		$ 20,000
Trucks	100,000	
Accumulated depreciation—trucks		10,000
Accounts payable		4,000
Transfer-in from General Fund—capital contribution		500,000
Revenues—vehicle charges		57,000
Gasoline and oil expense	9,500	
Maintenance expense	4,500	
Salaries expense	10,000	
Rent expense	2,000	
Depreciation expense—automobiles	20,000	
Depreciation expense—trucks	10,000	
	$591,000	$591,000

Financial Statements Illustration

The individual financial statements for Internal Service Funds are a statement of revenues, expenses, and changes in fund net assets; a statement of net assets; and a statement of cash flows. These statements are illustrated for 2004 in Tables 7-2, 7-3, and 7-4. The overall reporting process is discussed in Chapters 9 and 10.

Governmental units should use a classified balance sheet for their proprietary funds. Using this format, assets and liabilities are grouped into classifications similar to those used on a commercial balance sheet.

The general format for the statement of revenues, expenses, and changes in fund net assets is presented as follows:

Operating revenues (detailed)
  Total operating revenues
Operating expenses (detailed)
  Total operating expenses
    Operating income (loss)

Table 7-2

Statement of Revenues, Expenses, and Changes in Fund Net Assets—Internal Service Fund

CITY OF ANGUSVILLE
INTERNAL SERVICE FUND
MOTOR POOL FUND
STATEMENT OF REVENUES, EXPENSES, AND CHANGES IN FUND NET ASSETS
FOR THE YEAR ENDED DECEMBER 31, 2004

Operating revenues:		
Vehicle charges		$ 57,000
Operating expenses:		
Gas and oil expense	$ 9,500	
Maintenance expense	4,500	
Salaries expense	10,000	
Rent expense	2,000	
Depreciation expense—automobiles	20,000	
Depreciation expense—trucks	10,000	
Total operating expenses		56,000
Operating income		1,000
Capital contribution from General Fund		500,000
Change in net assets		501,000
Net assets at beginning of year		-0-
Net assets at end of year		$501,000

Nonoperating revenues and expenses (detailed)
    Income before other revenues, expenses, gains, losses, and transfers
Capital contributions and transfers (detailed)
    Increase (decrease) in net assets
Net assets—beginning of period
Net assets—end of period[3]

On a statement of net assets, GASB requires that the net assets section be reported in three components: (1) net assets invested in capital assets, net of related debt; (2) restricted net assets; and (3) unrestricted net assets. The simplest way to comply with these requirements is to close all nominal accounts to a Net assets account and then analyze that account to determine its components for financial reporting purposes. Notice that in the statement of net assets for the Motor Pool Fund (Table 7-3), only components (1) and (3) are reported, because the fund has no restricted net assets. Restricted assets result from contractual and other restrictions

---

[3] GASB Cod. Sec. 2200.167.

Table 7-3

Statement of Net Assets—Internal Service Fund

CITY OF ANGUSVILLE
INTERNAL SERVICE FUND
MOTOR POOL FUND
STATEMENT OF NET ASSETS
DECEMBER 31, 2004

Assets		
Current assets:		
Cash	$123,000	
Due from departments	12,000	
Total current assets		$135,000
Noncurrent assets:		
Automobiles (net of accumulated depreciation of $20,000)	280,000	
Trucks (net of accumulated depreciation of $10,000)	90,000	
Total noncurrent assets		370,000
Total assets		$505,000
Liabilities		
Current liabilities:		
Accounts payable		4,000
Net Assets		
Invested in capital assets, net of related debt	370,000	
Unrestricted net assets	131,000	
Total net assets		$501,000

placed on the use of the assets by outside parties or by law. Restricted assets are discussed in greater detail in the next section of this chapter.

For the Motor Pool Fund, the net assets invested in capital assets, net of related debt, is equal to $370,000 − $0, or $370,000. Nothing is deducted from the net capital (noncurrent) assets because they have no related debt. The remainder of the net assets $131,000 ($501,000 − $370,000) is reported as unrestricted.

The combined totals for all internal service funds should be reported in a separate column on the face of the Proprietary Fund financial statements to the right of the total Enterprise Funds column.[4] This aggregate information is supported by a combining statement for Internal Service Funds in the annual report.

A discussion of the cash flow statement is beyond the scope of this text. It is, however, presented to complete the financial disclosure for proprietary-type funds. More information is provided about this statement in the next section of this chapter.

---

[4] GASB Cod. Sec. 2200.162.

Table 7-4

Statement of Cash Flows—Internal Service Fund

CITY OF ANGUSVILLE
INTERNAL SERVICE FUND
MOTOR POOL FUND
STATEMENT OF CASH FLOWS
FOR THE YEAR ENDED DECEMBER 31, 2004

Cash Flows from Operating Activities

Receipts from customers	$ 45,000	
Payments to suppliers	(10,000)	
Payments to employees	(10,000)	
Payments for rent	(2,000)	
Cash flows from operations		$ 23,000

Cash Flows from Capital and Related Financing Activities

Purchase of capital assets	$(400,000)	
Capital contributed by municipality	500,000	
Cash flows from capital and related financing activities		100,000
Net increase in cash		123,000
Cash balance at beginning of year		-0-
Cash balance at end of year		$123,000

Reconciliation of operating income to net cash provided by operating activities:

Operating income	$ 1,000	
Adjustments to reconcile operating income to net cash provided by operating activities:		
Depreciation expense	30,000	
Changes in assets and liabilities:		
Due from departments	(12,000)	
Accounts payable	4,000	
Net cash provided by operations		$ 23,000

GOVERNMENTAL ACCOUNTING IN PRACTICE
The City of Columbus, Ohio

The City of Columbus, Ohio, uses Internal Service Funds to account for employee benefits, a central purchasing function, telecommunications, land acquisition, information services, and fleet management. For illustrative purposes, we will use the land acquisition fund. The financial statements for this fund are presented in Tables 7-5, 7-6, and 7-7. Notice that the statement of net assets contains only two subdivisions of net assets like our example.

Table 7-5

Statement of Revenues, Expenses, and Changes in Fund Net Assets—Internal Service Fund—City of Columbus, Ohio

CITY OF COLUMBUS, OHIO
INTERNAL SERVICE FUND
LAND ACQUISITION FUND
STATEMENT OF REVENUES, EXPENSES, AND CHANGES IN FUND NET ASSETS
FOR THE YEAR ENDED DECEMBER 31, 20X4
(AMOUNTS IN THOUSANDS)

Operating revenues:		
Charges for services		$477
Operating expenses:		
Personal services	$486	
Materials and supplies	6	
Contractual services	32	
Depreciation	16	
Total operating expenses		540
Operating loss (change in net assets)		$ (63)
Net assets at beginning of year		439
Net assets at end of year		$376

Source: Adapted from a recent annual report of the City of Columbus, Ohio.

ENTERPRISE FUNDS

Definition of Fund

An *Enterprise Fund* is used when a governmental unit provides goods or services to consumers who are not part of the governmental unit. Although it is possible that other governmental departments, agencies, or other units will use these goods or services, the factor that separates use of Enterprise Funds from use of Internal Service Funds is the presence of consumers outside the governmental unit.

According to GASB, Enterprise Funds may be used to report any activity for which a fee is charged to external users for goods or services. Activities are required to be reported as Enterprise Funds if any one of the following criteria is met. Governments should apply each of these criteria in the context of the activity's principal revenue sources.

a. The activity is financed with debt that is secured solely by a pledge of the net revenues from fees and charges of the activity. Debt that is secured by a pledge of net revenues from fees and charges *and* the full faith and credit of a related primary government or component unit—even if that government is not expected to make any payments—is not payable solely from fees and charges of the activity.

Table 7-6

Statement of Net Assets—Internal Service Fund—City of Columbus, Ohio

CITY OF COLUMBUS, OHIO INTERNAL SERVICE FUND LAND ACQUISITION FUND STATEMENT OF NET ASSETS DECEMBER 31, 20X4 (AMOUNTS IN THOUSANDS)		
Assets		
Current assets:		
Cash and investments with treasurer	$361	
Due from other funds	31	
Total current assets		$392
Noncurrent assets:		
Capital assets:		
Property, plant, and equipment, at cost	96	
Less accumulated depreciation	(82)	
Net property, plant, and equipment		14
Total assets		$406
Liabilities		
Current liabilities:		
Accounts payable	5	
Accrued wages and benefits	18	
Accrued vacation and sick leave	7	
Total current liabilities		30
Net Assets		
Invested in capital assets, net of related debt		14
Unrestricted		362
Total net assets		$376

Source: Adapted from a recent annual report of the City of Columbus, Ohio.

b. Laws or regulations require that the activity's costs of providing services including capital costs (such as depreciation or debt service) be recovered with fees and charges, rather than with taxes or similar revenues.

c. The pricing policies of the activity establish fees and charges designed to recover its costs, including capital costs (such as depreciation or debt service).[5]

When applying these criteria, a governmental unit is not required to use an Enterprise Fund if an insignificant activity (activities) is (are) funded by user charges.

---

[5] GASB Cod. Sec. 1300.109.

Table 7-7

Statement of Cash Flows—Internal Service Fund—City of Columbus, Ohio

CITY OF COLUMBUS, OHIO	
INTERNAL SERVICE FUND	
LAND ACQUISITION FUND	
STATEMENT OF CASH FLOWS	
DECEMBER 31, 20X4	
(AMOUNTS IN THOUSANDS)	

Operating Activities	
Quasi-external operating receipts	$488
Cash paid to employees	(500)
Cash paid to suppliers	(35)
Net cash used by operating activities	(47)
Decrease in cash and cash equivalents	(47)
Cash and cash equivalents at beginning of year	408
Cash and cash equivalents at end of year	$361
Reconciliation of operating loss to net cash used by operating activities	
Operating loss	$ (63)
Depreciation	16
Decrease (increase) in operating assets and increase (decrease) in operating liabilities:	
Due from other governments	17
Due from other funds	(7)
Accounts payable—net of items affecting property, plant, and equipment	3
Accrued wages and benefits	(15)
Accrued vacation and sick leave	2
Net cash used by operating activities	$ (47)

Source: Adapted from a recent annual report of the City of Columbus, Ohio.

The types of operations that normally require use of an Enterprise Fund(s) are those that perform services, such as those rendered by public utilities. However, Enterprise Funds are also used for the operations of ports, airports, public swimming pools, golf courses, and so forth.

As previously mentioned, goods and services provided by an Enterprise Fund are sometimes subsidized by the General Fund. By computing the activity's full cost of operations, and comparing these costs with the revenues earned, the extent of the subsidy needed can easily be determined.

Summary of Fund Activities

The operating cycle of an Enterprise Fund is similar to that of a business organization: Goods or services are provided to consumers, who must pay for them. During the operating period, the fund acquires assets such as supplies, property, and equipment. The cost of using these assets is recorded along with other operating expenses. Revenues from user charges must also be recorded. Thus we have the same cause-and-effect relationship that exists in a business organization: Expenses are incurred in order to earn revenues.

Control of Fund Activities

The operations of an Enterprise Fund are controlled by many different means. Because the functions of this type of activity are to supply goods or services to a general market, the consumer exercises some control. Whether a consumer decides to purchase a particular good or service is true "marketplace control." However, because many Enterprise Funds are public utilities, they possess *monopoly operating rights*. In many cases, therefore, no competitive goods or services are available. Control must be achieved through governing boards that determine the rates the utility can charge. These boards use outside consultants and operating data extensively to determine reasonable service charges. In these cases, accounting data are invaluable for measuring the results of operations.

Flexible budgets are used for the measurement and control of operations in Enterprise Funds in the same manner as in Internal Service Funds. They provide an additional element of control. The use of flexible budgets precludes recording the budget in the accounts, so the direct spending control found in the General Fund is not present in Enterprise Funds. In addition, because of the lack of absolute spending control, encumbrance accounting generally is not used for Enterprise Funds.

Still another method of control lies in the budgets of those funds that use the goods or services provided by the fund. Although it is an indirect method of control, it is still effective, especially for those funds that follow a current financial resources measurement focus.

The economic resources measurement focus is used in Enterprise Fund accounting because of the need to determine the full cost of operations. Thus, as with Internal Service Funds, the current financial resources measurement focus is replaced by a much more comprehensive approach. The provisions of GASB *Statement No. 20*, as discussed in the section "Internal Service Funds," also apply to accounting for Enterprise Funds. The economic resources focus is combined with the computation of expenses (including depreciation) and revenues, which are recorded under the accrual basis of accounting. Therefore, revenues are recorded when earned and expenses are recorded when incurred in earning the revenues. Because of the use of these procedures, the financial statements for Enterprise Funds include all the assets used in the operations of the funds: liquid assets (cash, receivables, inventory, and so on) and fixed assets (property, plant, and equipment). In addition, both current and long-term liabilities are carried on the balance sheet.

Accounting for Fund Activities

Operating Entries

For illustrative purposes, assume the City of Angusville owns and operates the French Market Corporation. This governmental unit was established to operate as a local tourist attraction a large open market like those used by the early colonists. Individuals and businesses can rent space in the market to sell anything from fresh fruits and vegetables to clothing and jewelry. A beginning trial balance for the fund is presented in Table 7-8.

The Cash—restricted for debt service account represents the amounts the corporation is required to set aside each year according to a bond indenture. This amount will be held in escrow until the bonds are retired and all interest is paid. Refer to the trial balance in Table 7-8. Notice that the total of the net assets is $1,182,000. This total consists of the following elements:

1. Net assets invested in capital assets (net of related debt) in the amount of $1,010,000. This total includes land ($500,000), equipment ($200,000), and buildings ($1,500,000), less the accumulated depreciation ($90,000 + $600,000), less the related debt of $500,000.
2. Net assets that are restricted in the amount of ($150,000). This total equals the restricted assets ($150,000) less the liabilities payable with restricted assets ($0). Any liabilities in this category would account for the difference between the restricted assets and the liabilities payable from restricted assets, which would be reported as Net assets—restricted.
3. Net assets—unrestricted of $22,000. This total represents the net assets not included in the first two categories.

Notice that we accumulated these amounts in one account: Net assets. At the end of each year all nominal accounts are closed into the Net assets account and

Table 7-8
Trial Balance—Enterprise Fund

CITY OF ANGUSVILLE
ENTERPRISE FUND
FRENCH MARKET CORPORATION FUND
POST CLOSING TRIAL BALANCE
DECEMBER 31, 2003

	DEBITS	CREDITS
Cash	$ 25,000	
Accounts receivable	15,000	
Supplies	2,000	
Cash—restricted for debt service	150,000	
Land	500,000	
Equipment	200,000	
Accumulated depreciation—equipment		$ 90,000
Buildings	1,500,000	
Accumulated depreciation—buildings		600,000
Accounts payable		20,000
Revenue bonds payable		500,000
Net assets		1,182,000
	$2,392,000	$2,392,000

then, for reporting purposes, the total is segregated into the three elements previously described.

If billings to the retailers during 2004 totaled $500,000, and $5,000 of that amount is for space provided to the city, the following entry should be made:

Accounts receivable	495,000	
Due from General Fund	5,000	
Revenue from rentals		500,000
To record rental revenue for the year.		

Collections during the year total $490,000, of which $5,000 is from the General Fund. They are recorded as follows:

Cash	490,000	
Accounts receivable		485,000
Due from General Fund		5,000
To record collections from customers.		

The appropriate entries in the books of the General Fund for these two events are

Entries in the books of the General Fund

Expenditures—rentals	5,000	
Due to French Market Corporation Fund		5,000
To record cost of rentals of 2004.		

Due to French Market Corporation Fund	5,000	
Cash		5,000
To record payment made to French Market Corporation Fund.		

Operating expenses (exclusive of depreciation) total $400,000. Of this amount, $50,000 is paid in cash and the remainder is on credit. The entry to record this information is

Personal services expense	280,000	
Utilities expense	50,000	
Repairs and maintenance expense	40,000	
Other expenses	30,000	
Cash		50,000
Accounts payable		350,000
To record operating expenses for 2004.		

These expenses do not include depreciation. Because we are accumulating the full cost of operating the market, depreciation must be recorded. Assuming the appropriate amounts are as indicated in the entry, the following is recorded:

Depreciation expense—equipment	15,000	
Depreciation expense—buildings	50,000	
Accumulated depreciation—equipment		15,000
Accumulated depreciation—buildings		50,000
To record depreciation for 2004.		

Payments to creditors total $350,000 during the year. These payments are recorded as follows:

Accounts payable	350,000	
Cash		350,000
To record payments on accounts payable.		

The account generally used to record the long-term debt is called Revenue bonds payable. *Revenue bonds* are debt securities that are serviced by the revenues generated by the fund. The entry to record interest of $40,000 for the current year on the long-term debt is

Interest expense	40,000	
Cash		40,000
To record bond interest paid for the year.		

In this illustration, it is assumed the bond interest is all paid in cash; that is, $20,000 is payable on June 30 and December 31 of each year. If the interest is not due at the end of the year, a proportionate amount is still recorded as an expense. When this happens, however, Interest payable (a liability payable with restricted assets) is credited.

Notice the difference in treatment of the accrued interest under the accrual basis of accounting as opposed to that followed by the modified accrual basis of accounting used in the Debt Service Funds. In most governmental-type funds, interest generally is not recorded until it legally matures and becomes payable.

In this illustration, $50,000 of revenue bonds are paid this year and another $50,000 will be paid next year; however, the $50,000 that will become due next year is listed as a current liability (as shown in Table 7-11). The entry in the Enterprise Fund to record the 2004 payment of principal is:

Revenue bonds payable	50,000	
Cash		50,000
To record payment of principal of revenue bonds due in 2004.		

Assume that during the year the French Market management begins a policy of requiring a $50 deposit from each customer. This policy is designed to reduce the losses suffered in prior years due to customers not paying their bills. The offsetting liability is Customers' deposits. If $20,000 is collected, the actual entry appears as follows:

Cash	20,000	
Customers' deposits		20,000
To record amounts received for customers' deposits.		

Also assume that in addition to requiring deposits, management establishes a provision for uncollectible accounts. The proper amount for 2004 is $5,000, which is recorded as follows:

Uncollectible accounts expense	5,000	
Estimated uncollectible accounts		5,000
To record the estimated uncollectible accounts at December 31, 2004.		

The Estimated uncollectible accounts account is reported as a deduction from Accounts receivable on the balance sheet. The Uncollectible accounts expense is reported on the operating statement. Notice the treatment afforded uncollectible accounts expense for proprietary-type funds as opposed to that used for governmental-type funds. Remember that in governmental-type funds, the provision for uncollectible accounts is treated as a direct reduction from revenue rather than as an expenditure.

During the year the fund used $1,000 of supplies. The entry to record this usage is

| Supplies expense | 1,000 | |
| Supplies | | 1,000 |

To record supplies used during 2004.

Although additional entries can be made, these summary journal entries reflect the type of activities and the recording of revenues and expenses normally incurred by Enterprise Funds.

A trial balance for the French Market Corporation Fund at December 31, 2004, is presented in Table 7-9.

Table 7-9
Trial Balance—Enterprise Fund

CITY OF ANGUSVILLE
ENTERPRISE FUND
FRENCH MARKET CORPORATION FUND
PRECLOSING TRIAL BALANCE
DECEMBER 31, 2004

	DEBITS	CREDITS
Cash	$ 45,000	
Accounts receivable	25,000	
Estimated uncollectible accounts		$ 5,000
Supplies	1,000	
Cash—restricted for debt service	150,000	
Land	500,000	
Equipment	200,000	
Accumulated depreciation—equipment		105,000
Buildings	1,500,000	
Accumulated depreciation—buildings		650,000
Accounts payable		20,000
Customers' deposits		20,000
Revenue bonds payable		450,000
Net assets		1,182,000
Revenue from rentals		500,000
Personal services expense	280,000	
Utilities expense	50,000	
Repairs and maintenance expense	40,000	
Other expense	30,000	
Depreciation expense—equipment	15,000	
Depreciation expense—building	50,000	
Interest expense	40,000	
Uncollectible accounts expense	5,000	
Supplies expense	1,000	
	$2,932,000	$2,932,000

Financial Statements Illustration

Individual financial statements for Enterprise Funds are an operating statement, a statement of net assets, and a statement of cash flows. These statements are illustrated for 2004 in Tables 7-10, 7-11, and 7-12. The overall reporting process is discussed in Chapters 9 and 10.

The financial reporting format for the assets and liabilities may be presented in either a typical assets equals liabilities plus net assets format or in a net asset format. The latter is illustrated in Table 7-11. The general format for the statement of revenues, expenses, and changes in fund net assets is presented in the Internal Service Fund section of the chapter.

Refer to the balance sheet in Table 7-11. The total of the net assets is $1,171,000. This total consists of the following elements:

1. Net assets invested in capital assets net of related debt ($995,000). This amount is equal to the sum of the land $500,000 plus the buildings $850,000 ($1,500,000 − $650,000) plus the equipment $95,000 ($200,000 − $105,000) less the debt of $450,000.

Table 7-10

Statement of Revenues, Expenses, and Changes in Fund Net Assets—Enterprise Fund

CITY OF ANGUSVILLE
ENTERPRISE FUND
FRENCH MARKET CORPORATION FUND
STATEMENT OF REVENUES, EXPENSES, AND CHANGES IN FUND NET ASSETS
FOR THE YEAR ENDED DECEMBER 31, 2004

Operating revenues:		
Charges for services		$ 500,000
Operating expenses:		
Personal services expense	$280,000	
Utilities expense	50,000	
Repairs and maintenance expense	40,000	
Depreciation expense	65,000	
Uncollectible accounts expense	5,000	
Supplies expense	1,000	
Other expenses	30,000	
Total operating expenses		471,000
Operating income		29,000
Nonoperating expenses:		
Interest expense		(40,000)
Change in net assets		(11,000)
Total net assets at beginning of year		1,182,000
Total net assets at end of year		$1,171,000

Table 7-11

Statement of Net Assets—Enterprise Fund

<table>
<tr><td colspan="3" align="center">CITY OF ANGUSVILLE
ENTERPRISE FUND
FRENCH MARKET CORPORATION FUND
STATEMENT OF NET ASSETS
DECEMBER 31, 2004</td></tr>
<tr><td colspan="3">Assets</td></tr>
<tr><td colspan="3">Current assets:</td></tr>
<tr><td>Cash</td><td>$ 45,000</td><td></td></tr>
<tr><td>Accounts receivable (net of estimated uncollectible accounts of $5,000)</td><td>20,000</td><td></td></tr>
<tr><td>Supplies</td><td>1,000</td><td></td></tr>
<tr><td>Total current assets</td><td></td><td>$ 66,000</td></tr>
<tr><td>Noncurrent assets:</td><td></td><td></td></tr>
<tr><td>Cash—restricted for debt service</td><td></td><td>150,000</td></tr>
<tr><td>Capital assets:</td><td></td><td></td></tr>
<tr><td>Land</td><td>500,000</td><td></td></tr>
<tr><td>Buildings (net of accumulated depreciation of $650,000)</td><td>850,000</td><td></td></tr>
<tr><td>Equipment (net of accumulated depreciation of $105,000)</td><td>95,000</td><td></td></tr>
<tr><td>Total noncurrent assets</td><td></td><td>1,445,000</td></tr>
<tr><td>Total assets</td><td></td><td>1,661,000</td></tr>
<tr><td colspan="3">Liabilities</td></tr>
<tr><td colspan="3">Current liabilities:</td></tr>
<tr><td>Accounts payable</td><td></td><td>20,000</td></tr>
<tr><td>Customers' deposits</td><td></td><td>20,000</td></tr>
<tr><td>Current portion of revenue bonds payable</td><td></td><td>50,000</td></tr>
<tr><td>Total current liabilities</td><td></td><td>90,000</td></tr>
<tr><td>Noncurrent liabilities:</td><td></td><td></td></tr>
<tr><td>Revenue bonds payable</td><td></td><td>400,000</td></tr>
<tr><td>Total liabilities</td><td></td><td>490,000</td></tr>
<tr><td colspan="3">Net Assets</td></tr>
<tr><td>Invested in capital assets net of related debt</td><td></td><td>995,000</td></tr>
<tr><td>Restricted for debt service</td><td></td><td>150,000</td></tr>
<tr><td>Unrestricted</td><td></td><td>26,000</td></tr>
<tr><td>Total net assets</td><td></td><td>$1,171,000</td></tr>
</table>

Table 7-12

Statement of Cash Flows—Enterprise Fund

CITY OF ANGUSVILLE
ENTERPRISE FUND
FRENCH MARKET CORPORATION FUND
STATEMENT OF CASH FLOWS
FOR THE YEAR ENDED DECEMBER 31, 2004

Cash Flows from Operating Activities		
Receipts from customers	$490,000	
Customers' deposits	20,000	
Payments to suppliers	(120,000)	
Payments to employees	(280,000)	
Cash flows from operations		$110,000
Cash Flows from Capital and Related Financing Activities		
Payments for debt service		(90,000)
Net increase in cash		20,000
Unrestricted cash and restricted cash balance at beginning of year		175,000
Unrestricted cash and restricted cash balance at end of year		$195,000
Reconciliation of operating income to net cash provided by operating activities:		
Operating income	$ 29,000	
Adjustments to reconcile operating income to net cash provided by operating activities:		
Depreciation expense	65,000	
Changes in assets and liabilities:		
Supplies	1,000	
Customers' deposits	20,000	
Accounts receivable (net)	(5,000)	
Net cash provided by operations		$110,000

2. Net assets that are restricted ($150,000). This amount is equal to the restricted assets for the revenue bonds.
3. Net assets—unrestricted ($26,000). This total represents the net assets that have no restrictions on their use, or the net assets not included in previous two categories ($1,171,000 − $995,000 − $150,000).

Closing Entry

The closing process for Enterprise Funds involves transferring the balances of the revenues, expenses, and other temporary accounts to the unrestricted net asset account. The entry, using the data given in the example, is:

Revenues from rentals	500,000	
Net assets	11,000	
Personal services expense		280,000
Utilities expense		50,000
Repairs and maintenance expense		40,000
Other expenses		30,000
Depreciation expense—building		50,000
Depreciation expense—equipment		15,000
Interest expense		40,000
Uncollectible accounts expense		5,000
Supplies expense		1,000
To close the revenue and expense accounts for the period.		

Notice the debit to Net assets, which results from the use of one net assets account in the accounting records. The total in the Net assets account is segregated into its three components for financial reporting purposes as discussed.

GOVERNMENT ACCOUNTING IN PRACTICE
The City of Columbus, Ohio

The City of Columbus, Ohio, uses three Enterprise Funds: Water, Sewer, and Electricity. The use of each fund is explained by their titles. Table 7-13 contains the statement of revenues, expenses, and changes in net assets for the Electricity Fund.

The statement of net assets used by the city is similar to that used by a business organization. Notice that the total of the net assets invested in capital assets, net of related debt, is $6,221 [($1,739 + $71,108) − ($1,830 + $64,796)] The restricted net assets total $6,737 [$7,034 − ($288 + $9)]. Notice also that the City of Columbus specifically identifies the assets and liabilities that are restricted. One account

is used in the text illustrations for simplicity. The traditional way of reporting these items is illustrated in Table 7-14.

The direct format is used for the statement of cash flows by the City of Columbus. As mentioned earlier in our discussion of Internal Service Funds, the direct approach should be used. For reporting purposes, as shown in the statement of cash flows in Table 7-15, cash receipts and disbursements are classified into four categories: operating activities, noncapital financing activities, capital and related financing activities, and investing activities. Notice that Columbus did not have any noncapital financing activities.

USE OF SPECIAL ASSESSMENTS

Special assessments are a means of financing services or capital improvements that benefit one group of citizens more than the general public. Taxpayers who receive the benefits of these activities are assessed for their share of the cost. Examples of special assessment activities include projects such as special police protection, paving streets, and building parking structures.

If a governmental unit wishes to charge a full-cost price for the services to determine the "true" subsidy provided to the citizens, an Enterprise Fund should be used

Table 7-13

Statement of Revenues, Expenses, and Changes in Fund Net Assets—Enterprise Fund—City of Columbus, Ohio

CITY OF COLUMBUS, OHIO
ENTERPRISE FUND
ELECTRICITY FUND
STATEMENT OF REVENUES, EXPENSES, AND CHANGES IN FUND NET ASSETS
FOR THE YEAR ENDED DECEMBER 31, 20X4
(AMOUNTS EXPRESSED IN THOUSANDS)

Operating revenues:		
Charges for services	$51,677	
Other	883	
Total operating revenue		$52,560
Operating expenses:		
Personal services	7,430	
Materials and supplies	200	
Contractual services	5,398	
Purchased power	33,217	
Depreciation	4,412	
Other	101	
Total operating expenses		50,758
Operating income		1,802
Nonoperating revenue (expenses)		
Investment income	421	
Interest expense	(3,138)	
Other, net	(92)	
Total nonoperating expenses		(2,809)
Loss before transfers		(1,007)
Operating transfers in		2,000
Change in net assets		993
Net assets at beginning of year		13,027
Net assets at end of year		$14,020

Source: Adapted from a recent annual report of the City of Columbus, Ohio.

to account for the service. Because the accrual basis of accounting is used, this approach includes a calculation of a charge for depreciation.

Use of an Enterprise Fund for service activities that are financed with special assessments results in entries similar to those previously presented in this chapter. The only major change is that the term *special assessment* is generally used to describe the receivable for the charge. Special assessment-type projects are discussed further in Chapter 8.

Table 7-14
Statement of Net Assets—Enterprise Fund—City of Columbus, Ohio

CITY OF COLUMBUS, OHIO
ENTERPRISE FUND
ELECTRICITY FUND
STATEMENT OF NET ASSETS
DECEMBER 31, 20X4
(AMOUNTS EXPRESSED IN THOUSANDS)

Assets		
Current assets:		
Cash and investments with treasurer	$ 342	
Receivables (net of allowance for uncollectibles)	5,352	
Due from other funds	321	
Inventory	922	
Total current assets		$ 6,937
Noncurrent assets:		
Restricted assets:		
Cash and cash equivalents with treasurer and other		7,034
Capital assets:		
Land and construction in progress	1,739	
Other capital assets, net of accumulated depreciation	71,108	
Net capital assets		72,847
Total assets		$86,818
Liabilities		
Current liabilities:		
Accounts payable	2,752	
Customer deposits	321	
Due to other:		
Governments	334	
Funds	227	
Others	73	
Total current liabilities		3,707
Noncurrent liabilities:		
Payable from restricted assets:		
Accounts payable	288	
Due to others	9	
Deferred revenue and other	664	
Accrued interest payable	658	
Accrued wages and benefits	218	
Accrued vacation and sick leave	628	
Notes payable	1,830	
Bonds and loans payable	64,796	
Total noncurrent liabilities		69,091
Total liabilities		72,798
Net Assets		
Invested in capital assets, net of related debt		6,221
Restricted for construction		6,737
Unrestricted		1,062
Total net assets		$14,020

Source: Adapted from a recent annual report of the City of Columbus, Ohio.

Table 7-15
Statement of Cash Flows—Enterprise Fund—City of Columbus, Ohio

CITY OF COLUMBUS, OHIO
ENTERPRISE FUND
ELECTRICITY FUND
STATEMENT OF CASH FLOWS
DECEMBER 31, 20X4
(AMOUNTS EXPRESSED IN THOUSANDS)

Operating activities:		
Cash received from customers	$52,084	
Cash paid to employees	(7,563)	
Cash paid to suppliers	(37,813)	
Other receipts	842	
Other payments	(317)	
Net cash provided by operating activities		$ 7,233
Capital and related financing activities:		
Proceeds from sale of land	42	
Purchases of property, plant, and equipment	(5,114)	
Proceeds from issuance of bonds, loans, and notes	36,624	
Principal payments on bonds and loans	(52,799)	
Interest paid on bonds, loans, and notes	(1,900)	
Operating transfers in	2,000	
Net cash used in capital and related financing activities		(21,147)
Investing activities:		
Proceeds from maturity of investment securities	4,509	
Interest received on investments	827	
Net cash provided by investing activities		5,336
Decrease in cash and cash equivalents		(8,578)
Cash and cash equivalents at beginning of year (including restricted accounts)		15,954
Cash and cash equivalents at end of year (including restricted accounts)		$ 7,376
Reconciliation of operating income to net cash provided by operations:		
Operating income		$ 1,802
Adjustments to reconcile operating income to net cash provided by operating activities:		
Depreciation		4,412
Amortization, net		(109)
		(continued)

Table 7-15

Continued

Decrease (increase) in operating assets and increase (decrease) in operating liabilities:	
Receivables	365
Due from other governments	148
Due from other funds	3
Inventory	(7)
Accounts payable—net of items affecting property, plant, and equipment	889
Customer deposits	(3)
Due to other funds	51
Deferred revenue	(185)
Accrued wages and benefits	(121)
Accrued vacation and sick leave	(12)
Net cash provided by operating activities	$ 7,233
Supplemental information:	
Change in fair value of investments	$ 36

Source: Adapted from a recent annual report of the City of Columbus, Ohio.

REVIEW QUESTIONS

Q7-1   What is the cause-and-effect relationship between the revenues and expenses of a proprietary fund?

Q7-2   Why are the revenues and expenditures of governmental-type funds "independent" of each other?

Q7-3   When should an Internal Service Fund be used?

Q7-4   What is a flexible budget?

Q7-5   How does the fund balance (net assets) section of a balance sheet of an Internal Service Fund differ from that of a governmental-type fund?

Q7-6   Why is depreciation recorded as an expense in Internal Service Funds, but not as an expenditure in governmental-type funds?

Q7-7   What is the difference between an Enterprise Fund and an Internal Service Fund?

Q7-8   Is there a cause-and-effect relationship between the revenues and expenses of an Enterprise Fund? Explain your answer.

Q7-9   Why is depreciation considered to be an expense for Enterprise Funds?

Q7-10 What are revenue bonds?

CASES

C7-1   The City of Iota recently incorporated and, therefore, became a separate legal entity in Bower County. As the first chief administrative officer, your task is to determine how to account for the various activities in which the government is involved.

  The first activity is a hotel-motel tax that is dedicated to providing resources for building a new sports arena. The mayor, Phinius T. Bower, feels that these activities should be accounted for in a Capital Projects Fund. He said that he remembered from his college days at Old War-Horse U. that Capital Projects Funds are used for construction of major fixed assets. After examining the situation, you find that the city has arranged temporary financing from the Only National Bank in Cut-Off. Permanent financing will be achieved through a bond issue when the project is completed.

  The second activity is a printing office. This office has extensive up-to-date facilities and prepares documents for the city. In addition, to help finance the cost of the equipment and operating costs, the city also does private printing and copying for various companies and citizens. Mayor Bower suggests that you use a Special Revenue Fund for these activities because the revenues from the outside will be used for a specific purpose.

  The third is a central purchasing function. In order to ensure that the city obtains the best possible price for its supplies and equipment, all purchases must be made through the Purchasing Department. Mayor Bower also stated that he felt the city could use its Purchasing Department for control purposes. He said that when he attended a meeting of mayors in Gulfberg last year, one of the speakers discussed controlling purchases through a centralized purchasing function.

  Write a report to the mayor that offers your suggestions for these items.

C7-2   You recently were asked by your alma mater to make a presentation to an accounting class. After a lengthy thought process, you decide to discuss governmental financial reporting. Carefully review the financial statements for the Internal Service Funds (Tables 7-5 through 7-7), and contrast them with the statements prepared for the Capital Projects Funds (Tables 6-9 and 6-10). Identify similarities and differences. Write a paper to present to the students.

C7-3   Mary Ann LaPlace, the president of the city council of West Sunview, asked you to assist the council in setting the pricing policy for its only Internal Service Fund. The fund is the Motor Pool Fund, and its operations are similar to those described in the illustration in this chapter.

  Write a report to President LaPlace and outline the options the city has with respect to pricing the use of the vehicles in the Motor Pool Fund. After you complete your report, write a recommendation for one of your choices and justify it.

EC7-1 Iber Township is in need of resources to finance its operations for the remainder of 2004. Poor internal control procedures under the previous administration created a serious funding problem for the new administration. Walter Buckhouse, the new mayor, feels that if he can get through the current year, he can develop a new budget and control future expenditures to create a surplus. After reviewing the township's financial statements, Buckhouse feels that the only possible source of money is borrowing from restricted assets in an Enterprise Fund. As the chief financial officer, you listen as Buckhouse discusses his plan with you. His main argument is his certainty that future surpluses from the township's operating budget will allow him to replace the borrowed funds in 3 to 5 years. How would you respond to the mayor?

EXERCISES

E7-1 (Interpreting the operating statement for an Internal Service Fund)
Angusville maintains a policy that its Internal Service Funds operate on a break-even basis, that is, revenues must equal expenses. Did the Motor Pool Fund illustrated in this chapter operate at a break-even level during 2004? Explain.

E7-2 (Journal entries for an Internal Service Fund)
The following transactions were incurred in establishing a central purchasing fund (an Internal Service Fund):
1. The General Fund made a permanent transfer of $100,000 to establish the fund.
2. The Purchasing Fund billed revenues of $200,000.
3. The Purchasing Fund incurred expenses of $300,000. *Hint:* Credit Cash for $250,000 and Accumulated depreciation for $50,000.
4. The General Fund subsidized the operations of the Purchasing Fund by transferring an additional $100,000 to the fund.

Required: Record the preceding entries and identify the fund(s) used.

E7-3 (Relationship of a fixed asset to depreciation)
Considering that the Motor Pool Fund illustrated in this chapter records the acquisition of an automobile by debiting an asset account, does the cost of that automobile ever enter into the determination of income? Explain.

E7-4 (Fill in the blanks)
1. An Internal Service Fund is used when goods and/or services are furnished to _____ .

2. A budget that is based on the level of activity attained in a fund is called a _____ .
3. The _____ basis of accounting is used in Internal Service Funds.
4. A permanent transfer of equity to an Internal Service Fund is credited to _____ in the Internal Service Fund.
5. When an Internal Service Fund acquires a truck, the account that is debited is _____ .

E7-5 (True or false)
Indicate whether the following statements are true or false. For any false statements, indicate why it is false.
1. A direct cause-and-effect relationship exists between the revenues and expenses of an Internal Service Fund.
2. Internal Service Funds are used to account for activities that involve providing services and/or products to the general public.
3. Internal Service Funds use the modified accrual basis of accounting.
4. All capital contributions received by an Internal Service Fund are credited directly to the Net assets account.
5. A fixed budget is used to control an Internal Service Fund.
6. The budget is not usually recorded for an Internal Service Fund.
7. Fixed assets used in an Internal Service Fund are not reported in the fund-level statements.
8. Depreciation expense is not recorded in an Internal Service Fund that uses fixed assets.
9. A net change in fund balance is calculated for Internal Service Funds.
10. Internal Service funds do not have restricted net assets accounts.

E7-6 (True or false)
Indicate whether the following statements are true or false. For any false statements, indicate why it is false.
1. Enterprise Funds are not used to account for the construction of major highways.
2. User charges must be assessed if an Enterprise Fund is to be used for accounting purposes.
3. Flexible budgets are used to control Enterprise Fund operations.
4. Depreciation is recorded in an Enterprise Fund.
5. Estimated bad debts are charged to an expense account in an Enterprise Fund.
6. Restricted assets are separately reported on an Enterprise Fund balance sheet.

E7-7 (Billings and collections between an Enterprise Fund and the General Fund)
A city used an Enterprise Fund to provide services to the General Fund and its citizens. A total of $50,000 was billed to the General Fund and collected 30 days later. Prepare the journal entries necessary to record this information and label the fund(s) used.

E7-8   (Closing entries for an Enterprise Fund)
The Municipal Park Fund for Valley View Township had the following pre-closing trial balance:

Valley View Township
Enterprise Fund
Municipal Park Fund
Preclosing Trial Balance
June 30, 2004

	Debits	Credits
Cash	$ 1,500	
Membership dues receivable	1,200	
Land	7,600	
Equipment	2,000	
Accumulated depreciation—equipment		$ 400
Accounts payable		200
Revenues from fees		5,000
Salaries expense	3,000	
Depreciation expense—equipment	300	
Utilities expense	400	
Miscellaneous expense	400	
Net assets invested in capital assets, net of related debt		9,200
Net assets unrestricted		1,600
	$16,400	$16,400

Required: 1. Prepare the closing entry or entries necessary at June 30, 2004.
2. Did the fund earn a profit during FY 2003–2004? How can you tell?

E7-9   (Fill in the blanks)
1. A _____ is used to account for goods and/or services provided only to other governmental units.
2. The activities of a government-owned utility usually are accounted for in a(n) _____ .
3. Enterprise Fund accounting follows a(n) _____ measurement focus.
4. Bonds that are serviced from specific revenues are called _____ .
5. Customers' deposits may be classified as _____ .

E7-10 (Comparison of accounting for long-term debt and acquisition of fixed assets, using governmental-type funds and proprietary-type funds)

The Village of d'East acquired a computer for $300,000. The computer was financed through a bond issue. Prepare the journal entries necessary to record these events assuming the computer was acquired using (1) the General Fund and (2) an Enterprise Fund. Also label the fund(s) used.

PROBLEMS

P7-1 (Journal entries and financial statements for an Internal Service Fund)
The following entries and financial statements relate to Thomasville. (Assume a voucher system is used.)

1. The General Fund made a transfer of capital to the Data Processing Fund (an Internal Service Fund). This fund will provide data-processing services to all governmental units for a fee. The initial transfer was $2 million.
2. The fund paid $1.9 million for a Tops computer.
3. Supplies costing $1,500 were purchased on credit.
4. Bills totaling $650,000 were sent to the various city departments.
5. Repairs to the computer were made at a cost of $400. A voucher was prepared for that amount.
6. Collections from the departments for services were $629,000.
7. Salaries of $180,000 were paid to the employees.
8. Vouchers totaling $1,900 were paid.
9. As of the end of the period, $300 of supplies had not been used.
10. Depreciation on the computer was $250,000.
11. The city charged the computer center $2,000 for the rental of office space and $500 for the rental of office equipment for the year. This amount was not paid at the end of the year.
12. Miscellaneous expenses not paid by the end of the year totaled $700. These amounts were owed to businesses outside the governmental unit.

Required: 1. Prepare the journal entries necessary to record the preceding information in the Data Processing Fund.
2. Prepare a statement of revenues, expenses, and changes in net assets for the Data Processing Fund for 2004 and a statement of net assets as of December 31, 2004.

P7-2 (Journal entries for several funds)
The following transactions were incurred by the City of Mountain View. Record the journal entry (entries) necessary for each and identify the fund(s) used. If no entry is required, write "None" next to the transaction number.

1. The mayor hired a new chief financial officer for the city.
2. The police department ordered 10 new cruisers at a cost of $14,000 each.
3. The Central Computer Fund billed the General Fund for $2,000 of services.
4. The Central Computer Fund acquired a new computer at a cost of $450,000. The old computer was sold for $50,000; it originally cost $245,000 and had a book value of $45,000 at the time of the sale.
5. The fund used to account for the construction of a new bridge over the Miss River received a progress billing from the contractor for $500,000. The bill, less an 8 percent retainage, was paid.
6. Interest of $100,000 and principal of $1,000,000 were paid on general obligation bonds. The bond indenture required a separate accounting for these types of transactions.

7. The police cruisers ordered in part (2) arrived. The total invoice cost was $139,000. This amount was paid to the dealer.
8. The city collected $200,000 of gasoline taxes. These taxes must be used to repair city streets. A separate accounting is required.
9. The mayor was paid a salary of $5,000.
10. The General Fund budget was amended. The appropriation for supplies was increased $45,000.

P7-3 (Journal entries for several funds and statements for an Internal Service Fund) The following transactions relate to Sunset Village for the fiscal year ended June 30, 2004:
1. The city established a Central Supplies Fund for the purpose of handling the acquisition and disbursement of supplies for the entire governmental unit. The General Fund made an initial capital contribution of $60,000 to the fund.
2. The Police Department ordered equipment at a total cost of $34,000.
3. The Central Supplies Fund purchased supplies for $25,000. This amount will be paid later.
4. The Debt Service Fund paid $120,000 of interest not previously recorded.
5. Central Supplies Fund billings to departments totaled $30,000. These supplies cost $22,000. Record the cost of the supplies as an expense: Cost of sales.
6. A Capital Projects Fund paid a contractor $100,000 for a previously submitted progress billing of $110,000. The difference between the billing and the amount paid is the retained percentage. The billing was properly recorded when received by the fund.
7. The Central Supplies Fund acquired office equipment for $2,000. A 90-day note was signed for that amount.
8. Collections from the departments by the Central Supplies Fund totaled $28,000.
9. Collections of current special assessments for debt service totaled $50,000.
10. Salaries paid to Central Supplies Fund employees were $20,000.
11. The police department equipment ordered in part (2) was delivered at a cost of $35,000. The invoice price will be paid later. Assume the excess was approved.
12. Depreciation on the office equipment of the Central Supplies Fund was $400.
13. Old office furniture used by the governmental unit was scrapped, with no cash received. The furniture originally cost $2,800.
14. The Central Supplies Fund paid $25,000 to various creditors outside the governmental unit.
15. Interest expense of $50 was accrued by the Central Supplies Fund.

Required: 1. Prepare all the journal entries necessary to record the preceding transactions and identify the fund(s) used.
2. Prepare a statement of revenues, expenses, and changes in net assets for the Central Supplies Fund for fiscal 2003–2004 and a statement of net assets as of June 30, 2004.

P7-4 (Journal entries and financial statements for an Enterprise Fund)
The following transactions relate to Walton City's Municipal Airport Fund for
the fiscal year ended June 30, 2004:

1. The General Fund made a permanent contribution of $3 million for working capital to start a municipal airport. The city used part of that money, together with the proceeds from a $25 million revenue bond issue, to purchase an airport from a private company. The fair value of the assets and liabilities was as follows:

Accounts receivable	$ 8,000
Land	21,000,000
Buildings	5,000,000
Equipment	1,800,000
Accounts payable	12,000

   The city purchased the airport for the fair market value of its net assets.
2. Airlines were billed $3,700,000 for rental rights to use ticket counters and landing and maintenance space. Of this amount, $3,690,000 is expected to be collectible.
3. Supplies totaling $1,500 were purchased on credit.
4. Collections from airlines totaled $3,680,000.
5. Salaries of $200,000 were paid to airport personnel employed by the city.
6. Utility bills totaling $100,000 were paid.
7. A notice was received from the Last District Bankruptcy Court. Air Lussa was declared bankrupt. The airport collected only $1,000 on its bill of $5,000.
8. The airport obtained $3 million of additional permanent contributions from the city to help finance improvements at the airport.
9. Interest of $2,125,000 was paid to the bondholders.
10. Supplies used during the year totaled $1,200.
11. The General Fund made an advance to the airport of $2 million. This amount must be repaid within 5 years. Airport management plans to begin repaying the advance in 2005.
12. A contract was signed with The Construction Company for the new facilities for a total price of $5 million.
13. Airport management invested $2 million in certificates of deposit
14. Airport management received $315,000 upon redeeming $300,000 of the certificates of deposit mentioned in part (13).
15. The airport purchased additional equipment for $300,000 cash.
16. Interest expense of $500,000 was accrued at the end of the year.
17. Other accrued expenses totaled $50,000.
18. Depreciation was recorded as follows:

Buildings	$500,000
Equipment	180,000

19. Paid $13,000 of Accounts payable.
20. Received $150,000 of interest revenue.
21. Excess cash of $4.3 million was invested in certificates of deposit.

Chapter 7   The Governmental Fund Accounting Cycle   303

Required: 1. Prepare the journal entries necessary to record the preceding transactions in the Municipal Airport Fund.
2. Prepare a trial balance at June 30, 2004.
3. Prepare a statement of revenues, expenses, and changes in net assets for the 2003–2004 fiscal year and a statement of net assets as of June 30, 2004.

P7-5   (Journal entries for several funds)
1. The city council of Bellview approved its General Fund budget for the year July 1, 2003–June 30, 2004. The budget contained the following: revenues, $3,500,000; transfers from other funds, $200,000; transfers to other funds, $500,000; and expenditures, $4,000,000. The city had a fund balance of $2,300,000 at the beginning of the year.
2. During the year, interest of $400,000 and principal of $2,000,000 were paid from resources accumulated for that purpose.
3. T. J. Construction submitted a progress billing for work done on a new city hall. The bill was for $800,000. This billing was for work done to the end of the year. Bonds were used to finance this project. The contract contained a 10 percent retainage clause.
4. The Airport Fund submitted a bill to the city and to Mid-West Airlines for $200,000 each. The bill was for landing fees for aircraft owned by the two entities.
5. The city sold surplus equipment. The equipment originally cost $45,000. Only $500 was received from the sale. There are no restrictions placed on the use of the $500.
6. The Airport Fund paid the bill received from T. J., less the 10 percent retainage.
7. Bellview paid the bill received from the Airport Fund.
8. Books R Us won a suit against the city. Bellview attempted to revoke the store's license so that it could sell the land used by Books to a local theater group. The court gave Books an award of $400,000. This amount will be paid from general tax revenues. An encumbrance was not set up.
9. A bridge over the East River was completed at a total cost of $5,000,000. In previous years, costs of $4,500,000 were recorded. The bridge was paid for from bond proceeds. After paying all bills, including the retainage percentage, $200,000 remained in the construction fund. The bond indenture requires that this amount be transferred into the fund that will service the bonds.
10. The Electric Utility Fund paid $1,200,000 to contractors for various construction jobs currently in process. This amount was not previously recorded. Assume encumbrance accounting is not used.

Required: Prepare the journal entries to record this information. Identify each fund used.

(Journal entries for several funds and a statement of revenues, expenses, and changes in net assets for an Internal Service Fund and an Enterprise Fund)

Bacchus City has one Internal Service Fund, a central purchasing fund, and one Enterprise Fund, an Electric Utility Fund. During 2004 the following events occurred.

1. Police department salaries of $30,000 were paid.
2. The General Fund collected $100,000 of taxes previously levied against property holders in the city.
3. The Electric Fund mailed bills of $400,000 to the residents.
4. The Central Purchasing Fund ordered supplies for its inventory totaling $15,000.
5. Two years ago, the city began to construct several housing units. Currently the Iberville Street units are under construction. The contractor submitted a progress billing for $300,000. The total contract price was $1 million. Encumbrance accounting is used. Record the progress billing. Bonds were used to finance this project. The contract provides for a 5 percent retainage.
6. Salaries paid to Electric Fund and Central Purchasing Fund employees totaled $130,000 and $10,000, respectively.
7. Collections of electric bills were $385,000.
8. The Electric Fund issued $150,000 of 2-year notes.
9. The Central Purchasing Fund acquired various pieces of office equipment for cash, $55,000.
10. The Central Purchasing Fund billed the Electric Fund $20,000; the cost of the supplies was $19,000.
11. To provide funds for the construction of new housing units on Fifth Street, $1,500,000 of general obligation bonds were issued.
12. Other operating expenses of the Electric Fund were $150,000. Of this amount, $130,000 was paid in cash.
13. Homeowners were billed $12,000 for electric service.
14. Depreciation on Central Purchasing Fund equipment totaled $5,500.
15. The Central Purchasing Fund invested $25,000 in interest-bearing notes.
16. Depreciation on plant and equipment for the Electric Fund was $50,000.
17. Supplies ordered by the Internal Service Fund in part (4) were received. The actual cost was $14,000.
18. Interest accrued on Central Purchasing Fund investments totaled $250.

Required: 1. Prepare all the journal entries necessary to record these transactions; identify the fund(s) involved.

2. Prepare a statement of revenues, expenses, and changes in net assets for the Electric Fund and the Central Purchasing Fund for 2004. (Assume that the beginning net assets in the Electric Fund and the Central Purchasing Fund were $31,400 and $15,000, respectively).

P7-6 **(Explanation of basis of accounting and fixed assets for different funds)**
The accounting system of the municipality of Kemp is organized and operated on a fund basis. Among the types of funds used are a General Fund, a Special Revenue Fund, and an Enterprise Fund.

a. Explain the basic differences in revenue recognition between the accrual basis of accounting and the modified accrual basis of accounting, as it relates to governmental accounting.

b. What basis of accounting should be used in fund-level accounting for each of the following funds?
   - General Fund
   - Special Revenue Funds
   - Enterprise Funds

   Why?

c. How should fixed assets and long-term liabilities related to the General Fund and to the Enterprise Fund be accounted for in the funds?

(AICPA adapted)

P7-7 **(Budget for an internal service fund)**
The City of Black Plains uses an Internal Service Fund to provide printing services to its various departments. It bills departments on the basis of an estimated rate per page of printed material, computed on the accrual basis of accounting. From the following information, compute the total cost that will be used to develop the cost per page. Assume that the equipment in part (6) was contributed by the city, and that the pricing objective was to recoup the cost of equipment in the rate charged over the life of the equipment.

1. Inventory of paper on hand at beginning of year, $10,000
2. Estimated paper purchases during the year, $60,000
3. Estimated amount of paper to be consumed during the year, $55,000
4. Estimated salaries to be paid during the year, $255,000
5. Estimated salaries earned during the year, including both what was paid and what was owed at year-end, $265,000
6. Cost of equipment on hand at beginning of the year (estimated life was 10 years), $1,000,000

P7-8 **(Continuation of P7-7)**
Assume the information presented in P7-7, except that the city did not contribute the equipment. Instead, the manager of the Internal Service Fund arranged to buy the equipment, paying for it over a period of 5 years. The terms of the acquisition required annual payments of $200,000 at the end of each year, with interest of 8 percent on the unpaid balance. The first payment was made, and it is in the second year of operations. Assume also that the fund has just enough cash on hand to finance its working capital needs, such as inventory requirements. Using these assumptions, would you make a different calculation of the total cost to be recouped in the billing rate? If so, explain why you would make a different calculation and how it would change.

Chapter 8

The Governmental Fund Accounting Cycle
Fiduciary Funds and Special Assessment Accounting

After completing this chapter, you should be able to:

➤ *Explain why and how Pension Trust Funds are used in governmental accounting.*

➤ *Prepare the journal entries normally used in Pension Trust Funds.*

➤ *Prepare financial statements for Pension Trust Funds.*

➤ *Explain why and how Investment Trust Funds are used in governmental accounting.*

➤ *Prepare the journal entries normally used in Investment Trust Funds.*

➤ *Prepare financial statements for Investment Trust Funds.*

➤ *Explain why and how Private Purpose Trust Funds are used in governmental accounting.*

➤ *Prepare the journal entries normally used in Private Purpose Trust Funds.*

➤ *Prepare financial statements for Private Purpose Trust Funds.*

➤ *Explain why and how Agency Funds are used in governmental accounting.*

➤ *Prepare the journal entries normally used in Agency Funds.*

➤ *Prepare a financial statement for Agency Funds.*

➤ *Define special assessments.*

➤ *Explain how special assessments are used in governmental units.*

➤ *Explain how special assessments are reported in governmental financial statements.*

*F*iduciary funds are used to account for assets held in a trustee or agency capacity and, therefore, cannot be used to finance the government's own programs. The four types of funds included in this group are Employee Pension Trust Funds, Investment Trust Funds, Private Purpose Trust Funds, and Agency Funds. The first three differ from Agency Funds in that a trust is established and the government is acting in a fiduciary capacity for individuals, private organizations, or other governments. In addition to these funds, we will discuss special assessment accounting in more detail than in Chapter 6.

FIDUCIARY-TYPE FUNDS: PENSION TRUST FUNDS

Definition of Fund

Public Employee Retirement Systems (PERS) operated by governmental units are accounted for in Pension Trust Funds. These systems provide retirement benefits for governmental employees. The employee groups can be defined as narrowly as the employees of a particular department of a governmental unit, or as broadly as the employees of an entire state. The expenditures (or expenses) associated with the contributions to the pension plans generally are recorded in the particular funds from which the employees are paid.

Summary of Fund Activities

The normal activities of a PERS include the accumulation of direct contributions made by the governmental units, withholdings from the salaries of their employees, or both. In addition, the investment of assets that generate income in the form of interest or dividends are accounted for in these funds. One unique activity to PERS is the making of periodic payments to employees who are retired from the governmental unit. In summary, Pension Trust Funds account for resources accumulated in PERS and the payment of retirement benefits.

Control of Fund Activities

Pension fund activities are controlled by pension agreements, and local and state laws. These laws cover the operations of retirement systems in general and PERS in particular. They vary in scope, ranging from laws that limit the types of investments that can be made with fund assets to laws that require specified periods of service before employees can qualify for pension benefits.

The financial statements of Pension Trust Funds include a statement of plan net assets and a statement of changes in plan net assets. In addition, a governmental unit must prepare two supplementary schedules: (1) a schedule of funding progress, and (2) a schedule of employer contributions. The financial statements are prepared using the economic resources measurement focus and the full accrual basis of accounting, with the exception that plan liabilities for benefits and refunds should be recognized when due and payable in accordance with the terms of the plan. This exception does not mean that the liabilities as reported are only current liabilities. It is possible for a plan to report some noncurrent liabilities such as a mortgage loan or a capital lease. The required supplementary schedules are designed to provide funding information to the reader of the financial statements.

Types of Pension Funds

Local governmental units have their own pension plans or participate in state-sponsored plans. These plans can be grouped in two major categories: defined benefit plans and defined contribution plans. *Defined benefit plans* are retirement plans that guarantee specific benefits when employees retire. These benefits are usually determined by a formula. A relatively common formula is one that gives employees a specific percentage credit (e.g., 2 percent) of their average salary over some period, such as the employee's highest 3 years. This credit would be computed as follows: assume an employee works for 25 years and her highest 3 consecutive years' salaries are $45,000, $47,000, and $49,000. Using the formula, she would be entitled to retirement benefits of $23,500 [$47,000 × (25 × .02)] per year.

Defined contribution plans are retirement plans that do not guarantee specific benefits. Instead, the employee's retirement benefits are determined when he or she retires, based on the amount accumulated in the plan. In most instances, the government and the employees contribute to both types of plans, but any combination of relative contributions is possible.

Because benefits are not guaranteed under a defined contribution plan, the only obligation the governmental unit has to a member depends on the amount of the member's contributions, earnings on investments of those contributions, and forfeitures of contributions made for other members that may be allocated to the member's account.[1] Contributions made by the government are expenses or expenditures of the period and, if the amount required is paid to the plan, the governmental unit has no further obligation.

Defined benefit plans specifically identify the amount the employee is to receive upon retirement. As a result, the calculations are quite complex because they must take into consideration expected salary increases, mortality rates, plan funding, investment gains and losses, administrative costs, and other related items. Due to the popularity of defined benefit plans, we have assumed that type of plan is used by the City of Angusville in the illustrations in this text. Both types of plans, however, are accounted for in fiduciary funds. Due to the other controls used in pension accounting, there is no budget and encumbrance accounting is not used.

Accounting for Fund Activities

Operating Entries

State and local governments base their accounting entries and financial reports on GASB *Statement No. 25* "Financial Reporting for Defined Benefit Pension Plans and Note Disclosures for Defined Contribution Plans," and *Statement No. 27*, "Accounting for Pensions by State and Local Governmental Employers." For illustrative purposes, assume that the City of Angusville has had a PERS in operation for several years. The PERS trial balance as of December 31, 2003, is presented in Table 8-1.

The following transactions are incurred by the PERS of Angusville during 2004 and form the basis for the statement of changes in plan net assets that took place during the period and the statement of plan net assets at the end of the period. The operating items will be reported on the statement of changes in plan net assets as either additions or deductions to net assets held in trust for pension benefits.

Assume that investment income of $500,000 is received in cash. This amount includes income accrued at the beginning of the year, $55,000. This investment income is recorded as follows:

Cash	500,000	
Interest receivable		55,000
Additions—interest on investments		445,000
To record the receipt of interest from investments.		

If retirement annuities of $230,000 are paid, a "deduction" is recorded:

Deductions—retirement annuities	230,000	
Cash		230,000
To record retirement annuities.		

Some PERS have their own administrative staffs. In other instances the operating costs of a PERS are borne by the General Fund, and no operating costs appear on the financial statements of the Pension Trust Fund. In our illustration, however, it is

---

[1] GASB Cod. Sec. Pe5.533.

Table 8-1

Trial Balance—Pension Trust Fund

CITY OF ANGUSVILLE
PENSION TRUST FUND
PUBLIC EMPLOYEES RETIREMENT SYSTEM
TRIAL BALANCE
DECEMBER 31, 2003

	DEBITS	CREDITS
Cash	$ 15,000	
Interest receivable	55,000	
Investments—U.S. government securities	2,000,000	
Investments—corporate stocks	3,067,000	
Building	500,000	
Accumulated depreciation—building		$ 100,000
Equipment	50,000	
Accumulated depreciation—equipment		10,000
Accounts payable		65,000
Net assets held in trust for pension benefits		5,512,000
	$5,687,000	$5,687,000

assumed that General Fund employees administer the PERS and that the PERS reimburses the General Fund for its share of the accounting and investment management costs. If accounting costs are $12,000 and investment management costs amount to $8,000, the following entries are made:

Entry in the books of the Pension Trust Fund	Deductions—administrative costs	12,000	
	Deductions—investment management costs	8,000	
	Due to General Fund		20,000
	To record operating costs for the current year.		

Entry in the books of the General Fund	Due from PERS	20,000	
	Expenditures—administrative costs		12,000
	Expenditures—investment management costs		8,000
	To record reimbursement of operating costs from PERS.		

Because full accrual accounting is used, investment income of $50,000 earned but not received at the end of the year is recorded as follows:

Interest receivable	50,000	
Additions—interest on investments		50,000
To record interest earned but not received.		

Dividends received during the year from investments are recorded as follows:

Cash	10,000	
Additions—dividends		10,000
To record dividends received during the year.		

Assume that sales of investments in corporate stocks result in a gain of $10,000 and the amount collected from these sales is $50,000.

Cash	50,000	
Investments—corporate stocks		40,000
Additions—net appreciation in fair value of investments		10,000
To record the sale of investments.		

Investments are reported at fair market value. Assuming the value of the investment portfolio increased by $25,000, the following entry is made:

Investments—corporate stocks	25,000	
Additions—net appreciation in fair value of investments		25,000
To record increase in fair value of investments.		

Notice that the realized gains and the unrealized gains are reported in a single account called Additions—net appreciation in fair value of investments. If losses were involved, the net amount would be reported. The realized gains and losses may be separately disclosed in the notes to the financial statements, subject to certain restrictions imposed by GASB. For financial reporting purposes, investments must be grouped by type.

During the year, the fund incurred maintenance costs on its building totaling $5,000 and purchased new computer equipment at a cost of $30,000. Depreciation on all of the equipment owned by the PERS is $1,000, plus $10,000 for the building. These are recorded as follows:

Deductions—building maintenance costs	5,000	
Cash		5,000
To record building maintenance costs.		

Equipment	30,000	
Cash		30,000
To record purchase of new equipment.		

Deductions—depreciation on equipment	1,000	
Deductions—depreciation on building	10,000	
Accumulated depreciation—equipment		1,000
Accumulated depreciation—building		10,000
To record depreciation for the year.		

During the year additional administrative costs of $15,000 are incurred that will be paid in the following year. These are recorded as follows:

Deductions—administrative costs	15,000	
Accounts payable		15,000
To record accrued administrative expenses.		

Payments on accounts payable during the year are recorded as follows:

Accounts payable	75,000	
Cash		75,000
To record payments on accounts payable.		

The retirement plan illustrated requires equal contributions by the employees and the government. When the amount of each contribution is determined, $200,000 in this case, the following entry is made:

Due from General Fund	400,000	
Additions—pension contributions—plan members		200,000
Additions—pension contributions—employer		200,000
To record amount due from the General Fund for pension contributions.		

In this illustration, it is assumed that the General Fund is the only fund that is financing pension expenditures. If any other funds become involved, a separate receivable is established for each fund.

Collections from the General Fund of $400,000 are recorded as follows:

Cash	400,000	
Due from General Fund		400,000
To record payment received from the General Fund.		

The entries on the books of the General Fund are (amounts assumed):

Expenditures—personal services	997,000	
Due to U.S. government		120,000
Due to PERS		200,000
Cash		677,000
To record payroll and the liability for the employees' share of pension contributions.		
Expenditures—retirement benefits	200,000	
Due to PERS		200,000
To record retirement contributions of government.		
Due to PERS	400,000	
Cash		400,000
To record payment to PERS.		

If cash of $600,000 is invested in corporate stocks, the entry to record this investment on the books of the PERS is as follows:

Investments—corporate stocks	600,000	
Cash		600,000
To record investment of excess cash.		

Although additional journal entries can be illustrated, these summary entries are sufficient to reflect the type of activities normally incurred by a typical PERS.

A trial balance for the fund as of the end of the fiscal year is shown in Table 8-2.

Closing Entry

At the end of the accounting period the books must be closed and financial statements prepared. The following closing entry is generally used for Pension Trust Funds:

Table 8-2
Trial Balance—Pension Trust Fund

CITY OF ANGUSVILLE
PENSION TRUST FUND
PUBLIC EMPLOYEES RETIREMENT SYSTEM
TRIAL BALANCE
DECEMBER 31, 2004

	DEBITS	CREDITS
Cash	$ 35,000	
Interest receivable	50,000	
Investments—U.S. government securities	2,000,000	
Investments—corporate stocks	3,652,000	
Building	500,000	
Accumulated depreciation—building		$ 110,000
Equipment	80,000	
Accumulated depreciation—equipment		11,000
Due to General Fund		20,000
Accounts payable		5,000
Net assets held in trust for pension benefits		5,512,000
Additions—interest on investments		495,000
Additions—net appreciation in fair value of investments		35,000
Additions—dividends		10,000
Additions—pension contributions—employer		200,000
Additions—pension contributions—plan members		200,000
Deductions—retirement annuities	230,000	
Deductions—administrative costs	27,000	
Deductions—investment management costs	8,000	
Deductions—building maintenance	5,000	
Deductions—depreciation on equipment	1,000	
Deductions—depreciation on building	10,000	
	$6,598,000	$6,598,000

Additions—interest on investments	495,000	
Additions—net appreciation in fair market value of investments	35,000	
Additions—dividends	10,000	
Additions—pension contributions—employer	200,000	
Additions—pension contributions—plan members	200,000	
Deductions—retirement annuities		230,000
Deductions—administrative costs		27,000
Deductions—investment management costs		8,000
Deductions—building maintenance		5,000
Deductions—depreciation on equipment		1,000
Deductions—depreciation on building		10,000
Net assets held in trust for pension benefits		659,000

To close the nominal accounts for 2004.

Financial Statements Illustration

The individual financial statements for Pension Trust Funds are a statement of changes in fiduciary net assets and a statement of fiduciary net assets. These statements are illustrated in Tables 8-3 and 8-4. GASB also requires two supplementary schedules for defined benefit pension plans. These two schedules are (1) a schedule of funding progress (see Table 8-5), and (2) a schedule of employer contributions (see Table 8-6). Notice that a statement of cash flows is not required.

The schedule of funding progress was prescribed to help financial statement users determine whether the financial status of the pension trust fund is improving

Table 8-3
Statement of Changes in Fiduciary Fund Net Assets—Pension Trust Fund

CITY OF ANGUSVILLE
PENSION TRUST FUND
PUBLIC EMPLOYEES RETIREMENT SYSTEM
STATEMENT OF CHANGES IN FIDUCIARY FUND NET ASSETS
FOR THE YEAR ENDING DECEMBER 31, 2004

Additions		
Contributions		
Employer	$200,000	
Plan members	200,000	
Total contributions		$ 400,000
Investment income		
Interest income	495,000	
Net appreciation in fair value of investments	35,000	
Dividends	10,000	
	540,000	
Less investment expense	(8,000)	
Net investment income		532,000
Total additions		932,000
Deductions		
Benefits	230,000	
Administrative costs	27,000	
Building maintenance	5,000	
Depreciation on equipment	1,000	
Depreciation on buildings	10,000	
Total deductions		273,000
Change in net assets		659,000
Net assets held in trust for pension benefits—beginning of year		5,512,000
Net assets held in trust for pension benefits—end of year		$6,171,000

Table 8-4

Statement of Fiduciary Fund Net Assets—Pension Trust Fund

CITY OF ANGUSVILLE
PENSION TRUST FUND
PUBLIC EMPLOYEES RETIREMENT SYSTEM
STATEMENT OF FIDUCIARY FUND NET ASSETS
DECEMBER 31, 2004

Assets		
Cash	$ 35,000	
Interest receivable	50,000	
Investments at fair value	5,652,000	
Building (less accumulated depreciation, $110,000)	390,000	
Equipment (less accumulated depreciation, $11,000)	69,000	
Total assets		$6,196,000
Liabilities		
Due to General Fund	20,000	
Accounts payable	5,000	
Total liabilities		25,000
Net assets held in trust for pension benefits		$6,171,000

Table 8-5

Schedule of Funding Progress

CITY OF ANGUSVILLE
PENSION TRUST FUND
PUBLIC EMPLOYEES RETIREMENT SYSTEM
SCHEDULE OF FUNDING PROGRESS
DECEMBER 31, 1999–2004
(AMOUNTS IN THOUSANDS)

ACTUARIAL VALUATION DATE	ACTUARIAL VALUE OF ASSETS	ACTUARIAL ACCRUED LIABILITY (AAL)— ENTRY AGE	UNFUNDED AAL (UAAL)	FUNDED RATIO	COVERED PAYROLL	UAAL AS A PERCENTAGE OF COVERED PAYROLL
12/31/99	$5,000	$5,750	$750	87.0%	$ 998	75.2%
12/31/00	5,100	5,800	700	87.9	997	70.2
12/31/01	5,350	6,100	750	87.7	995	75.4
12/31/02	5,700	6,300	600	90.5	998	60.1
12/31/03	6,000	6,400	400	93.8	1,000	40.0
12/31/04	6,200	6,500	300	95.4	997	30.1

Table 8-6

Schedule of Employer Contributions

CITY OF ANGUSVILLE
PENSION TRUST FUND
PUBLIC EMPLOYEES RETIREMENT SYSTEM
SCHEDULE OF EMPLOYER CONTRIBUTIONS
DECEMBER 31, 2004

YEAR ENDED DECEMBER	ANNUAL REQUIRED CONTRIBUTION	PERCENTAGE CONTRIBUTED
1999	$197,000	100.0%
2000	193,000	100.0
2001	197,500	100.0
2002	202,000	100.0
2003	197,000	100.0
2004	200,000	100.0

over time, through a report of the trend in the funded ratio [actuarial value of assets (AVA) divided by actuarial accrued liability (AAL)]. The schedule also shows the trend in the unfunded actuarial accrued liability (UAAL) as a percentage of covered payrolls. As a general rule, the financial status of the pension fund is improving if the first ratio increases over time and if the second ratio decreases.

Notice that in developing these ratios, actuarial information is used. The AVA may be similar to the asset values reported in the statement of plan net assets, but may be somewhat different if the actuary's method of computing asset values is different from the accountant's method. The AAL is a by-product of the method used by the actuary to compute the funding requirement for the particular pension fund. It provides a rough measure of the present value of the pension benefit earned to date by retired and active members of the plan.

The AAL, however, is not a uniform measure of the earned pension benefit, because the AAL would be different for different actuarial funding methods. Thus, the trend in funded ratio is useful for measuring the status of the trust fund itself but is less useful for comparing the funded status of one plan against another. (An earlier GASB standard did, in fact, require computation of a standardized measure of the earned pension benefit because all pension systems had to use the same actuarial method to compute the "pension benefit obligation.")

The schedule of employer contributions is based on the notion that, even though actuaries have options in how they compute the required pension contribution, a system that is funded in accordance with an actuary's calculation will have sufficient funds available to pay pension benefits when due. Hence, an analyst would look favorably on 100 percent numbers in that table.

The notes to the financial statements for defined benefit plans must include (1) a description of the plan, (2) a summary of significant accounting policies, (3) information about contributions and reserves, and (4) identification of concentrations of investments in certain organizations.

Measurement of Annual Pension Cost

Generally annual pension cost is reported as an expense (expenditure) in the fund that receives the services of the employees covered by the plan. Because the format of the plan can be quite complex, we will assume that the City of Angusville has a single employer plan, and provide an overview discussion of the calculation of the annual amount.

The two components to the actuary's calculation of the annual required contribution are (1) normal cost and (2) amortization of the UAAL. Although actuaries have options in how they make the calculation, the normal cost is generally the present value of the pension benefit earned by each employee for the year. The unfunded actuarial accrued liability results from a variety of factors, such as previous underfunding and benefit increases attributable to earlier years of service that have not yet been fully funded. The GASB prescribes certain "parameters" or constraints on the means of calculating these two components, such as the period over which the UAAL must be amortized. Together, these two components represent the annual required contribution (ARC).

If the government has an excess of required contributions over actual contributions it has a net pension obligation (NPO). If this amount exists, the annual pension cost will include three elements: (1) the ARC, (2) interest on the NPO, and (3) an adjustment to the ARC. If the NPO is positive (a net liability), interest is added to the calculation and the adjustment to the ARC is deducted. If the NPO is negative (a net asset), interest is deducted from the calculation and the ARC adjustment is added. Detailed calculation of the pension expense (expenditure) amount is beyond the scope of this text. Although the GASB does not prescribe specific methods for making these calculations, it does provide certain parameters within which those methods used must fall.

Reporting Pension Expense (Expenditure)

Governmental-type funds report a pension expenditure equal to the amount calculated previously, less any amount that will be paid in future years. The amount of the expenditure, therefore, is the amount that will be satisfied by available spendable resources. In proprietary-type funds and trust funds, the entire amount, as calculated previously, is reported as an expense. Any amount not paid during the current period is reported as a liability.

Financial Reporting for Defined Contribution Plans

Under defined contribution plans, the governmental unit does not commit itself to paying specified benefits, but merely making payments from the amount accumulated for the employee or distributing the total amount to the employee for his/her investment. The governmental unit does not have a specified liability, so financial reporting for these plans is much simpler. For these types of plans, the GASB requires notes disclosing the following: (1) a description of the plan, (2) a summary of significant accounting policies, and (3) identification of concentrations of investments in certain organizations.

Other Postemployment Benefits

Our discussion of pension benefits does not include other postemployment benefits. The GASB has a separate project on its agenda to address these other benefits, including health care benefits, as part of pension plans. "The GASB adopted this approach of separating these topics because additional or different measurement standards from those in this section may be needed in accounting for postemployment health care benefits.[2] Financial reporting for postemployment health care benefits included in pension plans is currently covered by GASB *Statement No. 26*, "Financial Reporting for Postemployment Healthcare Plans Administered by

GOVERNMENTAL ACCOUNTING IN PRACTICE
The City of Baton Rouge and Parish of East Baton Rouge Employees' Retirement System

The City of Baton Rouge and the Parish of East Baton Rouge, Louisiana, accounts for its employees' retirement system (the System) using GASB *Statement No. 25*. Tables 8-7 through 8-10 illustrate the financial statements and supporting schedules described in this chapter for the System. Notice that the System identifies the major classes of investments on its statement of plan net assets. These investments have a broad base, from U.S. government obligations to real estate. Strict rules govern what types of investments are permissible. These rules are described in the notes to the statements and include, among other provisions, a prohibition against the use of certain types of investments and a limit on the size of an investment that can be held in any individual organization. The Pending trades and Pending trades payable reported on the statement of plan net assets represent the receivable (payable) related to trades made by the System. Purchases and sales of investments are recorded on a "trade date" basis. Because the final accounting is determined on the "settlement date," usually three business days later, an asset or liability account results.

The statement of changes in plan net assets format presented in Table 8-7 is exactly like that presented in the text. In addition, Tables 8-9 and 8-10 present the supplementary schedules as required by GASB *Statement No. 25*.

---

[2] GASB Cod. Sec. Pe5 fn3.

Table 8-7

Statement of Changes in Fiduciary Net Assets—Pension Trust Fund—City of Baton Rouge and Parish of East Baton Rouge

CITY OF BATON ROUGE AND
PARISH OF EAST BATON ROUGE
EMPLOYEES' RETIREMENT SYSTEM
STATEMENT OF CHANGES IN FIDUCIARY FUND NET ASSETS
FOR THE YEARS ENDED DECEMBER 31, 20X4 AND 20X3

	20X4 COMBINED TOTAL	20X3 COMBINED TOTAL
Additions:		
Contributions:		
Employee	$ 8,672,779	$ 9,273,287
Employer	11,634,531	13,648,350
Severance contributions from employees	344,953	—
Total contributions	20,652,263	22,921,637
Investment income:		
Net appreciation in fair value of investments	(25,849,218)	9,459,899
Interest	9,140,808	9,458,887
Dividends	2,287,755	2,378,005
Total investment income	(14,420,655)	21,296,791
Less investment expenses	1,184,537	1,375,172
Net investment income	(15,605,192)	19,921,619
Total additions	5,047,071	42,843,256
Deductions:		
Benefit payments	44,051,754	44,803,115
Refunds and withdrawals	2,000,368	1,760,184
Administrative expenses	1,091,294	1,198,053
Total deductions	47,143,416	47,761,352
Net decrease	(42,096,345)	(4,918,096)
Net assets held in trust for pension benefits:		
Beginning of year	839,965,938	844,884,034
End of year	$797,869,593	$839,965,938

Source: Adapted from a recent annual report of the City of Baton Rouge and Parish of East Baton Rouge, Louisiana, Employees' Retirement System.

Table 8-8

Statement of Fiduciary Net Assets—Pension Trust Fund—City of Baton Rouge and Parish of East Baton Rouge

CITY OF BATON ROUGE AND
PARISH OF EAST BATON ROUGE
EMPLOYEES' RETIREMENT SYSTEM
STATEMENT OF FIDUCIARY FUND NET ASSETS
YEARS ENDED DECEMBER 31, 20X4 AND 20X3

	20X4 COMBINED TOTAL	20X3 COMBINED TOTAL
Assets		
Cash	$ 630,708	$ 64,311
Receivables:		
Employer contributions	917,728	820,592
Employee contributions	756,131	626,240
Interest and dividends	1,747,430	1,813,625
Pending trades	10,321,898	1,366,052
Other	2,386,865	344,844
Total receivables	16,130,052	4,971,353
Investments (at fair value):		
U.S. government obligations	68,259,778	56,853,146
Bonds—domestic	61,986,427	71,439,334
Bonds—Index Fund	152,447,365	146,107,737
Equity securities—domestic	399,981,638	437,734,515
Equity securities—international	84,014,529	106,147,731
Cash equivalents	28,200,000	18,111,000
Total investments	794,889,737	836,393,463
Land and buildings at cost, net of accumulated depreciation of $616,652 and $587,632, respectively	814,168	837,077
Total assets	812,464,665	842,266,204
Liabilities		
Accrued expenses and benefits	617,416	650,818
Pending trades payable	13,977,656	1,649,448
Total liabilities	14,595,072	2,300,266
Net assets held in trust for pension benefits	$797,869,593	$839,965,938

Source: Adapted from a recent annual report of the City of Baton Rouge and Parish of East Baton Rouge, Louisiana, Employees' Retirement System.

Table 8-9

Schedule of Funding Progress—Pension Trust Fund—City of Baton Rouge and Parish of East Baton Rouge

CITY OF BATON ROUGE AND
PARISH OF EAST BATON ROUGE
EMPLOYEES' RETIREMENT SYSTEM
REQUIRED SUPPLEMENTARY INFORMATION UNDER GASB *STATEMENT NO. 25*
SCHEDULE OF FUNDING PROGRESS

ACTUARIAL VALUATION DATE	ACTUARIAL VALUE OF ASSETS (A)	ACTUARIAL ACCRUED LIABILITY (AAL) (B)	UNFUNDED AAL $(B-A)$	FUNDED RATIO (A/B)	ANNUAL COVERED PAYROLL (C)	UAAL AS A PERCENTAGE OF COVERED PAYROLL $[(B-A)/C]$
12/31/W7	$480,505,268	$657,162,178	$176,656,910	73.1%	$100,596,231	175.6%
12/31/W8	551,301,959	718,277,070	166,975,111	76.8%	104,601,384	159.6%
12/31/W9	587,193,233	773,936,127	186,742,894	75.9%	109,658,886	170.3%
12/31/X0	635,463,896	811,977,242	176,513,346	78.3%	114,102,750	154.7%
12/31/X1	740,257,038	875,075,687	134,818,649	84.6%	118,742,991	113.5%
12/31/X2*	741,562,144	809,012,654	67,450,510	91.7%	96,744,086	69.7%
12/31/X3	786,941,507	855,994,379	69,052,872	91.9%	99,510,155	69.4%
12/31/X4**	813,977,773	902,821,264	88,843,491	90.2%	102,793,456	86.4%

* These results are adjusted to reflect the impact of the February 26, 20X2, police transfers out to MPERS and the actuarial assumption changes adopted by the Retirement Board.
** These results reflect the impact of the change in Asset Valuation Method described in the Summary of Actuarial Assumptions and Methods.
Source: Adapted from a recent annual report of the City of Baton Rouge and Parish of East Baton Rouge, Louisiana, Employees' Retirement System.

Defined Benefit Pension Plans." Because that reporting is similar to what GASB prescribes for pensions, we will not explore this issue any further.

Concluding Comment

This discussion of pension plan accounting is, by design, an overview. We described the basic concepts involved in the area of accounting and financial reporting for Pension Trust Funds. Because of the complexities involved in pension plan accounting, users of the financial statements must be supplied with notes that fully disclose the provisions of the plan together with its actuarial status. These notes are described earlier in this section. The authors feel that not providing the actuarial status of the plan on the statement of plan net assets is a serious deficiency in GASB *Statement No. 25*. This statement, however, is the current guidance for financial reporting for Pension Trust Funds. The authors also feel that the failure of the GASB to require a standardized measure of the pension benefit obligation in reporting on the funded status of the plan is another serious deficiency.

Table 8-10

Schedule of Employer Contributions—Pension Trust Fund—City of
Baton Rouge and Parish of East Baton Rouge

CITY OF BATON ROUGE AND
PARISH OF EAST BATON ROUGE
EMPLOYEES' RETIREMENT SYSTEM
REQUIRED SUPPLEMENTARY INFORMATION UNDER GASB STATEMENT NO. 25, CONTINUED
SCHEDULES OF EMPLOYER CONTRIBUTIONS
CPERS TRUST

YEAR ENDED	ANNUAL REQUIRED CONTRIBUTION	PERCENTAGE CONTRIBUTED
12/31/W8	$17,845,851	80.0%
12/31/W9	17,773,028	91.3%
12/31/X0	19,510,792	94.3%
12/31/X1	17,967,514	112.0%
12/31/X2	15,658,856	129.9%
12/31/X3*	11,240,695	120.9%
12/31/X4	13,708,997	84.0%

*These results are adjusted to reflect the impact of the February 26, 20X3, police
transfers out to MPERS and the actuarial assumption changes adopted by the
Retirement Board.
Note: Only 7 years of data are available.

POLICE GUARANTEE TRUST

YEAR ENDED	ANNUAL REQUIRED CONTRIBUTION	PERCENTAGE CONTRIBUTED
12/31/X3	$0	—%
12/31/X4	$0	—%

Note: Police Guarantee Trust was fully funded at inception effective February 26,
20X3.
Source: Adapted from a recent annual report of the City of Baton Rouge and Parish
of East Baton Rouge, Louisiana, Employees' Retirement System.

FIDUCIARY-TYPE FUNDS:
INVESTMENT TRUST FUNDS

Definition of Fund

Some governments maintain *external investment pools,* an arrangement that pools the
monies of more than one legally separate entity and invests them on behalf of the
participants. By definition, an external investment pool can include the monies of
the sponsoring government, but one or more of the participants must be a legally

separate government that is not part of the same reporting entity as the sponsoring government.

External investment pools are created, for example, when state laws authorize a state treasurer to hold and invest temporarily idle cash deposited by local governments with the state treasurer, or when state laws require legally separate local school districts to deposit temporarily idle cash with a county treasurer for investment. In such instances, a fiduciary relationship develops between the entity that manages the external investment pool and the participating governments.

Although the resources of external investment pools are commingled, the portion of the investment pool that belongs to the sponsoring government should be reported in an appropriate fund of the sponsoring government. The portion of the resources belonging to the *other participants* should be reported in a fiduciary-type fund called an *Investment Trust Fund*.

Summary of Fund Activities

Investment Trust Funds receive resources from the participating governments. These resources are then invested in securities. Income from these securities is accounted for using the economic resources measurement focus and the full accrual basis of accounting. Gains and losses incurred in trading securities and adjusting them to fair value are accumulated during the period in addition to any expenses incurred. Once the income is determined for the period, it is allocated to each participant depending on the trust agreement, usually based on the amount invested.

Control of Fund Activities

Like any other trust fund, Investment Trust Funds are controlled primarily by the trust agreement. This legal document specifies what type of investments can be made, how the income will be measured and distributed, and how much the sponsoring government can charge for managing the fund. A key element that should be specifically identified is how much income can be distributed. In most instances a net figure is used (Investment income − Investment losses − Expenses). The trust agreement should be specific regarding how much, if any, of the investment net income must be retained as a protection against possible future losses. Due to the other controls that are used, budgets are usually not found in these funds and encumbrance accounting is not used.

Accounting for Fund Activities

Operating Entries

To illustrate an Investment Trust Fund, assume that two small cities (Tinyville and Microville) each deposit $50,000 in the City of Angusville external investment pool. Even though Angusville could participate in the fund, for illustrative purposes we will assume it does not. Instead, Tinyville and Microville are seeking to use the fund management skills of Angusville's finance staff. The entry to record the receipt of the money on the books of Angusville's Investment Trust Fund is:

Cash	100,000	
Additions—net assets of Tinyville		50,000
Additions—net assets of Microville		50,000
To record the receipt of deposits made by Tinyville and Microville.		

The entry on the books of each of the participating governments is:

Equity in Angusville's investments pool	50,000	
Cash		50,000
To record investment of cash in a pool managed by the City of Angusville.		

Investments of pool cash should be separated into various categories (e.g., U.S. government obligations, municipal obligations, etc.). If $40,000 is invested in U.S. government securities and $55,000 in corporate securities, the following entry is needed on the books of the investment pool:

Investments—U.S. government securities	40,000	
Investments—corporate securities	55,000	
Cash		95,000
To record investment of pool cash.		

Notice that no entry is made on either the books of Tinyville or Microville at this time.

During the year, the fund earns $5,000 of interest, of which $4,000 is received in cash. The entry to record this interest income on the books of the investment pool is:

Cash	4,000	
Interest receivable	1,000	
Additions—interest		5,000
To record interest earned and received during 2004.		

As previously discussed, securities are reported at fair value. If the corporate investments increased by $3,000 during the year, the following entry is needed on the investment pool books:

Investments—corporate securities	3,000	
Additions—net increase in fair value of investments		3,000
To record the increase in the fair value of investments for 2004.		

Administrative expenses incurred by the fund during 2004 totaled $800. Assuming these expenses are paid in cash, they are recorded on the books of the investment pool as follows:

Deductions—administrative expenses	800	
Cash		800
To record administrative expenses for 2004.		

During 2004 corporate securities totaling $6,000 were sold for $7,000. These transactions are recorded on the books of the investment pool as follows:

Cash	7,000	
Investments—corporate securities		6,000
Additions—net increase in fair value of investments		1,000
To record sale of investments.		

Notice that no entry for the preceding four events is made on either the books of Tinyville or Microville at this time. They are only recorded in the investment pool on Angusville's books.

If $1,600 is distributed to Tinyville and Microville the following entry is made on Angusville's books:

Deductions—distributions to pool participants	3,200	
Cash		3,200
To record the distribution of part of the fund's resources to its participants.		

Each of the pool's participants would record the receipt of cash as follows:

Cash	1,600	
Revenues—increase in value of investments		1,600
To record a partial distribution of cash from Angusville's external investment pool.		

Although many other entries could be illustrated, the preceding entries are typical of an investment trust fund.

Closing Entry

The closing entry on the books of the Investment Trust Fund is as follows:

Additions—net assets of Tinyville	50,000	
Additions—net assets of Microville	50,000	
Additions—interest	5,000	
Additions—net increase in fair value of investments	4,000	
Deductions—administrative expenses		800
Deductions—distributions to pool participants		3,200
Net assets		105,000
To close the operating accounts of the external investment pool.		

In this illustration all items of revenue, expense, gain, or loss are divided based on the share of investments each participant had at the beginning of the year. Because both are equal, each of the cities would record the following:

Equity in Angusville's investments pool	2,500	
Revenues—increase in value of investments		2,500
To record a city's share of pooled investment changes during 2004.		

A trial balance for Angusville's Investment Trust Fund is presented in Table 8-11.

Financial Statements Illustration

The financial statements normally prepared for Investment Trust Funds are a statement of changes in net assets and a statement of net assets. These statements are illustrated in Tables 8-12 and 8-13. Notice that no cash flow statement is prepared.

Table 8-11

Trial Balance—Investment Trust Fund

CITY OF ANGUSVILLE
TRIAL BALANCE
INVESTMENT TRUST FUND
DECEMBER 31, 2004

	DEBITS	CREDITS
Cash	$ 12,000	
Interest receivable	1,000	
Investments—U.S. government securities	40,000	
Investments—corporate securities	52,000	
Additions—net assets of Tinyville		$ 50,000
Additions—net assets of Microville		50,000
Additions—interest		5,000
Additions—net increase in fair value of investments		4,000
Deductions—administrative expenses	800	
Deductions—distribution to pool participants	3,200	
	$109,000	$109,000

Table 8-12

Statement of Changes in Fiduciary Net Assets—Investment
Trust Fund

CITY OF ANGUSVILLE
FIDUCIARY FUND
STATEMENT OF CHANGES IN FIDUCIARY NET ASSETS
INVESTMENT TRUST FUND
DECEMBER 31, 2004

Additions		
Net assets of participating governments		$100,000
Investment earnings:		
Interest	$5,000	
Increase in fair value of investments	4,000	
Less investment expense	(800)	
Net investment earnings		8,200
Total additions		108,200
Deductions		
Distributions to fund participants		(3,200)
Change in net assets		105,000
Net assets—beginning of the year		-0-
Net assets—end of the year		$105,000

Table 8-13
Statement of Fiduciary Net Assets—
Investment Trust Fund

CITY OF ANGUSVILLE
FIDUCIARY FUND
STATEMENT OF FIDUCIARY NET ASSETS
INVESTMENT TRUST FUND
DECEMBER 31, 2004

Assets	
Cash	$ 12,000
Interest receivable	1,000
Investments	92,000
Total assets	105,000
Net assets	
Net assets held in trust	$105,000

GOVERNMENTAL ACCOUNTING IN PRACTICE
The State of Wisconsin Local Government Pooled Investment Fund

The State of Wisconsin maintains a Local Government Pooled Investment Fund similar to that used by the City of Angusville. The statement of changes in fiduciary net assets is presented in Table 8-14 and the statement of fiduciary net assets is presented in Table 8-15. The State of Wisconsin follows the same accounting and measurement focus procedures as Angusville.

FIDUCIARY-TYPE FUNDS: PRIVATE PURPOSE TRUST FUNDS

Definition of Fund

Private Purpose Trust Funds are used to account for resources held by a government, in a trustee capacity, that must be maintained intact and whose beneficiaries must be "outside" of the government. These beneficiaries may be other governments, individuals, or private organizations. A typical fund of this type is one used to report escheat property.[3] These funds follow an economic resources measurement focus and a full accrual basis of accounting.

---

[3] GASB Cod. Sec. 1300.113.

Table 8-14

Statement of Changes in Fiduciary Net Assets—Investment Trust Fund

STATE OF WISCONSIN
STATEMENT OF CHANGES IN FIDUCIARY NET ASSETS
LOCAL GOVERNMENT POOLED INVESTMENT FUND
FOR THE FISCAL YEAR ENDED JUNE 30, 20X4

Additions		
Deposits		$11,113,321
Investment income of investment trust funds	$ 182,250	
Less: Investment expense	(1,705)	
Net investment income		180,545
Total additions		11,293,866
Deductions		
Distributions	10,040,381	
Administrative expenses	166	
Total deductions		10,040,547
Net increase in net assets		1,253,319
Net assets—Beginning of year		2,563,920
Net assets—End of year		$ 3,817,239

Source: Adapted from a recent annual report of the State of Wisconsin.

Table 8-15

Statement of Net Assets—Investment Trust Fund

STATE OF WISCONSIN
STATEMENT OF FIDUCIARY NET ASSETS
LOCAL GOVERNMENT POOLED INVESTMENT FUND
JUNE 30, 20X4

Assets	
Cash and cash equivalents	$3,817,266
Liabilities and Net Assets	
Due to other funds	27
Net assets held in trust for pooled participants	$3,817,239

Source: Adapted from a recent annual report of the State of Wisconsin.

Summary of Fund Activities

The activities incurred by Private Purpose Trust Funds are similar to those of Investment Trust Funds. They entail the receipt of resources from direct contributions made by private individuals or organizations. These resources are invested and the income and/or principal is disbursed from the trust fund according to the trust agreement.

Control of Fund Activities

Control of Private Purpose Trust Funds is attained through the trust agreement, and to some extent, state laws. Due to the use of these controls, budgets are not usually found in these funds and encumbrance accounting is not normally used.

Accounting for Fund Activities

Operating Entries

Activities accounted for in Private Purpose Trust Funds generally are similar to those detailed in Chapter 5 for Permanent Funds and Special Revenue Funds. However, the full accrual basis of accounting and the economic resources measurement focus are followed.

As an example of the accounting procedures for Private Purpose Trust Funds, assume a prominent citizen of Angusville establishes an educational trust fund for children of police and fire department employees killed in the performance of their duties. The trust agreement provides for an initial contribution of $2 million. This amount is to be invested, and income generated by the investments is to be spent on college scholarships for the children of qualified employees.

The entries to record receipt of the gift and the original investment of the monies are as follows:

Cash	2,000,000	
Additions—donations		2,000,000
To record the receipt of donations during 2004.		

Investments—municipal bonds	500,000	
Investments—U.S. government securities	1,500,000	
Cash		2,000,000
To record investments made during 2004.		

If the earnings on the investments amount to $60,000, the following entry would be recorded:

Cash	60,000	
Additions—investment earnings		60,000
To record investment earnings during 2004.		

During the year, scholarships totaling $55,000 are awarded, and recorded with the following entry:

Deductions—scholarships	55,000	
Cash		55,000
To record scholarships for 2004.		

During 2004, operating costs of $1,000 are incurred, of which $600 is paid in cash. The entry to record these costs follows:

Deductions—operating costs	1,000	
Accounts payable		400
Cash		600
To record operating costs for 2004.		

Investments in municipal bonds totaling $200,000 are redeemed for $225,000 and the total proceeds are immediately reinvested in the same type of securities. The entries to record these events follow:

Cash	225,000	
Investments—municipal bonds		200,000
Additions—net appreciation in fair value of investments		25,000
To record redemption of investments.		

Investments—municipal bonds	225,000	
Cash		225,000
To record additional investments made in 2004.		

Additional income earned on investments, but not received by year-end, is recorded as follows:

Investment income receivable	10,000	
Additions—investment earnings		10,000
To record accrual of investments earnings at the end of 2004.		

If the fair value of the municipal bonds held by the fund increased in value by $15,000 by the end of 2004, the following entry is made:

Investments—municipal bonds	15,000	
Additions—net appreciation in fair value of investments		15,000
To record the increase in fair value of investments at the end of 2004.		

Closing Entry

At the end of the year, the following entry is made to close the books:

Additions—donations	2,000,000	
Additions—investment earnings	70,000	
Additions—net appreciation in fair value of investments	40,000	
Deductions—scholarships		55,000
Deductions—operating costs		1,000
Net assets		2,054,000
To close the books for 2004.		

Financial Statements Illustration

The financial statements for a Private Purpose Trust Fund are a statement of changes in fiduciary net assets and a statement of fiduciary net assets. These statements are illustrated for the City of Angusville in Tables 8-16 and 8-17.

Table 8-16

Statement of Changes in Fiduciary Net Assets—Private Purpose Trust Fund

CITY OF ANGUSVILLE
PRIVATE PURPOSE TRUST FUND
SCHOLARSHIP FUND
STATEMENT OF CHANGES IN FIDUCIARY NET ASSETS
FOR THE YEAR ENDED DECEMBER 31, 2004

Additions		
Contributions		
Donations		$2,000,000
Investment earnings:		
Net increase in fair value of investments	$ 40,000	
Income from investments	70,000	
Total investment earnings	110,000	
Less investment expense	(1,000)	
Net investment earnings		109,000
Total additions		2,109,000
Deductions		
Scholarships		55,000
Change in net assets		2,054,000
Net assets—beginning of year		-0-
Net assets—end of year		$2,054,000

Table 8-17

Statement of Fiduciary Net Assets—Private Purpose Fund

CITY OF ANGUSVILLE
PRIVATE PURPOSE TRUST FUND
SCHOLARSHIP FUND
STATEMENT OF FIDUCIARY NET ASSETS
DECEMBER 31, 2004

Assets		
Cash	$ 4,400	
Investment income receivable	10,000	
Investments—U.S. Government securities	1,500,000	
Investments—municipal bonds	540,000	
Total assets		$2,054,400
Liabilities		
Accounts payable		400
Net assets in trust for scholarships		$2,054,000

GOVERNMENTAL ACCOUNTING IN PRACTICE
The State of Michigan Private Purpose Trust Fund

The State of Michigan uses five Private Purpose Trust Funds: (1) Escheats Fund, (2) Gifts, Bequests, and Deposits Investment Fund, (3) Hospital Patients' Trust Fund, (4) Michigan Education Savings Program, and (5) Workers' Disability Compensation Trust Fund. The Michigan Education Savings Program Fund is illustrated here. This fund is a college-tuition savings plan, designed to collect and invest deposits made by contribu- tors, for purposes of financing tuition on behalf of future students. Investment earn- ings held in trust by the fund are federal and state tax-deferred until the student is ready to attend college. The federal government and the state both offer tax deductions for contri- butions made each year. Tables 8-18 and 8-19 show statements for this fund. Note in Table 8–19 the numbers do not add up because of rounding.

Table 8-18
Statement of Changes in Fiduciary Net Assets—Private Purpose Trust Fund—State of Michigan

MICHIGAN
STATEMENT OF CHANGES IN FIDUCIARY NET ASSETS
PRIVATE PURPOSE TRUST FUND
MICHIGAN EDUCATION SAVINGS PROGRAM
FISCAL YEAR ENDED SEPTEMBER 30, 20X4
(AMOUNTS IN THOUSANDS)

Additions		
Contributions from participants		$62,849
Investment income:		
Net depreciation in fair value of investments	$(6,704)	
Interest, dividends, and other	843	
Less investment expense:		
Investment activity expense	(119)	
Net investment loss		(5,980)
Miscellaneous income		1
Total additions		56,869
Deductions		
Benefits paid to participants		888
Refunds and transfers to other systems		1
Total deductions		889
Net increase		55,980
Net assets held in trust for others—Beginning of fiscal year		—
Net assets held in trust for others—End of fiscal year		$55,980

Source: Adapted from a recent annual report of the State of Michigan.

Table 8-19

Statement of Fiduciary Net Assets—Private Purpose Trust Fund—
State of Michigan

MICHIGAN
STATEMENT OF FIDUCIARY NET ASSETS
PRIVATE PURPOSE TRUST FUND
MICHIGAN EDUCATION SAVINGS PROGRAM
SEPTEMBER 30, 20X4
(AMOUNTS IN THOUSANDS)

Assets		
Cash		$ 355
Investments at fair value:		
Mutual funds	$51,314	
Pooled investment funds	4,437	
Total investments		55,751
Other current assets		339
Total assets		56,444
Liabilities		
Accounts payable and other liabilities		464
Net Assets		
Net assets held in trust for others		$55,980

Source: Adapted from a recent annual report of the State of Michigan.

FIDUCIARY-TYPE FUNDS: AGENCY FUNDS

Definition of Fund

An *Agency Fund* is a fiduciary-type fund used when a governmental unit is the custodian of resources that belong to some other organization. Agency Funds typically involve only the receipt, temporary investment, and remittance of fiduciary resources to individuals, private organizations, or other governments.[4] This type of fund is used when a single fund is established to perform a central collection or distribution function for the resources of other funds of the governmental unit and a trust fund does not exist. Because an Agency Fund does not have title to or control over these resources, there is no fund balance for this type of fund. Instead, all the resources held are balanced against the liabilities to be paid from those resources. Therefore, the accounting equation for agency funds is Assets = Liabilities.

A typical Agency Fund is one used as a *clearing account* to record the collection of property taxes. After the taxes have been collected at a central location, they are

---

[4] GASB Cod. Sec. 1300.114.

disbursed to the legally authorized recipients. It is also possible to use an Agency Fund to record FICA and other payroll deductions before these amounts are sent to the appropriate recipients. Agency Funds are also used for resources held in escrow and deposits from contractors doing business with the government. A key factor in determining whether an Agency Fund should be used is whether the governmental unit disburses the assets according to a previously agreed-upon formula, legal requirement, or instruction by the "owner." The key elements requiring use of an Agency Fund are that the government does not have discretionary use of the resources in these funds, and no trust agreement is established.

Summary of Fund Activities

If the City of Angusville establishes a Property Tax Collection Fund and the fund is used to account for the taxes collected, an Agency Fund would be created. (The actual levy would still be recorded in the General Fund, Special Revenue Fund, and so forth.) In addition, this fund is used to record the distribution of the taxes to the legal recipients, for example, school boards, levee districts, and so forth.

   If the resources received by an Agency Fund are not disbursed immediately, the governmental unit should invest them. Any income or expenses produced by these investments or the operations of the fund are generally recorded in the General Fund of the custodian, unless the laws or local policies require all or a portion of the earnings to go to the entity for which the collecting government is the custodian.

Control of Fund Activities

The primary element of control over an Agency Fund is the agreement between the governmental unit and the legal "owner" of the resources. As a result, a budget is not usually legally adopted, nor is encumbrance accounting needed.

   The full accrual basis of accounting is used to determine the timing of the transactions recorded and the economic resources measurement focus is used to determine the value assigned to each transaction. Depending on the legal or contractual problems involved, a separate Agency Fund may be required for each unique relationship. However, related situations can often be combined into a single fund.

Accounting for Fund Activities

Operating Entries

For illustrative purposes, assume the City of Angusville uses a Property Tax Collection Fund and that the city collects all property taxes and distributes two-thirds of the collections to other governments (the local school board and a levee district) and one-third to the General Fund of the city, respectively. Also assume that the local school board and the levee district are not part of the Angusville government. The levy of the tax is recorded by each governmental unit. To keep the example manageable, however, we will illustrate only the General Fund and the Agency Fund for Angusville. Entries similar to those for the General Fund are made by the other governmental units. The appropriate entry on the General Fund books is as follows, assuming the amounts as given:

Property taxes receivable—current	5,000,000	
Estimated uncollectible property taxes—current		1,000
Revenues—property taxes		4,999,000
To record levy of property taxes for 2004.		

The entry on the books of the Agency Fund is as follows:

Property taxes receivable for the city and other governmental units—current	15,000,000	
Due to the city and other governmental units		15,000,000
To record levy of 2004 property tax.		

Because of the services provided, the city charges the school board and the levee district a 2 percent fee. This amount is deducted from the amount owed to them when the taxes are collected. Any amounts earned by an Agency Fund are usually recorded as revenues of the General Fund. If $9 million is collected during 2004, the school board and the levee district will each receive $2,940,000 ($3,000,000 × .98), and the General Fund will receive $3,120,000 ($3,000,000 + $60,000 + $60,000). The entries in the Agency Fund necessary to record the collection and the distribution on the Agency Fund books are as follows:

Cash	9,000,000	
Property taxes receivable for the city and other governmental units—current		9,000,000
To record the collection of part of the 2004 property tax.		

Due to the city and other governmental units	9,000,000	
Due to General Fund		3,120,000
Due to School Board		2,940,000
Due to Levee District		2,940,000
To record allocation of taxes collected.		

Due to General Fund	3,120,000	
Due to School Board	2,940,000	
Due to Levee District	2,940,000	
Cash		9,000,000
To record distribution of 2004 property taxes collected.		

The entry on the books of the General Fund to record the receipt of its share of the property taxes and the collection fee is

Cash	3,120,000	
Property taxes receivable—current		3,000,000
Revenues—miscellaneous		120,000
To record receipt of part of the 2004 property tax plus a collection fee.		

The other governmental uniits will recognize the difference between the debit to Cash and the credit to Property taxes receivable—current as a debit to an expenditure or an expense account, as appropriate. To illustrate, the entry that would be recorded on the books of the Levee District is

Cash	2,940,000	
Expenditure—fee for collection of property taxes	60,000	
Property taxes receivable—current		3,000,000
To record receipt of part of the 2004 property tax.		

When uncollectible accounts are written off, the appropriate entry in the books of the Agency Fund is as follows:

Due to the city and other governmental units	300	
Property taxes receivable for the city and other governmental units—current (delinquent or lien)		300
To record the write-off of uncollectible property taxes.		

In addition, the appropriate entry or entries, as discussed in Chapter 5, are made on the books of the City of Angusville's General Fund and in the funds of the other governments. Notice that the activities described do not result in either a revenue or an expenditure to the Agency Fund.

A trial balance for the fund at the end of the year is presented in Table 8-20.

Closing Entry

Because only balance sheet accounts are involved in the activities of an Agency Fund, a closing entry is not needed.

Financial Statement Illustration

The financial statement of Agency Funds is a statement of net assets. The statement for the City of Angusville is illustrated in Table 8-21. In the statement of net assets,

Table 8-20
Trial Balance—Agency Fiduciary Fund

CITY OF ANGUSVILLE
AGENCY FIDUCIARY FUND
TAX AGENCY FUND
TRIAL BALANCE
DECEMBER 31, 2004

	DEBITS	CREDITS
Property taxes receivable for the city and other governmental units—current	$5,999,700	
Due to the city and other governmental units		$5,999,700
	$5,999,700	$5,999,700

Table 8-21

Statement of Fiduciary Net Assets—Agency Fund

CITY OF ANGUSVILLE FIDUCIARY FUND AGENCY FUND TAX AGENCY FUND STATEMENT OF FIDUCIARY NET ASSETS DECEMBER 31, 2004	
Assets	
Property taxes receivable	
for other governmental units—current	$3,999,800
	$3,999,800
Liabilities	
Due to other governmental units	$3,999,800
	$3,999,800

assets must equal liabilities. Therefore, there is no fund balance (net assets). The fact that Agency Funds do not have a fund balance cannot be overemphasized.

Notice that the statement of net assets does not include the amounts in the Agency Fund trial balance. The portion of the Agency Fund accounts that pertains to other funds of the governmental unit is not reported in the agency fund. Rather, these amounts are reported as assets and liabilities in the appropriate funds.[5] In this instance they are reported in the General Fund for the City of Angusville.

GOVERNMENTAL ACCOUNTING IN PRACTICE
The City of Columbus, Ohio, Agency Fund

The City of Columbus, Ohio, has 17 individual agency funds. They range from a Payroll Deposit Fund to a Police Property Room Deposit Fund. The city reports a statement of fiduciary net assets (see Table 8-22). In addition, the city provides a schedule of changes in assets and liabilities for each fund. This schedule is prepared based on the total assets and the total liabilities of each fund. No separate identification of the causes of the changes is made, except for the general categories of "additions" and "deductions."

---

[5] GASB Cod. Sec. 2200.176.

Table 8-22

Statement of Fiduciary Net Assets—City of Columbus, Ohio

CITY OF COLUMBUS, OHIO
STATEMENT OF FIDUCIARY NET ASSETS
AGENCY FUNDS
DECEMBER 31, 20X1
(AMOUNTS IN THOUSANDS)

Assets

Cash and cash equivalents:

Cash and investments with treasurer	$38,523
Cash and investments with trustee	20
Investments	31
Receivables (net of allowances for uncollectibles)	20
Total assets	$38,594

Liabilities

Due to:

Other governments	$27,156
Other	11,438
Total liabilities	$38,594

Source: Adapted from a recent annual report of the City of Columbus, Ohio.

SPECIAL ASSESSMENT PROJECTS

Description of Project Activities

Special assessments are a means of financing services or capital improvements that benefit one group of citizens more than the general public. Taxpayers who receive the benefits of these activities are assessed for their share of the cost. Examples of these activities include projects such as special police protection, paving of city streets, and building parking structures. Prior to the issuance of GASB *Statement No. 6,* "Accounting and Financial Reporting for Special Assessments," these activities were accounted for and reported in separate governmental-type funds called Special Assessments Funds. GASB *Statement No. 6* requires that Special Assessments Funds be discontinued as a reporting entity and that these activities be reported as any other service or capital improvement-type project.

Local laws sometimes require that special assessment projects be accounted for and reported as separate entities. Because these types of situations are not consistent with current GAAP, additional supplemental information must be disclosed by the governmental unit. Current GAAP is presented in the financial statements, and the special assessment accounting procedures form the basis for the supplemental reports. In many situations, the accounting procedures covered in previous chapters can be followed, and special assessment data can be gleaned from the accounts if they are needed for supplemental reporting. It is also possible to follow the "old" accounting procedures and reclassify the data to comply with current GAAP.

Control of and Accounting for Project Activities

Service Assessments

Service assessments generally include activities such as special police protection, storm sewer cleaning, and snow plowing. If these activities are financed by user charges in the form of special assessments, the reporting should be done in the General Fund, a Special Revenue Fund, or an Enterprise Fund, whichever best reflects the nature of the transactions.

Control over these activities is accomplished in the same manner as any other activity included in the particular fund type. In the governmental-type funds, control is accomplished through state and local laws and budgetary authorizations for the activities. When these funds are used, immediate control is achieved through a comparison of budget and actual data for revenues, expenditures, and other financing sources. Use of encumbrance accounting is generally found in those instances in which the General Fund or a Special Revenue Fund is used. When an Enterprise Fund is used, a flexible budget is the central control feature. In general, a flexible budget is prepared based upon the level of activity of the fund, and this budget is compared with the actual results of the period. Revenues and expenditures (expenses) are recognized according to the basis of accounting and measurement focus rules that are applicable to the particular fund type being used. Examples of this type of accounting and reporting can be found in Chapters 4 and 5 for the General Fund and Special Revenue Funds and Chapter 7 for Enterprise Funds.

To illustrate the use of the General Fund to account for service assessment activities, assume that the City of Angusville levies a special assessment on the property holders in the central business district (CBD) to provide for special police protection. Assume further that these activities will be accounted for in the police department budget within the General Fund. The entries to levy the assessment and collection of part of the receivables are as follows (amounts assumed):

Special assessment receivables—current	200,000	
Revenues—special assessments		200,000
To record levy of assessments for special police protection in the CBD.		
Cash	190,000	
Special assessment receivables—current		190,000
To record collection of assessments for special police protection in the CBD.		

If any of the receivables are not expected to be collected, a provision for uncollectible receivables should be established. If these receivables are not collected within a specific time period, they usually become delinquent and eventually are classified as a lien against the property in question. In these instances, the accounting would be the same as that illustrated in Chapter 5 for property taxes. Any expenditures associated with these activities are recorded in the fund involved. Unless the ordinance establishing the assessment requires a separate accounting, these activities should not be segregated from the other activities of the police department.

Capital Improvements Assessments

Capital improvements assessments generally include construction projects, such as street improvements and sidewalks. If these activities are financed by a special assessment, and the governmental unit is obligated in some manner, the reporting is done in two funds. The construction phase of the project is accounted for in a Capital Projects Fund and the debt service phase of the project is accounted for in a Debt Service Fund. A governmental unit is "obligated in some manner" for the special assessment debt ". . . if (a) it is legally obligated to assume all or part of the debt in the event of default or (b) the government may take certain action to assume secondary liability for all or part of the debt—and the government takes, or has given indication that it will take, those actions."[6]

Accounting for capital improvements assessments in which the government is "obligated in some manner" is exactly like that previously illustrated in Chapter 6 for capital projects. If you are not familiar with those procedures, review that material before continuing.

In those instances in which the governmental unit is not obligated in any manner, the construction phase is still accounted for in a Capital Projects Fund. The only significant difference is that the debt service phase of the project is reported in an Agency Fund (in the statement of fiduciary net assets) ". . . to reflect the fact that the government's duties are limited to acting as an agent for the assessed property owners and the bondholders."[7] In addition, the proceeds from the issuance of the special assessment bonds is reported as "Contribution from property owners" rather than "Bond proceeds" in the Capital Projects Fund.

When special assessments are collected over a period of years, a problem arises as to the amount of revenue that should be recognized. Here we assume that applying the current financial resources concept results in recognition of revenue when the special assessment installments become current assets. Thus, if an assessment of $1 million is levied, of which $100,000 is current, the following entries are appropriate in the Debt Service Fund:

Special assessment receivables—current	100,000	
Special assessment receivables—deferred	900,000	
Revenues—special assessments		100,000
Deferred revenues		900,000
To record the levy of special assessments.		

Collections of the assessments are recorded in the normal manner for receivables. When the second payment becomes a current asset, a proportionate amount of revenue is recognized (amounts assumed):

Special assessment receivables—current	100,000	
Special assessment receivables—deferred		100,000
To record the current status of the second installment of the receivable.		

---

[6] GASB Cod. Sec. S40.115.
[7] GASB Cod. Sec. S40.119.

| Deferred revenues | 100,000 | |
| Revenues—special assessments | | 100,000 |

To record the revenue from current special assessments.

Financial Statements

As mentioned previously, reporting for special assessment activities can take one of several forms. Now that the GASB has aligned special assessment accounting with that of other types of funds, these activities are reported in the manner described in this and previous chapters, depending on the type of activity involved and the extent to which the governmental unit is obligated for any debt. As a result, you should review the accounting and reporting requirements for the General Fund, Special Revenue Funds, Debt Service Funds, and Capital Projects Funds.

REVIEW QUESTIONS

Q8-1 When are Pension Trust Funds used?

Q8-2 How are the operations of a Pension Trust Fund controlled?

Q8-3 Distinguish between a defined benefit pension plan and a defined contribution pension plan.

Q8-4 What financial statements are prepared for Pension Trust Funds?

Q8-5 Identify and explain the schedules that are prepared for Pension Trust Funds?

Q8-6 What are other postemployment benefits?

Q8-7 Can the governmental unit sponsoring an external investment pool participate in it?

Q8-8 What financial statements are prepared for an Investment Trust Fund?

Q8-9 How are investments in an Investment Trust Fund valued? How are changes in value treated?

Q8-10 When are Private Purpose Trust Funds used?

Q8-11 How are Private Purpose Trust Funds controlled?

Q8-12 What financial statements are used for Private Purpose Trust Funds?

Q8-13 Assume a freshman approached you and asked you to define an agency relationship. How would you respond?

Q8-14 Is an operating statement prepared for an Agency Fund? Why or why not?

Q8-15 Does an Agency Fund have a fund balance? Why or why not?

Q8-16 If the activities of an Agency Fund produce revenues, where are these revenues usually accounted for?

Q8-17 The bookkeeper of the City of New Sherman recently made the following statement: "A Capital Projects Fund should be used for all special assessment projects." Do you agree or disagree? Why?

Q8-18 Lakefront Township recently assessed property holders for the cost of removing snow from the streets in each subdivision. What type of accounting would you recommend for this activity?

Q8-19 Has the GASB eliminated the Special Assessment Fund as an accounting entity?

Q8-20 Explain how the financing of capital projects with special assessments differs from the use of general obligation bonds.

CASES

C8-1 J. S. Moneybaggs wants to include a provision in her will that will assure her that her life's work of caring for small children will continue after her death. She is concerned that any resources given to the city might be used for some other purpose. Moneybaggs hires you as her financial consultant. How will you advise her?

C8-2 The city council of Largeville is facing a growing crime problem in its central shopping district (CSD). The council wants to increase the presence of police in the CSD, but the current year's budget lacks the funds to provide for the extra protection. One alternative would be to levy a special tax on the merchants in the CSD but, based on the Largeville City Charter, a tax would require a vote of the merchants and that would take time and additional resources. Joe del Puerto, the city manager for Largeville, asks you to help find a solution to this problem. What suggestions might you offer?

C8-3 A new employee of the City of Kashime was working with the accounting records of several of its funds. This employee, John Fergie, wanted to set up a Permanent Fund for the principal of some donations to the library and use a Special Revenue Fund to account for the earnings of the investment and their use. Another employee argued that a Private Purpose Trust Fund should be used for both principal and income. Do you agree with either of these individuals, or do you have a better suggestion?

C8-4 The City of Macroville hires you as a consultant to help establish a procedure to simplify its property tax collection processing and make the process more efficient. Currently the city and six special districts receive money from a property tax. Each district and the city has its own billing, recording, and collection functions. In addition, the taxpayers are upset about paying seven different tax bills. At a recent town hall–type meeting, several citizens spoke and demanded that the city do something to simplify the process. As a consultant, how would you advise the city?

ETHICS CASES

EC8-1 Aaronsborough's city manager, Thomas Smith, is facing a financial dilemma. The General Fund will not have enough revenues to cover the current year's expenditures. Because the city is too small to have a separate financial manager, Smith has the responsibility of balancing the budget. After an all-night session, he reduced the expenditures by only 5 percent, which is not enough to balance the budget. His wife, Jane Smith, mentioned to him that whenever they did not have enough money to meet their bills for a particular month, she merely borrowed money from the local bank. At that time, Smith decided to borrow part of the principal of a Pension Trust Fund. His intention was to repay the loan as soon as possible. Will the loan solve his problem? Explain. Is an ethical problem raised here? Explain.

EC8-2 Assume the same facts as stated in EC8-1, except that the Pension Trust Fund is operated by a five-member board of directors. Before the end of the current fiscal year, three of the board members' terms expire. If Smith appoints three new board members who are sympathetic to his plan, do you see a potential ethical problem?

EXERCISES

E8-1 (True or false)
Indicate whether the following statements are true or false. For any false statements, indicate why it is false.
1. If GASB *Statement No. 25* is used to account for a Pension Trust Fund, there is not an actual "fund balance" account.
2. "Net assets held in trust for pension benefits" represents an excess of the liabilities of the fund over its assets.
3. On the financial statements of a Pension Trust Fund, contributions from members of the PERS are reported differently from those of the governmental unit.
4. Retirement annuity payments increase the assets of a Pension Trust Fund.
5. Financial reporting for a defined contribution pension plan is the same as that of a defined benefits plan.
6. The liability a government has for unpaid pension contributions is reported the same whether the General Fund or an Enterprise Fund is involved.
7. Financial reporting for defined benefit pension plans involves only a statement of plan net assets and a statement of changes in plan net assets.

E8-2 (Financial reporting for a PERS)
Obtain a copy of a set of financial statements for a PERS and a governmental unit that reports the PERS as part of its Comprehensive Annual Financial Report. Compare the reporting with that described in the text.

E8-3 (Financial reporting for a PERS)
Is the present value (actuarially computed) status of a pension plan disclosed in the required financial reporting prescribed by GASB? If so, describe how it is reported and how the information may be used.

E8-4 (Journal entries for a PERS)
The Pension Trust Fund maintained by the city of Greensville incurred the following transactions during 2004. Record each transaction in the Pension Trust Fund. Ignore any other funds that may be involved in a transaction.
1. Contributions of $500,000 were received from General Fund employees and the General Fund contributed its share of $100,000.
2. The fund paid $500 for investment management fees.
3. Investments held by the fund increased in value by $3,500.
4. Depreciation on fund assets totaled $800.
5. Retirement benefits of $5,000 were paid to retirees.
6. Interest of $2,500 and dividends of $1,400 were received from investments.

E8-5 (Terminology)
Define the following terms as they apply to pension plans and postretirement benefit plans:
1. Defined benefit plan
2. Defined contribution plan
3. Postretirement benefits
4. Net assets held in trust for pension benefits
5. Unfunded actuarial accrued liability
6. Net pension obligation

E8-6 (Journal entries for an Investment Trust Fund)
Prepare the journal entries to record the following transactions in an Investment Trust Fund.
1. Turtle Creek and Pineview contributed $50,000 and $30,000, respectively, to an investment trust fund operated by Seggen County during 2004.
2. Investments totaling $75,000 were purchased.
3. Income from the investments during the year totaled $8,000.
4. The fund paid $1,500 to the county for investment management fees.
5. The investments increased in value by $3,000.
6. Income of $6,000 is paid to the two cities based on the relative amount of their initial investment.

E8-7 (Financial statements for an Investment Trust Fund)
Based on the information in E8-6, prepare a statement of changes in fiduciary fund net assets and a statement of fiduciary fund net assets.

E8-8 (Discussion)
Why would one entity permit another entity to invest its resources?

E8-9 (Journal entries for a Private Purpose Trust Fund)
Record the following journal entries in the Children's Book Fund, a Private Purpose Trust Fund that supplies books for children in privately owned battered women's shelters.
1. A wealthy citizen donated $500,000 to a Private Purpose Trust Fund. The trust specified that this money was to be used to acquire children's books for battered women's shelters.
2. The fund invested $420,000 in certificates of deposit.
3. Books costing $45,000 were acquired.
4. Income of $20,000 was received in cash from the investments.
5. The accounts were closed for the year.

E8-10 (Multiple choice)
1. Which of the following types of funds use the modified accrual basis of accounting?
   a. Capital Projects Funds
   b. Debt Service Funds
   c. General Fund
   d. Special Revenue Funds
   e. All of the above

2. Which of the following funds can be used to account for the spendable income from a Private Purpose Trust Fund?
   a. Agency Fund
   b. General Fund
   c. Capital Projects Fund
   d. Pension Trust Fund
   e. None of the above

3. Which of the following funds does not follow the current resources measurement focus?
   a. Private Purpose Trust Funds
   b. General Fund
   c. Special Revenue Funds
   d. Capital Projects Funds
   e. All of the above

4. To what provisions must the use of assets accumulated in a trust fund conform?
   a. State and local laws
   b. The trust agreement
   c. Both (a) and (b)
   d. The modified accrual basis of accounting
   e. None of the above

5. A citizen donated $1 million to a city upon her death. Her will provided that these resources be maintained in a trust and spent to provide free tickets to local baseball games for schoolchildren. In which fund is accounting for these activities done?
   a. General Fund
   b. Special Revenue Fund
   c. Investment Trust Fund
   d. Private Purpose Trust Fund
   e. Both (c) and (d)

E8-11   (Fill in the blanks)
   1. Private Purpose Trust Funds are controlled through _____ and _____ .
   2. Private Purpose Trust Funds follow a(n) _____ measurement focus and a(n) _____ basis of accounting.
   3. Amounts originally contributed to a Private Purpose Trust Fund are recorded as _____ .
   4. The following financial statements are prepared for a Private Purpose Trust Fund: _____ and _____ .
   5. The operations of a Private Purpose Trust Fund are usually (more or less) _____ complex than those of the General Fund.
   6. The most important document, with respect to a Private Purpose Trust Fund, is the _____ .

Chapter 8   The Governmental Fund Accounting Cycle   347

E8-12 (Compare and contrast an Investment Trust Fund with a Private Purpose Trust Fund)

Identify the major similarities and differences between an Investment Trust Fund and a Private Purpose Trust Fund. Be sure to include when each is used.

E8-13 (True or false)

Indicate whether the following statements are true or false. For any false statements, indicate why it is false.

1. Private Purpose Trust Funds use a capital maintenance measurement focus for recording events.
2. Investment Trust Funds use the full accrual basis of accounting for recording events.
3. The receipt of a gift by a Private Purpose Trust Fund is recorded as a direct entry to a contributed capital account.
4. A fixed budget is used to control expenditures of a Pension Trust Fund.
5. A statement of cash flows is prepared for a Private Purpose Trust Fund.
6. A statement of cash flows is prepared for a Pension Trust Fund.
7. A net income figure is calculated for a Private Purpose Trust Fund.
8. The activities of a Private Purpose Trust Fund may encompass the operation of a business.
9. All of the trust funds discussed in this chapter may be used interchangeably.

E8-14 (Discussion of alternatives for use of trusts)

You were recently approached by a wealthy individual who wants to set up a trust for the education of children of deceased schoolteachers. That person asked you to explain the best method of achieving his goal. Prepare a written statement regarding your response.

E8-15 (Multiple choice)

1. The principal amount of a gift held in a trust that cannot be spent should be accounted for in which of the following funds?
   a. General Fund
   b. Special Revenue Fund
   c. Capital Projects Fund
   d. Private Purpose Trust Fund

2. In what way can the amounts in an Investment Trust Fund be invested?
   a. Any way the government that operates the fund wishes
   b. Only in corporate stocks and bonds
   c. Only as provided in the trust agreement
   d. Only in governmental bonds

3. To what type of account are contributions to a Pension Trust Fund usually credited?
   a. A revenue account
   b. An expenditure account
   c. An additions account
   d. A net assets account

4. How are proceeds on the sale of an investment in excess of its book value handled in a Private Purpose Trust Fund?
   a. May be credited to the asset account
   b. May be debited or credited to the asset account
   c. Must be credited to an additions account
   d. May be debited to the assets or an additions account

5. Financial statements for a Pension Trust Fund
   a. Are not reported in governmental fund financial statements.
   b. Must be reported in governmental fund financial statements.
   c. Are included in the General Fund for financial reporting purposes.
   d. Are included in the Special Revenue Fund for financial reporting purposes.

E8-16 (Fill in the blanks)
   1. Agency Funds are classified as _____ type funds.
   2. An Agency Fund is used when the governmental unit is the _____ of resources that belong to some other organization.
   3. Agency Funds (do or do not) _____ have title to the resources in the fund.
   4. The financial statement for an Agency Fund is _____ .
   5. Revenues generated by the activities recorded in an Agency Fund are usually recorded in the _____ Fund.
   6. Agency Funds (are or are not) _____ used only as tax collection funds.

E8-17 (Multiple choice)
   1. The fee for the collection of property taxes by an Agency Fund will result in revenue in which of the following funds?
      a. General Fund and Agency Fund
      b. Agency Fund
      c. Capital Projects Fund
      d. Special Revenue Fund and Agency Fund
      e. None of the above

   2. Blaken Township established an Agency Fund to account for the collection and distribution of a general sales tax. The tax is collected for the General Fund, an independent school district, and several independent drainage districts. The school district and the drainage districts are entities that are separate from the city. During the year, $500,000 was collected in sales taxes. Entries to record the collection and distribution of the resources for the city should be made in the books for which of the following funds?
      a. General Fund
      b. Agency Fund
      c. General Fund and Agency Fund
      d. Special Revenue Fund and Agency Fund
      e. None of the above

   3. Collection of resources that must be distributed to other funds should be recorded in an Agency Fund as a debit to Cash and a credit to which account?

a. Revenues
b. Expenditures
c. Other financing sources
d. Other financing uses
e. None of the above

4. Which of the following funds does not have a fund balance account or net assets account?
   a. General Fund
   b. Special Revenue Fund
   c. Capital Projects Fund
   d. Permanent Fund
   e. Agency Fund

5. For what activities might an Agency Fund be used?
   a. Revenue generated from a property tax levy
   b. Expenditures of the General Fund
   c. Debt service for Enterprise Fund debt
   d. Debt service of general obligation bonds used to finance an addition to city hall
   e. None of the above

6. According to GAAP for Pension Trust Funds, which of the following is true?
   a. Revenues must be transferred to a Permanent Fund.
   b. Payments of resources are recorded as deductions.
   c. There is no concept of fund balance or net assets.
   d. All disbursements must be made to the General Fund.
   e. None of the above

E8-18 (Journal entries for an Agency Fund)
Prepare the following journal entries in the Bid Deposits Fund, an Agency Fund. This fund is used to record all deposits made by contractors doing work for the city. Any earnings on these resources are required to be paid to the depositing companies.
1. Deposits totaling $750,000 were received.
2. The amount received in part (1) was invested in certificates of deposit.
3. Income from the investments totaling $70,000 was received.
4. Deposits of $93,750 were returned to contractors upon successful completion of the projects on which they were working. In addition, these contractors received $8,750 of earnings on their deposits (their share of the earnings of the fund for the year). *Hint:* Do not forget to liquidate some of the investments.
5. The books were closed for the year.

E8-19 (Fill in the blanks—general terminology)
1. When special assessment bonds are issued to finance the cost of paving streets, the principal (is or is not) _____ recorded as a liability in the fund financial statements.

2. The project described in part (1) is called a _____ by the GASB.
3. If a city used a special assessment to finance the cost of storm sewer clean-ing, the project would be called a _____ by the GASB.
4. The accounting procedures used to record the activities involved in installing street lighting, using special assessments for funding, in a neigh-borhood are the same as those used in a(n) _____ .
5. The activities involved in a "service assessment" should be accounted for in _____ , _____ , or _____ as appropriate.
6. If a governmental unit is not "obligated in some manner" for the debt resulting from a special assessment construction project, the debt service activities should be accounted for in a(n) _____ .
7. In the situation described in part (6), the construction activities would be accounted for in a(n) _____ .

E8-20 (Discussion of "obligated in some manner")
Explain the term *obligated in some manner* as it is used by the GASB, and indi-cate how it affects special assessment accounting.

E8-21 (Multiple choice for various funds)
1. The construction of a new criminal courts building, using a federal grant for three-quarters of the cost, would be accounted for in which of the fol-lowing funds?
   a. General Fund
   b. Special Assessment Fund
   c. Capital Projects Fund
   d. Investment Trust Fund
   e. None of the above

2. The City of Milta financed the construction of a new street-lighting system through special assessments. The resulting asset (streetlights) should be reported in the fund financial statements in which of the following funds?
   a. General Fund
   b. Streetlight Fund (a Special Assessment Fund)
   c. Streetlight Fund (a Capital Projects Fund)
   d. Special Revenue Fund
   e. None of the above

3. When must a comparison of budgetary and actual data be reported for the General Fund?
   a. When the actual amounts exceed the budgeted amounts
   b. When the budgeted amounts exceed the actual amounts
   c. Always
   d. Never
   e. None of the above

4. When is the Special assessments receivable—deferred account used?
   a. To record the amount of revenue recognized from special assessments in a particular period

b. To offset any deficit arising from a special assessment project

c. As a budgetary account

d. To record the amount of assessments that will be collected in future periods

e. None of the above

5. In what fund are the activities of the police department of the City of Brent recorded?

a. General Fund

b. Capital Projects Fund

c. Special Assessments Fund

d. A combination of (b) and (c)

e. None of the above

6. What is the minimum number of funds a city may use for accounting purposes?

a. One

b. Two

c. Three

d. Four

e. Eight

PROBLEMS

P8-1 (Journal entries and statements for a Pension Trust Fund)

The City of Saintsville has had an employee pension fund for several years. The following is a trial balance for the fund at December 31, 2003, and several transactions that occurred during 2004:

City of Saintsville
Pension Trust Fund
Employees Retirement Fund
Trial Balance
December 31, 2003

	Debits	Credits
Cash	$ 52,500	
Investment income receivable	210,000	
Investments—corporate stocks	20,000,000	
Investments—U.S. government securities	30,575,000	
Accrued expenses		$ 12,000
Net assets held in trust for pension benefits		50,825,500
	$50,837,500	$50,837,500

1. Contributions from the General Fund totaled $750,000; included in this amount was $258,750 from the employees and $491,250 from the city.

2. Investments in corporate stocks costing $500,000 were purchased.
3. The fund collected interest accrued at December 31, 2003. Investment income for 2004 totaled $4,800,000, of which $4,290,000 was collected in cash. Investment income earned in 2004 included dividends of $850,000 and the remainder was interest.
4. Employee retirement benefits of $3,500,000 were paid.
5. Additional U.S. government securities totaling $1,100,000 were acquired.
6. Costs of operating the plan were $175,000; of this amount $150,000 was paid in cash and the remainder was accrued. The accrued expenses at the beginning of the year were also paid. These expenses are administrative in nature.
7. U.S. government securities that had a book value of $500,000 were redeemed for $600,000.
8. The market value of the corporate stocks at the end of the year increased by $1,000,000.

Required: 1. Prepare the journal entries necessary to record these transactions.
2. Prepare a statement of changes in fiduciary net assets for the fund for 2004.
3. Prepare a statement of fiduciary net assets as of December 31, 2004.

P8-2 (Journal entries for several funds)
Following are several transactions for the Village of Sol during 2004:
1. Supplies of $15,000 were ordered by the General Fund.
2. Property taxes of $325,000 were assessed through a Special Revenue Fund. Of this amount, $290,000 is expected to be collected.
3. Contributions to the PERS from the General Fund were $150,000. An equal amount was deducted from the salaries of the city workers. Assume that the entire payroll was $1 million and that $200,000 was withheld and recorded as "Due to U.S. government." The entire amount due was paid to the pension fund.
4. Collections of water bills by the Water Utility Fund were $1,300,000. Of this amount, $100,000 was from the General Fund. Assume that any revenue/expenditure was recorded previously.
5. The General Fund made its annual payment to a Debt Service Fund, $250,000 of which $200,000 was for principal. Assume that this amount was not encumbered.
6. Interest of $100,000 and principal of $100,000 were paid by a Debt Service Fund. Assume that no previous entries were made for these amounts.
7. Interest of $50,000 was paid by the Electric Utility Fund on outstanding bank loans.
8. New furniture was received for the mayor's office. The actual cost was $30,000. An encumbrance was set up for $30,000 when the order was placed.
9. Benefits paid to retired employees were $50,000.

10. Property tax receivables totaling $500 were written off as uncollectible in the Special Revenue Fund.

Required: Prepare all the journal entries necessary to record these transactions and identify the fund(s) used.

P8-3 (Preparation of a statement of fiduciary net assets for a Pension Trust Fund) The following information is available for Russellville at June 30, 2004:

Additions—interest	$ 250,000
Member contributions	340,000
Loss on sale of investments	30,000
Cash	180,000
Accrued expenses	56,000
Interest receivable	20,000
Accounts payable	33,000
Due to other funds	54,000
Investments	10,000,000
Deductions—operating costs	42,000
Retirement annuities paid	987,000

Required: Prepare a statement of fiduciary net assets for Russellville's Pension Trust Fund as of June 30, 2004.

P8-4 (Adjusting and correcting entries for several funds)
With the exception of the following events, the City of Lizabethville's books were maintained according to GAAP. Prepare any necessary adjusting or correcting entries based upon the information given and identify the fund(s). The current year is 2004.
1. Interest of $149,000 was earned by general obligation bondholders. This amount, together with $21,000 more, would be paid in February 2004. No entries were made for these amounts.
2. The General Fund paid $200,000 in cash to the PERS for the governmental employees. The city contributed $165,000 of the total. The entry in the PERS to record the receipt was

Cash	200,000	
Pension liability		200,000

3. A general obligation bond issue was sold by a Capital Projects Fund for $3,050,000. The face value of the bonds is $3 million. Local laws permit the fund to use the premium for construction costs. The only entry made for the sale of the bonds was recorded in the Capital Projects Fund as follows:

Cash	3,050,000	
Bonds payable		3,000,000
Premium on bonds payable		50,000

4. The city purchased 10 police cars for a total of $200,000. The only entry made for the purchase was recorded in the General Fund as follows:

Automobiles	200,000	
Cash		200,000

5. Revenue bonds with a face value of $8,000,000 were issued by the Municipal Electric Fund, an Enterprise Fund. The entries made for the issuance were recorded as follows:

EF	Cash	8,000,000	
	Proceeds from bond issue		8,000,000
GF	Bonds in Municipal Electric Fund	8,000,000	
	Bonds payable		8,000,000

P8-5 (Journal entries and financial statements for an Investment Trust Fund) Dryrock County operates an Investment Trust Fund for cities located in the county. The following entries are associated with the fund during 2004:
1. The cities of Bushville and Clintonville contributed assets, $75,000 and $50,000, respectively.
2. The entire amount received in part (1) was invested: $65,000 in certificates of deposit (CDs) and $60,000 in Treasury notes.
3. Interest income of $37,500 was received.
4. CDs totaling $40,000 and Treasury notes totaling $30,000 matured. Interest income of $1,000 was also received.
5. The money received in part (4) was reinvested in CDs.
6. Additional interest income was received, $17,500.
7. The General Fund charged the Investment Trust Fund $500 for administrative expenses. This amount was paid in cash.
8. The income of $50,000 was distributed to the participating cities according to the trust agreement (Bushville 60%, Clintonville 40%).

Required: 1. Prepare journal entries to record the 2004 entries in the Investment Trust Fund.
2. Prepare a statement of changes in fiduciary net assets for the fund for 2004.
3. Prepare a statement of fiduciary net assets for the fund as of December 31, 2004.

P8-6 (Journal entries and financial statements for an Investment Trust Fund) The City of Titanville established an Investment Trust Fund for Bay Town and Valley City. The cities contributed $200,000 and $100,000, respectively, to the fund. During 2004 the following transactions took place:
1. Bay Town contributed certificates of deposit (CDs) valued at $200,000, and Valley City contributed $100,000 to the fund.
2. The cash contributed by Valley City was invested in U.S. government securities.
3. The CDs matured. The principal was $70,000. Interest on the CDs was $3,000.
4. The principal amount received in part (3) was reinvested in municipal bonds.
5. The fund incurred internal administrative expenses totaling $700, of which $500 was paid in cash.

6. The General Fund charged the Investment Trust Fund $500 for managing the investments. This amount was paid in cash.
7. The trust fund income of $1,800 ($3,000 − $700 − $500) was distributed as provided in the trust agreement: two-thirds to Bay Town and one-third to Valley City.

P8-7 (Journal entries and financial statements for a Private Purpose Trust Fund) Landslot City received a gift from J. R. Landslot. Landslot wished to provide operating resources for a parade in her husband's honor. The gift was $2 million. To guarantee proper use of the money, Landslot made the donation in the form of a trust—a private purpose trust. The following events took place during 2004:
  1. Landslot gave Landslot City $2 million with the stipulations mentioned previously.
  2. The city paid $500,000 to a local advertising agency to publicize the parade.
  3. The city sponsored a float in the parade. The total cost of building the float was $200,000. Based on the trust agreement, this expenditure from the gift is acceptable.
  4. The police department spent $100,000 for extra police to control the traffic and crowds at the parade. The trust reimbursed the department for these costs.
  5. The sanitation department incurred $75,000 of costs in cleaning up after the parade. The trust reimbursed the department for these costs.
  6. The city paid $300,000 to various school bands and marching groups to participate in the parade.
  7. A "kick-off dinner" was held 2 months before the parade to start the parade season. The cost of the dinner was $123,000.
  8. An office was established to oversee the parade preparations. The total cost of running the office was $35,000, of which $25,000 was paid in cash.
  9. The cost of permits and other legal obligations totaled $500.
  10. The remaining cash, except for $10,000, was invested in certificates of deposit. According to the trust agreement, this money would be invested and used to provide for the 2005 parade.

Required: 1. Record these entries in the Landslot Parade Fund—a Private Purpose Trust Fund.
    2. Prepare a statement of changes in fiduciary net assets for 2004 and a statement of fiduciary net assets as of December 31, 2004, for the fund.

P8-8 (Journal entries for a Private Purpose Trust Fund)
  1. The City of Newfonia received $2 million from the First Tire Company. The company required the city to maintain the principal of the gift and any income to be used to provide resources to improve a privately owned automobile racetrack.
  2. The city invested the entire gift in certificates of deposit (CDs).
  3. Investment income of $100,000 was received in cash.

4. Because plans to improve the racetrack were incomplete, the $100,000 from part (3) was reinvested in short-term CDs.
5. After the improvement plans were completed and the short-term CDs matured, the city used the $100,000 of investments and the interest income of $1,000 to pay for part of the racetrack improvements.
6. As part of a continuing campaign, the city received an additional $300,000 gift from the First Tire Company. The same restrictions, as indicated in part (1), applied to this gift. The proceeds of the gift were immediately invested in CDs.
7. Investment income of $112,000 was received in cash.
8. Additional work on the racetrack totaling $97,000 was paid for.
9. Interest income of $2,300 was accrued at the end of 2004.
10. The General Fund charged the Racetrack Fund $3,000: $2,000 for managing the investments and $1,000 for administering the fund. The entire amount was paid in cash.

Required: 1. Prepare the journal entries necessary to record these events on the books of the Automobile Racetrack Fund.
2. Prepare a statement of changes in fiduciary fund net assets for 2004 for the Automobile Racetrack Fund.
3. Prepare a statement of fiduciary fund net assets for the Automobile Racetrack Fund at December 31, 2004.
4. Prepare the closing entry (entries) for the Automobile Racetrack Fund.

P8-9   (Journal entries for three Agency Funds and a trial balance for each fund)
Assume that the Town of Boonsville maintains an Agency Fund for its employees' insurance withholdings, another for its employees' income tax withholdings, and a third for its employees' pension contributions. The following are selected transactions, incurred during 2004, related to these funds:
1. The town recorded its monthly payroll. Salaries totaled $350,000. The withholdings were as follows: $70,000 for employees' income taxes, $30,000 for employees' insurance, $15,000 for employees' pension contributions, and $25,000 for miscellaneous deductions. The General Fund paid the appropriate amount to each Agency Fund.
2. The Employees' Insurance Deposits Fund made a payment of $25,000 to the various insurance companies providing insurance coverage to the employees.
3. The town recorded its monthly payroll. Salaries totaled $375,000. The withholdings were as follows: $75,000 for employees' income taxes, $20,00 for employees' insurance, $18,000 for employees' pension contributions, and $26,000 for miscellaneous deductions. The General Fund paid the appropriate amount to each Agency Fund.
4. The town recorded its monthly payroll. Salaries totaled $350,000. The withholdings were as follows: $70,000 for employees' income taxes, $30,000 for employees' insurance, $15,000 for employees' pension contributions, and $25,000 for miscellaneous deductions. The General Fund paid the appropriate amounts to the appropriate Agency Fund.

5. The General Fund matched the employees' payments to the Employees' Pension Agency Fund.
6. The appropriate Agency Funds made a payment of $215,000 to the U.S. government and $50,000 to the Pension Trust Fund.
7. The town recorded its monthly payroll. Salaries totaled $375,000. The withholdings were as follows: $75,000 for employees' income taxes, $20,000 for employees' insurance, $18,000 for employees' pension contributions, and $26,000 for miscellaneous deductions. The General Fund paid the appropriate amounts to the appropriate Agency Fund.
8. The General Fund matched the employees' payments to the Employees' Pension Agency Fund.

Required: Prepare the journal entries necessary to record these events on the books of the Employees' Insurance Agency Fund, Employees' Income Tax Agency Fund, and the Employees' Pension Agency Fund and prepare a trial balance for each fund.

P8-10 (Journal entries and financial statements for a street-lighting project financed with a special assessment)

The following entries were incurred between July 1, 2003, and June 30, 2004, for Brown Township:

1. The managing board approved the capital budget for the fiscal year July 1, 2003–June 30, 2004. Included in this budget was a drainage project that would be funded through special assessments and a contribution from the township. Intermediate financing was furnished by a bond issue that would be repaid with collections of the special assessments. The managing board also approved the budget for the project. Included in the budget were estimated revenues of $200,000 for the current year and appropriations of $1,600,000 for the project. The township's share of the cost for this project was $40,000. Assume the township guaranteed payment of the special assessment bonds used to finance the project.
2. A construction contract with Jorge Construction Company was approved for $1,400,000. The contract had a 10 percent retainage clause.
3. Special assessments totaling $1,360,000 were levied against the property holders that would benefit from the project. Of this amount, $100,000 was considered to be current and recognized as revenue. This same amount will become current next year.
4. Collections from property holders totaled $90,000.
5. Special assessment bonds totaling $1,360,000 were issued for $1,360,000.
6. A progress billing was received from the contractor for $500,000.
7. The contractor was paid the amount of the billing, less a 10 percent retainage. (Assume the city does not use a voucher system.)
8. Short-term securities were purchased for $900,000, using Capital Projects Fund resources.
9. An additional billing was received from the contractor for $600,000.
10. Investments that cost $600,000 were redeemed for $620,000. The difference was interest revenue.

11. The contractor was paid, less the agreed-upon retainage.
12. Investments that cost $300,000 were redeemed for $330,000. The difference was interest revenue.
13. The contractor completed the project and submitted a final bill for $300,000. After an examination of the work, it was accepted by the city and the full amount of the billing, plus all previously retained amounts, was paid.
14. Interest of $140,000 was paid on the special assessment bonds.
15. The township's share of the project was paid to the fund where the construction was recorded.

Required: 1. Prepare the journal entries necessary to record these events and indicate the fund(s) used. (Assume there is no interest on the assessments for 2003.)
2. Prepare a trial balance for the fund where the construction accounting was recorded.
3. Prepare all necessary year-end entries and closing entries in the Capital Projects Fund. After the project has been completed, any fund balance should be transferred to the Debt Service Fund. (Hint: Do not forget the status of the receivables in the Debt Service Fund at year-end.)
4. Prepare a statement of revenues, expenditures, and changes in fund balance and a balance sheet for the fund where the construction was recorded.

CONTINUOUS PROBLEMS

Pension Trust Fund

Bacchus City maintains a Pension Trust Fund for its employees. The following is a trial balance for the fund at December 31, 2003, and several transactions that occurred during 2004:

	Bacchus City Pension Trust Fund Employees' Retirement Fund Trial Balance December 31, 2003	
	Debits	Credits
Cash	$ 78,750	
Investment income receivable	315,000	
Investments—U.S. government securities	25,287,500	
Investments—corporate stocks	50,575,000	
Accrued expenses		$ 18,000
Net assets held in trust for pension benefits		76,238,250
	$76,256,250	$76,256,250

The following transactions took place during 2004:

1. The fund contributions from the General Fund totaled $1,000,000; included in this amount was $500,000 from the employees and $500,000 from the city.
2. Investments in certificates of deposit (CDs) costing $600,000 and U.S. government securities costing $400,000 were purchased.
3. Collected interest accrued at December 31, 2003. Interest income for 2004 totaled $7,000,000, of which $6,000,000 was collected in cash.
4. Employee retirement benefits of $6,100,000 were paid.
5. Additional U.S. government securities of $200,000 were acquired.
6. Costs of operating the plan were $180,000; of this amount $100,000 was paid in cash and the remainder was accrued. The accrued expenses at the beginning of the year were also paid. These expenses are administrative in nature.
7. CDs with a book value of $500,000 were redeemed for $510,000.
8. The fair value of the corporate stocks increased by $50,000 by the end of 2004.

Required: 1. Prepare the journal entries necessary to record these transactions.
2. Prepare a statement of changes in fiduciary net assets for the fund for 2004.
3. Prepare a statement of fiduciary net assets as of December 31, 2004.

Investment Trust Fund

Bacchus City established an Investment Trust Fund for the cities of Zeus and Comusville. The cities contributed $500,000 each to the fund. During 2004 the following transactions took place:

1. Bacchus City received the contributions from Zeus and Comusville.
2. The cash was immediately invested in U.S. government securities.
3. Some of the investments matured. The principal was $300,000. Interest on the securities was $5,000.
4. The principal amount received in part (3) was reinvested in municipal bonds.
5. The fund incurred internal administrative expenses totaling $1,000, of which $700 were paid in cash.
6. The Investment Trust Fund paid $900 to an investment advisor for managing the investments. This amount was paid in cash.
7. Accrued interest income at the end of the year totaled $30,000.
8. Cash in the amount of $1,800 was distributed as provided in the trust agreement: one-half to the City of Zeus and one-half to Comusville.

Required: 1. Prepare the journal entries to record the preceding events.
2. Prepare a statement of changes in fiduciary net assets for 2004.
3. Prepare a statement of fiduciary net assets at December 31, 2004.

Private Purpose Trust Fund

Bacchus City received a gift from Vera Thomas. Thomas wished to provide resources for scholarships for underprivileged children in memory of her husband. These scholarships would provide resources for books and tuition for up to 10 students per year at an in-state university. The total amount of the gift was $50 million. To guarantee proper use of the money, Thomas made the donation in the form of a trust—a private purpose trust that would be operated by Bacchus City. The following events took place during 2004:

1. Thomas gave Bacchus City the $50 million principal for the fund.
2. The city immediately awarded 10 scholarships and paid the recipients $8,000 each for the first year of their education.
3. The city invested $49,900,000 in U.S. government securities.
4. Securities in the amount of $1 million matured and produced $50,000 of interest income.
5. The $1,050,000 was immediately invested in certificates of deposit (CDs).
6. The students submitted bills for room and board for $27,000 while they attended classes. These expenses are valid expenses under the terms of the trust.
7. One student dropped out of college and had to repay the amount of his scholarship, $7,500.
8. Interest income of $1,997,000 was earned in 2004. Of this amount, $1,970,000 was received in cash.

Required: 1. Record these entries in the Thomas Scholarship Fund, a Private Purpose Trust Fund.
2. Prepare a statement of changes in fiduciary net assets for 2004 and a statement of fiduciary net assets as of December 31, 2004, for the fund.

Agency Fund

Bacchus City recently hosted a state fair. The city levied a special 1 percent sales tax on all sales made at the fair; the proceeds of the tax and all investment income were to be used to provide resources to the county to build new roads. The tax was collected by Bacchus City and disbursed to the county as provided in the agreement between the two. The dates of the fair spanned two fiscal periods. The following trial balance is available at the end of 2003:

Bacchus City
Fiduciary Fund
Agency Fund
State Fair Sales Tax Fund
Trial Balance
December 31, 2003

	Debits	Credits
Cash	$ 3,500	
Investments—certificates of deposit	46,600	
Due to other governmental funds		$50,100
	$50,100	$50,100

The following transactions took place during 2004:

1. Investments costing $15,000 were redeemed for a total of $18,000; the difference was investment revenue.
2. The Agency Fund collected $150,000 of sales taxes.
3. Contractors were paid $1,000 by the county after receiving a distribution of that amount from the Agency Fund.
4. The Agency Fund collected $800 in interest on investments.
5. An additional $13,500 was paid to the county.
6. Another contractor was hired by the county to build a road. The total cost of the road was $100,000.
7. The second contractor was paid $35,000 on the contract by the county.
8. The remaining investments were redeemed by the Agency Fund for $36,000.
9. The remainder in the Agency Fund was transferred to the county.

Required: 1. Prepare the entries necessary for the Agency Fund during 2004.
2. Prepare the statement of fiduciary net assets for the Agency Fund at the end of 2004.

Special Assessment Transactions

The following transactions were incurred by Bacchus City during 2004:

1. A street-lighting project was approved by the city manager of Bacchus City; the total cost was $750,000. Revenues of the Capital Projects Fund relating to this project for the current year are estimated to be $50,000, and special assessment bonds will be used to finance the remainder. Interest on outstanding bonds payable is estimated to be $75,000 for the year. (Assume a budget is not recorded in the Debt Service Fund; however, a budget is recorded in the Capital Projects Fund.) Bacchus City meets the "obligated in some manner" standard for this debt.
2. Special assessment bonds were issued for the street-lighting project. The bonds were issued for their face value of $700,000.
3. A contract was let with Old Iron Construction Company for the street-lighting project at a total cost of $750,000.
4. A special assessment of $750,000 was levied to pay for the cost of the street-lighting project. The current portion of the installment was $50,000. Revenue of $50,000 was recorded at that time.
5. Old Iron submitted a progress billing for $200,000. The retainage on this billing was $10,000.
6. Old Iron was paid $190,000; the remainder was retained until the completion of the project.
7. Construction cash from the street-lighting project totaling $500,000 was invested in certificates of deposit.
8. Special assessments totaling $50,000 were collected.
9. Interest of $75,000 was paid on the special assessment bonds outstanding.
10. The next installment of the special assessment was $50,000.

Required: Prepare all the journal entries necessary to record these transactions. In addition, identify the fund(s) in which each entry is recorded.

Chapter 9

Reporting Principles and Preparation of Fund Financial Statements

Preparing Fund Financial Statements
    Focus on Major Funds
    Measurement Focus and Basis of Accounting
    Special and Extraordinary Items
Preparing Fund Financial Statements for Governmental Funds
    Balance Sheet
    Statement of Revenues, Expenditures, and Changes in
        Fund Balances
Preparing Fund Financial Statements for Proprietary Funds
    Statement of Net Assets (or Balance Sheet)
    Statement of Revenues, Expenses, and Changes in Fund
        Net Assets
    Statement of Cash Flows
Preparing Fund Financial Statements for Fiduciary Funds
Preparing Budgetary Comparison Schedules
Preparing Notes to the Financial Statements
Preparing Statistical Tables
Auditor's Report
Review Questions
Cases
Ethics Case
Exercises
Problems
Summary Problems

After completing this chapter, you should be able to:

➤ *Describe the objectives of governmental financial reporting.*

➤ *Explain how governmental accountants define the "reporting entity."*

➤ *Describe how financial data for component units is incorporated in the financial statements of a reporting entity.*

➤ *Identify the major components of a Comprehensive Annual Financial Report (CAFR).*

➤ *Identify and describe the seven fund financial statements.*

➤ *Describe the content of Management's Discussion and Analysis.*

➤ *Discuss the measurement focus and basis of accounting used in the fund financial statements.*

➤ *Explain the relationship between fund financial statements and combining statements.*

➤ *Describe the content of budgetary comparison schedules.*

➤ *Explain how notes are used for financial statement reporting.*

➤ *Describe the content of the statistical tables.*

*G*overnmental financial reporting has undergone significant change in recent years. Until the year 2001, governmental financial reporting was fund-oriented, just like the underlying accounting. The basic financial statements were prepared in a multicolumn format, with financial data for individual funds aggregated into totals for each fund type. Balance sheets contained groups of columns for the three fund categories (governmental, proprietary, and fiduciary), with each fund category further subdivided by fund type (for example, General Funds, Special Revenue Funds, and so forth within the governmental fund category).

Because different bases of accounting were used for the fund categories, separate sets of operating statements were prepared for governmental and proprietary funds. Both sophisticated and unsophisticated readers criticized governmental financial reporting because financial statements were hard to understand, did not present a clear picture of the operating results and financial position of the entity as a whole, and might be misleading in some respects.

FINANCIAL REPORTING OBJECTIVES (GASB *CONCEPTS STATEMENT NO. 1*)

The Governmental Accounting Standards Board (GASB) started work on a new financial reporting model shortly after the GASB was created. As a framework for the new model, the GASB first determined the objectives of governmental financial reporting. The GASB concluded that financial reports need to be responsive specifically to three major groups of external users of those reports:

- Those to whom government is primarily accountable (the citizenry)
- Those who directly represent the citizens (legislative and oversight bodies)
- Those who lend or participate in the lending process (lenders and creditors)

The GASB believed the needs of other external users, such as higher-level governmental units, could be encompassed within the needs of these three groups.

A user needs study led to GASB *Concepts Statement No. 1*, "Objectives of Financial Reporting." The GASB concluded in that statement that governmental financial reports should provide information to assist users in assessing accountability and in making economic, social, and political decisions; specifically the following:

a. Financial reporting should assist in fulfilling government's duty to be publicly accountable and should enable users to assess that accountability by:
   (1) providing information to determine whether current-year revenues were sufficient to pay for current-year services;
   (2) demonstrating whether resources were obtained and used in accordance with the entity's legally adopted budget, and demonstrating

compliance with other finance-related legal or contractual requirements; and

   (3) providing information to assist users in assessing the service efforts and accomplishments of the governmental entity.

  b. Financial reporting should assist users in evaluating the operating results of the governmental entity for the year by:

   (1) providing information about sources and uses of financial resources;

   (2) providing information about how it financed its activities and met its cash requirements; and

   (3) providing information necessary to determine whether its financial position improved or deteriorated as a result of the year's operations.

  c. Financial reporting should assist users in assessing the level of services that can be provided by the governmental entity and its ability to meet its obligations as they become due by:

   (1) providing information about its financial position and condition;

   (2) providing information about its physical and other non-financial resources having useful lives that extend beyond the current year, including information that can be used to assess the service potential of those resources; and

   (3) disclosing legal or contractual restrictions on resources and the risk of potential loss of resources.[1]

Meeting those objectives would require changes to the reporting model then in existence, because the existing model focused on reporting by fund type and on flows and balances of current financial resources within the governmental-type funds.

THE NEW REPORTING MODEL (GASB *STATEMENT NO. 34*)

After many years of study, the GASB issued GASB *Statement No. 34*, "Basic Financial Statements—and Management's Discussion and Analysis—for State and Local Governments." The standard was issued in June 1999, to be phased in as follows:

- Governments with annual revenues of $100 million or more—financial statements for periods beginning after June 15, 2001
- Governments with annual revenues of $10 million or more but less than $100 million—financial statements for periods beginning after June 15, 2002
- Governments with annual revenues of less than $10 million—financial statements for periods beginning after June 15, 2003

Earlier implementation was permitted.

    GASB *Statement No. 34* fundamentally changed the nature of governmental financial reporting. In essence, GASB *Statement No. 34* retained the previous fund-

---

[1] GASB Cod. (2001) App. B, para. 77–79.

oriented reporting requirement (albeit in somewhat different form), and added a new highly aggregated top layer of financial reports. The fund-oriented layer is referred to as *fund financial statements,* and the new top layer is referred to as *government-wide financial statements.* The purpose of the government-wide layer of statements is to help statement users to do the following more readily:

- Assess a government's finances in its entirety.
- Determine if its overall financial position improved or deteriorated.
- Evaluate whether its current-year revenues were sufficient to pay for current-year services.
- Ascertain the way in which it financed its programs, that is, through user fees, other program revenues, or general tax revenues.[2]

Accomplishing government-wide reporting under the GASB *Statement No. 34* model requires the following major adjustments to the fund financial statements, as well as a number of other adjustments:

- To prepare a single operating statement that aggregates governmental-type and proprietary-type funds, a single basis of accounting must be used. The GASB concluded that the reporting objectives of government-wide financial statements could be achieved best by using an economic resources measurement focus and the full accrual basis of accounting. As a result, financial data reported in the fund financial statements using the current financial resources measurement focus and modified accrual basis of accounting needs to be adjusted to the full accrual basis to prepare government-wide statements.
- To avoid potential confusion caused by reporting resources for which the government has a fiduciary responsibility but which it cannot legally use to finance its own activities, fiduciary-type funds are omitted from the government-wide financial statements.

This chapter covers the general principles of financial reporting for state and local governments, as well as the details of the fund financial statements. Chapter 10 covers the government-wide financial statements, the adjustments that need to be made to the fund financial statements to produce government-wide financial statements, and certain other provisions of GASB *Statement No. 34.*

Financial reporting in both chapters will be illustrated by reference to the Comprehensive Annual Financial Report (CAFR) issued by the Village of Grafton, Wisconsin, for calendar year 2000. The Village of Grafton (year 2000 population of 10,541) was one of the first municipalities in the nation to implement GASB *Statement No. 34.* Grafton has received the Certificate of Achievement for Excellence in Financial Reporting from the Government Finance Officers Association of the United States and Canada. It has also received a Certificate of Commendation from GRATE (Governmental Reporting Awards through Evaluation), sponsored by the Wisconsin Institute of Certified Public Accountants and Marquette University.

---

[2] GASB *Statement No. 34,* "Basic Financial Statements—and Management's Discussion and Analysis—for State and Local Governments," Preface.

THE FINANCIAL REPORTING ENTITY

Defining the Reporting Entity (GASB *Statement No. 14*)

Until now, the discussion of state and local governmental accounting focused on funds, which are accounting subdivisions *within* a governmental entity. For financial reporting purposes, however, a broader focus is needed, because many reporting governments have such close organizational and financial ties with other legally separate governmental organizations. Excluding the separate organizations would make the reporting government's statements incomplete or misleading. Many of these legally separate organizations take the form of public authorities or public benefit corporations (such as toll roads, toll bridges, and special financing agencies) that are controlled in some manner by a parent government.

The *reporting entity* defines the boundaries of a particular financial reporting unit by identifying *whose* assets, liabilities, revenues, expenses, and equities are embraced within that organization's financial statements. The GASB developed standards for state and local governments on this subject in GASB *Statement No. 14*, "The Financial Reporting Entity." The main governmental unit is called the *primary government*. Other governmental units whose financial activities are included in the primary government's financial statements are called *component units*.

All state governments and general-purpose local governments, such as counties, cities, towns, and villages, are primary governments. A special-purpose government (such as a local school board or a hospital district) is also defined as a primary government, provided it has a separately elected governing body, is legally separate (for example, it is created as a body corporate and politic), *and* is fiscally independent of other state and local governments. To be considered fiscally independent, as defined by the GASB, the organization must be authorized to do three specific things without the approval of another government: (1) determine its budget, (2) levy taxes or set user charges, and (3) issue bonded debt.[3]

Component units are legally separate organizations for which the elected officials of a primary government are *financially accountable*. A primary government is financially accountable for a legally separate organization if:

1. The primary government can appoint a voting majority of the organization's governing body; *and*
2. a. The primary government is able to impose its will on that organization; *or*
   b. There is a potential for the organization to provide specific financial benefits to, or to impose specific financial burdens on, the primary government.[4]

A primary government has the ability to impose its will on an organization if it can significantly influence its day-to-day operations, including its programs, its activities, or the level of services it provides. For example, a mayor can impose his or

---

[3] GASB Cod. (2001) Sec. 2100.112 and 2100.115.
[4] GASB Cod. (2001) Sec. 2100.120a.

her will on an organization if he or she has the ability to remove members of the organization's governing board at will, or to modify or approve its budgets or the fees it charges for services.

A primary government has a financial benefit or burden relationship with an organization if (1) the primary government is legally entitled to or can otherwise access the organization's resources; (2) is legally obligated or has otherwise assumed the obligation to finance the deficits of, or provide financial support to, the organization; or (3) the primary government is obligated in some manner for the organization's debt.[5]

Notice that two elements must be met in assessing whether a legally separate organization is a component unit of a primary government: (1) appointment of a voting majority of the component unit's governing board, and (2) either ability to impose will or benefit/burden. The following examples illustrate circumstances under which the second element is met:

- A state lottery and off-track betting corporation, where the benefit/burden criterion is met because the law provides that the corporation's net revenues must be remitted to the state
- A city toll bridge authority, where the "imposition of will" criterion is met because the law provides that the city council must approve toll rates, or because the law allows the mayor to remove any board member at will
- A county building construction authority, where the benefit/burden criterion is met because the law provides that the county will guarantee payment of principal and interest on the debt issued by the authority

A primary government's financial reporting entity also includes organizations that, if omitted, would cause the primary government's financial statements to be misleading or incomplete. New York City's financial statements, for example, include the financial activities of a state-created financing agency whose governing board consists primarily of state officials or state-appointed officials. The agency was created during the City's fiscal crisis for the sole purpose of refinancing a portion of the City's debt. Interest and principal on the agency's debt, which replaced the City's debt, is paid with City sales taxes diverted by law to the state agency.

Reporting Component Units in the Reporting Entity's Financial Statements

After all the organizations to be included in the reporting entity are identified, a decision needs to be made as to *how* these organizations should be included in the financial statements. The two methods for inclusion are blending and discrete presentation. *Blending* is the process of treating the funds used by the component unit as if they were the funds of the primary government. *Discrete presentation* of a component

---

[5] GASB standards take a broad view of when a primary government is "obligated in some manner" for the debt of a legally separate entity. The standards provide that the obligation may be either expressed or implied by certain indications that make assumption of the debt probable (GASB Cod. Sec. 2100.132.).

unit involves reporting the component unit's funds in a separate column in the reporting entity's financial statements.

Blending is used when the component unit, although legally separate from the primary government, is so intertwined with the primary government that it is substantively the same as the primary government. This occurs when the primary government's governing body is represented on the component unit's governing body to such an extent that it can completely control the component unit. It also occurs when the goods or services provided by the component unit are all or almost all for the primary government itself.[6]

Blending should be used, for example, when a specially created, legally separate financing agency issues debt solely to finance construction for the primary government, and pays off the debt with rental payments received from the primary government. The financing agency, a component unit, is, in substance, a Debt Service Fund of the primary government and should be treated that way for financial reporting purposes.

Discrete presentation is more common than blending. The typical discretely presented organization is one that provides services to the general public, similar to an enterprise fund. It may, for example, operate a toll road, a toll bridge, a lottery, an electric utility, or a public hospital.

In accordance with the reporting requirements of GASB *Statement No. 34*, the financial information of blended component units is reported in both the fund financial statements and the government-wide financial statements. As a general rule, financial information of discretely presented component units is reported only in the government-wide statements, as discussed in Chapter 10.

Notes to the reporting entity's financial statements should contain an identification of the component units, the criteria for including them in the financial statements, and how they are reported.

OVERVIEW OF THE COMPREHENSIVE ANNUAL FINANCIAL REPORT

In previous chapters we discussed the process of accumulating financial information for governmental units. This information is communicated to users of financial information through a *Comprehensive Annual Financial Report (CAFR)*. A CAFR should be prepared and published by all governmental entities as a matter of public record. Based on the GASB *Statement No. 34* requirements, the major components of a CAFR are as follows:

  I. Introductory Section
  II. Financial Section

    A. Auditor's Report
    B. Management's Discussion and Analysis (MD&A)
    C. Basic Financial Statements
      1. Government-Wide Financial Statements
      2. Fund Financial Statements
      3. Notes to the Financial Statements

---

[6] GASB Cod. (2001) Sec. 2600.113.

    D. Required Supplementary Information (other than MD&A)

    E. Combining Statements and Individual Fund Statements and Schedules

III. Statistical Section

Preparing the CAFR is basically an aggregation process. Using the individual fund and component unit financial statements as building blocks, you first prepare certain combining statements (level II.E). (A combining statement aggregates the elements of individual fund statements into totals that are carried forward to higher-level statements.) Then, the fund financial statements (level II.C.2) are prepared. The fund financial statements then must be adjusted to prepare the government-wide financial statements (level II.C.1). The notes, which are an integral part of the financial statements, are often prepared as the financial statements are developed. Once the financial statements are done, the MD&A can be prepared, using the fund financial statements, the government-wide statements, and other financial, economic, and demographic data.

Because CAFRs are often lengthy (Grafton's CAFR runs 144 pages), governmental units sometimes issue *general purpose financial reports* separately from the CAFR for external purposes. The *minimum requirements* established by the GASB for general purpose external financial reports are MD&A, the basic financial statements, and required supplementary information other than MD&A (levels II.B, II.C, and II.D). Exhibit 9-1 illustrates these minimum requirements and shows how they relate to each other.[7]

The components of the CAFR are discussed briefly in the next few pages. They are then covered in greater detail and illustrated in the rest of this chapter and in Chapter 10.

Introductory Section

The CAFR begins with an introductory section that includes a table of contents and a transmittal letter containing comments that the management of the government unit feels are important to the reader. This section might include comments on the economic outlook, significant initiatives undertaken by the government, and an analysis of the entity's finances. As a result of the new requirement for MD&A, however, this section is likely to diminish in scope to avoid duplication.

Financial Section

Auditor's Report

The financial section of the CAFR starts with the auditor's report, which contains the auditor's opinion on the entity's financial statements. After describing the scope of their audit, the auditors state whether, in their opinion, the *basic financial statements* present fairly, in all material respects, the financial position and results of operations of the entity, in conformity with generally accepted accounting principles. The auditors generally express no opinion on MD&A, which is classified as required

---

[7] GASB Cod. (2001) Sec. 2200.103.

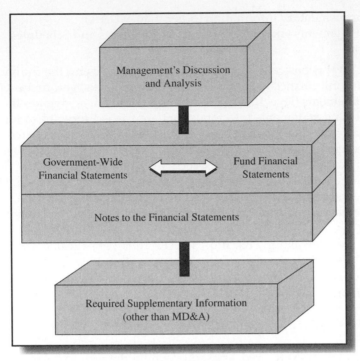

Exhibit 9-1
Minimum
External
Financial
Reporting
Requirements

supplementary information, and is therefore subjected only to limited audit inquiry. The auditors also indicate the extent to which they examined the other data contained in the CAFR, and the nature of their opinion on the other data.

Management's Discussion and Analysis

MD&A introduces the basic financial statements and provides an objective analysis of the government's financial operations and financial position, based on facts known to management as of the date of the auditor's report. MD&A should be easily readable and help the reader understand the fiscal policies, the economic factors, and other matters that affect the data reported in the financial statements.

Basic Financial Statements

As previously mentioned, auditors express their opinion about the basic financial statements. The basic financial statements are also generally included in official statements issued by governmental entities when selling bonds. The basic financial statements consist of the following:

1. Government-Wide Financial Statements
   a. Statement of net assets
   b. Statement of activities

2. Fund Financial Statements
   a. Governmental funds
      (1) Balance sheet
      (2) Statement of revenues, expenditures, and changes in fund balances
   b. Proprietary Funds
      (1) Statement of net assets (or balance sheet)
      (2) Statement of revenues, expenses, and changes in fund net assets or fund equity
      (3) Cash flows statement
   c. Fiduciary Funds
      (1) Statement of fiduciary net assets
      (2) Statement of changes in fiduciary net assets

Notes to the financial statements provide information that is essential for fair presentation of the financial statements but not shown on the face of the statements. Notes are therefore an integral part of the statements themselves.

Required Supplementary Information Other Than MD&A

Required supplementary information includes schedules, statistical data, and other information determined by the GASB to be essential for financial reporting and that should be presented with, but not as part of, the basic financial statements. For example, in addition to MD&A, the GASB requires that governmental units report a comparison of the budget with actual results, as well as certain data on pensions.

Combining Statements, Individual Fund Statements, and Schedules

Combining financial statements are needed if the primary government has more than one nonmajor fund or the reporting entity has more than one nonmajor component unit. Because the focus of the fund financial statements is on *major* funds, financial information for the total nonmajor funds is presented in a single column of the fund statements. Combining financial statements for nonmajor funds and component units provide details on each of those funds. Although they are presented in the CAFR, combining statements are not classified as basic financial statements.

Schedules included in the CAFR provide useful details not otherwise included in the basic financial statements. Schedules might, for example, be prepared to present additional details regarding sources of revenues and object of expenditure data for each department. Schedules could also be used to pull together into a more useful format data that might be spread throughout the various financial statements.

Statistical Section

The *statistical section* of the CAFR provides the reader with additional financial, economic, and demographic data to help in assessing the government's financial condition. Although the GASB recommends certain specific tables for inclusion, where applicable, the governmental unit can add any additional information that management feels is useful to the reader.

PREPARING MANAGEMENT'S DISCUSSION AND ANALYSIS

GASB *Statement No. 34* requires that the basic financial statements be preceded by an objective analytical commentary, called Management's Discussion and Analysis (MD&A). MD&A details for the reader of the statements an analysis of the government's financial activities and financial position, based on facts, decisions, and conditions known to management as of the date of the auditor's report. It should focus on the primary government, compare the current year with the previous year, and discuss both the positive and negative aspects of that comparison. MD&A should cover the following aspects:

- *Brief discussion of the basic financial statements.* It includes a discussion of how the government-wide and fund financial statements relate to each other, and why the results reported in the two sets of statements either reinforce each other or provide additional information.
- *Condensed financial information from the government-wide statements comparing the current year and the prior year.* Condensed financial information (such as current assets and long-term assets, current liabilities and long-term liabilities, total revenues, total expenses, excess of revenues over expenses before special items, extraordinary items, and transfers) supports the analysis of financial position and results of operations, discussed in the next point.
- *Analysis of the government's overall financial position and results of operations.* The objective of this analysis is to help users assess whether the government's financial position improved or deteriorated as a result of the year's operations. It covers both governmental and business-type activities as reported in the government-wide financial statements. Most important, the analysis covers the reasons for significant change from the previous year, such as changes in tax rates and numbers of government employees. Major economic factors affecting operating results (such as changes in tax bases and employment rates) should also be discussed.
- *Analysis of balances and transactions of individual funds.* This analysis covers reasons for significant changes in fund balances or fund net assets. It also addresses restrictions and other limitations on the availability of fund resources for future use.
- *Analysis of budgetary variations.* A discussion of significant variances between the original budget, the final budget, and actual results on a budgetary basis for the General Fund is important. Currently known reasons for variations that might significantly affect future services or liquidity are also mentioned.
- *Capital asset and long-term debt activity.* The analysis covers significant transactions and events affecting capital assets and long-term debt (such as capital expenditure commitments, credit rating changes, and debt limitations) that might affect the financing of planned facilities or services.
- *Infrastructure assets.* For governments using the modified approach to reporting infrastructure assets (covered in Chapter 10), the discussion includes significant changes in the condition assessment of the assets from previous assessments,

how the current condition assessment compares with the desired condition level established by the government, and significant differences between estimated and actual amounts spent during the year to maintain the assets.

- *Future impacts.* A description of facts, decisions, or conditions currently known to management that are expected to significantly affect the financial position or results of operations of the government needs to be included.

Exhibit 9-2 contains excerpts from the MD&A prepared by the Village of Grafton, Wisconsin, for its fiscal year 2000 annual report.

Exhibit 9-2
Management's Discussion and Analysis

Village of Grafton, Wisconsin
Management's Discussion and Analysis (Excerpts)
December 31, 2000

GENERAL FUND BUDGETARY HIGHLIGHTS

Differences between the original budget and the final amended budget were relatively minor. There were no additional appropriations. When the annual program budget is adopted, the only increases in salaries and wages and related fringe benefits are for those full-time employees within labor unions with contracts in place for the following year. However, a wage reserve account is included within a nondepartmental section of the general fund budget to provide anticipated funds for increases in salaries and wages as approved during the year. As contracts are approved, budget transfers are made to the appropriate expense category to reflect increases in salaries and wages and related fringe benefits.

In addition to the adjustments for salary and wage adjustments, an amount of $4,329 was transferred to the conservation and development budget (specifically for community development) and the amount of $6,000 was transferred to the community enrichment services budget for a replacement pool heater at the Family Aquatics Center.

As identified earlier, actual revenues and other sources exceeded budgeted revenues by $270,264 primarily in development related revenues. Actual expenditures were less than budgeted expenditures by $41,613. This amount was approximately equivalent to the remaining reserve for contingency budget, which is provided annually for unforeseen expenditures.

Because revenues exceeded budgetary estimates, the need to draw upon existing fund balance was decreased. The 2000 program budget for the general fund anticipated the use of $375,000 of fund balance. However, $64,032 of fund balance was actually used.

CAPITAL ASSET AND DEBT ADMINISTRATION

Capital assets. The Village of Grafton's investment in capital assets for its governmental business-type activities as of December 31, 2000, amounts to $28,768,449 net of accumulated depreciation. This investment in capital assets includes land, buildings, improvements other than buildings, machinery and equipment, infrastructure, and construction in progress. The total increase in the Village of Grafton's investment in capital assets for the current fiscal year was a total of approximately $2,126,837 net of depreciation or a 7.9 percent increase. As mentioned earlier, the infrastructure installed prior to 2000 is not included within these statements.

(continued)

Exhibit 9-2
Continued

VILLAGE OF GRAFTON'S CAPITAL ASSETS

	GOVERNMENTAL ACTIVITIES		BUSINESS-TYPE ACTIVITIES		TOTAL	
	2000	1999	2000	1999	2000	1999
Land	$ 2,287,133	$ 1,498,959	$ 448,852	$ 448,852	$ 2,735,985	$ 1,947,811
Buildings and system	7,673,058	7,252,675	973,194	935,792	8,646,252	8,188,467
Improvements other than buildings	1,054,732	587,299	204,821	219,452	1,259,553	806,751
Machinery and equipment	3,332,287	3,047,208	8,081,541	8,085,212	11,413,828	11,132,420
Infrastructure	398,746		14,858,517	14,169,526	15,257,263	14,169,526
Construction in progress	117,421	378,595	160,272		277,693	378,595
Total Capital Assets	14,863,377	12,764,736	24,727,197	23,858,834	39,590,574	36,623,570
Less Accumulated Depreciation	(3,846,097)	(3,482,989)	(6,976,028)	(6,498,969)	(10,822,125)	(9,981,958)
Capital Assets Net of Depreciation	$11,017,280	$ 9,281,747	$17,751,169	$17,359,865	$28,768,449	$26,641,612

Several major additions to capital assets in governmental fund activities include the acquisition of five properties at the intersection of Twelfth Avenue and Washington Street for redevelopment purposes of the downtown area ($642,414), the 8,500-square-foot build-out of the lower level of the library for a youth library department ($420,383), the first phase in developing 26-acre Centennial Park including ball diamonds, lighting, parking lot, etc. ($445,273), several public works infrastructure projects ($399,746), and other additions of equipment, machinery, etc. ($191,825).

Long-term debt. At the end of the current fiscal year, the Village of Grafton has total bonded debt outstanding of $13,155,000 entirely backed by the full faith and credit of the government.

The Village of Grafton issued $2,730,000 in general obligation bonds dated July 1, 2000. This debt was issued for various infrastructure projects, renovation of the existing library building to provide for a youth library in an unused section of the lower level, and $1,040,000 for various infrastructure projects, purchase of property, and preliminary engineering and consulting expenses related to the redevelopment of the downtown district of the Village of Grafton.

VILLAGE OF GRAFTON'S OUTSTANDING DEBT

	GOVERNMENTAL ACTIVITIES		BUSINESS-TYPE ACTIVITIES		TOTAL	
	2000	1999	2000	1999	2000	1999
General obligation bonds and notes	$12,460,262	$10,731,843	$694,738	$754,816	$13,155,000	$11,486,659
Total	$12,460,262	$10,731,843	$694,738	$754,816	$13,155,000	$11,486,659

The Village of Grafton maintains an "A1" rating from Moody's for general obligation debt.

Exhibit 9-2
Continued

State statutes limit the amount of general obligation debt a governmental entity may issue to 5 percent of its total equalized valuation. The current debt limitation for the Village of Grafton is $34,141,280, which significantly exceeds the Village of Grafton's current outstanding general obligation debt. The Village Board has established a policy whereby the Village will not issue debt in excess of 55 percent of the state authorized debt limit. As of December 31, 2000, the Village of Grafton's outstanding debt equaled 39% of the state authorized debt.

ECONOMIC FACTORS AND NEXT YEAR'S BUDGETS AND RATES

- The unemployment rate as of December 31, 2000, for Ozaukee County which includes the Village of Grafton is 1.7 percent. This compares with an unemployment rate of 3.0 percent for the State of Wisconsin and a national unemployment rate of 4.0 percent.

- The rate of inflation for the Milwaukee, Wisconsin metro area was 3.1 percent for 2000, while the 2001 tax rate increased by 1.14 percent.

- $354,546 of the unreserved fund balance in the general fund was appropriated for spending in the 2001 budget. It is intended that the use of available fund balance will lessen the required tax levy yet meet Village of Grafton guidelines to maintain a minimum unreserved fund balance of 15 percent of general fund expenses.

- The water and wastewater rates were not increased for 2001.

Source: Excerpted from Comprehensive Annual Financial Report, Year 2000, Village of Grafton, Wisconsin.

GOVERNMENT FINANCIAL REPORTING IN PRACTICE:
How New York City Covered the 9/11 Disaster in Its MD&A

MD&As contain a discussion of facts, decisions, or conditions known to management as of the date of the auditor's report that are expected to have a significant effect on financial position or results of operations. The following excerpt from its MD&A included in its comprehensive annual financial report for the fiscal year ended June 30, 2001 (dated October 30, 2001), shows how New York City covered the events of September 11, 2001.

On September 11, 2001, two hijacked passenger jetliners flew into the World Trade Center, resulting in a substantial loss of life, destruction of the World Trade Center and damage to other buildings in the vicinity. Continuing recovery, cleanup and repair efforts will result in substantial expenditures. The U.S. Congress passed emergency legislation which appropriates $40 billion for increased disaster assistance, increased security costs, rebuilding infrastructure systems and other public facilities, and disaster recovery and related activities, at least $20 billion of which is for disaster recovery activities and assistance in New York, Pennsylvania and Virginia. In addition, the State legislature increased the financing capacity of the TFA [Transitional Finance Authority, a component unit of New York City] by $2.5 billion to fund the City's costs related to or arising from the September 11 attack, and has authorized TFA to issue debt without limit as to principle amount that is payable solely from State or Federal aid received on account of the disaster. The amount of City costs resulting from the September 11 attack is expected to substantially exceed the amount of Federal aid and State resources which, to date, have been identified by the Federal and State governments as available for these purposes.

(continued)

Prior to September 11, the national and local economies had been weakening, reflecting lower business investment, increased unemployment and, recently, a decline in consumer confidence. It is expected that the destruction of the World Trade Center will have substantial impact on the City and its economy. Reduced economic activity is expected to lower corporate profits, increase job losses and reduce consumer spending, which would result in reduced personal income and sales tax receipts and other business tax revenues for the City and could negatively affect real property values. The events of September 11 increased the risk of a recession and a delay in recovery. It is not possible to quantify at present with any certainty the short-term or long-term adverse impact of the September 11 events on the City and its economy, any offsetting economic benefits which may result from recovery and rebuilding activities and the amount of additional resources from Federal, State, City and other sources which will be required.

Source: The City of New York, New York, Comprehensive Annual Report of the Comptroller, for the fiscal year ended June 30, 2001.

PREPARING FUND FINANCIAL STATEMENTS

Focus on Major Funds

The focus of the *fund financial statements* is on the primary government's *major* funds. Each major fund needs to be presented in a separate column in all of the fund financial statements. Nonmajor funds should be aggregated and displayed in a single column. Combining statements for the nonmajor funds may be presented as supplementary information to the basic statements, but would ordinarily be shown in the combining statements part (level 2.E.) of the CAFR.

What is a major fund? GASB *Statement No. 34* defines a major fund as:

a. The General Fund; and

b. A governmental or enterprise fund (including a blended component unit) whose total assets, liabilities, revenues, *or* expenditures/expenses are at least 10 percent of the corresponding element for all funds of that category or type (that is, total governmental or total enterprise funds), *and* the same element that met the 10 percent criterion is also at least 5 percent of the corresponding element total for all governmental and enterprise funds combined; and

c. Any other governmental or enterprise fund that governmental officials believe is particularly important (for example, because of public interest) to financial statement users.[8]

Grafton's statement of revenues, expenditures, and changes in fund balances, discussed later in this chapter, will be used to illustrate the calculations to be made in determining whether to classify a fund as major or nonmajor.

---

[8] GASB Cod. (2001) Sec. 2200.150.

Major fund reporting requirements do not apply to Internal Service Funds. Instead, the combined totals for all Internal Service Funds should be presented in a single column to the right of the total Enterprise Funds column. A combining statement should be prepared to report the details of the individual Internal Service Funds.

Measurement Focus and Basis of Accounting

Financial statements for governmental funds should be presented using the current financial resources measurement focus and the *modified accrual basis of accounting*, as described in Chapters 2, 4, 5, and 6. This approach means, among other things, that general capital assets acquired with governmental fund resources should not be reported as assets in the financial statements prepared for governmental funds. It also means that general long-term liabilities, such as the unmatured principal of bonds or other forms of long-term indebtedness should not be reported as liabilities in the governmental fund financial statements. These assets and liabilities should, however, be reported in the government-wide financial statements, where the measurement focus is on economic resources and where the full accrual basis of accounting is used.

Financial statements for proprietary funds should be presented using the economic resources measurement focus and the *accrual basis of accounting*, as discussed in Chapter 7. Financial statements of fiduciary funds should generally be reported using the economic resources measurement focus and the *accrual basis of accounting*. The exception regarding fiduciary funds pertains to certain liabilities of defined benefit plans and postemployment health care plans, discussed in Chapter 8.

Special and Extraordinary Items

To aid the report user in assessing a governmental entity's financial condition, GASB *Statement No. 34* requires that special and extraordinary items be displayed in a separate caption on operating statements. *Extraordinary items* are defined as transactions that are *both* unusual in nature *and* infrequent in occurrence. *Special items* are significant transactions or other events within the control of management that are *either* unusual in nature *or* infrequent in occurrence. Assume, for example, that a government encountering fiscal stress decides to balance its budget in form, though not in substance, with a "one-shot" financial resource resulting from the sale and leaseback of capital assets through one of its public authorities. That type of transaction would probably meet the definition of "special," although it might not rise to the level of being "extraordinary."

PREPARING FUND FINANCIAL STATEMENTS FOR GOVERNMENTAL FUNDS

Balance Sheet

The governmental funds balance sheet in the fund financial statements should report information about the current financial resources of each major governmental fund and for the total of the nonmajor funds. Resources and claims against the resources should be presented in balance sheet format (Assets = Liabilities + Fund Balance). Governmental fund balances should be segregated between reserved and unreserved amounts.

Table 9-1 contains the governmental funds balance sheet for the Village of Grafton, Wisconsin, as of December 31, 2000. Table 9-2 shows the combining balance sheet for Grafton's nonmajor governmental funds. (Even though the combining statement is not a basic statement, as previously mentioned, it is presented here to illustrate its relationship to the basic statement.)

Notice in Table 9-1 that three of Grafton's governmental funds meet the GASB's criteria to be classified as major, the General, Debt Service, and Capital Improvements Funds. Grafton also has 11 nonmajor funds (seven Special Revenue Funds, three Capital Projects Funds, and one Permanent Fund), which are reported in Table 9-2, the separate combining balance sheet. The amounts reported in the column captioned "other governmental funds" (Table 9-1) are the sums of the amounts for the 11 nonmajor funds combined (Table 9-2).

Notice also that the caption "total fund balances" (in the lower part of the balance sheet) is reconciled to "net assets of governmental funds." The latter is the net asset amount shown in the governmental activities column of the government-wide statement of net assets, which will be discussed in Chapter 10. Also, notice the nature of the reconciling items, including the fact that the governmental fund balance sheets lack both capital assets (because they are not financial resources) and long-term debt (because the debt is not due and payable in the current period).

Finally, notice the significant amounts of "deferred revenues–tax roll" in the General and Debt Service Funds. Grafton has deferred revenues because it levies property taxes and mails the tax bills in advance of the year for which the taxes are budgeted.

Statement of Revenues, Expenditures, and Changes in Fund Balances

The statement of revenues, expenditures, and changes in fund balances included in the fund financial statements shows information about inflows, outflows, and balances of resources, based on the current financial resources measurement focus and the modified accrual basis of accounting. This statement contains a separate column for each major fund and for the total of the nonmajor governmental funds. This statement is sequenced as follows:

> Revenues (by type)
> − Expenditures (by program or function)
> = Excess (deficiency) of revenues over expenditures
> ± Other financing sources and uses (such as proceeds of debt and transfers)
> ± Special and extraordinary items
> = Net change in fund balances
> + Fund balances at beginning of period
> = Fund balances at end of period[9]

---

[9]   GASB Cod. (2001) Sec. 2200.156.

Table 9-1
Governmental Funds Balance Sheet

	GENERAL	DEBT SERVICE	CAPITAL IMPROVEMENTS	OTHER GOVERNMENTAL FUNDS	TOTAL GOVERNMENTAL FUNDS
ASSETS					
Cash and investments	$2,988,047	$1,033,140	$2,286,089	$2,737,317	$ 9,044,593
Receivables					
Taxes	1,489,878	524,267	99,254	215,063	2,328,462
Delinquent personal property taxes	1,030	—	—	—	1,030
Accounts	39,966	—	58,933	—	98,899
Special assessments	—	—	246,072	—	246,072
Delinquent special assessments	—	—	3,722	—	3,722
Interest	1,194	—	—	2,072	3,266
Loans	—	—	—	622,151	622,151
Due from other funds	82,089	4,760	—	—	86,849
Advances to other funds	—	—	451,812	—	451,812
Prepaid items	28,812	—	—	2,677	31,489
Total Assets	$4,631,016	$1,562,167	$3,145,882	$3,579,280	$ 12,918,345
LIABILITIES AND FUND BALANCES					
Liabilities					
Accounts payable	$ 102,538	$ —	$ 19,174	$ 44,805	$ 166,517
Accrued liabilities	66,412	—	—	4,838	71,250
Deposits	13,874	—	—	138,867	152,741
Due to other funds	—	—	66,589	47,773	114,362
Due to plan participants	8,432	—	—	—	8,432
Advances from other funds	—	—	—	451,812	451,812
Deferred revenues—tax roll	3,168,430	1,115,000	211,000	457,179	4,951,609
Deferred special assessments	—	—	249,794	—	249,794
Total Liabilities	3,359,686	1,115,000	546,557	1,145,274	6,166,517
Fund Balances					
Reserved	29,842	447,167	617,080	669,291	1,763,380
Unreserved, reported in:					
General fund	1,241,488	—	—	—	1,241,488
Special revenue funds	—	—	—	1,573,797	1,573,797
Capital project funds	—	—	1,982,245	190,918	2,173,163
Total Fund Balances	1,271,330	447,167	2,599,325	2,434,006	6,751,828
Total Liabilities and Fund Balances	$4,631,016	$1,562,167	$3,145,882	$3,579,280	

Amounts reported for governmental activities in the statement of net assets are different because:

Capital assets used in governmental funds are not financial resources and therefore are not reported in the funds.	11,017,280
Other long-term assets are not available to pay for current-period expenditures and therefore are deferred in the funds.	279,380
Some liabilities, including long-term debt, are not due and payable in the current period and therefore are not reported in the funds.	(12,742,026)
NET ASSETS OF GOVERNMENTAL FUNDS (See Chapter 10, Table 10-1, page 425)	$ 5,306,462

See accompanying notes to financial statements.

Source: Comprehensive Annual Financial Report, Year 2000, Village of Grafton, Wisconsin.

Table 9-2
Nonmajor Governmental Funds Combining Balance Sheet

VILLAGE OF GRAFTON
NONMAJOR GOVERNMENTAL FUNDS
COMBINING BALANCE SHEET
DECEMBER 31, 2000

	SPECIAL REVENUE FUNDS				
	PARK AND OPEN SPACE	REVOLVING LOAN	WOODLAWN CEMETERY CAPITAL	PARK AND RECREATIONAL FACILITIES	LIBRARY
ASSETS					
Cash and investments	$51,454	$ 55,535	$28,149	$456,546	$46,227
Taxes receivable	13,999	—	—	—	—
Accounts receivable	—	—	—	—	—
Accrued interest	—	2,072	—	—	—
Loans receivable	—	622,151	—	—	—
Prepaid items	—	—	—	—	2,472
Due from other funds	—	—	—	—	—
Total Assets	$65,453	$679,758	$28,149	$456,546	$48,699
LIABILITIES AND FUND BALANCES					
Liabilities					
Accounts payable	$ —	$ —	$ —	$ —	$ 7,704
Accrued liabilities	—	—	—	—	4,838
Deposits	—	—	—	—	—
Due to other funds	—	—	—	—	—
Deferred revenues—tax roll	30,000	—	—	—	—
Advance from other funds	—	—	—	—	—
Total Liabilities	30,000	—	—	—	12,542
Fund Balances					
Reserved	—	622,151	—	—	—
Unreserved (deficit)	35,453	57,607	28,149	456,546	36,157
Total Fund Balances	35,453	679,758	28,149	456,546	36,157
Total Liabilities and Fund Balances	$65,453	$679,758	$28,149	$456,546	$48,699

Table 9-2
Continued

| Environmental | Police Retirement Health | Capital Projects Funds | | | Permanent Fund | Total Nonmajor Funds |
		TID No. 2	TID No. 3	Equipment	Cemetery Perpetual Care	
$948,459	$36,502	$219,428	$703,960	$143,917	$47,140	$2,737,317
—	—	105,206	17,020	78,838	—	215,063
—	—	—	—	—	—	—
—	—	—	—	—	—	2,072
—	—	—	—	—	—	622,151
—	205	—	—	—	—	2,677
—	—	—	—	—	—	—
$948,459	$36,707	$324,634	$720,980	$222,755	$47,140	$3,579,280
$ 25,281	$ —	$ 331	$ 11,089	$ 400	$ —	$ 44,805
—	—	—	—	—	—	4,838
—	—	138,867	—	—	—	138,867
—	—	—	3,378	44,395	—	47,773
—	—	223,510	36,169	167,500	—	457,179
—	—	—	451,812	—	—	451,812
25,281	—	362,708	502,448	212,295	—	1,145,274
—	—	—	—	—	47,140	669,291
923,178	36,707	(38,074)	218,532	10,460	—	1,764,715
923,178	36,707	(38,074)	218,532	10,460	47,140	2,434,006
$948,459	$36,707	$324,634	$720,980	$222,755	$47,140	$3,579,280

Source: Comprehensive Annual Financial Report, Year 2000, Village of Grafton, Wisconsin.

Table 9-3 contains the Village of Grafton's governmental funds statement of revenues, expenditures, and changes in fund balances for the year ended December 31, 2000. Table 9-4 shows Grafton's combining statement of revenues, expenditures, and changes in fund balances for the nonmajor governmental funds. Notice again that the totals in Table 9-4 agree with the totals for "other governmental funds" column in Table 9-3.

How did Grafton determine which funds were major and which were nonmajor? As previously discussed, four elements need to be considered: assets, liabilities, revenues, and expenditures. Using just the expenditures criterion, a fund would have had at least $965,002 of expenditures (10 percent of total governmental fund expenditures of $9,650,019, shown in Table 9-3) to be classified as major. The fund's expenditures would *also* have had to be at least $568,089 (5 percent of total expenditures/expenses for the governmental and enterprise funds combined—$9,650,019 plus $1,711,753, as shown in Table 9-6). Table 9-3 shows that Grafton's Debt Service

Table 9-3
Governmental Funds Statement of Revenues, Expenditures, and Changes in Fund Balances

VILLAGE OF GRAFTON
GOVERNMENTAL FUNDS
STATEMENT OF REVENUES, EXPENDITURES, AND CHANGES IN FUND BALANCES
FOR THE YEAR ENDED DECEMBER 31, 2000

	GENERAL	DEBT SERVICE	CAPITAL IMPROVEMENTS	OTHER GOVERNMENTAL FUNDS	TOTAL GOVERNMENTAL FUNDS
REVENUES					
Taxes	$2,914,658	$1,024,584	$ 100,000	$ 380,636	$4,419,878
Intergovernmental	1,438,519	78,193	13,449	335,592	1,865,753
Licenses and permits	364,728	—	—	—	364,728
Fines, forfeitures and penalties	108,557	—	—	—	108,557
Public charges for services	219,684	—	7,200	13,043	239,927
Intergovernmental charges for services	39,888	—	—	90,077	129,965
Special assessments	—	—	435,409	163,689	599,098
Investment income	203,445	110,820	95,478	148,263	558,006
Miscellaneous	30,867	—	203,905	78,223	312,995
Total Revenues	5,320,346	1,213,597	855,441	1,209,523	8,598,907
EXPENDITURES					
Current					
General government	577,022	—	2,618	2,308	581,948
Public safety	2,629,858	—	3,038	—	2,632,896
Public works	1,470,894	—	94,215	8,545	1,573,654
Community enrichment services	535,776	—	34,360	391,250	961,386
Conservation and development	66,064	—	9,380	274,980	350,424
Capital outlay	—	—	1,114,167	826,103	1,940,270
Debt service					
Principal retirement	—	1,001,581	—	—	1,001,581
Interest and fiscal charges	—	578,274	—	—	578,274
Debt issuance costs	—	—	18,314	11,272	29,586
Total Expenditures	5,279,614	1,579,855	1,276,092	1,514,458	9,650,019
Excess (deficiency) of revenues over expenditures	40,732	(366,258)	(420,651)	(304,935)	(1,051,112)
OTHER FINANCING SOURCES (USES)					
Proceeds of long-term debt	—	—	1,690,000	1,040,000	2,730,000
Transfers in	181,079	524,259	234,009	430,779	1,370,126
Transfers out	(285,843)	—	(461,001)	(444,941)	(1,191,785)
Total Other Financing Sources (Uses)	(104,764)	524,259	1,463,008	1,025,838	2,908,341
Excess (deficiency) of revenues and other sources over expenditures and other uses	(64,032)	158,001	1,042,357	720,903	1,857,229
FUND BALANCES—					
Beginning of Year	1,335,362	289,166	1,556,968	1,713,103	4,894,599
FUND BALANCES— END OF YEAR	$1,271,330	$ 447,167	$2,599,325	$2,434,006	$6,751,828

See accompanying notes to financial statements.
Source: Comprehensive Annual Financial Report, Year 2000, Village of Grafton, Wisconsin.

Table 9-4

Governmental Funds Combining Statement of Revenues, Expenditures, and Changes in Fund Balances

VILLAGE OF GRAFTON
NONMAJOR GOVERNMENTAL FUNDS
COMBINING STATEMENT OF REVENUES, EXPENDITURES, AND CHANGES IN FUND BALANCES
FOR THE YEAR ENDED DECEMBER 31, 2000

	SPECIAL REVENUE FUNDS				
	PARK AND OPEN SPACE	REVOLVING LOAN	WOODLAWN CEMETERY CAPITAL	PARK AND RECREATIONAL FACILITIES	LIBRARY
REVENUES					
Taxes	$30,000	$ —	$ —	$ —	$ —
Intergovernmental	—	—	—	—	11,297
Public charges for services	—	—	—	—	13,043
Intergovernmental charges for services	—	—	—	—	90,077
Impact fees	—	—	—	163,689	—
Investment income	1,779	28,633	1,548	31,131	319
Miscellaneous	15,449	—	3,900	—	—
Total Revenues	47,228	28,633	5,448	194,820	114,736
EXPENDITURES					
General government	—	—	—	—	—
Public works	—	—	—	—	—
Community enrichment services	29,288	—	1,721	—	360,241
Conservation and development	—	1,655	—	—	—
Capital outlay	—	—	—	—	—
Debt service					
Debt issuance costs	—	—	—	—	—
Total Expenditures	29,288	1,655	1,721	—	360,241
Excess (deficiency) of revenues over expenditures	17,940	26,978	3,727	194,820	(245,505)
OTHER FINANCING SOURCES					
Proceeds of long-term debt	—	—	—	—	—
Transfers in	3,560	—	—		281,662
Transfers out	—	—	—	(283,134)	—
Total Other Financing Sources (Uses)	3,560	—	—	(283,134)	281,662
Excess (deficiency) of revenues and other sources over expenditures	21,500	26,978	3,727	(88,314)	36,157
FUND BALANCES (DEFICIT)—Beginning of Year	13,953	652,780	24,422	544,860	—
FUND BALANCES (DEFICIT)— END OF YEAR	$35,453	$679,758	$28,149	$456,546	$ 36,157

(*continued*)

Table 9-4
Continued

| ENVIRONMENTAL | POLICE RETIREMENT HEALTH | CAPITAL PROJECTS FUNDS | | | PERMANENT FUND | TOTALS |
		TID No. 2	TID No. 3	EQUIPMENT	CEMETERY PERPETUAL CARE	
$ —	$ —	$174,636	$ —	$176,000	$ —	$ 380,636
324,000	—	295	—	—	—	335,592
—	—	—	—	—	—	13,043
—	—	—	—	—	—	90,077
—	—	—	—	—	—	163,689
41,591	1,587	9,484	24,597	4,856	2,738	148,263
40,000	—	—	—	14,974	3,900	78,223
405,591	1,587	184,415	24,597	195,830	6,638	1,209,523
—	2,308	—	—	—	—	2,308
—	—	—	—	8,545	—	8,545
—	—	—	—	—	—	391,250
126,803	—	3,845	142,677	—	—	274,980
—	—	—	642,414	183,689	—	826,103
—	—	—	11,272	—	—	11,272
126,803	2,308	3,845	796,363	192,234	—	1,514,458
278,788	(721)	180,570	(771,766)	3,596	6,638	(304,935)
—	—	—	1,040,000	—	—	1,040,000
141,376	4,181	—	—	—	—	430,779
(41,588)	—	(117,481)	—	—	(2,738)	(444,941)
99,788	4,181	(117,481)	1,040,000	—	(2,738)	1,025,838
378,576	3,460	63,089	268,234	3,596	3,900	720,903
544,602	33,247	(101,163)	(49,702)	6,864	43,240	1,713,103
$923,178	$36,707	$(38,074)	$(218,532)	$ 10,460	$47,140	$2,434,006

Source: Comprehensive Annual Financial Report, Year 2000, Village of Grafton, Wisconsin.

and Capital Improvements Funds had expenditures greater than $965,002, and Table 9-4 shows that the nonmajor funds had expenditures less than $965,002. As previously discussed, Grafton also considered the assets, liabilities, and revenue criteria to determine which of the other funds should be classified as major.

Notice also the relatively large amounts of transfers among the funds. The amounts shown for transfers in and transfers out do not agree because of the transfer from a proprietary fund (shown in the separate proprietary funds statement of revenues, expenses, and changes in fund net assets; see Table 9-6) to a governmental fund. Interfund transfers are detailed in a note to the financial statements.

Just as the fund and the government-wide balance sheets are reconciled with each other, so are the two operating statements for governmental activities reconciled with each other. This reconciliation will be discussed and illustrated in Chapter 10.

PREPARING FUND FINANCIAL STATEMENTS FOR PROPRIETARY FUNDS

Statement of Net Assets (or Balance Sheet)

Fund financial statements for proprietary funds should be presented using the economic resources measurement focus and the accrual basis of accounting. As a result, proprietary fund statements of net assets normally show both capital assets and long-term debt. This statement may be prepared either in the statement of net assets format (Assets − Liabilities = Net Assets) or in the balance sheet format (Assets = Liabilities + Net Assets).

The assets and liabilities should be presented in *classified* format, so as to distinguish between those that are current and those that are noncurrent. (Current assets are assets that are expected to be converted to cash or consumed in operations within 1 year, and current liabilities are liabilities that are due to be paid within 1 year.)

Regardless of whether the statement is prepared in net assets or balance sheet format, the net assets should be classified in three components: (1) invested in capital assets, net of related debt, (2) restricted, and (3) unrestricted. The component *invested in capital assets, net of related debt* represents the capital assets of the proprietary funds, minus accumulated depreciation and outstanding balances of bonds, notes, or other borrowings attributable to acquiring, constructing, or improving those assets.

Net assets are reported as *restricted* when constraints are imposed on the use of the assets either externally (by creditors, grantors, or laws or regulations of other governments) or by the entity's constitution or enabling legislation. For example, restrictions may be imposed by a debt covenant or by higher-level government that provides resources that may be used only for a specific purpose, such as a specific capital project.

Table 9-5 contains the proprietary funds statement of net assets for the Village of Grafton at December 31, 2000. Grafton has a single proprietary fund, the Water and Wastewater Utility Fund. If the Village had more than one proprietary fund, this statement would need to show financial information for each major fund and a total for nonmajor funds.

Notice that Table 9-5 is presented in classified format, with current assets and liabilities separated from noncurrent ones. Therefore, the amount of long-term debt due in 1 year is classified as current. Notice also that the net assets section of the statement is classified as invested in capital assets, net of related debt; restricted; and unrestricted. The amount shown as restricted ($595,175) is equal to the amount reported as Restricted assets—replacement fund.

Statement of Revenues, Expenses, and Changes in Fund Net Assets

The proprietary funds operating statement is called the statement of revenues, expenses, and changes in fund net assets. This statement should be prepared in a format that distinguishes between operating and nonoperating revenues and expenses,

Table 9-5
Proprietary Funds Statement of Net Assets

VILLAGE OF GRAFTON
PROPRIETARY FUNDS
STATEMENT OF NET ASSETS
DECEMBER 31, 2000

	WATER AND WASTEWATER UTILITY
ASSETS	
CURRENT ASSETS	
Cash and investments	$ 3,147,152
Customer accounts receivable	331,745
Other accounts receivable	13,049
Due from other funds	36,387
Materials and supplies	4,471
Total Current Assets	3,532,804
NON-CURRENT ASSETS	
Restricted Assets	
Replacement fund	595,175
Construction account	25
Capital Assets	
Water	
Plant in service	10,780,239
Accumulated depreciation	(2,040,359)
Construction work in progress	84,300
Wastewater	
Plant in service	13,786,686
Accumulated depreciation	(4,935,669)
Construction work in progress	75,972
Other Assets	
Unamortized debt discount	7,235
Total Non-Current Assets	18,353,604
Total Assets	21,886,408
LIABILITIES	
CURRENT LIABILITIES	
Current portion of general obligation debt	62,721
Accounts payable	86,807
Due to other funds	8,874
Other current liabilities	11,158
Total Current Liabilities	169,560

Table 9-5
Continued

NON-CURRENT LIABILITIES	
General obligation debt	632,018
Accrued compensated absences	35,457
Other long-term liabilities	11,609
Accrued revenues	13,200
Total Non-Current Liabilities	692,284
Total Liabilities	861,844
NET ASSETS	
Invested in capital assets, net of related debt	17,056,430
Restricted	595,175
Unrestricted	3,372,959
Total Net Assets	$21,024,564

See accompanying notes to financial statements.
Source: Comprehensive Annual Financial Report, Year 2000, Village of Grafton, Wisconsin.

and provides separate captions for *operating income* and income before other revenues, expenses, gains, losses, and transfers. The statement should be presented in the following format:

> Operating revenues (show details and total)
> − Operating expenses (show details and total)
> = Operating income (loss)
> ± Nonoperating revenues and expenses (show details)
> = Income before other revenues, expenses, gains, losses, and transfers
> ± Capital contributions, additions to endowments, special items, extraordinary items, and transfers
> = Change in net assets
> + Net assets at beginning of period
> = Net assets at end of period[10]

For an illustration, see Table 9-6 for the proprietary funds statement of revenues, expenses, and changes in fund net assets for the Village of Grafton for the year ended December 31, 2000. Notice that the transfer out ($178,341) is equal to the difference between the transfers in and out shown in Table 9-3.

Statement of Cash Flows

GASB *Statement No. 34* also requires preparation of a statement of cash flows for proprietary activities, using the direct method of presenting cash flows from operating activities.

---

[10] GASB Cod. (2001) Sec. 2200.167 (adapted).

Table 9-6

Proprietary Funds Statement of Revenues, Expenses, and Changes in Fund Net Assets

VILLAGE OF GRAFTON
PROPRIETARY FUNDS
STATEMENT OF REVENUES, EXPENSES, AND CHANGES IN FUND NET ASSETS
FOR THE YEAR ENDED DECEMBER 31, 2000

	ENTERPRISE FUNDS
OPERATING REVENUES	$ 2,251,533
OPERATING EXPENSES	
Operation and maintenance	1,125,518
Depreciation	552,592
Taxes	33,643
Total Operating Expenses	1,711,753
Operating Income	539,780
NON-OPERATING REVENUES (EXPENSES)	
Investment income	186,597
Interest expense	(35,697)
Total Non-Operating Revenue	150,900
Income Before Capital Contributions and Transfers	690,680
Capital Contributions	635,812
Transfers out	(178,341)
Change in Net Assets	1,148,151
Total Net Assets—Beginning of Year	19,876,413
Total Net Assets—End of Year	$21,024,564

Source: Comprehensive Annual Financial Report, Year 2000, Village of Grafton, Wisconsin.

Table 9-7 presents the proprietary funds statement of cash flows for the Village of Grafton for the year ended December 31, 2000. Discussion of this statement is generally outside the scope of this text. Note, however, that this statement supplements the accrual-basis statement of revenues, expenses, and changes in fund net assets by giving the reader a more complete understanding of the nature of the fund's financial activities. For example, the statement of cash flows shows how much the fund spent to acquire capital assets and how much it spent to pay debt principal, neither of which are evident from the accrual-basis financial statements. It also demonstrates that, because depreciation did not require a cash outlay, the net cash flows from operating activities ($1,060,076) helped provide cash resources to acquire capital assets.

Table 9-7
Proprietary Funds Statement of Cash Flows

VILLAGE OF GRAFTON
PROPRIETARY FUNDS
STATEMENT OF CASH FLOWS
FOR THE YEAR ENDED DECEMBER 31, 2000

	ENTERPRISE FUNDS
CASH FLOWS FROM OPERATING ACTIVITIES	
Cash received from customers	$1,977,478
Cash received from other funds for services	210,000
Cash paid to suppliers for goods and services	(695,771)
Cash paid to employees for services	(431,631)
Net Cash Flows From Operating Activities	1,060,076
CASH FLOWS FROM NONCAPITAL FINANCING ACTIVITIES	
Transfers out to other funds	(178,341)
CASH FLOWS FROM INVESTING ACTIVITIES	
Investment income received	186,597
Net Cash Flows From Investing Activities	186,597
CASH FLOWS FROM CAPITAL AND RELATED FINANCING ACTIVITIES	
Acquisition and construction of capital assets	(540,738)
Salvage on retirement of capital assets	—
Principal paid	(60,078)
Interest paid	(34,563)
Capital contributions received	145,937
Net Cash Flows From Capital and Related Financing Activities	(489,442)
Net Increase in Cash and Cash Equivalents	578,890
Cash and Cash Equivalents—	
Beginning of Year	3,163,462
Cash and Cash Equivalents— End of Year	$3,742,352

Noncash Investing, Capital and Related Financial Activities

During 2000, developers contributed improvements totaling $459,900 to the water and waste-water systems and the village contributed $29,975.

(continued)

Table 9-7

Continued

CASH FLOWS FROM OPERATING ACTIVITIES	
Operating income	$539,780
Adjustments to Reconcile Operating Income to Net Cash Flows From Operating Activities	
Noncash items included in income	
Depreciation	552,592
Depreciation charged to other accounts	1,315
Change in Noncash Components of Working Capital	
Accounts receivable	(61,033)
Due from other funds	2,598
Other accounts receivable	(5,620)
Inventories	(2,355)
Accounts payable	8,999
Due to other funds	8,519
Accrued sick leave	15,122
Other liabilities	159
Net Cash Flows from Operating Activities	$1,060,076
RECONCILIATION OF CASH AND CASH EQUIVALENTS PER COMBINED BALANCE SHEET TO COMBINED STATEMENT OF CASH FLOWS	
Proprietary Funds	
Amounts per Statement of Net Assets—Proprietary Funds	
Unrestricted cash and investments	$3,147,152
Restricted cash and investments	595,200
Cash and Cash Equivalents per Combined Statement of Cash Flows	$3,742,352

Source: Comprehensive Annual Financial Report, Year 2000, Village of Grafton, Wisconsin.

PREPARING FUND FINANCIAL STATEMENTS FOR FIDUCIARY FUNDS

GASB *Statement No. 34* requires two fiduciary fund financial statements, a statement of fiduciary net assets and a statement of changes in fiduciary net assets. These statements should provide information about all fiduciary funds of the primary government, as well as component units that are fiduciary in nature. The statements should have separate columns for each fund type, that is, Pension and Other Employee Benefit Trust Funds, Investment Trust Funds, Private Purpose Trust Funds, and Agency Funds.

The requirement for showing individual major funds does not extend to the Fiduciary Fund basic financial statements. Financial statements for individual pen-

Table 9-8

Fiduciary Funds Statement of Fiduciary Net Assets

VILLAGE OF GRAFTON
FIDUCIARY FUNDS
STATEMENT OF FIDUCIARY NET ASSETS
DECEMBER 31, 2000

	AGENCY TAX COLLECTION FUND
ASSETS	
Cash and investments	$ 5,551,160
Taxes receivable	5,154,834
Total Assets	10,705,994
LIABILITIES	
Due to other taxing units	10,705,994
Total Liabilities	$10,705,994

See accompanying notes to financial statements.
Source: Comprehensive Annual Financial Report, Year 2000, Village of Grafton, Wisconsin.

sion and postemployment health care plans, however, must be presented in the notes to the financial statements if separate GAAP financial statements have not been issued, but if such statements have been issued, the notes need only contain information about how to obtain these statements.

The statement of fiduciary net assets should have information about the assets, liabilities, and net assets for each fund type. The statement of changes in fiduciary net assets contains the information about the additions to, deductions from, and net increase (or decrease) for the year in net assets. The reporting requirements for Pension Funds are described in Chapter 8.

The Village of Grafton has a single fiduciary fund—a Tax Collection Agency Fund. As discussed in Chapter 8, Agency Funds are custodian accounts that collect and disburse resources. They have only assets and liabilities, and no net assets. Therefore, the only financial statement that needs to be prepared for Agency Funds is the statement of fiduciary net assets. Table 9-8 presents the Village of Grafton's statement of fiduciary net assets at December 31, 2000.

PREPARING BUDGETARY COMPARISON SCHEDULES

In addition to the basic fund financial statements, state and local governments are required to present fund-level budgetary comparison schedules for the General Fund and for each major Special Revenue Fund with a legally adopted annual budget.

These schedules should be presented as required supplementary information (RSI). Governments may choose, however, to present them as basic financial statements, rather than as RSI.

Budgetary comparison schedules compare the original appropriated budget, the final appropriated budget, and the actual inflows, outflows, and balances for the year, stated on the government's *budgetary* basis of accounting. GASB *Statement No. 34* defines the original budget as the first appropriated budget. This budget includes any modifications, such as transfers, allocations, and other legally authorized legislative and executive changes made before the start of the fiscal year. The final budget includes all other legally authorized legislative and executive changes applicable to the fiscal year, whenever signed into law or legally authorized.

Before GASB *Statement No. 34* became effective, budgetary comparison schedules showed only the final budget. Adding a requirement for presenting the original budget gives the reader a more complete picture of the factors causing actual results to vary from the budget, and the way in which management adapted to change. For example, if economic factors caused a reduction in tax collections, the budgetary comparison statement provides a clue about the actions taken to keep expenditures in line with the reduced revenues.

In presenting the budgetary comparison schedules, governments may choose to use either the format, terminology, and classifications used in the budget document or the same format as used in the statement of revenues, expenditures, and changes in fund balances. In either event, the entity should reconcile the actual data on the budgetary basis of accounting, as shown in the budgetary comparison schedules, with the data presented in the fund financial statements of revenues, expenditures, and changes in fund balances.

The general fund budgetary comparison schedule for the Village of Grafton for the year ended December 31, 2000, is shown in Table 9-9. Notice that Grafton presents expenditures in greater detail in its budgetary comparison schedule than in its statement of revenues, expenditures, and changes in fund balances (Table 9-3).

Notice also that the amounts shown in the "actual" columns are the same in both statements. Grafton's budgetary basis of accounting is effectively the same as that used in the fund financial statement for the General Fund—modified accrual. If the amounts shown in the "actual" columns differed, however, Grafton would be required to show a reconciliation of the amounts. A common reconciling item results from the fact that encumbrances are reported as outflows in the budgetary comparison schedule, but not in the statement of revenues, expenditures, and changes in fund balances.

PREPARING NOTES TO THE FINANCIAL STATEMENTS

At the bottom of each financial statement is the notation "See accompanying notes to the financial statements." *Notes to the financial statements* contain information essential to a user's understanding of the financial position and changes in financial position of the reporting unit, but that either does not meet the criteria for recognition in a financial statement or provides more detail than can appropriately be included in

Table 9-9
General Fund Budgetary Companion Schedule

VILLAGE OF GRAFTON
GENERAL FUND
BUDGETARY COMPARISON SCHEDULE
FOR THE YEAR ENDED DECEMBER 31, 2000

| | BUDGETED AMOUNTS | | | VARIANCE WITH FINAL |
	ORIGINAL	FINAL	ACTUAL	BUDGET
REVENUES				
General property tax for local purposes	$2,907,095	$2,907,095	$2,907,094	$ (1)
Taxes—penalties and interest	5,500	5,500	7,564	2,064
Intergovernmental	1,394,177	1,394,177	1,438,519	44,342
Licenses and permits	212,430	212,430	364,728	152,298
Fines, forfeitures, and penalties	116,682	116,682	108,557	(8,125)
Public charges for services	190,240	190,240	219,684	29,444
Intergovernmental charges for services	39,976	39,976	39,888	(88)
Investment income	150,010	150,010	203,445	53,435
Miscellaneous	24,126	24,126	30,867	6,741
TOTAL REVENUES	5,040,236	5,040,236	5,320,346	280,110
EXPENDITURES				
GENERAL GOVERNMENT				
Village board, administration, and promotions	176,221	183,103	176,664	6,439
Village clerk and elections	115,570	122,838	116,581	6,257
Finance	140,845	150,004	141,100	8,904
Assessing	60,809	61,564	60,112	1,452
Legal	18,500	18,500	23,884	(5,384)
Miscellaneous	86,365	85,739	58,681	27,058
TOTAL GENERAL GOVERNMENT	598,310	621,748	577,022	44,726
PUBLIC SAFETY				
Police	2,069,204	2,100,193	2,087,984	12,209
Fire department	402,482	400,902	400,878	24
Emergency government	4,742	4,742	1,213	3,529
Inspection	133,269	136,784	139,783	(2,999)
TOTAL PUBLIC SAFETY	2,609,697	2,642,621	2,629,858	12,763
PUBLIC WORKS				
Public works administration and engineering	232,864	239,466	240,282	(816)
Street repair and maintenance	641,595	630,927	688,744	(57,817)
Forestry	33,042	33,042	42,982	(9,940)
Equipment repair and maintenance	187,591	187,361	191,244	(3,883)
Sanitation and recycling	311,820	311,619	307,642	3,977
TOTAL PUBLIC WORKS	1,406,912	1,402,415	1,470,894	(68,479)

(continued)

Table 9-9

Continued

COMMUNITY ENRICHMENT SERVICES				
Recreational programs	$243,521	$238,177	$222,204	$ 15,973
Community activities administration	129,127	132,314	130,370	1,944
Aquatics	154,434	160,208	158,113	2,095
Cable TV	10,157	10,157	20,302	(10,145)
Cemetery	3,515	3,515	4,787	(1,272)
TOTAL COMMUNITY ENRICH-MENT SERVICES	540,754	544,371	535,776	8,595
CONSERVATION AND DEVELOPMENT				
Community development	56,135	60,464	66,064	(5,600)
TOTAL CONSERVATION AND DEVELOPMENT	56,135	60,464	66,064	(5,600)
NONDEPARTMENTAL				
Contingency and other	111,000	49,305	—	49,305
TOTAL DEPARTMENTAL	111,000	49,305	—	49,305
TOTAL EXPENDITURES	5,322,808	5,320,924	5,279,614	41,310
Excess (deficiency) of revenues and other sources over expenditures and other uses	(282,572)	(280,688)	40,732	321,420
OTHER FINANCING SOURCES (USES)				
Transfers in	190,925	190,925	181,079	(9,846)
Transfers out	(284,262)	(286,146)	(285,843)	303
Total Other Financing Sources (Uses)	(93,337)	(95,221)	(104,764)	(9,543)
Excess (deficiency) of revenues and other sources over expenditures and other uses	(375,909)	(375,909)	(64,032)	311,877
Fund Balances—Beginning of Year	1,335,362	1,335,362	1,335,362	—
Fund Balances—End of Year	$ 959,453	$ 959,453	$1,271,330	$311,877

Source: Comprehensive Annual Financial Report, Year 2000, Village of Grafton, Wisconsin.

the body of a financial statement.[11] The focus of the notes should be on the primary government, but certain information should also be included on the major component units. Notes tend to be lengthy and may run 30 to 40 pages. The discussion that follows covers some, but by no means all, of the disclosure requirements.

The notes generally start with a summary of the primary government's significant accounting policies. Significant accounting policies include the following:

- A description of the government-wide financial statements
- The component units of the financial reporting entity, the criteria for including them in the reporting entity, and their relationships with the primary government

---

[11] GASB *Statement No. 38,* "Certain Financial Statement Note Disclosures," para. 34.

- A description of the activities accounted for in certain columns (that is, major funds, Internal Service Funds, and fiduciary fund types) presented in the basic financial statements (for example, the transportation fund accounts for constructing, maintaining, and policing state highways)
- The measurement focus and basis of accounting used in the government-wide statements, and the revenue recognition policies (such as length of time used to define "available") in the fund financial statements
- The policy for capitalizing assets and estimating their useful lives
- The policy for defining operating and nonoperating revenues of proprietary funds

Governments are also required to make note disclosure of material violations of finance-related legal and contractual provisions, as well as the actions taken to address the violations. A government might, for example, violate a statute that prohibits incurring a deficit in a particular fund, or it might violate the debt service coverage requirements of a bond covenant. In these cases, the government would need to disclose not only the violation, but also the nature of the action (such as an increase in user charges) taken to overcome the violation.

A note requirement of particular concern to analysts of a government's financial condition concerns short-term and long-term debt. A schedule of short-term debt shows beginning balances, increases, decreases, and ending balances, as well as the purposes for which the debt was issued. For long-term debt and obligations under capital and noncancelable operating leases, governments need to disclose details of debt requirements to maturity, including principal and interest requirements, stated separately, for each of the 5 subsequent fiscal years, and in 5-year increments thereafter. (The significance of this requirement is discussed in Chapter 14.)

Some governments have significant dollar amounts of interfund transfers and year-end interfund balances. The nature of interfund transactions and balances is generally not apparent from data shown on the face of the financial statements. Many transfers are routine in nature, for example, to move revenues from a collecting fund to another fund (such as a Debt Service Fund) required by statute to expend them. Other transfers, however, are not routine and may be indicators of fiscal stress. Required disclosures therefore include such matters as (1) interfund balances that are not expected to be repaid within 1 year from the date of the financial statements, and (2) interfund transfers that are not consistent with the activities of the fund that makes the transfer.[12]

For illustrative purposes, several notes to the Village of Grafton's financial statements are included in Exhibit 9-3. Note 1.D describes the basis of accounting used in Grafton's financial statements. This note includes Grafton's tax calendar (fourth paragraph), and explains the reason (third paragraph) for the deferred revenues in its balance sheet. Note 1.E describes the measurement focus used in the government-wide and fund financial statements. Note 4 is a schedule of interfund transfers. Note 7 is an excerpt from the note on long-term obligations, showing the debt service requirements to maturity.

---

[12] GASB *Statement No. 38*, para. 14 and 15.

Exhibit 9-3
Notes to Financial Statements

VILLAGE OF GRAFTON
NOTES TO FINANCIAL STATEMENTS (EXCERPTS)
DECEMBER 31, 2000

NOTE 1—SUMMARY OF SIGNIFICANT ACCOUNTING POLICIES (CONT.)

D. BASIS OF ACCOUNTING

In the government-wide Statement of Net Assets and Statement of Activities both governmental and business-type activities are presented using the economic resources measurement focus and the accrual basis of accounting. Under the accrual basis of accounting, revenues are recognized when earned and expenses are recorded when the liability is incurred or economic asset used. Revenues, expenses, gains, losses, assets, and liabilities resulting from exchange and exchange-like transactions are recognized when the exchange takes place. Property taxes are recognized as revenues in the year for which they are levied. Grants and similar items are recognized as revenue as soon as all eligibility requirements imposed by the provider have been met.

The current financial resources measurement focus and the modified accrual basis of accounting is followed by the governmental funds. Under the modified accrual basis of accounting, revenues are recorded when susceptible to accrual, i.e., both measurable and available. Available means collectible within the current period or soon enough thereafter to be used to pay liabilities of the current period. For this purpose, the village considers revenues to be available if they are collected within 60 days of the end of the current fiscal period. Expenditures are recorded when the related fund liability is incurred, except for unmatured interest on long-term debt, claims, judgments, compensated absences, and pension expenditures, which are recorded as a fund liability when expected to be paid with expendable available financial resources.

Property taxes are recorded in the year levied as receivables and deferred revenues. They are recognized as revenues in the succeeding year when services financed by the levy are being provided. In addition to property taxes for the village, taxes are collected for and remitted to the state and county governments as well as the local school districts and technical college district. Taxes are levied in December on the assessed value as of the prior January 1.

Property tax calendar—2000 tax roll:

Lien date and levy date	December 2000
Tax bills mailed	December 2000
Payment in full, or	January 31, 2001
First installment due	January 31, 2001
Second installment due	March 31, 2001
Third installment due	May 31, 2001
Final settlement with county	August 2001
Personal property taxes in full	January 31, 2001
Tax sale—2000 delinquent real estate taxes	October 2004

Intergovernmental aids and grants are recognized as revenues in the period the related expenditures are incurred, if applicable, or when the village is entitled to the aids.

Exhibit 9-3

Continued

In the government-wide financial statements, special assessments are recognized as revenues when levied against the benefiting properties. In governmental fund financial statements, special assessments are recorded as revenues when they become measurable and available as current assets. Annual installments due in future years are reflected as receivables and deferred revenues. Delinquent special assessments being held for collection by the county are reported as receivables and deferred revenues in the capital improvements fund.

Revenues susceptible to accrual include property taxes, intergovernmental revenue, miscellaneous taxes, public charges for services, special assessments, and interest.

Other general revenues such as fines and forfeitures, inspection fees, recreation fees, and miscellaneous revenues are recognized when received in cash or when measurable and available under the criteria described above.

The village reports deferred revenues on its statement of net assets and its governmental funds balance sheet. For government-wide financial statements, deferred revenues arise from taxes levied in the current year which are for subsequent year's operations. For governmental fund financial statements, deferred revenues arise when a potential revenue does not meet both the "measurable" and "available" criteria for recognition in the current period. Deferred revenues also arise when resources are received before the village has a legal claim to them, as when grant monies are received prior to the incurrence of qualifying expenditures. In subsequent periods, when both revenue recognition criteria are met, or when the village has a legal claim to the resources, the liability for deferred revenue is removed from the combined balance sheet and revenue is recognized.

Proprietary funds are accounted for on the accrual basis. Revenues such as user fees are recognized in the accounting period in which they are earned; expenses are recognized in the period incurred.

The proprietary funds have elected to follow Financial Accounting Standards Board pronouncements issued before November 30, 1989, and all pronouncements of the Governmental Accounting Standards Board.

E. MEASUREMENT FOCUS

On the government-wide Statement of Net Assets and Statement of Activities both governmental and business-type activities are presented using the flow of economic resources measurement focus as defined below.

The measurement focus of all governmental funds is the flow of current financial resources concept. Under this concept, sources and uses of financial resources, including capital outlays, debt proceeds and debt retirements are reflected in operations. Resources not available to finance expenditures and commitments of the current period are recognized as deferred revenue or a reservation of fund equity. Liabilities for claims, judgments, compensated absences and pension contributions which will not be currently liquidated using expendable available financial resources are included as liabilities in the government-wide and proprietary fund financial statements but are excluded from the governmental funds financial statements. The related expenditures are recognized in the governmental fund financial statements when the liabilities are liquidated.

The measurement focus of proprietary funds is the flow of economic resources. Under this concept, revenues and expenses are matched using the accrual basis of accounting. All fixed assets are capitalized at historical cost and depreciated over their useful lives.

(continued)

Exhibit 9-3
Continued

NOTE 4—INTERFUND TRANSFERS

The following is a schedule of interfund transfers:

Fund Transferred To	Fund Transferred From	Amount
General fund	Woodlawn Cemetery Perpetual Care	$ 2,738
General fund	Water and wastewater utility	178,341
Park and open space	Park and recreational facilities	3,560
Library	General fund	281,662
Environmental	Capital improvement fund	141,376
Police retirement health insurance	General fund	4,181
Debt service fund	Park and recreational facilities	45,566
Debt service fund	Environmental fund	41,587
Debt service fund	Tax incremental district No. 2	117,481
Debt service fund	Capital improvement fund	319,625
Capital improvement fund	Park and recreational facilities	234,009
Total		$1,370,126

NOTE 7—LONG-TERM OBLIGATIONS

Debt service requirements to maturity are as follows:

YEARS	GOVERNMENTAL-TYPE LONG-TERM DEBT		BUSINESS-TYPE LONG-TERM DEBT	
	PRINCIPAL	INTEREST	PRINCIPAL	INTEREST
2001	$ 862,279	$ 694,373	$ 62,721	$ 32,015
2002	1,399,636	594,794	65,364	29,310
2003	1,101,993	524,929	68,007	26,440
2004	1,104,211	467,796	60,789	23,421
2005	1,139,806	410,436	65,194	20,685
2006–2010	5,657,337	1,207,646	372,663	55,180
2011–2014	1,195,000	138,824	—	—
Totals	$12,460,262	$4,038,798	$694,738	$187,051

In accordance with Wisconsin Statutes, total general obligation indebtedness of the village may not exceed 5 percent of the equalized value of taxable property within the village's jurisdiction. The debt limit as of December 31, 2000, was $34,141,280. Total general obligation debt outstanding at year end was $13,155,000.

Source: Excerpted and adapted from Comprehensive Annual Financial Report, Year 2000, Village of Grafton, Wisconsin.

PREPARING STATISTICAL TABLES

As previously mentioned, *statistical tables* provide economic, demographic and additional financial information useful in assessing a governmental unit's financial condition. The statistical tables recommended by the GASB are as follows (items a through g and items j, k, and m are to be presented for the last 10 fiscal years):

a. General governmental expenditures by function
b. General revenues by source
c. Property tax levies and collections
d. Assessed and actual value of taxable property
e. Property tax rates—all overlapping governments
f. Special assessment billings and collections (if the government is obligated in some manner for the related special assessment debt)
g. Ratio of net general bonded debt to assessed value and net bonded debt per capita
h. Computation of legal debt margin
i. Computation of overlapping debt
j. Ratio of annual debt service for general bonded debt to total general expenditures
k. Revenue bond coverage
l. Demographic statistics
m. Property value, construction, and bank deposits
n. Principal taxpayers
o. Miscellaneous statistics[13]

Illustrations of statistical tables are presented in Tables 9-10 and 9-11. Table 9-10 shows the 10-year trend in Grafton's revenues (by source), and Table 9-11 shows Grafton's 10-year trend in expenditures (by function). Additional illustrations of Grafton's statistical tables are presented in Chapter 14.

AUDITOR'S REPORT

One purpose of an independent audit is to lend credibility to the financial statements prepared by an entity's management. Exhibit 9-4 is the independent auditor's report that the firm of Virchow, Krause & Company issued on the financial statements of the Village of Grafton, Wisconsin, for the year ended December 31, 2000.

Notice the nature and scope of the audit, as well as the opinions expressed in the auditor's report. Notice particularly the third paragraph, wherein the auditor opines that ". . . the basic financial statements . . . present fairly, in all material respects, the financial position of the Village of Grafton . . . and the results of its operations . . . in conformity with accounting principles generally accepted. . . ." This type of opinion is often called a "clean opinion."

---

[13] GASB Cod. (2001) Sec. 2800.103.

Table 9-10
Statistical Tables—General Governmental Revenues by Source

VILLAGE OF GRAFTON
GENERAL GOVERNMENTAL REVENUES BY SOURCE
LAST 10 FISCAL YEARS

FISCAL YEAR	TAXES		INTER-GOVERNMENTAL		LICENSES AND PERMITS		FINES, FORFEITURES, AND PENALTIES		PUBLIC CHARGES FOR SERVICES	
1991	$2,739,818	51.3%	$1,450,486	27.2%	$122,104	2.3%	$ 51,703	1.0%	$ 83,772	1.6%
1992	2,926,718	54.5%	1,427,304	26.6%	118,561	2.2%	61,966	1.2%	166,361	3.1%
1993	3,519,525	57.7%	1,365,286	22.4%	160,290	2.6%	68,451	1.1%	179,583	2.9%
1994	3,693,853	53.5%	1,419,917	20.6%	218,242	3.2%	65,942	1.0%	195,095	2.8%
1995	3,780,396	50.5%	1,782,757	23.8%	252,070	3.4%	64,494	0.9%	242,759	3.2%
1996	4,068,573	53.7%	1,568,901	20.7%	249,739	3.3%	95,773	1.3%	218,013	2.9%
1997	3,691,704	54.2%	1,449,832	21.3%	285,951	4.2%	106,169	1.6%	250,058	3.7%
1998	4,007,070	49.0%	1,513,110	18.5%	328,697	4.0%	101,811	1.2%	235,171	2.9%
1999	4,288,079	46.4%	1,466,071	15.8%	427,171	4.6%	111,082	1.2%	265,797	2.9%
2000	4,598,219	52.4%	1,865,753	21.3%	364,728	4.2%	108,557	1.2%	239,927	2.7%

FISCAL YEAR	INTER-GOVERNMENTAL CHARGES FOR SERVICES		SPECIAL ASSESSMENTS		INVESTMENT INCOME		MISCELLANEOUS REVENUES		TOTAL REVENUES
1991	$ 168,159	3.1%	$ 254,437	4.8%	$341,437	6.4%	$129,262	2.4%	$5,341,178
1992	105,687	2.0%	192,682	3.6%	296,636	5.5%	76,687	1.4%	5,372,613
1993	99,730	1.6%	60,941	1.0%	470,505	7.7%	171,813	2.8%	6,096,124
1994	97,750	1.4%	222,470	3.2%	524,289	7.6%	462,307	6.7%	6,899,865
1995	103,175	1.4%	233,636	3.1%	419,020	5.6%	611,940	8.2%	7,490,247
1996	107,015	1.4%	479,999	6.3%	305,193	4.0%	482,830	6.4%	7,576,036
1997	112,105	1.6%	436,209	6.4%	386,879	5.7%	93,587	1.4%	6,812,494
1998	121,922	1.5%	742,170	9.1%	535,404	6.6%	590,303	7.2%	8,175,658
1999	134,946	1.4%	1,330,932	14.4%	432,038	4.7%	793,339	8.6%	9,249,455
2000	129,965	1.5%	599,098	6.8%	558,006	6.4%	312,995	3.6%	8,777,248

Includes General, Special Revenue, Debt Service, and Capital Projects Funds. GASB *No. 34* was implemented in 2000. Therefore, general governmental revenues for the year 2000 include funds presented as Trust Funds in previous years.

Source: Comprehensive Annual Financial Report, Year 2000, Village of Grafton, Wisconsin.

Table 9-11
Statistical Tables—General Expenditures by Function

VILLAGE OF GRAFTON
GENERAL GOVERNMENTAL EXPENDITURES BY FUNCTION
LAST 10 FISCAL YEARS

FISCAL YEAR	GENERAL GOVERNMENT		PUBLIC SAFETY		PUBLIC WORKS		COMMUNITY ENRICHMENT SERVICES	
1991	$467,939	7.5%	$1,735,753	28.0%	$1,138,839	18.4%	$572,801	9.2%
1992	426,573	6.5%	1,862,166	28.3%	1,063,182	16.2%	682,009	10.4%
1993	452,327	6.2%	1,909,855	26.0%	1,142,076	15.6%	681,516	9.3%
1994	470,680	6.8%	2,063,075	30.0%	1,158,200	16.8%	678,591	9.9%
1995	446,651	6.0%	2,051,078	27.5%	1,210,335	16.2%	797,362	10.7%
1996	509,109	4.8%	2,201,546	20.6%	1,241,954	11.6%	730,022	6.8%
1997	497,948	6.0%	2,281,354	27.5%	1,286,370	15.5%	810,442	9.8%
1998	573,701	6.4%	2,402,398	26.8%	1,261,016	14.0%	855,984	9.5%
1999	526,138	4.5%	2,525,620	21.6%	1,351,724	11.5%	903,255	7.7%
2000	581,948	6.0%	2,632,896	27.3%	1,573,654	16.3%	961,386	10.0%

FISCAL YEAR	CONSERVATION AND DEVELOPMENT		CAPITAL OUTLAYS		DEBT SERVICE		TOTAL EXPENDITURES
1991	$43,579	0.7%	$1,259,934	20.3%	$ 984,519	15.9%	$ 6,203,364
1992	74,288	1.1%	1,281,785	19.5%	1,179,816	18.0%	6,569,819
1993	56,709	0.8%	1,825,369	24.9%	1,274,248	17.4%	7,342,100
1994	191,016	2.8%	1,004,451	14.6%	1,318,933	19.2%	6,884,946
1995	47,228	0.6%	1,521,451	20.4%	1,378,397	18.5%	7,452,502
1996	40,595	0.4%	2,006,790	18.8%	3,932,262	36.9%	10,662,278
1997	56,326	0.7%	2,176,240	26.3%	1,174,466	14.2%	8,283,146
1998	85,771	1.0%	2,273,354	25.3%	1,526,888	17.0%	8,979,112
1999	67,829	0.6%	4,172,593	35.6%	2,171,047	18.5%	11,718,206
2000	350,424	3.6%	1,940,270	20.1%	1,609,441	16.7%	9,650,019

Includes General, Special Revenue, Debt Service, and Capital Projects Funds. GASB No 34 was implemented in 2000. Therefore, general government expenditures for the year 2000 include funds presented as Trust Funds in previous years.

Debt service for 1996 includes defeasance of the 1992 G.O. refunding bonds of $2,520,000.

In 1999, the Village of Grafton called $600,000 of the 1989 G.O. refunding bonds maturing 12/1/2001.

Source: Comprehensive Annual Financial Report, Year 2000, Village of Grafton, Wisconsin.

Exhibit 9-4

Independent Auditor's Report

Virchow, Krause & Company, LLP

Certified Public Accountants & Consultants

Independent Auditors' Report

To the Village Board
Village of Grafton
Grafton, Wisconsin

We have audited the accompanying basic financial statements of the Village of Grafton, Wisconsin, as of and for the year ended December 31, 2000, as listed in the table of contents. These basic financial statements are the responsibility of the village's management. Our responsibility is to express an opinion on these basic financial statements based on our audit.

We conducted our audit in accordance with auditing standards generally accepted in the United States of America. Those standards require that we plan and perform the audit to obtain reasonable assurance about whether the financial statements are free of material misstatement. An audit includes examining, on a test basis, evidence supporting the amounts and disclosures in the financial statements. An audit also includes assessing the accounting principles used and significant estimates made by management, as well as evaluating the overall financial statement presentation. We believe that our audit provides a reasonable basis for our opinion.

In our opinion, the basic financial statements referred to above present fairly, in all material respects, the financial position of the Village of Grafton, Wisconsin, at December 31, 2000, and the results of its operations and the cash flows of its proprietary funds for the year then ended in conformity with accounting principles generally accepted in the United States of America.

As discussed in Note 1.B, the Village of Grafton, Wisconsin, adopted the provisions of Governmental Accounting Standards Board Statement No. 33, *Accounting and Financial Reporting for Nonexchange Transactions* and Governmental Accounting Standards Board Statement No. 34, *Basic Financial Statements— Management's Discussion and Analysis—For State and Local Governments* as of January 1, 2000.

Information included under Management's Discussion and Analysis is not a required part of the basic financial statements but is supplemental information required by the Governmental Accounting Standards Board. We have applied certain limited procedures, consisting principally of inquiries of management regarding methods of measurement and presentation to this information. However, we did not audit the supplemental information and express no opinion on it.

Our audit was made for the purpose of forming an opinion on the basic financial statements taken as a whole. The combining and individual fund financial statements and supplemental schedules for the year ended December 31, 2000, and the individual fund statements for the year ended December 31, 1999, listed in the table of contents, are presented for purposes of additional analysis and are not a required part of the general purpose financial statements of the Village of Grafton, Wisconsin. The information has been subjected to the auditing procedures applied in the audit of the general purpose financial statements for the years ended December 31, 2000 and 1999, and, in our opinion, is fairly stated in all material respects in relation to the general purpose financial statements taken as a whole.

Exhibit 9-4

Continued

The financial and statistical information in the accompanying table of contents under "Introductory" and "Statistical Section" is presented for purposes of additional analysis and is not a required part of the basic financial statements of the Village of Grafton. The information has not been audited by us and, accordingly, we express no opinion on such information.

Virchow, Krause & Company, LLP

Madison, Wisconsin
February 28, 2001

Source: Comprehensive Annual Financial Report, Year 2000, Village of Grafton, Wisconsin.

REVIEW QUESTIONS

Q9-1   Which groups are the major external users of governmental financial reports?

Q9-2   How can financial reporting assist in fulfilling government's duty to be publicly accountable and assist users in assessing that accountability?

Q9-3   Define the term *reporting entity.*

Q9-4   Under what circumstances is a primary government considered to be financially accountable for a legally separate organization?

Q9-5   When reporting component units in a governmental organization's financial statements, what is the difference between blending and discrete presentation?

Q9-6   What are the major components of a comprehensive annual financial report?

Q9-7   What are the minimum requirements established by the GASB for general purpose external financial reports?

Q9-8   What are the components of the basic financial statements?

Q9-9   What is the purpose of Management's Discussion and Analysis?

Q9-10 What is the difference between fund financial statements and government-wide financial statements?

Q9-11 Define the term *major fund* in fund financial statements.

Q9-12 What measurement focus and basis of accounting should be used in reporting each of the three fund categories in fund financial statements?

Q9-13 What is a *special item* in financial reporting?

Q9-14 Describe the format of the governmental funds statement of revenues, expenditures, and changes in fund balances.

Q9-15 What are the three components of net assets in the proprietary funds statement of net assets?

Q9-16 What kind of information is compared in a budgetary comparison schedule?

Q9-17 Describe and illustrate the kind of information that should be reported in notes to the financial statements.

Q9-18 Describe and illustrate the kind of information that should be reported in statistical tables.

CASES

C9-1 The Building Authority was created by the city and organized as a separate legal entity. The authority is governed by a five-person board appointed for 6-year terms by the mayor, subject to city council approval. The authority uses the proceeds of its tax-exempt bonds to finance the construction or acquisition of general capital assets for the city only. The bonds are secured by the lease agreement with the city and will be retired through lease payments from the city. How should the city report the financial activities of the Building Authority?

(GASB *Statement 14*, para. 134)

C9-2 The Municipal Electric Utility (MEU) was created as a separate legal entity in accordance with state law to own, manage, and operate an electric utilities system in the city. The MEU's governing body consists of five members. It is a self-perpetuating board composed of four citizens (customers) and the mayor of the city serving ex officio. The four citizen board members provide representation from each of the MEU's main service areas. When a board vacancy occurs, the remaining board members must nominate the successor. The MEU board chooses the nominee from a list of candidates proposed by an independent citizens' committee. The MEU's board may reject these candidates for any reason and request additional candidates. The MEU's nomination is then subject to confirmation by the city council. The council's confirmation procedure is essentially a formality. After confirmation, the council cannot remove a member for any reason.

The MEU uses various services provided by departments of the city, including insurance, legal, motor pool, and computer services. The MEU is billed for these services on a proportionate cost basis with other user departments and agencies. The MEU provides customer service and related functions to the city's water department. The estimated cost of providing these services is paid by the water department. The MEU also provides electric service to the city and its agencies and bills the city for those services using established rate schedules. The MEU selects and employs its executives, controls the hiring of its employees, and is responsible for rate setting and its overall fiscal management. The city is not legally or morally obligated for the MEU's debt. The MEU receives no appropriations from the city. In compliance with its charter, the MEU is required to make a payment in lieu of taxes annually to the General Fund, calculated according to a formula based on kilowatt-hour sales for the preceding 12-month period. How should the city report the financial activities of the MEU?

(GASB *Statement 14*, para. 141)

C9-3   The State Turnpike Commission (STC) was established by the state to construct, operate, and maintain the state turnpike system. The STC was created as an instrumentality of the state as a separate legal entity with powers to issue revenue bonds payable from tolls and other revenues. The governing body of the STC consists of eight members appointed by the governor for fixed 10-year terms and three state officials serving ex officio—the elected state treasurer, the elected state controller, and the appointed superintendent of highways.

    The STC is financially self-sufficient, and the state cannot access its assets or surpluses and is not obligated to subsidize deficits of the STC. The STC sets its own rates and approves its own budget. The bond agreement states that the debt of the STC is not an obligation of the state. However, state statutes authorize the state's budget director to include in the budget submitted to the legislature an amount sufficient to make the principal and interest payments on the STC bonds in the event STC revenues are insufficient to meet debt service requirements. How should the state report the financial activities of the STC?

(GASB *Statement 14*, para. 142)

C9-4   The Board of Education (BOE) is a separately elected body that administers the public school system in the city. The BOE is not organized as a separate legal entity and does not have the power to levy taxes or issue bonds. Its budget is subject to approval by the city council to the extent that, under state law, the BOE has the discretionary authority to expend the amount appropriated to it by the city. The BOE requests a single amount to fund its operations; the city council can reject the BOE's requested budget.

    How should the city report the financial activities of the BOE?

(GASB *Statement 14*, para. 144)

ETHICS CASE

EC9-1 Several years ago the citizens of Jefferson Heights approved a $\frac{1}{4}$ percent increase in the sales tax dedicated to law enforcement. The legislation provided that a Special Revenue Fund be established to account for the collection and disbursement of the tax resources. In addition, the legislation specifically included a provision that prohibited any other use of these funds. John Morris, the chief financial officer of Jefferson Heights, discovered that the General Fund does not have enough resources to meet the final payroll of the fiscal year. Morris presented a proposal to the mayor, Jane Dufrend, that the Special Revenue Fund loan resources to the General Fund until the General Fund can repay the loan. The county attorney, Jerry Carson, gave Morris and Dufrend a legal opinion that indicated that such a loan was against the wording and the spirit of the Special Revenue Fund and the city's charter. Morris told Dufrend that no one could tell because he could combine the resources of all of the smaller Special Revenue Funds in the financial statements and the loan would not show up as being specifically related to this fund. How would you advise Dufrend? Explain.

EXERCISES

E9-1   (Organization of the CAFR)
You are asked to explain the organization of the Comprehensive Annual Financial Report, as specified in GASB *Statement No. 34*. Outline your talk.

E9-2   (Analysis of the MD&A section of a CAFR)
Obtain a CAFR from a governmental unit and read Management's Discussion and Analysis. Describe three significant comments made by management.

E9-3   (Analysis of the notes to the financial statements in a CAFR)
Obtain a CAFR from a governmental unit and read the statement of significant accounting policies in the notes to the financial statements. Write a brief report summarizing those policies.

E9-4   (Analysis of the notes to the financial statements in a CAFR)
Obtain a CAFR from a governmental unit and read the notes other than the statement of significant accounting policies. Write a brief report summarizing three of the notes.

E9-5   (Analysis of a budgetary comparison statement in a CAFR)
Obtain a CAFR from a governmental unit and read the budgetary comparison statement. Also, read what management says in its MD&A, if anything, about the results of its budgetary activities for the year. What conclusions can you reach from reading the budgetary comparison statement? How do management's comments in the MD&A improve your understanding of the budgetary comparison statement?

E9-6   (Multiple choice)
1. In governmental financial reporting, what is blending?
   a. A method of preparing the notes to the CAFR
   b. The process of including the financial data of a component unit with the financial data of the primary government
   c. The process of reporting the financial data of a component unit as a separate column in the reporting entity's financial statements
   d. The process of combining intergovernmental revenues with the revenues of the reporting government
2. In financial reporting, which of the following meets the requirement for a primary government to be financially accountable for a legally separate organization?
   a. The primary government can appoint one-half of the organization's governing body.
   b. The government's chief executive can appoint a long-time political ally to the organization's governing body.
   c. The primary government can appoint a voting majority of the organization's governing body.
   d. The chief executive and the chief of both houses of the legislature each can appoint one member of the organization's 12-person governing body.

3. What are the *minimum* requirements established by the GASB for general purpose external financial reports?
   a. A CAFR
   b. Fund financial statements and government-wide financial statements
   c. Basic financial statements and notes to the financial statements
   d. MD&A, basic financial statements, and required supplementary information other than MD&A
4. In fund financial statements, for which funds is depreciation reported?
   a. Only for governmental-type funds
   b. Only for proprietary-type funds
   c. For both governmental-type and proprietary-type funds
   d. For neither governmental-type nor proprietary-type funds

5. In fund financial statements, which of the following funds are reported using the economic resources measurement focus?
   a. General Fund
   b. Debt Service Funds and Capital Projects Funds
   c. All funds that meet the definition of *major*
   d. Enterprise Funds

E9-7   (Fill in the blanks)
1. The annual financial report of a governmental unit is called a _____ .
2. Government-wide financial statements include a statement of _____ and a statement of _____ .
3. Fund financial statements for fiduciary funds generally include a statement of _____ and a statement of _____ .
4. Budgetary comparison schedules should always have at least three columns for _____ , _____ , and _____ .
5. In fund financial statements, governmental funds should be presented using the _____ measurement focus and the _____ basis of accounting.

E9-8   (True or false)
State whether each of these statements is true or false. For any false statement, indicate why it is false.
1. In fund financial statements, the General Fund should always be reported as a major fund.
2. In fund financial statements, Enterprise Funds are reported using the economic resources measurement focus and the modified accrual basis of accounting.
3. When an auditor states that an entity's financial statements present fairly its financial position and results of operations, it is reasonable to assume that the entity's financial condition is healthy.
4. Notes to the financial statements are a form of required supplementary information.
5. Nonmajor funds may be combined and presented in a single column in the fund financial statements.

P9-1 (Multiple choice—theory)

1. In fund financial statements, for which of the following funds are financial statements prepared using the current financial resources measurement focus and the modified accrual basis of accounting?
   a. Both Enterprise Funds and Special Revenue Funds
   b. Both the General Fund and Debt Service Funds
   c. Both Capital Projects Funds and Pension Trust Funds
   d. Both Permanent Funds and Private Purpose Trust Funds

2. In fund financial statements, for which of the following funds are you most likely to see the category Long-term bonds payable?
   a. General Fund
   b. Capital Projects Fund
   c. Enterprise Fund
   d. Debt Service Fund

3. Which basis of accounting is used in preparing the budgetary comparison statement?
   a. The budgetary basis
   b. The accrual basis
   c. The modified accrual basis
   d. The cash receipts and disbursements basis

4. In fund financial statements, where are the revenues and expenditures (expenses) of governmental-type and proprietary-type funds reported?
   a. On different financial statements
   b. On the same financial statement
   c. Not on any financial statement
   d. On the same financial statement where fiduciary funds are reported

5. For which fund categories are fund financial statements required to have columns?
   a. Major funds only
   b. All funds
   c. Each major fund plus a column for nonmajor funds combined
   d. Only the combined total of all funds

6. Which of the following best expresses the accounting equation for Agency Funds?
   a. Assets = Liabilities
   b. Assets = Liabilities + Net Assets
   c. Assets − Liabilities = Net Assets
   d. Assets = Net Assets

7. Which of the following is part of the *minimum requirements* established by the GASB for general-purpose external financial reports?
   a. An introductory section
   b. Management's Discussion and Analysis
   c. A statistical section
   d. A schedule of cash receipts and disbursements for all funds

8. The process of *blending* is accomplished by reporting a component unit's funds in which manner?
   a. In the notes to the primary government's financial statements
   b. In a separate column to the left of the primary government's funds
   c. As if they were always fiduciary funds of the primary government
   d. As if they were the funds of the primary government
9. Which of the following situations would be defined as a *special item?*
   a. The amount of a revenue or an expenditure item increased by at least 10 percent over the previous year
   b. A significant transaction within the control of management is either unusual in nature or infrequent in occurrence
   c. A significant event outside the control of management causes the expenses or expenditures of a fund to exceed its revenues
   d. A vibrant economy causes an entity's tax revenues to rise by an extraordinary amount over the budgetary estimate
10. When preparing a fund statement of revenue, expenditures, and changes in fund balances for the Capital Projects Fund, how should proceeds of debt be reported?
    a. As a revenue
    b. As a transfer
    c. As an other financing source
    d. As bonds payable
11. In fund financial statements, where are the categories Capital assets, less accumulated depreciation, and Long-term bonds payable likely to appear?
    a. The General Fund, but not an Enterprise Fund
    b. An Enterprise Fund, but not a Capital Projects Fund
    c. Both an Enterprise Fund and a Capital Projects Fund
    d. An Enterprise Fund and Capital Projects Fund or a Debt Service Fund

P9-2   (Preparation of a governmental funds balance sheet)
The following information is available for the governmental funds of Tom's Village:

Account	General	Debt Service	Special Revenue Funds Fund A	Special Revenue Funds Fund B
Cash	$10,000	$5,000	$600	$1,000
Taxes receivable	5,000			
Due from other funds		2,000		
Accounts payable	9,000		200	400
Due to other funds	2,000			
Reserved for encumbrances	1,000			
Reserved for debt service		7,000		
Unreserved fund balance	3,000		400	600

Required: Prepare the governmental funds balance sheet for Tom's Village. The Tom's Village officials do not consider either Special Revenue Fund as particularly important to financial statement users.

P9-3   (Multiple choice: mini-problems)

The following information relates to questions 1, 2, and 3. A village levied property taxes in the amount of $800,000 for calendar year 2004. By year-end, the village had collected $770,000. It expected to collect $20,000 more in January and February of 2005 and the remaining $10,000 after February but before September 2005. Answer the following questions regarding the fund financial statements for the General Fund at December 31, 2004, and for the calendar year 2004.

1. What amount of property tax revenues should be recognized for calendar year 2004?
   a. $770,000
   b. $780,000
   c. $790,000
   d. $800,000

2. What amount of property taxes receivable should be reported at December 31, 2004?
   a. $0
   b. $10,000
   c. $20,000
   d. $30,000

3. What amount of deferred property tax revenues should be reported at December 31, 2004?
   a. $0
   b. $10,000
   c. $20,000
   d. $30,000

4. A city operates on a calendar year basis. On April 1, 2004, the city issues general obligation bonds in the amount of $1,000,000 to build a new city hall. The debt is to be paid off at the rate of $100,000 a year, with interest of 6 percent per annum on the outstanding debt, starting April 1, 2005. Although it maintains a Debt Service Fund, it has not transferred any resources to that fund to pay any interest or principal on the debt. When it prepares its governmental fund financial statements as of December 31, 2004, how much should the city report as Debt Service Fund expenditures?
   a. $0
   b. $45,000
   c. $60,000
   d. $120,000

5. Assume the same set of facts as in problem 4, except that the debt had been issued by the Water Enterprise Fund to extend water mains. When it prepares its proprietary fund financial statements, how much should the city report as interest expense?

a. $0
b. $45,000 $60 000 X $\frac{9}{12}$ = 45000
c. $60,000
d. $120,000

P9-4 (Net asset classification)
Nuevo York County maintains the Metro Bus Enterprise Fund to account for the activities of its municipal bus service. The following information is reported in the assets and liabilities sections of the proprietary funds statement of net assets.

Cash and investments	$ 250,000
Buses and bus garage	2,500,000
Accumulated depreciation, buses and garage	470,000
Accounts payable	62,000
Current amount of long-term bonds payable	250,000
Long-term bonds payable—noncurrent amount	1,500,000
Other long-term liabilities	50,000

Required: Compute the amount Nuevo York County should report as Invested in capital assets, net of related debt in the proprietary funds statement of net assets. Assume the long-term debt was issued to finance acquisition of the buses.

P9-5 (Preparation of proprietary funds statement of revenues, expenses, and changes in fund net assets)
The City of Breukelen maintains a rapid transit system, which is accounted for in a proprietary fund called Breukelen RTS. The following excerpt from the trial balance shows all the information needed to prepare an operating statement.

Revenues from fares	$3,050,000
Train operating expenses	2,430,000
Track and train maintenance expenses	565,000
Depreciation	325,000
Investment income	50,000
Interest expense on long-term debt	320,000
Cash subsidy from the City of Breukelen	500,000
Net assets, January 1, 2004	7,430,000

Required: Prepare a statement of revenues, expenditures, and changes in fund net assets for the Breukelen RTS for the year ended December 31, 2004, using the appropriate format.

SUMMARY PROBLEMS

Summary Problem 1. (Fund accounting and preparation of financial statements)
Part A. (Identification of funds)

Coco City established funds to account for the following activities:

1. To account for its day-to-day operating activities
2. To acquire or construct major capital assets
3. To accumulate resources to service long-term debt
4. To operate a municipal swimming pool

Required: State the names of the funds that Coco City will use for each of these activities.

Part B. (Budgetary accounting for the General Fund)

1. Coco City opened the year beginning January 1, 2004, with cash of $40,000, vouchers payable of $35,000, and unreserved fund balance of $5,000.
2. The Coco City Council adopted the following budget for the General Fund at the beginning of the year:

Revenues—property taxes	$400,000
Revenues—sales taxes	70,000
Revenues—parks admission fees	10,000
Appropriations:	
Police salaries	300,000
Police supplies	40,000
Parks salaries	80,000
Transfer to Debt Service Fund	45,000

3. Two purchase orders, one for $35,000 and one for $4,000, were placed against the appropriation for police supplies.
4. Because the unit price was lower than anticipated, an invoice for $33,000 was received and approved for supplies that had been ordered for $35,000.
5. The invoice for $33,000 was paid.

Required: Record the opening account balances; prepare journal entries to record transactions 2–5; post the journal entries to T-accounts; post the Police supplies budgetary transactions to an appropriation, encumbrance, and expenditure ledger.

Part C. (Other General Fund transactions)

1. Property taxes were levied in the amount of $404,000 in order to provide revenues of $400,000. Tax bills were sent to the property owners.
2. The account of a taxpayer who owed $3,000 was written off as uncollectible.
3. Property taxes of $370,000 were collected in cash.
4. At year-end, all uncollected taxes were declared delinquent. The Coco City finance director concluded that all the property taxes would be collected, so there was no need for any allowance for uncollectible taxes. She estimated that $21,000 of the delinquent taxes would be collected in January and February of 2005 and that the rest of the taxes would be collected later in the year.
5. The state collects sales taxes on behalf of all cities in the state. During the year, Coco City received $68,000 in sales taxes from the state. The state

also advised Coco that it would remit an additional $6,000 in sales taxes by January 20.

6. Coco City collected parks admissions fees of $18,000 during the year.
7. The unpaid vouchers of $35,000 at the beginning of the year were paid.
8. Salaries in the amount of $360,000 ($290,000 for the police department and $70,000 for the parks department) were paid.
9. The payroll for the period ended December 31, 2004 ($8,000 for the police department and $5,000 for the parks department), which was included in the year 2004 budget, will be paid on January 5, 2005.
10. A police department sedan accidentally sideswiped a citizen's vehicle in November 2004. Coco City's corporation counsel estimated that the City would ultimately settle the citizen's claim for about $4,000. It usually takes about 18 months to settle cases of this kind.

Required: Prepare journal entries, as appropriate, to record these transactions, and post the journal entries to T-accounts.

Part D. (Capital Projects Fund and Debt Service Fund transactions)

1. To provide financing for a new police station, Coco City sold bonds on April 1, 2004, in the amount of $500,000. Bond principal is payable over a 10-year period in 20 equal semiannual installments of $25,000, with interest of 6 percent per annum on the unpaid balance. The first payment is due on October 1, 2004.
2. Coco City purchased a prefabricated police station and paid $500,000 for it on delivery. The building, ready for occupancy on July 1, 2004, was expected to have a useful life of 25 years.
3. The General Fund transferred $45,000 to the Debt Service Fund in anticipation of the first installment of debt service.
4. The first installment of debt service became due and payable on October 1, 2004.
5. The first installment of debt service was paid.

Required: Prepare journal entries for all funds, as appropriate, to record these transactions, and post the journal entries to T-accounts for each fund.

Part E. (Enterprise Fund transactions)

1. Coco City operates a municipal swimming pool. It started the year with cash of $5,000; net capital assets of $510,000 (the swimming pool cost $600,000 and the accumulated depreciation was $90,000); and outstanding bonds of $480,000 (the original debt of $600,000 was being paid off over 15 years in equal annual installments of $40,000 at December 31 of each year, with interest of 5 percent per annum on the outstanding balance).
2. Coco received swimming pool admissions fees of $70,000.
3. Salaries totaling $8,000 were paid to a lifeguard and a clerk.
4. Coco paid the annual debt service requirement on the swimming pool bonds.
5. Coco recorded depreciation on the swimming pool. The cost of the pool is amortized over 20 years.

Required: Record the opening balances in T-accounts, prepare journal entries to record the transactions, and post the journal entries to T-accounts.

Part F. (Preparation of fund financial statements)

Required: Prepare preclosing trial balances for all funds. Prepare the following fund financial statements:

1. Governmental funds balance sheet
2. Governmental funds statement of revenues, expenditures, and changes in fund balances
3. Proprietary funds statement of net assets
4. Proprietary funds statement of revenues, expenses, and changes in fund net assets

Part G. (Preparation of journal entries for government-wide financial statements and preparation of government-wide financial statements) See Summary Problem at the end of Chapter 10 for remainder of this problem, to be done after reading Chapter 10.

Summary Problem 2. (Adjusting and correcting journal entries for several funds)

You are hired to examine the financial statements of the City of Rego for the year ended December 31, 2004. Your examination disclosed that, due to the inexperience of the town's new bookkeeper, all transactions for the year 2004 were recorded in the General Fund. The following General Fund trial balance, as of December 31, 2004, was furnished to you.

City of Rego
General Fund
Trial Balance
December 31, 2004

	Debits	Credits
Cash	$ 20,800	
Short-term investments	180,000	
Accounts receivable	11,500	
Taxes receivable—current	30,000	
Tax anticipation notes payable		$ 58,000
Appropriations		927,000
Expenditures	795,200	
Estimated revenues	927,000	
Revenues		750,000
General city property	98,500	
General obligation bonds payable	52,000	
Unreserved fund balance		380,000
	$2,115,000	$2,115,000

Note: 1. Single control accounts were used for items such as Appropriations and Expenditures.
2. The budget is only recorded for the General Fund.

Your audit disclosed the following additional information:

1. During the year, equipment with a book value of $9,000 was removed from service and sold for $6,400. In addition, new equipment costing $104,900 was purchased. These transactions were recorded in the General city property account. No other amounts were recorded relative to these events.

2. During the year, 100 acres of land were donated to the town for use as an industrial park. The land had a value of $125,000. No recording of this donation had been made.

3. To service other municipal departments, the town, at the beginning of the year, authorized the establishment of a central supplies warehouse (an Internal Service Fund). During the year, supplies totaling $90,000 were purchased and charged to Expenditures in the General Fund. A physical inventory of supplies on hand on December 31, 2004, was taken; this count disclosed that supplies totaling $84,000 had been used. Other records indicate that departments using the supplies were billed $92,400. No entries were made for the billings. The General Fund acquired and used all the supplies mentioned previously.

4. Outstanding purchase orders at December 31, 2004, not recorded in the accounts, amounted to $22,000. Although encumbrance accounting is required by city charter, it was not used during the year.

5. On December 31, 2004, the State Revenue Department informed the town that its share of a state-collected, locally shared tax would be $58,500. No entry was made for this information.

6. The Accounts receivable of $11,500 includes $2,000 due from Rego's electric utility for the sale of old equipment on behalf of the town. Accounts for the municipal electric utility operated by the town are maintained in a separate fund. The scrap was sold to K.R., Inc., which will pay for it in July. The old equipment originally cost $15,000. The entry made on the books of the General Fund to record the sale was

Accounts receivable	2,000	
Revenues		2,000

No entries were made on the books of the utility for this transaction.

7. The balance in Taxes receivable—current is now considered delinquent, and the town estimates that $4,000 will be uncollectible.

8. On December 31, 2004, the town retired, at face value, 6 percent general obligation serial bonds totaling $40,000. The bonds were issued on January 1, 2003, at a face value of $200,000. Interest of $12,000 was paid during 2004 and debited to General obligation bonds payable. A Debt Service Fund was established in 2003.

Required: 1. Prepare all the entries necessary to correct the town's records. Identify the funds used. *Hint:* If an item is recorded in an incorrect fund, it will require an entry to remove it from that fund and a separate entry to record it in the proper fund.

2. Prepare a revised trial balance for the General Fund.

(AICPA adapted)

Summary Problem 3. (Journal entries for several funds and a balance sheet for a Capital Projects Fund)

The City of Peak's Kill had the following transactions during the calendar year 2004. The transactions relate to financing and constructing a new city hall. Peak's Kill uses budgetary accounting in its Capital Projects Fund.

1. Peak's Kill adopted a budget for the Capital Projects Fund on January 1, based on the following assumptions:
   Bonds would be issued for $10 million.
   Interest earned on investment of idle cash would be $300,000.
   Contracts would be awarded for $10 million.
2. On April 1, Peak's Kill issued $10 million of 6 percent general obligation bonds to build a new city hall. Principal and interest payments are made each June 30 and December 31 for 20 years, starting December 31, 2004. Principal is amortized in equal semi-annual payments of $250,000. The bonds were sold for $10,100,000. The premium of $100,000 was transferred to the Debt Service Fund, to be used to defray the first payment of principal and interest.
3. On May 1, Peak's Kill contracted with Howard Architects for $500,000 to design the building and supervise construction.
4. On July 1, the Capital Projects Fund invested $7,500,000 in a certificate of deposit.
5. On September 1, Peak's Kill entered into a contract with Eddie Construction to build a new city hall for $9,300,000.
6. On December 10, Eddie Construction billed Peak's Kill $2 million for work done through November 30. Peak's Kill paid the bill, after approval by Howard Architects, less 10 percent retainage pending completion of construction.
7. On December 30, the General Fund transferred to the Debt Service Fund an amount sufficient to pay the December 31 installment of principal and interest on the bonds, after considering the $100,000 cash already in the Debt Service Fund.
8. On December 30, the city received a bill from Howard Architects for $175,000. The bill was approved and scheduled for payment on January 10, 2005.
9. On December 31, the Debt Service Fund paid the first installment of principal and interest on the bonds issued to construct city hall.
10. On December 31, in anticipation of preparing financial statements, the accountant accrued interest at the rate of 3 percent per annum on the certificate of deposit.

Required: 1. Prepare journal entries to record the transactions and identify the fund(s) used.
   2. Prepare a balance sheet for the City of Peak's Kill Capital Projects Fund as of December 31, 2004.
   3. Prepare closing entries for the Capital Projects Fund.

Summary Problem 4. (Journal entries for several funds)

Following are several transactions that relate to Weaverstown for 2004:

1. The general operating budget was approved as follows:

Appropriations	$5,200,000
Estimated revenues	5,000,000
Estimated other financing sources	300,000

2. Plans for a new criminal courts building were approved. General obligation bonds with a face value of $7 million were issued for $7,200,000. Local laws stipulate that any premium must be transferred to the appropriate Debt Service Fund. In addition, a federal grant of $8 million was received.

3. The fire department ordered new equipment to replace outdated equipment. The new equipment was expected to cost $35,000. The old equipment cost $23,000 but was sold for $750.

4. The city received $400,000 from the state. This amount represents the city's share of the state gasoline tax. This money can only be spent to repair streets, and a separate accounting is required by the state.

5. General obligation bonds of $5 million were retired by a Debt Service Fund. At this time, interest of $150,000 was also paid to the bondholders.

6. The 2004 property tax was levied by the city. The total amount was $3,000,000, of which $2,990,000 was expected to be collected.

7. Salaries of governmental employees were paid, totaling $800,000. Of this amount, $65,000 was withheld and included in an account called Due to federal government as income tax payments. In addition, the city paid its share of retirement premiums, $100,000, and the employees' share, $50,000, to the city's PERS. Assume that all employees were paid through the General Fund. (Salaries and related costs are not encumbered.)

8. The Central Supplies Fund, an Internal Service Fund, billed the General Fund $15,000 and the Gas Service Fund, an Enterprise Fund, $8,000 for supplies. Assume that the General Fund previously encumbered $15,500 for supplies.

9. The Gas Service Fund billed the General Fund for $2,500, the Central Supplies Fund for $1,000, and the remainder of its customers for $2,500,000. The General Fund had encumbered $2,600 for this expenditure.

10. The General Fund made its annual contribution of $200,000 to the Debt Service Fund. Assume that $150,000 was for interest.

11. The contract for the new court building was signed with Excell Construction Company for $14,500,000. It contained a 10 percent retainage clause.

12. The fire equipment ordered in part (3) arrived. The total cost was $36,000. The city paid the bill upon delivery. (Assume the excess expenditure was approved.)

13. Excell Construction Company sent a progress billing for $1,500,000.

14. Property taxes of $2,800,000 were collected and $5,000 was written off as uncollectible. The remainder became delinquent.

15. Suzanne Night gave the city $500,000 of marketable securities. The securities were to be used as the principal of a trust that must be maintained

intact. The income earned from these investments can only be used for purchasing library books.

16. A property tax bill from 2003 for $200 was written off as uncollectible. At this time the receivable was in a delinquent state.

17. Special assessment bonds with a face value of $345,000 were issued for a drainage project. The total assessment was $345,000. Of this amount, $30,000 was considered to be current and to be revenue of 2004. (Assume the city guaranteed the bonds.)

18. Income of $14,000 was received by the Night Principal Trust Fund, set up in part (15). This amount was immediately transferred to the Night Library Special Revenue Fund, and $12,600 was used to purchase library books.

Required: Prepare the journal entries necessary to record these transactions and indicate the fund(s) used.

Chapter 10

Government-Wide Financial Statements

After completing this chapter, you should be able to:

➤ *Describe the major differences between fund financial statements and government-wide statements.*

➤ *Discuss how Interfund and Internal Service Fund balances and activity are handled in government-wide statements.*

➤ Discuss accrual accounting principles for major revenue sources.

➤ Describe and prepare the major basis of accounting adjustments needed to convert fund financial statements to government-wide statements.

➤ Describe and prepare the major measurement focus adjustments needed to convert fund financial statements to government-wide statements.

➤ Discuss the requirements for reporting capital assets in government-wide statements and the "modified approach" for reporting infrastructure assets.

➤ Describe and prepare the government-wide financial statements.

➤ Describe and explain the content of the reconciliations between fund financial statements and government-wide statements.

TYPES OF GOVERNMENT-WIDE FINANCIAL STATEMENTS

Basic Principles for Required Financial Statements

GASB *Statement No. 34* requires preparation of two government-wide financial statements, a statement of net assets and a statement of activities. Government-wide financial statements should be prepared using the following basic principles:

a. Information should be reported about the *overall* government, without showing individual funds or fund types.
b. Assets, liabilities, revenues, and expenses should be reported using the economic resources measurement focus and the accrual basis of accounting for all activities, regardless of the types of funds used to account for them.
c. Financial statements should be formatted in such a way as to distinguish between the primary government and its discretely presented component units; also, for the primary government, the formatting should distinguish between governmental and business-type activities.
d. Information about fiduciary activities should be excluded from the statements.[1]

Format of the Statement of Net Assets

The *statement of net assets* shows all financial and capital resources. The statement may be formatted either in the form of Assets − Liabilities = Net Assets or in the traditional balance sheet form of Assets = Liabilities + Net Assets. Either way, the difference between assets and liabilities should be shown as *net assets*, not fund balance or equity.

---

[1] GASB Cod. (2001) Sec. 2200.110.

The statement of net assets generally has four columns of financial data, although it could have more or fewer columns, depending on the structure of the reporting entity and choice of reporting methods. If the reporting entity has no discretely presented component units, it will usually have three columns: one for governmental activities, one for business-type activities, and a total column. A column for discretely presented component units is presented to the right of the total column.

Reporting on Liquidity

Governments are encouraged to provide information on the relative liquidity of the assets and liabilities. This disclosure may be done in two ways:

1. By presenting asset and liability elements in order of their relative liquidity
2. By preparing the statement of net assets in classified form

Relative liquidity regarding assets means nearness in time to conversion to cash; for liabilities, it means nearness in time to payment. *Classified statements* of net assets distinguish between current and noncurrent. Current assets include cash and assets that the entity expects to convert to cash or to be consumed in operations within 1 year. Current liabilities are those that are due to be paid within 1 year, including the portion of long-term bonds payable due to be paid in the year following the date of the statement of net assets.

Classification of Net Assets

The difference between assets and liabilities—the net assets—should be separated into three components: (1) invested in capital assets, net of related debt, (2) restricted, and (3) unrestricted. The net asset component *invested in capital assets, net of related debt* represents the entity's capital assets, minus accumulated depreciation and outstanding balances of bonds, notes, or other borrowings attributable to acquiring, constructing, or improving those assets. The calculation of this net asset component will be illustrated later in the chapter.

Net assets are reported as *restricted* when constraints are imposed on the use of assets, either externally (by creditors, grantors, or laws or regulations of other governments) or by the entity's constitution or in enabling legislation. For example, restrictions may be imposed by debt covenants or by higher-level governments when they provide resources with the explicit requirement that they be used only for a specific purpose, such as a particular capital project or a particular operating function.

The amount reported as *unrestricted* net assets in the governmental activities column of the government-wide statement of net assets can differ significantly from the total unreserved fund balances reported in the governmental funds balance sheet. Possible causes of the difference include the use of different bases of accounting in the two statements and outstanding debt issued to finance prior-year operating deficits.

Table 10-1 presents the government-wide statement of net assets for the Village of Grafton, Wisconsin, at December 31, 2000. Notice that Grafton's assets and liabilities are shown in order of relative liquidity. Noncurrent liabilities due within 1 year are separated from those due in more than 1 year. Grafton has no discretely presented component units, so its statement of net assets has only three columns: governmental activities, business-type activities, and a total.

Table 10-1

Government-Wide Statement of Net Assets

VILLAGE OF GRAFTON
STATEMENT OF NET ASSETS
DECEMBER 31, 2000

	GOVERNMENTAL ACTIVITIES	BUSINESS TYPE ACTIVITIES	TOTAL
ASSETS			
Cash and investments	$ 9,044,593	$ 3,742,352	$12,786,945
Receivables (net)			
Taxes	2,328,462	—	2,328,462
Loans	622,151	—	622,151
Other	352,989	344,794	697,783
Internal balances	(27,513)	27,513	
Prepaid items and inventories	31,489	4,471	35,960
Other assets	29,586	7,235	36,821
Capital assets			
Capital assets not being depreciated	2,404,554	609,124	3,013,678
Other capital assets, net of depreciation	8,612,726	17,142,045	25,754,771
Total Assets	23,399,037	21,877,534	45,276,571
LIABILITIES			
Accounts payable and accrued expenses	511,180	97,965	609,145
Deferred revenues—tax roll	4,951,609	—	4,951,609
Noncurrent liabilities			
Due within 1 year	862,280	62,721	925,001
Due in more than 1 year	11,767,506	692,284	12,459,790
Total Liabilities	18,092,575	852,970	18,945,545
NET ASSETS			
Invested in capital assets, net of related debt	10,124	17,056,430	17,066,554
Restricted for:			
Loan programs	679,758	—	679,758
Park and recreational impact fees	456,546	—	456,546
Debt service	447,167	—	447,167
Permanent fund	47,140	—	47,140
Equipment replacement	—	595,175	595,175
Unrestricted	3,665,727	3,372,959	7,038,686
Total Net Assets	$ 5,306,462	$21,024,564	$26,331,026

Source: Comprehensive Annual Financial Report, Year 2000, Village of Grafton, Wisconsin.

Format of the Statement of Activities

The operations of a governmental reporting entity are reported in a *statement of activities*, presented in a format that first shows the *net* expense or revenue of each governmental function or program. To make this report, gross expenses are listed in the upper part of the financial statement, with reductions shown for revenues directly related to each function or program. Taxes, other general revenues (such as investment earnings and grants not restricted to specific purposes), and special items (such as gains on the sale of capital assets) are displayed in the lower part of the statement. The purpose of this format is to show the extent to which each function is "self-financing" (through fees and intergovernmental financing) and the extent to which it draws on the government's general revenues.

Table 10-2 presents the government-wide statement of activities for the Village of Grafton, Wisconsin, for the year ended December 31, 2000. Notice that expenses and related program revenues are displayed in the upper half of the financial statement, with governmental activities separated from business-type activities. Taxes, other general revenues, and special items are shown in the lower part of the statement.

If Grafton had component units, captions for each function/program would be shown on the left side of the page after business-type activities, and a component units column would be included after the total column on the right side of the page.

Reporting Expenses

Governmental units report expenses by function or program (such as public safety and culture and recreation), except for expenses that meet the definition of special or extraordinary, which need to be shown separately as discussed in Chapter 9. At a minimum, the statement of activities should show the *direct* functional expenses—those that are clearly identifiable to a particular function. Although not required to do so, governmental units may allocate certain indirect expenses (such as general government and support services) among the functions.

Depreciation expense for capital assets that can be specifically identified with a function (for example, a police station or a fire house) should be included with the direct expenses of the function. Depreciation expense for general infrastructure assets (such as water mains) may be reported either as a direct expense of the function (such as public works) that acquires and maintains the assets or as a separate line item in the statement of activities. Interest on general long-term debt should generally be shown separately.

Notice that Grafton's statement of activities (Table 10-2) shows the same five functions in its governmental activities that it reports in its governmental funds statement of revenues, expenditures, and changes in fund balances (Table 9-3 on page 384). In reporting on business-type activities in its statement of activities, it separated the Proprietary Fund operating statement (Table 9-6 on page 390) into two functions, water and sewer.

Reporting Net Functional Expenses

The statement of activities must be displayed in a manner that shows the net functional/program expense or revenue. For this reason, the statement of activities uses columns for three types of revenues associated directly with each function. They

Table 10-2
Government-Wide Statement of Net Assets

VILLAGE OF GRAFTON
STATEMENT OF ACTIVITIES
FOR THE YEAR ENDED DECEMBER 31, 2000

		Program Revenues			Net (Expenses) Revenues and Changes in Net Assets		
Functions/Programs	Expenses	Charges for Services	Operating Grants and Contributions	Capital Grants and Contributions	Governmental Activities	Business-Type Activities	Totals
Governmental Activities							
General government	$ 622,960	$ 24,068	$ 100	$ —	$ (598,792)	$ —	$ (598,792)
Public safety	2,751,610	443,172	49,667	6,995	(2,251,776)	—	(2,251,776)
Public works	1,681,084	495,201	609,166	14,518	(562,199)	—	(562,199)
Community enrichment services	1,050,305	436,162	28,772	179,131	(406,740)	—	(406,740)
Conservation and development	350,424	47,647	352,633	148,595	198,451	—	198,451
Interest and fiscal charges	618,656	—	—	—	(618,656)	—	(618,656)
Total Governmental Activities	7,075,539	1,446,250	1,040,338	349,239	(4,239,712)	—	(4,239,712)
Business-Type Activities							
Water	713,943	1,039,780	—	292,457	—	618,294	618,294
Sewer	997,810	1,211,753	—	343,355	—	557,298	557,298
Interest and fiscal charges	35,697	—	—	—	—	(35,697)	(35,697)
Total Business-Type Activities	1,747,450	2,251,533	—	635,812	—	1,139,895	1,139,895
Total	$8,822,989	$3,697,783	$1,040,338	$985,051	(4,239,712)	1,139,895	(3,099,817)

(continued)

Table 10-2
Continued

General Revenues:			
Taxes:			
Property taxes, levied for general purposes	2,937,094	—	2,937,094
Property taxes, levied for debt service	1,024,584	—	1,024,584
Property taxes, capital assets including TIF	450,636	—	450,636
Intergovernmental revenues not restricted to specific programs	794,872	—	794,872
Investment income	502,353	186,597	688,950
Miscellaneous	163,980	—	163,980
Gains on disposal/sale of capital assets	53,416	—	53,416
Transfers	178,341	(178,341)	—
Total General Revenues	6,105,276	8,256	6,113,532
Change in Net Assets	1,865,564	1,148,151	3,013,715
Net Assets—Beginning of Year	3,440,898	19,876,413	23,317,311
Net Assets—End of Year	$ 5,306,462	$21,024,564	$26,331,026

See accompanying notes to financial statements.
Source: Comprehensive Annual Financial Report, Year 2000, Village of Grafton, Wisconsin.

are charges for services, program-specific operating grants and contributions, and program-specific capital grants and contributions.

Charges for services are revenues based on exchange or exchange-like transactions. They include fees for specific services (such as garbage collection, water use, or parks admissions fees), licenses and permits (such as liquor licenses and building permits), and other amounts charged to service recipients. Charges for services also include fines and forfeitures (such as parking fines and fines arising out of inspections) because they are revenues generated by specific programs. Although charges for services tend to defray only a small part of the expenses of governmental activities, they often exceed the expenses of business-type activities.

Program-specific operating grants and contributions arise out of revenues received from other governments, organizations, or individuals that are restricted for use in a particular program. Grants and contributions reported in this column are those received for operating purposes or either operating or capital purposes at the receiving government's discretion. Program-specific operating grants and contributions include the typical program-oriented state aid programs such as aid for education or health purposes.

Program-specific capital grants and contributions are reported in a separate column. In analyzing financial statements, amounts in this column need to be considered carefully because they can distort the amounts shown as net expenses or revenues. For example, a grant may cover the full amount of a capital expenditure, but the expense will show only the depreciation. (It can be argued that the proprietary funds operating statement— Table 9-6 on page 390—displays the financial results of business-type activities more realistically than the business-type activity section of the statement of activities.)

Examine the upper part of Grafton's statement of activities (Table 10-2). Notice the amounts in the three columns headed Program Revenues, as well as the amounts shown in the Net (Expenses) Revenues and Changes in Net Assets columns. Notice that the amounts in the governmental activities column are generally net expenses and the amounts in the business-type activities columns are generally net revenues. The aggregate of the net expenses in the governmental activities column ($4,239,712) is the amount that is financed by taxes and other general revenues of the reporting government.

Interfund and Internal Service Fund Balances and Activity

As discussed in previous chapters, fund accounting often results in transfers among, charges to, and balances due to and from the various funds. As a general rule, these types of *internal* activities and balances—reported in the fund financial statements— should be eliminated when preparing the government-wide statement of net assets and statement of activities. Unless the eliminations are made, totals for the entity as a whole would be inflated. How should these eliminations be made?

Interfund Receivables and Payables

Amounts due between individual governmental funds, as reported in the governmental funds balance sheet, should be eliminated against each other and not carried forward to the governmental activities column of the government-wide statement of net assets. The same should be done for amounts due between individual proprietary funds. Amounts due between the two fund categories (that is, governmental and proprietary) should be carried forward to the respective columns for governmental and business-type activities in the statement of net assets, and reported as internal balances. The internal balances should be eliminated against each other within the statement of net assets.

To see how to make these adjustments, turn to Grafton's governmental funds balance sheet (Table 9-1 on page 381) and statement of net assets (Table 10-1). In Table 9-1, Due from other funds shows $86,849 in the Total Government Funds column, and Due to other funds shows $114,362. Amounts due to and due from the various governmental-type funds ($86,849) are offset against each other. The difference ($27,513), which is the net amount due to proprietary funds, is reported as a negative amount next to the caption Internal balances in the Governmental Activities column of the statement of net assets (Table 10-1). Grafton's proprietary funds statement of net assets (Table 9-5) also shows amounts due from and to other funds ($36,387 and $8,874), which net to a debit of $27,513. This amount is reported next to the caption Internal balances in the Business-Type Activities column of the statement of net assets (Table 10-1). The debits and credits of $27,513 offset each other so that the total column of Table 10-1 shows zero.

Interfund Transfers

In the statement of activities, the same treatment just described should be given to interfund transfers and charges. Trace the elimination of the interfund activity by using Tables 9-3, 9-6, and 10-2 of the Grafton illustration. Notice that transfers in ($1,370,126) and transfers out ($1,191,785) in Table 9-3 net to $178,341, and that transfers out of $178,341 are reported in Table 9-6. Notice also that the two items for $178,341 then cancel each other out in the lower part of Table 10-2, so that all the internal activity is eliminated in the government-wide activity statement.

The fact that interfund transfers are eliminated in the statement of activities does not mean that they should be ignored when analyzing governmental financial statements. Some transfers may be considered as routine transfers from a resource-collecting fund to a fund authorized by law to incur expenditures or expenses. Other interfund transfers, however, may indicate that a particular activity is experiencing financial difficulties and requires continuing subsidies.

Internal Service Fund Activity

To avoid artificial inflation of activity reported in the government-wide statements, Internal Service Fund activity also requires certain eliminations. This is because Internal Service Fund operating statements show both revenues (from sales to other funds) and expenses. The fund buying services from an Internal Service Fund reports expenditures or expenses as a result of the billings. From a government-wide perspective, only one expense occurred—the costs incurred by the Internal Service Fund. Further, Internal Service Funds often generate artificial profits or losses by billing other funds in amounts more or less than their costs.

To illustrate the nature of the elimination, assume an Internal Service Fund had costs of $20,000 and revenues of $25,000, for a net profit of $5,000 (20 percent of revenues). Its revenues came from billing two governmental activities (police for $12,500; fire for $7,500) and the Sewer Enterprise Fund for $5,000. To avoid the duplication and artificial profit, the Internal Service Fund costs ($20,000) and revenues ($25,000) should be eliminated and total expenditures or expenses of the activities billed should be reduced by $5,000. To make this change, each activity's billing would be reduced by 20 percent, so that the police activity expenditures, for example, would be reduced by $2,500 (20 percent of $12,500).

How should the net assets of the Internal Service Fund be reported? Although Internal Service Funds are classified as proprietary funds, they usually provide all or most of their services to governmental-type funds. Therefore, when preparing the government-wide statement of net assets, the net assets of Internal Service Funds are generally aggregated with those of the governmental activities.

MEASUREMENT FOCUS AND BASIS OF ACCOUNTING FOR GOVERNMENT-WIDE FINANCIAL STATEMENTS

One of the most significant changes made by GASB *Statement No. 34* is the requirement for using the economic resources measurement focus and the accrual basis of accounting for *all* activities—including governmental activities—when preparing the government-wide financial statements. As a result, financial information used in preparing fund financial statements for governmental funds (which is based on the current financial resources measurement focus and the modified accrual basis of accounting) must be adjusted to prepare the government-wide financial statements. In general, adjustments need to be made to accommodate the following points:

- Revenues, expenses, assets, and liabilities resulting from exchange and exchange-like transactions are recognized when the exchange takes place.
- Revenues, expenses, assets, and liabilities resulting from nonexchange transactions (such as taxes and intergovernmental grants) are recognized in accordance with the accrual-basis requirements of GASB *Statement No. 33*, "Accounting and Reporting for Non-exchange Transactions."
- Capital assets, including infrastructure assets, are reported as assets and depreciated, subject to certain permitted modifications for infrastructure assets.
- Proceeds from issuing long-term debt are reported as liabilities, and payments of debt principal are reported as reductions of liabilities.

Because proprietary fund financial statements are prepared using the economic resources measurement focus and accrual basis of accounting, no measurement focus or basis of accounting adjustments are needed when they are incorporated in the government-wide financial statements. (Notice that the net assets shown in Grafton's proprietary fund statement of net assets—Table 9-5 in Chapter 9—is $21,024,564, the same as the net assets for business-type activities shown in Grafton's government-wide statement of net assets in Table 10-1. Notice also that the change in net assets reported in Grafton's proprietary funds statement of revenues, expenses, and changes in fund net assets in Table 9-6 is $1,148,151, the same as that reported in Grafton's government-wide statement of activities in Table 10-2.) Therefore, most of the material covered in the rest of this chapter deals with the incorporation of financial information for governmental-type funds into the government-wide financial statements.

Implications of Using Accrual Basis of Accounting

Revenues

For revenues, the most significant difference between the modified accrual basis of accounting and the accrual basis lies in the measurement and recognition of taxes. Under modified accrual accounting, taxes are recognized as revenues in the accounting period in which they become available and measurable. For accrual accounting, the GASB adopted specific rules for taxes and other nonexchange revenues in GASB *Statement No. 33*. These rules are summarized as follows:

Derived Tax Revenues.   Derived tax revenues are those that result from assessments imposed by the government on external exchange transactions engaged in by individuals, corporations and other entities. They include, for example, personal income taxes levied by the government on wages and other earnings of individuals as well as sales taxes and motor fuel taxes levied by the government on purchases made by consumers.

The accrual accounting rule for these types of taxes is that assets should be recognized either when the exchange transaction on which the tax is imposed occurs or when the resources are received, whichever occurs first. Revenues should be recognized (net of estimated refunds and estimated uncollectible amounts) in the same period the assets are recognized, provided the underlying transaction has occurred. Resources received before the underlying exchange transaction has occurred should be reported as deferred revenues.[2]

To illustrate, suppose a local government that operates on a calendar-year basis levies sales taxes on consumer purchases. The merchant is required to send both the state and local government shares of the sales taxes to the state within 10 days after the end of each quarter. The state takes several months, however, to complete the administrative work on the tax returns. As a result, the state remits the sales taxes for the October 1–December 31, 2004, quarter to the local government on March 30, 2005. Under accrual accounting, the local government would accrue the March 30, 2005, receipts as receivables at December 31, 2004, and as revenues for calendar-year 2004.

Imposed Nonexchange Revenues.   These revenues result from taxes and other assessments levied on individuals and others, without underlying external exchange transactions. The most common revenue of this kind is the real property tax, which is imposed by many governments on residential, commercial, and industrial real property. Other examples are fines and penalties. The accrual accounting rule for real property taxes and other imposed nonexchange revenues is that assets should be recognized either in the period when an enforceable legal claim to the assets arises, or when the resources are received, whichever occurs first. Property tax revenues

---

[2]   GASB Cod. (2001) Sec. N50.113.

should be recognized (net of estimated refunds and estimated uncollectible amounts) in the *period for which* the taxes are levied, even if the enforceable legal claim arises or the due date for payment occurs in a different period.[3]

Notice the absence of the "available and measurable" rule for property tax revenue recognition under accrual accounting. The implications of the absence of "available and measurable" will be illustrated later in this chapter in the discussion of adjustments needed for accrual basis accounting. Because of the Village of Grafton's tax calendar and its virtual lack of tax delinquencies, its property tax accounting under the modified accrual basis of accounting and the accrual basis is similar. Notice that Grafton reported deferred tax revenues of $4,951,609 at December 31, 2000 (Table 10-1), because Grafton levied property taxes and mailed tax bills at the end of the year 2000 to provide services for the year 2001. These revenues are recognized in 2001, the period for which the taxes were levied.

Notice also the requirement for recognizing property tax revenues net of both estimated refunds and uncollectible amounts. Because unresolved taxpayer appeals on assessments could result in refunds, allowances for uncollectible property taxes need to be carefully evaluated to ensure that receivables and revenues are not overstated.

Government-Mandated Nonexchange Transactions.   These transactions (generally referred to as intergovernmental aid) occur when a government at one level provides resources to a government at another level, to be used for specific purposes set forth in the providing government's enabling legislation. In addition to the purpose restrictions, a provider may also establish other eligibility requirements, such as time requirements and expenditure-incurrence requirements. The general rule here is that the aid recipient should recognize receivables and revenues (net of estimated uncollectible amounts) when all the eligibility requirements, including the time requirements, are met.[4]

To illustrate, assume that, in accordance with legislation, a state mandates that counties undertake a specific health program. The law provides that the state will reimburse counties 50 percent of all allowable costs incurred by them, subject to maximum amounts specified by the state health department in annual contracts with the counties. Counties should recognize receivables and revenues as they incur allowable costs—the point when they meet the eligibility requirements—up to the maximum amount specified in the contracts.

Expenses

Reporting expenses when using the economic resources measurement focus and the accrual basis of accounting requires consideration of the processes known as accruals, deferrals, and amortizations. These distinctions create certain significant differences from reporting expenditures when using the current financial resources measurement focus and modified accrual basis of accounting. Although certain accruals must be made when using the modified accrual basis, many departures from accrual accounting, as well as allowable options, also occur. The most significant differences

---

[3]   GASB Cod. (2001) Sec. N50.114–.115.
[4]   GASB Cod. (2001) Sec. N50.118.

regarding expenditure/expense recognition between the two measurement focuses and accounting bases are as follows:

Expenses Incurred, But Not Currently Due and Payable.   When preparing fund financial statements using modified accrual accounting, certain specific expenditures are recognized as fund liabilities and expenditures only to the extent the liabilities are "normally expected to be liquidated with expendable available resources." In effect, they are recognized as expenditures when the liabilities come due for payment. The items involved include compensated absences, claims and judgments, special termination benefits, and landfill closure and postclosure costs. Under accrual accounting, these expenses are recognized when the liabilities are incurred, regardless of when the cash outflows take place, for example, when compensated absences are earned, and when information regarding claims indicates that it is probable a liability has been incurred and the amount of the loss can be reasonably measured. Therefore, when preparing government-wide financial statements, it is likely that additional expenses will need to be accrued and additional liabilities (probably noncurrent) will need to be recognized.

"Stub Period" Interest on Long-Term Debt.   Under modified accrual accounting, a special rule provides that debt service on bonds and capital leases is specifically recognized only when the debt service matures. Interest for the stub period (the period between the last payment in the reporting year and the first payment in the next year) is not accrued when preparing fund financial statements for governmental-type funds, except under certain conditions (discussed in Chapter 6) where an accrual is permitted, but not required. For government-wide financial reporting using accrual accounting, an accrual for the stub period interest is required.

Accounting for Inventories and Prepayments.   Under modified accrual accounting, purchases of materials and supplies are generally recorded as expenditures when they are acquired under the "purchases" method discussed in Chapter 5 even though they are not consumed until a later period. Financial statement preparers, however, may use the accrual-basis "consumption" method, under which the cost of materials, supplies, and services is recorded when the items are used. The same accounting method and option applies to prepayments. Under accrual accounting, however, the "consumption" method of accounting for purchases and prepayments is required.

Implications of Using Economic Resources Measurement Focus

Reporting Capital Assets
One of the most significant changes (in terms of dollar effect) resulting from the adoption of the economic resources measurement focus and accrual basis of accounting for governmental activities in government-wide financial statements concerns capital expenditures and depreciation. Under the current financial resources measurement focus, expenditures for capital assets are recognized as expenditures, rather than as assets. Further, because the assets have not been recognized as such, they are not depreciated. Under the economic resources measurement focus and accrual basis of accounting used in preparing government-wide statements, how-

ever, capital asset expenditures are recognized as assets. Unless the assets are inexhaustible (such as land), they need to be depreciated over their estimated useful lives in a systematic and rational manner.

GASB *Statement No. 34* provides, however, that infrastructure assets that are part of a network or subsystem of a network, such as roads and street lighting systems, need not be depreciated under certain circumstances. This "modified approach" is discussed later in this chapter.

Reporting Long-Term Debt

Switching to the economic resources measurement focus when preparing government-wide financial statements for governmental activities also has a major effect on reporting long-term debt. Issuing long-term debt when reporting on the economic resources measurement focus results in recognizing a liability, not a financing source. Repaying the debt results in a reduction of the liability, not an expenditure. This treatment also affects other forms of long-term debt, such as liabilities incurred under capital leases.

Adjustments Needed for Preparing Government-Wide Financial Statements

Adjusting amounts reported for governmental-type funds in fund financial statements to amounts reported for governmental activities in government-wide financial statements requires taking account of the way transactions were previously recorded (or not recorded) in the funds. The remainder of this section shows typical adjustments required for preparing the government-wide financial statements.

Acquiring and Depreciating Capital Assets

When capital assets are acquired with governmental fund resources, they are recorded in the funds as capital outlay expenditures, rather than as assets. Further, the capital assets are not depreciated in the funds. Therefore, to report using the economic resources measurement focus and accrual basis of accounting, expenditures need to be decreased, capital assets need to be recorded, and depreciation expense needs to be recorded. For example, assume that a city, which operates on a calendar-year basis, acquires fire-fighting equipment on May 1, 2004, at a cost of $300,000. The equipment is expected to have a useful life of 10 years and will have no salvage value. The following *adjusting entries* are needed to prepare government-wide financial statements.

Capital assets—equipment	300,000	
Expenditures—capital outlay		300,000
To reduce expenditures and record capital assets.		
Depreciation expense—equipment	20,000	
Accumulated depreciation—equipment		20,000
To record 8 months' depreciation expense.		

If these capital assets had been acquired with tax resources, the $280,000 net increase in assets at December 31, 2004, would be reported in the net asset section of the government-wide statement of net assets as invested in capital assets, net of related debt. (By December 31, 2005, the accumulated depreciation would be $50,000, so the amount reported as invested in capital assets, net of related debt, would be $250,000.) Notice that using the caption "invested in capital assets, net of related debt" calls attention to the fact that a portion of the net assets is "tied up" in capital assets and is not available for other purposes.

Issuing Long-Term Debt to Acquire Capital Assets

When proceeds of general long-term debt are recorded in governmental funds, they are recorded as other financing sources, rather than as fund liabilities. Repayments of principal are recorded as expenditures, rather than as reductions of the liability. Further, interest on the outstanding debt generally is not recorded until it is due and payable. To report on the economic resources measurement focus and accrual basis of accounting, other financing sources and expenditures must be decreased and liabilities must be recorded. Also, interest expense on outstanding long-term debt must be accrued if it has been incurred, even though it is not yet due and payable.

To illustrate, assume the city in the previous illustration issued $300,000 of bonds on April 1, 2004, to finance acquisition of the fire-fighting equipment. Repayment of the bonds began October 1, 2004, with the first of 10 semiannual installments of principal (each $30,000), with 6 percent interest on the outstanding debt. To prepare government-wide financial statements, the following adjusting entries would be needed.

Proceeds from bond issue	300,000	
Bonds payable		300,000
To reverse recording of other financing source on April 1 and to record bonds payable.		
Bonds payable	30,000	
Expenditures—bond principal		30,000
To reverse recording of expenditure on October 1 and to record repayment of bonds payable.		
Interest expense	4,050	
Interest payable		4,050
To accrue interest on $270,000 of debt at 6 percent for October 1–December 31.		

No adjustment needs to be made for the October 1 interest payment, except that for government-wide reporting on the accrual basis of accounting, the term *interest expense* should be used, rather than *interest expenditure*.

The fire-fighting equipment would be reported at the net asset value of $280,000, as calculated in the previous illustration. Outstanding debt in the amount of $270,000 (original debt of $300,000, less repayment of $30,000) related to this asset remains. Therefore, the net asset section of the government-wide statement of net assets would show $10,000 as invested in capital assets, net of related debt ($280,000 minus $270,000). At the end of the following year, the net investment in capital assets would be $40,000 (net asset value $250,000 minus outstanding debt of $210,000).

Accruing Tax Revenues

As discussed in Chapter 5, tax revenues are recognized in governmental funds when they are measurable and available. When applying the "available" criterion, governments generally recognize tax revenues if they receive the cash within the year or within 60 days after the end of the year. Depending on the nature of the tax, different types of year-end adjusting entries are needed when preparing fund financial statements. Because property tax receivables and revenues are initially recognized when the taxes are levied, revenues that do not meet the "available" criterion need to be deferred. Self-assessed taxes, such as sales and income taxes, are generally recognized when received in cash, so accruals are needed to report additional revenues that are "available." The previously made year-end adjustments must be considered when reporting on the accrual basis of accounting for the government-wide financial statements.

To illustrate, assume a small city has property tax and sales tax revenues, and at the beginning of calendar year 2004, it levies property taxes of $850,000. If the city expects to collect all the taxes, it should record property taxes receivable and property tax revenues of $850,000. Assume also that it receives $800,000 in cash during the year and expects to collect $35,000 in the first 60 days of 2005 and the remaining $15,000 later in 2005. It should defer revenue recognition for $15,000 of taxes it does not expect to collect during the first 60 days of 2005 when preparing its fund financial statements at the end of 2004. To prepare the government-wide financial statements using the accrual basis of accounting, this deferral needs to be reversed, as follows:

Deferred revenues—property taxes	15,000	
Revenues—property taxes		15,000
To recognize property taxes on the accrual basis of accounting.		

Now, assume the city receives $500,000 of sales taxes during 2004, and expects to collect $25,000 of 2004 taxes in the first 60 days of 2005 and another $5,000 of 2004 taxes later in 2005. To prepare the 2004 fund financial statements, it should accrue $25,000 of tax receipts, rather than $30,000. To prepare the accrual-basis government-wide financial statements, an additional $5,000 should be accrued, as follows:

Sales taxes receivable	5,000	
Revenues—sales taxes		5,000
To recognize additional sales taxes.		

Accruing Expenses

As discussed in Chapter 5, the standards for measuring expenditures under the modified accrual basis of accounting were clarified in GASB *Interpretation No. 6*, "Recognition and Measurement of Certain Liabilities and Expenditures in Governmental Fund Financial Statements." Certain expenditures, such as compensated absences and judgments and claims, are recognized in the fund financial statements when they are "normally expected to be liquidated with expendable available financial resources." When that rule is applied to compensated absences, an expenditure accrual is needed only to the extent that the amounts due to employees who resigned or retired during the year were not paid before the end of the year.

Governmental employees generally accrue compensated absences throughout their working lives, so the accrual basis liability to be reported in the government-wide financial statements is likely to be significantly greater than the amount shown in the fund financial statements. In addition to recognizing a liability on transition to the new reporting model, an annual accrual will probably need to be made when the compensated absences liability is calculated at the end of each year, as follows (amount assumed):

Expenses—compensated absences	30,000	
Compensated absences payable		30,000
To accrue liability for compensated absences.		

REQUIRED RECONCILIATION BETWEEN FUND AND GOVERNMENT-WIDE FINANCIAL STATEMENTS

GASB *Statement No. 34* requires that the fund financial statements be reconciled in summary form with the government-wide financial statements, to allow users to assess the relationship between the two sets of statements. The reconciliation may be presented either at the bottom of the fund financial statements or in an accompanying schedule. Virtually all the reconciling items result from the accruals and other adjustments discussed in the preceding section. For example, typical reconciling items between the two sets of activity statements result from the following:

- Reporting annual depreciation expense instead of expenditures for capital outlays
- Reporting long-term debt proceeds as liabilities rather than other financing sources, and reporting debt principal repayments as reductions of liabilities rather than expenditures
- Reporting revenues on the accrual, rather than modified accrual, basis of accounting
- Reporting expenses on the accrual, rather than modified accrual, basis of accounting
- Adjusting for the net revenue (expense) of internal service funds

The Village of Grafton, Wisconsin, used its governmental funds balance sheet (see Table 9-1 on page 381) to reconcile the fund balances ($6,751,828) to the net assets of governmental activities reported in its government-wide statement of net assets ($5,306,462). Notice that the major reconciling items relate to reporting capital assets and long-term debt in the government-wide statement, but not in the funds statement.

Grafton's reconciliation between the fund and the government-wide operating statements is shown in Table 10-3. Notice that the net change in fund balances reported in the governmental funds operating statement (Table 9-3 on page 384) was $1,857,229, while the change in net assets for governmental activities reported in the government-wide operating statement (Table 10-2) was $1,865,564. Although the difference between the two numbers is not significant in this situation, the difference can be much larger in other situations. Review the reconciling items and relate them to the discussion earlier in this chapter about the differences in the measurement focuses and bases of accounting. Trace as many of the reconciling items as you can back to the amounts reported in Table 9-3.

Table 10-3

Reconciliation of Fund and Government-Wide Operating Statements

VILLAGE OF GRAFTON
RECONCILIATION OF THE STATEMENT OF REVENUES, EXPENDITURES, AND CHANGES
IN FUND BALANCES OF GOVERNMENTAL FUNDS
TO THE STATEMENT OF ACTIVITIES
FOR THE YEAR ENDED DECEMBER 31, 2000

Net Change in Fund Balances—Total Governmental Funds	$ 1,857,229
Amounts reported for governmental activities in the statement of activities are different because:	
Governmental funds report capital outlays as expenditures. However, in the statement of activities the cost of these assets is allocated over their estimated useful lives and reported as depreciation expense. This is the amount by which capital outlays ($2,026,449) exceeded depreciation ($425,853) in the current period.	1,600,596
Debt proceeds provide current financial resources to governmental funds, but issuing debt increases long-term liabilities in the statement of net assets. Repayment of debt principal is an expenditure in the governmental funds, but the repayment reduces long-term liabilities in the statement of net assets. This is the amount by which proceeds ($2,730,000) exceeded payments ($1,001,581).	(1,728,419)
Revenues in the statement of activities that do not provide current financial resources are not reported as revenues in the funds.	163,855
Some expenses reported in the statement of activities do not require the use of current financial resources and therefore are not reported as expenditures in the governmental funds.	(57,283)
Governmental funds report debt discount and issuance costs as expenditures. However, in the statement of net assets these are reported as deferred charges. These are allocated over the period the debt is outstanding in the statement of activities and are reported as amortization expense. This is the amount by which debt discount and issuance costs of the current year ($29,586), exceeded amortization expense ($-0-).	29,586
Change in Net Assets of Governmental Activities—Statement of Activities	$ 1,865,564

See accompanying notes to financial statements.
Source: Comprehensive Annual Financial Report, Year 2000, Village of Grafton, Wisconsin.

REPORTING ON CAPITAL ASSETS, INCLUDING INFRASTRUCTURE ASSETS

GASB *Statement No. 34* prescribes standards for reporting on capital assets and provides for special treatment of certain infrastructure assets. The basic rule is that:

- capital assets of proprietary funds should be reported in both the government-wide and fund financial statements;

- capital assets of fiduciary funds should be reported only in the statement of fiduciary net assets; and
- all other capital assets are general capital assets, which should *not* be reported as assets in governmental funds, but should be reported in the governmental activities column in the government-wide statement of net assets.[5]

Capital assets should be reported at their historical cost. Capital assets costs include ancillary charges necessary to place the asset into its intended location and condition for use, such as freight and transportation costs and site preparation costs. They should be depreciated over their estimated useful lives, unless they are inexhaustible (such as land) or are infrastructure assets that are reported using the "modified approach" described in subsequent paragraphs.

Reporting on Infrastructure Assets

Infrastructure assets are defined as

> . . . long-lived capital assets that normally are stationary in nature and normally can be preserved for a significantly greater number of years than most capital assets. Examples of infrastructure assets include roads, bridges, tunnels, drainage systems, water and sewer systems, dams, and lighting systems. Buildings, except those that are an ancillary part of a network of infrastructure assets, should not be considered infrastructure assets.[6]

Because governmental accounting standards in existence before the GASB adopted *Statement No. 34* did not require reporting infrastructure assets, many governments lacked financial inventories of those assets. GASB *Statement No. 34* therefore permitted the following phase-in period for reporting infrastructure assets:

- Infrastructure assets acquired during the year GASB *Statement No. 34* was adopted, and thereafter, must be reported in the financial statements.
- Major general infrastructure assets acquired before implementation of the new financial reporting requirements must be capitalized retroactively and reported, depending on the size of government, as follows:
  a. Governments with annual revenues of $100 million or more—starting fiscal years beginning after June 15, 2005
  b. Governments with annual revenues of $10 million or more but less than $100 million—starting fiscal years beginning after June 15, 2006
  c. Governments with total annual revenues less than $10 million—may, but are not required to, capitalize infrastructure assets acquired before implementation of the new reporting requirements.

Notice that, in the Capital assets section of Grafton's *statement of net assets* (Table 10-1), Grafton separates its capital assets between those that are depreciable and those that are not. In a note to the financial statements, Grafton states that infra-

---

[5] GASB Cod. (2001) Sec. 1400 Statement of Principle.
[6] GASB Cod. (2001) Sec. 1400.103.

structure assets put into service before the year 2000 are not included in the report, but management's goal is to include the historical cost of its existing infrastructure in subsequent financial statements.

Once they are capitalized, infrastructure assets must be depreciated over their estimated useful lives, unless the government adopts the so-called "modified approach."

"Modified Approach" for Infrastructure Assets

Under the modified approach, infrastructure assets need not be depreciated, provided the government has an asset management system and documents that the assets are being preserved at or above a condition level that it establishes and discloses. This approach was developed in response to concerns about the usefulness of depreciation based on historical cost for assets likely to have long lives if appropriately maintained.

To meet the requirement for having an asset management system, the government would need to do the following:

- have an up-to-date inventory of the infrastructure assets,
- make periodic assessments of the physical condition of the assets and summarize the results using a measurement scale, and
- estimate each year the annual amount needed to maintain and preserve the assets at the condition level that it establishes and discloses.[7]

Governments would also need to document that:

- complete condition assessments are made at least every 3 years, and
- the results of the three most recent condition assessments give reasonable assurance that the assets are indeed being preserved approximately at or above the established condition levels.[8]

If these sets of requirements are met and the infrastructure assets are not depreciated, all expenditures made for the assets (except for additions and improvements) should be treated as expenses in the year they are incurred. Additions or improvements (which increase the capacity or efficiency of the assets, rather than preserve their useful lives) should be capitalized.

Documentation regarding the management and preservation of infrastructure assets needs to be provided in the financial report as required supplementary information (RSI). To illustrate, a government might rate the condition of its roads on a scale of 1 to 7, based on various distress factors found in the pavement surfaces. To make the ratings, it might use pavement distress measurement techniques, such as special machines and visual inspections compared with pictures that describe various degrees of distress. It might consider a rating of 5 as good and 7 as perfect. Its policy might be that sufficient repair and maintenance will be scheduled each year so

---

[7] GASB Cod. (2001) Sec. 1400.105.
[8] GASB Cod. (2001) Sec. 1400.106.

that at least 90 percent of the road miles will be rated 5 or better. It could demonstrate in RSI that it is complying with its condition assessment standards by showing:

- for the three most-recent condition assessments, the percentage of lane-miles of streets and roads that is rated 5 or better, and the percentage that is rated 4 or less, and
- for the last five reporting periods, the estimated dollar requirement to maintain and preserve the streets and roads at the established condition level (at least 90 percent of road miles rated 5 or better), and the amounts actually expensed in each period.

CREATING GOVERNMENT-WIDE FINANCIAL STATEMENTS FROM FUND FINANCIAL DATA: A COMPREHENSIVE ILLUSTRATION

This section illustrates how government-wide financial statements can be prepared from the fund financial statements. The major objective of this illustration is to show the types of adjustments needed to convert data that were originally reported in statements prepared using the current financial resources measurement focus and modified accrual basis of accounting to statements using the economic resources measurement focus and accrual basis financial statements. The illustration is limited to governmental-type funds, because proprietary-type funds are reported on the economic resources measurement focus and accrual basis of accounting in both government-wide and fund financial statements.

Statement of the Transactions

Assume, for simplicity, that Eunee City has only three governmental funds: a General Fund, a Debt Service Fund, and a Capital Projects Fund. Assume further that all three funds meet the definition of "major fund." The General Fund has two programs: Public Safety and Parks. To further simplify the illustration, budgetary accounting is not shown.

Following is a listing of transactions affecting Eunee City for calendar year 2004.

1. On January 1, the City levies property taxes of $710,000. It expects to collect all the taxes, though not necessarily during 2004.
2. During the year, the City collects property taxes in the amount of $660,000.
3. The City pays cash for salaries and supplies. The expenditures are charged to Public Safety ($470,000) and to Parks ($140,000).
4. The City collects parking fees of $20,000 for parking in its parks.
5. On April 1, the City sells $400,000 of 6 percent serial bonds, to be used solely to acquire capital assets. It will repay the debt over a 5-year period, in 10 semi-annual payments of $40,000, plus interest, starting October 1, 2004.
6. On July 1, the City pays $300,000 for fire-fighting equipment, using resources of the Capital Projects Fund.

7. On September 25, the General Fund transfers $60,000 to the Debt Service Fund for payment of debt service on outstanding debt.
8. On October 1, the Debt Service Fund makes the first installment of debt service—$40,000 of principal and $12,000 of interest.
9. To prepare fund financial statements, the City makes an adjustment for property taxes. It expects to collect $30,000 in the first 60 days of 2005 and the remaining $20,000 later in the year.

Journal Entries to Record Transactions

Journal entries to record the foregoing transactions in the three governmental-type funds are as follows.

Entry in General Fund	1. Property taxes receivable
	    Revenues—property taxes
	  To record property tax levy.
		710,000	710,000

Entry in General Fund	2. Cash
	    Property taxes receivable
	  To record collection of property taxes.
		660,000	660,000

Entry in General Fund	3. Expenditures—public safety
	  Expenditures—parks
	    Cash
	  To record cash disbursements.
		470,000
		140,000
			610,000

Entry in General Fund	4. Cash
	    Revenues—parking fees
	  To record parking fee revenue.
		20,000	20,000

Entry in Capital Projects Fund	5. Cash
	    Proceeds of bonds
	  To record debt proceeds.
		400,000	400,000

Entry in Capital Projects Fund	6. Expenditures—capital outlay
	    Cash
	  To record payment for fire-fighting equipment.
		300,000	300,000

Entry in General Fund	7. Transfer out to Debt Service Fund
	    Cash
	  To record transfer out.
		60,000	60,000

Entry in Debt Service Fund	7. Cash
	    Transfer in from General Fund
	  To record transfer in.
		60,000	60,000

Entry in Debt Service Fund	8. Expenditures—bond principal
	  Expenditures—bond interest
	    Cash
	  To record debt service payment.
		40,000
		12,000
			52,000

Adjusting Entry in General Fund	9. Revenues—property taxes
	    Deferred revenues
	  To adjust for unavailable property taxes.
		20,000	20,000

Preclosing Trial Balances and Fund Financial Statements

Preclosing trial balances, based on the foregoing journal entries, are shown in Table 10-4. Fund financial statements, prepared from the trial balances, are shown in Tables 10-5 (balance sheet) and 10-6 (statement of revenues, expenditures, and changes in fund balances).

Preparing Government-Wide Financial Statements

To prepare government-wide financial statements from the fund financial statements, adjustments must be made for certain transactions previously recorded using the current financial resources measurement focus and modified accrual basis of

Table 10-4
Preclosing Trial Balances

EUNEE CITY
GENERAL FUND
PRECLOSING TRIAL BALANCE
DECEMBER 31, 2004

	DEBITS	CREDITS
Cash	$ 10,000	
Property taxes receivable	50,000	
Deferred revenues		$ 20,000
Revenues—property taxes		690,000
Revenues—parking fees		20,000
Expenditures—public safety	470,000	
Expenditures—parks	140,000	
Transfer out to Debt Service Fund	60,000	
Totals	$730,000	$730,000

Debt Service Fund

	DEBITS	CREDITS
Cash	$ 8,000	
Expenditures—bond principal	40,000	
Expenditures—bond interest	12,000	
Transfer in from General Fund		$ 60,000
Totals	$ 60,000	$ 60,000

Capital Projects Fund

	DEBITS	CREDITS
Cash	$100,000	
Expenditures—capital outlay	300,000	
Proceeds of bonds		$400,000
Totals	$400,000	$400,000

Table 10-5

Fund Financial Statement—Balance Sheet

EUNEE CITY
BALANCE SHEET
GOVERNMENTAL FUNDS
DECEMBER 31, 2004

	GENERAL	DEBT SERVICE	CAPITAL PROJECTS	TOTAL
Assets				
Cash	$10,000	$8,000	$100,000	$118,000
Property taxes receivable	50,000			50,000
Total assets	$60,000	$8,000	$100,000	$168,000
Liabilities				
Deferred revenues	$20,000	$	$	$ 20,000
Total liabilities	20,000			20,000
Fund Balances				
Reserved for debt service		8,000		8,000
Unreserved	40,000		100,000	140,000
Total fund balances	40,000	8,000	100,000	148,000
Total liabilities and fund balances	$60,000	$8,000	$100,000	$168,000

accounting. These transactions need to be recorded using the economic resources measurement focus and accrual basis of accounting. The adjusting entries and the explanations for them follow. When reading them, refer back to the related original transactions, as appropriate, and to the entries made to record them.

a. Property tax revenues need to be recognized for the full amount of taxes expected to be collected, regardless of when they are collected. Therefore, the deferral made to prepare the fund statements (entry 9) must be reversed.

Deferred revenues	20,000	
Revenues—property taxes		20,000

b. Bond proceeds were recorded as other financing sources in entry 5, and the bond principal repayment was recorded as an expenditure in entry 8. The original transactions need to be adjusted to record the bond liability and the repayment.

Proceeds of bonds	400,000	
Expenditures—bond principal		40,000
Bonds payable		360,000

Table 10-6

Fund Financial Statement—Statement of Revenues, Expenditures, and Changes in Fund Balances

EUNEE CITY

STATEMENT OF REVENUES, EXPENDITURES, AND CHANGES IN FUND BALANCES

GOVERNMENTAL FUNDS

FOR THE YEAR ENDED DECEMBER 31, 2004

	GENERAL	DEBT SERVICE	CAPITAL PROJECTS	TOTAL
Revenues				
Property taxes	$690,000			$690,000
Parking fees	20,000			20,000
Total revenues	710,000			710,000
Expenditures				
Current:				
Public safety	470,000			470,000
Parks	140,000			140,000
Debt service:				
Principal		$ 40,000		40,000
Interest		12,000		12,000
Capital outlay			$300,000	300,000
Total expenditures	610,000	52,000	300,000	962,000
Excess (deficiency) of revenues over expenditures	100,000	(52,000)	(300,000)	(252,000)
Other Financing Sources (Uses)				
Proceeds of bonds			400,000	400,000
Transfers in		60,000		60,000
Transfers out	(60,000)			(60,000)
Total	(60,000)	60,000	400,000	400,000
Net change in fund balances	40,000	8,000	100,000	148,000
Fund balances—beginning	0	0	0	0
Fund balances—ending	$ 40,000	$ 8,000	$100,000	$148,000

c. An accrual needs to be made for interest at the rate of 6 percent on the outstanding debt ($360,000), for the period October 1–December 31, 2004 (see entries 5 and 8):

Interest expense	5,400	
Interest payable		5,400

d. The capital asset expenditure was recorded as an expenditure in entry 6. An adjustment is needed to record it as an asset.

Capital assets	300,000	
Expenditures—capital outlay		300,000

e. Depreciation for 6 months needs to be recorded on the $300,000 of capital assets acquired in entry 6. Assume the equipment has a useful life of 10 years.

Depreciation expense	15,000	
Accumulated depreciation—equipment		15,000

Table 10-7 illustrates a work sheet showing a trial balance of the financial data reported in the fund financial statements, the preceding adjusting entries, and the effect of the adjustments on the account balances.

After making the adjustments, the government-wide financial statements and the reconciliation between those statements and the fund financial statements can be prepared. When preparing the statements, several additional things need to be considered:

a. GASB *Statement No. 34* encourages presentation of the assets and liabilities in the Statement of net assets in order of relative liquidity. Regarding bonds payable, amounts due in 1 year (in this problem, $80,000) should be separated from amounts due in more than 1 year.

Table 10-7
Work Sheet for Preparing Government-Wide Financial Statements

	Aggregated Balances Fund Statements		Adjustments		Adjusted Balances	
	Debit	Credit	Debit	Credit	Debit	Credit
Cash	$ 118,000				$ 118,000	
Property taxes receivable	50,000				50,000	
Capital assets			d. $300,000		300,000	
Accumulated depreciation				e. $ 15,000		$ 15,000
Deferred revenues		$ 20,000	a. 20,000			
Interest payable				c. 5,400		5,400
Bonds payable				b. 360,000		360,000
Revenues:						
Property taxes		690,000		a. 20,000		710,000
Parking fees		20,000				20,000
Expenditures:						
Public safety	470,000				470,000	
Parks	140,000				140,000	
Debt service principal	40,000			b. 40,000		
Debt service interest	12,000		c. 5,400		17,400	
Capital outlay	300,000			d. 300,000		
Depreciation expense			e. 15,000		15,000	
Other financing items:						
Proceeds of bonds		400,000	b. 400,000			
Transfers in		60,000				60,000
Transfers out	60,000				60,000	
Totals	$1,190,000	$1,190,000	$740,400	$740,400	$1,170,400	$1,170,400

b. Interfund activity (in this problem, the $60,000 transfer between the governmental funds) should be eliminated.

c. Depreciation expense should be considered as an expense of the appropriate program (in this problem, the public safety program) in the statement of activities.

d. In preparing the statement of net assets, net assets need to be displayed in three components: invested in capital assets, net of related debt; restricted; and unrestricted. In this problem, $400,000 of debt was issued to finance capital assets, but only $300,000 was used to acquire fire-fighting equipment. The other $100,000 may be spent only for additional capital assets. Therefore, outstanding debt related to the investment in capital assets is $260,000 (original investment of $300,000, less repayment of $40,000).

The amount to be reported as invested in capital assets, net of related debt is $25,000 [capital assets net of accumulated depreciation ($285,000) less *related* debt ($260,000)]. The $100,000 of additional bond proceeds is restricted for capital projects. However, because the related $100,000 of bonds payable is reported as a liability, the net assets restricted for capital projects is zero. To avoid misleading inferences from the face of the statement of net assets, this restriction on the use of assets should be covered in a note to the statements.

The government-wide statement of net assets for Eunee City (prepared from the adjusted trial balance) is shown in Table 10-8 and the government-wide statement of activities is shown in Table 10-9.

Reconciliations of the fund financial statements and the government-wide financial statements are presented in Table 10-10. Because this problem did not contain opening balances, the same numbers necessarily appear in both reconciliations. Notice, however, that the explanations in Reconciliation A are presented from a balance sheet perspective, and the explanations in Reconciliation B are presented from an operating statement perspective.

CARRYOVER ACCOUNT BALANCES

To simplify the presentation in this chapter, the illustrations of the adjustments needed to prepare government-wide statements did not have beginning-of-year account balances. In actual practice, once government-wide financial statements are prepared, the opening asset and liability account balances need to be considered when preparing the adjusting entries for the subsequent year's financial statements. For example, existing capital assets and long-term debt need to be recorded in the adjustments made for preparing the initial set and subsequent sets of government-wide statements. This section illustrates the way opening account balances are considered in making adjusting entries for government-wide statements. As you read, keep the following things in mind:

- The fund-level financial statements provide the starting point for preparing the government-wide statements.
- The adjustments made for preparing government-wide statements, such as adding capital assets, ultimately increase or decrease the net assets reported on the government-wide statements.

Table 10-8

Government-Wide Statement of Net Assets

<table>
<tr><td colspan="2" align="center">EUNEE CITY
STATEMENT OF NET ASSETS
DECEMBER 31, 2004</td></tr>
<tr><td></td><td align="right">GOVERNMENTAL
ACTIVITIES</td></tr>
<tr><td>Assets</td><td></td></tr>
<tr><td>Cash</td><td align="right">$118,000</td></tr>
<tr><td>Property taxes receivable</td><td align="right">50,000</td></tr>
<tr><td>Capital assets, net of $15,000
   accumulated depreciation</td><td align="right">285,000</td></tr>
<tr><td>   Total assets</td><td align="right">$453,000</td></tr>
<tr><td>Liabilities</td><td></td></tr>
<tr><td>Interest payable</td><td align="right">$ 5,400</td></tr>
<tr><td>Bonds payable:</td><td></td></tr>
<tr><td> Due within 1 year</td><td align="right">80,000</td></tr>
<tr><td> Due in more than 1 year</td><td align="right">280,000</td></tr>
<tr><td>   Total liabilities</td><td align="right">365,400</td></tr>
<tr><td>Net Assets</td><td></td></tr>
<tr><td>Invested in capital assets, net of related debt</td><td align="right">25,000</td></tr>
<tr><td>Restricted for:</td><td></td></tr>
<tr><td> Capital projects (see note)</td><td></td></tr>
<tr><td> Debt service</td><td align="right">8,000</td></tr>
<tr><td>Unrestricted</td><td align="right">54,600</td></tr>
<tr><td> Total net assets</td><td align="right">87,600</td></tr>
<tr><td> Total liabilities and net assets</td><td align="right">$453,000</td></tr>
</table>

Note: Cash and bonds payable include $100,000 of proceeds from bonds that are required to be spent for capital projects, but that have not yet been spent.

Capital Assets and Long-Term Debt

When the first set of government-wide financial statements is prepared, existing capital assets and outstanding long-term debt need to be reported. Reporting capital assets increases the government-wide net assets and reporting outstanding debt decreases the net assets. In preparing subsequent-year government-wide statements, the balances in these accounts are carried over to the worksheet used for preparing the statements. For example, if Eunee City (in Table 10-7) had started the year with $800,000 of capital assets, that amount (offset by a credit to net assets) should be shown in the worksheet. In preparing the following year's statements, the amount carried over would be $1,100,000 ($800,000 + $300,000 acquired in the year 2004).

Table 10-9

Government-Wide Statement of Activities

EUNEE CITY

STATEMENT OF ACTIVITIES

FOR THE YEAR ENDED DECEMBER 31, 2004

PROGRAMS:	EXPENSES	CHARGES FOR SERVICES	NET (EXPENSE) REVENUE
Public safety	$485,000		$(485,000)
Parks	140,000	$20,000	(120,000)
Interest on long-term debt	17,400		(17,400)
Total governmental activities	$642,400	$20,000	(622,400)
General revenues—property taxes			710,000
Change in net assets			87,600
Net assets—beginning			0
Net assets—ending			$ 87,600

Liability for Operating Expenses Not Due and Payable

Because they use the modified accrual basis of accounting, governmental-type funds do not accrue certain operating-type liabilities that are not immediately due and payable, such as vacation pay, judgments, and claims. As a result, although the short-term portion of the liabilities for those expenditures is reported on the fund-level balance sheets, the longer-term portion is not. Therefore, adjusting entries are required for the long-term liabilities when government-wide statements are prepared.

The first time government-wide statements are prepared, recording the aggregate long-term liabilities for vacation pay, judgments, and claims reduces the entity's net assets. These liabilities (offset by a debit to net assets) are carried forward on the worksheet for preparing the next year's government-wide statements, similar to what is done for capital assets and long-term debt. At the end of the year, a worksheet adjustment is made to record an increase or decrease in the long-term liabilities. For example, if the long-term estimated liability for judgments and claims was $180,000 at the beginning of the year and $195,000 at the end of the year, the following entry is made on the worksheet for preparing the government-wide statements:

Expenses (identified to a function)	15,000	
Judgments and claims liabilities		15,000
To adjust for increase in long-term liability.		

Property Tax Revenue Deferral

Governments that collect property taxes are likely to report deferred revenues in the fund financial statements. For example, in the Eunee City comprehensive illustration (see Table 10-5), the fund balance sheet at December 31, 2004, shows deferred reve-

Table 10-10

Financial Statement Reconciliations

A. *Reconciliation of Funds Balance Sheet to Government-Wide Statement of Net Assets*

Total fund balances (Table 10-5)	$148,000
Amounts reported in the statement of net assets are different because:	
Capital assets used in governmental activities are not financial resources and therefore are not reported in the funds.	285,000
A portion of the revenues is not available to pay for current-period expenditures and therefore is deferred in the funds.	20,000
Bonds payable are not due and payable in the current period and therefore are not reported in the funds.	(360,000)
Interest on long-term debt is not due and payable in the current period and therefore is not reported in the funds.	(5,400)
Net assets of governmental activities (Table 10-8)	$ 87,600

B. *Reconciliation of Funds Statement of Revenues, Expenditures, and Changes in Fund Balances to Government-Wide Statement of Activities*

Net change in fund balances (Table 10-6)	$148,000
Amounts reported in the statement of activities are different because:	
Governmental funds report capital outlays as expenditures. In the statement of activities, the costs of capital assets are allocated over their useful lives as depreciation. The amount by which capital outlays in the current period ($300,000) exceeded depreciation ($15,000) is	285,000
Bond proceeds provide current financial resources (and debt repayments are expenditures) in governmental funds. Issuing debt increases liabilities (and repaying debt decreases them) in the statement of net assets. The amount by which bond proceeds ($400,000) exceeded repayments ($40,000) is	(360,000)
Revenues in the statement of activities that do not provide current resources are not reported as revenues in the funds.	20,000
Some expenses in the statement of activities do not require use of current financial resources and are not shown as expenditures in funds.	(5,400)
Change in net assets (Table 10-9)	$ 87,600

---

nues of $20,000. The adjustment made to prepare the government-wide financial statements had the effect of taking the deferred revenues into revenue, correspondingly increasing net assets by $20,000.

Now, let's expand the illustration to cover calendar year 2005. Because Eunee City keeps its books on the modified accrual basis of accounting, it will record the December 31, 2004, deferral of $20,000 as revenues in 2005. Assume that, on December 31, 2005, Eunee City reports deferred revenue of $25,000. From the government-wide reporting perspective, revenues for the year 2005 were only $5,000 greater than those reported in the fund-level statements. That amount represents the difference between the two year-end deferral amounts. Therefore, the adjusting journal entry needed for the government-wide financial statements for the year ended December 31, 2005, should have the effect of both eliminating the deferred revenues account and reporting only $5,000 more revenues than that reported in the fund statements. The adjusting entry is as follows:

Deferred revenues	25,000	
Revenues—property taxes		5,000
Net assets		20,000

To adjust for net increase in deferred revenues over previous year.

Expense Accrual

The effect of previous-year adjustments also needs to be considered for expense-type accruals. To illustrate, refer to adjusting entry c in Table 10-7. For purposes of preparing the government-wide statements, that entry records a $5,400 expense and liability for accrued interest for the period October 1 through December 31, 2004. The entry has the effect of reducing Eunee City's net assets by $5,400 in the government-wide statements.

In the year 2005, Eunee City will pay two semiannual installments on its outstanding serial bonds, together with $10,800 interest on April 1, 2005, and $9,600 interest on October 1, 2005. The fund financial statements, prepared on the modified accrual basis of accounting, will show interest expenditures of $20,400 ($10,800 + $9,600) and no liability for interest payable. The government-wide financial statements, prepared on the accrual basis of accounting, must show interest expense of only $19,200 ($5,400 for January 1 through March 31, 2005, + $9,600 for April 1 through September 30, 2005, + $4,200 for October 1 through December 31, 2005). Therefore, interest expense reported in the government-wide statements will be $1,200 less than the interest expenditure shown on the fund statements. The government-wide financial statements must also show accrued interest payable of $4,200 not reported in the fund-level financial statements. The resulting adjusting entry is as follows:

Net assets	5,400	
Interest payable		4,200
Interest expense/expenditure		1,200

To adjust for net decrease in accrued liability from previous year.

As a result of the interest adjustments, the cumulative effect on net assets at December 31, 2005, is that net assets will be $4,200 less in the government-wide statements than that shown in the fund-level statements.

CAPITAL INVESTMENT ACCOUNT GROUP

In Chapter 6, we referred to the use of memorandum accounts to improve accountability for capital assets and to provide data for the government-wide financial statements. There are several ways to construct such a set of accounts. The simplest is to limit the number of accounts used to those needed for controlling the details of capital assets. A second approach is to add accounts to keep track of the amount reported as invested in capital assets, net of related debt, as well as asset disposals during the year.

We will use the second approach in this text and call it the Capital Investment Account Group (CIAG). Maintaining a CIAG requires journal entries each time a transaction occurs that affects the amount reported as invested in capital assets, net of related debt. This net asset subdivision is affected when the governmental unit acquires, depreciates, or disposes of capital assets and when it uses or repays debt issued to acquire capital assets.

To illustrate the nature of the journal entries, assume a governmental entity uses tax resources to purchase a police cruiser for $20,000 on January 1, 2004, and sells it on January 1, 2005, for $13,000. Because it uses the current financial resources measurement focus and modified accrual basis of accounting, entries are made in the General Fund only to record the financial resource inflows and outflows—the $20,000 purchase and the $13,000 revenue from the sale. For government-wide reporting, however, depreciation and the gain or loss on disposal of the cruiser need to be reported.

The CIAG entries parallel the adjustments for the government-wide statements. The entries shown below as increases and decreases are to the amount reported as invested in capital assets, net of related debt. The journal entries for 2004 are as follows:

Jan. 1	Equipment	20,000	
	Increases—capital outlay expenditures		20,000
	To record capital outlay.		
Dec. 31	Decreases—depreciation expense	5,000	
	Accumulated depreciation—equipment		5,000
	To record depreciation for the year, assuming a useful life of 4 years.		

At December 31, the increases and decreases would be closed to the account Invested in capital assets, net of related debt, so that the amount reported in that account would be $15,000 ($20,000 − $5,000). On January 1, 2005, when the police cruiser is sold, the following entry in the CIAG would provide the basis for the worksheet adjusting entry needed to record the accrual-basis economic results of the transaction—a $2,000 loss on the disposal, rather than a revenue of $13,000.

Jan. 1	Accumulated depreciation—equipment	5,000	
	Decreases—loss on disposal of equipment	2,000	
	Decreases—realized on sale of equipment	13,000	
	Equipment		20,000
	To record disposal of equipment.		

Use of CIAG in Comprehensive Illustration

We can illustrate the use of a CIAG by referring to the Eunee City transactions in this chapter. If Eunee City kept a CIAG, it would record capital asset and debt transactions in the CIAG when related entries are made in the funds. The numbers shown to the left of the following CIAG entries are the transaction numbers used in the illustration.

5. Available for investment in capital assets	400,000	
Bonds payable		400,000
To record issuance of debt.		

6. Capital assets	300,000	
Increases—capital outlay expenditures		300,000
To record increase in net assets invested in capital assets.		

Decreases—debt used to acquire capital assets	300,000	
Available for investment in capital assets		300,000
To record decrease in net assets invested in capital assets.		

8. Bonds payable	40,000	
Increases—repayment of debt		40,000
To record increase in investment through payment of bond principal.		

In addition, the following entry is needed to record depreciation on the capital assets.

Decreases—depreciation expense	15,000	
Accumulated depreciation—equipment		15,000
To record depreciation.		

Notice that when the CIAG increase and decrease accounts are closed into Invested in capital assets, net of related debt, the balance in that account is $25,000, which is the amount reported in the Eunee City government-wide statement of net assets. Notice also that the journal entries in the CIAG are constructed so that the account balances readily show the $100,000 available for additional investment in capital assets, as reported in the note to Table 10-8.

In summary, the CIAG, though not essential for external financial reporting, improves internal control over the governmental entity's capital assets and provides additional details for preparing the government-wide financial statements.

REVIEW QUESTIONS

Q10-1   What are the four basic principles for preparing government-wide statements?

Q10-2   Describe the column headings generally used in the government-wide statement of net assets.

Q10-3   Describe the three components of net assets in the government-wide statement of net assets.

Q10-4   What is the purpose of a *classified* statement of net assets?

Q10-5   What are the three categories of revenues that are deducted from expenses to compute the net expenses or revenues for each function or program shown in the government-wide statement of activities?

Q10-6 How are interfund activities and balances reported in government-wide financial statements?

Q10-7 How is Internal Service Fund activity reported in government-wide statements?

Q10-8 When should personal income tax revenues and property tax revenues be recognized for governmental activities in the government-wide statement of activities?

Q10-9 Describe the difference between expenditure recognition and measurement in the governmental funds financial statements and expense recognition for governmental activities in government-wide financial statements.

Q10-10 Describe the difference in reporting capital assets and long-term debt in the governmental funds financial statements and reporting those elements for governmental activities in government-wide financial statements.

Q10-11 Describe the major items that require reconciliation between fund financial statements and government-wide financial statements.

Q10-12 Define and give illustrations of infrastructure assets.

Q10-13 Discuss under what circumstances a governmental unit may choose not to depreciate infrastructure assets.

ETHICS CASE

EC10-1 Mayor Meier served for many years as the chief executive officer of a city. During that time he used his red pencil liberally when reviewing the draft of the introductory section of the CAFR, prepared by finance director Ted Gee. For example, when Ted made reference to large amounts of accumulating leave and unsettled claims that might affect future General Fund expenditures, Meier struck it out. When Ted discussed the implications of the city's recent issuance of large amounts of general obligation debt, with debt service payments scheduled to begin 10 years after the bonds were issued, Meier crossed it out. When Ted mentioned in the introductory section that the city had been neglecting to maintain its capital assets, Meier struck that out also. Ted never even bothered to mention that the city's credit rating had been gradually reduced during Meier's tenure, knowing that the mayor would surely delete it.

Last year, the city implemented the requirements of GASB *Statement No. 34*. Ted Gee read its requirements carefully. He made the necessary accruals when he prepared the government-wide financial statements. He also concluded that many of the comments he had made in previous years' drafts of the introductory section (which Meier had crossed out) and other comments that he didn't make (because he knew Meier would cross them out) should be made in Management's Discussion and Analysis (MD&A). Ted made all the comments he felt were needed to comply with the MD&A requirements of GASB *Statement No. 34*, and gave his draft of the MD&A to the mayor. The mayor applied his red pencil in the usual manner and dumped the draft on Ted's desk. What should Ted do?

E10-1 (Analysis of financial statements)

Obtain a CAFR from a governmental unit. Examine the governmental fund financial statements, the governmental activities sections of the government-wide financial statements, and the reconciliations between the two sets of statements. Trace the items comprising the reconciliations back to the financial statements as best you can. Write a brief report explaining the nature of each item of the reconciliation.

E10-2 (Analysis of the MD&A)

Obtain a CAFR from a governmental unit. Review all financial statements carefully. Read the MD&A. Consider the comments made in the MD&A in light of the financial statements. Write a brief report assessing the quality of the MD&A based on the data in the financial statements.

E10-3 (Multiple choice)

1. In government-wide financial statements, when is depreciation reported?
   a. Only for governmental activities
   b. Only for business-type activities
   c. For both governmental and business-type activities
   d. For neither governmental nor business-type activities
2. In government-wide financial statements, for which activities is the economic resources measurement focus and accrual basis of accounting used?
   a. Only for governmental activities
   b. Only for business-type activities
   c. For both governmental and business-type activities
   d. For neither governmental nor business-type activities
3. Where are fiduciary-type funds reported?
   a. Only in the fund financial statements
   b. Only in the government-wide financial statements
   c. In both fund and government-wide financial statements
   d. In neither fund nor government-wide financial statements
4. The General Fund makes a transfer to the Debt Service Fund. How should the transfer be reported in the financial statements?
   a. The transfers in and out should be reported in both the fund operating statement and the government-wide operating statement.
   b. The transfers in and out should be reported in neither the fund operating statement nor the government-wide operating statement.
   c. The transfers in and out should be reported in the fund operating statement, but not in the government-wide operating statement.
   d. The transfers in and out should be reported in the government-wide operating statement, but not in the fund operating statement.
5. In government-wide financial statements, how are the net assets of Internal Service Funds generally treated?
   a. They are ignored.
   b. They are aggregated with business-type activities.

c. They are aggregated with fiduciary-type activities.

d. They are aggregated with governmental activities.

6. A city issues $100,000 of 10-year general obligation bonds on April 1, 2004. It is required to pay debt service of $10,000 on April 1 of each year, starting April 1, 2005, with interest of 5 percent on the unpaid principal. How much interest expenditure or expense should the city recognize in its operating statements for the calendar year 2004?

	Fund Statement	Government-Wide Statement
a.	$3,750	$ 0
b.	3,750	3,750
c.	0	3,750
d.	0	0

7. A village issues $3,000,000 of general obligation bonds to build a new firehouse. How are the debt proceeds reported?

a. As a liability in the government-wide statement of net assets

b. As a liability in the fund financial statement

c. As proceeds of debt in the government-wide statement of activities

d. As a liability in the net assets section of the government-wide statement of net assets

8. A village levies property taxes in the amount of $940,000 for the fiscal year ended June 30, 2005. It collects $900,000 during the year. Regarding the $40,000 of delinquent receivables, it expects to collect $25,000 in July and August of 2005 and another $10,000 after August but before March of 2006. It expects to write off $5,000 as uncollectible. How much should the village recognize as property tax revenue in its government-wide statement of activities for the fiscal year ended June 30, 2005?

a. $940,000

b. $935,000

c. $925,000

d. $900,000

E10-4 (True or false) For any false statement, indicate why it is false.

1. In government wide financial statements, information about fiduciary funds should be presented in a discrete column to the right of the business-type activities.

2. In government-wide financial statements, expenses for each program should be presented in such a way that charges for services directly related to the programs are shown to reduce the gross expenses of the programs.

3. In government-wide financial statements, interest on long-term general obligation debt should be recognized in the period that the interest is due and payable.

4. The "consumption" method of accounting for inventories may be used when preparing governmental fund financial statements, but must be used when reporting on governmental activities in the government-wide statements.

5. The economic resources measurement focus and accrual basis of accounting are used in reporting on enterprise funds in both the fund statements and the government-wide statements.
6. The existence of Internal Service Funds is not likely to affect amounts reported as expenses in the governmental activities column of government-wide financial statements.
7. Fiduciary funds are reported in fund financial statements, but are not reported in government-wide financial statements.
8. Only the major proprietary funds are reported in government-wide financial statements.

E10-5 (Adjustments for fund and government-wide financial statements)
Oliver City had the following transactions and events during calendar-year 2004.
1. The state collects sales taxes on behalf of all cities. During the year 2004, the state collected and remitted $530,000 of sales taxes to Oliver. On January 20, 2005, the state sent Oliver the following letter: "We have collected $30,000 of sales taxes on your behalf based on December 2004 sales in your city and will send you a check for that amount on or about February 10, 2005."
2. During 2004 Oliver hired several inexperienced truck drivers who sideswiped some privately owned vehicles while driving city sanitation trucks. The City settled one of the claims in late December 2004 for $3,000, and expected to pay the claim in early January 2005. The other accidents occurred in December 2004. The City corporation counsel thought the City could settle the claims for about $50,000, but expected negotiations to drag on until late 2005 or early 2006.
3. Oliver City uses the purchases method to account for materials and supplies. Its inventory at December 31, 2003, was not material. At December 31, 2004, Oliver considered its $65,000 inventory to be material and decided to make an appropriate adjustment when preparing its calendar-year 2004 financial statements.

Required: 1. Prepare journal entries to record the year-end adjustments needed for preparing the fund financial statements for the year ended December 31, 2004.
2. Prepare adjusting entries needed for preparing the governmental activities column of the government-wide statements for the year ended December 31, 2004.

E10-6 (Reporting Internal Service Fund financial information)
The Village of Delmar is preparing its government-wide statement of activities for the year ended December 31, 2004. Analysis of the data accumulated thus far shows the following expenses for each of its programs.

Program	Salaries	Supplies	ISF Billings	Total Expenses
General	$ 250,000	$ 45,000	$ 20,000 *20%*	$ 315,000 *311*
Police	675,000	75,000	35,000 *20%*	785,000 *778*
Fire	380,000	40,000	30,000 *20%*	450,000 *444*
Parks	200,000	35,000	15,000 *20%*	250,000 *247*
Totals	$1,505,000	$195,000	$100,000 *20%*	$1,800,000

80000

The Internal Service Fund (ISF) billings are from the Village's Motor Pool ISF. The Internal Service Fund column of the proprietary funds statement of revenues, expenses, and changes in fund net assets, prepared by the Village of Delmar, shows the following:

Charges for services	$100,000
Operating expenses:	
Personal services	60,000
Repairs and maintenance	5,000
Depreciation	15,000
Total operating expenses	80,000
Operating income	20,000
Total net assets—beginning	45,000
Total net assets—ending	$ 65,000

Required: Calculate the amounts that the Village of Delmar should report as expenses for each of its programs in its government-wide statement of activities for the year ended December 31, 2004.

PROBLEMS

P10-1 (Accounting for and reporting on capital assets acquired using governmental funds)

Marilyn County operates on a calendar-year basis. It uses a Capital Projects Fund to account for major capital projects and a Debt Service Fund to accumulate resources to pay principal and interest on general obligation debt. It does not use encumbrance accounting in the Capital Projects Fund. The following transactions occur:

1. On January 1, 2004, Marilyn County issues general obligation bonds in the amount of $900,000 to build a community center. The debt will be paid off in 30 equal semiannual installments of $30,000 over a 15-year period commencing October 1, 2004, with interest of 6 percent on the outstanding debt.

2. The Village realizes that the community center will cost more than it originally anticipated. On May 1, the Village transfers $20,000 from its General Fund to its Capital Projects Fund to help meet project costs.

3. Construction is completed on July 1, 2004, and the community center is ready for occupancy. The Village pays the contractor a total of $920,000 on July 1. The County anticipates that the community center will have a useful life of 20 years.
4. On September 30, 2004, the General Fund transfers an amount to the Debt Service Fund that is sufficient to pay the first debt service installment, which is due October 1.
5. The Village pays the debt service due on October 1.

Required: 1. Prepare journal entries to record the foregoing transactions in the Capital Projects Fund, the General Fund, and the Debt Service Fund.
2. Prepare adjustments needed to develop the governmental activities column of the government-wide financial statements.
3. Calculate the amount that Marilyn County will report in its December 31, 2004, government-wide statement of net assets as "invested in capital assets, net of related debt." Also, assuming all debt service installments are paid when due in 2005, calculate the amount "invested in capital assets, net of related debt" at December 31, 2005.

P10-2 (Preparation of statement of activities)
The following information is taken from Hamilton Township's December 31, 2004, trial balance after all adjustments had been made for preparation of the government-wide financial statements. Hamilton Township has governmental activities, but no business-type activities.

Revenues—property taxes	$3,250,000
Revenues—sales taxes	2,175,000
State operating aid—police program	410,000
State operating aid—town road maintenance	250,000
State capital aid—town road maintenance	50,000
Fees—sanitation	75,000
Fees—programs for youth and seniors	65,000
Fees—parks admissions	85,000
Revenue from disposal of donated property	425,000
General government expenses	625,000
Police program expenses	2,615,000
Road maintenance program expenses	975,000
Sanitation program expenses	1,410,000
Parks and recreation programs expenses	525,000
Youth and senior programs expenses	325,000
Net assets—beginning of year	3,125,000

Required: Prepare, using the appropriate format, a statement of activities for the Town of Hamilton for the year ended December 31, 2004.

P10-3 (Property tax revenue transactions and measurement in financial statements) A village levies property taxes in March of each year to help finance the General Fund expenditures for the calendar year. Property owners are required to pay the taxes in equal installments in April and October. Taxes remaining uncollected are declared delinquent at the end of the year. The facts regarding property taxes levied and collected for calendar-years 2004 and 2005 are as follows:

2004: The village levied property taxes of $700,000, anticipating the entire amount to be collected. It actually collected $650,000 during the year. When the village prepared its financial statements, it assumed all the delinquent taxes would be collected during 2005, $40,000 in the first 60 days and the remaining $10,000 later in 2005.

2005: The village levied property taxes of $730,000, again expecting the entire amount to be collected. It actually collected $690,000 in the year of the levy. When it prepared its 2005 financial statements, the village assumed all delinquent 2005 taxes would be collected during 2006, $25,000 in the first 60 days and the remaining $15,000 later in 2006. Regarding the $50,000 of delinquent 2004 taxes, it collected $38,000 in the first 60 days of 2005, $7,000 during the rest of 2005, and wrote off the remaining $5,000 as uncollectible.

Required: Prepare journal entries as follows:
1. Record the year 2004 transactions in the General Fund, including the year-end adjustment needed to prepare the fund financial statements.
2. Make the adjustment needed to prepare the governmental activities column of the government-wide statements.
3. Record the year 2005 transactions in the General Fund, including the year-end adjustment needed to prepare the fund financial statements.
4. Make the adjustment needed to prepare the governmental activities column of the government-wide statements.

Also, calculate the amount of property tax revenues that the village should recognize in its fund financial statements and in its government-wide financial statements for both 2004 and 2005.

P10-4 (Conversion to government-wide financial statements) Harlan City, a small city with revenues less than $10 million a year, is planning to issue its first set of government-wide financial statements for the year ended December 31, 2004. To prepare for the transition, the city comptroller wants to have a government-wide statement of net assets as of January 1, 2004, the beginning of the year. The available information includes extracts from the governmental funds portion of the balance sheet prepared as of

December 31, 2003, together with other data necessary to construct a government-wide statement of net assets for governmental activities, using the economic resources measurement focus and accrual basis of accounting.

The balance sheet for the combined governmental funds as of December 31, 2003, is as follows:

Assets

Cash	$175,000
Property taxes receivable	85,000
Due from other governments	40,000
Total assets	$300,000

Liabilities

Accounts payable	$ 43,000
Accrued salaries and other expenses	14,000
Deferred property tax revenues	18,000
Total liabilities	75,000

Fund Balances

Unreserved	225,000
Total fund balances	225,000
Total liabilities and fund balances	$300,000

The following additional information is available as of December 31, 2003:

Capital assets: Harlan's capital asset records show that the total cost of the assets in use as of December 31, 2003, is $8,400,000. Estimated accumulated depreciation on the assets is $4,600,000.

Bonds payable: Harlan has outstanding bonds payable at December 31, 2003, of $2,600,000. Of this amount, principal due to be paid during the calendar year 2004 is $150,000. Analysis of the outstanding bonds shows that all of the debt had been sold to finance the acquisition of capital assets, except for $200,000 that had been sold in 2001 to provide cash for an unanticipated operating expense.

Interest on long-term debt: In its fund statements, Harlan recognizes interest on bonds payable when it is due and payable. It does not accrue interest for year-end "stub periods" that will be paid early in the following year. Stub period interest at December 31, 2003, was $20,000.

Property taxes: Harlan expects that all of its property taxes receivable will be collected in 2004. Property tax revenues of $18,000 were deferred because Harlan did not expect to collect them during the first 60 days of 2004.

Other expenses: Employees may accumulate vacation pay, subject to certain limits, that they may receive in cash on retirement. Accrued expenses of $14,000 include $2,000 of accrued vacation pay that the city will pay early in 2004 to retired employees. Other employees have accumulated vacation pay of $42,000 that Harlan expects to pay when they retire in future years. No accrual has been made for this amount.

Required: 1. Prepare a six-column worksheet similar to that shown in Table 10-7, showing the balances in the fund accounts, the adjusting entries needed to prepare a government-wide statement of net assets as of January 1, 2004, and the adjusted balances. Make the adjustments needed to prepare a government-wide statement of net assets, and support the adjustments with journal entries. (Hint: Reclassify the fund balance to net assets. Because no statement of activities is required, the adjustments to report the additional assets and liabilities will directly affect net assets.)

2. Prepare a statement of net assets as of January 1, 2004, in classified format. Show the net assets either as invested in capital assets, net of related debt, or as unrestricted.

3. Prepare a reconciliation of the funds balance sheet to the government-wide statement of net assets in a format similar to that shown in Table 10-10, Part A.

SUMMARY PROBLEM

Summary Problem 1. (Preparation of government-wide financial statements) This problem is a continuation of Summary Problem 1 at the end of Chapter 9. It is Part G of the problem.

Required: 1. Prepare journal entries needed to convert the governmental funds financial statements to the governmental activities column of the government-wide financial statements. Post the journal entries to a six-column work sheet similar to that shown on page 447 of this chapter.

2. Prepare Coco City's financial statements: the government-wide statement of net assets and the government-wide statement of activities.

Chapter

11

Federal Government Accounting and Reporting

After completing this chapter, you should be able to:

➤ *Explain the federal budgetary process.*

➤ *Discuss the federal Anti-Deficiency Act.*

➤ Discuss the similarities and differences between federal government accounting and state and local government accounting.

➤ List the funds used by the federal government.

➤ Explain the function of the Federal Accounting Standards Advisory Board and discuss four standards promulgated by that organization.

➤ Compare and contrast budgetary and proprietary accounting as used by the federal government.

➤ Discuss commitment accounting.

➤ Prepare entries for the accounting cycle of a federal agency.

➤ Describe the financial statements used by federal agencies.

*T*he federal government of the United States is a large consumer of resources. With a budget of more than $2 trillion, it is the largest accounting entity in existence. Its activities affect literally everyone in the United States and almost everyone in the world. Therefore, it is important to understand the accounting system developed to control this monolith.

Like the accounting systems used by state and local governmental units, the federal accounting system is heavily influenced by both legal and economic considerations. Budgetary accounting is so heavily integrated into the federal accounting process that federal agencies literally use a two-track accounting system—one with budgetary accounts and another with financial (called proprietary) accounts. The federal government has several fund types, and generally uses the accrual basis of accounting. Federal accounting standards are established by the Federal Accounting Standards Advisory Board (FASAB).

In this chapter we will briefly cover the procedures used by federal agencies to account for and report on their resources. Before we begin this discussion, however, let us review the federal budgetary process and roles of various parties involved.

THE FEDERAL BUDGETARY PROCESS

The federal budgetary process begins about 18 months before the beginning of a fiscal year (October 1). At this time overall policy issues are identified, budget projections are made, and preliminary program plans are presented to the president. The president reviews this information, along with data on projected revenues and economic conditions. On the basis of this review, the president establishes general budgetary and fiscal policy guidelines for the fiscal year under discussion and for the 4 fiscal years that follow.

Using presidential guidelines, agencies prepare their budgetary requests. These requests are reviewed in detail by the departments of which the agencies are a part (e.g., the U.S. Forest Service is a part of the Department of Agriculture) and by the Office of Management and Budget (OMB).[1] After differences between OMB, the departments, and the agencies are resolved, revised agency budgets are presented to the president, who reviews them in light of the latest economic data and revenue estimates. Last-minute revisions are made, and the various agency budgets are combined into one document, which is presented to the Congress. The budgetary document represents the president's recommendations for new and existing programs, as well as projections of receipts and expenditures.

Formal congressional review of the budget begins shortly after the president transmits it to the Congress, about 8 or 9 months before the fiscal year begins. The Congress considers the president's budget proposals and may change funding levels of individual programs, add or eliminate programs, and add or eliminate taxes and other sources of receipts. Before passing *appropriations* for specific programs, however, the Congress passes a budget resolution that sets levels for budgetary receipts and for budgetary authority and outlays, in total and by functional category.

Requests for appropriations and for changes in revenue laws are first considered in the House of Representatives. The House Ways and Means Committee reviews proposed revenue measures, and the House Appropriations Committee studies requests for appropriations. These committees then make their report to the entire House of Representatives, which acts on the revenue and appropriations bills. After the bills are approved, they are sent to the Senate, where the process is repeated. If the two houses of Congress cannot agree on the various fiscal measures, a conference committee (consisting of members of both houses) resolves the issues and submits a report to both houses for approval.

After approval by the Congress, the various revenue and appropriations measures are transmitted to the president in the form of enrolled bills. The president then approves or vetoes these bills. If appropriations bills are not passed by the beginning of the fiscal year, the Congress passes a *continuing resolution.* This resolution provides the authority for affected agencies to continue spending until a specified date, or until their regular appropriations are approved. When the appropriations bill is signed by the president, *appropriations warrants* are sent to the various agencies by the Treasury. Each agency then revises its budget in accordance with the appropriations bill and, within 30 days, submits a request for apportionment to the OMB.

It should be noted that congressional appropriations are not based directly on expenditures. Rather, each agency is given *budget authority,* which is the authority to obligate the government to ultimately make disbursements for expenditures, repayment of loans, and the like.[2] A congressional appropriation is really nothing more

---

[1] The OMB is an agency within the Executive Office of the President, which has responsibility for the overall financial management of the federal government. It is ultimately responsible for preparing the executive budget and for apportioning appropriate resources to the various departments and agencies.

[2] Budget authority may take several forms, the most common of which is appropriations. Budget authority may also take the form of borrowing authority, contract authority (which generally requires a subsequent appropriation), and authority to spend from offsetting collections.

than a spending authority or limit for that fiscal year. It does not mean that cash is immediately available for spending. Availability of cash depends on many factors, such as inflows of tax revenues and the level of surplus funds from prior years.

Most appropriations are for 1 year only. If they are not spent or obligated by the end of the fiscal year, they must be returned. In some cases, however, Congress makes multiyear or indefinite appropriations. Examples of this latter type of appropriation include those used to fund Social Security and to service public debt. The remainder of this chapter will be devoted to 1-year appropriations.

When the OMB receives a request for *apportionment* from an agency, it apportions a part of the agency's appropriation to the department of which the agency is a part, based on a time period (usually quarterly) or activity. The purpose of the apportionment system is to help prevent agencies from obligating or spending more than their appropriations, to enable the Treasury to better match revenues and disbursements (cash management), and to restrict expenditures in areas in which the president believes that amounts appropriated by the Congress are excessive.

The last-mentioned use of the apportionment system, presidential impounding, has generated a great deal of controversy over the years. In 1974, Congress passed the Impoundment Control Act of 1974. This law provides that the president must report to the Congress any administrative action to postpone or eliminate spending authorized by law. *Deferrals,* which are temporary withholdings of authority to spend, cannot extend beyond the end of the fiscal year and may be overturned by either house of the Congress at any time. *Rescissions,* which are permanent cancellations of spending authority, must be approved by the full Congress. If both houses of Congress do not approve, the withheld resources must be made available to the agency.

When a department receives its apportionment from OMB, the department head (or his or her representative) *allots* all or a part of the amount of the apportionment intended for each agency under the department's control. Each agency can only obligate (and spend) the allotted portion of its appropriation.

When an agency receives its allotment, it is free to spend up to that amount of money, within budgetary guidelines. Agency personnel, however, cannot spend more than the amount appropriated for (and allotted to) that agency without violating the *Anti-Deficiency Act* (31 U.S.C. 1517 of the Revised Statutes). The main purposes of this act are to prevent the incurring of obligations, and making of disbursements, in excess of appropriations and to fix responsibility within each agency for the incurrence of obligations and expenditures. Agency personnel who violate this law are subject to both civil and criminal penalties.

Before an agency makes a disbursement, it generally "obligates" the resources. An obligation, which is recorded as an "undelivered order," is similar to an encumbrance. It represents resources earmarked for a specific purpose. When the goods are received, the undelivered orders become "expended authority." Instead of making direct payment, however, the agency sends a *disbursement schedule* to the Treasury. The Treasury then sends a check to the vendor. The payments of obligations become "outlays." This process, which results primarily in budgetary accounting entries, is illustrated in Exhibit 11-1.

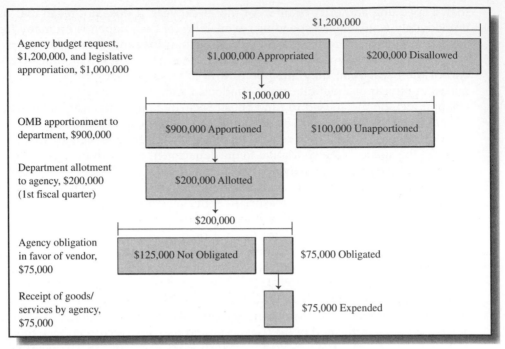

Exhibit 11-1
The Federal Budgetary Accounting Cycle

FEDERAL VERSUS STATE AND LOCAL GOVERNMENTAL ACCOUNTING

Both similarities and differences can be noted between federal accounting and state and local governmental accounting. The introduction to state and local government financial reporting of government-wide reporting on the full accrual basis of accounting, however, reduced the number of differences. Some differences relate to the degree to which one or the other has adopted a particular practice. Other differences relate to the size and scope of the U.S. government. The following is a comparison of some of the accounting and financial reporting practices.

1. *Integration of budgetary accounting.* Both the federal government and state and local governments integrate budgetary accounting into their financial accounting systems. Federal use of budgetary accounting, however, is more pervasive than state and local government use. As discussed subsequently, the federal government uses a two-track accounting system, one for budgetary transactions and the other for financial accounting transactions.

2. *Use of funds and basis of accounting within the funds.* Both the federal government and state and local governments use funds, many of which are similar in nature. In its financial accounting system, however, the federal government

uses a greater degree of accrual accounting within the funds than do state and local governments. Because of certain practical limitations, the federal government recognizes tax revenues on what might best be characterized as a "modified cash" basis. Expenses, however, are generally recognized on the full accrual basis. For example, inventories are recognized when consumed and certain fixed assets are capitalized and depreciated. State and local governments use the modified accrual basis of accounting within some funds and the full accrual basis in others at the fund level of reporting.

3. *Financial reporting practices.* In the federal government, separate accounting records are maintained and financial statements are issued for each agency and/or fund. In most cases, the agency statements cover a portion of a particular fund (e.g., the General Fund), not the entire fund. The U.S. government also issues consolidated financial statements. Further, federal government reporting is based on a single set of integrated financial reports. State and local government reporting, on the other hand, covers all agencies of the government, rather than just a single department. Although individual departments of state and local governments sometimes issue departmental financial statements, they are usually for internal use only. Finally, state and local governments have a dual set of reports, one based on government-wide data using the full accrual basis of accounting and another based on fund-level data using the modified accrual basis for some funds and the full accrual basis for others.

4. *Treatment of fund balances.* Residual balances of funds used by state and local governmental units (assets minus liabilities, or "net assets") are shown in the fund balance accounts of those funds. They represent, among other things, the amount available for expenditures. In federal accounting, activities of many different agencies can be recorded in a "common" fund. Because each agency is an accounting entity, it is necessary to use terms to identify the portion of each common fund that represents that agency's net assets. Terms used for this purpose are *net position, unexpended appropriations,* and *cumulative results of operations.* It should be noted that, unlike those of governmental-type funds used by state and local governmental units, net assets of federal funds are not always liquid.

5. *Treatment of cash.* Most funds used by state and local governmental units use a cash-in-bank account. Checks are drawn against this account to make disbursements, and the governmental unit has a direct relationship with the bank. Because of the size and nature of the federal government, individual agencies do not generally deal directly with banks. Rather, the Treasury acts as their banker. At the beginning of a fiscal year, each agency is provided with an account with the Treasury for each appropriation. The size of this account is equal to the agency's appropriation plus any amounts left over from previous periods that the agency has not been required to return. When an agency makes a disbursement, it sends a disbursement schedule to the Treasury. The Treasury writes a check for the amount of the schedule. The account used by federal agencies to record their claims against the Treasury is "Fund balance with U.S. Treasury." When agencies receive resources from the Treasury, this account is debited. When the disbursements ordered by the agencies are made by the Treasury, this account is credited.

TYPES OF FUNDS USED IN FEDERAL ACCOUNTING

Federal agency activities are financed through federal funds—General Fund, Special Funds, Public Enterprise (Revolving) Funds, Intragovernmental Funds, and Trust Funds. Unlike the accounting procedures within the state and local government fund types, transactions in the funds used by the federal government are generally recorded in a similar manner in all funds.

1. *The General Fund.* This fund comprises the greater part of the federal budget. It is used to account for receipts that are not earmarked for a specific purpose, such as almost all income tax receipts and the proceeds of general borrowing. General Fund expenditures are recorded in General Fund appropriation accounts. As with state and local governmental units, one General Fund is used for the entire federal government. However, General Fund appropriations are made to individual agencies and programs. From the perspective of the individual agencies within the federal government, each appropriation is treated as a separate fund, as if it were a separate accounting entity.

2. *Special Funds.* These funds are similar to Special Revenue Funds used by state and local governmental units. They are used to account for resources received from specific sources earmarked by law for special purposes, and spending in accordance with specific legal provisions.

3. *Public Enterprise (Revolving) Funds.* These funds are used for programs authorized by law to conduct business-type activities, primarily with the public. Outlays from these funds generate collections that are credited directly to the fund and are available for expenditure without further congressional action. They are thus similar to Enterprise Funds used by state and local governments.

4. *Intragovernmental Funds.* These funds are used to conduct business-type operations, based on user charges, primarily within and between governmental agencies. They are also revolving-type funds whose operations are financed from collections that are credited directly to the fund. They are similar to Internal Service Funds used by state and local governmental units.

5. *Trust Funds.* These funds are used to account for receipts and expenditures of resources to carry out specific purposes and programs in accordance with the terms of a statute that designates the fund as a Trust Fund or for carrying out the purposes of a trust agreement. Examples are the Old Age and Survivors and Disability Insurance Trust Funds (commonly called Social Security) and the Highway Trust Fund. The federal budget meaning of the term *trust* differs significantly from private sector usage. The federal government owns the assets of most federal Trust Funds, and there is no substantive difference between a Trust Fund and a Special Fund.

The federal government also maintains certain accounts outside the budget, known as *Deposit Funds*. Deposit Funds are established to record amounts held temporarily until ownership is established and to account for monies for which the federal government acts as a banker or agent for others. They are similar to Agency Funds used by state and local governmental units.

As with state and local governmental units, most of the activities of federal agencies are recorded in the General Fund. Therefore, the remainder of this chapter will be devoted to a discussion of procedures used by federal agencies to account for their General Fund activities.

FEDERAL ACCOUNTING STANDARDS

In October 1990 the Secretary of the Treasury, the Director of the Office of Management and Budget (OMB), and the Comptroller General established the Federal Accounting Standards Advisory Board (FASAB), a nine-member board whose purpose is to consider and recommend accounting principles for the federal government.

The FASAB considers financial and budgetary information needs of executive agencies, congressional oversight groups, and others who use federal financial information. The FASAB proposes accounting standards after appropriate due process, which includes publication of "exposure drafts" of proposed standards and, sometimes, public hearings. After considering the comments received in response to the due process, the FASAB submits proposed standards to the Secretary of the Treasury, the Director of the OMB, and the Comptroller General for their review. If, within 90 days after submission, none of these officials object to the proposed standard, it becomes a final statement of the Board. If any of them object to the proposed standard, it is returned to the FASAB for further consideration.

The FASAB completed a basic set of accounting and financial reporting standards, which provided the basis for issuing audited consolidated federal government financial statements starting in 1997. As of this writing, the FASAB has issued three concepts statements and more than 20 Statements of Federal Financial Accounting Standards (SFFAS). Some highlights of these standards follow:

1. *Inventory and related property.* SFFAS No. 3 covers inventory (items held for sale), operating materials and supplies, stockpile materials, seized and forfeited property, and certain other property.
   - Inventory held for sale includes personal property held for sale within the same organization or agency. Such inventory must be valued at historical cost or by any other valuation method that approximates historical cost. Latest acquisition cost may also be used as a valuation method, provided it is adjusted for unrealized holding gains and losses.
   - Operating materials and supplies (personal property to be consumed in the normal course of operations) are also valued at historical cost or any other method that approximates it. They are normally accounted for using the consumption method. Purchases may be expensed immediately, however, if the amounts are not significant, are in the hands of the end user, and the consumption method is not cost-beneficial.

2. *Property, plant, and equipment (PP&E).* SFFAS No. 6, as amended, establishes four categories of federal PP&E: general PP&E, national defense PP&E, heritage assets, and stewardship land. General PP&E provides general government services or goods. National defense PP&E covers the huge federal investment in

Department of Defense weapons systems. Heritage assets possess significant educational, cultural, or natural characteristics, such as the White House, the Library of Congress, and the Washington Monument. Stewardship land covers most federal land, such as park land.

General PP&E is capitalized on the balance sheet at acquisition cost and depreciated. Annual expenditures to acquire, replace, or improve national defense PP&E, heritage assets, and stewardship land, however, are not shown on the balance sheet. Instead, the costs are reported as expenses in the period incurred. For accountability purposes, capital assets not shown on the balance sheet (referred to collectively as stewardship PP&E) must be reported as "required supplemental stewardship information," a report unique to the federal government. (At the time of this writing, the FASAB was considering a proposal to treat national defense PP&E as general PP&E. In that event, national defense PP&E would be capitalized and depreciated.)

The standards also require disclosure of deferred maintenance, which is maintenance that was not performed when it should have been and was, therefore, delayed to a future period. Deferred maintenance may be estimated by several methods including condition assessment surveys, which are periodic inspections that assess the condition of capital assets and estimate the costs to restore the assets to acceptable operating condition.

SFFAS No. 6 also requires estimating (and periodically reestimating) and recognizing liabilities and expenses for cleanup costs. Cleanup costs are costs incurred in removing, containing, and disposing of hazardous waste. Such costs include the cost of decontaminating and decommissioning nuclear submarines, other nuclear facilities, and toxic chemical sites. Cleanup costs for general PP&E are recognized as expenses systematically over the useful life of the PP&E. Consistent with accounting for the acquisition cost of stewardship PP&E (e.g., a nuclear submarine), cleanup costs for stewardship PP&E are recognized in the period the asset is placed in service.

3. *Accounting for federal liabilities.* Although many transactions and events that create federal liabilities are similar to those encountered by state and local government and business enterprises, some are unique to the federal government. As a general rule, federal liabilities arising from exchange transactions (in which each party to the transaction sacrifices value and receives value in return) are accounted for on the accrual basis of accounting. The federal reporting entity recognizes a liability when it receives goods or services in return for a promise to pay in the future.

The federal government also engages, however, in many nonexchange transactions, in which it promises to provide benefits pursuant to law or grant without directly receiving value in return. An example is payments to health care providers for services under the Medicaid program. In those cases, the federal reporting entity recognizes a liability for any unpaid amounts as of the reporting date. The liability includes an estimate for services rendered by providers but not yet reported to the federal entity.

4. *Accounting for social insurance programs.* Perhaps the most controversial issue dealt with by the FASAB concerned Social Security and similar social insurance

programs. Some believed that a liability for Social Security ought to be reported only for amounts due but unpaid as of the reporting date. They argued that Social Security was enacted as a compulsory intergenerational transfer program and that the government has the ability to cancel or significantly reduce program benefits. Others believed a liability should be reported (similar to a pension plan) for the unfunded present value of amounts due in the future to current Social Security beneficiaries, as well as for amounts earned by active future beneficiaries. They argued that the Social Security program has elements of exchange transactions, and the commitments, expectations, and political climate affecting the program make future payment so highly probable as to meet the liability definition.

The issue was resolved with the publication of SFFAS No. 17, *Accounting for Social Insurance,* in 1999. SFFAS No. 17 requires that liabilities for social insurance programs be recognized only for benefits that are *due and payable at the end of the reporting period*—basically, the amount due for the month of September. The standard also requires that extensive disclosures be made to facilitate assessment of long-term program sustainability, including the ability of the nation to raise resources from future program participants to pay for benefits promised to present participants. Required disclosures include projections of future cash inflows and outflows, projections of ratios of number of contributors to number of beneficiaries, actuarial present values of future contributions from or for and expenditures to or on behalf of current participants who have attained retirement age and for participants who have not attained retirement age, and a discussion of the significant assumptions used in making projections. (See comment on "Social Security Administration's Financial Statements" later in this chapter.)

THE FEDERAL AGENCY ACCOUNTING CYCLE

Accounting systems used by federal agencies must provide information for two purposes:

1. To help agency managers avoid overexpending or overobligating appropriations—actions that carry legal penalties.
2. To account for assets entrusted to the care of agencies and for the equities in those assets—liabilities and capital.

As a result, federal agencies use a *two-track accounting system.* One track is a self-balancing set of *budgetary accounts,* which demonstrate budgetary compliance. The other track is a self-balancing set of *proprietary accounts,* which is used for financial management. Differences between budgetary-track and proprietary-track accounting, with respect to recognition of events that constitute transactions, are found in Table 11-1. Notice the similarities between proprietary accounting used by federal agencies and accounting used by commercial organizations. Key entries prepared by federal agencies are summarized in Table 11-2.

Table 11-1

Summary of Key Differences Between Budgtetary and Proprietary Accounting
in Recognition of Events that Constitute Transactions

BUDGETARY ACCOUNTING	PROPRIETARY ACCOUNTING
Entries are made for commitment of funds in advance of preparing orders to procure goods and services.	Entries are not made for commitments.
Entries are made for obligation of funds at the time goods and services are ordered.	Entries are not made for obligations.
Entries are made to expend appropriations when goods and services chargeable to the appropriation are received, regardless of when they are used and regardless of when they are paid for.	Goods and services that will last more than a year and otherwise meet the criteria to qualify as assets are capitalized and expensed when consumed, regardless of what appropriation funded them and when they are paid for.
Entries are made only against an appropriation for transactions funded by the appropriation.	Goods and services consumed in the current period for which payment is to be made from one or more subsequent appropriations are recognized as expenses in the current period.
Entries are not made against an appropriation for transactions not funded by the appropriation.	Goods and services consumed in the current period, but paid for in prior periods, are expensed in the current period.

Source: U.S. General Accounting Office, *GAO Accounting Guide: Basic Topics Relating to Appropriations and Reimbursables* (Washington, DC: GAO, 1990), p. 3-2.

Illustrative Entries

Opening Entries

The accounting cycle of a federal agency begins at the start of the fiscal year when the Congress makes (and the president approves) an appropriation. If the appropriation is $150,000, entries on the books of the agency are as follows:

Budgetary entry	Other appropriations realized	150,000	
	Unapportioned authority—available		150,000
	To record receipt of appropriation authority.		
Proprietary entry	Fund balance with Treasury	150,000	
	Unexpended appropriations		150,000
	To record receipt of appropriation warrant.		

The first entry establishes initial accountability by the agency for its appropriation. The debit to Other appropriations realized distinguishes the agency's basic operating appropriation from other special purpose appropriations it might have received. The second entry records the establishment of a "line of credit" with the Treasury. The account Fund balance with Treasury is the equivalent of a cash

Table 11-2

Summary of Key Entries Prepared by Federal Agencies

WHO ACTS?	WHAT ACTION?	BUDGETARY ENTRY	PROPRIETARY ENTRY
Congress	Appropriates	Other appropriations realized Unapportioned authority—available	Fund balance with Treasury Unexpended appropriations
OMB	Apportions	Unapportioned authority—available Apportionment	None
Department	Allots	Apportionment Allotments—realized resources	None
Agency	Commits	Allotments—realized resources Commitments	None
Agency	Obligates	Commitments Undelivered orders	None
Agency	Receives services	Undelivered orders Expended authority	Operating/program expenses Accounts payable Unexpended appropriations Appropriations used
Agency	Receives goods or equipment	Undelivered orders Expended authority	Assets Accounts payable Unexpended appropriations Appropriations used
Agency	Requests payment for goods or equipment	None	Accounts payable Disbursements in transit
Agency	Uses goods	None	Operating/program expenses Assets
Agency	Records depreciation	None	Operating/program expenses Accumulated depreciation

account, and Unexpended appropriations represents the increase in the equity of the agency.

After Congress makes the appropriation, the OMB apportions it to the department of which the agency is a part. As was mentioned earlier, OMB is an agency within the Executive Office of the President and has broad financial management powers. Among its responsibilities are the apportionment of appropriations among departments and the establishment of "reserves" in anticipation of cost savings, contingencies, and so on. Thus, the fact that an agency is appropriated a given amount of resources by Congress does not always mean that the agency will have that amount to spend.

If all of the agency's appropriation is apportioned by OMB to the department of which the agency is a part, the entry on the books of the agency is

Budgetary entry   Unapportioned authority—available   150,000
                              Apportionment   150,000
                            To record apportionment of resources by OMB.

Proprietary entry None

The amount of its apportionment that an agency can actually use is up to departmental management, which will allot a part of, or the entire, apportionment to the agency. Allotments are usually made each quarter. However, for simplicity, we will assume that the agency in this illustration receives its entire allotment at the beginning of the fiscal year. If departmental management allots $148,000 to the agency, the entry on the books of the agency is

Budgetary entry   Apportionment   148,000
                              Allotments—realized resources   148,000
                            To record allotment of resources to finance operations.

Proprietary entry None

The account Allotments—realized resources is particularly important. The balance of this account represents the amount of resources available for the agency to carry out its operations. If the agency has not expended or obligated its apportionment and its allotments by the end of the fiscal year, it must return these resources to the Treasury. All of the preceding entries are made as of October 1, the first day of the fiscal year. This record is made even if the appropriation bill has not been enacted by that date.

Operating Entries

When an agency receives notice of its allotment, it can begin (or continue) its fiscal operations. To enhance planning and fund control, many agencies use what is known as "commitment accounting." *Commitments* reserve budgetary authority from an allotment for the estimated amount of orders to be placed. They do not legally encumber the allotment. Rather, they formally disclose purchase requests before actual orders are placed. If requests are made by agency personnel to spend $100,000 of the agency's allotment on supplies and $12,000 on outside services, the entry to record the commitments is

Budgetary entry   Allotments—realized resources   112,000
                              Commitments   112,000
                            To record purchase requests placed for supplies and services.

Proprietary entry None

When a purchase order is issued, an *obligation* is created. Obligations are the federal equivalent of encumbrances used by state and local governmental units. They charge the allotment with the most recent estimate of the cost of items ordered and release any related prior commitments. If the agency places formal purchase orders for supplies whose cost is expected to be $95,000, the entry is

Budgetary entry	Commitments	95,000	
	Undelivered orders		95,000
	To obligate funds for supplies ordered but not delivered.		

Proprietary entry None

The debit in the budgetary entry represents the reduction of outstanding commitments. The credit represents the actual obligation and is similar to the Reserve for encumbrances account used by state and local governmental units.

When goods arrive or services are performed, the following entries are made. The budgetary entry removes the obligation in favor of the vendor. It also records the amount of the appropriation expended at this time. Assume that the actual cost of supplies ordered amounts to $94,000.

Budgetary entry	Undelivered orders	95,000	
	Expended authority		94,000
	Allotments—realized resources		1,000
	To record expenditure of portion of allotment.		

Notice that because the actual cost of the supplies is less than the amount estimated, the difference is returned to Allotments—realized resources, from where it was first taken.

Proprietary entries	Inventory of supplies	94,000	
	Accounts payable		94,000
	To record receipt of supplies.		
	Unexpended appropriations	94,000	
	Appropriations used		94,000
	To record financing source of supplies.		

The first proprietary entry records the receipt of supplies and the resulting liability. It is similar to the entry that would be made by a commercial organization. The second proprietary entry records the reduction in unexpended appropriations as a result of the acquisition of supplies.

In addition, when goods arrive or services are performed, a *disbursement schedule* is sent to the Treasury ordering it to pay the vendors. This does not reduce the agency's balance with the Treasury until checks are actually issued. As a result, the processing of payables is recorded in two steps. When the disbursement schedule is sent to the Treasury, the entry, assuming that the preceding purchase of supplies is the only transaction on the schedule, is

Budgetary entry None
Proprietary entry	Accounts payable	94,000	
	Disbursements in transit		94,000
	To record request to Treasury for check(s).		

When the agency is notified by the Treasury that the check(s) requested was issued, the entry on the agency's books is

Budgetary entry None
Proprietary entry	Disbursements in transit	94,000	
	Fund balance with Treasury		94,000
	To record issuance of check by the Treasury.		

Chapter 11 Federal Government Accounting and Reporting

If supplies costing $50,000 are used by the agency, their cost is recorded as an expense. No budgetary entry is necessary because the expending of the appropriation has already been recorded.

Budgetary entry None

Proprietary entry Operating/program expenses—supplies   50,000
                  Inventory of supplies   50,000
             To record supplies used.

Purchases of services are treated in the same manner as purchases of supplies except that, because they are used immediately upon receipt, an entry is needed to record the use of the appropriation. Entries recording the commitment and obligation are similar to those shown for the purchase of supplies; when services (expected to cost $12,000) are received, the entries are

Budgetary entry   Undelivered orders   12,000
                   Expended authority   12,000
             To record expenditure of portion of allotment.

Proprietary   Operating/program expenses—contractual services   12,000
entries   Accounts payable   12,000
             To record receipt of contractual services.

             Unexpended appropriations   12,000
                   Appropriations used   12,000
             To record financing source of outside services.

If a disbursement schedule is sent to the Treasury listing this expense, the entry is

Budgetary entry None

Proprietary entry Accounts payable   12,000
                   Disbursements in transit   12,000
             To record request to Treasury for check.

Items such as salaries, rent, and utilities are also recorded as expenses, just as they are in commercial organizations. However, entries recording the sources of financing and the expenditure of budgetary authority are also required. In many cases (as in this example) these items have not been previously obligated. Assume that the agency incurs the following costs:

Rent	$ 6,000
Utilities	2,000
Miscellaneous	1,500
Salaries and benefits	22,000
Total	$31,500

The salaries will be paid immediately, and liabilities will be set up for the other costs. The entries to record these costs are

Budgetary entry	Allotments—realized resources	31,500	
	Expended authority		31,500
	To record expenditure of portion of allotment.		
Proprietary entries	Operating/program expenses—rent	6,000	
	Operating/program expenses—utilities	2,000	
	Operating/program expenses—miscellaneous	1,500	
	Operating/program expenses—salaries and benefits	22,000	
	Accounts payable		9,500
	Fund balance with Treasury		22,000
	To record certain operating expenses.		
	Unexpended appropriations	31,500	
	Appropriations used		31,500
	To record financing source of operating expenses.		

Agencies of the federal government record the cost of certain fixed assets. They also record depreciation on these assets. The entries to record the purchase of fixed assets are similar to those shown previously to record the purchase of supplies.

Because depreciation is not chargeable against an appropriation, a budgetary entry is not necessary. However, proprietary entries are necessary to record the expense and increase in accumulated depreciation and to record the reduction of the book value of the assets. If depreciation of $8,000 is recorded, the entries are

Budgetary entry	None		
Proprietary entry	Operating/program expenses—depreciation	8,000	
	Accumulated depreciation		8,000
	To record depreciation on fixed assets.		

If year-end entries are made to record accrued, but unpaid, salaries and benefits of $3,500, the entries are

Budgetary entry	Allotments—realized resources	3,500	
	Expended authority		3,500
	To record expenditure of portion of allotment.		
Proprietary entries	Operating/program expenses—salaries and benefits	3,500	
	Accrued funded payroll		3,500
	To record accrual of year-end payroll.		
	Unexpended appropriations	3,500	
	Appropriations used		3,500
	To record financing source of operating expenses.		

Closing Entries

At the end of the year, most appropriations lapse unless they are classified as multi-year or no-year (permanent). To "lapse" means that any resources not spent or formally obligated by this time must be returned to the Treasury. These amounts cannot be carried forward to finance operations of the following year. Resources formally obligated by the end of the year, however, may be carried forward to meet given obligations. If these resources are not expended within 5 years, they must be returned to the Treasury.

After the transactions of the year are recorded and appropriate adjusting entries are prepared, budgetary entries are made to close accounts representing expired budget authority and Expended authority. Proprietary entries are made to close expense accounts and Appropriations used.

Budgetary entries	Apportionment	2,000	
	Allotments—realized resources	2,000	
	Commitments	5,000	
	Other appropriations realized		9,000
	To close Apportionment, Allotment, and Commitment accounts and to record expiration of budgetary authority.		
	Expended authority	141,000	
	Other appropriations realized		141,000
	To close Expended authority account.		
Proprietary entries	Appropriations used	141,000	
	Operating/program expenses—supplies		50,000
	Operating/program expenses—contractual services		12,000
	Operating/program expenses—salaries and benefits		25,500
	Operating/program expenses—rent		6,000
	Operating/program expenses—utilities		2,000
	Operating/program expenses—miscellaneous		1,500
	Operating/program expenses—depreciation		8,000
	Cumulative results of operations		36,000
	To close proprietary accounts.		

Notice that the differences between Appropriations used and the expense accounts is closed to Cumulative results of operations, an equity account.

FINANCIAL STATEMENTS USED BY FEDERAL AGENCIES

To meet the objectives of federal financial reporting, FASAB *Concepts Statement No. 2,* "Entity and Display," suggests that all federal reporting entities issue a financial report that would include the following basic financial statements:

1. Balance sheet
2. Statement of net costs
3. Statement of changes in net position
4. Statement of financing
5. Statement of budgetary resources

Federal reporting entities would also issue a statement of custodial activities, when appropriate, and a statement of program performance measures. (The latter is not considered a basic financial statement. It is still being developed while federal agencies implement the Government Performance and Results Act, which requires performance reporting.) Both of these statements are beyond the scope of this text.

To begin, a preclosing trial balance would be prepared as shown in Table 11-3. From it, the other basic statements are drawn. All the figures in the five basic statements illustrated in Tables 11-4 through 11-8 are based on the entries previously discussed. The figures assume that the agency's opening balance sheet showed furniture

Table 11-3
Preclosing Trial Balance

FEDERAL OVERSIGHT AGENCY
PRECLOSING TRIAL BALANCE
SEPTEMBER 30, 2004

BUDGETARY ACCOUNTS

Other appropriations realized	$150,000	
Unapportioned authority—available		$ —
Apportionment		2,000
Allotments—realized resources		2,000
Commitments		5,000
Undelivered orders		—
Expended authority		141,000
Totals	$150,000	$150,000

PROPRIETARY ACCOUNTS

Fund balance with Treasury	$ 34,000	
Inventory of supplies	44,000	
Furniture	65,000	
Accumulated depreciation—furniture		$ 30,000
Disbursements in transit		12,000
Accounts payable		9,500
Accrued funded payroll		3,500
Unexpended appropriations		9,000
Cumulative results of operations		43,000
Appropriations used		141,000
Operating/program expenses—salaries and benefits	25,500	
Operating/program expenses—contractual services	12,000	
Operating/program expenses—supplies	50,000	
Operating/program expenses—rent	6,000	
Operating/program expenses—utilities	2,000	
Operating/program expenses—depreciation	8,000	
Operating/program expenses—miscellaneous	1,500	
Totals	$248,000	$248,000

Table 11-4

Balance Sheet of Federal Agency

FEDERAL OVERSIGHT AGENCY
BALANCE SHEET
SEPTEMBER 30, 2004

Assets

Fund balance with U.S. Treasury		$ 34,000
Inventory of supplies		44,000
Furniture	$65,000	
Less: Accumulated depreciation	(30,000)	35,000
Total assets		$113,000

Liabilities and Net Position

Liabilities:

Disbursements in transit	12,000	
Accounts payable	9,500	
Accrued funded payroll	3,500	
Total liabilities		$ 25,000

Net Position:

Unexpended appropriations	9,000	
Cumulative results of operations	79,000	
Total net position		88,000
Total liabilities and net position		$113,000

Table 11-5

Statement of Net Costs of Federal Agency

FEDERAL OVERSIGHT AGENCY
STATEMENT OF NET COSTS
FOR FISCAL YEAR ENDED SEPTEMBER 30, 2004

Operating/program expenses:

Salaries and benefits	$ 25,500
Contractual services	12,000
Supplies	50,000
Rent	6,000
Utilities	2,000
Depreciation	8,000
Miscellaneous	1,500
Net cost of operations	$105,000

Table 11-6
Statement of Changes in Net Position

FEDERAL OVERSIGHT AGENCY STATEMENT OF CHANGES IN NET POSITION FOR FISCAL YEAR ENDED SEPTEMBER 30, 2004	
Net cost of operations	$105,000
Financing sources:	
Appropriations used	141,000
Other (not illustrated)	—
Net change in cumulative results of operations	36,000
Increase (decrease) in unexpended appropriations	9,000
Change in net position	45,000
Net position, beginning of period	43,000
Net position, end of period	$ 88,000

Table 11-7
Statement of Financing

FEDERAL OVERSIGHT AGENCY STATEMENT OF FINANCING FOR FISCAL YEAR ENDED SEPTEMBER 30, 2004	
Resources Used to Finance Activities:	
Obligations incurred	$141,000
Other (not illustrated)	—
Total resources used to finance activities	141,000
Resources that Do Not Fund Net Cost of Operations:	
Change in amount of goods and services ordered but not yet received (not illustrated)	—
Costs capitalized on the balance sheet (purchases of supplies)	(94,000)
Costs that Do Not Require Resources:	
Depreciation	8,000
Use of supplies	50,000
Financing Sources Yet to Be Provided (not illustrated):	—
Net Cost of Operations	$105,000

Table 11-8

Statement of Budgetary Resources

FEDERAL OVERSIGHT AGENCY STATEMENT OF BUDGETARY RESOURCES FOR FISCAL YEAR ENDED SEPTEMBER 30, 2004	
Budgetary Resources Made Available:	
Budget authority	$150,000
Other (not illustrated)	—
Total budgetary resources made available	$150,000
Status of Budgetary Resources:	
Obligations incurred	$141,000
Unobligated balances available for obligation	—
Unobligated balances—not available	9,000
Total, status of budgetary resources	$150,000
Outlays:	
Obligations incurred	$141,000
Less: obligated balance, end of period	25,000
Total outlays	$116,000

of $65,000, accumulated depreciation of $22,000, and cumulative results of operations of $43,000. These statements reflect the opening balance sheet and the entries shown or discussed in the previous pages.

Notice that the net position ($88,000) shown on the balance sheet (Table 11-4) is the difference between proprietary account assets and liabilities. Net position generally consists of the entity's unexpended appropriations and cumulative results of operations. Cumulative results of operations represents amounts accumulated by the entity over the years from its financing sources, less expenses and losses. Cumulative results of operations in this illustration ($79,000) equals the inventory of supplies and the net furniture account, because they required previous financing sources but have not yet become expenses.

The *statement of net costs* (Table 11-5) shows the costs of programs that are supported with taxes. Costs are presented on the accrual basis of accounting, so, for example, the illustration shows the amount of supplies used ($50,000) rather than the amount purchased ($94,000). If the entity earned revenues (e.g., through fees charged for services), they would be deducted in determining net cost of operations.

The statement of net costs presented here shows objects of account because those accounts were used in the illustrative journal entries. In practice, however, this financial statement would be presented on a program basis in a matrix format, showing program costs incurred by each suborganization in the department. Eventually, this statement will support the department's performance measurement statistics, showing how net costs relate to program outputs and outcomes.

The *statement of changes in net position* (Table 11-6) shows the factors that caused the entity's net position to increase or decrease during the period. Notice that, in this illustration, the net position increased from $43,000 to $88,000. The major cause of the $45,000 increase was the $36,000 net change in cumulative results of operations. This change occurred because appropriations used to finance operations (such as the inventory buildup) exceeded the net cost of operations.

The *statement of financing* (Table 11-7) explains how budgetary resources used in the period (obligations incurred) relates to net cost of operations. Obligations incurred consists of expended authority ($141,000) plus undelivered orders ($0). (Trace those numbers to the trial balance.) Three factors reconcile the budgetary resources used with the accrual-based net cost of operations: (1) resources that do not fund net cost of operations (e.g., amounts spent to acquire supplies and equipment that are capitalized on the balance sheet); (2) operating costs that do not require resources (e.g., depreciation of equipment previously acquired and use of supplies from inventory); and (3) financing not yet provided (e.g., for costs accrued but not yet financed). Another major reconciling item (no amount shown in this illustration) is the change in undelivered orders (goods and services ordered but not yet received).

The *statement of budgetary resources* (Table 11-8) contains three elements: (1) budgetary resources made available to the entity, (2) status of budgetary resources, and (3) outlays. Notice from the trial balance of the budgetary accounts in Table 11-3 that the left side shows the budgetary resources and the right side shows the status of the resources. You have already traced the obligations incurred (expended authority plus undelivered orders). Unobligated balances—not available ($9,000) are the balances in the other three accounts on the right side of the trial balance: Apportionments, Allotments—realized resources, and Commitments. They are not available for future obligation because they expire at year-end.

Outlays are payments to liquidate obligations. In this illustration, all obligations incurred were liquidated by Treasury disbursements, except for the $25,000 reported as liabilities on the balance sheet.

FEDERAL FINANCIAL REPORTING IN PRACTICE
Social Security Administration's Financial Statements

If you want to learn about the financial position of the Social Security Administration (SSA)—the federal agency that administers the social security system—start with the SSA's Performance and Accountability Report available at www.ssa.gov. The financial statements contained in that report give you only part of the story, because federal accounting standards do not require reporting the long-term obligation to Social Security beneficiaries on the face of the financial statements. For a more complete understanding of the long-term solvency of Social Security, you also need to read the supplementary information in either the SSA report or in the annual report of the federal government.

(continued)

SSA administers the combined Old Age and Survivors and Disability Insurance (OASDI) programs, commonly known as Social Security. These programs are financed through the two Social Security trust funds. The SSA also administers several smaller programs, which are financed by governmental appropriations. For the year ended September 30, 2000, the Social Security trust funds received tax revenues of $502 billion and interest of $62 billion. It made Social Security benefit payments of $404 billion and had operating expenses of $4 billion. The major asset of the trust funds at September 30, 2000, was in the form of investments: $1,007 billion in federal government I.O.U.s. These numbers come from SSA's program financial statements, shown here in highly condensed form (in billions of dollars) for the two Social Security programs combined.

BALANCE SHEET		STATEMENT OF CHANGES IN NET POSITION	
Assets:		Net Cost of Operations	$408
Investments	$1,007		
Other	65	Financing Sources:	
Total Assets	$1,065		
		Tax revenues	502
		Interest and other	62
		All other	(3)
Total liabilities	$ 81	Total financing sources	561
Net position	984	Change in net position	153
		Net position, beginning	832
Total liabilities and Net position	$1,065	Net position, ending	$1,065

Social Security is not financed like a pension system. Although most pension systems are advance-funded during the working life-time of the employees, Social Security is financed essentially on a "pay-as-you-go" basis. The amount paid into the trust fund during one's work life is used to pay the pension benefits of those already retired. Note that the ratio of trust fund assets to Social Security benefits in fiscal year 2000 was only about 2½ to 1 (net assets of $984 billion versus benefit payments of $404 billion). By contrast, the ratio of net assets to pension benefits in well-funded state and local government pension systems is 15 to 1 and greater.

In accordance with the FASAB's requirements, the financial reports of the federal government and the SSA contain extensive supplementary information about the financial status of Social Security. Following are some facts that can be obtained from reading that data. It is important to remember, however, that the status of Social Security is highly sensitive to economic and demographic factors, such as birthrates, mortality rates, and economic growth rates, making financial projections extremely complex.

• Starting in the year 2010, as the baby-boom generation reaches retirement age, benefit payments will increase rapidly. As a result, benefit payments will exceed tax revenues starting in about the year 2016.

• Starting in about the year 2025, making Social Security payments will require drawing down some of the assets of the trust fund. Unless changes are made in the Social Security structure, the assets of the Social Security fund will be fully exhausted in about the year 2038.

• The present value of future benefit payments to Social Security recipients who are already receiving benefits is

$4,020 billion—four times the amount of the trust fund net assets. (This ratio demonstrates clearly that the Social Security system is based on having current workers pay for the benefits of those who are retired.)

- In the year 1960, for every 100 workers, there were about 20 Social Security beneficiaries. By the year 2000, 100 workers covered only about 30 recipients. The number of Social Security recipients is expected to rise dramatically, however, so that by the year 2020, 100 workers will cover only 40 recipients. The worker-beneficiary ratio is expected to continue to worsen.

REVIEW QUESTIONS

Q11-1   Briefly outline the budgetary process used by the federal government.

Q11-2   What is the difference between an appropriation, an apportionment, and an allotment?

Q11-3   What are deferrals? Rescissions?

Q11-4   In federal government accounting, a commonly used term is *obligation*. What is an obligation and what is its equivalent in state and local governmental accounting?

Q11-5   What is the Anti-Deficiency Act?

Q11-6   What is "expended authority"?

Q11-7   What is the Office of Management and Budget?

Q11-8   If at the beginning of FY 2004, Congress appropriates $2,000,000 to the Bureau of Bird Management, can the director of this bureau immediately order $2,000,000 worth of telescopes? If not, why not?

Q11-9   List the various types of federal funds and the municipal fund type that comes closest to matching each.

Q11-10 Compare the use of accrual accounting within the funds used by the federal government and the funds used in municipal accounting.

Q11-11 How is depreciation handled in federal accounting and financial reporting? How does this treatment differ from that given to depreciation in municipal accounting and financial reporting?

Q11-12 What is the purpose of the Federal Accounting Standards Advisory Board?

Q11-13 List and discuss three standards promulgated by the Federal Accounting Standards Advisory Board.

Q11-14 List and briefly describe five financial statements used by federal agencies.

Q11-15 How does the financing of Social Security differ from the financing of most state and local government pension plans? If you think the financing of Social Security should be changed, how would you do it?

C11-1 Financial reporting of Social Security has been a controversial subject in the federal government. Current federal accounting standards require that liabilities be reported only for Social Security payments that are currently due and payable, but that no liability be reported for the unfunded actuarial present value of amounts due to retirees or their beneficiaries or the unfunded actuarial present value of benefits earned by other participants in the Social Security system. However, the standard does require various disclosures regarding the financial status of Social Security. Give arguments for and against the current financial reporting standard and state your opinion about the soundness of the standard.

C11-2 A federal agency receives a separate appropriation for supplies. A large number of purchase orders, marked "Rush," are processed in August. Because several clerks are on vacation, however, they are not recorded as obligations. The supplies are received in early September, before the end of the fiscal year. After matching the invoices with the receiving reports, the accountant finds the agency has insufficient funds to process many of the payments. On further inquiry, the accountant locates the batch of unrecorded purchase orders. He also finds that the supplies were used immediately upon receipt. He explains the problem to his immediate supervisor, who says, "Forget it. Just charge the bills to next year's appropriation." Explain the nature of the accountant's dilemma and discuss what you think he should do.

C11-3 Recently your manager expressed concern about a lack of planning and control in the placement of purchase orders by your agency. He felt that orders were placed on a first-come, first-served basis and when the allotment was used up there would be no money for the agency to continue operations vital to its mission. At an Association of Government Accountants meeting, a friend of yours employed by the National Finance Center mentioned that his agency uses commitment accounting to enhance planning and fund control. You become curious and call him for more information. Write a brief report explaining what commitment accounting is, what it does, how it works, and any negative factors that should be taken into consideration before implementing it.

EXERCISES

E11-1 (Multiple choice)
   1. What funds are used by federal agencies to account for receipts of resources from specific sources, earmarked by law for special purposes?
      a. Special Revenue Funds
      b. Special Funds
      c. Revolving Funds
      d. Deposit Funds

2. What funds are used to account for revenues derived primarily from user charges received from nonfederal sources?
   a. Special Funds
   b. Trust Funds
   c. Internal Service Funds
   d. Public Enterprise Funds
3. Who sets federal accounting standards?
   a. The Congress
   b. The Financial Accounting Standards Board (FASB)
   c. The Federal Accounting Standards Advisory Board (FASAB)
   d. The Governmental Accounting Standards Board (GASB)
4. What does an unliquidated obligation represent?
   a. Resources that cannot be spent for any purpose
   b. Resources that have already been disbursed
   c. Resources that must be returned to the Treasury
   d. Resources earmarked for a specific purpose
5. Who makes apportionments of appropriations to an agency?
   a. The Congress
   b. The Office of Management and Budget (OMB)
   c. The agency
   d. The department of which the agency is a part
6. What is the function of commitments?
   a. To legally encumber an allotment
   b. To formally disclose purchase requests before actual orders are placed
   c. To represent the authority to spend money for a particular project
   d. To represent legally enforceable promises to specific vendors
7. What account is used to show that an agency has requested payment by the Treasury to a certain vendor(s)?
   a. Fund balance with Treasury
   b. Accounts payable
   c. Disbursements in transit
   d. Processed invoices
8. Which of the following statements is *not* prepared by federal agencies?
   a. A balance sheet
   b. A statement of revenues, expenditures, and changes in fund balance
   c. A statement of net costs
   d. A statement of financing

E11-2 (Matching)
Match the items in the following right column with those in the left column.

_____ 1. An act of Congress that gives a department and/or agency authority to obligate the federal government to make disbursements for goods and services

_____ 2. Document sent to the Treasury ordering it to pay vendors and employees

a. Rescission
b. Obligation
c. Disbursement schedule
d. GASB
e. Appropriation

_____ 3. Sets standards for federal government accounting

_____ 4. Funds used to account for commercial-type operations of federal agencies

_____ 5. Action by which OMB distributes amounts available for obligation to agencies

_____ 6. Permanent cancelation of authority to spend

_____ 7. Reserves budgetary authority from an allotment for the estimated amount of orders to be placed

_____ 8. Federal equivalent of encumbrances used by state and local governmental units

_____ 9. Temporary withholding of authority to spend

f. Revolving funds
g. Apportionment
h. FASAB
i. Allotment
j. Trust funds
k. Deferral
l. Commitment

E11-3 (Use of the budgetary accounts)

In federal accounting the most frequently used budgetary accounts are the following:

> Other appropriations realized
> Unapportioned authority—available
> Apportionment
> Allotments—realized resources
> Commitments
> Undelivered orders
> Expended authority

Required: Determine which of these account titles best describes each of the following situations:

_____ 1. Spending authority allotted but not yet committed

_____ 2. Resources obligated but not yet expended

_____ 3. Spending authority apportioned, but not yet allotted, to an agency

_____ 4. The portion of an agency's appropriation that has been used

_____ 5. Spending authority appropriated, but not yet apportioned, by OMB

_____ 6. Spending authority reserved for the estimated amount of orders to be placed

E11-4 (Federal accounting cycle)

Geological Resources Agency is an agency within the Department of Resources. The following transactions took place in October, the first month of FY 2005.

1. The Agency was notified that its FY 2005 appropriation was $2,500,000.
2. OMB apportioned $600,000 to the Department of Resources for the first quarter of the fiscal year.
3. The Department of Resources' CEO allotted $200,000 to the Agency for its October operations.

4. Purchase orders placed during the month for materials and supplies were $150,000. (The Agency does not use commitment accounting.) The materials and supplies arrived during the month, along with an invoice for $148,000.
5. Materials costing $100,000 and supplies costing $20,000 were used during the month. In addition, salaries amounting to $48,000 were paid on the last day of the month.
6. A disbursement schedule was sent to the Treasury ordering payment for the materials and supplies.

Required: Make appropriate journal entries to record these transactions.

E11-5 (Monthly accounting cycle)
The Bureau of Canine Affairs was established as a part of the Department of Wildlife by an act of Congress and began operations on October 1. Following are the bureau's transactions for its first month of operation.
1. Congress passed and the president approved a $400,000 appropriation for the bureau.
2. The Office of Management and Budget apportioned $350,000 of this appropriation for use by the bureau.
3. The Secretary of Wildlife allotted $100,000 to the bureau for October operations.
4. Purchase orders for equipment and supplies estimated to cost $70,000 were requested.
5. An order was placed with the Margaret Company for equipment expected to cost $25,000.
6. An order was placed with the Erica Company for supplies expected to cost $40,000.
7. The supplies ordered from the Erica Company were received, along with an invoice for $40,000.
8. A disbursement schedule was sent to the Treasury requesting payment of Erica's invoice.
9. The Treasury informed the bureau that the Erica Company invoice had been paid.
10. Employees of the agency were paid $30,000.

Required: Prepare journal entries to record these transactions.

E11-6 (Journal entries—emphasis on budgetary entries and statements)
Central Think Tank (CTT) receives a separate appropriation from the Congress for the acquisition of advanced intelligence gathering components. The following is a summary of transactions affecting CTT's intelligence gathering component appropriation for the year ended September 30, 2005.
1. CTT received an appropriation of $400,000.
2. OMB apportioned to the agency the entire amount that Congress appropriated.
3. To keep control over its rate of expenditures, the agency used an allotment system. During the year, the entire apportionment was allotted.

4. Commitments placed during the year for intelligence gathering components totaled $390,000.
5. Purchase orders issued against the commitments totaled $375,000.
6. Of the intelligence gathering components ordered, $360,000 worth was delivered this year; the remaining $15,000 worth will be delivered next year. The delivered components were accepted and placed in inventory.
7. During the year, intelligence gathering components of $140,000 were consumed in operations.

Required: 1. Prepare journal entries to record these transactions. State which entries are budgetary and which are proprietary.
2. Prepare a statement of budgetary resources. Assume that all funds not obligated by year-end are not available for future spending. Also, assume that the Treasury paid the bill in transaction (6).

E11-7   (Journal entries—relationship of statements of net costs and financing)
Central Think Tank (CTT) receives a separate appropriation from the Congress for the purpose of testing advanced intelligence gathering components. The appropriation covers salaries, supplies, equipment, and rent and utilities. Assume that entries to record appropriations, apportionments, allotments, and obligations have been made. The following transactions affect the agency's net costs for the year ended September 30, 2005:
1. Salaries amounting to $425,000 were paid.
2. Salaries of $15,000 were unpaid at year-end and had to be accrued.
3. Rent and utilities bills amounting to $65,000 were received and payables set up.
4. Supplies of $35,000, acquired in previous years and placed in inventory, were consumed in testing the intelligence gathering components.
5. Depreciation on testing equipment acquired in previous years was $75,000.

Required: 1. Prepare journal entries to record these transactions and events. State which journal entries are budgetary and which are proprietary.
2. Prepare a statement of net costs for the year.
3. Prepare a statement of financing for the year. (*Hint:* Obligations incurred equal the expended authority in this problem.)
4. Explain the relationship of the statement of net costs and the statement of financing.

PROBLEMS

P11-1   (Accounting cycle for 1 month)
The Federal Commission on Governmental Performance was formed on October 1, 2004. This agency does not use commitment accounting. Among the transactions that took place that year were the following:
1. An appropriation of $6,500,000 was passed by the Congress and approved by the president. The resources are to be used for operating purposes.

2. The OMB notified the Department of Administration, of which the agency is a part, of the following schedule of apportionments:

First quarter	$2,000,000
Second quarter	2,000,000
Third quarter	1,500,000
Fourth quarter	1,000,000

3. The Department of Administration allotted $700,000 to the commission for its operations in October.

4. Purchase orders were placed in October for the following:

Materials	$150,000
Rent	50,000
Supplies	40,000

5. The payroll for the first 2 weeks of October amounted to $200,000. It was paid on October 15.

6. Invoices approved by the agency for payment were as follows:

XYZ Widget Co.—materials	$120,000
Scrooge Realty Co.—October rent	50,000
NOLA Office Supply—supplies	20,000
L & K Supply—supplies	10,000

The Treasury informed the commission that the invoices from XYZ Widget and L & K Supply were paid in full and one-half of the Scrooge Realty bill had been paid. Supplies and rent are expensed upon approval for payment. Materials are inventoried when purchased and expensed when used.

7. The payroll for the remainder of October was $200,000. It was paid on October 31.

8. Materials costing $85,000 were used during October.

Required:
1. Prepare appropriate journal entries for the transactions of October 2004.
2. Prepare appropriate monthly closing entries. (*Hint:* Do not close out the budgetary accounts.)
3. Prepare the following month-end statements:
   a. Balance sheet
   b. Statement of net costs
   c. Statement of changes in net position
   d. Statement of financing
   e. Statement of budgetary resources (*Note:* Consider amounts not yet allotted as balances not available.)

P11-2 (Accounting cycle for 1 month)

The Star Exploration Agency, a unit of the Space Department, was established by Congress to begin operations at the beginning of FY 2004. Following are the agency's transactions during October, its first month of operations:

October 1   Congress passed and the president approved a $1,000,000 appropriation for this agency for FY 2004.

October 1   Of the amount appropriated, $950,000 was apportioned by OMB.

October 1 The Space Department allotted the agency $100,000 to carry out its October operations.

October 1 Purchase requests were made for materials and telescopes, estimated to cost $88,000.

October 4 Purchase orders were placed for materials and telescopes, estimated to cost $85,000.

October 10 Materials and telescopes previously ordered were received, together with invoices for $88,000 ($70,000 for materials and $18,000 for telescopes). The agency accepted the items despite the higher price. All the items were considered as program expenses because they would be consumed within 1 year.

October 14 A disbursement schedule was sent to the Treasury, requesting that it pay invoices amounting to $60,000.

October 31 The Treasury informed the agency that it had paid invoices amounting to $55,000. It also told the agency it had issued checks in the amount of $10,000 for October salaries.

Required:
1. Prepare journal entries to record the events of October.
2. Post the journal entries.
3. Prepare a preclosing trial balance.
4. Prepare appropriate closing entries. (*Hint:* Do not close out the budgetary accounts.)
5. Prepare a postclosing trial balance.
6. Prepare the following month-end statements:
   a. Balance sheet
   b. Statement of net costs
   c. Statement of changes in net position
   d. Statement of budgetary resources (*Note:* Consider amounts not yet allotted as balances not available.)

P11-3 (Financial statements after initial month of operations)

The Bureau of Astrology, a unit of the Space Department, was established October 1, 2004. Its purpose is to provide astrological services to the general public. It is financed by an appropriation from Congress. Following are the transactions of the agency during October 2004.

October 1 The agency received a certified copy of an appropriation warrant from the Department of the Treasury for $900,000.

October 1 Of the amount available for apportionment, $850,000 was apportioned by the OMB.

October 1 Of the amount apportioned, $120,000 was allotted to the agency by the Space Department to finance its October operations.

October 1 Purchase requests were made for materials and equipment, estimated to cost $48,000.

October 3 Purchase orders were placed for materials, estimated to cost $30,000, and for equipment, estimated to cost $15,000.

October 15   All the equipment ordered October 3 was received with an invoice for $14,800.

October 16   Some of the materials ordered October 3 were received with an invoice for $22,000. The cost estimate used to record the obligation on October 3 was $22,500. The materials were recorded as inventory. A disbursement schedule for this invoice was sent to the Treasury.

October 27   The Treasury paid the $22,000 invoice for the materials.

October 31   Materials costing $18,000 were used by the agency during October.

October 31   Salaries for October totaled $50,000. The agency's FICA contributions were $2,000.

October 31   Depreciation of $1,200 was recorded by the agency.

Required: 1. Record these transactions in general journal form.
2. Post the journal entries to the general ledger and compute the account balances.
3. Prepare a preclosing trial balance.
4. Prepare month-end closing entries. (*Hint:* Because it is month-end, you need not close the budgetary accounts.)
5. Prepare a postclosing trial balance.
6. Prepare the following financial statements:
   a. Balance sheet
   b. Statement of net costs
   c. Statement of changes in net position
   d. Statement of financing
   e. Statement of budgetary resources (*Note:* Consider amounts not yet allotted as balances not available.)

Chapter

12

Accounting for Not-for-Profit Organizations

After completing this chapter, you should be able to:

➤ Describe the characteristics that distinguish not-for-profit organizations (NFPOs) from for-profit organizations and from governmental entities.

➤ Identify the types of organizations classified as voluntary health and welfare organizations (VHWOs) and as other not-for-profit organizations (ONPOs).

➤ Name and discuss the financial statements prepared by NFPOs.

➤ Discuss the characteristics of the three classifications of net assets reported on the statement of financial position.

➤ Describe the nature of donor-imposed restrictions and how they are reported.

➤ Discuss the nature of and the difference in accounting for unconditional and conditional promises to give.

➤ Discuss accounting for contributed services.

➤ Discuss accounting for collections of works of art, rare books, and similar assets.

➤ Discuss how investments are measured for financial reporting purposes.

➤ Discuss the journal entries needed when resources are released from restrictions.

➤ Prepare journal entries to record the activities of VHWOs and ONPOs.

➤ Describe the major types of funds used by NFPOs.

➤ Prepare financial statements for VHWOs and ONPOs.

DESCRIPTION OF NOT-FOR-PROFIT ORGANIZATIONS

The distinction between not-for-profit, for-profit, and governmental organizations is not always clear. Hospitals, for example, can be organized as not-for-profit, for-profit, or governmental entities, as can colleges and universities. Whether an organization is not-for-profit, for-profit, or governmental depends not on the activities they perform, but rather on such factors as the source of their revenues, their intention to earn profits, and their ownership.

Generally, the major characteristics that distinguish not-for-profit from for-profit entities are that not-for-profit entities (1) receive significant amounts of resources in the form of contributions from providers who do not expect to receive monetary benefits in return; (2) operate for purposes other than to earn profits; and (3) lack defined ownership interests that can be sold, transferred, or redeemed.[1] Not-for-profit entities possess these characteristics in varying degrees.

Entities such as states, cities, counties, and towns (including public corporations and "bodies corporate and politic") are clearly governmental, rather than not-for-profit. However, some entities created by charter under state corporation or not-for-profit corporation laws perform activities so closely related to what governments do that it may not be clear what kind of entity they are. As distinguished from not-for-profit entities, governmental entities have one or more of these characteristics: (1) their officers are either popularly elected or a controlling majority of their governing boards are appointed or approved by entities that are clearly governmental; (2) they may have the power to tax; (3) they may have the power to issue tax-exempt debt; or (4) they can be dissolved unilaterally by a government and their net assets assumed by it without compensation.[2]

Accounting Standards Jurisdiction

For accounting purposes, the distinctions among not-for-profit, for-profit, and governmental organizations are important. As discussed in Chapter 1, jurisdiction for setting accounting and financial reporting standards is shared by several organiza-

---

[1] FASB *Concepts Statement No. 4*, "Objectives of Financial Reporting by Nonbusiness Organizations," (Norwalk, CT: FASB, 1980), para. 6.

[2] *AICPA Audit and Accounting Guide—Health Care Organizations* (New York: AICPA, 2001), para. 1.02.c.

tions. The Governmental Accounting Standards Board (GASB) sets the standards that apply to state and local governmental entities, and the Financial Accounting Standards Board (FASB) sets the standards for for-profit and not-for-profit entities. The GASB's standards are not always the same as the FASB's standards.

Until recently, not-for-profit organizations followed the accounting principles and reporting practices recommended by "industry" audit and accounting guides issued by the American Institute of Certified Public Accountants (AICPA) for transactions not covered in FASB pronouncements. The FASB, which has final authority over accounting and financial reporting principles used by not-for-profit organizations, recognized that inconsistencies had developed over the years among the guides and that the guides were not always followed. To provide consistency in accounting and financial reporting among all not-for-profit organizations, it addressed the major issues in three documents effective in 1995 and 1996. They are FASB *Statement No. 116*, "Accounting for Contributions Received and Contributions Made," FASB *Statement No. 117*, "Financial Statements of Not-for-Profit Organizations," and FASB *Statement No. 124*, "Accounting for Certain Investments Held by Not-for-Profit Organizations." The AICPA updates its guides periodically to conform to the FASB requirements.

Examples of Not-for-Profit Entities

Four broad categories of not-for-profit organizations include voluntary health and welfare organizations, health care organizations, colleges and universities, and other not-for-profit organizations. This chapter covers basic accounting and financial reporting principles applicable to all four not-for-profit categories. When referring to principles that apply to all four, the acronym NFPOs will be used. However, the illustrations in this chapter relate primarily to *voluntary health and welfare organizations (VHWOs)* and *other not-for-profit organizations (ONPOs)*. Not-for-profit colleges and universities are discussed in an appendix to this chapter. Health care entities, as well as discussions of accounting and reporting matters unique to them, are covered in Chapter 13.

VHWOs are entities formed for the purpose of providing voluntary services for various segments of society, in the fields of health, welfare, and other social services. They obtain resources primarily from voluntary contributions from the general public. They may also receive grants and contracts from governmental agencies to provide specific social services. Because they are organized for the benefit of the public, they are exempt from many taxes. Well-known examples of VHWOs are the American Cancer Society, the Boy Scouts of America, the National Urban League, and the Young Women's Christian Association of the U.S.A. A VHWO may provide such services as family counseling, recreation and work for youth, and meals for the elderly, often at no charge or low charge to the service recipients.

The category ONPOs includes other types of not-for-profit organizations that are not VHWOs, colleges and universities, or health care entities. Some of them provide services similar to those provided by VHWOs, and charge user fees. Many of them, however, are organized to provide benefits to their members, and hence derive their revenues primarily from membership dues and fees. Examples of ONPOs include the following:

- Cemetery organizations
- Civic and community organizations
- Labor unions
- Nongovernmental libraries and museums
- Performing arts organizations
- Political parties
- Private foundations
- Private not-for-profit elementary and secondary schools
- Professional associations and trade associations
- Religious organizations
- Research and scientific organizations
- Social and country clubs

OVERVIEW OF INTERNAL ACCOUNTING VERSUS EXTERNAL REPORTING

Though not required to do so, NFPOs generally use fund accounting for internal accounting purposes. They normally have resources whose use is restricted by donors as well as resources whose use is unrestricted. Maintaining separate funds for resources whose use is restricted helps to ensure that the resources are used in accordance with donor restrictions.

External financial reporting for NFPOs, however, focuses on the organization as a whole, rather than on the individual funds. To prepare financial statements for these organizations, you must aggregate the resources of the individual funds and classify the net assets (that is, the difference between the assets and liabilities) as either unrestricted, temporarily restricted, or permanently restricted. (For example, if a donor contributes $1,000 with the stipulation that it must be used for a specific purpose, the resulting net asset is classified as temporarily restricted until it is used for that purpose.) All expenses are reported in the financial statements as if financed from unrestricted net assets. To facilitate financial reporting, accounting within the funds is designed to accommodate the three classifications of net assets, as well as the reclassifications among the three.

FASB *Statement No. 117* permits disclosure of fund-type data in external financial reports, provided the required organization-as-a-whole data are also reported.

To simplify the presentation in this chapter, we will first discuss the general principles of accounting and financial reporting for NFPOs, without reference to fund accounting. We will then discuss the funds generally used by NFPOs and illustrate accounting within the funds.

FINANCIAL STATEMENTS

Due to the intangible nature of many of the services offered by VHWOs and ONPOs, it is practically impossible to place a monetary value on them. Thus it is impossible to prepare financial statements that can measure the results of operations in the same sense as those used for business enterprises. The basic functions of the financial reporting process for VHWOs and ONPOs are therefore limited to (1) providing information on how the resources of the organization were obtained and used during the period, (2) presenting the resources available for future use at the end of the period, and (3) reporting on the organization's ability to continue to supply services in the future.

The financial statements of VHWOs and ONPOs are prepared for four general types of users of financial information: (1) the management group of the organization (e.g., directors and other individuals who are responsible for carrying out day-to-day operations of the organization); (2) government officials who have oversight responsibility for such organizations; (3) individuals who contribute resources to the organization; and (4) constituents of the organization.[3]

To provide financial information to this diverse group, three basic financial statements are prepared: (1) a statement of financial position, (2) a statement of activities, and (3) a statement of cash flows.[4] In addition, VHWOs are required to provide information in a separate financial statement about expenses by their natural classifications.[5] (Such information breaks down the broad functional categories, such as major programs and administrative support expenses, into components, such as salaries, supplies, and depreciation.)

Statement of Financial Position

A statement of financial position provides important information about the assets, liabilities, and net assets of the organization and their relationship to each other (see Table 12-1). This information, when used with information on other financial statements and related disclosures, helps interested parties to assess the organization's ability to continue operations and its liquidity, financial flexibility, ability to meet obligations, and future financing needs.[6] It focuses on the organization as a whole, as opposed to individual funds, and reports total assets, total liabilities, and net assets. Because of the emphasis on the organization as a whole, the term *net assets* is used rather than the term *fund balance.*

---

[3] An in-depth discussion of these objectives and users is included in *Statement of Financial Accounting Concepts No. 4*, "Objectives of Financial Reporting by Nonbusiness Organizations" (Norwalk, CT: FASB, 1980).

[4] FASB *Statement No. 117*, "Financial Statements of Not-for-Profit Organizations" (Norwalk, CT: FASB, 1994), para. 6.

[5] Ibid., para. 26.

[6] Ibid., para. 9.

Table 12-1

Statement of Financial Position

NOT-FOR-PROFIT ORGANIZATION
STATEMENT OF FINANCIAL POSITION
JUNE 30, 2005 AND 2004
(AMOUNTS IN THOUSANDS)

	2005	2004
Assets		
Cash and cash equivalents	$ 75	$ 460
Accounts and interest receivable	2,130	1,670
Inventories and prepaid expenses	610	1,000
Contributions receivable	3,025	2,700
Short-term investments	1,400	1,000
Assets restricted to investment in land, buildings, and equipment	5,210	4,560
Land, buildings, and equipment	61,700	63,590
Long-term investments	218,070	203,500
Total assets	$292,220	$278,480
Liabilities and Net Assets		
Liabilities:		
Accounts payable	$ 2,570	$ 1,050
Refundable advance		650
Grants payable	875	1,300
Notes payable		1,140
Annuity obligations	1,685	1,700
Long-term debt	5,500	6,500
Total liabilities	10,630	12,340
Net assets:		
Unrestricted	115,228	103,670
Temporarily restricted (Note B)	24,342	25,470
Permanently restricted (Note C)	142,020	137,000
Total net assets	281,590	266,140
Total liabilities and net assets	$292,220	$278,480

Accompanying notes to financial statements not included.
Source: Adapted from FASB *Statement No. 117,* "Financial Statements of Not-for-Profit Organizations" (Norwalk, CT: FASB, 1994), para. 156.

Under FASB *Statement No. 117*, net assets must be reported as permanently restricted, temporarily restricted, and unrestricted, depending on the existence and nature of *donor-imposed restrictions*. The existence and nature of these restrictions must be reported on the face of the statement of financial position or in the notes to the financial statements or both.

Permanently restricted net assets are ones "resulting

(a) from contributions and other inflows of assets whose use by the organization is limited by donor-imposed stipulations that neither expire by passage of time nor can be fulfilled or otherwise removed by actions of the organization,

(b) from other enhancements and diminishments subject to the same kinds of stipulations, and

(c) from reclassifications from (or to) other classes of net assets as a consequence of donor-imposed stipulations."[7]

Temporarily restricted net assets are ones "resulting

(a) from contributions and other inflows of assets whose use by the organization is limited by donor-imposed stipulations that either expire by passage of time or can be fulfilled and removed by actions of the organization pursuant to those stipulations,

(b) from other asset enhancements and diminishments subject to the same kinds of stipulations, and

(c) from reclassifications to (or from) other classes of net assets as a consequence of donor-imposed stipulations, their expiration by passage of time, or their fulfillment and removal by actions of the organization pursuant to those stipulations."[8]

Unrestricted net assets are ones that are neither permanently nor temporarily restricted. The only limits on their use are ones resulting from the nature of the organization and the environment in which it operates and contractual agreements with creditors, suppliers, and others entered into in the ordinary course of business. Information about such limits should be disclosed in the notes to the financial statements. Because they are not donor-imposed, those limitations do not meet the FASB's definition of restrictions.

FASB *Statement No. 117* does not specify or preclude any one format of financial statement. As a result, both vertical and horizontal formats are permitted, as are single and multicolumn and single and multipage formats. Notice that assets in Table 12-1 are presented in order of liquidity, whereas liabilities are presented in order of anticipated liquidation. The refundable advance shown on this statement refers to a donor's conditional promise to give, whose conditions have not been met. Net assets are presented by type and are disclosed in detail in the notes to the financial statements (not included in Table 12-1).

Statement of Activities

A statement of activities provides information "about

(a) the effects of transactions and other events and circumstances that change the amount and nature of net assets,

---

[7] Ibid., para. 168.
[8] Ibid.

(b) the relationships of those transactions and other events and circumstances to each other, and

(c) how the organization's resources are used in providing various programs or services."[9]

Like the statement of financial position, it focuses on the organization as a whole and reports the change in net assets, by level of restriction, for the period. Year-end net assets reported for each net asset classification in this statement should be the same as that reported in the statement of financial position.

A statement of activities can be prepared in a single column or a multicolumn format. The latter is preferred because it enables the reader to observe, at a glance, the effects of revenues, gains, other support, expenses, and losses on each category of net assets. It also enables the reader to observe, at a glance, the effect on net assets of changes in levels of restrictions. A statement of activities prepared in a multicolumn format is shown in Table 12-2.

Notice that the first caption in Table 12-2 is Revenues, Gains, and Other Support. What is the distinction among those terms from the perspective of an NFPO? *Revenues* are inflows from selling goods and providing services that constitute the organization's ongoing major or central operations, such as fees for providing child care services, college and university tuitions, and services to hospital patients. *Gains* are inflows from peripheral or incidental transactions, such as profits from selling securities or operating a parking lot in conjunction with an NFPO's major activities. It is possible that an activity considered by one organization to produce "revenues" will be considered by another organization to produce "gains." Donor contributions received by NFPOs may be considered revenues or gains, depending upon whether they are actively sought and frequently received, but *support* is a more descriptive term and is used throughout the FASB's literature on NFPOs.

Expenses incurred by NFPOs must be reported on the statement of activities or in the notes to the financial statements "by their functional classification such as major classes of program services and supporting activities."[10] When functional classifications are used, individual expenses are reported by function or program. Thus, such items as salaries and supplies used by each program are reported as expenses of those activities. Functional classifications are required because they enable the reader to determine the cost of various programs offered by the organization. The organization's programs should also be described in the notes to the financial statements.

For financial reporting purposes, a *program* is considered to be an activity that is directly related to the purpose(s) for which the organization was established. Although most organizations are involved in many programs, it is possible that an organization may have only one such activity.

Expenses identified as management and general are those associated with the overall direction and management of the organization, in addition to those associated with record keeping, the annual report, and so forth. Fund-raising and other supporting services are associated with the solicitation of money, materials, and the like, for which the individual or organization making the contribution receives no direct economic benefit.

---

[9] Ibid., para. 17.
[10] Ibid., para. 26.

Table 12-2

Statement of Activities

NOT-FOR-PROFIT ORGANIZATION
STATEMENT OF ACTIVITIES
YEAR ENDED JUNE 30, 2005
(AMOUNTS IN THOUSANDS)

	UNRESTRICTED	TEMPORARILY RESTRICTED	PERMANENTLY RESTRICTED	TOTAL
Revenues, Gains, and Other Support				
Contributions	$ 8,640	$ 8,110	$ 280	$ 17,030
Fees	5,400			5,400
Income on long-term investments (Note E)	5,600	2,580	120	8,300
Other investment income (Note E)	850			850
Net unrealized and realized gains on long-term investments (Note E)	8,228	2,952	4,620	15,800
Other	150			150
Net assets released from restrictions (Note D):				
Satisfaction of program restrictions	11,990	(11,990)		
Satisfaction of equipment acquisition restrictions	1,500	(1,500)		
Expiration of time restrictions	1,250	(1,250)		
Total revenues, gains, and other support	43,608	(1,098)	5,020	47,530
Expenses and Losses				
Program A	13,100			13,100
Program B	8,540			8,540
Program C	5,760			5,760
Management and general	2,420			2,420
Fund-raising	2,150			2,150
Total expenses (Note F)	31,970			31,970
Fire loss	80			80
Actuarial loss on annuity obligations		30		30
Total expenses and losses	32,050	30		32,080
Change in net assets	11,558	(1,128)	5,020	15,450
Net assets at beginning of year	103,670	25,470	137,000	266,140
Net assets at end of year	$115,228	$24,342	$142,020	$281,590

Accompanying notes to financial statements not included.

Source: Adapted from FASB *Statement No. 117,* "Financial Statements of Not-for-Profit Organizations" (Norwalk, CT: FASB, 1994), para. 159.

They include such items as printing, personnel, the cost of maintaining a mailing list, and the cost of any gifts that are sent to prospective contributors. The distinction between program expenses and other expenses is useful to those interested in knowing the percentage of total expenses that an NFPO devotes to program activities.

In the statement of activities, notice that revenues, gains, and other support are reported as increases in either unrestricted or restricted assets, depending on whether the use of assets is limited by donor-imposed restrictions. However, all expenses are reported as decreases in unrestricted net assets, even if they were financed with restricted resources. This is accomplished by means of journal entries that reduce restricted assets and increase unrestricted assets, as resources are released from restrictions through their satisfaction (such as incurring program expenses) or the expiration of time. (See the activity reported under Net assets released from restrictions in Table 12-2.)

Statement of Functional Expenses

All VHWOs are required to prepare both a statement of activities and a statement of functional expenses. The statement of functional expenses is presented in matrix format. For each program or function, this statement identifies the expenses by natural or object classification (e.g., salaries, grants to other organizations, supplies, depreciation, and occupancy expense). A statement of functional expenses is shown in Table 12-3. Notice how the expenses by natural classification are associated with each of the programs and functions shown in the statement of activities. Although

Table 12-3
Statement of Functional Expenses

NOT-FOR-PROFIT ORGANIZATION
STATEMENT OF FUNCTIONAL EXPENSES
YEAR ENDED JUNE 30, 2005
(AMOUNTS IN THOUSANDS)

	TOTAL	A	B	C	MANAGEMENT AND GENERAL	FUND-RAISING
Salaries, wages, and benefits	$15,115	$ 7,400	$3,900	$1,725	$1,130	$ 960
Grants to other organizations	4,750	2,075	750	1,925		
Supplies and travel	3,155	865	1,000	490	240	560
Services and professional fees	2,840	160	1,490	600	200	390
Office and occupancy	2,528	1,160	600	450	218	100
Depreciation	3,200	1,440	800	570	250	140
Interest	382				382	
Total expenses	$31,970	$13,100	$8,540	$5,760	$2,420	$2,150

Source: Adapted from FASB Statement No. 117, "Financial Statements of Not-for-Profit Organizations" (Norwalk, CT: FASB, 1994), para. 161.

they are not required to prepare a statement of functional expenses, many ONPOs elect to do so because the statement is useful to managers and others concerned with the way resources are spent.

Statement of Cash Flows

A statement of cash flows provides the user of the financial statements with information on cash receipts and cash payments of the organization during the same period as the statement of activities. The statement is organized so that the effect of operating, investing, and financing activities on cash flows is clearly shown. Such a statement is shown in Table 12-4.

CONTRIBUTIONS

General Rule for Contributions Other Than Services and Collections

Not-for-profit organizations may receive contributions in many forms, such as cash, pledges of cash, investments, materials, supplies, facilities, use of facilities or utilities, personal services, and collections. The general rule for contributions other than services and collections is that they must be

    (a) reported as revenues or gains in the period received,

    (b) reported as assets, decreases of liabilities, or expenses, depending on the form the benefits take,

    (c) measured at the fair value of the contribution received, and

    (d) reported as either restricted support or unrestricted support.[11]

For example, if an NFPO receives free use of a building that normally leases for $15 per square foot, the NFPO would recognize the fair value of the contribution ($15 per square foot) as a revenue and as an expense. If a utility provides free electricity, the NFPO would also recognize the fair value of the electricity as a revenue and as an expense. If a pharmaceutical company provides free drugs, the NFPO would recognize the fair value of the drugs as a revenue and as an asset. All three are forms of contributed resources.

Contributions may be received with or without donor-imposed restrictions. Unrestricted contributions should be reported on the statement of activities as unrestricted revenues or gains (unrestricted support), which increase unrestricted net assets. Expenses incurred from unrestricted net assets are reported as decreases in those assets.

Contributions Received with Donor-Imposed Restrictions

A donor-imposed restriction limits the use of contributed assets beyond the broad limits resulting from the nature of the organization and the purposes for which it was organized. For example, a contributor to a performing arts entity may stipulate that

---

[11] FASB *Statement No. 116,* para. 8.

Table 12-4

Statement of Cash Flows

Cash flows from operating activities:	
Change in net assets	$15,450
Adjustments to reconcile change in net assets to net cash used by operating activities:	
Depreciation	3,200
Fire loss	80
Actuarial loss on annuity obligations	30
Increase in accounts and interest receivable	(460)
Decrease in inventories and prepaid expenses	390
Increase in contributions receivable	(325)
Increase in accounts payable	1,520
Decrease in refundable advance	(650)
Decrease in grants payable	(425)
Contributions restricted for long-term investment	(2,740)
Interest and dividends restricted for long-term investment	(300)
Net unrealized and realized gains on long-term investment	(15,800)
Net cash used by operating activities	(30)
Cash flows from investing activities:	
Insurance proceeds from fire loss on building	250
Purchase of equipment	(1,500)
Proceeds from sale of investments	76,100
Purchase of investments	(74,900)
Net cash used by investing activities	(50)
Cash flows from financing activities	
Proceeds from contributions restricted for:	
Investment in endowment	200
Investment in term endowment	70
Investment in plant	1,210
Investment subject to annuity agreements	200
	1,680
Other financing activities:	
Interest and dividends restricted for reinvestment	300
Payments of annuity obligations	(145)
Payments on notes payable	(1,140)
Payments on long-term debt	(1,000)
	(1,985)
Net cash used by financing activities	(305)
Net decrease in cash and cash equivalents	(385)
Cash and cash equivalents at beginning of year	460
Cash and cash equivalents at end of year	$ 75

Accompanying notes to financial statements not included.
Source: Adapted from FASB *Statement No. 117*, "Financial Statements of Not-for-Profit Organizations" (Norwalk, CT: FASB, 1994), para. 160.

his or her contribution be used only for a clarinet and flute duet. This type of restriction, a temporary restriction, is satisfied by the action of the performing arts entity in giving the concert. Another donor may require that his or her contribution to the performing arts entity be maintained permanently, with the income from the contribution used to train future ballet artists. The permanent restriction can never be removed by action of the entity, but the income from the contribution is classified as temporarily restricted until it is used for the training program.

Contributions received with donor-imposed restrictions must be reported as *restricted support*. These contributions will increase either temporarily restricted or permanently restricted net assets. As an option, however, in the case of donor-restricted contributions whose restrictions are met in the same reporting period the contributions are received, the contribution may be reported as unrestricted support, provided the entity reports similar types of contributions that way consistently from one period to another.

An NFPO must recognize the expiration of a donor-restricted contribution in the period that the restriction expires. This expiration occurs when the stipulated purpose for which the contribution was made has been fulfilled, when the stipulated time period has elapsed, or both. FASB *Statement No. 117* requires that all expenses be reported in the statement of activities as decreases in unrestricted net assets, even though the original contribution that financed the expense was reported as an increase in temporarily or permanently restricted net assets. Through journal entries, restricted net assets are reclassified as unrestricted net assets.

Unconditional and Conditional Promises to Give

Unconditional Promises

A *promise to give* (sometimes called a pledge or a charitable subscription) is a written or oral agreement to contribute cash or other assets to another entity. The FASB concluded that *unconditional promises to give*—those that depend only on the passage of time or demand by the receiver of the promise—meet the definition of assets because promise makers generally feel bound to honor them. Therefore, unconditional promises to give should be recognized in the financial statements as receivables and as revenues or gains when the promises are received. An appropriate allowance for uncollectible promises should be established.

Receipts of unconditional promises to give, whose payments are due in *future periods,* must be reported as restricted support, generally as temporarily restricted assets. However, a promise should be reported as unrestricted if "explicit donor stipulations or circumstances surrounding the receipt of a promise make clear that the donor intended it to be used to support activities of the current period."[12] When reporting pledges, the following must be disclosed:

(a) Amounts of promises receivable within one year, from one to five years, and in more than five years, and

(b) The allowance for uncollectible pledges.[13]

---

[12] Ibid., para. 15.
[13] Ibid., para. 24.

Conditional Promises

Conditional promises to give are promises that bind the promisor on the occurrence of a specified future and uncertain event. For example, a donor promises to give $15,000 in cash to an NFPO provided the NFPO raises an equal amount from other contributors by a specific date. As another example, a donor promises to contribute $20,000 as soon as the NFPO establishes a daycare center and starts admitting children.

Conditional promises to give are not recognized as receivables and as revenues (or gains) until the conditions on which they depend are substantially met. At that point, the conditional promise becomes unconditional and should be recognized as a receivable and a revenue. When an NFPO receives conditional promises to give, it must disclose the total amount promised, and describe each group of promises having similar characteristics, such as amounts of promises conditioned on completing a new building and raising matching gifts by a specified date.

If a donor were to actually transfer assets to an NFPO simultaneously with a conditional promise, the NFPO could not recognize revenues. Instead, the receipt of the assets would be accounted for as a refundable advance (deferred revenue) until the conditions were substantially met.

Notice how the accounting treatment of *conditions* differs from that regarding *restrictions*. Conditions may involve significant uncertainty, including events outside the organization's control. Recognizing assets before the uncertainty is sufficiently resolved may cause the information to be unreliable. Therefore, judgment must be exercised in determining when a condition is "substantially met." Suppose, for example, a donor promised a gift of $50,000 in the year 2004 on condition that the entity raises matching gifts totaling $50,000. The NFPO wants to recognize the gift in its year 2004 financial statements. Would the condition be "substantially met" if the NFPO raised $25,000 by year-end and the matching gifts were dwindling? Not likely. Would the condition be "substantially met" if it had raised $45,000 by year-end and matching gifts were being received at a strong pace? Perhaps.

If a promise is received with ambiguous donor stipulations, the promise should be presumed to be conditional until the ambiguities are resolved. On the other hand, if a donor attaches a condition to a promise and the possibility that the condition will not be met is remote, the promise should be considered to be unconditional. (An example of the latter is an administrative requirement to file a routine annual report.)

Contributed Services

The rule regarding contributed services is somewhat different from the general rule regarding contributions. An NFPO must record the fair value of contributed services, provided the services received (1) create or enhance nonfinancial assets or (2) require specialized skills, *and* are provided by individuals who possess those skills, *and* would typically need to be purchased if the services were not donated. Services requiring "specialized skills" are those provided by professionals and craftspeople, such as accountants, architects, carpenters, doctors, electricians, lawyers, nurses, plumbers, and teachers.[14] When these criteria are met, a contribu-

---

[14] Ibid., para. 9.

tion should be recorded for the fair value of the services donated, along with an off-setting expense.

The rule regarding contributed services is intended to be restrictive, so that contributed services that do not meet the enumerated criteria may not be recognized. For example, assume a lawyer donates five hours of time to a performing arts center. She spends three hours preparing contracts with artists and two hours selling tickets at the box office. The fair value of the time she spends drawing up contracts should be recognized as a contribution and as an expense. The two hours she spends selling tickets should not be recognized, however, because the work—even though needed by the center—does not require specialized skills.

An NFPO that receives contributed services must describe, in notes to its financial statements, the nature and extent of services received, programs or activities for which they were used, and the amount recognized as revenues. If practicable, the fair value of contributed services received but not recognized should also be disclosed. For example, a note to the financial statements of a performing arts center might say: "Donated service revenues and program expenses include the fair value of professional services contributed by performing artists. During the year, performing artists contributed services valued at $60,000 for the free summer concert series."

Contributions to Collections

A museum in dire financial straits is about to receive a gift of a painting, valued at $1 million, that it plans to display. The museum thinks it would be misleading to report the contribution as a revenue and as an asset because other potential donors, noting the revenue, might conclude that the museum does not need financial support for day-to-day operating purposes. Must the museum recognize the contribution as a revenue and as an asset?

The FASB resolved this controversial issue by giving NFPOs the option of not recognizing donated works of art, historical artifacts, rare books, and similar assets as revenues or gains and assets, *provided* the donated items are added to collections and the collections meet all of the following conditions:

(a) Are held for public exhibition, education, or research in furtherance of public service rather than financial gain,

(b) Are protected, kept unencumbered, cared for, and preserved, and

(c) Are subject to an organizational policy that requires the proceeds from sales of collection items to be used to acquire other items for collections."[15]

Thus, NFPOs, such as museums, art galleries, and similar entities that have collections meeting all three of these conditions, have a choice when new items are added. If they choose to capitalize their collections, they must recognize new items as revenues or gains. If they choose not to capitalize their collections, their revenues or gains cannot be recognized. Furthermore, they must follow a consistent policy. They cannot capitalize selected collections or items within a collection.

---

[15] Ibid., para. 11.

City Harvest, Inc., a not-for-profit corporation, rescues and distributes surplus and donated food to social service agencies, soup kitchens, homeless shelters, and other agencies that provide free meals to the hungry and homeless in New York City. Its statement of activities for the year ended June 30, 2001, shows total public support and revenue of $17.2 million, which includes contributions of donated food ($8.7 million) as well as cash and in-kind contributions from corporations, foundations, and individuals ($6.7 million). Its expenses were $16.5 million—$13.5 million for food distribution and operations and $3.0 million for supporting services. Its largest item of expense (which can be found in its statement of functional expenses) was Food rescued—the same $8.7 million of donated food included in public support.

As discussed previously in the text, contributions received by NFPOs need to be reported as revenues or gains and measured at the fair value of the contribution received.

The notes to the financial statements describe how City Harvest measured the fair value of the food donated by restaurants, corporations, and individuals. These organizations contributed 12.6 million pounds of perishable and packaged food in fiscal year 2001. City Harvest valued the food at 69 cents a pound, a number derived from the average cost to feed an individual under the U.S. Department of Agriculture "thrifty food plan." The notes to the statements also point out that City Harvest also received donations of prepared food, but did not report it on the face of the financial statements because it did not have a determinable market value.

The notes also state that City Harvest's reported public support and expenses include the fair value of donated legal services ($84,000) and advertising services ($145,000), but the services of a substantial number of unpaid volunteers were not recognized in the financial statements because those services did not meet the FASB's recognition criteria.

Source: City Harvest, Inc. (New York, NY) Financial statements, June 30, 2001 and 2000.

On the other hand, contributions of works of art, historical treasures, and similar items that are *not* part of a collection must be recognized as revenues or gains and assets when received. For example, suppose an NFPO holds a collection of art that meets all three criteria for triggering the choice to either capitalize or not capitalize the collection. The NFPO chooses not to capitalize. However, it receives a donation of three works of art that it does not intend to add to its collection. In that situation, the NFPO must recognize the donation as revenues or gains and assets when the three works of art are received.

If an organization does not capitalize its collections, it must report the following information "on the face of its statement of activities, separately from revenues, expenses, gains, and losses:

(a) Costs of collection items purchased as a decrease in the appropriate class of net assets

(b) Proceeds from sale of collection items as an increase in the appropriate class of net assets

(c) Proceeds from insurance recoveries of lost or destroyed collection items as an increase in the appropriate class of net assets."[16]

It must also describe its collections, "including their relative significance, and its accounting and stewardship policies for collections."[17] If items in the collection are deaccessed (removed from the collection) during the period, the organization must also "(a) describe the items given away, damaged, destroyed, lost, or otherwise deaccessed during the period or (b) disclose their fair value."[18] In addition, these disclosures must be referred to in a line item shown on the face of the statement of financial position.

Accounting for Reclassifications

As previously noted, reporting net assets as either unrestricted, temporarily restricted, or permanently restricted requires journal entries reclassifying net assets from one classification to another as resources are released from restrictions.

Reclassifications have an effect similar to interfund transfers in governmental accounting. They increase net assets of one net asset class and correspondingly reduce net assets of another. As shown in the statement of activities (Table 12-2), reclassification transactions are reported as "revenues, gains, and other support" under the caption "net assets released from restrictions." The journal entry to record these transactions should be prepared in sufficient detail to enable reporting the cause of the reclassification, such as satisfaction of program restrictions or expiration of time restrictions.

To illustrate, assume an individual donated $5,000 in 2004, to be used only for a specific purpose. The gift is used in 2005. As discussed in the section "Contributions Received with Donor-Imposed Restrictions," the contribution would be reported initially as temporarily restricted net assets. When the gift is used as intended, the purpose restriction has been satisfied. At that point, the resources are released from the restrictions and become unrestricted; at the same time, the expense is reported as a reduction of unrestricted net assets.

Financial reporting of the reclassification transactions is shown in the statement of activities illustrated in Table 12-2 on page 505. The debit to Reclassifications out is reported as a negative amount under Net assets released from restrictions, in the temporarily restricted column. The credit to Reclassifications in is reported as a positive amount—alongside the negative amount—under Net assets released from restrictions in the unrestricted column.

From an organization-wide perspective, the reclassifications cancel each other. Also, viewed organization-wide, the revenue is recognized at the time of the donation

---
[16] Ibid., para. 26.
[17] Ibid., para. 27.
[18] Ibid.

and the expense is recognized when incurred. However, when viewed from the perspective of changes in unrestricted net assets, the inflow (reported by means of the reclassification) and the outflow (the expense) occur in the same accounting period.

ILLUSTRATIONS OF CONTRIBUTIONS TRANSACTIONS

An NFPO operates a clinic that provides services to substance abusers. It has the following transactions.

1. It receives cash donations of $15,000 that may be used for any purpose. Also, a pharmaceutical company donates medical supplies having a fair market value of $10,000.

Cash	15,000	
Inventory—medical supplies	10,000	
Unrestricted support—contributions		15,000
Unrestricted support—supplies		10,000
To record unrestricted contributions.		

2. It receives two cash donations. One is for $5,000 from a donor who stipulates that it may be used only for research into a new method for treating substance abusers. The other is for $25,000 from a donor who stipulates the gift must be maintained in perpetuity, with the income from the gift to be used for any purpose.

Cash	30,000	
Temporarily restricted support—contributions		5,000
Permanently restricted support—contributions		25,000
To record temporarily and permanently restricted gifts.		

3. In response to its annual fund-raising campaign, the NFPO receives pledges of $50,000 to be used during the current period for any purpose. Based on past experience, the NFPO expects to collect 90 percent of the pledges. Later in the year, the NFPO receives $10,000 of promises to give cash during the following year, all of which it expects to collect.

Contributions receivable	50,000	
Allowance for uncollectible contributions		5,000
Unrestricted support—contributions		45,000
To record receipt of pledges to give cash this year,		
less provision for estimated uncollectible pledges.		

Contributions receivable	10,000	
Temporarily restricted support—contributions		10,000
To record receipt of pledges to give cash next year.		

4. A donor promises to contribute $50,000 to the NFPO's new building fund, provided the NFPO raises an equal amount from other donors.

No entry should be made until the donor's conditional promise is substantially met.

5. A psychiatrist donates 10 hours counseling patients. She also spends 5 hours serving food at lunchtime. The NFPO would have purchased both services if the psychiatrist had not donated her time. She normally gets $150 an hour when counseling her patients.

Expenses—counseling services	1,500	
Unrestricted support—services		1,500

    To record donation of professional services. (*Note:* No entry should be made for serving meals because it requires no "specialized skills.")

6. Research is conducted into a new method for treating substance abusers, using the gift made in transaction (2).

Expenses—special research programs	5,000	
Cash		5,000
Temporarily restricted asset reclassifications out—		
satisfaction of program restrictions	5,000	
Unrestricted asset reclassifications in—		
satisfaction of program restrictions		5,000

    To record disbursement of cash for research program and satisfaction of program restrictions.

OTHER ACCOUNTING MATTERS

Investments: Valuation, Income, Gains, and Losses

As a general rule, investments held by NFPOs in equity securities that have readily determinable fair values, and all investments in debt securities, must be reported at fair value (market price) in the statement of financial position. Thus, although investments are initially recorded at cost (if purchased directly by the NFPO) and at fair value (if received by the NFPO through a contribution), the carrying amount of the investments will usually need to be adjusted so that fair values are reported in the financial statements.

Because investments must be reported at fair value, unrealized gains and losses resulting from changes in the market price of securities held need to be recognized in the statement of activities. If unrealized gains and losses have been recognized in previous reporting periods on investments sold in the current period, the amount of gain or loss reported in the current period should exclude the amount previously reported in the statement of activities.

To illustrate, assume an NFPO purchased 100 shares of an equity security for $5,000 on March 1, 2004. On December 31, 2004, the date of its financial statements, the security had a market value of $5,600. On April 15, 2005, it sold the security for $5,800. In its 2004 financial statements, the NFPO should report a gain of $600 and value the security at $5,600. In its 2005 financial statements, the NFPO should report a gain of $200. The $200 gain may be reported either at the net amount of $200 or by its components; that is, as a realized gain of $800, less the previously recognized unrealized gain of $600. If the NFPO chooses to report both unrealized and realized gains and losses in a single account, it would credit both realized and unrealized gains in this illustration to the account "net unrealized and realized investment gains and losses." If it chooses the latter method, the journal entries would be as follows:[19]

Investment valuation account	600	
Change in net unrealized gains and losses on investments		600
To record unrealized gain in the year 2004.		
Cash	5,800	
Realized gain on investments		800
Investments		5,000
Change in net unrealized gains and losses on investments	600	
Investment valuation account		600
To record realized gain and reverse unrealized gain in the year 2005.		

Investment income, such as interest and dividends, should be recognized as the income is earned. Such income should be reported on the statement of activities as increases in unrestricted net assets, unless use of the income is limited by donor-imposed restrictions. For example, a donor may stipulate that investment income from a permanently restricted contribution be used to support a particular program. In that case, the investment income would be reported as an increase in temporarily restricted net assets. As the income is used in support of the program, a reclassification from temporarily restricted to unrestricted net assets would be necessary.

Depreciation

NFPOs must recognize the cost of using up the service potential of their long-lived tangible assets, which includes property acquired by the NFPO through both exchange transactions and through donation. Depreciation expense is reported as a decrease in unrestricted net assets. If the asset being depreciated is reported as temporarily restricted, because of donor-imposed restrictions on its use, reclassifications from temporarily restricted to unrestricted must be recorded. Disclosures regarding long-lived assets and depreciation methods are also required.

Separate rules apply to works of art, historical treasures, and collections. The circumstances under which NFPOs are permitted to not capitalize these assets were discussed previously. But suppose NFPOs elect to capitalize works of art, historical treasures, and collections. If they capitalize them, must they depreciate them? The answer is not necessarily. Consistent with practice regarding land used as a building site, depreciation need not be recognized on individual works of art or historical treasures "whose economic benefit or service potential is used up so slowly that their estimated useful lives are extraordinarily long."[20] A work of art or historical treasure is deemed to have this characteristic only if verifiable evidence indicates that the NFPO has the technological and financial capacity to preserve the asset.

---

[19] *AICPA Audit and Accounting Guide—Health Care Organizations* (New York: AICPA, 2001), Sect. 4.19.
[20] FASB *Statement No. 93*, "Recognition of Depreciation by Not-for-Profit Organizations," para. 6.

Subscription and Membership Income

For many ONPOs, subscription and membership income are the primary basis of support for their operating activities. In general, these items are recognized as revenue in the period or periods in which they can be used to pay for services rendered by the organization. For example, membership dues that are collected in September of each year, but apply to calendar-year memberships, are recognized as revenue during the period in which the individual receives membership privileges—in this case the calendar year.

Items such as nonrefundable initiation fees and life membership fees can cause some measurement problems. Like membership dues, the key factor for revenue recognition lies in the period over which these fees pay for services rendered by the organization. Thus, these items should be recognized as revenue on a basis that reflects the services available to the members during this period of time. If, in fact, the items are not related to services rendered but are actually contributions, they should be recognized as revenue in the period or periods in which the organization is entitled to them.

Revenues and Receivables from Exchange Transactions

Many NFPOs obtain revenues from exchange-type transactions, for example, when they charge fees for services such as day care for children, care for the elderly, or care for the infirm. NFPO accounting for exchange revenues and receivables is similar to that used by for-profit entities. Revenues from exchange transactions should be recognized using accrual accounting principles. Estimated bad debts should be recognized as an expense, and accounts receivable should be reported net of allowances for uncollectible amounts.

Fund-Raising Activities

Not-for-profit entities conduct fund-raising activities to induce potential donors to contribute resources to the entity. Costs that relate solely to fund-raising are reported separately as fund-raising expenses. Sometimes, however, an NFPO may incur joint costs; that is, costs that relate to both fund-raising and a program activity. Joint costs may occur, for example, when an NFPO distributes a brochure containing both information about the entity's programs and an appeal for funds.

As a general rule, if the joint activity criteria of purpose, audience, and content are met, the joint costs should be allocated between fund-raising and the program or function. If any of the three criteria are not met, however, all costs of the joint activity should be reported as fund-raising.

The *purpose* and *content* criteria of the rule are met if the solicitation for support also calls on the audience to take specific action that will help accomplish the organization's mission. For example, if an organization's mission is to improve individuals' physical health, sending a brochure that urges the audience to stop smoking and that suggests specific methods that may be used to stop smoking is an activity that helps accomplish the mission. The presumption is that the *audience* criterion is not met if the audience includes prior donors or was selected based on the likelihood of their contributing to the organization, but this presumption can be overcome if the audience was also selected for other reasons, such as a need to take the specific action called for in the brochure.

For example, suppose the mission of an NFPO is to prevent drug abuse. It mails information to the parents of junior high school students explaining the dangers of drug abuse, describing methods for counseling children about drug abuse, and showing how the parents can detect drug abuse. The mailing also appeals for contributions. In this illustration, the nature of the action requested and the audience contacted are such that the three criteria are met. Therefore, the cost of the mailing should be allocated between fund-raising and program expenses, using appropriate cost-accounting techniques.[21]

FUNDS USED

Although not required to do so for financial reporting purposes, many NFPOs use fund accounting for internal record-keeping purposes. When using fund accounting, it may be necessary for the organization to divide the fund balances into more than one net asset class. NFPOs generally use the following types of funds:

1. *Unrestricted Current Fund* (also called Unrestricted Operating Fund, General Fund, or Current Unrestricted Fund). Unrestricted Current Funds are used to account for resources over which governing boards have discretionary control, so that the resources are available for the general operations of the organization. Unrestricted Current Funds obtain resources primarily from unrestricted donor contributions; exchange transactions with members, clients, students, customers and others; and unrestricted investment income. Unrestricted Current Fund resources that are designated by a governing board for a specific purpose either remain in that fund or are transferred to some fund other than a restricted fund (such as a Plant Fund). Because land, buildings, and equipment are usually accounted for in a separate fund, the Unrestricted Current Fund is generally used to account for current assets that can be used in the organization's operations at its management's discretion. For financial reporting purposes, Unrestricted Current Fund balances are generally classified as unrestricted net assets in the statement of financial position.

2. *Restricted Current Funds* (also called Restricted Operating, Specific-Purpose, or Current Restricted Funds). The fund accounting notion of "restricted" is somewhat broader than the definition of restricted that is used for financial reporting by net asset classification. As previously stated, temporarily restricted net assets

---

[21] Further coverage of this subject is beyond the scope of this text. For extensive discussion, see *AICPA Audit and Accounting Guide—Not-for-Profit Organizations* (New York: AICPA, 2001), Sec. 13.43–13.56 and appendices.

for financial reporting purposes are those whose restrictions are imposed only by donors. However, Restricted Current Funds may include not only contributions from donors for specific operating purposes, but also resources (such as grants and contracts) whose use is limited by other external parties. Therefore, for financial reporting purposes, if fund accounting is used, the fund balances need to be separated between net assets restricted by donors (classified as temporarily restricted net assets) and net assets restricted by contract or other limitations (classified as unrestricted net assets).

3. *Endowment Funds.* These funds are used to account for resources required by the donor to be maintained in perpetuity (permanent or pure endowment) or to be maintained for a specific time period or until the occurrence of a specified event (term endowment). For financial reporting purposes, Permanent Endowment Funds are classified as permanently restricted net assets. Term Endowment Funds are generally classified as temporarily restricted net assets, until the term expires or the specified future event occurs. Colleges and universities often have a third type of Endowment Fund, called *Quasi-Endowment Funds.* These are funds that have been set aside by the organization's governing board for specific purposes for long but unspecified time periods. They are classified as unrestricted because the designation is not donor-imposed.

4. *Land, Building, and Equipment Funds* (or Plant Funds). These funds are used to account for land, buildings, and equipment currently in use in the operations of the organization, together with any associated depreciation and long-term debt. In addition, they are used to account for resources whose use is restricted to the acquisition of land, buildings, or equipment. Colleges and universities sometimes divide their Plant Funds into four sub-fund account groups: Unexpended Plant Funds, Funds for Renewal and Replacement, Funds for Retirement and Indebtedness, and Net Investment in Plant. Depending on the circumstances (such as the nature of restrictions imposed by donors on use of the assets), these funds may need to be separated among unrestricted, temporarily restricted, or permanently restricted for financial reporting purposes.

Some NFPOs also use other types of funds, such as Loan Funds, Annuity Funds, and Agency Funds. Colleges and universities, for example, commonly use Loan Funds to account for loans made to students. Loan Fund resources are classified as unrestricted or restricted depending on whether the resources were designated by governing boards for use as Loan Funds or whether they were restricted by donors. Further, restricted Loan Funds may be temporarily or permanently restricted, depending on the nature of the donor-imposed restrictions.

Interfund Transfers

Using fund accounting may cause reclassification transactions from one net asset classification to another to affect more than one fund; for example, both a Restricted Current Fund and the Unrestricted Current Fund. In addition, using fund accounting may cause interfund transactions other than those resulting in net asset reclassifications. For example, the Unrestricted Current Fund might transfer cash to the

Land, Buildings, and Equipment Fund to acquire equipment. This transaction is referred to as a *transfer*. For fund accounting purposes, the fund transferring cash would debit a "Transfer to . . ." account, and the fund receiving cash would credit a "Transfer from . . ." account.

Colleges and universities classify their interfund transfers as either nonmandatory or mandatory. *Nonmandatory transfers* are those made at the discretion of the governing board for such purposes as additions to Loan Funds, Plant Funds, or Quasi-Endowment Funds. *Mandatory transfers* are those arising out of binding legal agreements, such as setting aside amounts for debt retirement or for meeting legal requirements to match gifts or grants.

FUND ACCOUNTING TRANSACTIONS AND FINANCIAL REPORTING BY NOT-FOR-PROFIT ORGANIZATIONS

Assume that the Kezar Fund, a VHWO, is formed at the beginning of 2004. It receives its support from the public at large, as well as through the United Way. Kezar intends to buy a building and some equipment to carry out its services, which are counseling and education programs.

This organization uses an Unrestricted Current Fund (UCF); a Restricted Current Fund (RCF); an Endowment Fund (EF); and a Land, Buildings, and Equipment Fund (LBEF). Kezar's accounting practices require donor contributions with time or purpose restrictions to be recorded in the RCF, except for those related to land, buildings, and equipment, which are recorded in the LBEF. All expenses financed by donor-restricted contributions, initially recorded in the RCF, are recorded in the UCF. However, Kezar uses the LBEF to account for all capital asset transactions, so depreciation and mortgage interest expenses are recorded in the LBEF. Donor contributions required to be maintained in perpetuity are recorded in the EF.

Unrestricted Current Fund   The following transactions pertain to the UCF for 2004:

1. Unrestricted pledges of $130,000, which apply to the current period, are made by various people. Of this amount, $15,000 is not expected to be collected.

Contributions receivable	130,000	
Allowance for uncollectible contributions		15,000
Unrestricted support—contributions		115,000
To record pledges receivable and estimated uncollectibles.		

2. Contributions receivable of $110,000 are collected, and contributions of $12,000 are written off as uncollectible.

Cash	110,000	
Allowance for uncollectible contributions	12,000	
Contributions receivable		122,000
To record collection and write-off of certain pledges.		

3. Kezar's allocation from the United Way, which may be used for any purpose, is $65,000. From this amount, United Way deducts a share ($5,000) of its fund-raising costs.

Cash	60,000	
United Way fund-raising costs	5,000	
Unrestricted support—United Way		65,000
To record 2004 allocation from United Way.		

4. Membership dues of $15,000 are collected during the year.

Cash	15,000	
Revenues—membership dues		15,000
To record receipt of membership dues.		

5. A fund-raising book sale is held. The event raises $12,000. Out of this amount, however, $3,000 of related costs are incurred and paid.

Cash	9,000	
Expenses—fund-raising	3,000	
Revenue—special events		12,000
To record revenues and expenses from special fund-raising book sale.		

[*Note:* Under some circumstances, this transaction might be defined as a gain (resulting from an entity's peripheral or incidental transactions) rather than as a revenue (resulting from its ongoing major or central activities). Such events, however, are often ongoing activities.]

6. Kezar invests $20,000 of its unrestricted resources in equity securities that have a readily determinable fair value and in debt securities.

Investments	20,000	
Cash		20,000
To record purchase of equity and debt securities.		

7. Income of $2,000 is earned during the year from the investment of unrestricted resources. Of this amount, $1,500 is received by year-end.

Cash	1,500	
Accrued interest receivable	500	
Unrestricted revenue—investment income		2,000
To record income from the investment of unrestricted net assets.		

8. At year-end, investments with a carrying value of $20,000 have a fair (market) value of $24,000. The following adjustment is made to record their fair value.

Investments (or Investment Valuation Account)	4,000	
Unrestricted net unrealized and realized investment gains/losses		4,000
To record appreciation in the fair value of investments.		

9. Services donated to Kezar are as follows:

   a. A psychologist provides counseling services at no cost. The services are valued at $3,000.

   b. A certified public accounting firm provides audit services without charge. The firm would normally charge $2,000 for these services.

   c. Several professors sell books at the fund-raising event in transaction (5). If they had been teaching, their time would have been worth $1,000.

Expenses—counseling services		3,000	
Expenses—administration		2,000	
Unrestricted support—donated services			5,000
To record receipt of donated services.			

(*Note:* The book-selling services of the professors are not recognized as revenues and expenses because they do not require specialized skills.)

10. Supplies, with a market value of $800, are donated to the society by a local accounting firm. They are used in the general operation of the organization.

Expenses—administration		800	
Unrestricted support—donated supplies			800
To record receipt of donated supplies.			

11. Salaries and wages incurred during the year (including fringe benefits) are allocated as follows:

Administration	$25,000
Counseling services	60,000
Education	50,000
Fund-raising	5,000

By year-end all salaries, wages, and fringe benefits have been paid.

Expenses—administration		25,000	
Expenses—counseling services		60,000	
Expenses—education		50,000	
Expenses—fund-raising		5,000	
Cash			140,000
To record salaries, wages, and fringe benefits for 2004.			

12. Other expenses are allocated as follows:

Contractual services:		
Counseling services	$10,000	
Education	5,000	$15,000
Supplies (all education)		10,000
Miscellaneous expenses:		
Administration	5,000	
Counseling services	2,000	
Education	3,000	
Fund-raising	1,000	11,000
Total		$36,000

Of this amount, all but $4,000 has been paid by year-end.

Expenses—administration	5,000	
Expenses—counseling services	12,000	
Expenses—education	18,000	
Expenses—fund-raising	1,000	
Accounts payable		4,000
Cash		32,000
To record expenses incurred in 2004 and payment of vouchers.		

Restricted Current Fund Transactions pertaining to the RCF for 2004 are as follows:

1. Pledges of $20,000 and cash gifts of $10,000 are received, with the stipulation by the donors that they be used only for special educational programs. Twenty percent of the pledges are estimated to be uncollectible.

Cash	10,000	
Contributions receivable	20,000	
Allowance for uncollectible contributions		4,000
Temporarily restricted support—contributions		26,000
To record temporarily restricted gifts and pledges.		

2. Restricted-purpose pledges of $15,000 are collected and another $2,000 are written off as uncollectible.

Cash	15,000	
Allowance for uncollectible contributions	2,000	
Contributions receivable		17,000
To record collection and write-off of restricted pledges.		

3. Special educational expenses of $21,000 are paid by this fund in 2004.

Restricted Current Fund		
Temporarily restricted asset reclassifications out—satisfaction of program restrictions	21,000	
Cash		21,000
To record payment of special education program expenses and reclassification of temporarily restricted assets due to satisfaction of program restrictions.		

Unrestricted Current Fund		
Expenses—special education	21,000	
Unrestricted asset reclassifications in—satisfaction of program restrictions		21,000
To record reclassification of temporarily restricted assets to unrestricted due to satisfaction of program restrictions, and to record special education expenses.		

(*Note:* The reclassification transaction requires an entry in the UCF because Kezar's fund accounting practices require all program expenses to be recorded in that fund. The use of funds causes these journal entries to be organized somewhat differently from the entries shown on page 515, where fund accounting was not used.)

4. Jim Antonio pledges $1,000 to Kezar, provided Kezar is able to raise $4,000 more to send certain professors on a fishing expedition to Arkansas. (No entry.

For this conditional promise, neither the receivable nor the support should be recognized until the condition attached to the pledge is met by Kezar's raising of $4,000 for the fishing expedition.)

5. At year-end, Kezar undertakes a special fund-raising drive. Prospective donors are told that the contributions will be used in 2005 for general activities. Kezar obtains pledges of $10,000, all of which are expected to be collected.

Contributions receivable	10,000	
Temporarily restricted support—contributions		10,000
To record receipt of pledges, to be used for 2005 activities.		

(*Note:* At the beginning of 2005, the time restriction will expire and journal entries will be made reclassifying the asset as unrestricted. For fund accounting purposes, the receivable will be transferred to the UCF. The account Unrestricted asset reclassifications in—satisfaction of time restrictions will be credited in the UCF. A corresponding debit will be made to a reclassifications out account in the RCF.)

Endowment Fund   The following transaction pertains to the EF for 2004. At year-end a donor contributes investments with a fair market value of $25,000. The donor requires Kezar to maintain the gift in perpetuity but permits the income from the gift to be used for any purpose the Kezar trustees desire.

Investments	25,000	
Permanently restricted support—contributions		25,000
To record permanently restricted contribution.		

Land, Building, and Equipment Fund   The following transactions pertain to the LBEF for 2004.

1. The organization receives a grant of $250,000 from the Weller Foundation, to be used for the purchase of a building and equipment. Weller stipulates that the grant may also be used to make payments of mortgage principal and interest on the building, and that any income earned on investment of the grant must be used for the stipulated purposes.

Cash	250,000	
Temporarily restricted support—contributions		250,000
To record contribution for purchase of building and equipment.		

2. An investment of $100,000 is made in government securities.

Investments	100,000	
Cash		100,000
To record investment in government securities.		

3. Equipment costing $50,000 is purchased, using the Weller-donated resources.

Equipment	50,000	
Cash		50,000
To record acquisition of equipment with donor-restricted resources.		

Temporarily restricted asset reclassifications out—satisfaction of plant acquisition restrictions	50,000	
Unrestricted asset reclassifications in—satisfaction of plant acquisition restrictions		50,000
To record satisfaction of plant acquisition restrictions.		

(*Note:* Even though the equipment remains in the LBEF, in accordance with Kezar's fund accounting practices, a reclassification entry is needed to record the satisfaction of plant acquisition restrictions for financial reporting purposes.)

4. A building is purchased for $400,000. A down payment of $80,000 is made from Weller-donated resources and a mortgage is taken out for the remainder.

Building	400,000	
Mortgage payable		320,000
Cash		80,000
To record purchase of building with donated resources and mortgage.		

Temporarily restricted asset reclassifications out—satisfaction of plant acquisition restrictions	80,000	
Unrestricted asset reclassifications in—satisfaction of plant acquisition restrictions		80,000
To record use of Weller Foundation resources for purchase of building and satisfaction of plant acquisition restrictions.		

5. Interest of $8,000 is received on the investment in government securities.

Cash	8,000	
Temporarily restricted revenue—investment income		8,000
To record earnings on investments acquired with Weller donation, restricted to plant acquisition.		

6. Payments of $10,000 are made during the year, of which $8,000 is for interest and $2,000 is for principal.

Mortgage payable	2,000	
Expenses—interest	8,000	
Cash		10,000
To record payments on mortgage with donor-restricted resources.		

Temporarily restricted asset reclassifications out—satisfaction of plant acquisition restrictions	10,000	
Unrestricted asset reclassifications in—satisfaction of plant acquisition restrictions		10,000
To record satisfaction of plant acquisition restrictions through mortgage payment.		

7. Depreciation for the year amounts to $20,000 on the building and $10,000 on the equipment. It is allocated as follows:

Administration	$ 3,000
Counseling services	10,000
Educational services	16,000
Fund-raising	1,000

Depreciation expense—administration	3,000	
Depreciation expense—counseling services	10,000	
Depreciation expense—educational services	16,000	
Depreciation expense—fund-raising	1,000	
Accumulated depreciation—building		20,000
Accumulated depreciation—equipment		10,000

To record depreciation on building and equipment for 2004.

Preparing Financial Statements from Fund Records

The preclosing trial balances for the UCF, the RCF, the EF, and the LBEF are set forth in Tables 12-5, 12-6, 12-7, and 12-8, respectively. The financial statements can be prepared from these trial balances. The Statement of Activities is shown in Table 12-9 and the Statement of Financial Position in Table 12-10.

Remember that the required financial statements focus on information for the entity as a whole and on net assets and changes in net assets, classified as either unrestricted, temporarily restricted, or permanently restricted. (Statements may also be presented by fund group, provided entity-as-a-whole statements are also prepared.) For the entity-as-a-whole statements, based on Kezar's accounting policies, all account balances in the UCF are classified as unrestricted; all balances in the RCF are classified as temporarily restricted; all Endowment Fund balances are classified as permanently restricted; and balances in the LBEF are separated between unrestricted and restricted.

The required entity-as-a-whole financial statements could be prepared from the fund-based trial balances with the help of a multicolumn spreadsheet. The spreadsheet would show the trial balances for the four funds in the first eight columns. Another set of columns would be used to help prepare the Statement of Activities and another set would be used for the Statement of Financial Position.

Statement of Activities

As you trace the information from the fund trial balances shown in Tables 12-5 through 12-8 to the statement of activities presented in Table 12-9, notice the following:

1. All the nominal accounts in the UCF are included in the unrestricted column of the statement of activities. The nine UCF accounts, starting with Unrestricted support—contributions and ending with Unrestricted asset reclassifications in—satisfaction of program restrictions, total $239,800. That amount is part of the $379,800 total revenues, gains, and other support reported in the unrestricted column. The six UCF expense accounts total $210,800, which is part of the $248,800 total expenses reported in the unrestricted column. The difference between the nominal account credits ($239,800) and debits ($210,800) is a net credit of $29,000. This $29,000 net credit will be the fund balance of the UCF after the nominal accounts are closed. It is also a part of the unrestricted net assets in the statement of financial position, as discussed in the next section.
2. Both nominal accounts of the RCF contain "temporarily restricted" in the caption, so they are included in the temporarily restricted column of the statement

Table 12-5

Trial Balance—UCF

KEZAR FUND
UNRESTRICTED CURRENT FUND
PRECLOSING TRIAL BALANCE
DECEMBER 31, 2004

Cash	$ 3,500	
Contributions receivable	8,000	
Allowance for uncollectible contributions		$ 3,000
Accrued interest receivable	500	
Investments	24,000	
Accounts payable		4,000
Unrestricted support—contributions		115,000
Unrestricted support—United Way		65,000
Unrestricted support—donated services		5,000
Unrestricted support—supplies		800
Revenues—membership dues		15,000
Revenues—special events		12,000
Unrestricted revenues—investment income		2,000
Unrestricted net unrealized and realized investment gains and losses		4,000
Unrestricted asset reclassifications in—satisfaction of program restrictions		21,000
Expenses—counseling	75,000	
Expenses—education	68,000	
Expenses—special education	21,000	
Expenses—administration	32,800	
Expenses—fund-raising	9,000	
Expenses—United Way fund-raising	5,000	
Totals	$246,800	$246,800

of activities. The $36,000 credit for contributions is part of the $286,000 contributions reported in the temporarily restricted column. The $21,000 debit for temporarily restricted reclassifications out is reported in the temporarily restricted column as a negative net asset released from program restrictions. It offsets the corresponding reclassification in, shown in the unrestricted column. The difference between nominal account debits and credits is a net credit of $15,000. The $15,000 net credit will be the fund balance of the UCF after the nominal accounts are closed. It is also a part of the temporarily restricted net assets, as discussed in the next section.

3. The $25,000 permanently restricted contribution in the EF is reported in the permanently restricted column of the statement of activities. That amount will

Table 12-6

Trial Balance—RCF

KEZAR FUND		
RESTRICTED CURRENT FUND		
PRECLOSING TRIAL BALANCE		
DECEMBER 31, 2004		
Cash	$ 4,000	
Contributions receivable	13,000	
Allowance for uncollectible contributions		$ 2,000
Temporarily restricted support—contributions		36,000
Temporarily restricted asset reclassifications out— satisfaction of program restrictions	21,000	
Totals	$38,000	$38,000

be the fund balance of the EF when the accounts are closed. It is also the amount of the permanently restricted net assets reported in the statement of financial position.

4. The five accounts in the LBEF that contain expense captions total $38,000. Remember that, for financial reporting purposes, all expenses are shown as reductions of unrestricted net assets. Therefore, they are included in the unrestricted column of the statement of activities. The $38,000 and the $210,800 from the UCF, as in part (1), total $248,800, which equals the total expenses shown in the unrestricted column.

The four nominal accounts in the LBEF that contain "temporarily restricted" or "unrestricted" in their captions are included in the related columns in the statement of activities. Temporarily restricted support—contributions ($250,000) is part of the $286,000 contributions reported in the temporarily restricted column. The two $140,000 reclassification items are shown side-by-side in the unrestricted and tem-

Table 12-7

Trial Balance—EF

KEZAR FUND		
ENDOWMENT FUND		
PRECLOSING TRIAL BALANCE		
DECEMBER 31, 2004		
Investments	$25,000	
Permanently restricted support—contributions		$25,000
Totals	$25,000	$25,000

Table 12-8

Trial Balance—LBEF

KEZAR FUND
LAND, BUILDING, AND EQUIPMENT FUND
PRECLOSING TRIAL BALANCE
DECEMBER 31, 2004

Cash	$ 18,000	
Investments	100,000	
Building	400,000	
Accumulated depreciation—building		$ 20,000
Equipment	50,000	
Accumulated depreciation—equipment		10,000
Mortgage payable		318,000
Temporarily restricted support—contributions		250,000
Temporarily restricted revenues—investment income		8,000
Unrestricted asset reclassifications in—satisfaction of plant acquisition restrictions		140,000
Temporarily restricted asset reclassifications out— satisfaction of plant acquisition restrictions	140,000	
Expenses—counseling	10,000	
Expenses—education	16,000	
Expenses—administration	3,000	
Expenses—fund-raising	1,000	
Expenses—interest	8,000	
Totals	$746,000	$746,000

porarily restricted columns. The $220,000 difference between the three LBEF nominal account credits ($398,000) and the six debits ($178,000) will be the fund balance of the LBEF. As discussed in the next section, part of that amount will be reported as unrestricted net assets and part as restricted.

Statement of Financial Position

Now, trace the information from the four trial balances to the statement of financial position, shown in Table 12-10.

1. The asset and liability accounts from the four funds have been aggregated, but other formats (such as segregations between unrestricted, temporarily restricted, and permanently restricted) are permitted. The LBEF has $118,000 of financial resources (cash of $18,000 and investments of $100,000) that must be used, in accordance with donor-imposed restrictions (Weller donation), for long-term plant investment. Notice that the $118,000 is shown separately

Table 12-9

Statement of Activities—Kezar Fund

KEZAR FUND
STATEMENT OF ACTIVITIES
FOR THE YEAR ENDED DECEMBER 31, 2004

	UNRESTRICTED	TEMP. RESTRICTED	PERM. RESTRICTED	TOTAL
Revenues, Gains, and Other Support				
Contributions	$115,000	$286,000	$25,000	$426,000
Contributions—United Way	65,000			65,000
Donated services and supplies	5,800			5,800
Membership dues	15,000			15,000
Special events	12,000			12,000
Investment income	2,000	8,000		10,000
Unrealized and realized investment gains	4,000			4,000
Net assets released from restrictions:				
Satisfaction of program restrictions	21,000	(21,000)		
Satisfaction of plant acquisition restrictions	140,000	(140,000)		
Total revenues, gains, other support	379,800	133,000	25,000	537,800
Expenses				
Counseling	85,000			85,000
Education	84,000			84,000
Special education	21,000			21,000
Administration	35,800			35,800
Fund-raising	15,000			15,000
Interest	8,000			8,000
Total expenses	248,800			248,800
Change in net assets	131,000	133,000	25,000	289,000
Net assets at beginning of year	—	—	—	—
Net assets at end of year	$131,000	$133,000	$25,000	$289,000

from the other assets to inform the reader that it is not available for operating activities. Notice also that the $25,000 of EF investments is reported as restricted for endowment because it too is not available for operating purposes.

2. Net assets must be classified as unrestricted, temporarily restricted, or permanently restricted. Notice that the amount of unrestricted net assets ($131,000) is the same as the "bottom line" net assets shown in the statement of activities. The temporarily restricted net assets ($133,000) have been separated into three components to inform the reader how those assets must be used. (As an alternative, that information could be presented in the notes.) The $25,000 of Endowment Fund net assets is reported as permanently restricted.

Table 12-10
Statement of Financial Position—Kezar Fund

KEZAR FUND
STATEMENT OF FINANCIAL POSITION
DECEMBER 31, 2004

Assets:	
Cash	$ 7,500
Contributions receivable, less allowance for uncollectibles of $5,000	16,000
Accrued interest receivable	500
Investments, at fair value	24,000
Assets restricted for investment in plant	118,000
Building, net of accumulated depreciation of $20,000	380,000
Equipment, net of accumulated depreciation of $10,000	40,000
Investments restricted for endowment	25,000
Total assets	$611,000
Liabilities and net assets:	
Liabilities:	
Accounts payable	$ 4,000
Mortgage payable	318,000
Total liabilities	322,000
Net assets:	
Unrestricted	131,000
Temporarily restricted:	
For special educational programs	5,000
For next year's activities	10,000
For plant purposes	118,000
Permanently restricted	25,000
Total net assets	289,000
Total liabilities and net assets	$611,000

3. Now, let us return to the individual funds and reconcile their fund balances with the three net asset classifications shown in the statement of financial position.

	Net Asset Classifications			
Funds	Unrestricted	Temp. Restricted	Perm. Restricted	Fund Balances
UCF	$ 29,000			$ 29,000
RCF		$ 15,000		15,000
EF			$25,000	25,000
LBEF	102,000	118,000		220,000
Totals	$131,000	$133,000	$25,000	$289,000

As previously discussed, based on Kezar's accounting policies, the fund balances of the UCF, RCF, and EF fall readily into the restricted, temporarily restricted, and permanently restricted net asset classifications. The allocation of the LBEF fund balance of $220,000 between unrestricted and temporarily restricted may not be so readily apparent. As previously noted, the LBEF has $118,000 of unexpended financial resources from the original Kezar donation and related investment income, which are temporarily restricted net assets available for plant acquisition. The other $102,000 represents the net other assets in the LBEF (building and equipment of $450,000, less accumulated depreciation of $30,000 and mortgage payable of $318,000). It is also the amount reclassified during the year to unrestricted net assets ($140,000), less the amount "consumed" through depreciation and other expenses.

REVIEW QUESTIONS

Q12-1 What characteristics distinguish NFPOs from for-profit organizations? What characteristics distinguish government organizations from NFPOs?

Q12-2 What body has the final authority for determining the accounting procedures for NFPOs?

Q12-3 Identify several organizations that would be classified as VHWOs. Identify several types of organizations that would be classified as ONPOs.

Q12-4 What financial statements must be prepared by all VHWOs and ONPOs? What additional financial statements must be prepared by VHWOs?

Q12-5 Identify and briefly describe the three classifications of net assets on the financial statements of NFPOs.

Q12-6 Illustrate the kinds of restrictions that donors may impose on the use of resources they contribute to NFPOs.

Q12-7 Discuss the differences between a donor-imposed restriction and a conditional promise to give. How is each reported in the financial statements?

Q12-8 How are pledges that are expected to be uncollectible reported in the financial statements of NFPOs?

Q12-9 Describe the circumstances under which contributed services must be recognized as revenues and expenses in the financial statements.

Q12-10 Under what circumstances must an NFPO recognize a contributed work of art as revenue? Under what circumstances does the organization have an option not to recognize it as revenue?

Q12-11 When is a reclassification made and what is its purpose?

Q12-12 Identify and briefly describe the major funds used by NFPOs.

EXERCISES

E12-1 (Funds used by VHWOs)
Using the following coding system, indicate which fund or funds would be used to record each of the transactions described.

UCF   Unrestricted Current Fund
RCF   Restricted Current Fund
LBEF   Land, Building, and Equipment Fund
EF   Endowment Fund

1. The organization received unrestricted pledges of $400,000, to be used in the current year. Of this amount, $390,000 is expected to be collected.
2. Jane Public gave the organization securities with a market value of $1.2 million. The gift provided that the principal must be maintained intact; however, the income could be spent for any purpose approved by the governing board.
3. John Dough gave the organization $50,000, stipulating that his gift could be used only for a specific research project.
4. Salaries of employees involved in rendering services to the public totaled $75,000.

E12-2 (Identifying appropriate classification of net assets)
For each of the transactions in E12-1, state which of the following net asset classifications would be affected in the organization's financial statements.
Unrestricted net assets
Temporarily restricted net assets
Permanently restricted net assets

E12-3 (Recording journal entries for VHWOs)
Prepare the journal entries necessary to record the data given in E12-1. In addition, indicate which fund is used for each entry.

E12-4 (Multiple choice)
1. How should expenses be reported in an NFPO's statement of activities?
   a. As decreases in the net asset classification where the revenues were reported
   b. As decreases of permanently restricted net assets
   c. As decreases of temporarily restricted net assets
   d. As decreases of unrestricted net assets
2. Which of the following is a general rule established by the Financial Accounting Standards Board regarding contributions received in the form of investments by an NFPO?
   a. They must be recorded either in a restricted fund or in an unrestricted fund.
   b. They must be reported either as restricted support or unrestricted support.
   c. They must be recorded as the amount paid by the donor for the investment.
   d. They must be reported in an endowment fund.
3. Which of the following financial statements is required for VHWOs but not for ONPOs?
   a. Statement of financial position
   b. Statement of activities
   c. Statement of functional expenses
   d. Statement of cash flows

4. If a donor provides that interest earned on an endowment must be used to finance a particular program, how should the interest revenue be classified?
   a. As unrestricted
   b. As temporarily restricted
   c. As permanently restricted
   d. As quasi-endowment income
5. In which fund is a mortgage on the land and buildings owned by a VHWO recorded?
   a. Unrestricted Current Fund
   b. Restricted Current Fund
   c. Land, Building, and Equipment Fund
   d. Loan Fund
6. Which of the following net asset classifications may have one or more items of donor support?
   a. Unrestricted net assets
   b. Temporarily restricted net assets
   c. Permanently restricted net assets
   d. All of the above
7. The Prevent Cancer Organization incurred several expenses during 2004. Which of the following would not be classified as program support?
   a. Instruction for cancer prevention to the general public
   b. Pamphlets mailed to the general public regarding the "danger signals of cancer"
   c. Postage for announcements of the 2004 Kickoff Dinner
   d. Salaries of personnel who perform cancer research
8. As a result of its annual fund-raising program, an NFPO receives pledges in the amount of $300,000 during December 2004, the last month of its reporting period. Based on its previous history regarding pledges, the NFPO believes that about $250,000 will be collected in the first 60 days of 2005, some will trickle in during the rest of 2005, and 10 percent will not be collected at all. How much should the NFPO report as contribution revenue on its 2004 financial statements?
   a. $0
   b. $250,000
   c. $270,000
   d. $300,000
9. Mae Wood, a certified public accountant, donated 60 hours of her time to Food Kitchen, an NFPO that serves food to needy people. She spent 20 hours auditing Food Kitchen's books and 40 hours serving food to the needy. Mae normally earns $200 an hour as a CPA, and Food Kitchen normally pays $5 an hour to students when it can't find volunteers to serve the needy. How much should Food Kitchen report as contribution revenue for Mae's services?
   a. $0
   b. $200
   c. $4,000
   d. $4,200

E12-5 (Statement of activities for a country club)

The following information was taken from the records of the Land's End Country Club. All account balances are as of the end of the accounting year, June 30, 2005.

Cash	$ 12,000
Dues	631,000
Locker room rentals to members	20,000
Expenses associated with the golf course	255,000
Expenses associated with the tennis courts	105,000
Initiation fees	78,000
Prepaid expenses	8,000
Administration expenses	65,000
Fees: Golf course	87,000
Swimming pool	44,000
Tennis courts	12,000
Expenses associated with the swimming pool	31,000
Land, buildings, and equipment	800,987
Investments	56,000
Assessments against members for capital improvements	200,000
Net assets—6/30/04 (unrestricted)	97,000

Required: Prepare a statement of activities for the Land's End Country Club.

E12-6 (Journal entries for an NFPO)

The Society to Save Humankind from Its Ills, a VHWO, was founded in 2004. This organization conducts two types of programs: education and testing. It maintains three funds: Unrestricted Current; Restricted Current; and Land, Buildings and Equipment. During 2004, the following events took place:

1. Pledges amounting to $200,000 were received. Of this amount, $50,000 was restricted for the use of a special research program. All of the restricted pledges and $140,000 of the unrestricted pledges are expected to be collected.

2. Les Miller made a $1,000 cash contribution to be used as the directors of the society see fit. However, Mr. Miller stipulated that it not be used until 2005.

3. The restricted pledges were all collected. With respect to the unrestricted pledges, $120,000 was collected and $5,000 was written off.

4. The society received a $10,000 allocation from the United Fund. Of this amount, $2,000 was deducted for fund-raising costs.

5. The society invested $10,000 of unrestricted funds in government securities. Earnings on these resources amounted to $500 in 2004.

6. During the year, $40,000 of restricted funds was spent on the special research program.

7. A grant of $500,000 was made to the society by the Allen Company. The grant was to be used to purchase equipment and for a down payment on a building. Cash donations of $10,000, for the purpose of debt service (paying interest and principal on the mortgage), were also received.

8. Equipment was purchased for $75,000, using resources donated by the Allen Company.
9. A down payment of $400,000 was made on a building costing $1,000,000. A 20-year mortgage was taken out for the remainder.
10. The following services were donated to the society, all of which should be recorded:
    a. Free accounting work by a local accounting firm—$500
    b. Free tests by a national testing laboratory—$1,000
    c. The services, at no cost, of several teachers, from a local junior college, who conducted physical fitness and wellness programs—$2,000
    In addition, the accounting firm donated supplies worth $200.
11. Salaries, wages, and other operating expenses for 2004 amounted to $135,000. They were paid with unrestricted monies and were allocated as follows:

Administration	$20,000
Education	90,000
Testing	15,000
Fund-raising	10,000

12. Interest of $8,000 was paid on the mortgage during the year.
13. Depreciation amounted to $50,000 on the building and $10,000 on the equipment. It was allocated as follows:

	Building	Equipment
Administration	$10,000	—
Education	20,000	$3,000
Testing	20,000	7,000

14. Revenues from membership dues amounted to $18,000 in 2004.

Required: Prepare journal entries for the preceding transactions by fund, identifying increases and decreases by net asset classification as appropriate.

E12-7 (Journal entries using classifications of net assets)
The Mon Elisa Museum of Fine Arts is an NFPO that derives most of its resources from wealthy patrons. Mon Elisa has recently changed its accounting system to eliminate the use of separate funds. All journal entries are made so as to indicate which of the three net asset classifications are affected. The following transactions and events occurred during 2004:
1. Cash of $40,000 was received from donors, who stated that it may be used for any purpose desired by the museum.
2. A donor gave the museum $10,000, stipulating that the money may be used only to acquire fine examples of Weller Dickensware pottery.
3. Elias Gotbucks sent Mon Elisa a letter, stating he would donate $15,000 to the museum to purchase examples of Sara Dawn's quilt work, provided the museum conducted a special campaign that raised at least $25,000 to buy additional examples.
4. The museum spent $4,000 to acquire a fine Weller Dickensware vase. (Assume that Mon Elisa capitalizes its art collections.)

5. Mon Elisa contacted wealthy patrons to raise funds to buy Sara Dawn's quilt work. It obtained $30,000 in pledges, all likely to be paid. Mon Elisa then wrote to Elias Gotbucks, advising him it had raised $30,000.

6. Attorney Ted Floot donated his services to the museum. He spent 4 hours on museum legal matters and 3 hours as a salesperson in the museum shop. Ted bills $250 an hour when he works as an attorney.

7. A wealthy patron donated "The Portrait of Samantha," which had a fair value of $6,000, to the museum. The museum accepted the gift with the understanding that it would be sold at auction and the proceeds used for any purpose the museum wished.

Required: Prepare journal entries for these transactions and events and identify the affected classification of net assets.

PROBLEMS

P12-1 (Journal entries for a VHWO)

Eye Institute (EI) accounts for its activities by means of a UCF, an RCF, and an LBEF. All resources of the LBEF had been previously transferred to it from the UCF, so that the LBEF contains no restrictions that need to be satisfied. EI's accounting policies require that contributions containing program or time restrictions be recorded initially in the RCF and reclassified to the UCF upon satisfaction of the restrictions. Following are some of the transactions for the EI during 2004.

1. Pledges were received as follows:

Unrestricted	$3,000,000
Restricted to research	1,000,000

2. During the year, 90 percent of all pledges were collected.

3. Amounts received from the United Fund totaled $1.5 million.

4. The EI paid $20,000 to the United Fund as its share of the fund-raising costs for the year.

5. Salaries for the year totaled $500,000, and the related payroll costs were $100,000. The entire amount was paid in cash.

6. An additional parcel of land and a small building were acquired, using assets segregated for that purpose. The land was appraised for $75,000 and the building was appraised for $160,000. The institute paid $23,500 down and financed the remainder of the appraised value with a mortgage.

7. Depreciation for the year was $246,000.

8. The following general operating costs were paid:

Professional management fees	$ 75,000
Professional fees for research	500,000
Supplies	5,000
Printing	15,000
Utilities	100,000
Miscellaneous	15,000

9. Restricted resources were used as follows to conduct research:

Research salaries	$300,000
Payroll cost	30,000
Supplies	20,000
Postage	150,000

10. Unrestricted contributions received in 2004, but designated for use in 2005, totaled $35,000.
11. Equipment that cost $3,000 was acquired with unrestricted funds.
12. At the end of the year, management estimates that all the pledges outstanding in the RCF will be collected; however, $10,000 of the pledges in the UCF will probably not be collected.
13. At the end of the year, supplies that cost $500 were still on hand (see item 8).
14. Interest paid on the mortgage on the land and building was $20,000.
15. The distribution of expenses into functional categories in the UCF was as follows:*

Fund-raising	$ 152,000
Management and general	88,500
Research	1,155,000
Public service	414,000
Total	$1,809,500

16. The distribution of depreciation and the interest on the mortgage was as follows:*

Management and general	$ 22,000
Fund-raising	6,000
Research	215,000
Community service	23,000
Total	$266,000

*Assume journal entries are made for the distribution.

Required: Prepare the journal entries necessary to record these data; also indicate the fund used for each entry.

P12-2 (Journal entries for an NFPO)

Oliver's Place is a not-for-profit entity that cares for dogs until they are adopted. It uses a UCF, an RCF, and an EF. It charges expenses to the care of animals program, special programs, and administrative expenses. Following are some of its transactions for 2004:

1. During the year, it received unrestricted pledges of $100,000. It estimated that 95 percent of the pledges would be collected in cash.
2. Oliver's Place received the following gifts from various donors:
   a. Donor A made a gift of common stock that had a fair market value of $20,000. Donor A stated that the gift may be used for any purpose.
   b. Donor B made a cash gift of $5,000, stipulating that it may be used only for a new program to take calm dogs to visit elderly people.
   c. Donor C made a gift of common stock that had a fair market value of $50,000. Donor C stipulated that the gift, and any gains on the sale of

the stock, shall be maintained in perpetuity, and that the dividends received on the investment may be used for any purpose.
3. Volunteers contributed their time to Oliver's Place, as follows:
   a. Dr. D, a veterinarian, spent 10 days caring for medical needs of the dogs. Those services would normally cost Oliver's Place $10,000.
   b. Dr. E, a kidney surgeon, spent 12 days feeding the dogs, keeping them occupied, and placing them for adoption. He earns $2,000 a day as a surgeon.
4. Oliver's Place received dividends of $400 on the common stock donated by Donor A and $600 on the common stock donated by Donor C.
5. At year-end, the stock donated by Donor A had a fair value of $22,000 and the stock donated by Donor C had a fair value of $47,000.
6. During the year, Oliver's Place collected $80,000 in cash on the pledges made in transaction (1).
7. Oliver's Place spent $3,000 on the special program designed to take calm dogs to visit elderly people.
8. Oliver's Place paid the following expenses:

Care of animals	$40,000
Administrative expenses	30,000

9. Cash gifts of $12,000 were received from various donors who stipulated that the resources must be used in 2005.

Required: Prepare the journal entries needed to record these transactions; also, indicate the fund used for each entry. (You can check the accuracy of your work by preparing a trial balance and comparing it with the trial balances in P12-3.)

P12-3 (Preparation of financial statements for an NFPO)
Following are the preclosing fund trial balances as of December 31, 2004, for Oliver's Place, an NFPO. (The trial balances are based on the transactions contained in P12-2.)

Oliver's Place
Preclosing Trial Balances
December 31, 2004
Unrestricted Current Fund

	Debit	Credit
Cash	$ 11,000	
Contributions receivable	20,000	
Investments	22,000	
Allowance for uncollectible contributions		$ 5,000
Unrestricted support—contributions		115,000
Unrestricted support—donated services		10,000
Unrestricted revenue—investment income		1,000
Unrestricted gains—unrealized investment gains		2,000
Unrestricted asset reclassifications in—satisfaction of program restrictions		3,000
Care of animals expense	50,000	
Special programs expense	3,000	
Administrative expenses	30,000	
	$136,000	$136,000

Restricted Current Fund

	Debit	Credit
Cash	$14,000	
Temporarily restricted support—contributions		$17,000
Temporarily restricted asset reclassifications out— satisfaction of program restrictions	3,000	
	$17,000	$17,000

Endowment Fund

	Debit	Credit
Investments	$47,000	
Permanently restricted support—contributions		$50,000
Permanently restricted losses—unrealized investment losses	3,000	
	$50,000	$50,000

Required: 1. Prepare a statement of activities for the year ended December 31, 2004.

2. Prepare a statement of financial position as of December 31, 2004.

P12-4 (Journal entries for a VHWO)

Youth Services Agency (YSA) is a VHWO that provides counseling and recreation programs for youthful offenders. YSA's programs are financed through a contract with the county in which it is located and through contributions from local citizens. Its contract with the county provides for reimbursement of allowable costs based on monthly billings to the county. YSA does not use fund accounting, but does identify all revenues by net asset class. The following transactions occurred during 2004:

1. YSA received pledges of gifts in the amount of $20,000, to be used as the YSA trustees consider appropriate. Based on previous experience, YSA's CEO believed that 90 percent of the pledges would be collected.

2. YSA collected $17,000 cash on the pledges received in transaction (1). It also wrote off $1,500 of the pledges as uncollectible.

3. YSA received a gift of 50 shares of General Electric stock that had a fair value of $1,300 at the time of the gift. The donor sent the CEO a letter with the gift, saying that proceeds of the stock should be used only to purchase athletic equipment for the basketball team.

4. YSA realized $1,400 in cash from the sale of the stock received in transaction (3).

5. YSA paid $800 cash for athletic equipment, using the proceeds received in transaction (4). The expense was charged to Recreation programs.

6. YSA spent $12,000 cash on the following:

Counseling programs	$ 8,000
Recreation programs	3,000
Administration expense	1,000
Total	$12,000

7. YSA billed the county $6,500 for costs incurred under its contract.

Required: Prepare journal entries to record these transactions. Identify all revenues within the journal entries as unrestricted, temporarily restricted, or permanently restricted.

P12-5 (Preparation of financial statements for a VHWO)

Following are the preclosing trial balances of Marilyn Township Senior Citizens Center at December 31, 2004.

	Unrestricted		Temporarily Restricted	
	Debit	Credit	Debit	Credit
Cash	$ 3,000		$1,600	
Pledges receivable	1,000		500	
Allowance for uncollectible pledges		$ 300		
Investments	3,200			
Accrued interest receivable	100			
Net assets, January 1, 2004		6,700		$2,000
Contributions		1,000		500
Membership dues		1,500		
Program service fees		3,000		
Grant from county		2,500		
Grant from state		2,500		
Unrealized and realized gains on investments		200		
Investment income		100		
Luncheon program expenses	7,200			
Recreation program expenses	3,400			
Administration expenses	300			
Temporarily restricted asset reclassifications out—satisfaction of program restrictions			400	
Unrestricted asset reclassifications in—satisfaction of program restrictions		400		
	$18,200	$18,200	$2,500	$2,500

Required: Prepare a statement of financial position and a statement of activities as at and for the year ended December 31, 2004.

P12-6 (Discussion problems for specific not-for-profit transactions)

For each of the following transactions, discuss the issues and state the appropriate accounting solution:

1. The Society to Eliminate Hunger spent $8,000 to prepare and mail a two-page brochure to potential contributors. The brochure contained general information about the Society, described its accomplishments, pointed out that a contribution of $25 would provide 25 dinners, and urged recipients to contribute. The Trustees want the accountant to charge the cost of preparing and mailing the brochures to the Distribution of Food Program.

The executive director thinks the expenses should be charged to fund-raising expenses.

2. Professional lawyers and accountants volunteered to perform all the legal and audit services required by Youth Services, an NFPO. The Trustees of the NFPO take great pride in their low overhead rate. They tell the accountant: "We didn't pay for these services, so there's really no point in recording any expenses for them."

3. Sam Rich made annual contributions of $100,000 for the past 3 years to Cardinal House, a not-for-profit drug treatment center. On December 20, 2004, Cardinal House received a letter from Sam, promising to contribute $500,000 if the organization would change the name of the entity to Rich House. The Trustees debated the name change until it was time to issue the annual financial report but could not decide whether to make the change. They told the accountant: "We'd really like to report Sam's pledge as a receivable, because it will cause other donors to contribute. Besides, Sam has been a major supporter in the past and will probably contribute even if we don't change the name. We think we ought to recognize Sam's offer of $500,000 as a revenue and a receivable."

4. A wealthy individual donated a valuable work of art to a museum. The museum intends to keep the work, protect it from harm and deterioration, and hang it in a location so all can see it. The accountant sees no need either to recognize the asset or to depreciate it. However, one of the newer trustees, the chief executive of a large business entity, said, "In our company, we depreciate everything. And we know that, ultimately, everything turns to dust. So, why don't we recognize the work of art as an asset and depreciate it?"

5. On March 1, 2004, Rebecca Mantha promised to contribute $15,000, which was 50 percent of the estimated cost of a special program to be undertaken by the Shelley Center, an NFPO. Rebecca stated, however, that she would make the contribution only if the Center would raise the rest of the needed funds from other donors during the next 12 months. By December 31, 2004, the Center had raised $6,000 of the additional amount needed. The Center expected to mount a special campaign to obtain the other $9,000 and thought it would be successful. Should the Center recognize Rebecca's promise as a revenue for the year ended December 31, 2004?

P12-7 (Journal entries for a not-for-profit college)

Manny Saxe College is a small, not-for-profit college known for its excellence in teaching accounting. The college uses fund accounting and has an Unrestricted Current Fund, a Restricted Current Fund, a Plant Fund, and an Endowment Fund. It charges its expenses to Instruction and research, Student services, Plant operations, and Auxiliary enterprises. It had the following transactions and events during 2004:

1. Revenues from student tuition and fees were $2.5 million, all of which were collected.

2. Revenues from auxiliary enterprises were $400,000 in cash.

3. Salaries and wages, all of which were paid, were $1.8 million, chargeable as follows:

Instruction and research	$1,200,000
Student services	200,000
Plant operations	250,000
Auxiliary enterprises	150,000

4. Materials and supplies costing $800,000 were purchased on account and placed in inventory during the year.
5. Materials and supplies used during the year were $700,000, chargeable as follows:

Instruction and research	$300,000
Student services	50,000
Plant operations	150,000
Auxiliary enterprises	200,000

6. A cash transfer of $100,000 was made from the Unrestricted Current Fund to the Plant Fund to start the design work on a new student services building.
7. The college received a cash gift of $20,000 from K. Schermann, to finance a 3-year research project on governmental service efforts and accomplishments reporting.
8. The college paid B. Chaney $7,000 to do research on the project in transaction (7).
9. P. Defliese donated $1 million in equity securities to the college, stipulating that the corpus and all gains and losses on the sale of the securities remain intact in perpetuity. He also stipulated that income on the investments be used solely to finance a chair in governmental accounting.
10. At year-end, the securities donated by Defliese in transaction (9) had a fair value of $1,030,000. Income earned on the investments during the year was $45,000.
11. Antonio Harmer sent a letter to the college at the end of the year, promising to contribute $25,000 to equip the new student services building if the college raised an equal amount from other contributors. The college planned to write to the alumni to seek additional funds.

Required: Prepare the journal entries necessary to record these transactions, identifying the net asset classification as appropriate. Show which fund is used to record each transaction.

Not-for-Profit Colleges and Universities

Not-for-profit colleges and universities are required to follow the same accounting standards used by other not-for-profit organizations, as discussed in this chapter. They also prepare financial statements using the unrestricted, temporarily restricted, and permanently restricted net asset classifications. Those that use fund accounting also use the fund types previously discussed.

The major functional expense categories used by colleges and universities in financial reporting are instruction, research, public service, academic support, student services, auxiliary enterprises, and institutional support. Auxiliary enterprises include the operation of bookstores, residence halls, dining services, and intercollegiate athletics. Institutional support includes management and general and fund-raising expenses. Costs of operating and maintaining the physical plant (including depreciation) are generally allocated to the other functions.

FINANCIAL STATEMENTS OF NOT-FOR-PROFIT COLLEGES AND UNIVERSITIES

Not-for-profit colleges and universities, like other not-for-profit organizations, are required to prepare a statement of financial position, a statement of activities, and a cash flow statement. Tables 12A-1 through 12A-4 illustrate not-for-profit college and university financial reporting, using the year 2001 financial statements of The Johns Hopkins University.

The Johns Hopkins University calls its statement of financial position a balance sheet (Table 12A-1). The assets are arrayed generally in order of nearness to cash, and liabilities are arrayed generally in order of payout. Net assets are separated among the three net asset classifications, just like any other not-for-profit entity.

Notice that The Johns Hopkins University statement of activities distinguishes between operating revenues and expenses and nonoperating revenues, gains and losses (Table 12A-2). The caption "excess of operating revenues over expenses" provides a measure of *operating results* from the university's basic operations—a "bottom line" in addition to the caption "Increase (decrease) in net assets." The use of such intermediate captions was explored by the FASB in deliberations leading to FASB *Statement No. 117.* The FASB decided not to prescribe specific operating measures, but to allow them to evolve for the various types of not-for-profit organizations.

NOTES TO THE FINANCIAL STATEMENTS

The notes to financial statements are an important part of the statements and need to be read carefully to increase one's understanding of the statements. Space limitations preclude presentation of all the notes to The Johns Hopkins University statements, but some of them are discussed here to provide additional details on matters covered elsewhere in this chapter.

Table 12A-1

Balance Sheet—Not-for-Profit University

THE JOHNS HOPKINS UNIVERSITY
BALANCE SHEETS
JUNE 30, 2001 AND 2000
(AMOUNTS IN THOUSANDS)

	2001	2000
Assets		
Cash and cash equivalents	$ 248,819	$ 226,721
Accounts receivable, net	195,498	179,387
Prepaid expenses, deferred charges, and other assets	41,450	25,171
Contributions receivable, net	201,776	136,926
Loans receivable, net	35,648	34,585
Investments	2,245,066	2,216,149
Deposits with bond trustees	59,184	86,624
Investment in plant assets, net	908,404	832,715
Interests in trusts and endowment funds held by others	71,848	79,310
Total assets	**$4,007,693**	**$3,817,588**
Liabilities:		
Accounts payable, deferred revenues, and accrued expenses	$ 266,159	$ 226,693
Payables and deferred revenues under split-interest agreements	54,535	52,676
Debt	554,717	539,958
Obligations under deferred compensation agreements and other long-term liabilities	178,247	196,818
Total liabilities	1,053,658	1,016,145
Net assets:		
Unrestricted	1,828,524	1,846,706
Temporarily restricted	342,874	224,572
Permanently restricted	782,637	730,165
Total net assets	2,954,035	2,801,443
Total liabilities and net assets	**$4,007,693**	**$3,817,588**

Accompanying notes to financial statements not included.
Source: The Johns Hopkins University, Financial Report, 2001.

Notice (Table 12A-1) that the University has a significant amount of contributions receivable at June 30, 2001, and that the amount increased from the previous year. *How soon are these receivables likely to be collected? Does the University expect difficul-* *ties in collecting them? Have donors made conditional promises, which are not recognized on the face of the financial statements?* The notes say the following:

Allowance is made for uncollectible contributions receivable based on management's

Table 12A-2

Statement of Activities—Not-for-Profit University

THE JOHNS HOPKINS UNIVERSITY
STATEMENT OF ACTIVITIES
YEAR ENDED JUNE 30, 2001
(AMOUNTS IN THOUSANDS)

	UNRESTRICTED NET ASSETS	TEMPORARILY RESTRICTED NET ASSETS	PERMANENTLY RESTRICTED NET ASSETS	TOTAL
Operating revenues:				
Tuition and fees, net of student financial aid	$ 210,452	—	—	$ 210,452
Grants, contracts, and similar agreements	1,190,958	—	—	1,190,958
Clinical services	194,538	—	—	194,538
Reimbursements from affiliated institutions	132,497	—	—	132,497
Contributions	51,393	$172,234	—	223,627
Investment income	109,846	—	—	109,846
Maryland State aid	17,680	—	—	17,680
Sales and services of auxiliary enterprises	42,703	—	—	42,703
Other	56,404	—	—	56,404
Net assets released from restrictions	51,441	(51,441)	—	—
Total operating revenues	2,057,912	120,793	—	2,178,705
Operating expenses:				
Compensation and benefits	1,159,727	—	—	1,159,727
Contractual services	418,104	—	—	418,104
Supplies, materials, and other	241,475	—	—	241,475
Depreciation of property and equipment	70,790	—	—	70,790
Travel	46,328	—	—	46,328
Interest	28,408	—	—	28,408
Total operating expenses	1,964,832	—	—	1,964,832
Excess of operating revenues over expenses	93,080	120,793	—	213,873
Nonoperating revenues, gains and losses:				
Contributions	—	23,461	$ 59,352	82,813
Investment loss	(131,033)	(502)	(5,024)	(136,559)
Loss on disposals of property and equipment	(2,368)	—	—	(2,368)
Net assets released from restrictions	27,595	(27,595)	—	—
Loss on extinguishment of debt	(585)	—	—	(585)
Other	(4,871)	2,145	(1,856)	(4,582)
Nonoperating revenues, gains and losses, net	(111,262)	(2,491)	52,472	(61,281)
Increase (decrease) in net assets	(18,182)	118,302	52,472	152,592
Net assets at beginning of year	1,846,706	224,572	730,165	2,801,443
Net assets at end of year	**$1,828,524**	**$342,874**	**$782,637**	**$2,954,035**

Accompanying notes to financial statements not included.
Source: The Johns Hopkins University, Financial Report, 2001.

Table 12A-3
Statement of Activities (Comparative)—Not-for-Profit University

THE JOHNS HOPKINS UNIVERSITY
STATEMENT OF ACTIVITIES
YEAR ENDED JUNE 30, 2000
(AMOUNTS IN THOUSANDS)

	UNRESTRICTED NET ASSETS	TEMPORARILY RESTRICTED NET ASSETS	PERMANENTLY RESTRICTED NET ASSETS	TOTAL
Operating revenues:				
Tuition and fees, net of student financial aid	$ 199,808	—	—	$ 199,808
Grants, contracts, and similar agreements	1,057,513	—	—	1,057,513
Clinical services	187,271	—	—	187,271
Reimbursements from affiliated institutions	123,433	—	—	123,433
Contributions	66,487	$ 23,638	—	90,125
Investment income	91,558	—	—	91,558
Maryland State aid	15,477	—	—	15,477
Sales and services of auxiliary enterprises	44,724	—	—	44,724
Other	71,290	—	—	71,290
Net assets released from restrictions	25,756	(25,756)	—	—
Total operating revenues	1,883,317	(2,118)	—	1,881,199
Operating expenses:				
Compensation and benefits	1,051,929	—	—	1,051,929
Contractual services	377,908	—	—	377,908
Supplies, materials, and other	222,407	—	—	222,407
Depreciation of property and equipment	75,254	—	—	75,254
Travel	40,896	—	—	40,896
Interest	25,773	—	—	25,773
Total operating expenses	1,794,167	—	—	1,794,167
Excess (deficiency) of operating revenues over expenses	89,150	(2,118)	—	87,032
Nonoperating revenues, gains and losses:				
Contributions	—	33,528	$ 82,124	115,652
Investment income	164,361	733	7,031	172,125
Loss on disposals of property and equipment	(3,292)	—	—	(3,292)
Net assets released from restrictions	36,600	(36,600)	—	—
Other	(3,211)	(2,744)	3,658	(2,297)
Nonoperating revenues, gains and losses, net	194,458	(5,083)	92,813	282,188
Increase (decrease) in net assets	283,608	(7,201)	92,813	369,220
Net assets at beginning of year	1,563,098	231,773	637,352	2,432,223
Net assets at end of year	$1,846,706	$224,572	$730,165	$2,801,443

Accompanying notes to financial statements not included.
Source: The Johns Hopkins University, Financial Report, 2001.

Table 12A-4

Statement of Cash Flows—Not-for-Profit University

<table>
<tr><td colspan="3" align="center">THE JOHNS HOPKINS UNIVERSITY
STATEMENTS OF CASH FLOWS
YEARS ENDED JUNE 30, 2001 AND 2000
(AMOUNTS IN THOUSANDS)</td></tr>
<tr><th></th><th>2001</th><th>2000</th></tr>
<tr><td>Cash flows from operating activities:</td><td></td><td></td></tr>
<tr><td>Increase in net assets</td><td>$ 152,592</td><td>$ 369,220</td></tr>
<tr><td>Adjustments to reconcile increase in net assets
to net cash provided by operating activities:</td><td></td><td></td></tr>
<tr><td>Depreciation and loss on disposals of property and equipment</td><td>73,158</td><td>78,546</td></tr>
<tr><td>Loss on extinguishment of debt</td><td>585</td><td>—</td></tr>
<tr><td>Decrease (increase) in accounts receivable, net</td><td>(16,111)</td><td>37,027</td></tr>
<tr><td>Increase in prepaid expenses, deferred charges, and other assets</td><td>(16,279)</td><td>(8,359)</td></tr>
<tr><td>Decrease (increase) in contributions receivable, net</td><td>(64,850)</td><td>36,967</td></tr>
<tr><td>Increase in accounts payable, deferred revenues, and accrued
expenses</td><td>40,612</td><td>1,490</td></tr>
<tr><td>Increase in payables and deferred revenues under split-
interest agreements</td><td>1,859</td><td>7,697</td></tr>
<tr><td>Contributions restricted for long-term investment</td><td>(86,975)</td><td>(142,996)</td></tr>
<tr><td>Net realized and unrealized (gains) losses from investments</td><td>96,015</td><td>(202,913)</td></tr>
<tr><td>Other, net</td><td>21</td><td>1,265</td></tr>
<tr><td>Net cash provided by operating activities</td><td>180,627</td><td>177,944</td></tr>
<tr><td>Cash flows from investing activities:</td><td></td><td></td></tr>
<tr><td>Purchases of investments</td><td>(1,996,016)</td><td>(2,603,490)</td></tr>
<tr><td>Proceeds from sales and maturities of investments</td><td>1,878,546</td><td>2,495,333</td></tr>
<tr><td>Purchases of property and equipment</td><td>(149,993)</td><td>(126,557)</td></tr>
<tr><td>Disbursements for student loans</td><td>(5,600)</td><td>(5,282)</td></tr>
<tr><td>Repayments of student loans</td><td>4,636</td><td>4,278</td></tr>
<tr><td>Decrease (increase) in deposits with bond trustees, net</td><td>27,440</td><td>(83,002)</td></tr>
<tr><td>Net cash used by investing activities</td><td>(240,987)</td><td>(318,720)</td></tr>
<tr><td>Cash flows from financing activities:</td><td></td><td></td></tr>
<tr><td>Contributions restricted for long-term investment</td><td>86,975</td><td>142,996</td></tr>
<tr><td>Proceeds from borrowings</td><td>71,372</td><td>127,560</td></tr>
<tr><td>Repayments of borrowings</td><td>(57,318)</td><td>(15,450)</td></tr>
<tr><td>Increase (decrease) in other long-term liabilities</td><td>(18,571)</td><td>13,193</td></tr>
<tr><td>Net cash provided by financing activities</td><td>82,458</td><td>268,299</td></tr>
<tr><td>Net increase in cash and cash equivalents</td><td>22,098</td><td>127,523</td></tr>
<tr><td>Cash and cash equivalents at beginning of year</td><td>226,721</td><td>99,198</td></tr>
<tr><td>Cash and cash equivalents at end of year</td><td>$ 248,819</td><td>$ 226,721</td></tr>
</table>

Accompanying notes to financial statements not included.
Source: The Johns Hopkins University, Financial Report, 2001.

judgment and analysis of the creditworthiness of the donors, past collection experience, and other relevant factors. Estimated collectible contributions to be received after one year are discounted using a risk-free rate for the expected period of collection.

In another note, the University shows how much of the contributions receivable are expected to be collected in less than 1 year, how much in 1 to 5 years, and how much in more than 5 years. The note also states the following:

At June 30, 2001, approximately 57% of the gross contributions receivable were due from ten donors. . . . Approximately 66%. . . . of contribution revenues for 2001. . . . were from ten donors. At June 30, 2001, the University had also received bequest intentions of approximately $85,675,000 and certain other conditional promises to give. These intentions and conditional promises to give are not recognized as assets and, if they are received, they will generally be restricted for specific purposes stipulated by the donors.

Notice (Tables 12A-2 and 12A-3) that some contributions are classified as operating revenues, while others are included in nonoperating revenues, gains and losses. Why? The University describes the distinction in the notes this way:

Contributions received for capital projects or perpetual or term endowment funds

and contributions under split-interest agreements or perpetual trusts are reported as nonoperating revenues. All other contributions are reported as operating revenues.[1]

Notice (Tables 12A-2 and 12A-3) that large amounts of investment income or loss are classified as operating revenues, but equally significant amounts are included in nonoperating revenues, gains and losses. What is the distinction? What is included in investment income or loss? According to the notes:

Investments are stated at their fair values. . . . Investment income included in operating revenues consists of income and *realized* gains and losses on investments. . . . All *unrealized* gains and losses. . . . are reported in nonoperating revenues. [Emphasis added.] (Additional details of the investment income and loss are presented in another note.)

Notice (Tables 12A-2 and 12A-3) that the operating expenses are presented by natural classification, rather than by function. FASB standards state that expenses by function may be presented either in the statement of activities or in the notes. The university chose to report the functional expense information in the notes.

---

[1] In a split-interest agreement, a donor makes a gift to the NFPO, but the NFPO is not the only beneficiary.

Chapter 13

Accounting for Health Care Organizations

After completing this chapter, you should be able to:

➤ *Identify the sources of generally accepted accounting principles for health care organizations.*

➤ *Identify the types of resources accounted for in the General Fund of health care organizations.*

➤ *Prepare journal entries related to patient service revenue and patient receivables.*

➤ *Prepare other journal entries normally used in the General Fund to record the operating activities of hospitals.*

➤ *Identify the Restricted Funds maintained by health care organizations.*

➤ *Prepare journal entries normally used in the Restricted Funds.*

➤ *Identify and prepare financial statements for not-for-profit and governmental hospitals.*

*B*ecause of the rising cost of health care and the growth of third-party health care insurers, a great amount of attention has been directed toward organizations providing health care services. Major third parties involved in financing the cost of health care include governments, private insurance companies, and health maintenance organizations (HMOs). Public programs that receive the most attention are Medicare and Medicaid. The Medicare program is financed primarily by the federal government. Medicaid is a public assistance-type program financed by the federal, state, and sometimes local governments.

The interest of third-party insurers, together with rising costs, results in emphasis on the accounting and financial reporting systems of health care entities. Accounting is important because third parties often base their payments to health care providers on allowable costs, some form of fixed-rate reimbursement, or a combination of both. Thus measurement and control of costs are critical, both to health care providers and to third-party payers.

HEALTH CARE SERVICE PROVIDERS

Health care services are provided not only in many different types of settings, but also by entities having different ownership structures and operating orientations. Health care services may be provided, for example, in hospitals, surgery centers, clinics, laboratories, group medical practices, nursing homes (that differ in the intensity of the medical care they provide), home health agencies, and continuing care retirement communities. Health care organizations may be organized as not-for-profit, governmental, or private for-profit entities. Not-for-profit health care entities may be classified as having either a business orientation or a non-business orientation. This chapter covers accounting and financial reporting by health care entities organized either as governmental or as not-for-profit with a business orientation.

The characteristics of governmental entities, as distinguished from not-for-profit entities, are discussed in Chapter 12. Some governmental health care providers are organized within departments of state or local governments. Other governmental health care providers are organized as legally separate corporations, governed by boards appointed by government officials. Legally separate governmental corporations may have the power to tax and to issue tax-exempt debt directly (rather than through a state or local government agency).

Not-for-profit health care providers, like other not-for-profit entities, have no ownership interests and thus do not operate to maximize profits for owners. Not-for-profit health care entities with a business orientation are basically self-supporting as a result of fees they charge for their services, but they may also receive relatively small amounts of contributions. Non–business-oriented not-for-profit health care entities are considered so because they obtain most of their revenues from contributions, grants, and other support. Non–business-oriented not-for-profit health care entities are included in the voluntary health and welfare organizations (VHWOs) discussed in Chapter 12.

SOURCES OF GENERALLY ACCEPTED ACCOUNTING PRINCIPLES

The Financial Accounting Standards Board (FASB) establishes accounting standards for for-profit and not-for-profit entities. The Governmental Accounting Standards Board (GASB) establishes them for governmental entities. Although some differences exist in the standards established for not-for-profit and government health care entities, the move for comparability among entities that perform similar functions has resulted in far more similarities than differences. The AICPA Audit and Accounting Guide—Health Care Organizations, which provides general accounting guidance for all health care entities except VHWOs, has been approved as a source of accounting principles by both the FASB and the GASB.[1]

In this chapter we will discuss health care entity transactions simultaneously for not-for-profit and governmental entities, pointing out differences where they exist. Most of the differences occur in accounting for certain contributions and in financial reporting. Keep the following factors in mind as you read this chapter:

- Governmental health care entities are subject to the accounting and reporting requirements for governmental *proprietary funds*, discussed in Chapter 7. Not-for-profit health care entities are subject to the accounting and reporting requirements for *not-for-profit organizations*, discussed in Chapter 12.
- Governmental health care entities use the economic resources measurement focus and the full accrual basis of accounting, as discussed in Chapter 7. They also tend to use fund accounting. The GASB permits governmental entities that use proprietary fund accounting to apply FASB standards, except for those that conflict with or contradict GASB standards.[2] For example, the GASB does not permit proprietary funds to apply FASB standards whose provisions are limited to or are developed primarily for not-for-profit entities, such as FASB *Statement Nos. 116 and 117*, discussed in Chapter 12.[3] The implications of that requirement will become clear later in this chapter.
- Not-for-profit business-oriented health care entities also use full accrual accounting and generally use fund accounting. Even though most of their revenues are obtained from fees and charges for services, they are subject to the accounting and financial reporting standards of FASB *Statement Nos. 116 and 117*, because they are not-for-profit entities.

---

[1]   American Institute of Certified Public Accountants, *AICPA Audit and Accounting Guide—Health Care Organizations* (New York, AICPA, 2001). As discussed in Chapter 1, AICPA Audit and Accounting Guides made applicable by the the FASB and the GASB are in the second level of the respective GAAP hierarchies.
[2]   GASB Cod. (2001), Sec. P80.102 and 103.
[3]   GASB Cod. (2001), Sec. P80.103.

HOSPITAL ACCOUNTING—THE GENERAL FUND

Governmental and not-for-profit hospitals[4] have traditionally used funds for internal accounting and managerial control purposes. Until recently, they also reported by fund type. As discussed in Chapter 12, however, the FASB now requires that all not-for-profit entities classify their funds into three broad net asset classes (unrestricted, temporarily restricted, and permanently restricted) for financial reporting purposes. Because many governmental and not-for-profit hospitals continue to use funds for internal accounting purposes, we will discuss the nature of those funds in this chapter.

Scope of the General Fund

Funds used by hospitals are categorized into two groups: General Fund and Restricted Funds. The *General Fund* (sometimes called Unrestricted Funds) accounts for the day-to-day operations of a hospital and its nonrestricted resources. The resources and liabilities of the General Fund fall into four broad categories: operating resources and liabilities, assets limited as to use, assets and liabilities in agency funds, and plant resources.

- *Operating resources* are assets and liabilities associated with the normal daily operations of a hospital. Thus, current assets used in operations are reported in this group. These assets include cash, receivables, inventories, and prepaid expenses. Current liabilities associated with daily operations (accounts payable, notes payable, accrued expenses, etc.) are also included in this group.
- *Assets limited as to use* are resources that are set aside either internally by the hospital's governing board or in accordance with an agreement with an external party other than a donor or grantor. To illustrate:
  - A hospital's governing board may decide to set aside funds for a specific project or function, such as a special training program or capital acquisition. Although the funds are segregated, the board's decision represents an internal designation rather than an external restriction, because the governing board can readily change its mind.
  - A hospital may issue revenue bonds and be required to maintain certain deposits with a trustee in accordance with the bond agreement. Or the hospital may be required by a third-party payer to fund depreciation on certain capital assets. Even though these requirements legally restrict the use of funds, they are reported as "limited as to use" because they were not imposed by donors or grantors.

---

[4] Although the basic principles discussed in this chapter cover all types of health care entities, most of the illustrations relate to hospitals. To avoid confusion, we will henceforth refer to hospitals throughout this chapter unless the point being made specifically relates to health care entities other than hospitals.

- *Agency resources* are resources a hospital holds that belong to other persons such as patients and doctors. They are similar in function to the resources found in Agency Funds used by governmental units.
- *Plant resources* are property, plant, and equipment used by a hospital in its general operations and any related liabilities. Thus, long-term debt issued to finance capital assets is included in the General Fund.

General Fund Revenue Sources

Hospital operating revenues come primarily from patient services (based on fees for nursing and other professional services) and health care insurance premiums (based on agreements to provide care). (Other types of health care entities may obtain significant revenues from resident services, based on maintenance or rental fees.) Hospitals often also obtain revenues (or gains) from investment income, education programs, contributions, and gift shops.

Hospitals obtain most of their revenues from third-party payers, including both public sources, such as Medicare and Medicaid, and private insurers, such as HMOs and Blue Cross. Third-party payers have developed various payment systems, under which they generally pay hospitals at amounts less than the hospital's established rates. (Differences between a hospital's established rates and the amounts "allowed" by third-party payers are referred to as *contractual adjustments*.) Hospitals also provide services to some patients without charge (charity cases) and provide courtesy discounts to others. The different payment arrangements affect the way hospitals account for revenues and receivables.

Nature of Hospital Payment Systems

Hospital payment systems have changed significantly in recent years. The systems include fees based on diagnosis-related groups; capitation premiums that are paid per member, per month (PMPM); fees based on negotiated bids; and cost-reimbursement methods. Some payment rates are established prospectively (i.e., in advance of service delivery) at fixed amounts. Other payment rates may be based on interim billing amounts, subject to retrospective (i.e., after the accounting period ends) adjustment.

Medicare generally pays hospitals prospectively, based on *diagnosis-related groups (DRGs)*. Under the DRG system, all potential diagnoses are classified into a number of medically meaningful groups, each of which has a different value. Each hospital in a specific geographic region receives the same amount for each DRG, depending on whether the hospital is classified as urban or rural. Thus an uncomplicated appendectomy results in the same basic reimbursement to all hospitals in a given urban or rural area. However, other factors, such as whether the entity is a teaching hospital, are also considered in the payments a hospital will receive. The more efficient hospital will benefit from the prospective payment, because it may keep any reimbursement in excess of cost.

Third-party payers that pay hospitals retrospectively reimburse hospitals initially on the basis of interim payment rates. The interim payment rates are then adjusted retrospectively based on stipulated allowable costs after the hospitals submit required cost reports to the third-party payers. The rates reached on final settlement may differ significantly from the interim payment rates. Therefore, to ensure that revenues and net assets are reported on the accrual basis of accounting, reasonable estimates of the amounts receivable from or payable to the third-party payers need to be made in the period that the services are rendered.

Under *capitation agreements* with HMOs, hospitals generally receive agreed-upon premiums per member, per month, based on the number of participants in the HMO. In exchange, the hospitals agree to provide all medical services to the HMO's subscribers. The hospitals thus earn these revenues from *agreeing to provide* care, and will receive the capitation payments regardless of the actual services they perform. The hospitals may also receive fees from the HMO for certain services. Revenues under capitation arrangements are reported as premium revenues, not as patient service revenues.

A variety of other payment methods are also in effect, including prospectively determined rates per discharge, prospectively determined daily rates, and discounts from established charges.

Accounting for Revenues from Patient Care

Revenues based on fees for services *actually provided* by hospitals are classified as *patient service revenues*. These revenues include those derived from Medicare and Medicaid beneficiaries. Revenues based on *agreements to provide* care (regardless of whether care is actually provided) are classified as premium revenues and would include revenues from capitation arrangements with HMOs. Patient service revenues are reported separately from premium revenues in the financial statements.

Hospitals record patient service revenues and receivables initially at their gross (established) rates, even if they do not expect to collect those amounts. As previously noted, several factors are likely to cause the amount realized from these services to be significantly less than the established rates. These factors include contractual rate adjustments with third-party payers, provision of charity care, discounts granted to various persons, bad debts, and retrospective adjustments.

For financial reporting purposes, patient service revenue is reported on the operating statement *net* of contractual rate adjustments, charity care, and similar items that the hospital does not expect to collect. Patient service revenue is not reduced, however, by a provision for uncollectible accounts (bad debts expense). Instead, bad debts expense is reported in the expenses section of the operating statement. Receivables resulting from health care services are reported on the balance sheet at the amount likely to be realized in cash. Therefore, gross receivables must be reduced by allowances needed to present the receivables at their *net realizable value*.

Gross Patient Service Revenues and Provision for Contractual Adjustments

To illustrate, assume that a hospital's regular charges (at established rates) for nursing and other professional services are $1,700,000. To record this information, the following entry is made:

| Patient accounts receivable | 1,700,000 | |
| Patient service revenue | | 1,700,000 |

To record gross patient service revenue.

Although we use one account for each type of revenue, remember that this *control account* is used in the same manner as a control account in general accounting. Subsidiary records are used to accumulate the revenues for the unit to which the patient was admitted or whose services were used—for example, general nursing services, surgery, pediatrics, and radiology.

As previously stated, payment rates may be established either prospectively or retrospectively. When established prospectively, the full contractual adjustment is known at billing time. When established retrospectively, the full adjustment may not be known until the following year. In that case, interim rates reflecting a tentative contractual adjustment may be used for billing purposes. Provision for further contractual adjustment (upward or downward), however, may be needed at year-end to report revenues and receivables from third-party payers at net realizable amounts.

For example, assume that under a prospective billing arrangement with third-party payer X, the hospital has contractual adjustments of $80,000. Under a retrospective rate arrangement with third-party payer Y, it has contractual adjustments of $40,000 based on interim rates, pending later negotiation of final rates. The hospital would make the following entry at the time of the billings:

| Provision for contractual adjustments | 120,000 | |
| Patient accounts receivable | | 120,000 |

To record adjustments to revenue and receivables, based on prospective
billing contract with payer X and interim rates negotiated with payer Y.

After reducing the patient accounts receivable by the provision for contractual adjustments, the outstanding receivables would include the amount the hospital expects to collect from third-party payers plus the amount it expects to collect directly from the patients.

Other types of adjustments to gross patient revenues are made for charity services and "discounts" granted to the clergy, volunteers, and employees. These adjustments also represent the amount of the established rates that the hospital will not collect. The only difference between these and the contractual adjustments lies in the reason they will not be collected. Assume, for example, that the hospital provides services of $50,000 to charity patients. As soon as the hospital classifies the patients as "charity patients," the following entry is made:

| Provision for charity services | 50,000 | |
| Patient accounts receivable | | 50,000 |

To record adjustment to revenues and receivables because of charity care.

If collections of receivables during the year total $1,400,000, they would be recorded as follows:

| Cash | 1,400,000 | |
| Patient accounts receivable | | 1,400,000 |

To record collection of receivables.

Provision for Uncollectible Receivables

Accounts receivable must be stated in the financial statements at their net realizable value. Therefore, patient accounts receivable need to be reviewed for likelihood of collectiblity. An estimate for uncollectible accounts receivable (usually made by the allowance method) is reported as a bad debts expense. Recall from previous discussions that an allowance for uncollectible accounts is reported as a contra to accounts receivable because it is not known which specific accounts will turn out to be "bad debts." If hospital management estimates uncollectible amounts to be $30,000, the following entry would be made:

Uncollectible accounts (or bad debts) expense	30,000	
Allowance for uncollectible accounts		30,000
To record allowance for uncollectible accounts.		

If $20,000 of individual patient accounts become uncollectible, patient accounts receivable and the allowance for uncollectible accounts are reduced, as follows:

Allowance for uncollectible accounts	20,000	
Patient accounts receivable		20,000
To record write-off of accounts determined to be uncollectible.		

Estimated Third-Party Settlements

As previously stated, arrangements with some third-party payers may call for billing at interim rates, subject to retrospective adjustment based on a review of cost reports submitted by the hospital. To ensure that amounts reported as net patient service revenues, receivables or payables in the financial statements are valid, estimates must be made of the settlement amounts for all billing arrangements that have not been settled as of the date of the financial statements. The adjustment takes the form of an additional contractual adjustment.

Regarding its retrospective rate arrangement with third-party payer Y, assume the hospital estimates at year-end that it will need to refund $15,000 because its analysis of reimbursable costs shows that the interim rates negotiated with Y were too high. If Y had paid all amounts previously billed by the hospital, the following entry would be needed at year-end:

Provision for contractual adjustments	15,000	
Estimated third-party payer settlements		15,000
To record provision for estimated refund to payer Y, pending		
negotiation of retrospective rate.		

Based on these journal entries, the amount reported on the hospital's operating statement as net patient service revenue would be $1,515,000 (gross billings of $1,700,000, less the $135,000 provision for contractual adjustments and the $50,000 provision for charity services). Net patient accounts receivable reported on the hospital's balance sheet would be $100,000 (gross outstanding receivables of $110,000, less $10,000 remaining in the contra account allowance for uncollectible accounts). The $15,000 estimated third-party payer settlements account would be reported as a liability. (Note that, in the previous journal entry, we assumed that third-party payer Y had paid all amounts previously billed by the hospital. If Y had not paid all amounts previously billed, the $15,000 estimated settlement would be reported as a reduction of the outstanding receivables in order to state the receivables at net realizable value.)

Capitation Premiums

In addition to billing fees for services, the hospital also has capitation agreements with various HMOs, wherein it receives agreed-upon premiums per member, per month. If the hospital receives $400,000 of capitation fees at the beginning of the month, it would make the following entry:

Cash	400,000	
Premium revenue		400,000
To record capitation premium revenues.		

Assume that, at the end of the month, hospital records show that it provided services to participants in these HMOs amounting to $375,000 at its established billing rates. Although this information is valuable for internal management purposes, no entry is made in the financial accounting records.

For an example of the effect of these entries on financial reporting, see Patient accounts receivable and Estimated third-party payer settlements in Table 13-1 (page 573) and Net patient service revenue and Premium revenue in Table 13-2 (page 574).

Notes to Financial Statements Regarding Patient Revenue Recognition

The nature of the third-party arrangements, revenue recognition practices, and charity care policies should be described in notes to the financial statements. The following is an illustration of a note regarding these arrangements that might be made in the summary of significant accounting policies.

> *Net Patient Service Revenue.* The hospital has agreements with third-party payers, providing for payments at amounts different from its established rates. The agreements provide both for prospectively and retrospectively determined rates. Net patient service revenue is reported at estimated net realizable amounts from patients, third-party payers, and others for services rendered, including estimated retroactive adjustments under agreements with third-party payers. Estimated retroactive adjustments are accrued in the period services are provided and adjusted in future periods as final settlements are made.
>
> *Premium Revenue.* The hospital has agreements with various health maintenance organizations to provide services to subscribing participants. In accordance with the agreements, the hospital receives monthly capitation payments based on the number of participants, regardless of the services the hospital actually performs.
>
> *Charity Care.* The hospital provides care to patients either without charge or at less than its established rates. These patients must meet the criteria under the hospital's charity care policy. The value of these services is not reported as revenue because the hospital does not seek to collect amounts that qualify as charity care.

Hospitals generally provide additional details regarding third-party payment arrangements and charity care (including the dollar amount of charges forgone for services provided under the charity care policy) in separate notes.

Investment Returns

Investment activities often provide a major source of revenue for hospitals. Not-for-profit hospitals account for investments in accordance with FASB *Statement No. 124*, "Accounting Guide for Certain Investments Held by Not-for-Profit Organizations," discussed in Chapter 12. Governmental hospitals account for investments in accordance with GASB *Statement No. 31*, "Accounting and Financial Reporting for Certain Investments and for External Investment Pools," discussed in Chapter 8. Both standards require that, in general, hospitals report investments in equity and debt securities at fair value on the balance sheet. Reporting investments at fair value on the balance sheet means that investment returns in the operating statement include dividends and interest, realized gains and losses, and unrealized gains and losses.

For financial reporting purposes, some prefer to distinguish realized investment gains and losses from unrealized gains and losses. Not-for-profit hospitals actually make such a distinction. As shown in Table 13-2, they report all realized investment gains and losses above the caption "excess of revenues over expenses," and report unrealized investment gains and losses on securities other than trading securities below that caption.[5] (A security is classified as *other than trading* if it is acquired without the intent to sell it in the near term.) GASB investment accounting standards, which are applicable to governmental hospitals, generally do not permit realized gains and losses to be displayed in the financial statements separately from the net increase or decrease in the fair value of investments.[6] This distinction in reporting affects the accounting treatment.

To illustrate, assume a governmental and a not-for-profit hospital each purchase a security for $100,000 on March 15, 2004. (The not-for-profit hospital considers it to be other than trading.) Both would make the following entry:

Investments	100,000	
Cash		100,000
To record purchase of investment.		

Both securities increase in value to $115,000 at December 31, 2004, the balance sheet dates, and both are sold in the year 2005 for $120,000. Both hospitals have an unrealized gain of $15,000 in 2004 and both have an additional gain of $5,000 in 2005. The $5,000 gain in 2005 can be separated into two components—a realized gain of $20,000 and a decrease in the unrealized gain of $15,000. The governmental hospital would carry the investment at fair value and report both the unrealized and the realized gain in a single account called "Net realized and unrealized gains and losses on investments." It would make the following entries to record the transactions:

---

[5] *AICPA Guide—Health Care Organizations* (2001), para. 4.07 and 4.19.
[6] GASB Cod. (2001), Sec. I50.111. (The GASB does, however, permit note disclosure of realized gains and losses.)

| Investments | 15,000 | |
| Revenues—net realized and unrealized gains and losses on investments | | 15,000 |

To record unrealized gain on investments in 2004.

Cash	120,000	
Investments		115,000
Revenues—net realized and unrealized gains and losses on investments		5,000

To record gain on sale of investments in 2005.

The governmental hospital would report investment revenue as nonoperating revenue in its operating statement.

The not-for-profit hospital would carry the investment at original cost and use an "investment valuation account" to record the adjustment to fair value. It would also use separate accounts for the unrealized gain and the realized gain. It would make the following journal entries.

| Investment valuation account | 15,000 | |
| Unrestricted revenue—change in net unrealized gains and losses on investments | | 15,000 |

To record unrealized gain on investments in 2004.

Cash	120,000	
Unrestricted revenue—realized gain on investments		20,000
Investments		100,000
Unrestricted revenue—change in net unrealized gains and losses on investments	15,000	
Investment valuation account		15,000

To record realized gain on investments and reverse unrealized gain in 2005.

For financial reporting purposes, the not-for-profit hospital would add the $15,000 balance in the investment valuation account to the investments account in order to report investments at fair value at the end of 2004. It would report the $15,000 unrealized gain below Excess of revenues over expenses. In 2005, the realized gain of $20,000 would be included with other investment income and reported above Excess of revenues over expenses. The negative $15,000 net change in unrealized gains and losses would be reported below that caption. Notice the presentation of these items in Table 13-2. (Despite the different presentation methods, the net effect for both hospitals is to increase net assets by $15,000 in 2004 and by $5,000 in 2005.)

Other Revenues, Gains, and Support

Hospitals may also derive revenues and gains from services and activities other than services to patients and investing. Other sources of revenue and gains include educational program fees (including tuition for schools), sales of medical and pharmaceutical supplies to doctors and others, parking fees, cafeteria sales, and gift shop sales. Contributions also provide a source of support for hospital activities. For analytical purposes, other forms of revenue, gains, and support are reported in captions separate from net patient service revenue and premium revenue.

There is a fine distinction between revenues and gains. Revenues are inflows from delivering goods, providing services or other activities that constitute the entity's ongoing major or central operations. Gains are increases in net assets from an entity's peripheral or incidental transactions. An activity peripheral to one entity might be a normal, ongoing activity of another. Depending on materiality of individual items, revenues and gains may be aggregated as Other revenues for reporting purposes.

Parking and Other Revenues or Gains

Revenues received from parking fees, the cafeteria, educational programs (such as nursing school tuition), and so forth are recorded as follows (amounts assumed):

Cash	245,000	
Other receivables	5,000	
Other revenues (or gains)		250,000
To record other revenues.		

Contributions of Cash and Supplies

Contributions to hospitals may take the form of unrestricted or restricted cash donations, supplies and commodities (such as medicines or materials) to cover the cost of charity services, and professional or nonprofessional services. Unrestricted contributions are recorded in the General Fund as other revenue or gains, measured at fair value. Restricted contributions are recorded initially in a donor-restricted fund.

Contributions received by not-for-profit hospitals are accounted for and reported in accordance with FASB *Statement Nos. 116 and 117*, as discussed in Chapter 12. Contributions received by governmental hospitals are accounted for and reported in accordance with GASB standards for voluntary nonexchange transactions, as described in GASB *Statement No. 33*. For example, a governmental hospital should recognize the fair value of donated commodities as revenue in the period when all eligibility requirements are met, which is usually in the period when the commodities are received.

To illustrate, assume a private organization makes an unrestricted cash donation of $100,000 and medicines having a fair value of $75,000 to both a not-for-profit hospital and a governmental hospital. Both hospitals would report both donations as revenues on receipt of the contributions. The not-for-profit hospital would report the contributions as increases in unrestricted net assets (other revenue), and the governmental hospital would report them as General Fund or unrestricted fund nonoperating income:

Cash	100,000	
Other revenue (or gains)—unrestricted support		100,000
To record receipt of unrestricted cash donation.		
Inventory—medicines and drugs	75,000	
Other revenue (or gains)—donated commodities		75,000
To record receipt of medicines at fair value.		

Contributed Services

Services donated to not-for-profit hospitals would be accounted for based on the criteria set forth in FASB *Statement No. 116,* discussed in Chapter 12. For example, if doctors and nurses donated professional services having a fair value of $10,000 to a not-for-profit hospital, and the services would typically need to be purchased, the following entry would be made:

Patient care expense	10,000	
Other revenue (or gains)—donated services		10,000
To record receipt of donated services.		

If donated services do not meet the criteria discussed in Chapter 12 (i.e., if they do not require specialized skills, are not provided by individuals who possess those skills, and would not need to be purchased), the hospital should not recognize expenses and revenues. Thus, a not-for-profit hospital should not recognize the value of many donated services that do not require specialized skills, such as moving wheelchairs and selling at gift shops.

GASB *Statement No. 33* does not apply to donated services. In the absence of standards regarding donated services, governmental hospitals often do not record them. Others record them if the hospital controls the employment and duties of the donors and the services are of significant value.

Expenses

Expenses related to the general operation of a hospital consist of nursing and other professional services, general services, fiscal services, and administrative services. The *Health Care Organization Guide* states that expenses may be reported on the face of the financial statements either by natural classification (e.g., salaries and benefits, medical supplies and drugs, insurance) or by function (e.g., patient care expense, dietary services).[7] Not-for-profit entities that report by natural classification on the face of the financial statements are required also to show expenses by functional classification in the notes. In this chapter, we illustrate expenses by functional classification. The entry used to record some of these expenses is (amounts assumed):

Patient care expense	750,000	
Dietary services expense	50,000	
General services expense	200,000	
Administrative services expense	145,000	
Interest expense	155,000	
Cash		1,100,000
Accounts payable, salaries payable, and so on		200,000
To record certain operating expenses.		

For simplicity, we combined the recording and payment of expenses in the preceding entry, and we combined several liability items. Because we are dealing with

---

[7] *AICPA Guide—Health Care Organizations,* para. 10.22.

summary journal entries that cover an entire year, this aggregation will have no effect on the results of our illustrations.

During the year, the acquisition and use of inventory items is recorded as follows (amounts assumed):

Inventories	150,000	
Accounts payable		150,000
To record purchase of inventory.		

Patient care expense	70,000	
Dietary services expense	50,000	
Administrative services expense	20,000	
Inventories		140,000
To record use of inventory.		

Because full accrual accounting is used for hospitals, items of property, plant, and equipment are recorded as assets when acquired and are depreciated over their useful lives. The entry to record this expense is as follows (amounts assumed):

Depreciation expense	200,000	
Accumulated depreciation—plant and equipment		200,000
To record depreciation for the year.		

Medical Malpractice Claims

Settlements and judgments on medical malpractice claims constitute a potential major expense for hospitals. Whether expenses and liabilities need to be recognized on malpractice claims depends on whether risk has been transferred by the hospital to third-party insurance companies or to public entity risk pools.

FASB *Statement No. 5*, "Accounting for Contingencies," and GASB *Statement No. 10*, "Accounting and Financial Reporting for Risk Financing and Related Insurance Issues," provide guidance regarding medical malpractice claims. The basic rule is: If risk of loss has not been transferred to an external third party, expenses must be recognized and liabilities reported if it is probable that a loss has been incurred and the amount of the loss can be reasonably estimated.

The basic rule applies whether or not claims for incidents occurring before the balance sheet date are known. These claims are called incurred but not reported (IBNR) claims. An estimate must be made for losses on IBNR claims if it is probable that claims will be asserted and losses can be reasonably estimated. Historical experience of both the entity and the industry may be used in estimating the probability of IBNR claims.

Estimates of losses from malpractice claims may be based on a case-by-case review of all claims, or by applying historical experience regarding losses (e.g., the ratio of settlement amounts to claimed amounts) to outstanding claims, or both. For example, if an uninsured hospital has 10 medical malpractice claims aggregating $1,000,000 and historical experience shows that claims have been settled for an average of 30 percent of the amount claimed, the hospital should accrue an expense and a liability for $300,000.

What if one patient has filed a claim for $500,000 and negotiations between the attorneys, though not complete, indicate that the claim probably can be settled for an amount within the range of $150,000 and $300,000? For that situation, the basic rule is: If it is probable that a loss has occurred, but analysis shows that the amount of loss is within a range of amounts, the most likely amount within the range should be accrued as an expense. If no amount in the range is more likely than any other, the minimum amount in the range should be accrued, and the potential additional loss should be disclosed in the notes if a reasonable possibility exists for loss greater than the amount accrued. (As a practical matter, care should be taken in presenting this disclosure to preserve the ability to negotiate an appropriate settlement.)

For financial reporting purposes, amounts accrued that are expected to be paid within 1 year after the date of the financial statements should be reported as current liabilities and the rest of the accrual should be reported as noncurrent. Hospitals should also disclose their programs of malpractice insurance coverage and their basis for recording accruals.

Other Transactions

The General Fund often borrows and repays loans. If a hospital repays $15,000 of short-term loans, pays $3,000 in interest, and accrues $1,000 of additional interest, the following entry is made:

Notes payable	15,000	
Interest expense	4,000	
Cash		18,000
Interest payable		1,000

To record payment made on the principal of notes outstanding and the interest expense for the year.

As previously mentioned, segregation of unrestricted funds by the managing board for a particular purpose does not create a restricted fund, because the board retains authority to change any previous actions. These segregated funds are, however, shown as Assets limited as to use. (See the Asset section in Table 13-1 for an example of the reporting of assets internally designated for capital acquisition purposes.)

To illustrate the recording of such a transaction, assume that the managing board of a not-for-profit hospital formally decides to set aside $50,000 of unrestricted resources in a fund for modernizing plant and equipment. During the year, the investments made by the fund earn $3,000, of which $2,000 is received in cash. The entries to record these events are:

Cash—board-designated for plant and equipment	50,000	
Cash		50,000

To record board designation of resources for plant and equipment replacement.

Cash—board-designated for plant and equipment	2,000	
Interest receivable—board-designated for plant and equipment	1,000	
Unrestricted revenues—investment income		3,000

To record income from board-designated investments.

Although not necessary for external financial reporting, an entry should also be made to separate unrestricted but designated net assets from other unrestricted assets for internal financial reporting.

During the year, the hospital issues $5 million of 20-year bonds to provide funds for the acquisition of new X-ray equipment. These resources are deposited directly with the First National Bank, as prescribed in the bond indenture. (Thus they are classified as Assets limited as to use.) The following entry should be made when the bonds are issued:

Cash—acquisition of equipment	5,000,000	
Bonds payable		5,000,000
To record the issuance of bonds and the deposit of the proceeds.		

Later in the year, the hospital uses some of the bond proceeds to acquire new equipment for its operating rooms. The following entry is necessary to record the acquisition.

Equipment	1,060,000	
Cash—acquisition of equipment		1,060,000
To record the purchase of operating room equipment.		

ACCOUNTING PROCEDURES FOR RESTRICTED FUNDS

Types of Restricted Funds

Restricted Funds are used to account for resources that must be used in compliance with the terms of an agreement, like those related to donor gifts or grants. Restricted Funds are used only when an external limitation is placed on the use of the resources and the resources are not related to a bond agreement or third-party reimbursement. Hospitals generally have Specific Purpose Funds, Plant Replacement and Expansion Funds, and Endowment Funds, and may also have Student Loan Funds, Annuity Funds, and Life Income Funds.

- *Specific Purpose Funds* consist of resources that are donor- or grantor-restricted for specific operating purposes. For example, if an individual donates funds to a hospital for cancer research, these funds are recorded in a Specific Purpose Fund. As the research expenses are incurred, they are recorded in the General Fund.
- *Plant Replacement and Expansion Funds* are used to accumulate resources contributed by outsiders that can only be used to replace existing plant assets or to expand the existing plant. Assets acquired with those resources are recorded in the General Fund.
- *Endowment Funds* may be either Term Endowment Funds or Permanent (Pure) Endowment Funds. *Term endowment funds* are used when a donor requires that the principal be maintained for a specific time period or imposes other restrictions. After the term restrictions have been satisfied, the principal can be unrestricted or restricted. *Permanent Endowment Funds* are used when the donor requires that the principal be maintained in perpetuity. Income from Endowment Funds may be restricted or unrestricted. If the income is restricted, it is usually recorded in a Specific Purpose Fund or a Plant Replacement and Expansion Fund. If it is unrestricted, the income is recorded in the General Fund.

- *Student Loan Funds* are resources used for making loans to students. These resources from donors or grantors are loaned to students who must repay them, usually with interest. The interest is used to cover operating expenses and bad debts, as well as to make additional loans.
- *Annuity Funds* and *Life Income Funds* enable donors to make a contribution, but to retain an interest in it. When Annuity Funds are used, a *specific dollar amount* is paid to the donor or some other party for a specified time period. When Life Income Funds are used, *all the income* earned from the donated resources is paid to the donor or other party for a specified time period, usually the lifetime of the person receiving the income. After the specified time period, the principal of both types of funds is available to the hospital either for restricted or unrestricted purposes.

A donor may create a legal trust that is independent of the hospital. In such a situation, the hospital has no control over the resources of the trust because the trust is administered by a third party. Income from such a trust is usually given to the hospital. Because the hospital does not have control over the principal of the trust, these resources are not reported on the hospital's balance sheet. The hospital is required, however, to disclose information about these funds in the notes to the financial statements. If the principal of the fund reverts to the hospital after some time or specified event, the hospital may report these assets on its financial statements.

Not-for-Profit Hospital Accounting for Restricted Funds

The notion of "restricted," as used in not-for-profit fund accounting, is somewhat broader than the FASB's definition of restricted for financial reporting. Specific Purpose Funds, for example, can be classified as either unrestricted or temporarily restricted, depending on whether the fund balances represent amounts contributed with donor-imposed restrictions or whether they are subject to limitations other than those imposed by donors. We will illustrate accounting procedures for the more commonly used restricted funds.

General Rules
The general rules for not-for-profit hospital accounting within each of the funds are similar to those discussed in Chapter 12 for other not-for-profit organizations. They are as follows:

- All donor-restricted contributions are recorded as either temporarily or permanently restricted revenues or gains when received.
- When temporarily restricted resources are released from restriction, not-for-profit hospitals record a reclassification out of temporarily restricted resources and a reclassification in to unrestricted net assets.
- Expenses resulting from use of the reclassified resources are reported as decreases in unrestricted net assets.

Specific Purpose Funds
Specific purpose funds are used to account for resources that are restricted for specific operating purposes. Restrictions on their use are temporary, expiring either with the passage of time or by fulfillment of the purpose stipulated by the donor. Assume a not-for-profit hospital receives a $500,000 gift, to be used specifically for research

into methods of counseling individuals who have become addicted to drugs. Later, the hospital incurs $25,000 in research program expenses. The entries to record those transactions and the funds used to record them are as follows:

Entries to accounts for Specific Purpose Funds	Cash	500,000	
	Temporarily restricted support—contributions		500,000
	To record contribution for research.		
	Temporarily restricted asset reclassifications out—net assets		
	released from restriction used for operations	25,000	
	Cash		25,000
	To record payment of research program expenses and net assets released from restriction.		
Entry to accounts for General Fund	Research program expenses	25,000	
	Unrestricted asset reclassifications in—net assets released		
	from restrictions used for operations		25,000
	To record research program expenses and net assets released from restriction.		

Plant Replacement and Expansion Funds

Plant replacement and expansion funds accumulate resources from donors or grantors that can be used only to replace or expand existing plant assets. Because hospital plant is reported in the General Fund, Plant Replacement and Expansion Funds contain only financial resources that will be used to acquire capital resources. To illustrate, assume that Rocky MacDuff donates $100,000 cash to a not-for-profit hospital and that the gift must be used to replace existing assets. Then, $80,000 of the contribution is used to acquire equipment, causing expiration of the temporary restriction. The entries to record these transactions are as follows:

Entries to accounts for Plant Replacement and Expansion Fund	Cash	100,000	
	Temporarily restricted support—contributions		100,000
	To record MacDuff gift for capital asset replacement.		
	Temporarily restricted asset reclassifications out—net assets		
	released from restriction for purchase of equipment	80,000	
	Cash		80,000
	To record release of net assets from restriction and payment for equipment.		
Entry to accounts for General Fund	Equipment	80,000	
	Unrestricted asset reclassifications in—net assets		
	released from restriction for purchase of equipment		80,000
	To record purchase of equipment and release of net assets from restriction.		

If fund resources are invested in marketable securities until plant is acquired, the recording of income from the securities is determined by the restrictions, if any, placed on that income. If no restrictions are placed on the use of the investment income, it is recorded in the General Fund as unrestricted. Assume income from the securities in this illustration must be used for the same purpose as the gift itself, which is what usually occurs. If $2,000 income accrues from investment of the MacDuff gift, the investment income is recorded in the Plant Replacement and Expansion Fund, as follows:

Interest receivable	2,000	
Temporarily restricted revenue—investment income		2,000
To record investment income from MacDuff gift.		

Endowment Funds

Endowment funds are used when a donor gives a hospital assets whose principal must be maintained intact. Income from the investment of the assets can be either restricted or unrestricted in use. Assume that Sam and Max Katz give, to a hospital, marketable securities with a fair market value of $500,000. The principal of the fund must be maintained in perpetuity (and is, therefore, considered as a Permanent or Pure Endowment Fund). The income from the endowment is restricted to finance the cost of cancer research. Income of $30,000 is received during the year. The entries to record those transactions are as follows:

Entry to accounts	Marketable securities	500,000	
for Endowment	Permanently restricted support—contributions		500,000
Fund	To record receipt of Sam and Max Katz gift.		
Entry to accounts	Cash	30,000	
for Specific	Temporarily restricted revenue—investment income		30,000
Purpose Fund	To record investment income from Sam and Max Katz fund to be		
	used for cancer research.		

(*Note:* In the preceding entry, the investment income was recorded directly in the Specific Purpose Fund. Some prefer to record the revenue initially in the Endowment Fund and establish a "due to" the Specific Purpose Fund, to provide control over the investment income. When the resources of the Specific Purpose Fund are used to conduct research, the expenses are reported in the General Fund and the temporarily restricted net assets are released from restrictions. This journal record is made with reclassification entries, as shown in the section on Specific Purpose Funds.)

If the contribution specified that the income from the endowment could be used for any purpose desired by the hospital's management, the investment income would be reported in the General Fund with a credit to Unrestricted revenue—investment income.

Financial Reporting Effect

The foregoing illustrations assume the use of fund accounting for internal control purposes. For external financial reporting, however, not-for-profit hospitals must report on the entity as a whole (distinguishing among unrestricted, temporarily restricted, and permanently restricted resources) just like any other not-for-profit entity.

To observe the financial reporting effect of the foregoing transactions, see Tables 13-2 and 13-3. Notice that donor-restricted contributions are reported in the Statement of Changes in Net Assets (Table 13-3) as increases in temporarily or permanently restricted net assets. Net assets released from restrictions are reported in that statement as decreases in temporarily restricted net assets. Net assets released from restrictions used for operations (reclassification in) and related program expenses are reported on the Statement of Operations (Table 13-2) and in the Statement of Changes in Net Assets. Net assets released from restrictions used for purchase of property and equipment (reclassification in) are also reported on both statements, but below the line showing Excess of revenues over expenses.

Governmental Hospital Accounting for Restricted Funds

General Rules

For financial reporting purposes, the GASB defines the term *restricted* differently from the FASB. The GASB does not distinguish between temporarily and permanently restricted and does not limit restricted net assets to those subject to donor-imposed restrictions. The GASB requires that net assets be reported as restricted when constraints are imposed either:

- Externally, by creditors (such as through debt covenants), grantors, contributors, or laws or regulations of other governments, or
- By law, through constitutional provisions or enabling legislation.[8] (Enabling legislation, as the term is used by the GASB, includes a legally enforceable requirement that resources be used only for the purposes stipulated in the legislation.)

Governmental hospitals engaged in business-type activities follow GASB standards for proprietary funds. Pursuant to GASB *Statement No. 34*, all proprietary fund revenues, including capital contributions and additions to permanent and term endowments, should be reported on the statement of revenues, expenses, and changes in net assets.[9]

Hospital transactions accounted for in restricted funds are often what the GASB defines as *voluntary nonexchange transactions.* They include certain governmental grants and entitlements as well as donations by nongovernmental entities, including individuals. Governmental hospitals receiving such grants and donations should recognize revenues when all applicable eligibility requirements, including time requirements, are met.[10]

GASB *Statement No. 33* distinguishes between time requirements and purpose restrictions. *Time requirements* specify the period when resources must be used or when use may begin. Time requirements affect revenue recognition. For example, if a hospital receives resources before it is eligible to use them, the grant or gift should be reported as deferred revenue. *Purpose restrictions* specify the purpose for which the resources are required to be used. They do not affect revenue recognition, but instead affect whether the net assets should be classified as restricted or unrestricted.

In addition to time requirements, other types of eligibility requirements affect the timing of revenue recognition. For example, a higher-level government may specify that the recipient of a hospital construction grant does not qualify for resources until allowable costs are incurred (as in the case of expenditure-driven grants). In those instances, revenues are recognized as allowable costs are incurred. Gifts received as endowments should be recognized as revenues upon receipt, provided all eligibility requirements are met.

When restricted fund resources are used for the intended purposes, expenses or assets should be recorded in the General Fund. The credit part of the entry to record

---

[8] GASB Cod. (2001), Sec. 1800.134.
[9] GASB Cod. (2001), Sec. P80.119.
[10] GASB Cod. (2001), Sec. N50.104d.

these transactions in the General Fund should be labeled "Amounts released from restriction," which is narrower and hence more descriptive than the term *transfers*.

Illustration of Private Donation with Purpose Restriction

A corporation makes a donation to a governmental hospital, stipulating that the donation must be used solely for the purpose of training nurses. For this voluntary nonexchange transaction, the hospital should recognize the entire amount as revenue (reported as nonoperating revenues) when the gift is received. The resulting net assets should be reported as restricted until the purpose restriction (training nurses) is fulfilled. If $50,000 is donated and $20,000 of that amount is used, the following entries would be made to record the transaction.

Entries to accounts for Specific Purpose Funds	Cash	50,000	
	Restricted revenue (nonoperating)—contributions		50,000
	To record contribution for nurse training.		
	Amounts released from restriction to General Fund	20,000	
	Cash		20,000
	To record fulfillment of purpose restriction for nurse training.		
Entry to accounts for General Fund	Training expenses	20,000	
	Amounts released from restriction from Specific Purpose Funds		20,000
	To record research expenses from contribution.		

Illustration of Construction Grant with Eligibility Requirement

A federal agency makes a cash grant of $500,000 to finance a governmental hospital's acquisition of special equipment. The grant agreement contains an eligibility requirement; namely, the hospital does not qualify for the grant without first incurring allowable costs. In this situation, the hospital should report the grant as deferred revenue until it incurs expenditures under the grant. If the hospital spends $200,000 to acquire equipment and sends an invoice to the federal agency for that amount, it would make the following entries:

Entries to accounts for Plant Replacement and Expansion Fund	Cash	500,000	
	Deferred revenue		500,000
	To record receipt of grant for equipment acquisition.		
	Amounts released from restriction to General Fund	200,000	
	Cash		200,000
	To record capital expenditure.		
	Deferred revenue	200,000	
	Revenue—capital contributions		200,000
	To record revenue recognition		
Entry to accounts for General Fund	Equipment	200,000	
	Amounts released from restriction from Plant Replacement and Expansion Fund		200,000
	To record purchase of equipment under federal grant.		

If the hospital does not receive an advance payment from the federal agency, it makes no entry until it incurs expenditures under the grant. When it incurs expenditures, it should recognize both receivables and revenues.

Financial Reporting Effect

Although the preceding illustrations assume the use of fund accounting for internal purposes, governmental hospitals prepare external financial reports on the entity as a whole, as illustrated in Tables 13-5 and 13-6 (pages 577 and 578). Therefore, when the hospital prepares its operating statement, amounts recorded in the funds as "released from restriction" are eliminated against each other. In the first illustration, the entire $50,000 contribution is reported as nonoperating revenue. At year-end, the unspent portion ($30,000) of the contribution is reported as restricted net assets. In the second illustration, the $200,000 of recognized revenue should be reported as capital contributions after Income before other revenues and expenses. For illustrations of the reporting of transactions such as these, see the appropriate captions in Tables 13-5 and 13-6.

FINANCIAL STATEMENTS

Although many similarities can be noted between the financial statements prepared by not-for-profit and governmental hospitals, some differences are also evident, as indicated in the preceding discussion. The differences result primarily from the fact that not-for-profit hospitals must meet the general standards established by the FASB for not-for-profit organizations in FASB *Statement No. 117* (discussed in Chapter 12), while governmental hospitals must meet the standards established by the GASB for proprietary funds in GASB *Statement No. 34* (covered in Chapter 7). The statements of both not-for-profit and governmental hospitals focus on the hospital as a whole, rather than on their individual funds. Both not-for-profit and governmental hospitals prepare balance sheets, operating statements, and cash flow statements. Not-for-profit hospital financial statements are illustrated in Tables 13-1 through 13-4 and governmental hospital financial statements are illustrated in Tables 13-5 through 13-7.

Balance Sheet

Table 13-1 is an example of a balance sheet for a not-for-profit hospital. In preparing the balance sheet, all the funds (General and Restricted) are consolidated. Notice that the fund types do not appear on the balance sheet. Instead, net assets of the individual funds, like those of other not-for-profit entities, must be classified into one or more of three broad net asset classifications: unrestricted, temporarily restricted, or permanently restricted. (General Funds have unrestricted net assets, Specific Purpose Funds might have both unrestricted and temporarily restricted net assets, and so on.) The purposes for which the restricted net assets may be used should be explained in the notes.

Table 13-1
Balance Sheet—Not-for-Profit Hospital

SAMPLE NOT-FOR-PROFIT HOSPITAL
BALANCE SHEETS
DECEMBER 31, 2005 AND 2004
(AMOUNTS IN THOUSANDS)

	2005	2004
Assets		
Current assets:		
Cash and cash equivalents	$ 4,758	$ 5,877
Short-term investments	15,836	10,740
Assets limited as to use	970	1,300
Patient accounts receivable, net of allowance for doubtful accounts of $2,500 in 2005 and $2,400 in 2004	15,100	14,194
Other current assets	2,670	2,856
Total current assets	39,334	34,967
Interest in net assets of Sample Hospital Foundation	510	462
Assets limited as to use:		
Internally designated for capital acquisition	12,000	12,500
Held by trustee	6,949	7,341
	18,949	19,841
Less amount required to meet current obligations	(970)	(1,300)
	17,979	18,541
Long-term investments	4,680	4,680
Long-term investments restricted for capital acquisition	320	520
Property and equipment, net	51,038	50,492
Other assets	1,185	908
Total assets	$115,046	$110,570
Liabilities and Net Assets		
Current liabilities:		
Current portion of long-term debt	$ 1,470	$ 1,750
Accounts payable and accrued expenses	5,818	5,382
Estimated third-party payer settlements	2,143	1,942
Other current liabilities	1,969	2,114
Total current liabilities	11,400	11,188
Long-term debt, net of current portion	23,144	24,014
Other liabilities	3,953	3,166
Total liabilities	38,497	38,368
Net assets:		
Unrestricted	70,846	66,199
Temporarily restricted	2,115	2,470
Permanently restricted	3,588	3,533
Total net assets	76,549	72,202
Total liabilities and net assets	$115,046	$110,570

See accompanying notes to financial statements.
Source: American Institute of Certified Public Accountants, *Audit and Accounting Guide—Health Care Organizations* (New York, AICPA, 2001), Appendix A. Copyright 2001 by American Institute of Certified Public Accountants, Inc. Reprinted with permission.

Table 13-2
Statement of Operations—Not-for-Profit Hospital

SAMPLE NOT-FOR-PROFIT HOSPITAL
STATEMENTS OF OPERATIONS
YEARS ENDED DECEMBER 31, 2005 AND 2004
(AMOUNTS IN THOUSANDS)

	2005	2004
Unrestricted revenues, gains, and other support:		
Net patient service revenue	$85,156	$78,942
Premium revenue	11,150	10,950
Other revenue	2,601	5,212
Net assets released from restrictions used for operations	300	
Total revenues, gains, and other support	99,207	95,104
Expenses:		
Operating expenses	88,521	80,585
Depreciation and amortization	4,782	4,280
Interest	1,752	1,825
Provision for bad debts	1,000	1,300
Other	2,000	1,300
Total expenses	98,055	89,290
Operating income	1,152	5,814
Other income:		
Investment income	3,900	3,025
Excess of revenues over expenses	5,052	8,839
Change in net unrealized gains and losses on other than trading securities	300	375
Net assets released from restrictions used for purchase of property and equipment	200	
Change in interest in net assets of Sample Hospital Foundation	283	536
Transfers to parent	(688)	(3,051)
Increase in unrestricted net assets, before extraordinary item	5,147	6,699
Extraordinary loss from extinguishment of debt	(500)	
Increase in unrestricted net assets	$ 4,647	$ 6,699

See accompanying notes to financial statements.
Source: American Institute of Certified Public Accountants, *Audit and Accounting Guide—Health Care Organizations* (New York, AICPA, 2001), Appendix A. Copyright 2001 by American Institute of Certified Public Accountants, Inc. Reprinted with permission.

Table 13-3

Statement of Changes in Net Assets—Not-for-Profit Hospital

SAMPLE NOT-FOR-PROFIT HOSPITAL
STATEMENTS OF CHANGES IN NET ASSETS
YEARS ENDED DECEMBER 31, 2005 AND 2004
(AMOUNTS IN THOUSANDS)

	2005	2004
Unrestricted net assets:		
Excess of revenues over expenses	$ 5,052	$ 8,839
Net unrealized gains on investments, other than trading securities	300	375
Change in interest in net assets of Sample Hospital Foundation	283	536
Transfers to parent	(688)	(3,051)
Net assets released from restrictions used for purchase of property and equipment	200	
Increase in unrestricted net assets before extraordinary item	5,147	6,699
Extraordinary loss from extinguishment of debt	(500)	
Increase in unrestricted net assets	4,647	6,699
Temporarily restricted net assets:		
Contributions for charity care	140	996
Net realized and unrealized gains on investments	5	8
Net assets released from restrictions	(500)	
Increase (decrease) in temporarily restricted net assets	(355)	1,004
Permanently restricted net assets:		
Contributions for endowment funds	50	411
Net realized and unrealized gains on investments	5	2
Increase in permanently restricted net assets	55	413
Increase in net assets	4,347	8,116
Net assets, beginning of year	72,202	64,086
Net assets, end of year	$76,549	$72,202

See accompanying notes to financial statements.
Source: American Institute of Certified Public Accountants, *Audit and Accounting Guide—Health Care Organizations* (New York, AICPA, 2001), Appendix A. Copyright 2001 by American Institute of Certified Public Accountants, Inc. Reprinted with permission.

Notice that current assets and current liabilities are presented separately from the other assets and liabilities on the balance sheet. Notice also that the assets whose use is limited are also shown separately. The purposes for which those assets will be used are described in greater detail in the notes. Finally, notice that the portion of those assets required to meet current obligations is classified with the other current assets.

The balance sheet (or statement of net assets) for a governmental hospital (see Table 13-5) is generally similar to that of a not-for-profit hospital. The major difference

Table 13-4
Cash Flow Statement—Not-for-Profit Hospital

SAMPLE NOT-FOR-PROFIT HOSPITAL
STATEMENTS OF CASH FLOWS (INDIRECT METHOD)
YEARS ENDED DECEMBER 31, 2005 AND 2004
(AMOUNTS IN THOUSANDS)

	2005	2004
Cash flows from operating activities:		
Change in net assets	$ 4,347	$ 8,116
Adjustments to reconcile change in net assets to net cash provided by operating activities:		
Extraordinary loss from extinguishment of debt	500	
Depreciation and amortization	4,782	4,280
Net realized and unrealized gains on investments, other than trading	(450)	(575)
Undistributed portion of change in interest in net assets of Sample Hospital Foundation	(48)	(51)
Transfers to parent	688	3,051
Provision for bad debts	1,000	1,300
Restricted contributions and investment income received	(290)	(413)
(Increase) decrease in:		
Patient accounts receivable	(1,906)	(2,036)
Trading securities	215	
Other current assets	186	(2,481)
Other assets	(277)	(190)
Increase (decrease) in:		
Accounts payable and accrued expenses	436	679
Estimated third-party payer settlements	201	305
Other current liabilities	(145)	(257)
Other liabilities	787	(128)
Net cash provided by operating activities	10,026	11,600
Cash flows from investing activities:		
Purchase of investments	(3,769)	(2,150)
Capital expenditures	(4,728)	(5,860)
Net cash used in investing activities	(8,497)	(8,010)
Cash flows from financing activities:		
Transfers to parent	(688)	(3,051)
Proceeds from restricted contributions and restricted investment income	290	413
Payments on long-term debt	(24,700)	(804)
Payments on capital lease obligations	(150)	(100)
Proceeds from issuance of long-term debt	22,600	500
Net cash used in financing activities	(2,648)	(3,042)
Net (decrease) increase in cash and cash equivalents	(1,119)	548
Cash and cash equivalents, beginning of year	5,877	5,329
Cash and cash equivalents, end of year	$ 4,758	$ 5,877

Source: American Institute of Certified Public Accountants, *Audit and Accounting Guide—Health Care Organizations* (New York, AICPA, 2001), Appendix A. Copyright 2001 by American Institute of Certified Public Accountants, Inc. Reprinted with permission.

Table 13-5
Balance Sheet—Governmental Hospital

COUNTY HOSPITAL AT CROTON
BALANCE SHEETS
DECEMBER 31, 2005 AND 2004
(AMOUNTS IN THOUSANDS)

	2005	2004
Assets		
Current assets:		
Cash and cash equivalents	$ 8,300	$ 6,800
Short-term investments	3,100	2,600
Patient accounts receivable, net of estimated uncollectibles—$2,300 in 2005; $2,200 in 2004	16,700	17,500
Medical supplies and drugs	2,300	2,200
Total current assets	30,400	29,100
Assets limited as to use:		
Internally designated	15,000	15,000
Noncurrent assets:		
Restricted investments	1,500	
Land	6,200	6,200
Buildings and equipment	52,400	49,000
Less, accumulated depreciation	(16,700)	(13,000)
Total noncurrent assets	43,400	42,200
Total assets	$88,800	$86,300
Liabilities		
Current liabilities:		
Current maturities of long-term debt	$1,300	$1,300
Accounts payable and accrued expenses	4,800	4,000
Estimated third-party settlements	2,100	2,100
Total current liabilities	8,200	7,400
Noncurrent liabilities:		
Long-term debt, net of current maturities	27,000	28,300
Other noncurrent liabilities	4,700	4,700
Total noncurrent liabilities	31,700	33,000
Total liabilities	39,900	40,400
Net assets:		
Invested in capital assets, net of related debt	13,600	12,600
Restricted—research grants	800	800
Restricted—endowment funds (nonexpendable)	1,500	
Unrestricted	33,000	32,500
Total net assets	48,900	45,900
Total liabilities and net assets	$88,800	$86,300

See accompanying notes to financial statements.

Table 13-6

Operating Statement—Governmental Hospital

COUNTY HOSPITAL AT CROTON
STATEMENT OF REVENUES, EXPENSES, AND CHANGES IN NET ASSETS
YEARS ENDED DECEMBER 31, 2005 AND 2004
(AMOUNTS IN THOUSANDS)

	2005	2004
Operating revenues:		
Net patient service revenue	$62,300	$60,600
Premium revenue	13,900	12,900
Other revenue	2,500	3,600
Total revenues	78,700	77,100
Operating expenses:		
Salaries and benefits	43,600	42,800
Medical supplies and drugs	12,100	11,800
Insurance	5,800	5,600
Other supplies	9,700	9,300
Provision for bad debts	2,100	2,000
Depreciation of buildings and equipment	3,700	3,500
Total operating expenses	77,000	75,000
Operating income	1,700	2,100
Nonoperating revenues (expenses)		
Interest and investment revenue	300	400
Interest on long-term debt	(1,500)	(1,600)
Total nonoperating expenses	(1,200)	(1,200)
Income before other revenues and expenses	500	900
Capital contributions	1,000	0
Endowment contributions	1,500	0
Change in net assets	3,000	900
Total net assets—beginning	45,900	45,000
Total net assets—ending	$48,900	$45,900

See accompanying notes to financial statements.

lies in the presentation of the net assets section. In accordance with the requirements of GASB *Statement No. 34*, governmental hospitals categorize net assets as either invested in capital assets (net of related debt), restricted, or unrestricted, rather than unrestricted, temporarily restricted, or permanently restricted. The category "restricted net assets" must be displayed by major category of restriction, and the amount restricted for endowments needs to be further segregated between expendable and nonexpendable amounts. (Notice the captions in the net assets section of Table 13-5.) Refer back to Chapter 7 (page 278) for discussion of the three components of proprietary fund net assets.

Table 13-7

Cash Flow Statement—Governmental Hospital

COUNTY HOSPITAL AT CROTON
CASH FLOW STATEMENT
YEAR ENDED DECEMBER 31, 2005
(AMOUNTS IN THOUSANDS)

Cash flows from operating activities:	
Receipts from patients	$61,000
Receipts from insurance premiums, other	16,400
Payments to employees	(43,600)
Payments to suppliers	(26,900)
Net cash provided by operating activities	6,900
Cash flows from capital and related financing activities:	
Capital contributions	1,000
Purchases of capital assets	(3,400)
Principal paid on capital debt	(1,300)
Interest paid on capital debt	(1,500)
Net cash (used) for capital and related financing activities	(5,200)
Cash flows from noncapital financing activities:	
None	
Cash flows from investing activities:	
Purchases of investments	(3,100)
Proceeds from maturity of investments	2,600
Interest received	300
Net cash (used) for investing activities	(200)
Net increase in cash and cash equivalents	1,500
Cash at beginning of year	6,800
Cash at end of year	$ 8,300
Reconciliation of Operating Income to Net Cash Provided by Operating Activities:	
Operating income	$1,700
Adjustments to reconcile operating income to net cash provided by operating activities:	
Depreciation expense	3,700
Changes in assets and liabilities:	
Decrease in net patient receivables	800
Increase in inventories	(100)
Increase in accounts payable	800
Net cash provided by operating activities	$6,900

Statements of Operations and Changes in Net Assets

Not-for-Profit Hospitals

FASB *Statement No. 117* permits differing formats for not-for-profit statements of activities, allowing entities to report information in what they consider to be the most meaningful way to financial statement users. For this reason, the *Health Care Organizations Guide* prescribes two statements of changes in net assets. One, called the statement of operations, covers only changes in unrestricted net assets and includes the details of revenues and expenses that constitute a *performance indicator*. The other, called a statement of changes in net assets, covers the changes in net assets for all three net asset classifications.

To emphasize the importance of the performance indicator within the statement of operations, the *Guide* calls for it to be clearly labeled, using terms such as *revenues over expenses, revenues and gains over expenses and losses, earned income,* or *performance earnings.*[11] The performance indicator should be presented in a statement that also presents the total changes in unrestricted net assets. To accomplish this purpose, changes in net assets other than those that affect the performance indicator are reported on the operating statement below the performance indicator line.

To illustrate, turn to Table 13-2. First, notice that this operating statement relates only to unrestricted net assets. Transactions affecting temporarily restricted and permanently restricted net assets are not included in a hospital's operating statement, except to the extent those net assets have been released from restrictions into unrestricted net assets.

Next, notice that patient service revenue is the main source of revenue for the operations of a hospital. As discussed in the section on General Fund revenues, Net patient service revenue is the excess of gross billings for services less provisions for charity care, contractual adjustments with third-party payers, and other similar items the hospital does not expect to collect. These adjustments do not include a provision for bad debts. Premium revenue is revenue derived from capitation payment arrangements with entities like HMOs, also discussed earlier in this chapter.

Other revenue is generated by normal day-to-day activities, other than patient care, that are related to the organization's central operations. Notice that in Table 13-2, all resource inflows that enter into the performance indicator (the performance indicator is the line captioned Excess of revenues over expenses) are reported under Unrestricted revenues, gains, and other support, except for investment income. Investment income, which is part of the performance indicator, could also be reported as part of Other revenue.

Finally, return to the performance indicator Excess of revenues over expenses ($5,052 in 2005). Notice that the performance indicator is separated from other factors causing the net increase in unrestricted net assets ($4,647). Now, consider the difference between transactions affecting the performance indicator and those presented below the performance indicator line. Notice that Net assets released from restrictions used for operations ($300) are part of the "Unrestricted revenues, gains,

---

[11]   *AICPA Guide—Health Care Organizations* (2001), para. 10.17.

and other support" used in computing the performance indicator. Those net assets can be matched with the related expenses. However, net assets released from restrictions used for the purchase of property and equipment ($200) are reported outside the performance measure. Because only the current year's depreciation on those assets is included in expenses, showing the entire amount released from restrictions as part of the performance indicator would overstate the hospital's performance.

The statement of changes in net assets is a summary reconciliation of the beginning and ending net assets of each of the three net asset classifications. Table 13-3 illustrates the statement of changes in net assets of a not-for-profit hospital. Notice that, for the unrestricted net assets, the details constituting the performance indicator Excess of revenues over expenses—which were in the operating statement—are not repeated in the statement of changes in net assets. Notice also, under Temporarily restricted net assets, that net assets released from restrictions (−$500) equals the amounts in the two related captions ($300 and $200) in the unrestricted net assets operating statement.

Governmental Hospitals

Governmental hospitals report in accordance with the GASB's standards for proprietary funds. GASB *Statement No. 34* requires that the proprietary fund operating statement take the form of an all-inclusive statement of revenues, expenses, and changes in fund net assets or fund equity, as illustrated in Chapter 7 (page 293). No provision is made in GASB *Statement No. 34* for separate "statements of operations" for unrestricted funds and "statements of changes in net assets" covering both unrestricted and restricted funds.

The statement of revenues, expenses, and changes in fund net assets, which distinguishes between operating and nonoperating revenues and expenses, requires a separate subtotal for operating income. It also requires that nonoperating revenues and expenses be reported after operating income, leading to a subtotal of Income before other revenues and expenses.

The GASB does not define "operating" and "nonoperating," but allows each government to establish and disclose definitions appropriate to the activity being reported. However, revenues from capital contributions, additions to the principal of permanent and term endowments, special and extraordinary items, and transfers must be reported separately, after nonoperating revenues and expenses. Based on the types of items normally included in "nonoperating" (for example, interest income and interest expense) and the types of items that must be reported separately, it would be reasonable to use the subtotal Income before other revenues and expenses as a performance indicator.

Table 13-6 illustrates a statement of revenues, expenses, and changes in fund net assets for a governmental hospital. Notice the captions of the various subtotals and the items comprising nonoperating income and expenses, such as interest on long-term debt. Notice also that capital contributions and endowment contributions are reported toward the end of the statement, just before Change in net assets. Because this statement is all-inclusive, covering both unrestricted and restricted funds, reporting of amounts released from restrictions is not necessary.

Statement of Cash Flows

Tables 13-4 and 13-7 illustrate the cash flow statements of not-for-profit and governmental hospitals, respectively. Cash flow statements describe the causes of increases and decreases in cash from the beginning of the year to the end of the year for all the funds. Notice that the end-of-year amounts for cash and cash equivalents, shown in the last line of the cash flow statements, are the same as the amounts reported for cash and cash equivalents on the balance sheets.

Because of differences in the standards adopted by the FASB and the GASB, several major differences can be found in the details of these two statements:

1. The not-for-profit hospital cash flow statement is presented using the indirect method, whereas the governmental cash flow statement is presented using the direct method.
2. The not-for-profit hospital cash flow statement presents three major classifications of cash flows: operating activities, investing activities, and financing activities. The governmental hospital cash flow statement provides four classifications: operating activities, noncapital financing activities, capital and related financing activities, and investing activities.
3. The starting point for the operating activity portion of the not-for-profit cash flow statement is the change in net assets. Notice that the first line of the 2004 statement is $4,347, which is the increase in net assets for the year, shown in the statement of changes in net assets. The reconciliation point for the governmental cash flow statement, however, is operating income (loss) for the year.

REVIEW QUESTIONS

Q13-1 Which major publications deal specifically with the application of GAAP for health care organizations?

Q13-2 To what extent does the GASB permit government-owned health care entities that use proprietary fund accounting to apply FASB accounting standards?

Q13-3 Distinguish between the kinds of resources accounted for in the General Fund and the kinds accounted for in Restricted Funds.

Q13-4 Describe the four broad categories of resources included in the General Fund.

Q13-5 What is a contractual adjustment?

Q13-6 A hospital has contractual adjustments, takes charity cases, grants discounts to clergy, and has bad debts. How does each affect net patient service revenue?

Q13-7 How do prospective and retrospective payment agreements affect net patient service revenue?

Q13-8 A not-for-profit hospital invests a $10,000 restricted donation in equity securities. At the date of its financial statements, the securities have a fair value of $12,000. How would the hospital handle the increased value in its financial statements? Would your answer be the same if it were a governmental hospital?

Q13-9 Under what circumstances, if any, would a not-for-profit hospital recognize donated services and donated drugs in its records?

Q13-10 Illustrate the difference between recording a hospital's expenses by natural classification and recording by function. Discuss which is more informative.

Q13-11 Describe the basic rule for recognizing expenses and liabilities for medical malpractice claims.

Q13-12 Describe the accounting process to record the segregation of resources by the managing board of a hospital.

Q13-13 A donor contribution for a specific operating purpose should be recognized by a not-for-profit hospital as _____ . A governmental hospital recognizes it as _____ . (For each blank, answer whether it is unrestricted revenue, temporarily restricted revenue, permanently restricted revenue, or restricted revenue.)

Q13-14 If a governmental hospital receives a cash grant that contains a time requirement, when should the hospital recognize revenues for the grant?

Q13-15 Discuss the differences in the kinds of information a user of a not-for-profit hospital's financial statements can obtain from the statement of operations, the statement of changes in net assets, and the statement of cash flows.

CASES

C13-1 Several young doctors banded together to start a small not-for-profit outpatient-type hospital in a poor neighborhood in their spare time. Because each of the doctors received his or her education free from the state in the form of scholarships, each feels a responsibility to help the citizens. These doctors plan to work at the hospital without pay. The chief administrative officer, Sara Stone, does not believe that the value of the donated services should appear in the financial statements of the hospital. The controller, Lucien LeDoux, feels that the conditions under which the services were donated require that they be recorded. Stone feels that if the revenue associated with the services is recorded it will look like the hospital has a great deal more revenue than it actually has, which may cause it a problem when seeking donations and grants. In addition, because of its simplistic operations, the doctors will look like they are taking large amounts out of the operating funds of the hospital in the form of salaries. On this latter point, the doctors are adamant; they do not want the value of their services recorded. How would you respond to this situation?

C13-2 The chief administrative officer of the East Jeff Hospital, Vera Thomas, is attempting to find resources to add a new wing to the hospital. For the past several years, many patients were turned away because of a lack of space. The hospital has a large endowment, but all earnings from these funds are restricted to various operating purposes; for example, providing continuing education for nurses and maintaining the parking lot. Thomas approached you and asked whether a recently received gift from T. W. Wealthy could be used to begin expansion. Wealthy donated $1 million to the hospital in his deceased wife's name. She recently died from cancer, and in her memory Wealthy established a cancer research fund. How would you respond to Ms. Thomas?

ETHICS CASES

EC13-1 Rodney de Fine, the chief administrative officer of the First Street Hospital, is having an argument with Jane Bronson, the hospital's controller. De Fine recently received a gift of $100,000 from a wealthy benefactor. He wants to put money into a board-designated fund to allow the board to do whatever it wants with the money. Bronson, however, feels that the hospital should talk with the donor to determine whether he wishes any particular use for his donation. De Fine is concerned that if the donor wishes to use the money in a manner that does not meet the hospital's immediate needs, the hospital may have to turn away some patients because of a lack of facilities. How would you handle this dilemma?

EC13-2 Kathy Joewalski, the controller of the Green Lawn Hospital, is working with Rose Gloro to plan the hospital's first development fund campaign. Gloro wants the drive to be successful, and she would like to have as few limitations on the use of the monies raised as possible. Joewalski, however, feels that the hospital must ask the donors whether they want to limit use of these funds because of the accounting and reporting restrictions with which she must comply. Rose Gloro is the wife of the chief administrative officer (CAO), and he and the managing board would like the money as free from restrictions as possible, even if it means overlooking restrictions placed on some donations. Joseph Gloro realizes that large donations are easily traced and the donor may wish to be informed of how his or her money was used, but smaller donations could easily be intermixed and the same explanation of use could be given to several of these types of donors. Besides, Joseph Gloro indicated that during his 7-year tenure as the hospital's CAO, not one small donor asked how his or her money was used. After all, he states, "If the gifts are used to further the hospital's operations, doesn't the entire community benefit?" How would you react to this situation?

EXERCISES

E13-1 (Fill in the blanks—general terminology)
1. The AICPA publishes the _____ as a source of information on hospital accounting.
2. FASB standards (always, sometimes, never)_____ apply to governmental hospitals.
3. Operating resources and board-designated resources are subdivisions of the _____ Fund.

4. Endowment Funds, Plant Replacement and Expansion Funds, and Specific Purpose Funds are _____ Funds.
5. The daily operations of a hospital are accounted for in the _____ Fund.
6. Parking fees, cafeteria revenues, and pharmacy revenues are reported on the _____ statement as _____ .
7. Hospitals use the _____ basis of accounting.

E13-2 (Use of funds)
The Brite-Hope Hospital uses the following types of funds:

GF   General Fund
EF   Endowment Funds
PREF   Plant Replacement and Expansion Funds
SPF   Specific Purpose Funds

Using these codes, identify which fund or funds would be used to account for the following events:

GF   1. The operations of the cafeteria.
SPF 2. A gift received from an individual for medical research (at this time consider only the receipt of the gift).
PREF 3. Income is earned on investments of money donated by the Manybucks Corporation (the original gift and all income earned must be used to provide up-to-date equipment for the hospital).
EF   4. The hospital received $1 million in securities from an individual. The principal of the gift must be maintained intact. (Consider only the receipt of the gift.)
GF   5. The managing board of the hospital decided to start a fund for cancer research. It transferred $30,000 into the fund. Which fund would be used to record the receipt of the money?
GF   6. The payment of salaries to the nursing staff.
GF   7. Depreciation is recorded on the equipment in use.
GF   8. The purchase of additional hospital equipment.

E13-3 (Identification of net asset classifications)
Assume that Brite-Hope Hospital, in E13-2, is a not-for-profit hospital. Using the following letters identify which net asset classification would be affected by the events listed in E13-2.
a. Unrestricted net assets
b. Temporarily restricted net assets
c. Permanently restricted net assets

E13-4 (Matching)
Match the items on the right with those on the left by placing the letter of the best match in the space provided.

a. All income required to be paid to the donor or other designated party for a period of time
b. Resources whose use is restricted by a third-party donor or grantor
c. Requires payments of specific amounts to be made to the donor

_____ 1. General Fund
_____ 2. Restricted Funds
_____ 3. Patient service revenue
_____ 4. Statement of changes in net assets
_____ 5. Life Income Funds
_____ 6. Gains and losses

or other party for a particular period of time

d. Reported as part of the General Fund

e. Used to report contributions of endowment funds to not-for-profit hospitals

f. Result from peripheral or incidental transactions of a hospital

g. Prepared for changes in unrestricted net assets of not-for-profit hospitals

h. Prepared for all funds

i. Main source of revenue for a hospital

j. Used to account for the day-to-day operations of a hospital

_____ 7. Assets limited as to use

_____ 8. Annuity Fund

_____ 9. Balance sheet

_____ 10. Statement of operations

E13-5 (General Fund transactions)

The following transactions were incurred by the Numb Hospital, a not-for-profit entity, during January 2004:

1. The hospital billed its patients for $250,000.
2. Nurses and doctors employed by the hospital were paid their salaries, $100,000.
3. The chief administrative officer was paid her salary of $10,000.
4. The hospital paid its utility bill, $5,000.
5. Depreciation on the equipment was $34,000.
6. Doctors donated services valued at $3,000.
7. The board transferred $1,000 into a Special Management Fund for contingencies.
8. An unrestricted donation of $4,000 was received.

Required: Record these entries in the General Fund of the Numb Hospital.

E13-6 (Accounting for board-designated funds)

On January 1, 2004, the managing board of a governmental hospital set aside $35,000 in a fund to upgrade the skills of its newly hired nurses. During the month of January, the hospital spent $15,000 to train the nurses. Prepare journal entries to record the transactions and identify the funds used.

E13-7 (Accounting for uncollectible patient accounts)

The Metro County Hospital could not collect the amount billed to a patient. The patient declared bankruptcy and had no assets with which to pay his debts. Assuming the patient owed the hospital $3,000, prepare the entry or entries necessary to record the uncollectible account if the hospital uses the allowance method. After preparing the necessary entry or entries, indicate what effect the write-off will have on the balance sheet.

E13-8   (Accounting for contractual adjustments)
A hospital arranges with a third-party payer to charge the third party 75 percent of its established billing rates. During January 2004, the hospital provided services amounting to $1 million at the established billing rates.
Prepare journal entries to record the January billings.

E13-9   (Accounting for premium revenues)
A hospital arranges with an HMO to provide hospital care to the HMO's
members at a specific rate per member, per month. During the month of
June, the HMO paid the hospital $850,000, in accordance with the agreement.
The hospital's cost accounting records showed that, if it had billed the HMO
in accordance with its established billing rates, it would have billed the HMO
$975,000. Prepare the appropriate journal entry (or entries) to record this
transaction.

E13-10 (Accounting for net patient service revenues)
Shelley Marder Hospital had the following transactions during the year
ended December 31, 2004:

1. The hospital provided services to third-party payer A amounting to $5 mil-
    lion at its established billing rates. The hospital's prospective billing
    arrangement with this third party stipulates payment to the hospital of
    80 percent of its established rates for services performed. All billings were
    paid during the year.

2. The hospital provided services to third-party payer B amounting to $4 mil-
    lion at its established billing rates. Its retrospective billing arrangement
    with this third party agrees that the hospital should receive payment at an
    interim rate of 90 percent of its established rates, subject to retrospective
    adjustment based on agreed-upon allowable costs. By year-end, B had paid
    all the billings. Before issuing its financial statements, the hospital calcu-
    lated that it would need to refund $250,000 to B based on allowable costs.

3. The hospital provided services to charity patients amounting to $1 million
    at its established billing rates.

Required: 1. Prepare journal entries to record these transactions.
              2. State the amount that Shelley Marder Hospital would report
                  as net patient service revenues in its operating statement.

E13-11 (Journal entries to record investment transactions)
A hospital purchased 100 shares of General Electric stock on June 30, 2004, for
$3,100, intending to hold the stock until needed for plant expansion purposes.
At December 31, 2004, the date of its financial statements, the stock's fair value
was $2,900. On November 30, 2005, the hospital sold the stock for $3,500.

Required: 1. Assuming it is a governmental hospital, prepare journal
                  entries to record all the transactions and events related to the
                  investment.
              2. Assuming it is a not-for-profit hospital, prepare journal
                  entries to record all the transactions and events related to the
                  investment.

E13-12 (Financial reporting of investment gains and losses)

Reread the material on reporting investment gains and losses in the section on "Investment Returns" and consider the journal entries you made in E13-11. Which of the two reporting methods (if either) do you think is the more informative? Which of the two reporting methods (if either) do you think better expresses the hospital's financial performance? Give reasons for your answers.

E13-13 (Journal entries to record the receipt and use of contributions by a not-for-profit hospital)

Mary Milligan Hospital, a not-for-profit hospital, had the following transactions during the year ended December 31, 2004. Prepare journal entries necessary to record the transactions and indicate which fund or funds would be used to record them.

1. Ed Glott, a high school senior, donated his services to the hospital for an entire summer, serving food to patients and performing general tasks. If paid for, these services would have cost the hospital $5,000.
2. D. Bean donated $20,000 to the hospital, stipulating that the funds be used only to update the skills of the nurses.
3. The hospital used D. Bean's donation for the stipulated purpose.
4. D. Lily Allen donated $500,000 to the hospital to help pay for new MRI equipment.
5. The hospital used D. Lily Allen's donation for new MRI equipment.

E13-14 (Use of funds)

The following transactions relate to the Tableaux Hospital, a not-for-profit hospital. Indicate which fund or funds would be used to record the data.

1. Collected $2,345 from a patient.
2. Received a $100,000 grant from Toosuups Drug Company for a study of the effects of morphine on female patients.
3. Received unrestricted gifts of $50,000.
4. Purchased equipment for $125,000 by using resources previously accumulated in the Plant Replacement and Expansion Fund.
5. Research expenses totaling $12,000 were incurred in studying the effects of morphine on female patients.
6. The board decided to begin a fund for nursing education. Initially $10,000 of general hospital resources was transferred to the fund.
7. Marketable securities with a fair value of $15,000 were donated by WFJ, Inc., to help the hospital acquire new equipment.
8. The securities in item (7) produced income of $5,000. Assume that the investment income is restricted in the same way as the original gift.

E13-15 (Transactions involving General Fund and restricted funds)

Using the same information given in E13-14, prepare the journal entries that would be used to record the data. Identify each type of fund used.

E13-16 (Financial statements)

Using the following codes, indicate which statement would be used to report each item for a not-for-profit hospital.

BS   Balance sheet
SO   Statement of operations

_____ 1. Land, buildings, and equipment
_____ 2. Unrestricted contributions
_____ 3. General services expense
_____ 4. Contributions receivable
_____ 5. Temporarily restricted net assets
_____ 6. Assets limited as to use
_____ 7. Restricted assets in Specific Purpose Funds
_____ 8. Estimated liability for malpractice costs
_____ 9. Fund-raising costs

PROBLEMS

P13-1 (Matching)
Match items on the right with those on the left by placing the letter of the best match in the space provided.

a. Restricted Funds
b. Prepared for a not-for-profit hospital's changes in unrestricted net assets only
c. Endowment Fund
d. _Audit and Accounting Guide— Health Care Organizations_
e. Used to account for resources that are donor-restricted for a particular operating purpose
f. General Fund
g. Assets whose use is limited
h. Reported on a not-for-profit hospital's statement of changes in net assets
i. Donor resources that require a specific amount to be paid to the donor or other party for a particular period of time
j. Life Income Funds

_____ 1. Used to account for day-to-day operations of a hospital
_____ 2. Annuity Funds
_____ 3. Used to account for resources that must be used in compliance with the terms of an agreement, like a gift or grant
_____ 4. Resources set aside for a specific purpose by a hospital's governing board
_____ 5. Revenues from restricted resources
_____ 6. Used to account for resources donated to a hospital for which the principal must be maintained intact
_____ 7. Specific Purpose Funds
_____ 8. AICPA audit guide for hospitals
_____ 9. Statement of operations
_____ 10. Donor resources that require all of the income earned by those resources to be paid to the donor or other party for a specified period of time

P13-2 (Multiple choice)
1. In accordance with its established billing rates, Alpha Hospital provided services amounting to $14 million during the year ended December 31, 2004. Included in the $14 million were contractual adjustments of $3 million and charity patient care of $1 million. What amount should Alpha report as net patient service revenue in its year 2004 financial statements?
   a. $10 million
   b. $11 million
   c. $13 million
   d. $14 million
2. Beta Hospital provided services to patients who were covered by the Eton Health Plan. Beta's arrangement with Eton called for interim billing rates at 25 percent less than the established rates, as well as a retrospective rate adjustment. Based on its established billing rates, Beta provided services amounting to $4 million to patients covered by Eton during the year ended December 31, 2004. At year end, Beta estimated that it would need to refund $150,000 to Eton in accordance with the cost standards set forth in the retrospective rate arrangement. What amount should Beta report as net patient service revenue in its year 2004 financial statements?
   a. $2,850,000
   b. $3,000,000
   c. $3,850,000
   d. $4,000,000
3. Gamma Hospital provided services amounting to $10 million at its established billing rates in the year ended December 31, 2004. Included in the $10 million were services of $8 million to Medicare patients. Medicare paid Gamma at 60 percent of Gamma's established rates. Also included in the $10 million were $2 million of services to self-pay patients. Gamma collected $1.5 million from the self-pay patients during the year and estimated that 40 percent of the uncollected amount would not be collected. What amount should Gamma report as net patient service revenue in its year 2004 financial statements?
   a. $6.3 million
   b. $6.6 million
   c. $6.8 million
   d. $10 million
4. On January 10, 2004, Delta Hospital received a bequest in the form of equity securities. Delta was required to hold the securities in perpetuity, but could spend the income. The securities had cost the donor $2.7 million, but their fair value was $3.4 million when Delta received them. The fair value of the securities fluctuated during the year, and Delta's comptroller calculated that the average fair value during the year was $3.1 million. When Delta prepared its financial statements as of December 31, 2004, the fair value of the securities was $3.3 million. At what amount should Delta report the securities in its financial statements at December 31, 2004?

a. $2.7 million
b. $3.1 million
c. $3.3 million
d. $3.4 million

5. Abbott and Costello Labs donated drugs to Epsilon Hospital, a not-for-profit entity, in January 2004. If Epsilon had purchased the drugs, it would have paid $600,000. During the year, Epsilon used all the drugs in providing services to patients. How should Epsilon report the donation in its financial statements for the year ended December 31, 2004?
   a. Report nothing
   b. Report the donation in a note to its financial statements
   c. Report $600,000 as other revenues (or gains)
   d. Report $600,000 as a reduction of operating expenses

6. Omicron Hospital, a not-for-profit entity, received $6 million in premium revenue under an agreement with Zeta HMO to provide services to subscribing participants. Its internal records showed that Omicron spent $5.6 million in caring for Zeta's subscribers. How should Omicron report the transactions with Zeta in its financial statements?
   a. Report $400,000 as unrestricted premium revenue
   b. Report $400,000 as temporarily restricted premium revenue
   c. Report $6 million as unrestricted premium revenue
   d. Report $6 million as temporarily restricted premium revenue

7. Which of the following is the most likely description of the resources reported by Kappa Hospital on its balance sheet as assets limited as to use?
   a. A donation that can be used only for cancer research
   b. A donation that must be held in perpetuity in an Endowment Fund
   c. An investment of unrestricted resources that is not readily marketable
   d. An amount designated by Kappa's governing board for plant expansion

8. In which part of its financial statements should Phi Hospital, a governmental hospital, report an increase in the fair value of its investments?
   a. Only in the notes to its statements
   b. As part of nonoperating revenues (expenses) in its statement of revenues, expenses, and changes in net assets
   c. As part of operating revenues in its statement of revenues, expenses, and changes in net assets
   d. As a direct addition to total net assets

P13-3 (Multiple choice)
1. A governmental hospital has not transferred risk on malpractice claims to a third-party insurer. Which of the following statements best expresses the general rule regarding the reporting of liabilities for malpractice claims on the face of the balance sheet (or statement of net assets)?
   a. They should be reported only to the extent that judgments and settlements are due and payable.
   b. Outstanding claims should be described in the notes to the statements; adjudicated and settled claims should be reported if they have not been paid.

c. They should be reported if it is highly likely that the disputes ultimately will be resolved in favor of the claimants.

d. They should be reported if it is probable that a loss has been incurred and the amount of the loss can be reasonably estimated.

2. Historical experience shows that a hospital sometimes receives malpractice claims in the year after the incident occurs. Which of the following statements best expresses the general rule for reporting liabilities for such claims, if risk of loss has not been transferred to a third-party insurer?

   a. No mention is required to be made of these claims anywhere in the financial statements.

   b. A note should be prepared discussing the likelihood that claims will be received after the balance sheet date, but no estimate needs to be made of the possibility of loss.

   c. Liabilities should be recognized in the statements if it is probable that claims will be asserted for incidents occurring before the balance sheet date and the losses can be reasonably estimated.

   d. Liabilities should be recognized in the statements if claims have been received before the statements are issued; a note should be prepared discussing the likelihood of receiving additional claims after the statements have been issued.

3. A not-for-profit hospital receives a gift from a donor who specifies that the gift must be used only to further its research into the treatment of Lyme disease. When the hospital incurs expenses on this program, in which classification of net assets should the expenses be reported?

   a. Unrestricted net assets

   b. Temporarily restricted net assets

   c. Permanently restricted net assets

   d. Assets limited as to use

4. A not-for-profit hospital sells long-term bonds in the amount of $25 million to finance the construction of a new hospital wing. The bond agreement requires the hospital to pay $1 million of this amount to a trustee as security until the debt is fully repaid. How should this payment be reported in the financial statements?

   a. As an expense, to be amortized over the life of the debt

   b. As assets limited as to use

   c. As non-current assets, with all other long-term investments

   d. As construction in progress

5. The balance sheet of a governmental hospital shows capital assets ($20 million), accumulated depreciation ($12 million), current maturities of long-term debt ($500,000), and long-term debt net of current maturities ($5.5 million). The long-term debt was issued to acquire capital assets. How much should the hospital report as invested in capital assets, net of related debt?

   a. $14 million

   b. $8 million

c. $2.5 million

d. $2 million

6. During the year ended December 31, 2004, a not-for-profit hospital had both unrealized and realized gains on investments made with its unrestricted net assets. How should these gains be reported in the hospital's statement of operations for the year 2004?

   a. Both the realized and the unrealized gains should be reported.

   b. Neither the realized nor the unrealized gains should be reported.

   c. Realized gains should be reported, but unrealized gains should not.

   d. Unrealized gains should be reported, but realized gains should not.

7. Under which of these circumstances would a not-for-profit hospital account for resources in restricted funds?

   a. Whenever there are external limitations on using the resources

   b. When a donor places limitations on using the resources

   c. When the hospital's board of directors sets resources aside for plant expansion

   d. When a bond agreement requires the hospital to set resources aside

P13-4 (Multiple choice—governmental hospital)

1. What are the components of the net asset section of a governmental hospital's balance sheet?

   a. Unrestricted; temporarily restricted; permanently restricted

   b. Assets limited as to use; assets unlimited as to use

   c. Invested in capital assets, net of related debt; restricted; unrestricted

   d. Restricted; unrestricted

2. A county hospital receives grants from higher-level governments to construct and equip a special trauma unit. How should the hospital report the grants in its financial statements?

   a. As nonoperating revenues

   b. As a separate item after nonoperating revenues (expenses) are added to (deducted from) operating income (loss)

   c. As a direct addition to "invested in capital assets, net of related debt"

   d. As an item of extraordinary or special revenue

3. A county hospital receives $1 million from the county's General Fund to help cover the hospital's annual operating deficit. How should the hospital report that receipt of cash?

   a. As operating revenues

   b. As nonoperating revenues

   c. As a separate item after nonoperating revenues (expenses) are added to (deducted from) operating income (loss)

   d. As a direct addition to unrestricted net assets

4. A county hospital receives a grant of $250,000 from the state health department, which specifies that the grant may be used for any purpose the trustees wish, provided it is used at the rate of $50,000 a year for 5 years, starting the following year. How should the hospital report the gift in its financial statements in the year the cash is received?

a. As deferred revenue
b. As revenue in the amount of $250,000
c. As revenue in the amount of $250,000, discounted at the government's borrowing rate over the 5-year period
d. As a direct addition to unrestricted net assets

5. How is interest on long-term bonds issued by a county hospital generally reported?
a. As operating expenses
b. As nonoperating expenses
c. As a separate item after nonoperating revenues (expenses) are added to (deducted from) operating income (loss)
d. As a direct reduction of beginning net assets

P13-5 (Accounting for and reporting patient service revenues)

The Andrew Gorman Hospital had the following transactions regarding its patient service billings during fiscal year 2004:

1. The total services provided by the hospital to all patients during the year amounted to $19 million at the hospital's established billing rates.
2. The hospital bills Medicare for services to program beneficiaries as included in item (1) at prospectively determined rates. Contractual adjustments under this program to the predetermined rates were $1.5 million.
3. An agreement with third-party payer X calls for retrospective final rates. Patient services included in item (1) under interim billing rates with X resulted in contractual adjustments of $1 million.
4. The hospital provided charity services included in item (1) valued at $500,000 under the established rates.
5. The hospital made a provision for bad debts in the amount of $300,000.
6. The hospital collected $13.5 million from third-party payers and direct-pay patients. The hospital also wrote off bad debts of $200,000.
7. The hospital estimated it would need to refund $100,000 to payer X in item (3), when retrospective rates are determined. (The hospital's receivables include no amounts due from payer X.)

Required: 1. Prepare the journal entries needed to record these transactions.
2. State (a) the amount of net patient service revenue the hospital will report on its operating statement, and (b) the amount of net patient accounts receivable the hospital will report on its balance sheet.

P13-6 (Accounting for medical malpractice claims)

Caire-Less Hospital carries no insurance for medical malpractice claims. Analysis of medical malpractice claims at year-end shows the following:

1. Claim A is for $500,000. The hospital's attorneys are 90 percent confident that the hospital will win the claim if it goes to trial. The hospital will not settle the claim for any amount and is awaiting trial.
2. Claim B is for $400,000. The hospital's attorneys are not confident of winning if the case goes to trial. They believe the claim can be settled out of court, within the range of $100,000 to $200,000.

3. The hospital also has 20 outstanding smaller claims. The average claim is for $10,000. Past experience shows that the hospital loses 60 percent of the claims, and the average loss on them is 30 percent of the amount claimed.
4. Experience also shows that two small claims, relating to incidents occurring before year-end, are likely to be received during the following year.

Required: 1. Compute the amount, if any, that the hospital ought to establish as a liability on its balance sheet for malpractice claims. Discuss the content of any note disclosures that the hospital should make.
2. Describe the accounting principles leading to your conclusions.

P13-7 (Journal entries and financial statements—General Fund)
New City Hospital was established in 2004. This not-for-profit hospital began operations by issuing bonds to acquire the assets of an existing hospital. The following transactions occurred during the year:
1. To supply cash to begin operations, long-term revenue bonds were issued. The proceeds were $4 million. The bonds were issued for their face value.
2. To provide security for payment of debt service on the bonds, the hospital was required by the bond agreement to deposit $200,000 of the proceeds in an escrow account with a trustee, to remain there until the debt is fully redeemed. The trustee immediately invested the cash in a certificate of deposit.
3. The physical assets of the existing hospital were purchased for $3,500,000 cash. The appraised values of the land, building, and equipment were $400,000, $2,600,000, and $500,000, respectively.
4. Services to Medicare program beneficiaries were billed at predetermined rates. Medicare program beneficiaries received services amounting to $4 million at the hospital's established billing rates. Contractual adjustments against the predetermined billing rates were $600,000. By year-end, the hospital had collected $3,100,000 against the billings.
5. The hospital has an agreement to provide services to members of an HMO at rates per member, per month. In accordance with this arrangement, the hospital received monthly cash premiums amounting to $1.4 million.
6. The hospital provided care to charity patients amounting to $300,000 at established billing rates.
7. The hospital provided care to self-pay patients amounting to $700,000 at established billing rates. The hospital collected $550,000 in cash against these billings. It also established an allowance for uncollected receivables of 5 percent of the amount billed, and subsequently wrote off $12,000 as uncollectible.
8. The hospital purchased medicines and other supplies for $80,000 cash. The medicines and supplies were placed in inventory.
9. Inventories were used as follows:

Nursing care	$60,000
Dietary services	10,000

10. Operating expenses of the hospital, all of which were paid in cash, were $4,750,000. The expenses should be charged as follows:

Nursing care	$3,200,000
Dietary services	500,000
Maintenance services	450,000
Administrative services	600,000

11. The hospital paid debt service on the bonds in the amount of $440,000 for the year. Of this amount, interest was $240,000 and payment of bond principal was $200,000.
12. In accordance with the bond agreement, the trustee—see item (2)— forwarded the interest on the certificate of deposit to the hospital for use in the hospital's general operations. The interest amounted to $10,000.
13. Nursing care salaries were accrued at year-end in the amount of $40,000.
14. Depreciation was recorded as follows: building $130,000; equipment, $50,000.
15. A journal entry was made to report $100,000 of the outstanding long-term debt as current.

Required: 1. Prepare all the journal entries necessary to record these transactions.
2. Prepare a statement of operations for 2004.
3. Prepare a statement of changes in net assets for 2004.
4. Prepare a balance sheet at December 31, 2004.

P13-8 (Journal entries and financial statements—General Fund)
Following is a trial balance for the Metro General Hospital, a governmental hospital:

Metro General Hospital
General Fund
Trial Balance
December 31, 2003

Cash	$ 6,000	
Patient accounts receivable	20,000	
Allowance for uncollectible receivables		$ 3,000
Inventories	5,000	
Land	300,000	
Building	2,000,000	
Accumulated depreciation—building		80,000
Equipment	500,000	
Accumulated depreciation—equipment		100,000
Accounts payable		8,000
Bonds payable		2,400,000
Net assets		240,000
	$2,831,000	$2,831,000

During 2004, the following transactions took place:

1. Services were provided to patients amounting to $3,300,000 at established billing rates. Following is an analysis of the billings:
   a. Medicare patients were billed for $2,000,000 at established rates. However, contractual allowances against these billings were $400,000.
   b. Billings under a retrospective arrangement with a third party were $600,000 at the established rates. However, the interim billing rates called for contractual adjustments of $100,000.
   c. Billings to self-pay patients were $500,000 at established rates. Based on previous experience, the hospital anticipated that $25,000 of the billings would not be collected.
   d. Services to charity patients were $200,000 at established rates.
2. Inventories of $56,000 were purchased on credit.
3. Operating expenses were incurred as follows:

Nursing services expense	$1,475,000
Other professional services expense	665,000
General services expense	200,000
Administrative services expense	90,000

   Assume that all the expenses were incurred on credit.
4. The board decided to set aside $30,000 cash in a separate account to provide for the continuing education of nurses.
5. The hospital entered into a capitation agreement with the county in which it was located, agreeing to provide hospital services to certain groups of county employees and their dependents. The agreement provided for the county to make a monthly payment for each covered county employee to the hospital. Cash payments received by the hospital under this agreement were $300,000.
6. Collections of patient receivables totaled $2,200,000. In addition, $13,000 of patient receivables was written off as uncollectible.
7. Payments of accounts payable totaled $1,900,000.
8. The use of inventories was recorded as follows:

Nursing services	$30,000
General services	20,000

9. Depreciation was recorded as follows: building, $40,000; equipment, $50,000.
10. During the year, the hospital paid debt service of $220,000 on the outstanding bonds, consisting of interest of $120,000 and principal of $100,000. At year-end, the hospital made an entry to report $100,000 of its outstanding long-term debt as current.
11. During the year, a self-pay patient instituted legal action in the amount of $200,000 against the hospital for medical malpractice. The hospital does not carry insurance. Hospital attorneys have started negotiations with the claimant and believe it is highly probable that the claim can be settled for $50,000.

12. At year-end, the hospital reviewed its cost accounting records in connection with the retrospective billing arrangement made with the third-party payer in item (1), part (b). The hospital believes it will need to refund $40,000 to that third party in accordance with that agreement. The third party paid all billings made by the hospital.

Required: 1. Prepare all the journal entries necessary to record these transactions.

2. Prepare a statement of revenues, expenses, and changes in fund net assets for 2004.

3. Prepare a balance sheet at December 31, 2004.

P13-9 (Journal entries for restricted funds and General Fund)
The not-for-profit West Street Hospital had the following transactions during 2004:

1. A gift of $100,000 was received from Warso Stores. The terms of the gift specified that the principal amount (and any appreciation from fund investments) must be maintained intact permanently. The income could be spent for any purpose that would help the hospital. The total amount of the gift was immediately invested in marketable securities.

2. First Construction Company gave the hospital a grant of $500,000 for cancer research. The proceeds from the grant were invested in marketable securities.

3. Paigekat Company donated $200,000 to the hospital for the construction of a building addition that would be devoted to dealing with mental patients.

4. Architectural fees for the building addition for the mental health unit were paid in cash, $30,000. The remainder of the Paigekat gift was invested in marketable securities.

5. During the year, the hospital began a fund-raising drive for the mental health unit. Pledges totaling $200,000 and cash donations totaling $30,000 were received. (*Hint:* Record the pledges as receivables.)

6. Investment income of $30,000 was received in cash on the First Construction Company Fund investments. In addition, $20,000 of investments matured. The hospital paid face value when purchasing these securities. Assume that the investment income is restricted in the same way as the original grant.

7. Cancer research costs of $45,000 were incurred and paid by the General Fund. The First Construction Company Fund reimbursed the General Fund for these expenditures.

8. Income of $8,000 was earned by the Warso Stores Fund investments. Of this amount, $7,000 was received in cash.

9. Collections of pledges during the year totaled $80,000.

10. At year-end, the fair value of the investments held in the Warso Stores Fund was $108,000.

Required: 1. Prepare all the journal entries necessary to record these transactions in the restricted funds and the General Fund of the West Street Hospital and identify each fund used.

2. Prepare a statement of changes in net assets for the temporarily and permanently restricted net assets for 2004.

P13-10 (Journal entries for hospitals)
Following is a trial balance for Darwin Memorial, a not-for-profit hospital:

Darwin Memorial Hospital
General Fund
Trial Balance
July 1, 2004

Cash	$ 12,000	
Patient accounts receivable	40,000	
Allowance for uncollectible patient accounts		$ 4,000
Land	600,000	
Buildings	2,500,000	
Accumulated depreciation—building		650,000
Equipment	2,000,000	
Accumulated depreciation—equipment		400,000
Accounts payable		15,000
Notes payable		100,000
Bonds payable		2,000,000
Unrestricted net assets		1,983,000
	$5,152,000	$5,152,000

During the 2004–2005 fiscal year, the following selected transactions took place:

1. Darwin had capitation agreements with several HMOs, wherein the HMOs agreed to pay monthly premiums per member at the beginning of every month in exchange for Darwin's agreement to provide hospital services to the HMO members. Darwin received premiums of $2 million in cash during the year. In addition, Darwin billed its self-pay patients a total of $100,000.

2. Several self-pay patient accounts were classified as uncollectible and written off. These accounts totaled $2,000.

3. The MVT Corporation gave the hospital a grant for research into the use of a verbally operated microscope. The grant was for $500,000. The entire amount was immediately invested in marketable securities.

4. Operating expenses were incurred as follows:

Nursing services	$550,000
Other professional services	300,000
General services	300,000
Administrative services	175,000
Dietary services	100,000

Assume that all expenses were incurred on credit.

5. Self-pay patient receivables of $110,000 were collected.

6. Accounts payable of $1,400,000 were paid.

7. Several individuals in the community contributed a total of $1 million for the expansion of the burn unit of the hospital. This money was invested in marketable securities until the plans for the unit were completed. The fund was titled the Burn Unit Fund.
8. Debt service of $210,000 on the outstanding debt was paid in cash. Of this amount, $110,000 was for interest and the rest was for debt principal.
9. The managing board decided to establish a fund for the development of its professional staff. The amount transferred from general hospital resources was $25,000. The new fund was called the Professional Improvement Fund.
10. The construction and planning costs incurred on the new burn unit totaled $200,000. This amount was paid from the Burn Unit Fund cash account. To make these payments, investments that originally cost $190,000 were sold for $205,000. In addition, $10,000 cash income was received on the investments. Assume that the income from the investments has the same restrictions as the original donation.
11. During the year, the hospital received $25,000 cash income from the investment of the MVT grant money. Assume that the investment income is restricted in the same way as the original grant.
12. Research costs associated with the MVT grant were $20,000. These costs were paid with cash generated by the investment of the original grant.
13. Jane Doe gave the hospital $15,000, which must be maintained intact. The income from the gift can be used in any way the managing board feels is helpful to the hospital. The money was immediately invested in marketable securities.
14. Investments in the Jane Doe Fund earned $2,000 during the year. Of this amount $1,900 was received in cash.
15. The fair value of the remaining investments in the Burn Unit Fund at the end of the year was $850,000.

Required: Prepare all the journal entries necessary to record these transactions and identify the fund or funds involved.

Chapter

14

Analysis of Financial Statements and Financial Condition

After completing this chapter, you should be able to:

➤ *Explain how financial statement format and content assist in financial analysis.*

➤ *Explain the need for using ratios to facilitate analysis of financial data.*

➤ *Explain how time-series analysis and comparative analysis facilitate assessment of financial condition.*

➤ *Describe and calculate various indicators of an entity's liquidity.*

➤ *Describe and calculate various indicators of an entity's asset turnover or efficiency.*

➤ Describe and calculate various indicators of an entity's budgetary solvency and operating results.

➤ Describe and calculate various indicators of an entity's debt burden and long-term financial flexibility.

➤ Describe the factors, other than ratios derived from financial statements, that are needed to assess an entity's financial condition.

$\mathcal{S}$ome accounting scandals that have shaken the financial markets in the past few years might have been more apparent to financial statement analysts than to others. Consider, for example, these *Wall Street Journal* reports:

- August 22, 2000. Managers of Boston Scientific Corp., a manufacturer of medical devices, had shipped about $75 million of unsold goods to Japanese warehouses in a scheme to report fake sales and profits.
- November 18, 1997. Bausch & Lomb's Asia-Pacific Division had overstated its earnings several years earlier by recording fictitious sales of sunglasses.

Why are these particular scams relevant to the analysis of financial statements? Consider how these scams might have been detected. Fake sales do not increase a company's cash; they increase accounts receivable. Perceptive financial statement analysts at company headquarters—both scams were detected by company personnel—might have wondered why the ratios of accounts receivable to sales were unusually high. Were credit terms becoming too lenient? Was follow-up on unpaid receivables becoming lax? Or, were the reported sales levels of medical instruments and Ray-Ban sunglasses just too good to be true? At Bausch & Lomb, the scheme did indeed start to unravel "when accounts receivable hit the roof."[1]

Financial statements provide the primary source of information both for internal managers and outside parties in assessing an entity's operating results and financial position. When various elements of the statements are converted to ratios (such as outstanding accounts receivable to sales), they can be used to spot deviations either from industry norms or previous-year company patterns. When combined with economic and demographic data, information can be developed to aid in assessing an entity's financial condition, providing some insight into its future financial health.

Some of the ratios developed for business-type entities can be adapted readily to the analysis of governmental and not-for-profit organizations, such as hospitals. Additional ratios have been developed

---

[1] *Business Week*, October 23, 1995, p. 90.

specifically to help in assessing the financial condition of governmental organizations.

In reading this chapter, remember that analyzing an organization's financial health is an art, not a science. No single ratio or "rule of thumb" drawn from nationwide data over time can be used to assess the financial health of a governmental or not-for-profit organization. Financial condition analysis, in particular, requires consideration of many factors—financial, economic, demographic and political—and the application of judgment to those factors.

INFORMATIONAL CONTENT OF FINANCIAL STATEMENTS: A FINANCIAL ANALYSIS PERSPECTIVE

Before discussing the techniques of financial statement and financial condition analysis, it is useful to reexamine the information content of the statements and related data covered in this text:

- *Statement of net assets,* also called the statement of financial position or the balance sheet
- *Statement of activities,* also called the statement of operations or the statement of revenues, expenses (expenditures), and changes in net assets (fund balances or fund equity)
- Notes to the financial statements and required supplementary information

Some differences in the financial statements and related data prepared by the various types of organizations covered in this text exist because of formatting requirements, prescribed measurements, and other accounting standards. Nevertheless, a sufficient number of similarities allow the following general observations about the purposes served by the statements and the related data.

Statement of Net Assets

The statement of net assets (or equivalent designation) provides information about an organization's assets, liabilities, and net assets as of the date of the statement. Because of the way the statement of net assets is presented and its information content, the analyst can learn something about an organization's liquidity and its financial flexibility.

Assets are generally listed in order of *liquidity,* or their nearness to cash and nearness to being consumed in operations. Liabilities are listed in terms of nearness to being paid. To provide further emphasis on liquidity, assets and liabilities are generally classified as *current* and *noncurrent.* Current assets include cash, those expected to be converted to cash in the following year, or those expected to be consumed in operations in the following year. Current liabilities are expected to be paid in the following year. For example, the portion of long-term bonds that is due to be paid in the following year is shown as current while the rest is reported as noncurrent.

Evidence of financial flexibility is provided by the captions attached to the various assets and liabilities, by the liquidity order in which the assets and liabilities are listed, and by the classifications shown in the net assets section of the statement of net assets. For example, both governmental and not-for-profit organizations show the extent to which the net assets are restricted as to use. When net assets are classified as unrestricted, they can be used for any purpose within the scope of the entity's charter that its management considers appropriate. When classified as restricted, the net assets are available only for the specific activity, function, or time period designated by law or by the party that restricted the use of the assets.

Obviously, management's financial flexibility is greater if its resources are relatively liquid and the level of its unrestricted net assets (or fund balance) is relatively high. How the analyst determines what is "relatively" liquid or high will be discussed shortly.

Statement of Activities

The statement of activities (or equivalent designation) shows both the details and the totals of an organization's revenues, expenses, and other elements leading to the change in net assets for the year. Thus, depending on such factors as the measurement focus and basis of accounting used in preparing the statements and the level of detail provided in the statements, the analyst can discover the following:

- Whether the resources were sufficient to cover the costs of the services provided during the year
- The various sources of revenues obtained during the year
- The nature of the services provided during the year
- Whether unusual factors, such as significant "one-time" items, influenced the operating results for the year

Separating revenues by source provides a clue as to the volatility and reliability of revenue streams available to finance future activities. In financing governments, for example, property taxes tend to be more stable from year to year than personal income taxes and sales taxes, which are more heavily influenced by economic factors. Also, revenues from higher-level governments tend to be less reliable than own-source revenues. Heavily endowed not-for-profit organizations can experience volatile revenues because of stock market fluctuations, even though unrealized gains and losses on securities in a particular year may not affect the organization's long-run financial health.

Subtotals and formats play a useful role in conveying information on the statement of activities. For example, the not-for-profit hospital's statement of operations (Table 14-3 on page 621) provides a measure of financial performance by separating the "excess of revenues over expenses" from other factors affecting the increase in unrestricted net assets for the year. The government-wide statement of activities (see page 427) measures the relative burden each function places on the taxpaying public by showing both the gross functional expenses and revenues directly related to those functions. A not-for-profit organization's statement of activities (see page 505) helps readers understand the sources and uses of resources by separating revenues into three net asset classifications, and by separating program expenses from administrative and fund-raising expenses.

A financial analyst needs to recognize that the statement of activities has limitations as an indicator of future events. Its limitations are particularly evident in government, where the statement of activities measures the cost of services provided but not the cost of unmet service needs. The fact that a governmental entity's net assets at year-end increased over the previous year does not necessarily mean that its financial condition improved. Unmet service needs that cannot be readily financed must be considered in examining a government's financial condition.

Notes to the Financial Statements and Required Supplementary Information

As previously stated, notes are an integral part of the financial statements, providing information not shown on the face of the statements but nevertheless essential to fair presentation of the statements. Required supplementary information also provides information considered essential to financial reporting. Although all notes and required supplementary information need to be read, some of the data is particularly important in assessing an organization's financial position and condition include the following:

- *Property Tax Calendar.* Some governments obtain large amounts of revenues from property taxes. Although property taxes are generally collected twice a year, 6 months apart, the first payment may be due before the fiscal year begins, at any time during the year, or even in the next year. The tax calendar can therefore affect an entity's cash flows, producing either interest income or interest expense, and may help explain the size of amounts reported as cash, taxes receivable, deferred revenues, and notes payable.
- *Debt Service Requirements to Maturity.* Debt service requirements affect an entity's financial flexibility. An entity that can balance its current budget and simultaneously redeem relatively large amounts of debt has greater financial flexibility than one that needs to push its debt redemption off to the long-term future. Governmental entities are required to disclose their debt service requirements to maturity, showing amounts due each year for the next 5 years and amounts due in 5-year increments thereafter.
- *Pension Plan Obligations.* Defined benefit pension plans and postemployment benefit plans create future debt-like commitments. As discussed in Chapter 8, governments with pension plans are required to disclose funding progress (ratio of actuarial value of assets to actuarial accrued liability, or "funded ratio") and actual compared to required pension contributions. If all other factors are the same, an entity that has a high funded ratio and is contributing 100 percent of its annual funding requirement is likely to be in better fiscal health than one with a low ratio and that is not contributing the full requirement.

AN APPROACH TO FINANCIAL STATEMENT AND FINANCIAL CONDITION ANALYSIS

The extent to which one might analyze financial statements depends on the purpose of the analysis. One analyst might be concerned only about a particular data element, such as the size of a not-for-profit organization's year-end unrestricted fund balance and how it compares with the previous year-end. Another analyst might be concerned with how a hospital's overall financial position at year-end and results of operations for the year compare with the previous year. A third analyst might want to review the overall financial condition of a governmental entity to assess its long-term ability to finance anticipated debt and expanded services.[2]

The first analyst is interested in a single element of an organization's financial position at two points in time, which can be obtained by reading that data element in the statement of financial position. The second one needs to read the statements and related notes, select certain data elements from the statements, convert them to useful financial ratios, do the same with the previous year's statements, and interpret the results. The third analyst needs to use a longer time period, select additional data elements (including economic and demographic data obtained outside the financial statements), and develop a frame of reference composed of other governments to aid in interpreting the results.

Converting Data to More Useful Formats

To aid in interpreting data for financial statement and financial condition analysis, the analyst needs to convert data elements to more useful formats. The numbers take on a different meaning when viewed in comparison with another relevant statistic. For example, an analyst may conclude that the accounts receivable collection process got worse if the accounts receivable balance at December 31, 2005, was $420,000, up from $400,000 at December 31, 2004. Considering the increase in revenues during 2005 by converting the accounts receivable balance to the number of days' revenue represented by the balance might show, however, that the collection process actually improved during the year.

Data formats used in financial analysis include ratios, per capita information, and common size statements. In addition, analyzing data can be made easier by developing percentage change information and location quotient information.

- *Ratios* are developed by relating one data element to another to produce an indicator of a particular characteristic. We just saw how relating the receivables

---

[2] Robert Berne defines financial condition as "the probability that a government will meet both (a) its financial obligations to creditors, consumers, employees, taxpayers, suppliers, constituents, and others as they become due and (b) the service obligations to constituents, both currently and in the future." Robert Berne, *The Relationships Between Financial Reporting and the Measurement of Financial Condition* (Norwalk, CT: GASB, 1992), p. 17.

balance to revenues provides the analyst with a good indicator of receivables collection efficiency. Using ratios also allows the analyst to assess trends for the entity itself and to compare the entity with other organizations—things that could not be done in a meaningful way using just the raw numbers.

- *Per capita information* is produced by dividing financial data elements by the entity's population. Converting financial data to per capita information also makes it easier to trace trends for the entity and to compare the entity with other organizations.
- *Common size statements* are obtained by converting financial statement elements to percentages of 100. Using common size statements allows the analyst to readily identify changes over time in the proportion that individual data elements bear to the total (for example, the share of total expenses consumed by a government's public safety expenses, or a not-for-profit entity's fund-raising expenses).
- *Percentage change information* is obtained by comparing data elements for a later year with data elements for an earlier year. For example, if the cash balance increased from $200,000 in 2004 to $250,000 in 2005, the percentage change was plus 25 percent. It provides another approach to showing comparisons over time within an entity or with other entities.
- *Location quotient information* is obtained by dividing a data element for the entity under study by the comparable data element for other entities, so that results revolve around 1. For example, if the cash balance for the entity under study was $200,000 and the average cash balance for a comparison entity was $250,000, the location quotient would be 0.8. It is a useful way of comparing data over time with other entities.

Time-Series Analysis

Financial statement and financial condition analysis require review of statements over a period of time for the organization under study, called *time-series analysis.* At a minimum, data (such as raw numbers, ratios, per capita information, or other formats) for the current year need to be compared with the previous year so that observations can be made about the nature and extent of improvement or deterioration. To assess financial condition, however, analysts generally study changes for 5 to 10 years. To ascertain the implications of trends in economic and demographic factors (such as population shifts), data for even longer periods of time are reviewed.

Comparative Analysis

Suppose the earnings margin (discussed later in this chapter) for a not-for-profit hospital increased from 2.2 percent to 2.5 percent from last year to the current year. The earnings margin improved, which seems to be a favorable factor. But, by what standard does 2.5 percent appear to be favorable? To answer this question, one might ask: "What is the median earnings margin of other not-for-profit hospitals of similar size and similar patient mix?" *Comparative analysis* is a valuable tool for the financial analyst because it provides an external reference point—a type of standard or norm—for assessing the data developed for the organization under study.

Analysts concerned with assessing operating results, financial position, and financial condition of individual organizations maintain extensive databases to facilitate comparative analysis among generally similar organizations. For example:

- The New York State Comptroller's Office publishes annually a special statistical report, organized by type of government in New York State, to assist in overseeing the fiscal affairs of local governments within the state.[3]
- Municipal bond-rating agencies maintain extensive nationwide databases to help in their bond-rating processes. These agencies often publish documents containing ratios that can serve as "rules of thumb" (general guidelines) for governmental entities seeking to compare their ratios with others.
- The Center for Healthcare Industry Performance Studies (CHIPS) publishes an *Almanac of Hospital Financial and Operating Indicators* to help health care entities compare their ratios with similar entities.

Information obtained from sources such as these can help in assessing the implications of ratios developed for a particular entity. If such information is not readily available, analysts should construct their own "reference groups" or "peer groups" for comparison purposes. Nevertheless, "rule of thumb" and reference group data need to be developed and used with care because of the potential for distortion caused by environmental differences, such as nature of functions performed, mix of population served, size of entity, revenue sources, and location.

Although nationwide data may serve as good frames of reference for some ratios, it is often better to compare the organization under study with a reference group of similar organizations. For example, if an analyst is studying the financial condition of a city, a reference group of about 10 other *city* governments *within the state* might be developed, because all the cities are likely to perform the same functions and be subject to the same laws. They should also be of generally similar population size. For some ratios, data on all local governments within the state and available nationwide "rules of thumb" will serve as a useful check on the ratios developed for the 10-city reference group.

In summary, financial statement and financial condition analysis is helped by (1) converting data elements to more useful formats such as ratios, (2) tracing data over time within the entity, and (3) comparing the entity with other similar organizations.

FINANCIAL STATEMENT AND FINANCIAL CONDITION ANALYSIS INDICATORS

Many indicators used for analyzing financial statements and financial condition are developed entirely from financial statement data elements or from the relationship of a financial statement element to a demographic or economic element. These indicators

---

[3] "Comptroller's Special Report on Municipal Affairs for New York State," Office of the State Comptroller, Albany, NY.

may be classified as liquidity indicators, asset turnover or efficiency indicators, budgetary solvency and operating results indicators, and debt burden and other long-term financial flexibility indicators. Other indicators (used in the more extensive financial condition analyses) come from economic and demographic elements and other factors.

The indicators covered in this text are illustrative of the many ratios suggested by writers on this subject. The authors focus on indicators that they have observed in practice or that they consider particularly useful. Some indicators are used for analyzing all three types of entities covered in the text: governmental, general not-for-profit entities, and not-for-profit hospitals. Others have been adapted to or developed for the operating peculiarities of a particular type of entity.

In considering these indicators, keep in mind that no single indicator taken alone can be used to measure an entity's financial position or condition. For example, ratios based on balance sheet information are as of a single point in time and may not be representative of what occurs throughout the year. Appropriate judgments can be made, however, when the indicators are considered as a group, examined over a period of years, and assessed in terms of a representative group of similar organizations.

Liquidity Indicators

New York City's fiscal crisis of the late 1970s was preceded by a sharp increase in short-term debt. Increased short-term borrowings and a buildup of unpaid bills are some of the first signs of fiscal stress. *Liquidity indicators* provide information on the ability of an organization to meet its short-term obligations.

Commonly used liquidity indicators are the *current ratio, quick ratio,* and *number of days' cash on hand.* The general formulae for calculating them are as follows:

$$\text{Current Ratio} = \frac{\text{Current Assets}}{\text{Current Liabilities}}$$

$$\text{Quick Ratio} = \frac{\text{Cash} + \text{Cash Equivalents} + \text{Short-Term Investments}}{\text{Current Liabilities}}$$

$$\frac{\text{Number of days'}}{\text{Cash on Hand}} = \frac{\text{Cash} + \text{Cash Equivalents} + \text{Short-Term Investments}}{(\text{Operating Expenses} - \text{Bad Debts} - \text{Depreciation}) / 365}$$

Current liabilities are obligations as of the balance sheet date that are due to be paid within 1 year. Depending on when they are due for payment, these obligations will be paid out of cash currently on hand, other current assets that will be converted to cash, and cash inflows from the next year's activities. The current ratio considers all current assets in assessing an entity's ability to pay current obligations. The quick ratio, sometimes called the "acid test," eliminates current assets that are less readily convertible to cash.

A conservative quick ratio is one comprised of cash, cash equivalents, and other short-term (or temporary) investments. *Cash equivalents* are short-term liquid investments readily convertible to known amounts of cash and are so close to maturity (having had an original maturity of 3 months or less) that there is little risk of loss in value. *Short-term investments* other than cash equivalents have slightly longer maturities, and include certificates of deposit, money market funds, and U.S. Treasury bills. Some analysts include accounts receivable in calculating the quick ratio.

From the perspective of the financial condition analyst, higher current and quick ratios signify a greater ability to meet current obligations. Historically, many organizations (including business enterprises) have found that a current ratio of 2.0 and a quick ratio of 1.0 provide reasonable margins for safety in meeting current obligations. These historical "rules of thumb," however, are not etched in stone. Many business enterprises have found more productive uses for their cash, and have current ratios well below 2.0. Hospitals that carry large amounts of slow-paying accounts receivable (from both self-pay patients and third-party payers) may need a current ratio higher than 2.0 to meet current obligations.

A quick ratio of 1.0 says enough cash is on hand to pay currently due bills, but a lower ratio may suffice if some current liabilities are not due for immediate payment and if cash received early in the next year from the next year's activities will help pay them. Monthly cash forecasts help supplement the liquidity ratios. Increasingly large amounts of notes payable due early in the next year can signal an onset of liquidity problems.

Number of days' cash on hand, often used as a liquidity indicator by not-for-profit hospitals, provides another perspective on liquidity. It is a quick ratio converted to another form, because it shows how many days the entity can continue to pay its regular operating expenses without new inflows of cash. In making this calculation, bad debts and depreciation are removed from the operating expenses because they do not require cash outlays. Some writers include debt principal repayments in the denominator.

Asset Turnover or Efficiency Indicators

Cash can be invested or used to pay bills, but accounts receivable cannot. Receivables can, of course, be sold or used as collateral to borrow cash, but both come at a price—the payment of interest. Generally, the more rapidly an entity can convert its receivables to cash, the more liquid it is.

Expressing receivables collection efficiency can be done in several ways. Hospitals and governmental business-type activities generally express *accounts receivable collection efficiency* in terms of number of days' revenue in receivables or average collection period. General governments measure property tax collection efficiency in terms of percentage of taxes collected (or *not* collected) in the year of the tax levy, or the ratio of property taxes receivable to property tax revenues. The general formulae for calculating these indicators are as follows:

$$\frac{\text{Days' Revenue in}}{\text{Receivables}} = \frac{\text{Net Patient Accounts Receivable}}{\text{Net Patient Service Revenue} / 365}$$

$$\frac{\text{Property Tax}}{\text{Collection Rate}} = \frac{\text{Current-Year Real Property Taxes Collected}}{\text{Current-Year Real Property Tax Levy}}$$

$$\frac{\text{Property Tax}}{\text{Receivable Rate}} = \frac{\text{Real Property Taxes Receivable}}{\text{Real Property Tax Revenues}}$$

The number of days' revenue in receivables can also be calculated using the *asset turnover* method. Accounts receivable turnover is calculated by dividing revenues by accounts receivable. Days' revenue in receivables (or average receivables collection period) is then determined by dividing 365 by the accounts receivable turnover.

Year-to-year changes in these rates may indicate weak administration, such as poor follow-up on slow payers or insufficient penalties for nonpayment of real property taxes. Increasing rates of real property tax delinquency, however, could also be a sign of the onset of fiscal stress, caused by an inability of property taxpayers to make their payments because of economic hardship. For example, referring again to the New York City fiscal crisis, analysis of the City's real property tax collection experience showed a gradual increase in delinquencies as the crisis of the 1970s worsened and better collections as the city emerged from the crisis.[4] Moody's suggests that a current tax collection rate of less than 95 percent or a declining trend is a potential sign of credit distress.[5]

Another common asset turnover or efficiency ratio is the *total asset turnover,* which is calculated as follows:

$$\frac{\text{Total Asset}}{\text{Turnover}} = \frac{\text{Unrestricted Revenues, Gains, and Other Support}}{\text{Unrestricted Net Assets}}$$

Total asset turnover is a good indicator of asset efficiency, particularly for hospitals. Assets used in producing revenues can be thought of as inputs, and the revenues can be considered as outputs. The greater the quantity of output for a given quantity of input (that is, the higher the asset turnover), the greater is the asset efficiency.

Budget Solvency and Operating Results Indicators

Budget solvency means being able to generate sufficient recurring revenues each year to meet recurring expenses (or expenditures) and having a sufficiently large "cushion" of unrestricted resources to weather unforeseen economic downturns and expenditure needs. Entities with relatively volatile revenue structures (such as governments that obtain large amounts of revenue from economy-sensitive taxes like personal income and sales taxes) should maintain a larger cushion than those with relatively stable revenue structures.

The general formulae for the ratios discussed in this section are as follows:

$$\frac{\text{Operating Margin or}}{\text{Earnings Margin}} = \frac{\text{Excess of Revenues over Expenses (or expenditures)}}{\text{Total Revenues, Gains, and Other Support (or total revenues, or other corresponding item)}}$$

$$\frac{\text{Operating Margin or}}{\text{Earnings Margin}} = \frac{\text{Change in Unrestricted Net Assets (or net assets)}}{\text{Total Revenues, Gains, and Other Support (or total revenues, or other corresponding item)}}$$

$$\text{Budgetary Cushion} = \frac{\text{Total Unreserved Fund Balance}}{\text{Total Revenues}}$$

$$\text{Program Service Ratio} = \frac{\text{Program Expenses}}{\text{Total Expenses}}$$

---

[4] "Comparative Analysis of New York City's Financial and Economic Indicators," Office of the Comptroller, Bureau of Financial Analysis, The City of New York, January 1982.

[5] "The Determinants of Credit Quality," Moody's Investors Service, November 1999, p. 8.

One indicator of budgetary solvency is the extent to which operating revenues exceed expenses/expenditures—which helps determine the *operating margin or earnings margin*. The AICPA *Audit and Accounting Guide—Health Care Organizations* emphasizes the need for statements of operations prepared by health care entities to have clearly labeled operating performance indicators, using terms such as "revenues over expenses" or "performance earnings." This indicator should be presented in a statement that also presents the total changes in unrestricted net assets.[6] Despite the value of this indicator, significant transactions or events reported below the performance indicator also warrant scrutiny in assessing the entity's financial health. An analyst might question, for example, whether unrealized securities losses might ultimately be realized.

Details of governmental operating statements (both fund statements and government-wide statements) also need to be understood to assess the quality of amounts reported as net change in fund balances or change in net assets. For example, amounts reported as special items may be one-time revenue sources used to help balance the budget, and could be evidence of fiscal stress. Causes of amounts reported as transfers in and out also need to be considered in assessing the quality of operating results, because both may be indicators of fiscal stress within the reporting entity.

A 1-year decline in operating results is not necessarily a cause for concern to the financial analyst. For example, a government may budget deliberately for an operating deficit in a particular year to use up a small portion of its unreserved fund balance or to avoid raising tax rates. The analyst thus needs to understand the reasons for the year-to-year change and to examine the longer-term trends in the operating results indicator.

A significant indicator for analysts of governmental financial statements is the ratio of unreserved fund balance to total revenues—the *budgetary cushion*. Moody's writes that it "likes to see a General Fund balance sufficient to address *normal* contingencies, which as a general guideline, is typically between 5 and 10 percent of annual revenues," but emphasizes that an appropriate level of fund balance depends on each government's operating environment.[7] Other factors that need to be considered in assessing the level of fund balance include the nature and extent of interfund transfers, and the historical relationship between budgets and actual financial performance.

Trends in the composition of revenues and expenses are also important to the analysis of budgetary solvency. For example, an increasingly high level of revenues from economy-sensitive taxes may warrant an increase in the budgetary cushion. Review of expenditure details may help to identify *why* they increased over the previous year, so as to draw managerial attention to the need for remedial action.

Examination of the composition of expenses of not-for-profit organizations is useful to those concerned with how donations are being spent. The FASB requirement to show program expenses separately from administrative and fund-raising expenses enables the reader to calculate the percentage of total expenses devoted to program— the *program services ratio*. The Better Business Bureau suggests that charities should

---

6 AICPA *Audit and Accounting Guide—Health Care Organizations* (2001), para. 10.17.
7 "The Determinants of Credit Quality," Moody's Investors Service, November 1999, p. 6.

spend no more than 50 percent of total available support and revenue on fund-raising and administrative costs combined.[8] A general rule of thumb is that not-for-profit organizations should strive for a program services ratio of at least 70 percent.

Debt Burden and Other Long-Term Financial Flexibility Indicators

Credit-rating agencies, credit enhancers (such as bond insurers), and investors are all concerned with whether entities that issue long-term debt are likely to have sufficient resources to meet the interest and principal payments on the debt. The general citizenry is also concerned with the strain on resources caused by the need to meet those payments. Outstanding debt, however, is not the only potential drain on an entity's future resources. Pension and postemployment health care obligations also have an impact on an entity's long-term financial condition. Analysts for public and not-for-profit entity employee unions are concerned with the ability of these entities to meet such obligations.

Debt Issued by Governments

The general formulae for calculating a government's debt and debt service burdens are as follows:

$$\text{Debt Burden} = \frac{\text{Outstanding Long-Term Debt}}{\text{Population (or full value of taxable real property or personal income)}}$$

$$\text{Debt Service Burden} = \frac{\text{Total Debt Service}}{\text{Total Revenues (or total expenditures)}}$$

As a general rule, governments issue long-term bonds to finance the acquisition of long-lived capital assets, although long-term debt may also be issued to finance operating needs in periods of fiscal stress. Governments that have a policy of financing a portion of their capital asset needs from tax revenues tend to have greater financial flexibility than those that finance all their capital asset needs by long-term borrowing.

State constitutions generally limit the amount of debt a local government can issue. Debt limits are usually expressed as a percentage of the full value of taxable real property. Therefore, the closer a government is to its maximum debt limit, the less flexibility it has to borrow for its capital needs. Further, even if it has the legal capacity to borrow, a government may still find it difficult to borrow at reasonable interest costs because of imbalances between its revenues and expenditures.

Common measures of a government's *debt burden* are those that relate outstanding long-term debt to bases that measure its ability to pay the debt, and that can be tracked over time and compared with other governments. They include debt per capita and debt as a percentage of full value of taxable real property. Debt per capita is a simple measure, but does not take account of the wealth of the government's citizens. Debt as a percent of full value of taxable real property provides a measure of

---

[8] "BBB Standards for Charitable Solicitations," New York Philanthropic Advisory Service, standard B-4, available at www.newyork.bbb.org/nypas/standards.html (March 2, 2002).

the wealth of the community and is therefore a better measure. Debt as a percent of personal income, though not often used, is an excellent measure of debt burden because it takes account of a community's ability to pay the debt service.

Outstanding debt for purposes of calculating debt burden includes the *net direct debt* of the government itself and *overlapping debt,* which is the proportionate share of debt issued by other governmental units that provide services to the citizens of the government. Net direct debt includes both general obligation debt and lease-purchase debt of the government, but, depending on the circumstances, may exclude "self-supporting" debt, such as debt supported by the revenues of an enterprise fund. Overlapping debt includes debt issued by related entities, such as school districts, park districts, cities, and counties. These entities tax the same real property base taxed by the government, thus placing a burden on its stream of resources.

A government's *debt service burden* is the portion of its revenues that is consumed by the annual payment of principal and interest on long-term debt and interest on short-term debt. Because refinancing outstanding debt may be costly, the annual debt service requirement is a relatively "fixed" expense. Therefore, the greater the portion of an entity's revenues that is consumed by its debt service requirements, the less flexibility it has to issue additional debt, to meet operating expenditure needs, and to weather the effects of an economic downturn. Bond rating agencies generally consider a debt service burden of 10 percent to be moderate and a burden of 15 to 20 percent as high.[9]

A factor closely related to the annual debt service burden is the rate of payback of debt principal. State constitutions generally limit the length of debt issuances. For example, some require that debt be issued for a period no greater than the useful life of the capital asset to be financed with the debt. Others require that debt be issued for no more than a specific number of years. To keep interest costs down, some governments establish debt repayment schedules faster than the legal requirements. On the other hand, a government may decide to stretch its debt repayment schedule further into the future by refinancing its outstanding debt, which is often a sign of fiscal stress.

Municipal bond-rating agencies consider a debt repayment schedule as "average" if 25 percent of the outstanding debt is paid off in 5 years and 50 percent is paid off in 10 years.[10] As long as it is not placing a strain on the operating budget, a faster rate of payback not only reduces interest costs, but also gives an entity greater flexibility in issuing additional debt to meet capital needs.

Debt Issued by Not-for-Profit Organizations

Debt analysis for not-for-profit organizations generally focuses on capital structure and on coverage. *Capital structure* concerns the extent to which the organization is leveraged, that is, the extent to which its assets are financed through the use of debt. As the use of debt increases, the entity's financial flexibility decreases and risks to financial solvency increase. Ratios may be calculated using just the long-term debt or the total liabilities as the numerator. Using total liabilities offers the advantage of

---

[9] Standard and Poor's Public Finance Ratings Criteria, 2000, p. 25.
[10] Ibid.

capturing the extent to which the organization is being financed by borrowing short-term and by not paying its creditors in a timely manner.

Coverage analysis focuses on the entity's ability to repay the debt, as demonstrated by its level of net earnings. Coverage indicators measure the number of times debt service (or interest on debt) is covered by the earnings. Thus, the greater number of times debt service (or interest on debt) is covered by earnings, the greater is the cushion against possible nonpayment. The commonly used ratios are calculated generally as follows:

$$\frac{\text{Debt to}}{\text{Equity}} = \frac{\text{Total Liabilities}}{\text{Total Net Assets}}$$

$$\frac{\text{Long-Term Debt}}{\text{to Equity}} = \frac{\text{Long-Term Debt, Net of Current Portion}}{\text{Total Net Assets}}$$

$$\frac{\text{Debt Service}}{\text{Coverage}} = \frac{(\text{Excess of Revenues over Expenses}) + \text{Depreciation} + \text{Interest}}{\text{Principal Payment} + \text{Interest Expense}}$$

$$\frac{\text{Times Interest}}{\text{Earned}} = \frac{(\text{Excess of Revenues over Expenses}) + \text{Interest Expense}}{\text{Interest Expense}}$$

Pension Obligations

Pension benefit and postemployment health care arrangements create long-term debt-like commitments. An adequately funded pension plan provides for annual employer (and employee, where required) contributions to a pension system, so that amounts contributed plus earnings on them will be sufficient to pay benefits earned by the employees as they come due. Failure to fund the pension plan appropriately each year as benefits are earned could place a future strain on an entity's operating budgets.

The most common measure of the adequacy of pension funding is the *funded ratio*, discussed in Chapter 8. Another good measure, particularly where different measures of the actuarial accrued liability make comparisons difficult, is *pension payout coverage*. These indicators are calculated as follows:

$$\text{Funded Ratio} = \frac{\text{Pension Fund Assets Available for Benefits}}{\text{Pension Benefit Obligation (actuarial accrued liability)}}$$

$$\frac{\text{Pension Payout}}{\text{Coverage}} = \frac{\text{Pension Fund Assets Available for Benefits}}{\text{Pension Benefits Paid Last Year}}$$

Table 14-1 presents a summary of the indicators previously discussed.

FINANCIAL CONDITION ASSESSMENT

The financial condition of state and local governments and other not-for-profit entities is assessed for a variety of reasons, as shown in the following examples:

- The New York State Comptroller's Office gathers financial information from all local governments in the state as part of its responsibility for overseeing local government fiscal affairs. The objective of this process is to detect early signals of fiscal stress so that prompt action may be taken to ward off serious fiscal crises.

Table 14-1
Summary of Financial Analysis Indicators

Liquidity Indicators

   Purpose: To help assess an entity's ability to meet its short-term obligations

   Common Indicators:

   Current ratio (current assets *divided by* current liabilities)

   Quick ratio (cash + cash equivalents + short-term investments *divided by* current liabilities)

   Number of days' cash on hand (cash + cash equivalents + short-term investments *divided by* cash needs per day)

Asset Turnover or Efficiency Indicators

   Purpose: To help assess an entity's efficiency in using its resources.

   Common Indicators:

   Number of days' revenue in accounts receivable (net patient accounts receivable *divided by* net patient service revenues per day)

   Property tax collection rate (current year property taxes collected *divided by* current year real property tax levy)

   Property tax receivable rate (real property taxes receivable *divided by* real property tax revenues)

   Total asset turnover (unrestricted revenues, gains, and other support *divided by* unrestricted net assets)

Budget Solvency and Operating Results Indicators

   Purpose: To help assess an entity's ability to generate sufficient recurring revenues to meet expenses and to meet unforeseen operating budget needs

   Common Indicators:

   Earnings margin (excess of revenues over expenses *divided by* total revenues, gains, and other support [or equivalent]) or (change in unrestricted net assets *divided by* total revenues, gains and other support [or equivalent])

   Budgetary cushion (total unreserved fund balance *divided by* total revenues)

   Program services ratio (program expenses *divided by* total expenses)

Debt Burden and Other Long-Term Financial Flexibility Indicators

   Purpose: To help assess an entity's likelihood of having sufficient resources to meet its long-term obligations and to finance long-term capital and other needs

   Common Indicators:

   Debt issued by governments:

      Debt burden (outstanding long-term debt *divided by* population or full value of taxable real property or personal income)

      Debt service burden (total debt service *divided by* total revenues or expenditures)

   Debt issued by not-for-profit organizations:

      Debt to equity (total liabilities *divided by* total net assets)

      Long-term debt to equity (long-term debt [net of current portion] *divided by* total net assets)

      Debt service coverage ([excess of revenues over expenses] + depreciation + interest expense *divided by* principal payment + interest expense)

      Times interest earned ([excess of revenues over expenses] + interest expense *divided by* interest expense)

   Pension obligations

      Funded ratio (pension fund assets available for benefits *divided by* pension benefit obligation)

      Pension payout coverage (pension fund assets available for benefits *divided by* pension benefits paid last year)

- Bond-rating agencies provide an independent, objective assessment of the relative creditworthiness of debt obligations. These assessments aid the issuer in obtaining capital and aid the investor in deciding whether to invest in a particular obligation.
- Credit enhancers assess the creditworthiness of debt obligations in deciding whether to insure the payment of debt service. Insurance lowers the net interest cost to the borrower and provides a guarantee of payment to the lender.

Assessment of an organization's financial condition for purposes of providing credit ratings and insuring payment of debt service requires procedures beyond the analysis of financial statements. Bond-rating agencies generally consider four groups of factors in developing their ratings: economic, financial, debt, and administrative.[11] They generally assess the risk of nonpayment of debt service over long future periods. Assessing whether the current financial condition carries the seeds of future fiscal crises involves shorter future time periods, but requires similar analytic procedures.

To understand the need for going beyond the data contained in financial statements when analyzing financial condition, it is important to keep in mind that the financial condition of governments, in particular, depends on these factors:

- the economic and demographic environment underlying the government
- the way in which governmental officials react to their environment

History shows that some governmental entities with a strong economic base have encountered fiscal stress because of the failure of political will, while other governments with a weaker economic base have been able to avoid a fiscal crisis because of careful budgeting and a history of sound fiscal policies.

Consideration of the economic and demographic environment involves such factors as business activity growth, risk of loss of business activity because of an excessive degree of concentration, tax base growth (such as personal income, property values, and sales), employment and unemployment levels, labor skills and education of the residents, and poverty levels. An illustration provided later in the chapter covers these items.

Consideration of the way governmental managers react to their environment includes such factors as the will to maintain budgets that are balanced both in form and substance, and the speed with which fiscal problems are recognized and dealt with. It also includes the professionalism of staff, as evidenced by the planning processes and the effectiveness of the accounting and financial reporting systems.

ILLUSTRATION OF ANALYSIS OF NOT-FOR-PROFIT HOSPITAL FINANCIAL STATEMENTS

Two of the financial statements of Sample Not-for-Profit Hospital for the years 2005 and 2004, originally used in Chapter 13, will be used to illustrate the calculations of the ratios used in financial statement analysis. For ease in reading, the statements are

---

[11] Moody's, pp. 3–6, and Standard and Poor's, pp. 22–26.

shown again in Tables 14-2 and 14-3. Trace the numbers used in developing the ratios to the financial statements. When tracing numbers for items containing groups of data elements, notice the captions of the details that comprise the totals. Remember that the raw numbers used in developing the ratios are in thousands of dollars.

Liquidity Indicators

Current Ratio

The balance sheet (Table 14-2) shows the current ratio at December 31, 2005, to be

$$\frac{\text{Current Assets}}{\text{Current Liabilities}} = \frac{\$39,334}{\$11,400} = 3.45$$

The ratio of 3.45 is an improvement over the ratio at the end of the previous year, when it was 3.13 ($34,967/$11,188).

Quick Ratio

The quick ratio at December 31, 2005, is 1.89. The numerator ($21,564) consists of cash and cash equivalents ($4,758), plus short-term investments ($15,836), plus cash and short-term investments included in assets limited as to use ($970). The denominator ($11,400) is the current liabilities. The ratio was 1.60 at December 31, 2004.

Number of Days' Cash on Hand

Calculating the number of days' cash on hand requires reference to both the balance sheet (Table 14-2) and the statement of operations (Table 14-3). The statement of operations is used to estimate the average amount of cash needed each day to pay operating expenses. Start with the total expenses for the year and subtract depreciation and provision for bad debts, because those expenses do not require cash outlays. Divide by 365 to get the cash needs per day. Then, divide the cash and short-term investments by the cash needed per day. Calculations for 2005 are as follows:

Total Expenses ($98,055) − [Depreciation and Amortization ($4,782) and Provision for Bad Debts ($1,000)] = $92,273

$92,273/365 = $252.8 (cash needed per day)

$$\frac{\text{Cash + Short-Term Investments}}{\text{Average Cash Needed per Day}} = \frac{\$4,758 + \$15,836 + \$970}{\$252.8} = 85.3 \text{ days}$$

Thus, the amount of cash on hand is sufficient to pay operating expenses for about 85.3 days. This indicator shows an improvement over the previous year, when the number of days' cash on hand was 78.1. Major elements of the year 2004 computation are as follows: Cash needed per day was $229.3 ($89,290 − $4,280 − $1,300 = $83,710; $83,710/365 = $229.3). Cash and short-term investments were $17,917 ($5,877 + $10,740 + $1,300).

Efficiency Indicator (Number of Days' Revenue in Receivables)

Calculating the number of days' revenue in receivables (or the average number of days required to collect receivables) also requires reference to both the balance sheet (Table 14-2) and the statement of operations (Table 14-3). First, determine the net

Table 14-2
Balance Sheet—Not-for-Profit Hospital

SAMPLE NOT-FOR-PROFIT HOSPITAL
BALANCE SHEETS
DECEMBER 31, 2005 AND 2004
(AMOUNTS IN THOUSANDS)

	2005	2004
Assets		
Current assets:		
Cash and cash equivalents	$ 4,758	$ 5,877
Short-term investments	15,836	10,740
Assets limited as to use	970	1,300
Patient accounts receivable, net of allowance for doubtful accounts of $2,500 in 2005 and $2,400 in 2004	15,100	14,194
Other current assets	2,670	2,856
Total current assets	39,334	34,967
Interest in net assets of Sample Hospital Foundation	510	462
Assets limited as to use:		
Internally designated for capital acquisition	12,000	12,500
Held by trustee	6,949	7,341
	18,949	19,841
Less amount required to meet current obligations	(970)	(1,300)
	17,979	18,541
Long-term investments	4,680	4,680
Long-term investments restricted for capital acquisition	320	520
Property and equipment, net	51,038	50,492
Other assets	1,185	908
Total assets	$115,046	$110,570
Liabilities and Net Assets		
Current liabilities:		
Current portion of long-term debt	$ 1,470	$ 1,750
Accounts payable and accrued expenses	5,818	5,382
Estimated third-party payer settlements	2,143	1,942
Other current liabilities	1,969	2,114
Total current liabilities	11,400	11,188
Long-term debt, net of current portion	23,144	24,014
Other liabilities	3,953	3,166
Total liabilities	38,497	38,368
Net assets:		
Unrestricted	70,846	66,199
Temporarily restricted	2,115	2,470
Permanently restricted	3,588	3,533
Total net assets	76,549	72,202
Total liabilities and net assets	$115,046	$110,570

See accompanying notes to financial statements.

Source: American Institute of Certified Public Accountants, *Audit and Accounting Guide—Health Care Organizations* (New York, AICPA, 2001), Appendix A. Copyright 2001 by American Institute of Certified Public Accountants, Inc. Reprinted with permission.

Table 14-3
Statements of Operations—Not-for-Profit Hospital

SAMPLE NOT-FOR-PROFIT HOSPITAL
STATEMENTS OF OPERATIONS
YEARS ENDED DECEMBER 31, 2005 AND 2004
(AMOUNTS IN THOUSANDS)

	2005	2004
Unrestricted revenues, gains, and other support:		
Net patient service revenue	$85,156	$78,942
Premium revenue	11,150	10,950
Other revenue	2,601	5,212
Net assets released from restrictions used for operations	300	
Total revenues, gains, and other support	99,207	95,104
Expenses:		
Operating expenses	88,521	80,585
Depreciation and amortization	4,782	4,280
Interest	1,752	1,825
Provision for bad debts	1,000	1,300
Other	2,000	1,300
Total expenses	98,055	89,290
Operating income	1,152	5,814
Other income:		
Investment income	3,900	3,025
Excess of revenues over expenses	5,052	8,839
Change in net unrealized gains and losses on other than trading securities	300	375
Net assets released from restrictions used for purchase of property and equipment	200	
Change in interest in net assets of Sample Hospital Foundation	283	536
Transfers to parent	(688)	(3,051)
Increase in unrestricted net assets, before extraordinary item	5,147	6,699
Extraordinary loss from extinguishment of debt	(500)	
Increase in unrestricted net assets	$ 4,647	$ 6,699

See accompanying notes to financial statements.

Source: American Institute of Certified Public Accountants, *Audit and Accounting Guide—Health Care Organizations* (New York, AICPA, 2001). Appendix A. Copyright 2001 by American Institute of Certified Public Accountants, Inc. Reprinted with permission.

Chapter 14   Analysis of Financial Statements and Financial Condition   621

patient service revenue per day. Then, divide the net patient accounts receivable by the net patient service revenue per day. Calculations for 2005 are as follows:

Net patient service revenue ($85,156)/365 = $233.3 (patient service revenue per day)

$$\frac{\text{Net Patient Accounts Receivable}}{\text{Net Patient Service Revenue per Day}} = \frac{\$15,100}{\$233.3} = 64.7 \text{ days}$$

Thus, Sample Hospital has 64.7 days of revenue tied up in accounts receivable at December 31, 2005. This indicator is slightly better than the previous year, when there were 65.6 days' revenue in accounts receivable ($78,942/365 = $216.3; $14,194/$216.3 = 65.6 days).

Operating Results Indicator (Earnings Margin)

The statement of operations (Table 14-3) provides the data for calculating the earnings margin. Sample Hospital's earnings margin in 2005 was 5.1 percent, calculated as follows:

$$\frac{\text{Excess of Revenues over Expenses}}{\text{Total Revenues, Gains, and Other Support}} = \frac{\$5,052}{\$99,207} = 5.1\%$$

This percentage is well below the earnings margin of 9.3 percent ($8,839/ $95,104) achieved in the year 2004. This decline is sufficiently large to require analysis of the revenue and expense components. Notice, for example, that other revenue declined from $5,212 to $2,601. What is the makeup of other revenue and why did it decline? Using the percentage change calculation discussed earlier in this chapter, notice that operating expenses increased by 9.8 percent (from $80,585 to $88,521), whereas net patient service revenue increased by only 7.1 percent (from $78,942 + $10,950 to $85,156 + $11,150). Why did the revenue increase fail to keep pace with the increase in expenses?

In addition to analyzing the causes of the year-to-year change in operating margin, the analyst needs to understand the implications of the items appearing below the caption "Excess of revenues, gains, and other support over expenses." It is possible that, for purposes of assessing the quality of the reported operating margin, some below-the-line items ought to be considered as revenues or expenses. For example, if a "transfer to parent" is in the nature of a continuing charge for services, it might be appropriate to consider it as a recurring expense.

Debt Burden and Other Financial Flexibility Indicators

Long-Term Debt-to-Equity Ratio

Sample's long-term debt-to-equity ratio at December 31, 2005, was 30.2 percent, calculated from data in Table 14-2 as follows:

$$\frac{\text{Long-Term Debt, Net of Current Portion}}{\text{Total Net Assets}} = \frac{\$23,144}{\$76,549} = 30.2\%$$

The 30.2 percent long-term debt-to-equity ratio is lower and therefore better than the ratio at December 31, 2004, when it was 33.3 percent ($24,014/$72,202).

Debt Service Coverage

Calculating debt service coverage requires reference to the statement of operations (Table 14-3) and the cash flow statement. The denominator of this ratio shows the amount of what was covered—debt principal and interest. Although the principal payment can usually be obtained from the cash flow statement, the amount shown in this cash flow statement is distorted by a debt refinancing. Therefore, for illustrative purposes, we will use the current portion of the long-term debt reported in the year 2004 balance sheet ($1,750), because that amount is what would have been paid had it not been for the refinancing. The interest shown in the statement of operations is $1,752.

The numerator shows the extent of the coverage—the hospital's earnings. The coverage represents the total of (1) the excess of revenues over expenses ($5,052); plus (2) depreciation ($4,782), which is available to pay debt service because it does not consume cash; plus (3) interest ($1,752), which is part of the amount covered and needs to be added back because it was previously included as an expense.

For purposes of this calculation, items below the amount reported as Excess of revenues over expenses should be considered. For example, additional information should be obtained regarding the amount shown as transfers to parent because that amount may indeed reduce the amount available to cover the debt service.

Sample's debt service coverage in the year 2005 was 3.31, calculated as follows:

$$\frac{\text{Excess of Revenues over Expenses} + \text{Depreciation} + \text{Interest Expense}}{\text{Principal Payment} + \text{Interest Expense}}$$

$$= \frac{\$5,052 + \$4,782 + \$1,752}{\$1,750 + \$1,752} = \frac{\$11,586}{\$3,502} = 3.31$$

Sample Hospital's interest coverage (times interest earned) for 2005 was 3.88, calculated as follows:

$$\frac{\text{Excess of Revenues over Expenses } (\$5,052) + \text{Interest Expense } (\$1,752)}{\text{Interest Expense } (\$1,752)} = 3.88$$

Comparison with Reference Group

Comparison of ratios with the previous year or longer demonstrates whether the entity's financial position and results of operations are improving or worsening. To get a broader perspective on these matters, however, it is also useful to see how the entity compares with its peers, a reference group of similar-sized entities in the same industry. For that purpose, Sample Hospital's ratios can be compared with the median ratios developed by The Center for Healthcare Industry Performance Studies (CHIPS). Table 14-4 compares Sample's 2005 ratios with CHIPS' 2000 medians for hospitals having revenues between $60 million and $100 million, which form Sample's peer group.[12] (For

---

[12] Source of CHIPS data: William O. Cleverley, *2000 Almanac of Hospital Financial & Operating Indicators*, The Center for Healthcare Industry Performance Studies; obtained directly from Dr. Cleverley.

Table 14-4
Comparison of Sample Hospital Financial Ratios with CHIPS'
Medians for Similar-Sized Hospitals

RATIO	SAMPLE	2000 MEDIAN
Current ratio	3.45	2.22
Days in patient accounts receivable	64.7	71.5
Days' cash on hand, all sources	85.3	45.9
Total margin (%)	5.1	2.9
Long-term debt to capitalization (%)	30.2	25.7
Times interest earned	3.88	2.86

this illustration, assume the ratios are for similar years. Also, we used the CHIPS captions in Table 14-4, which differ slightly from those used in the text.)

Comparison of Sample Hospital's financial indicators with those of the reference group shows that most of Sample's indicators are better than the reference group indicators. Some inferences and conclusions that may be drawn from an analysis of the indicators are as follows.

Liquidity Indicators, Efficiency Indicator
Sample's current ratio is significantly better than the industry median. Its number of days' cash on hand and its number of days' revenue in receivables are also better. Sample could improve its liquidity even more if it were to continue to improve the efficiency of its collection of patient receivables. Considering all three ratios and the improvements from the previous year, Sample should have no difficulty meeting its short-term obligations.

Operating Results Indicator
Sample's earning margin is down sharply from the previous year, but is nevertheless better than that of the reference group. Inquiry into the causes of the decline in Sample's earnings margin, as suggested in the earlier discussion of the year-to-year comparison, is clearly warranted. The reference group's earning margin is also down in recent years.

Debt Burden and Financial Flexibility Indicators
Sample's long-term debt-to-equity ratio is slightly worse than the reference group median, but the interest coverage ratio is better, primarily because of Sample's better earnings margin. Sample designated some resources for plant purposes, as its balance sheet shows. Sample also appears to have the financial capacity to support more debt for plant, if necessary. How much more debt it can issue depends partly on its future earnings margin and the amount of debt service required to pay off new debt.

ILLUSTRATION OF ANALYSIS OF GOVERNMENTAL FINANCIAL STATEMENTS

The following illustration of the calculations made in analyzing governmental financial statements is based on the financial statements prepared by the Village of Grafton, Wisconsin, for the year 2000. The ratios calculated in this illustration are developed primarily from the fund financial statements shown in Chapter 9, but we also use data from other parts of the CAFR and from the government-wide statements presented in Chapter 10. (Governments are still in the process of implementing GASB *Statement No. 34*. Therefore, as a practical matter, time-series data based on government-wide statements is not yet available and experience with using government-wide statements is still lacking.)

The ratios shown in the first part of this chapter have been adapted as necessary to the governmental environment and to the data provided in Grafton's financial statements. For ease in tracing the numbers, several statements from Chapter 9 are repeated here as Tables 14-5 and 14-6. Trace the numbers used in calculating the ratios to the financial statements and consider the nature of the items included in the detail of the numbers.

The Village of Grafton sold long-term bonds during the year 2001 to finance various capital projects and obtained a credit rating from Moody's in connection with that sale. To show how financial statement analysis is combined with economic, demographic, and other factors to assess an entity's financial condition, we added an excerpt from the credit report issued by Moody's (see the Financial Analysis in Practice feature at the end of this section).

Ratios can be developed for individual funds (particularly the General Fund), for the total of the General and Debt Service Funds, and for the total of the General, Debt Service, and Special Revenue Funds (often called the *governmental operating Funds* because they finance the basic day-to-day governmental operations). For financial analysis purposes, capital asset needs and Enterprise Funds are generally examined separately.

Interfund transfers need to be scrutinized carefully when developing ratios. When developing ratios based only on General Fund data, many transfers out (such as transfers to Debt Service Funds and to Library Special Revenue Funds) should be treated as if they were expenditures, because the funds receiving the transfers have no other significant source of income and cannot function without the transfers. Bond proceeds deposited in the General Fund need to be viewed as a potential indicator of fiscal stress.

Developing ratios based on the aggregated governmental operating funds provides a broader perspective than that obtained by using only the General Fund and Debt Service Funds. It also overcomes potential distortions caused by making transfers in amounts greater than actually needed by a particular fund. Transfers among the aggregated funds cancel each other when ratios based on aggregated operating funds are developed. However, to simplify this presentation, we have not used the governmental operating fund aggregation.

Table 14-5
Governmental Funds Balance Sheet

VILLAGE OF GRAFTON
BALANCE SHEET
GOVERNMENTAL FUNDS
DECEMBER 31, 2000

	GENERAL	DEBT SERVICE	CAPITAL IMPROVEMENTS	OTHER GOVERNMENTAL FUNDS	TOTAL GOVERNMENTAL FUNDS
Assets					
Cash and investments	$2,988,047	$1,033,140	$2,286,089	$2,737,317	$ 9,044,593
Receivables					
Taxes	1,489,878	524,267	99,254	215,063	2,328,462
Delinquent personal property taxes	1,030	—	—	—	1,030
Accounts	39,966	—	58,933	—	98,899
Special assessments	—	—	246,072	—	246,072
Delinquent special assessments	—	—	3,722	—	3,722
Interest	1,194	—	—	2,072	3,266
Loans	—	—	—	622,151	622,151
Due from other funds	82,089	4,760	—	—	86,849
Advances to other funds	—	—	451,812	—	451,812
Prepaid items	28,812	—	—	2,677	31,489
Total Assets	$4,631,016	$1,562,167	$3,145,882	$3,579,280	$12,918,345
Liabilities and Fund Balances					
Liabilities					
Accounts payable	$ 102,538	$ —	$ 19,174	$ 44,805	$ 166,517
Accrued liabilities	66,412	—	—	4,838	71,250
Deposits	13,874	—	—	138,867	152,741
Due to other funds	—	—	66,589	47,773	114,362
Due to plan participants	8,432	—	—	—	8,432
Advances from other funds	—	—	—	451,812	451,812
Deferred revenues—tax roll	3,168,430	1,115,000	211,000	457,179	4,951,609
Deferred special assessments	—	—	249,794	—	249,794
Total Liabilities	3,359,686	1,115,000	546,557	1,145,274	6,166,517
Fund Balances					
Reserved	29,842	447,167	617,080	669,291	1,763,380
Unreserved, reported in:					
General fund	1,241,488	—	—	—	1,241,488
Special revenue funds	—	—	—	1,573,797	1,573,797
Capital project funds	—	—	1,982,245	190,918	2,173,163
Total Fund Balances	1,271,330	447,167	2,599,325	2,434,006	6,751,828
TOTAL LIABILITIES AND FUND BALANCES	$4,631,016	$1,562,167	$3,145,882	$3,579,280	

Amounts reported for governmental activities in the statement of net assets are different because:

Capital assets used in governmental funds are not financial resources and therefore are not reported in the funds.	11,017,280
Other long-term assets are not available to pay for current-period expenditures and therefore are deferred in the funds.	279,380
Some liabilities, including long-term debt, are not due and payable in the current period and therefore are not reported in the funds.	(12,742,026)
NET ASSETS OF GOVERNMENTAL FUNDS	$ 5,306,462

See accompanying notes to financial statements.
Source: Comprehensive Annual Financial Report, Year 2000, Village of Grafton, Wisconsin.

Table 14-6

Governmental Funds Statement of Revenues, Expenditures, and Changes in Fund Balances

	GENERAL	DEBT SERVICE	CAPITAL IMPROVEMENTS	OTHER GOVERNMENTAL FUNDS	TOTAL GOVERNMENTAL FUNDS
Revenues					
Taxes	$2,914,658	$1,024,584	$ 100,000	$ 380,636	$4,419,878
Intergovernmental	1,438,519	78,193	13,449	335,592	1,865,753
Licenses and permits	364,728	—	—	—	364,728
Fines, forfeitures, and penalties	108,557	—	—	—	108,557
Public charges for services	219,684	—	7,200	13,043	239,927
Intergovernmental charges for services	39,888	—	—	90,077	129,965
Special assessments	—	—	435,409	163,689	599,098
Investment income	203,445	110,820	95,478	148,263	558,006
Miscellaneous	30,867	—	203,905	78,223	312,995
Total Revenues	5,320,346	1,213,597	855,441	1,209,523	8,598,907
Expenditures					
Current					
General government	577,022	—	2,618	2,308	581,948
Public safety	2,629,858	—	3,038	—	2,632,896
Public works	1,470,894	—	94,215	8,545	1,573,654
Community enrichment services	535,776	—	34,360	391,250	961,386
Conservation and development	66,064	—	9,380	274,980	350,424
Capital outlay	—	—	1,114,167	826,103	1,940,270
Debt service					
Principal retirement	—	1,001,581	—	—	1,001,581
Interest and fiscal charges	—	578,274	—	—	578,274
Debt issuance costs	—	—	18,314	11,272	29,586
Total Expenditures	5,279,614	1,579,855	1,276,092	1,514,458	9,650,019
Excess (deficiency) of revenues over expenditures	40,732	(366,258)	(420,651)	(304,935)	(1,051,112)
Other Financing Sources (Uses)					
Proceeds of long-term debt	—	—	1,690,000	1,040,000	2,730,000
Transfers in	181,079	524,259	234,009	430,779	1,370,126
Transfers out	(285,843)	—	(461,001)	(444,941)	(1,191,785)
Total Other Financing Sources (Uses)	(104,764)	524,259	1,463,008	1,025,838	2,908,341
Excess (deficiency) of revenues and other sources over expenditures and other uses	(64,032)	158,001	1,042,357	720,903	1,857,229
Fund Balances—Beginning of Year	1,335,362	289,166	1,556,968	1,713,103	4,894,599
Fund Balances—End of Year	$1,271,330	$ 447,167	$2,599,325	$2,434,006	$6,751,828

See accompanying notes to financial statements.

Source: Comprehensive Annual Financial Report, Year 2000, Village of Grafton, Wisconsin.

Using fund financial statements in combination with government-wide statements improves the overall analysis.

Liquidity Indicator (Quick Ratio)

The quick ratio provides a good, conservative measure of liquidity for general-purpose governments. Grafton's quick ratio can be computed from the general and debt service columns shown in the governmental funds balance sheet (Table 14-5).

Calculating the quick ratio is normally a simple process. The calculation of Grafton's quick ratio is somewhat complicated, however, because of its property tax billing policy, which results in billing at year-end for the following year's taxes, collecting a significant portion of them in December, and reporting deferred revenues in the balance sheet. These deferred revenues are not liabilities resulting from transactions related to the year just completed (year 2000), so the ratio would be distorted by considering them as liabilities. Therefore, both the deferred revenues and an equal amount of assets produced by them should be eliminated from the calculation.

For example, notice that the deferred revenues for Grafton's General Fund are $3,168,430 and taxes receivable are $1,489,878. The difference between the two is $1,678,552. To eliminate $3,168,430 from both the assets and liabilities, cash and investments should be reduced by this difference ($1,678,552). Actually, this difference is cash collected in December to finance the following year's activities. The resulting General Fund cash and investments, for purposes of this calculation, is $1,309,495 ($2,988,047 − $1,678,552). Based on a similar calculation, the Debt Service Fund cash and investments is $442,407 (deferred revenues of $1,115,000 minus taxes receivable of $524,267 = $590,733; cash and investments of $1,033,140 minus $590,733 = $442,407).

Grafton's quick ratio is calculated as follows:

$$\frac{\text{Cash and Investments}}{\text{Current Liabilities}} = \frac{\$1{,}309{,}495 \text{ (general)} + \$442{,}407 \text{ (debt service)}}{\$191{,}256 \text{ (general)} + \$0 \text{ (debt service)}}$$

$$= \frac{\$1{,}751{,}902}{\$191{,}256} = 9.2$$

The calculation shows that Grafton has a quick ratio of 9.2. Stated another way, Grafton has sufficient cash and investments on hand in its General and Debt Service Funds to cover its current liabilities 9.2 times. Clearly, Grafton has sufficient liquid assets to cover its current liabilities.

Efficiency Indicator (Tax Collection Rate)

Grafton's tax collection efficiency can be determined from the tax receivables shown in the balance sheet (Table 14-5, Total Governmental Funds column) and the tax revenues reported in the operating statement (Table 14-6, Total Governmental Funds column). The accrual-basis government-wide statements should be used normally for this ratio. Because delinquent taxes are reported separately in the fund statements, however, Grafton's fund statements provide more data than the government-wide statements. Information about tax collections may also be obtained from the Property Tax Levies and Collections table in the CAFR statistical section.

Grafton levies both a real property tax and a personal property tax. Its governmental funds balance sheet shows a negligible amount ($1,030) of delinquent personal property taxes, and its statistical tables show that it collected virtually 100 percent of its tax levies every year for the past 10 years. The tax collection efficiency indicator can be expressed in terms of either collection experience or delinquency experience. Because Grafton reports taxes in all of its governmental-type funds, including Capital Projects Funds, this indicator should be based on an aggregation of all governmental-type funds.

Grafton's tax delinquency rate is calculated as follows.

$$\frac{\text{Delinquent Taxes}}{\text{Tax Revenues}} = \frac{\$1,030}{\$4,419,878} = \text{Virtually zero \%}$$

Budgetary Solvency and Operating Results Indicators

Operating Margin

Both the fund financial statements and the government-wide statements need to be used with care when calculating operating margins. Fund statements for governmental-type funds, which are prepared on the modified accrual basis of accounting, can be misleading because they lack certain accruals. Care must also be taken in using the governmental activities column of the government-wide statements to compute operating margins for the following reasons:

- Depreciation information may be incomplete because governments are still phasing in capital asset accounting.
- The requirement to reduce program expenses by program-related *capital* grants and contributions can overstate the margin resulting from operating activities. Although these grants increase net assets, they are not "operating" revenues.
- The inclusion of other revenues restricted to capital projects can also overstate the margin resulting from operating activities.

As applied to the Village of Grafton, it is possible to use the amount reported as the "change in net assets" in the governmental activities column of the government-wide statement of activities ($1,865,564 in Table 10-2 in Chapter 10) as the starting point for determining the operating margin. For this exercise, however, it is simpler and more revealing to calculate the operating margin for Grafton's General Fund, using the fund financial statements. The implications of certain information provided in the government-wide statements, such as the reconciling accruals, should also be considered.

When working with the fund statements, what is the year's surplus or deficit for purposes of calculating the operating margin and what are its implications? To deal with this question, the analyst needs to look at the bottom part of the statement of revenues, expenditures, and changes in fund balances, starting with Excess (deficiency) of revenues over expenditures. Notice the data in the General Fund column for Grafton in Table 14-6. It contains a $40,732 excess of revenues over expenditures, some transfers in and out, a $64,032 deficiency for the year, and a year-end fund balance of $1,271,330. An analyst might raise the following questions about these numbers:

- What is the nature of transfers in and out? Should they be treated as revenues and expenditures for the purpose of this analysis? Analysis of the note disclosures shows that the transfers were recurring. The transfer in was an annual payment in lieu of taxes and the transfer out was mostly for the annual financing of library activities. Therefore, they should be treated as revenues and expenditures when computing Grafton's General Fund operating margin. If nonrecurring transfers in were involved, the operating margin would be computed both with and without them.
- What are the implications of the $64,032 deficiency for the year? Although this figure might be a concern, it need not be troublesome if the resulting fund balance was still high enough to provide a reasonable budgetary cushion for the future. For this reason, the budgetary cushion is calculated in the next section. In rating Grafton's bonds, Moody's noted (see the excerpt from Moody's report on page 633) that Grafton intended to use a portion of its accumulated fund balance when preparing its budget for the year. (Notice the deficit shown in the original budget column in Grafton's Budgetary Comparison Schedule in Table 9-9 in Chapter 9.)
- What additional information is available from the government-wide financial statements? Review the reconciliation of the operating statements (Table 10-3 in Chapter 10). Notice that, to prepare the government-wide operating statement, the revenue accruals ($163,855) exceeded the expense accruals ($57,283). Although it is not evident how the accruals relate specifically to the General Fund, it is likely that the effect would be positive if the General Fund operating statement had been prepared on the accrual basis of accounting.

Having considered the transfers in and out as revenues and expenditures for purposes of this analysis, we can use the Excess of revenues and other sources over expenditures and other uses to compute the operating margin for Grafton's General Fund, as follows:

$$\frac{\text{Excess of Revenues and Other Sources over Expenditures and Other Uses}}{\text{Total Revenues and Transfers In}} =$$

$$\frac{(\$64,032)}{\$5,320,346 + \$181,079} = \frac{(\$64,032)}{\$5,501,425} = (1.2\%)$$

The operating margin can also be computed for the total of the General and Debt Service Funds and for the total of the governmental operating funds to obtain a broader perspective on the operating results of the governmental activities on the modified accrual basis of accounting.

Budgetary Cushion

The budgetary cushion—the availability of accumulated financial resources from previous years' activities to finance future years' activities—is an important element of a governmental entity's financial condition. The larger the cushion, the more likely it is that the entity can withstand revenue shortfalls from economic problems and emergency expenditure needs. Grafton's General Fund budgetary cushion, which is the ratio of unreserved fund balance to revenues and transfers in, can be calculated from the balance sheet (Table 14-5) and operating statement (Table 14-6) as follows:

$$\frac{\text{Unreserved Fund Balance}}{\text{Revenues and Transfers In}} = \frac{\$1,241,488}{\$5,320,346 + 181,079} = 22.6\%$$

This calculation differs slightly from the one developed by Moody's (see excerpt from Moody's report on page 633), because we considered transfers in as part of the revenue base. Some analysts use expenditures as the denominator for this ratio. In any event, a budgetary cushion of 22.6 percent is considered favorable by analysts, particularly because of the Village's stated intent to maintain it at a level of at least 15 percent.

For a broader perspective on an entity's budgetary solvency, the budgetary cushion can also be based on the aggregations previously discussed.

Debt Burden and Other Financial Flexibility Indicators

Debt Burden

State laws generally limit the amount of long-term debt that its municipalities can have outstanding at any time. Wisconsin laws limit outstanding village long-term debt to 5 percent of the equalized value (full value) of taxable real and personal property within the jurisdiction. At December 31, 2000, Grafton's equalized value of real and personal property was $682.8 million, so its debt limit (at 5 percent) was $34,141,280. Against that limit, Grafton had total outstanding long-term debt of $13,155,000. Therefore, Grafton had a *legal debt margin* (the amount of additional long-term debt that it could legally issue) of almost $21 million. Financial condition analysis helps to determine its relative financial ability to issue that much additional debt.

Grafton's statistical tables include one that measures its 10-year debt burden trend. The trend shows that Grafton's net debt per capita increased by 46 percent since 1991. Because its revenue base (measured by full value of property) almost doubled since 1991, however, the ratio of net debt to full value of property declined almost 16 percent. As previously mentioned, property values provide some measure of wealth. By that measure, despite issuing additional debt, Grafton actually reduced its debt burden over the past 10 years. Grafton calculated its debt burden at December 31, 2000, as follows:

| | Based on | |
	Population	Property Value
Outstanding general obligation debt	$13,155,000	$ 13,155,000
Funds available for debt service	$ 447,167	$ 447,167
Net outstanding debt	$12,707,833	$ 12,707,833
Measurement base (population; full value)	10,541	$682,825,600
Ratio (net debt/measurement base)	$ 1,206	1.86%

Grafton's statistical tables also provide information on its overlapping debt—the proportional share of the debt of other governments (such as school districts) that service Grafton's citizens and tax the same property base. Including that debt in the calculations leads to the determination of the overall debt burden. Moody's report (page 633), prepared during the latter part of 2001 (after the overlapping school districts had issued significant amounts of debt), shows Grafton's overall debt burden to be 3.8 percent.

Debt Service Burden

As previously mentioned, debt service is a relatively fixed expenditure, which reduces the ability of a governmental entity to finance operating activities from taxes and other resources. Debt service burden can be calculated from the information reported in the general and debt service columns of the statement of revenues, expenditures, and changes in fund balance. Grafton's debt service burden (trace the numbers to Table 14-6) is calculated as follows:

$$\frac{\text{Debt Service Expenditures}}{\text{Revenues and Transfers In}} = \frac{\$1,001,581 \text{ (principal)} + \$578,274 \text{ (interest)}}{\$5,320,346 \text{ (general)} + \$1,213,597 \text{ (debt service)}}$$
$$+ \$181,079 \text{ (general)} + \$524,259 \text{ (debt service)}$$

$$= \frac{\$1,579,855}{\$7,239,281} = 21.8\%$$

In determining Grafton's debt service burden, note that not all the debt service affects its ability to finance services provided from General Fund resources. About one-third of the debt service ($524,259) is financed by transfers from other governmental funds, mostly, Capital Projects Funds. If the debt service financed by transfers were to be removed from the calculation, the debt service burden would drop to 15.7%.

As previously mentioned, the level of debt service expenditures is affected partly by the length of time over which debt is financed. Financing capital projects over periods less than their useful lives increases annual debt service expenditures, but reduces total interest expenditures. This practice may account for part of Grafton's seemingly high debt service burden. Examine the schedule of debt service requirements to maturity in Grafton's Notes to Financial Statements (Exhibit 9-3 in Chapter 9) and calculate the portion of debt principal that Grafton is scheduled to pay off in 5 years and in 10 years. Notice that Grafton will pay off 45 percent of debt principal in 5 years and 90 percent in 10 years, much better than what analysts generally consider as acceptable.

STATE AND LOCAL GOVERNMENT FINANCIAL ANALYSIS IN PRACTICE

How Moody's Rated the Bonds Issued by Grafton, Wisconsin

The following is an excerpt from the credit report issued by Moody's in connection with the sale by Grafton, Wisconsin, of $2.1 million general obligation capital improvement bonds in November 2001. The report illustrates the more significant matters considered by Moody's in assigning a credit rating to Grafton's bonds. Notice that assessing financial condition to rate a governmental entity's credit requires consideration not only of the financial statements, but also of the economic and demographic environment and the entity's budgeting and financing policies.

MOODY'S ASSIGNS A1 RATING TO THE VILLAGE OF GRAFTON'S (WI) GO CAPITAL IMPROVEMENT BONDS

Moody's has assigned an A1[13] rating to the Village of Grafton's $2,100,000 General Obligation Capital Improvement Bonds. . . . The bonds are secured by the Village's general obligation, unlimited tax pledge. The rating reflects the Village's strong financial position, growing tax base, and average debt levels.

STRONG FINANCIAL POSITION EXPECTED TO CONTINUE

Moody's expects the Village's financial position to remain strong due to conservative budgeting, sound fiscal policies, and growing property tax revenues. The Village experienced a modest

$64,000 operating deficit due to a budgeted drawdown to offset the tax levy. The Village's fiscal 2000 General Fund balance was $1.3 million, equal to 23.9% of General Fund revenues. According to Village policy, a minimum undesignated reserve level of 15% will be maintained and such reserve was 23.3% of fiscal 2000 General Fund revenues, or $1.2 million. . . . Although debt service comprises a significant 23.0% of operating expenditures, a significant portion is supported by nonlevy sources, mitigating the impact on the general levy.

GROWING TAX BASE NORTH OF MILWAUKEE

Moody's believes the Village's $748 million tax base will continue to benefit from its location twenty miles north of Milwaukee (general obligation rated Aa2) and the ability to do annexations. . . . Tax base growth has averaged 8.6% annually over the last eight years . . . Resident wealth levels exceeded the state averages . . . Ozaukee County's [Grafton is located in Ozaukee County] unemployment rate, 2.9% as of August 2001, has consistently been below the state's.

MODERATE DEBT BURDEN WITH RAPID PRINCIPAL RETIREMENT

Moody's expects the Village's average, 3.8% overall debt burden to remain manageable, given continued moderate tax base growth and rapid principal amortization of 85.8% in ten years.

---

[13] Moody's has nine basic rating categories for long-term obligations, ranging from Aaa (highest quality) to C (lowest quality). Bonds rated A possess many favorable investment attributes and are considered upper medium grade. Factors securing principal and interest are considered adequate, but other elements may suggest susceptibility to impairment some time in the future. A1-rated bonds have the strongest credit attributes among A-rated bonds.

Source: Excerpts from report prepared by Moody's Investors Service, dated October 31, 2001. Printed with the permission of Moody's.

REVIEW QUESTIONS

Q14-1   How does the organization of the statement of net assets help the reader assess an entity's financial position?

Q14-2   How does the organization of the statement of activities help the reader assess an entity's operating results?

Q14-3   How do the calculations of ratios and per capita information assist in assessing an entity's financial position and financial condition?

Q14-4   Why is it appropriate to use time-series analysis and comparative analysis in assessing an entity's operating results, financial position, and financial condition?

Q14-5   What is the purpose of preparing common size financial statements?

Q14-6   What is the purpose of calculating the current ratio and the quick ratio?

Q14-7   What is the purpose of calculating the number of days' revenues in accounts receivable?

Q14-8   How is the budgetary cushion calculated and why should a governmental entity maintain such a cushion?

Q14-9   What can a potential donor to a not-for-profit organization learn by calculating the organization's program services ratio?

Q14-10 Discuss why an analyst might prefer to calculate a governmental entity's debt burden as a percentage of full value of property rather than on a per capita basis.

Q14-11 Describe the relationship, if any, between a governmental entity's debt service burden and the rate at which it pays off debt principal.

Q14-12 What is the purpose of calculating debt service coverage?

Q14-13 What is the purpose of calculating a pension's funded ratio?

Q14-14 Why is it necessary to consider the economic and demographic environment in assessing a governmental entity's financial condition?

CASE

C14-1   Ken Mead, newly elected mayor of Bronson City, promised the citizens during his campaign that he would not raise taxes during his tenure as mayor. He asks his new commissioner of finance to analyze the city's financial statements to see whether the city has "any extra money laying around" to help keep taxes down. The commissioner of finance notices the caption "unreserved fund balance" in the city's General Fund balance sheet. The commissioner shows the financial statements to the mayor and says: "See that unreserved fund balance. Looks like a slush fund to me. Why don't we just use it to help keep taxes down?" How would you advise the mayor about this matter?

E14-1   Good Faith Hospital needs to sell bonds to finance major renovations and purchases of modern equipment. The hospital recently experienced difficulties, however, and its operating margin for the past 3 years fell below the median operating margin for hospitals of similar size. The hospital is preparing its financial statements, and preliminary indications are that its operating margin will continue its downward slide. The CFO is concerned that the bond-rating agency will lower the hospital's bond rating, resulting in an increase in the interest rate on the new bonds.

The CFO wants to report a higher operating margin than the previous year. He tells the chief accountant: "I don't want you to do anything you shouldn't do, but we both know that higher interest rates on the new bonds will reduce our operating margin even further. Just sharpen your pencil to see if you can reduce this year's provision for uncollectible patient receivables and estimated third-party settlements."

If you were the chief accountant, how would you react to the CFO's request?

EXERCISES

E14-1   (Multiple choice)
1. When common size statements are prepared, how are all data elements treated?
   a. Converted to amounts per capita
   b. Presented on a single page
   c. Shown as percentages of 100
   d. Shown in the form of location quotients
2. Which of the following is considered an asset in computing the quick ratio?
   a. Supplies inventory
   b. Prepaid insurance
   c. Investments in long-term bonds
   d. Certificates of deposit purchased with an original maturity of 30 days
3. Which of the following belongs in the numerator when computing the budgetary cushion of a municipal government?
   a. Infrastructure assets
   b. Unreserved fund balance
   c. Proceeds of bonds issued for capital construction purposes
   d. Deferred revenues

4. In computing the program services ratio, which of these expenses would *not* be considered part of the program service expenses?
   a. Donated services of an administrative nature, such as legal fees
   b. Depreciation of equipment used by a program
   c. Expenses of a program financed from temporarily restricted funds
   d. Donated services applicable to a program
5. What does the number of days' revenue in a hospital's receivables indicator reveal?
   a. Its bad debts expense for the year
   b. The amount of its charity services
   c. Its accounts receivable collection efficiency
   d. The amount of its net patient service revenue

E14-2 (Computation of current ratio and quick ratio)
The following information is extracted from Alpha Hospital's balance sheet:

Cash and cash equivalents	$ 2,432,000
Short-term investments	5,317,000
Long-term investments	15,641,000
Patient accounts receivable, net	15,903,000
Other current assets	3,815,000
Current portion of long-term debt	2,400,000
Long-term debt, net of current portion	22,600,000
Accounts payable and accrued expenses	4,615,000

Required: 1. Compute Alpha's current ratio.
2. Compute Alpha's quick ratio (without accounts receivable).

E14-3 (Computation of a hospital's debt service coverage)
The following information is extracted from Beta Hospital's financial statements:

Total revenues, gains, and other support		$78,458,000
Operating expenses	$62,490,000	
Depreciation and amortization	3,765,000	
Interest on long-term borrowings	2,200,000	
Provision for bad debts	3,000,000	71,455,000
Operating income		7,003,000
Investment income		2,000,000
Excess of revenues over expenses		$ 9,003,000
Principal payment on debt		$ 3,000,000

Required: Compute Beta's debt service coverage and times interest earned.

E14-4 (Computation of days' revenue in patient accounts receivable)
The following information is extracted from Gamma Hospital's financial statements:

Patient accounts receivable, net	$14,710,000
Patient service revenues, gross	97,478,000
Provision for contractual adjustments	12,609,000

Required: Compute the number of days' revenue in patient accounts receivable.

E14-5 (Computation of a not-for-profit organization's program services ratio)
A voluntary health and welfare organization obtains contributions to perform various social services. The following information is extracted from its statement of activities:

Expenses:
Youth services	$ 89,000
Senior citizens health services	312,000
Adult counseling services	248,000
Management and general	156,000
Fund-raising	68,000
Total expenses	$873,000

Required: Compute the organization's program services ratio.

E14-6 (Computation of a city's budgetary cushion)
The following information is extracted from the general fund column of a city's fund financial statements:

Fund balance:
Reserved for encumbrances	$ 46,376
Unreserved	647,864
Total fund balance	$ 694,240
Revenues	$22,582,000

Required: Compute the city's budgetary cushion.

E14-7 (Computation of a city's debt burden)
The following information is extracted from a city government's CAFR:
Net direct debt	$ 15,841,000
Overlapping debt	$ 12,142,000
Population	13,243
Full value of taxable real property	$484,481,000

Required: Compute the city's debt burden based on population and on property value. Make separate computations for (a) net direct debt and (b) combined net direct and overlapping debt.

E14-8 (Computation of a village's operating margin)
The following information is extracted from a village's governmental funds statement of revenues, expenditures, and changes in fund balances (amounts in thousands):

	General	Debt Service	Library
Total revenues	$8,640	$ 26	$ 15
Total expenditures	7,412	842	234
Excess (deficiency) of revenues over expenditures	1,228	(816)	(219)
Transfers in		850	225
Transfers out	(1,075)		
Net change in fund balances	$ 153	$ 34	$ 6

Required: Compute the village's operating margin (a) for the General Fund and (b) for the General, Debt Service, and Library Funds aggregated. (*Hint:* The transfers out are routine transfers to the other two funds, and should be considered as expenditures in calculating the General Fund's operating margin. Because the transfers in are from the aggregated funds, they should be ignored in calculating the denominator for the aggregated funds operating margin.)

PROBLEMS

P14-1 (Computation of financial analysis ratios for a hospital from a trial balance) Following is a condensed trial balance of the accounts of Palindrome Hospital at December 31, 2004 (amounts in thousands).

	Debits	Credits
Cash and cash equivalents	$ 4,700	
Short-term investments	5,400	
Patient accounts receivable	14,700	
Allowance for uncollectible receivables		$ 2,600
Drugs and supplies inventories	2,100	
Buildings and equipment	72,000	
Accumulated depreciation, buildings and equipment		22,000
Accounts payable and accrued expenses		5,400
Estimated third-party payer settlements		2,300
Long-term debt		37,000
Unrestricted net assets, beginning of year		27,600
Patient service revenues (gross)		66,300
Provision for contractual adjustments	7,100	
Provision for charity care	1,500	
Operating expenses	45,300	
Depreciation expense	4,200	
Interest expense	2,400	
Provision for bad debts	2,300	
Other expenses	1,700	
Investment income		200
Totals	$163,400	$163,400

Additional information (amounts in thousands): (a) the amount of long-term debt principal paid during the year ended December 31, 2004, was $1,800; and (b) the current portion of the long-term debt payable at December 31, 2004, is $2,000.

Required: 1. In preparation for calculating ratios, compute the net patient accounts receivable, the net patient service revenues, the excess of revenues over expenses, and the unrestricted net assets at end-of-year.

2. Compute the following liquidity indicators: current ratio, quick ratio (without patient accounts receivable), and number of days' cash on hand.
3. Compute the efficiency indicator, or number of days' revenue in receivables.
4. Compute the operating results indicator, or earnings margin.
5. Compute the debt burden and other financial flexibility indicators: long-term debt-to-equity ratio, debt service coverage, and times interest earned.

P14-2 (Assessment of hospital financial analysis ratios)
Palindrome Hospital wants to issue $25 million of additional long-term debt in order to expand its operations and modernize its equipment. It expects to pay off the new debt in equal annual installments of principal over 25 years, together with interest of 6 percent on the outstanding debt. The hospital's CFO believes the expanded capacity will increase gross patient service revenues by about $15 million annually and its earnings margin will remain at about the same rate as it was for the year 2004.

Required: 1. Prepare a schedule comparing the ratios calculated in P14-1 with the CHIPS' medians shown on page 624.
2. Write a brief assessment of the hospital's financial position based on the comparison in part (1), without considering the expansion plan.
3. Based on the assessment in part (2), and the data provided on the hospital's expansion plan, comment on the hospital's capacity to issue the additional debt.

P14-3 (Computation of financial analysis ratios for a county government)
Following are extracts from the financial statements of Elisa County for the year ended December 31, 2004. The funds shown are the governmental operating funds; Capital Projects Funds are omitted. All amounts are in thousands of dollars.

Balance Sheet			
	General	Special Revenue	Debt Service
Assets:			
Cash and cash equivalents	$ 6,700	$2,100	$100
Property taxes receivable (net)	19,500		
Other receivables	500	3,100	
Due from state government	3,500		
Total assets	$30,200	$5,200	$100
Liabilities:			
Accounts payable	$16,700	$1,100	
Accrued liabilities	1,800	300	
Matured bonds payable			$100
Total liabilities	18,500	1,400	100

(continued)

Fund balances:

	General	Special Revenue	Debt Service
Reserved for encumbrances	800	200	
Unreserved	10,900	3,600	
Total fund balances	11,700	3,800	
Total liabilities and fund balances	$30,200	$5,200	$100

Statement of Revenues, Expenditures, and Changes in Fund Balances

	General	Special Revenue	Debt Service
Revenues:			
Real property taxes	$ 46,000		
Sales taxes	45,000		
State and federal aid	36,500	$ 5,400	
Other revenues	27,200	9,400	$ 1,200
Total revenues	154,700	14,800	1,200
Expenditures:			
General government	15,100		
Public safety	26,600		
Public health	17,100		
Economic assistance	68,300		
Other expenditures	15,200	16,800	
Debt service:			
Principal			6,200
Interest	500		4,100
Total expenditures	142,800	16,800	10,300
Excess of revenues over expenditures	11,900	(2,000)	(9,100)
Other financing sources (uses):			
Transfers in		1,900	9,100
Transfers out	(11,000)		
Net change in fund balances	900	(100)	0
Fund balances—beginning	10,800	3,900	0
Fund balances—ending	$ 11,700	$ 3,800	$ 0

Note: The General Fund transfers out are routine transfers to finance county libraries (accounted for in a Special Revenue Fund) and debt service.

Required: Based on the data given, compute the following ratios for Elisa County:

1. Quick ratio (aggregated governmental operating funds)
2. Property tax receivable rate (*Note:* All taxes receivable are delinquent.)
3. Operating margin (separately, for General Fund and aggregated operating funds)
4. Budgetary cushion (separately, for General Fund and aggregated operating funds) (*Note:* Ignore transfers in when computing denominator.)
5. Debt service burden (aggregated General and Debt Service Funds)

P14-4 (Assessment of governmental financial analysis ratios)

The state in which Elisa County in P14-3 is located publishes certain financial analysis ratios for all counties within the state. To provide a reference group for assessing Elisa County's financial analysis ratios, the median county ratios are listed here:

Quick ratio	110%
Property tax receivable rate	47%
Operating margin	
General Fund	2.4%
Aggregated Funds	2.3%
Budgetary cushion	
General Fund	12.0%
Aggregated Funds	12.1%
Debt service burden	4.9%

Required: Based on the reference group ratios, prepare a brief report assessing the implications of the financial analysis ratios computed for Elisa County in P14-3.

P14-5 (Analyzing trends based on common size financial statements)

Table 9-10 in Chapter 9 shows Grafton's expenditures by function from 1991 through 2000. Review the data to determine whether any trends (upward and downward) or unusual occurrences in previous operating expenditures might be noted for discussion in assessing future expenditures. To aid your analysis, prepare common size statements, by converting the expenditure amounts to percentages of the total. To avoid distortions in making the analysis, (a) remove capital outlays from the total because they are not operating expenditures and tend to be volatile, and (b) reduce debt service expenditures by bond amounts shown as defeased (in 1996) and called (in 1999).

Chapter 15

Fundamentals of Accounting

After completing this chapter, you should be able to:

➤ *Define and distinguish among assets, liabilities, and equity.*

➤ *Explain the logic of the accounting equation.*

➤ *Analyze transactions to distinguish between those that affect only assets and liabilities and those that affect equity.*

➤ *Define and illustrate the accrual basis of accounting.*

➤ *State the rules of debit and credit for assets, liabilities, equity, revenues, and expenses.*

➤ *Record transactions in a general journal.*

➤ *Post transactions from a general journal to a general ledger.*

➤ *Prepare a trial balance from the general ledger.*

➤ *Prepare adjusting journal entries.*

➤ *Prepare an income statement, a statement of changes in owner's equity, and a balance sheet.*

➤ *Prepare closing journal entries.*

THE ACCOUNTING EQUATION: TRANSACTION ANALYSIS

All organizations, whether for-profit (business-type) or not-for-profit (nonbusiness-type), must keep records of their resources, their use of the resources, and claims against the resources. These resources, commonly called *assets*, represent items of value that are either owned or controlled by the entity as a result of past transactions and events. Assets might be financial in nature (like cash and accounts receivable) or nonfinancial (like buildings and equipment). An entity's operations are centered on using its resources for the purpose for which the entity was established.

A business-type entity obtains assets primarily from three sources: (1) investing by its owners, (2) incurring economic obligations (commonly called *liabilities*), and (3) earning profits from its operations. These activities can be illustrated as follows. First, an owner might provide additional assets (such as cash) by investing to expand operations. Second, an asset (cash) is created when a business incurs a liability (called a note payable) by borrowing from a bank. Third, an asset (merchandise inventory) is created when a business incurs a liability (an account payable) by buying merchandise on credit from a supplier. Fourth, a net increase in assets (which might take the form of cash or accounts receivable) occurs when merchandise inventory is sold or services are provided to a customer at a profit—a price that is greater than the cost of providing the goods or services.

The Accounting Equation

The difference between assets and liabilities is called *equity* or *capital*. Equity comes from investments in the business by its owners and from profits earned by the business. The relationship among these three elements can be expressed in the form of the following equation, known as the *accounting equation:*

$$\text{Assets} = \text{Liabilities} + \text{Equity}$$

This equation states that the assets (resources) of an entity are equal to the sources of those assets: liabilities and equity.

At any point in time, for example, at the beginning or at the end of the year, the assets, liabilities, and equity of a business can be presented in a financial statement. This statement is based on the accounting equation and is commonly called a *balance sheet*. The dollar value of the assets will always equal the dollar value of the liabilities plus the dollar value of the equity. The balance sheet is a status statement—a statement of financial position—at a particular point in time. In fact, most not-for-profit entities now refer to this statement as the statement of financial position.

Effect of Transactions and Events on the Accounting Equation

In the course of the year, an entity will engage in numerous transactions and be affected by many events that change one or more of the elements of the accounting equation: assets, liabilities, or equity. Changes that affect the equity of the entity are expressed in another financial statement, generally called an *income statement* or an operating statement. The income statement thus serves as a link between the balance sheet at one point in time (the beginning of the accounting period) and the balance sheet at a later point in time (the end of the period).

Some transactions or events affect only assets, only liabilities, or a combination of assets and liabilities. In those situations, no increase or decrease in the entity's equity occurs. Here are two examples of these types of situations: (1) If an entity buys equipment on credit, an asset (equipment) is increased and a liability (accounts payable) is increased; and (2) if an entity buys merchandise inventory for cash, an asset (merchandise inventory) is increased and another asset (cash) is decreased. Notice that, in both of these transactions, the accounting equation Assets = Liabilities + Equity is always in balance. In the first situation, an asset increase is offset by a liability increase; in the second, an asset increase is offset by an asset decrease. Equity is not affected in either case.

Other transactions may affect an asset or a liability and, at the same time, increase or decrease the entity's equity. For example, if an entity bills a customer for a service, an asset (accounts receivable) is increased and equity is increased because there is an increase in the entity's net assets. As a second example, if an entity pays an employee to provide the service just referred to, an asset (cash) is decreased and equity is decreased because of the decrease in the entity's net assets. If the price charged by the entity for the service is greater than the salary and other costs incurred by the entity, a net increase in the entity's equity will result.

Changes in Equity

Increases in assets generated through profit-oriented activities of a business (for example, by providing services to a customer) increase the owner's equity. These increases in equity are called *revenues*. On the other hand, assets used in or liabilities incurred through the profit-oriented activities of a business (for example, by paying an employee to provide the services) reduce the owner's equity. These decreases in equity are called *expenses*. When an owner adds capital to (or withdraws capital from) the business, however, it is neither a revenue nor an expense. It is a direct change in equity.

We can look upon revenues and expenses as temporary subsets of equity and thus broaden our equation to express both the point-in-time and the operating concepts:

$$\text{Assets} = \text{Liabilities} + \text{Equity [Opening Equity} + \text{(Revenues} - \text{Expenses)}$$
$$+ \text{(Owner Additions to} - \text{Withdrawals from Equity)]}$$

Recording Business Transactions

The process of accounting involves the following: first, analyzing economic transactions and events to see how they have affected assets, liabilities, and equity; and, second, recording the effects as changes (increases or decreases) to one or more of those elements. To understand this process, consider the following transactions of a computer service started on January 2, 2004, by Kyle Thomas. Thomas intends to provide computer education to individuals who purchase personal computers.

1. On January 2, Kyle deposited $10,000 of his personal cash into a bank account, to be used exclusively by the business.
2. On January 2, Kyle also purchased 10 computers. The computers cost $30,000. He made a down payment of $3,000 in cash and financed the remainder through the French Quarter bank. The agreement with the bank requires that Kyle pay back $9,000 on each succeeding January 2 for 3 years, together with interest of 10 percent a year on the unpaid balance of the loan.
3. In order to have an office for the operation of the business, Kyle rented office space on January 2 from the Mardi Gras Realty Company for $2,000 a month. Because the rental contract required payments at the beginning of each month, he immediately wrote a check for $2,000.
4. At the end of January, Kyle sent bills to his students. The amount due him for services performed in January was $5,000.
5. During the month, Kyle paid salaries of $1,500 to an employee who helped to train his students.
6. Kyle received a utility bill for $300 for the month of January. Because the due date on the bill is February 10, the bill will not be paid until then.

Now, let us analyze each transaction and show how the accounting equation applies to it.

1. The $10,000 Investment

The entity concept (which relates to the scope of the activities covered in financial reporting) requires that the operations of an organization be kept separate from the owner's personal financial records. Therefore, we will consider only those transactions that affect the assets, liabilities, and equity of the business. The $10,000 deposit causes an increase in the asset Cash. It also causes a corresponding increase in equity. To show the increase in equity, we will use the caption K. Thomas, Capital. This transaction is reflected in the accounting equation, as shown in Table 15-1.

Table 15-1

Effect of Owner Investment

		ASSETS	=	LIABILITIES	+	EQUITY
		CASH				K. THOMAS, CAPITAL
Owner invests cash in the business	+	$10,000	=		+	$10,000
		$10,000	=	-0-	+	$10,000

Two important observations about the transaction in Table 15-1 should be made:

1. The dollar amount of the items included in the transaction must balance in terms of the equation; that is, the net change in the assets must equal the net change in the liabilities plus (minus) the net change in equity.
2. The equation itself must balance after the transaction has been recorded.

2. The $30,000 Purchase of Computers

Recording this transaction causes the accounting equation to expand, as shown in Table 15-2.

Several observations should be made regarding this purchase:

1. The assets of the business increased by $27,000: Cash decreased by $3,000 and computers increased by $30,000.
2. The business now owes the bank $27,000. Thus a liability exists that must be reflected in the system.
3. The computers are recorded at their full cost, $30,000, even though Kyle borrowed $27,000 to purchase them.

In summary, the business now has assets totaling $37,000—that is, $27,000 contributed by creditors (the bank) and $10,000 contributed by the owner. Notice that the acquisition of the computers did not affect the owner's equity, because he did not contribute any additional assets to the business as a result of this transaction.

A simple method of analyzing a transaction in terms of its effect on the accounting equation is to ask four questions:

1. Did any assets increase or decrease?
2. Did any liability or liabilities increase or decrease?
3. Did the equity increase or decrease?
4. Does the transaction have a balanced effect on the equation?

Table 15-2
Effect of Computer Purchase

		ASSETS		=	LIABILITIES	+	EQUITY
		CASH	COMPUTERS		NOTES PAYABLE TO BANK		K. THOMAS, CAPITAL
Previous balances		$10,000		=			$10,000
The firm purchased computers	−	3,000	+ $30,000	=	+ $27,000		
		$ 7,000	+ $30,000	=	$27,000	+	$10,000

For example, consider the acquisition of the computers:

1. The asset Cash decreased by $3,000 and the asset Computers increased by $30,000.
2. The liability Notes payable to bank increased by $27,000.
3. No change in equity occurred.
4. The transaction increased assets by $27,000 and had a similar effect on total liabilities and equity. Therefore, the accounting equation is still in balance.

Although this type of analysis may seem cumbersome, it will be a great help when more complex transactions are encountered.

3. The $2,000 Office Rental

Applying the four-step analysis, the transaction has the following effects on the accounting equation:

1. The asset Cash decreased by $2,000. Because the business now has "control" over the use of office space for the month of January, another asset has been acquired. This type of asset is usually called Prepaid rent, and it increased by $2,000. No other assets changed as a result of this transaction.
2. Because the business does not owe any more or any less as a result of this transaction, no liabilities changed.
3. Because the net effect of this transaction resulted in a decrease in one asset and an increase in another, the owner's share of the total assets did not change. Therefore, no change in equity took place.
4. The transaction had a balanced effect on the accounting equation. The decrease in one asset was offset by an increase in another asset. Liabilities and equity were not affected by this transaction.

The result of this analysis on the accounting equation is shown in Table 15-3. Notice that the total of the assets ($37,000) is equal to the total of the liabilities plus equity ($37,000).

Table 15-3
Effect of Office Rental

			ASSETS				=	LIABILITIES	+	EQUITY
		CASH		COMPUTERS		PREPAID RENT		NOTES PAYABLE TO BANK		K. THOMAS, CAPITAL
Previous balances		$7,000	+	$30,000			=	$27,000	+	$10,000
The firm paid the rent for the month	−	2,000			+	$2,000	=			
		$5,000	+	$30,000	+	$2,000	=	$27,000	+	$10,000

4. The $5,000 Billings

By applying the four-step analysis, we can determine the following:

1. Sending out the bills is a formal recognition that Kyle's customers owe $5,000 for services he rendered. As a result, he has a claim against each of them. These claims are assets because they give him the right to collect the amounts due. The title usually given to these assets is *Accounts receivable.* No other assets changed as a result of this transaction.
2. Because the business does not owe any more or any less as a result of this transaction, no liabilities changed.
3. Because the $5,000 net increase in assets was generated by Kyle's profit-oriented activities—services provided to customers—his equity increases by $5,000. (We can also "back into" this conclusion by noting that steps 1 and 2 produce an increase in assets without any change in liabilities. Because each transaction must have a balancing effect on the equation, an increase in equity must occur.)
4. The transaction has a balanced effect on the accounting equation: assets increased by $5,000, and liabilities + equity increased by $5,000.

The results of this analysis on the accounting equation are shown in Table 15-4. Notice that the total of the assets ($42,000) is equal to the total of the liabilities plus equity ($42,000).

5. The $1,500 Salary Payment

Applying the four-step analysis, we find the following:

1. The asset Cash decreases by $1,500 as a result of the payment to the employee.
2. Technically, Kyle has a liability to his employee from the moment the employee starts to work. However, it is impractical to record that liability continuously. If he has not paid the employee, an increase in a liability rather than a decrease in an asset has occurred. But, because he has made the payment, there is no liability to record.

Table 15-4
Effect of Billing Customers

	ASSETS				=	LIABILITIES	+	EQUITY
	CASH	COMPUTERS	PREPAID RENT	ACCOUNTS RECEIVABLE		NOTES PAYABLE TO BANK		K. THOMAS, CAPITAL
Previous balances	$5,000 +	$30,000 +	$2,000		=	$27,000	+	$10,000
The firm billed customers				+ $5,000	=		+	5,000
	$5,000 +	$30,000 +	$2,000 +	$5,000	=	$27,000	+	$15,000

3. The salary is an expense of doing business and therefore a decrease in equity. (We can also "back into" this conclusion by noting that, because each transaction must have a balancing effect on the equation, and because steps 1 and 2 showed only a decrease in an asset, there must be a decrease in equity.)
4. The transaction has a balanced effect on the equation: assets decrease by $1,500 and liabilities + equity decrease by the same amount.

The result of this analysis is shown in Table 15-5. Notice that the total of the assets ($40,500) equals the total liabilities + equity ($40,500).

6. The $300 Utility Bill

The four-step analysis results in the following effects on the accounting equation:

1. Because the business does not have title to or control over any items of value that it did not have before this transaction, no changes in assets occur.
2. The business now owes money to an additional creditor. The receipt of the bill is a formal recognition of this fact. It necessitates recording a liability of $300. The title normally given to this account is *Accounts payable*.
3. The result of this analysis (steps 1 and 2) reflects an increase in liabilities with no corresponding increase in assets. Because each transaction must contribute to a balanced effect on the equation, a decrease in equity of $300 must occur.
4. The transaction had a balanced effect on the accounting equation: Assets did not change, and the net effect on liabilities + equity was zero (+ $300 − $300).

The result of this analysis on the accounting equation is shown in Table 15-6. Notice that the total of the assets ($40,500) is equal to the total of the liabilities plus equity ($40,500).

Although numerous other types of transactions could be illustrated for the operations of a business, those selected here should be sufficient to enable you to understand the process used for determining the effect of each transaction on the accounting equation.

Table 15-5
Effect of Salary Payment

	CASH		COMPUTERS		PREPAID RENT		ACCOUNTS RECEIVABLE	=	NOTES PAYABLE TO BANK	+	K. THOMAS, CAPITAL
					ASSETS			=	LIABILITIES	+	EQUITY
Previous balances	$5,000	+	$30,000	+	$2,000	+	$5,000	=	$27,000	+	$15,000
The firm paid salaries	−1,500							=		−	1,500
	$3,500	+	$30,000	+	$2,000	+	$5,000	=	$27,000	+	$13,500

Table 15-6
Effect of Receiving Utility Bill

	ASSETS				=	LIABILITIES		+	EQUITY
	CASH	COMPUTERS	PREPAID RENT	ACCOUNTS RECEIVABLE		NOTES PAYABLE TO BANK	ACCOUNTS PAYABLE		K. THOMAS, CAPITAL
Previous balances	$3,500 +	$30,000 +	$2,000 +	$5,000	=	$27,000		+	$13,500
The firm received a bill for utilities					=		+ $300	–	300
	$3,500 +	$30,000 +	$2,000 +	$5,000	=	$27,000 +	$300	+	$13,200

Review Exercise

The following exercise should be completed by using the approach previously described. After completing a work sheet, compare it with the solution that follows so that you can determine how well you understand the concepts involved.

In this exercise, assume that Paige Keith is an independent tour guide who works for several large tour companies. Her income is determined by the number of individuals on each tour she hosts. To start the business, Paige incurred the following transactions:

2004

June 1   Paige placed $5,000 cash into a bank account to be used in the operations of her business, Kaki Tours.

2   Paige signed a contract with Tel-Ans, a telephone-answering service. The service cost $50 per month, payable at the beginning of each month. Paige paid Tel-Ans $50.

4   Paige paid Print Faster $55 for stationery and the various forms she needed.

5   Paige purchased office equipment for $250. She paid $25 down and will pay the remainder in 30 days.

7   Paige purchased additional office supplies costing $125. She paid cash for these supplies.

10   Paige billed several tour companies for tours she conducted during the month. The total billing was $300.

15   Paige received $250 from companies she billed earlier that month.

18   Paige hired an assistant and agreed to pay him 25 percent of her revenue from the tours that he helped to organize.

20   Paige deposited $130 in her bank account. This amount was collected from various walking tours she conducted.

Table 15-7
Solution to Paige Keith's Transactions

	CASH	ACCOUNTS RECEIVABLE	PREPAID SERVICES	OFFICE SUPPLIES	OFFICE EQUIPMENT	=	ACCOUNTS PAYABLE	+	P. KEITH, CAPITAL
			ASSETS				LIABILITIES		EQUITY
2004									
June 1	+$5,000								+$5,000
2	−$ 50		+$50						
4	−$ 55			+$ 55					
5	−$ 25				+$250		+$225		
7	−$ 125			+$125					
10		+$300							+$ 300
15	+$ 250	−$250							
18	No transaction—no assets, liabilities, or equity have changed. Nothing is owed to the assistant until he completes some work.								
20	+$ 130								+$ 130
25	−$ 75								−$ 75
30		+$400							+$ 400
	$5,050	$450	$50	$180	$250		$225		$5,755

Total Assets[a] = $5,980

Total Liabilities + Equity[a] = $5,980

[a]Cumulative totals after each transaction were omitted in order to conserve space.

25   Paige shared an office with someone and she paid $75 for her share of the June rent (including utilities).

30   Paige billed several tour companies for a total of $400 for tours she conducted during the month.

Solution

The solution is found in Table 15-7.

THE ACCRUAL BASIS OF ACCOUNTING

Before moving on, you need to get a better understanding of the nature of assets, liabilities, expenses, and revenues, and of the purpose of accounting and financial reporting. Assume, for example, that you own a department store. You ask: "Can I find out how much profit I made last month just by seeing how much cash I had in the bank at the beginning of the month and at the end of the month?" If you think you can, then ask: "How about the unpaid bills for the merchandise I bought? What about the items I sold on credit for which customers have not yet paid? What about the new fixtures I bought that are likely to last 10 years?" Knowing your cash position is important, but it's not enough to let you know how much profit you made. It tells you nothing about your other assets and liabilities.

A major purpose of accounting is measuring performance (such as profitability) and financial position. To measure performance, an entity first needs to know what it is trying to measure, which is called its *measurement focus*. To achieve a particular measurement focus, accountants adopt what is called a *basis of accounting*. If an entity wants to measure inflows and outflows of cash, it uses the cash basis of accounting. But, as we have just seen, the cash basis of accounting will not provide a good measure of net income, because it recognizes the effect of transactions and events only when cash is received or disbursed. To measure net income, accountants use the *accrual* basis of accounting. Under the accrual basis of accounting, revenues are recorded when earned. Expenses are recorded when incurred, not necessarily when cash changes hands.

Accruals, Deferrals, and Amortizations

Accrual accounting is accomplished by certain processes, known as *accruals, deferrals,* and *amortizations.* An accrual recognizes assets, liabilities, revenues, and expenses attributable to one period but not expected to be received or paid in cash until a future period. A deferral has just the opposite effect. In a deferral, cash has been received or paid in the past, but the economic benefit lies in the future. Thus, the recognition of the revenue or expense is deferred to a future period. Amortization includes recognizing an expense by periodically writing down an asset. In the examples that follow, observe that every accrual, deferral, or amortization affects equity (either an expense or revenue) and either an asset or liability:

- If employees earn their salaries in year 1, but will be paid in year 2, a salary expense and a liability are *accrued* (added to) in year 1.
- If revenues are earned in year 1, but the cash will be received in year 2, a revenue and an asset are *accrued* (added to) in year 1.
- If cash is paid in year 1 for a 3-year insurance policy, payment for the insurance creates an asset called "prepaid insurance." Recognition of insurance expense is *deferred* into the years actually covered by the insurance, some of which might be in year 1, some in year 2, and so on.
- If cash is paid in year 1 for equipment that will last 10 years, the payment creates an asset called "equipment." The expense of using the equipment is *deferred* and recognized by means of *amortizing* the asset over its 10-year life.

The Matching Process

The discussion of accrual accounting allows us to broaden our concept of the nature of assets. As previously noted, some assets either are cash or will soon be converted to cash, like accounts receivable. But buildings and equipment, previously described as nonfinancial resources, can also be described as unexpired bundles of future services, awaiting recognition as expenses as they are used up with the passage of time.

Prepaid insurance and rent are also unexpired bundles of future services. So are inventories, which become expenses in the period they are sold. The notion of relating expenses to the same period of time that revenues are recognized is called "matching." Accrual accounting also helps broaden the notion of liabilities; that is, liabilities may result not only from borrowing and from not paying expenses, but also from receiving cash to provide services or products in the future.

Now, let us return to Kyle Thomas to see whether any of the transactions referred to previously require further consideration when applying the concepts of accrual accounting. Our analysis shows that, if Kyle requested financial statements to measure accurately his financial performance for the month of January and his financial position at the end of January, these matters must be taken into account:

1. Interest of $225 would need to be accrued because, even though he did not pay it, Kyle incurred interest expense for the month of January because of the loan from French Quarter Bank. The accrual decreases equity (Interest expense) and increases a liability (Interest payable). The calculation is $27,000 \times 10\% \times 1/12$.

2. The asset Computers (an unexpired bundle of future services) would need to be amortized to recognize an expense because 1 month of the computers' estimated useful lives has expired. Assuming the computers have estimated useful lives of 50 months, the expense for the month would be $600 ($30,000/50). This decrease in equity (an expense called *depreciation*) parallels the reduction in the asset Computers.

3. Rent expense of $2,000 would need to be recognized because the asset Prepaid rent (another unexpired bundle of future services) expired at the end of January. Recognizing rent expense decreases equity and also decreases the asset Prepaid rent.

The result of this analysis is shown in Table 15-8. Notice that the total assets ($37,900) equals the total of the liabilities ($27,525) plus equity ($10,375).

Table 15-8
Effect of Accrual Adjustments

	ASSETS				=	LIABILITIES			+	EQUITY
	CASH	COMPUTERS	PREPAID RENT	ACCOUNTS RECEIVABLE		NOTES PAYABLE TO BANK	ACCOUNTS PAYABLE	INTEREST PAYABLE		K. THOMAS, CAPITAL
Previous balances (Table 15-6)	$3,500 +	$30,000	+ $2,000 +	$5,000	=	$27,000 +	$300		+	$13,200
Accrual of interest								+ $225	−	225
Using up of computers		− 600							−	600
Expiration of prepaid rent			− 2,000						−	2,000
	$3,500 +	$29,400	− +	$5,000	=	$27,000 +	$300	+ $225	+	$10,375

RECORDING TRANSACTIONS: DEBITS AND CREDITS

Journals, Ledgers, and Accounts

In the previous sections we discussed how analysis of business transactions and events leads to the recording of increases and decreases to various components of assets, liabilities, and equity. The use of a work sheet to accomplish that procedure, however, is far too cumbersome. Consider, for example, the size of the work sheet that would be needed to record the huge number of transactions and the numerous kinds of assets, liabilities, revenues, and expenses of any large corporation.

Because of the awkwardness of the previously discussed systems of analysis and record keeping, a more efficient system has been developed. This system is based on the same concepts previously discussed: transactions and events are analyzed and recorded by increasing and decreasing components of the accounting equation. The actual recording of transactions, however, is accomplished through the use of journals, ledgers, and accounts. Transactions are analyzed and recorded in journals, from which they are then posted to a ledger that contains accounts. To explain these terms,

- *Journals* are books in which every transaction that affects the accounting equation is recorded in chronological order. Journals, often referred to as "books of original entry," are the permanent records of all the transactions of a business.
- *Posting* is the process of transferring information from the journals to the ledger.
- A *ledger* is a book with a separate page that accumulates transaction data (increases and decreases) for each account (component of assets, liabilities, or equity). For example, separate accounts are kept for cash, accounts receivable, and accounts payable. Each account is in the general form of a "T," with one side of the T representing increases to the account balance and the other representing decreases.

Double-Entry Accounting—Debits and Credits

Recall from the earlier sections of this chapter that every transaction resulted in changes to at least two components of assets, liabilities, and equity. For example, when Kyle Thomas sent bills to his students, an asset (accounts receivable) was increased and equity was increased. The practice of increasing or decreasing two or more accounts as a result of each transaction is known as double-entry accounting. We will now discuss how the T-form of the account facilitates the recording of increases and decreases.

As noted, rather than use columns on a work sheet, an *account* is used to accumulate the increases and decreases in assets, liabilities, and equity. It is much easier to accumulate changes if like items are grouped, so the increases are accumulated on one side of the account and the decreases on the other. Arbitrarily, the increases (+) in assets have been accumulated on the left and the decreases (−) on the right. As a result, it is much easier and faster to calculate the balance in an account at any point in time. This convention produces the following situation:

Assets

+	−

Because the system is based on the accounting equation, the following relationship develops:

$$\frac{\text{Assets}}{+\;|\;-} = \frac{\text{Liabilities}}{\qquad|\qquad} + \frac{\text{Equity}}{\qquad|\qquad}$$

When the account form is transferred to the right side of the equation and is used to accumulate changes in liabilities and equity, the signs must change. The increases are accumulated on the right side and the decreases on the left side. This maintains the mathematical integrity of the transaction analysis and of the system:

$$\frac{\text{Assets}}{+\;|\;-} = \frac{\text{Liabilities}}{-\;|\;+} + \frac{\text{Equity}}{-\;|\;+}$$

Debit and Credit Analysis

In accounting terminology the left side of an account is referred to as the *debit side* and the right side is referred to as the *credit side.* Note that the terms *debit* and *credit* refer only to position. Without any association with a particular account, these terms do not mean plus or minus. When a particular type of account has been considered, however, the terms do refer to plus or minus. For example, when assets are considered (see the previous illustration), increases are accumulated on the left, or debit side, and decreases are accumulated on the right, or credit side. Liabilities and equity, however, are increased or decreased in the opposite manner: Debits represent decreases, and credits represent increases. These rules are summarized in Table 15-9.

To complete the system, revenues and expenses must be analyzed in terms of their debit/credit effect. At the end of each period, it is important that management study the relative size of the individual revenues and expenses incurred in operating an organization. In the previous illustrations, revenues and expenses were recorded as direct increases or decreases in equity. To make such an analysis easier, however, we will begin to accumulate the changes in each revenue and expense in a separate account. This practice will avoid the rather cumbersome task of sorting out the revenues and expenses after they have been combined in the equity account.

Table 15-9
Debits and Credits

Type of Account	Increases	Decreases
Assets	Debits	Credits
Liabilities	Credits	Debits
Equity	Credits	Debits

The debit/credit analysis of revenues and expenses is based on the relationship of each to equity. Remember that revenues and expenses were defined as temporary subsets of the equity of a firm. Because revenues cause equity to increase, they are recorded as credits. Any reductions of revenues are recorded as debits, as shown in the following illustration:

Revenues	
Debits	Credits
−	+

Note the *direct* relationship with equity. Equity is increased with credits. Because revenues increase equity, *revenues* are increased with *credits*. Equity is decreased with debits. Because decreases in revenue are decreases in equity, revenues are decreased with debits.

Expenses follow the same logic. The analysis, however, is a bit more complex. *Expenses* have been defined as those decreases in equity associated with the profit-oriented activities of the business. Therefore, as expenses increase, the amount of equity decreases. A decrease in equity is recorded as a debit. Continuing with this logic, then, an increase in an expense must be recorded with a debit. This procedure reflects the decrease in equity that is taking place.

This analysis can be extended to include a decrease in an expense, which results in a credit to the expense account and reflects the increase in equity that is taking place, as shown in the following illustration:

Expenses	
Debits	Credits
+	−

To summarize, it is helpful to return to our earlier comment about considering revenues and expenses as temporary subsets of equity. In this context, revenues may be viewed as the increase side (credits) of equity and expenses as the decrease side (debits) of equity. Thus, an increase in expenses (a debit) is really a decrease in equity. This relationship is shown in the following illustration:

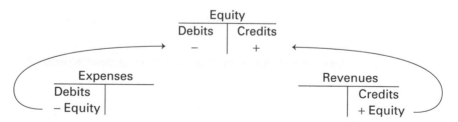

Notice that this system is based on the mathematical integrity of the accounting equation. As a result, the equality mentioned in the section "The Accounting Equation: Transaction Analysis" still exists—that is, the accounting equation must be balanced after the result of each transaction has been recorded. In terms of debits and credits, this equality can be stated as follows:

The total dollar amount of debits for any transaction must EQUAL the total dollar amount of credits.

This rule is critical because it affects the integrity of the entire accounting system.

Transaction Analysis Using Debits and Credits

The effects of a transaction can now be recorded in terms of debits and credits that reflect increases or decreases in the accounts. Following are several examples taken from the Review Exercise in the previous section.[1]

Transaction		Analysis	
June 1	Paige invested $5,000 cash into a bank account to be used in the operations of her business, Kaki Tours.	Debit:	Cash, $5,000—to reflect the increase in this asset.
		Credit:	P. Keith, Capital, $5,000—to reflect the increase in equity.
June 2	She signed a contract with Tel-Ans, a telephone-answering service. The service cost $50 per month, payable at the beginning of each month. She paid Tel-Ans $50.	Debit:	Prepaid services, $50—to reflect the increase in this asset.
		Credit:	Cash, $50—to reflect the decrease in this asset.
June 4	She paid Print Faster $55 for stationery and the various forms she needed.	Debit:	Office supplies, $55—to reflect the increase in this asset.
		Credit:	Cash, $55—to reflect the decrease in this asset.
June 5	She purchased office equipment for $250. She paid $25 down and will pay the remainder in 30 days.	Debit:	Office equipment, $250—to reflect the increase in this asset.
		Credit:	Cash, $25—to reflect the decrease in this asset.
		Credit:	Accounts payable, $225—to reflect the increase in this liability.

Review Exercise

Using the following information, prepare an analysis of the remaining transactions of Paige Keith's tour business similar to that presented previously. Compare your results with the solution that follows.

---

[1] The effects of the transactions on the individual accounts are summarized in Table 15-10.

Transaction	
June 7	Paige Keith purchased additional office supplies costing $125. She paid cash for these supplies.
June 10	She billed several tour companies for tours she conducted during the month. The total billing was $300.
June 15	She received $250 from companies she billed earlier that month.
June 18	She hired an assistant and agreed to pay him 25 percent of her revenue from the tours that he helped to organize.
June 20	Paige Keith deposited $130 in her bank account. This amount was collected from various walking tours she conducted.
June 25	She shared an office with someone and she paid $75 for her share of the June rent (including utilities).
June 30	She billed several tour companies for a total of $400 for tours she conducted during the month.

Solution

June 7	*Debit:*	Office supplies, $125—to reflect the increase in this asset.
	Credit:	Cash, $125—to reflect the decrease in this asset.
June 10	*Debit:*	Accounts receivable, $300—to reflect the increase in this asset.
	Credit:	Tour revenue, $300—to reflect the increase in equity from profit-oriented activities.
June 15	*Debit:*	Cash, $250—to reflect the increase in this asset.
	Credit:	Accounts receivable, $250—to reflect the decrease in this asset.
June 18		No transaction: no assets, liabilities, or equity have changed. Nothing is owed to the assistant until he completes some work.
June 20	*Debit:*	Cash, $130—to reflect the increase in this asset.
	Credit:	Tour revenue, $130—to reflect the increase in equity from profit-oriented activities.
June 25	*Debit:*	Office rent expense, $75—to reflect the decrease in equity from profit-oriented activities.
	Credit:	Cash, $75—to reflect the decrease in this asset.
June 30	*Debit:*	Accounts receivable, $400—to reflect the increase in this asset.
	Credit:	Tour revenue, $400—to reflect the increase in equity from profit-oriented activities.

The results of these transactions in the accounts are summarized in Table 15-10.

Table 15-10
Paige Keith Transactions—Ledger Accounts

Cash		Accounts Receivable		Prepaid Services		Office Supplies	
5,000	50	300	250	50		55	
250	55	400				125	
130	25	700	250			180	
	125	450					
	75						
5,380	330						
5,050							

Office Equipment		Accounts Payable		P. Keith, Capital		Tour Revenue	
250			225		5,000		300
							130
							400
							830

Office Rent Expense	
75	

Completion of Review Exercise

Table 15–10 covers each transaction in the Review Exercise in the section "The Accounting Equation: Transaction Analysis." Several transactions were omitted in that section, however, because we had not yet discussed accrual accounting. The items that follow are similar to those covered in the section "The Accrual Basis of Accounting":

1. The assistant was not paid for the services he performed. Because this amount is owed at the end of the month, the amount earned must be recorded. This entry will record the liability owed and the effect on equity of the services performed by the assistant. Assuming this amount is $40, the following entry is necessary:

    Debit: Salary expense, $40—to reflect the decrease in equity from profit-oriented activities.

    Credit: Salary payable, $40—to reflect the increase in liabilities.

2. By the end of June, the services performed by Tel-Ans for the month were "used up" and no longer had any value. The following entry, therefore, is necessary:

    Debit: Telephone-answering expense, $50—to reflect the decrease in equity from profit-oriented activities.

    Credit: Prepaid services, $50—to reflect the decrease in this asset.

Note: To save time, most companies record entries such as the payment for answering services directly in an expense account. This practice eliminates the need for a second entry like the one described here. If this procedure had been followed here, the June 2 entry would have required a debit to Telephone-answering expense and a credit to Cash for $50. Notice that the effect of these two procedures on the accounting equation is the same: Assets decrease and Equity decreases.

3. Office supplies totaling $180 were purchased in June. During the month some of these supplies were used. Assuming the cost of the supplies used was $30, the following entry is necessary:

Debit: Office supplies expense, $30—to reflect the decrease in equity from profit-oriented activities.

Credit: Office supplies, $30—to reflect the decrease in this asset.

4. The final item that must be considered is office equipment. Whenever a business purchases an asset, it is really buying a "bundle of future services." As these services are used up, an expense is recorded. (This process is explained in the preceding entry for the asset Office supplies.) Using the services of an asset such as Office equipment is generally referred to as *depreciation.* Because it is the using up of an asset in the profit-oriented activities of the business, it is recognized as an expense. The following entry is, therefore, necessary (assume the amount is $5):

Debit: Depreciation expense—office equipment, $5—to record the decrease in equity from profit-oriented activities.

Credit: Accumulated depreciation—office equipment, $5—to reflect the decrease in the asset. Accumulated depreciation is credited instead of the asset itself because it is important to maintain the original cost in a separate account. The Accumulated depreciation account is treated as a negative, or contra, asset—the effect is the same as crediting the Office equipment account directly (see Table 15-15 on page 672).

After these transactions have been entered into the system, the accounts will appear as shown in Table 15-11.

A More Complete Look at the Transaction Recording Process

Now that we have discussed the principles of recording transactions through the use of debits and credits, let us return to the actual process of maintaining accounting records by using journals and ledgers. We said that a journal is a permanent record of all the transactions of a business. The process of recording transactions in a journal is referred to as making journal entries or *journalizing.* Although there are various types of journals, the one we will illustrate is called a *general journal.* Exhibit 15-1 illustrates the form of a general journal. (To simplify the recording process, entities use separate journals—such as cash receipts, cash disbursements, sales, and purchase journals—to record similar types of transactions.)

Table 15-11
Paige Keith Transactions—Ledger Accounts

Cash		Accounts Receivable		Prepaid Services		Office Supplies	
5,000	50	300	250	50	50	55	30
250	55	400		-0-		125	
130	25	700	250			180	30
	125	450				150	
	75						
5,380	330						
5,050							

Office Equipment		Accumulated Depreciation—		Accounts Payable	
250			5		225

Salary Payable		P. Keith, Capital		Tour Revenue		Office Rent Expense	
	40		5,000		300	75	
					130		
					400		
					830		

Salary Expense		Telephone-Answering Expense		Office Supplies Expense		Depreciation Expense— Office Equipment	
40		50		30		5	

Exhibit 15-1
General Journal

		GENERAL JOURNAL				Page 1	
Date 2004		Description	P.R.	Debit		Credit	
June	1	Cash	101	5000 –			
		P. Keith, Capital	301			5000 –	
		Owner invested $5,000 in the business					

Continuing the example used in the previous two sections, let us reconsider the first transaction illustrated. The following steps are used when entering information in the journal (follow each step by referring to the journal entry in Exhibit 15-1):

1. The year is written at the top of each page in the Date column.
2. The month of the transaction is entered. As additional transactions are entered, the month is usually not rewritten unless the same journal page is used for more than 1 month.
3. The third item of information is the date of the transaction. Because this helps separate the transactions, the date for each transaction is usually entered—even if it is the same as that of the preceding transaction.
4. The debit account is entered next to the left-hand margin in the Description column. If more than one debit account is involved in a transaction, all the debit items must be entered before any credit items are entered.
5. Each debit amount is entered in the Debit money column.
6. The credit account or accounts are entered and are *slightly indented* to the right.
7. The respective credit amount or amounts are placed in the Credit money column.
8. The final part of the entry is the explanation. Here a brief description of the transaction is entered. It helps to explain the event that was recorded. It can be useful when attempting to analyze the events that caused a particular account to change.
9. A line is usually skipped between journal entries in order to help separate the entries and to make the information included in the journal easier to read.

The Ledger and Posting

Changes in the accounting equation are accumulated in the journal by transaction. To provide information to decision makers, these data must be summarized in useful categories. This summarization is provided in the ledger. We said earlier that the ledger is a book with a separate page for each account. The traditional two-column ledger account is shown in Exhibit 15-2. We also said that posting is the process of transferring information from the journal to the ledger. The following steps are used when posting a debit entry to the ledger (follow each step by referring to the ledger in Exhibit 15-2):

1. The year is entered as the first item in the Date column on the debit side of the account. As in the journal, it is entered only once.
2. The next item of information is the month. It is placed beneath the year and is entered only once unless the same ledger page is used for more than 1 month.
3. The date of the transaction is the next piece of information placed in the ledger.
4. The amount of the transaction is then entered in the Debit money column.
5. Finally, the P.R. (Posting Reference) column is used to enter the page number where the transaction is recorded in the journal.

GENERAL LEDGER

Cash   Account No. 101

Date 2004	Item	P.R.	Debit	Date	Item	P.R.	Credit
June 1		1	5000 –				

P. Keith, Capital   Account No. 301

Date	Item	P.R.	Debit	Date 2004	Item	P.R.	Credit
				June 1		1	5000 –

Exhibit 15-2
General Ledger

6. The account number (for Cash it is 101) is entered in the journal in the P.R. column (see Exhibit 15-1). Thus the cross-referencing system has been completed. The journal entry can be traced to the ledger, and the ledger entry can be traced back to the original transaction in the journal.

These steps follow the posting of a debit to the Cash account. The process is the same for each credit entry except that the recording is made on the credit side of the account. (See Exhibit 15-2 for the P. Keith, Capital account, and follow the steps previously listed.) The ledger referred to in Exhibit 15-2 is a *general ledger*.

Review Exercise

Record the entries for Kaki Tours, following the format in Exhibit 15-1; post the entries to the appropriate accounts, following the format in Exhibit 15-2. (The entries are described earlier in this section. Don't forget the four entries used to "complete the exercise.") After performing these steps, compare your answer with the solution provided on pages 665–668. You should begin by recording the first transaction—the deposit by Paige Keith—in the journal.

Solution

GENERAL JOURNAL					Page 1	
Date 2004		Description	P.R.	Debit	Credit	
June	1	Cash	101	5000 –		
		P. Keith, Capital	301		5000 –	
		Owner invested $5,000 in the business				
	2	Prepaid services	102	50 –		
		Cash	101		50 –	
		Paid Tel-Ans for telephone answering services.				
	4	Office supplies	104	55 –		
		Cash	101		55 –	
		Purchased stationery from Print Faster.				
	5	Office equipment	107	250 –		
		Cash	101		25 –	
		Accounts payable	201		225 –	
		Purchased office equipment.				
	7	Office supplies	104	125 –		
		Cash	101		125 –	
		Purchased office supplies.				
	10	Accounts receivable	103	300 –		
		Tour revenue	401		300 –	
		Billed tour companies for tours conducted.				
	15	Cash	101	250 –		
		Accounts receivable	103		250 –	
		Collected accounts receivable.				
	20	Cash	101	130 –		
		Tour revenue	401		130 –	
		Collected cash for tours conducted.				
	25	Office rent expense	501	75 –		
		Cash	101		75 –	
		Paid rent on office.				
	30	Accounts receivable	103	400 –		
		Tour revenue	401		400 –	
		Billed tour companies for tours conducted.				

GENERAL JOURNAL

Date 2004		Description	P.R.	Debit	Credit
June	30	Salary expense	502	40 –	
		Salary payable	202		40 –
		Recorded unpaid salary of assistant.			
	30	Telephone-answering expense	503	50 –	
		Prepaid services	102		50 –
		Recorded telephone answering services used.			
	30	Office supplies expense	504	30 –	
		Office supplies	104		30 –
		Recorded office supplies used.			
	30	Depreciation expense—office equipment	505	5 –	
		Accumulated depreciation—office equipment	108		5 –
		Recorded depreciation for June.			

GENERAL LEDGER

Cash   101

Date 2004		Item	P.R.	Debit	Date 2004		Item	P.R.	Credit
June	1		1	5000 –	June	2		1	50 –
	15		1	250 –		4		1	55 –
	20		1	130 –		5		1	25 –
		(5,050)		5380 –		7		1	125 –
						25		1	75 –
									330 –

Prepaid Services   102

Date 2004		Item	P.R.	Debit	Date 2004		Item	P.R.	Credit
June	2		1	50 –	June	30		2	50 –
		(Ø)							

Accounts Receivable   103

Date 2004		Item	P.R.	Debit	Date 2004		Item	P.R.	Credit
June	10		1	300 –	June	15		1	250 –
	30		1	400 –					
		(450)		700 –					

Office Supplies   104

Date 2004		Item	P.R.	Debit	Date 2004		Item	P.R.	Credit
June	4		1	55 –	June	30		2	30 –
	7		1	125 –					
		(150)		180 –					

Office Equipment   107

Date 2004		Item	P.R.	Debit	Date 2004	Item	P.R.	Credit
June	5		1	250 –				

Accumulated Depreciation—Office Equipment   108

Date 2004	Item	P.R.	Debit	Date 2004		Item	P.R.	Credit
				June	30		2	5 –

Accounts Payable   201

Date 2004	Item	P.R.	Debit	Date 2004		Item	P.R.	Credit
				June	5		1	225 –

Salary Payable   202

Date 2004	Item	P.R.	Debit	Date 2004		Item	P.R.	Credit
				June	30		2	40 –

P. Keith, Capital   301

Date 2004	Item	P.R.	Debit	Date 2004		Item	P.R.	Credit
				June	1		1	5000 –

Tour Revenue   401

Date		Item	P.R.	Debit	Date 2004		Item	P.R.	Credit
					June	10		1	300 –
						20		1	130 –
						30	(830)	1	400 –
									830 –

Office Rent Expense   501

Date 2004		Item	P.R.	Debit	Date		Item	P.R.	Credit
June	25		1	75 –					

Salary Expense   502

Date 2004		Item	P.R.	Debit	Date		Item	P.R.	Credit
June	30		2	40 –					

Telephone-Answering Expense   503

Date 2004		Item	P.R.	Debit	Date		Item	P.R.	Credit
June	30		2	50 –					

Office Supplies Expense   504

Date 2004		Item	P.R.	Debit	Date		Item	P.R.	Credit
June	30		2	30 –					

Depreciation Expense—Office Equipment   505

Date 2004		Item	P.R.	Debit	Date		Item	P.R.	Credit
June	30		2	5 –					

FINANCIAL STATEMENTS

The Accounting Cycle

Thus far, we have discussed the recording aspect of the accounting cycle, which consists of (1) analyzing transactions and events to see how they affect assets, liabilities, and equity; (2) recording the transactions and events by making entries in a journal; and (3) posting the journal entries to ledger accounts.

The ultimate purpose of accounting is to provide information to decision makers. Information about results of past operations and current financial position assists in making decisions about the future. Financial reporting organizes the mass of data that the accounting system has gathered into statements that can help users interpret the information. The financial reporting aspects of the accounting cycle are (1) preparing a trial balance, (2) adjusting the accounts as necessary, and (3) preparing financial statements. The final aspect of the accounting cycle is closing the temporary subsets of equity.

This cycle is repeated every accounting period. In specific cases, the cycle may be expanded or contracted to fit the particular circumstances facing the organization.

The Trial Balance

To help prepare financial statements and locate errors that may have been made in the recording or posting processes, a *trial balance* is usually prepared. The trial balance is a columnar listing of each ledger account, together with its balance. If the debit and credit columns equal each other, the system is in balance. (See Table 15-12, which was prepared from the ledger accounts on pages 666–668.)

Errors can occur within the system even if the debit and credit columns in the trial balance are equal. Examples of such errors include (1) entries that are not recorded, (2) amounts debited (credited) to incorrect accounts, and (3) complete entries recorded for incorrect amounts.

The financial statements are usually prepared directly from trial balance data. In some systems, a formal adjusting process must be completed before the statements can be prepared. Such a process is discussed next.

Adjusting Entries

After the trial balance has been prepared, *adjusting entries* may be needed to bring the financial records up-to-date before statements are prepared. Adjusting entries, as discussed previously, are needed if the books have not been adjusted continuously to the full accrual basis of accounting. A good example is depreciation. Recall that, in the Kaki Tours illustration, depreciation was recorded to recognize the fact that the services of the asset Office equipment were being "used up."

Logic would indicate that the "using up" process is gradual and does not occur suddenly at the end of an accounting period. If the books were to be maintained on a current basis, an entry for depreciation would need to be made daily. Because financial statements are prepared only periodically, however, it is not necessary to have the

Table 15-12

Trial Balance

<table>
<tr><td colspan="3" align="center">KAKI TOURS
TRIAL BALANCE
JUNE 30, 2004</td></tr>
<tr><td></td><td align="center">DEBITS</td><td align="center">CREDITS</td></tr>
<tr><td>Cash</td><td>$5,050</td><td></td></tr>
<tr><td>Accounts receivable</td><td>450</td><td></td></tr>
<tr><td>Office supplies</td><td>150</td><td></td></tr>
<tr><td>Office equipment</td><td>250</td><td></td></tr>
<tr><td>Accumulated depreciation—office equipment</td><td></td><td>$ 5</td></tr>
<tr><td>Accounts payable</td><td></td><td>225</td></tr>
<tr><td>Salary payable</td><td></td><td>40</td></tr>
<tr><td>P. Keith, Capital</td><td></td><td>5,000</td></tr>
<tr><td>Tour revenue</td><td></td><td>830</td></tr>
<tr><td>Office rent expense</td><td>75</td><td></td></tr>
<tr><td>Salary expense</td><td>40</td><td></td></tr>
<tr><td>Telephone-answering expense</td><td>50</td><td></td></tr>
<tr><td>Office supplies expense</td><td>30</td><td></td></tr>
<tr><td>Depreciation expense—office equipment</td><td>5</td><td></td></tr>
<tr><td></td><td>$6,100</td><td>$6,100</td></tr>
</table>

books fully up-to-date until the statements are prepared. Therefore, adjusting entries are made at the end of each period before the financial statements are prepared.

In addition to depreciation in the Kaki Tours illustration, Prepaid services must be adjusted. Although the services were used each day, it was not necessary to record the "using up" (or gradual expiration) of the asset until the end of the period. In the illustration, note that adjustments were also made for "using up" Office supplies, as well as for salaries earned by an employee but not yet paid to him. The section "The Accrual Basis of Accounting" discusses other examples of accruals, deferrals, and amortizations for which adjusting entries might be needed if not otherwise recorded.

Financial Statements

After adjusting entries have been made, we are ready to prepare financial statements. Statements commonly prepared are (1) an income (or operating or activity) statement, (2) a statement of changes in owner's equity, (3) a balance sheet, and (4) a statement of cash flows.

An income statement compares the revenues earned with the expenses incurred in earning those revenues, and it reports the resulting net income or net loss. For a profit-oriented organization, this statement is called an *income statement*. An income statement for Paige Keith's business—Kaki Tours—is shown in Table 15-13.

Table 15-13

Income Statement

KAKI TOURS		
INCOME STATEMENT		
FOR THE MONTH ENDED JUNE 30, 2004		
Revenue		
Tour revenue		$830
Expenses		
Office rent expense	$75	
Salary expense	40	
Telephone-answering expense	50	
Office supplies expense	30	
Depreciation expense—office equipment	5	200
Net Income		$630

The *statement of changes in owner's equity* provides a reconciliation of the beginning and ending owner's capital balance. Items that increase owner's capital include investments by the owner and net income for the period. Items that decrease the balance are owner's withdrawals and net losses. Owner's withdrawals are covered later in this chapter. A statement of changes in owner's equity is shown in Table 15-14.

The final statement that will be illustrated is the *balance sheet*. This statement reflects the balances of the asset, liability, and capital accounts at the end of the period (see Table 15-15).

An understanding of the accounting system requires an understanding of the relationship between the financial statements. Notice how the net income for the period is taken from the income statement and is used to determine the ending balance in the owner's capital account. Notice also how the ending balance in the owner's capital account is used to balance the balance sheet.

Table 15-14

Statement of Changes in Owner's Equity

KAKI TOURS	
STATEMENT OF CHANGES IN OWNER'S EQUITY	
FOR THE MONTH ENDED JUNE 30, 2004	
P. Keith, Capital, June 1, 2004	$ -0-
Investment during June	5,000
Income for June	630
P. Keith, Capital, June 30, 2004	$5,630

Table 15-15

Balance Sheet

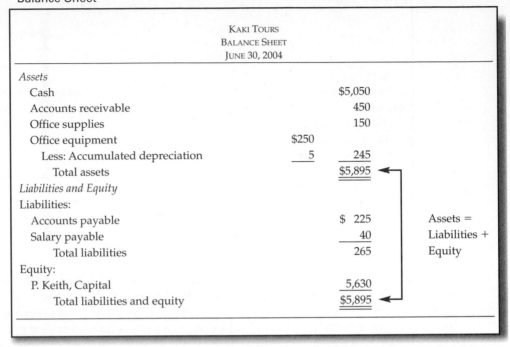

KAKI TOURS
BALANCE SHEET
JUNE 30, 2004

Assets

Cash		$5,050
Accounts receivable		450
Office supplies		150
Office equipment	$250	
Less: Accumulated depreciation	5	245
Total assets		$5,895

Liabilities and Equity

Liabilities:

Accounts payable		$ 225
Salary payable		40
Total liabilities		265

Equity:

P. Keith, Capital		5,630
Total liabilities and equity		$5,895

Assets =
Liabilities +
Equity

A *statement of cash flows* should also be prepared for a business, but a discussion of its preparation is beyond the scope of this text.

Financial Statement Work Sheet

To facilitate preparation of the financial statements, accountants use a *work sheet* that starts with the trial balance and spreads this information across columns for the income statement, the statement of changes in owner's equity, and the balance sheet. Often, the work sheet will contain 12 columns; the first two for the unadjusted trial balance, the next two for adjusting entries, the next two for the adjusted trial balance, and the last six for the financial statements. For Kaki Tours, a trial balance is shown in Table 15-12. This trial balance already contains the effect of the adjusting journal entries, so we will prepare an eight-column work sheet—starting with the adjusted trial balance. Preparing the work sheet requires an ability to distinguish between accounts that belong in the income statement and accounts that belong in the balance sheet.

When you review the work sheet (Table 15-16), notice the following:

- When you extend the income statement accounts from the adjusted trial balance columns into the income statement columns, the total of the credit amounts exceeds the total of the debit amounts by $630. This means that net revenues exceed net expenses, resulting in net income—an increase in owner's equity. To keep the statements in balance, the $630 net credit in the income statement

Table 15-16
Work Sheet for Preparing Financial Statements

KAKI TOURS
WORK SHEET FOR PREPARING FINANCIAL STATEMENTS
JUNE 30, 2004

	ADJUSTED TRIAL BALANCE		INCOME STATEMENT		CHANGES IN OWNER'S EQUITY		BALANCE SHEET	
	DEBITS	CREDITS	DEBITS	CREDITS	DEBITS	CREDITS	DEBITS	CREDITS
Cash	$5,050						$5,050	
Accounts receivable	450						450	
Office supplies	150						150	
Office equipment	250						250	
Acc. dep.—off. equip.		$ 5						$ 5
Accounts payable		225						225
Salary payable		40						40
P. Keith, Capital		5,000				$5,000		
Tour revenue		830		$830				
Office rent expense	75		$ 75					
Salary expense	40		40					
Tel. ans. expense	50		50					
Office supplies exp.	30		30					
Dep. exp.—off. equip.	5		5					
	$6,100	$6,100	200	830				
Net income			630			630		
			$830	$830		5,630		
P. Keith, Cap. 6/30					$5,630			5,630
					$5,630	$5,630	$5,900	$5,900

columns is extended into the credit column of the statement of changes in owner's equity by putting a $630 debit in the income statement columns and a corresponding credit in the statement of changes in owner's equity columns.

- The next step is to extend the owner's equity accounts from the trial balance into the columns for changes in owner's equity. As a result of this year's net income, the owner's equity now shows total credits of $5,630. Because there were no debits, the new owner's equity amount is $5,630. Now extend that net credit into the balance sheet, by putting a $5,630 debit into the columns for the statement of changes in owner's equity, and a corresponding credit into the balance sheet columns.
- Finally, you should extend the balance sheet accounts from the trial balance into the columns for the balance sheet. Notice that the original balance for P. Keith, Capital has been changed by the net effect of the "temporary" revenue and expense accounts. If you made no errors in extending the amounts from the adjusted trial balance into the appropriate columns, the amounts of the total debits and the total credits in the balance sheet would "balance."

Now, trace the figures from each column of the work sheet to the corresponding financial statements illustrated in Tables 15-13, 15-14, and 15-15.

CLOSING THE BOOKS AND OTHER MATTERS

Closing the Books

The final step in the accounting process is closing the books and getting them ready for the next year.

In this chapter the accounting equation was originally used to account for the acquisition and use of the resources of an organization. Table 15-1, which explained how transactions affect the equation, contained only three types of accounts: assets, liabilities, and equity. These accounts are generally referred to as the *permanent* or *real* *accounts*. They are labeled *permanent* because they are carried from one period to another. Thus the ending balance of Cash of one period will be the beginning balance of Cash for the next period.

As the illustrations in this chapter became more complex, the changes in equity resulting from operations of the business were accumulated in separate accounts called revenues and expenses. The purpose of these accounts was to identify the particular operating items causing equity to change. Thus these accounts became the source of the data that were presented on the activity (income) statement. These data were used to help decision makers evaluate the effectiveness of the use of the resources available to management.

After such an evaluation has been made for the current period, however, the data lose their importance. The generation of revenue and the incurrence of expenses are relative to a certain period of time. It serves little purpose to know that a business that has been in operation for 100 years has accumulated $500 million in revenue. Information on revenues and expenses is useful only for evaluating the operations of an organization on a period-by-period basis. As a result, revenue and expense accounts are generally referred to as *temporary* or *nominal accounts.*

If temporary (revenue and expense) accounts are to be used to generate information relative to certain periods, they must be closed out (reduced to a zero balance) at the end of each period; and the balances in those accounts must be transferred to equity. The ledger in Table 15-11 shows a balance in the P. Keith, Capital, account, of $5,000, the initial contribution by Paige Keith. Analysis of the balance sheet in Table 15-15, however, indicates a capital balance of $5,630. The reason for the difference between these two figures is that the former, the one found in the ledger, does not include the income for the period. Because the effects of operations have already been recorded in the asset and liability accounts, they must also be reflected in the capital account so that the balance sheet will balance.

In summary, the trial balance figure for capital does not include the effect of operating the business. Therefore, it must be updated. In addition, the revenue and expense accounts must be reduced to zero to begin accumulating data for the next period. The process of achieving these goals is referred to as *closing the books*. The closing entry for Kaki Tours at June 30, 2004, is shown in Exhibit 15-3.

The purpose of the closing process is to zero out the balances of the temporary accounts and transfer the net income for the period to the capital account. The steps involved in this process are as follows:

1. Debit each revenue account for the credit balance currently in the account.
2. Credit each expense account for the debit balance currently in the account.
3. Debit or credit the capital account for the amount needed to balance the journal entry—make the debits equal the credits—which provides the amount of the net income or loss.

After posting these entries to the accounts, the revenue and expense accounts will no longer have any balances. A double line should be drawn under the date and amount columns for each of those accounts, and the accounts are now ready for the next year's postings. The asset, liability, and equity accounts all have balances that will be carried into the next period as the beginning balances in those accounts.

Withdrawals by the Owner

At this point it is important to discuss another type of transaction that can be recorded in the system. Withdrawals by the owner are not treated as an expense of the operations of a business. Therefore, had Paige Keith taken money or other assets from the business, the entry would have required a reduction of assets (credit) and a debit to an account called P. Keith, Withdrawals. This latter account would have been closed at the end of the period into P. Keith, Capital; that is, the withdrawals account would have been credited and the capital account debited. This sequence of entries was omitted from the basic example because it has no counterpart in a non-business system.

Exhibit 15-3
Closing Entry

GENERAL JOURNAL						3
Date 2004		Description	Ref.	Dr.	Cr.	
June	30	Tour revenue	401	830 –		
		Office rent expense	501		75 –	
		Salary expense	502		40 –	
		Telephone—answering expense	503		50 –	
		Office supplies expense	504		30 –	
		Depreciation expense—office equipment	505		5 –	
		P. Keith, Capital	301		630 –	
		Record closing the revenue and expense accounts				
		and transfer the net income to capital.				

Control and Subsidiary Accounts

Until now, we have shown just single accounts for accounts receivable and for accounts payable. In practice, large entities will have thousands of individual accounts receivable and accounts payable, representing amounts owed by their customers and to their creditors. Maintaining separate accounts for each receivable and each payable in the general ledger would make the general ledger extremely unwieldy. To simplify record keeping, most entities maintain a separate accounts receivable ledger, with a page for each customer. They also keep a separate accounts payable ledger, with a page for each creditor. These ledgers are called *subsidiary ledgers* and the individual accounts are called *subsidiary accounts*.

To record individual receivable and payable transactions, postings are made to each affected account in the subsidiary ledger. Summary postings for the total of the amounts affecting the accounts receivable and accounts payable accounts are made to those accounts in the general ledger. The accounts receivable and accounts payable accounts maintained in the general ledger are referred to as *control accounts*. The totals of the control accounts must be equal at all times to the total of the individual accounts kept in the subsidiary ledgers.

Review Exercise

Using the information in Table 15-17, prepare the necessary closing entry in the general journal at December 31, 2004, and fill in the blanks that follow. Compare your results with the solution provided.

Table 15-17
Review Exercise

ACCOUNT	BALANCE
Cash	$12,000
Accounts receivable	15,000
Prepaid rent	1,000
Office equipment	30,000
Accumulated depreciation—office equipment	14,000
Accounts payable	5,000
Notes payable to bank	10,000
Amy Norris, Capital	25,000
Service revenue	40,000
Depreciation expense—equipment	7,000
Rent expense	15,000
Salary expense	14,000

After posting the closing entry, indicate the balance of each of the following accounts:

Cash $ _____

Accounts payable $ _____

Amy Norris, Capital $ _____

Service revenue $ _____

Rent expense $ _____

What was the net income for the period? _____

Solution

Date 2004		Description	P.R.	Debit	Credit
Dec.	31	Service Revenue		4000 –	
		Depreciation expense—equipment			700 –
		Rent expense			1500 –
		Salary expense			1400 –
		Amy Norris, Capital			400 –
		To record the closing of the revenue and expense			
		accounts and transfer the net income to capital.			

GENERAL JOURNAL — Page 5

Cash	$12,000
Accounts payable	$ 5,000
Amy Norris, Capital	$29,000 ($25,000 + $4,000)
Service revenue	$-0- (closed)
Rent Expense	$-0- (closed)

This income for the period was $4,000 (the amount closed into capital).

OTHER TRANSACTIONS

Credit Sales and Bad Debts

The U.S. economy is basically a credit economy. Instead of paying cash immediately, customers are allowed a certain period of time to pay. Although this practice may stimulate sales, selling on credit also has a cost. Some customers may not pay their bills, resulting in an expense called *bad debts expense*. When should you record this expense, in the year of the sale or in the year the bad debt is written off?

To determine the answer, think about the question in another way: Is this expense attributable to the year the sales were made or to the year the customer failed to pay the bill? Remember that, under accrual accounting, expenses need to be matched with the revenues to which the expenses relate. Therefore, the bad debts expense should be recorded in the year the sales revenue was recorded.

Recording this expense raises a few questions:

- If specific bad debts have not yet occurred, how do you know how much to record as an expense?

Answer: Make an estimate, generally based on past experience and calculated as a percentage of the year's sales or as a percentage of the unpaid accounts receivable.

- If bad debts have not yet occurred, how do you reduce the balance of the Accounts receivable account? Which specific account in the accounts receivable subsidiary ledger should you reduce, if you don't know who the bad debt will be?

Answer: Don't reduce any specific account receivable at the time you record the bad debts expense. Instead, create a special account, called Allowance for uncollectible accounts. This account stands in place of the credit to Accounts receivable until an actual bad debt becomes known. When an actual bad debt becomes known, reduce Accounts receivable, as well as the Allowance account.

To illustrate this process, return to the Kaki Tours illustration. Notice (from Table 15-13) that Kaki Tours had tour revenue of $830. Notice also (see Accounts receivable in Table 15-15) that some customers had not yet paid their bills. They owed Kaki a total of $450. These financial statements were based on the assumption that everyone would pay. Suppose, however, based on her previous experience, Paige Keith believes that not everyone will pay. She estimates that about 10 percent of the $450 owed to her on June 30, 2004, will not be paid. To record this estimate, the following entry is needed:

Bad debts expense   45
        Allowance for uncollectible accounts   45
     To record estimated bad debts.

The $45 bad debts expense would be reported as one of the expenses on the income statement, thereby reducing Kaki Tours' net income from $630 to $585. The Allowance for uncollectible accounts would be shown as a reduction of Accounts receivable on the balance sheet, so that the net accounts receivable would be reported as $405.

Now, assume one of the individuals included in Accounts receivable at June 30 goes bankrupt in August, after the statements are issued. Because he cannot pay, Accounts receivable must be reduced. Also, because the Allowance for uncollectible accounts had been set up for that purpose, that account is also reduced. The entry is as follows:

Allowance for uncollectible accounts   30
        Accounts receivable   30
     To record write-off of bad debt.

What is the financial reporting effect of these transactions? The account, Allowance for uncollectible accounts, is called a *contra-asset*. For financial reporting purposes, it serves to reduce the reported Accounts receivable balance, so that Accounts Receivable is stated at its net realizable value; that is, the amount expected to be realized in cash. A balance sheet prepared at June 30, 2004, would show Accounts receivable of $450, less Allowance for uncollectible accounts of $45, for a net asset of $405. A balance sheet prepared immediately after the write-off of the bad debt would show Accounts receivable of $420, less Allowance for uncollectible accounts of $15, leaving the same net asset of $405.

Buying and Selling Merchandise

For simplicity, the illustrations in this chapter deal with the sale of services. Much of what takes place in the U.S. economy, however, concerns the purchase (or manufacture) and sale of products. How would a retail store, for example, account for the purchase and sale of clothing? Assume Sammi's Dresses purchases 12 dresses on credit at a cost of $100 each. She sells five of them for cash at $160 each.

You can tell, from inspection, that Sammi made a profit of $300 on the sale, because she sold five dresses and made a profit of $60 on each. You reached that conclusion because you "matched" the selling price of each dress ($160) with the cost of each dress ($100). The accounting process follows the same matching process, as the following entries show:

Merchandise inventory	1,200	
Accounts payable		1,200
To record merchandise purchases (12 dresses @ $100).		
Cash	800	
Sales revenue		800
To record sales of merchandise (5 dresses @ $160).		
Cost of goods sold	500	
Merchandise inventory		500
To record cost of sales (5 dresses @ $100).		

Consider the effect of these transactions. Merchandise inventory is an asset account. After the journal entries were made, that account has a balance of $700, representing seven dresses that cost Sammi $100 each. Sales revenue and Cost of goods sold are equity accounts (a revenue and an expense account). Matching the Sales revenue ($800) with the Cost of goods sold ($500) shows that Sammi's gross profit was $300.

REVIEW QUESTIONS

Q15-1 Define the following terms:
    a. Assets
    b. Liabilities
    c. Equity
    d. Revenue
    e. Expense

Q15-2 Write the accounting equation.

Q15-3 Must the accounting equation always balance? Why?

Q15-4 Describe the difference between the cash basis of accounting and the accrual basis.

Q15-5 Describe and illustrate the difference between an accrual and a deferral.

Q15-6 Identify the rules of debit and credit with respect to assets, liabilities, equity, revenues, and expenses.

Q15-7 A student of basic accounting made the following statement: "For each account debited, there must be another account credited for the same amount." Do you agree? Why or why not?

Q15-8 Why do credits increase the equity account?

Q15-9 What is a journal and how is it used in the accounting process?

Q15-10 What is a ledger and how is it used in the accounting process?

Q15-11 How are journals and ledgers interrelated in an accounting system?

Q15-12 If the columns of a trial balance total to the same amount, the information included in the accounts must be correct. Do you agree or disagree? Why?

Q15-13 What are the three basic financial statements illustrated in the text?

Q15-14 Describe the interrelationship among the three statements in Q15-13.

Q15-15 Why is it important to put the appropriate date or time period on a financial statement?

Q15-16 What is the purpose of adjusting entries?

Q15-17 Which accounts are closed at the end of an accounting period? Why are these accounts closed?

EXERCISES

E15-1 (Preparing transactions)

For each of the following categories, compose a transaction that will cause that category to increase and one that will cause it to decrease:

1. Assets
2. Liabilities
3. Equity
4. Revenues
5. Expenses

E15-2 (Associating changes with specific accounts)

For each of the following transactions of the Kit-Kat Company, identify the accounts that would be increased and those that would be decreased:

1. The owner invested $25,000 in the business.
2. Rent for the month was paid to Jiffy Realty Company, $500.
3. A secretary was hired at a monthly salary of $550.
4. Customers were billed for services rendered, $700.
5. The utilities bill for the month was paid, $234.

E15-3 (Calculating the change in equity from balance sheet data)

The beginning and ending balances in certain account categories of the Release Company are as follows:

Account Categories	Beginning Balances	Ending Balances
Assets	$306,000	$307,000
Liabilities	$107,000	$110,000

Based upon this information, what was the change in equity for the period?

E15-4   (Associating accrual-type changes with specific accounts)

For each of the following events affecting the Kit-Kat Company in E15-2, identify the accounts that would be increased and those that would be decreased:

1. The month for which rent of $500 had been paid to Jiffy Realty Company expired.
2. The secretary worked for a full month and earned $550 but was not paid.

E15-5   (Associating accrual-type changes with specific accounts)

For each of the following events affecting Becca's Bootery, identify the accounts that would be increased and those that would be decreased on April 30 in order to accurately measure the results of her operations for the month of April:

1. Becca borrowed $10,000 on April 1 to provide working capital for her business. She promised to repay the loan in 12 months with interest at 8 percent a year.
2. Becca did not plan to use the entire $10,000 immediately. On April 1, she invested $2,000 in a 90-day Treasury bill that would pay her 6 percent interest.
3. Becca paid $1,800 on April 1 for a 3-year fire insurance policy.

E15-6   (Using debits and credits)

Identify the account(s) that would be debited and/or credited as a result of the following transactions:

1. The owner invested $10,000 in the business.
2. Supplies were purchased for cash, $800.
3. Service revenue of $1,000 was received in cash.
4. Customers were billed for services rendered, $500.
5. Employees were paid their salaries totaling $800.
6. Collections of accounts receivable totaled $300.
7. Rent for the month was paid, $350.
8. Salaries owed employees at the end of the month totaled $100.
9. Supplies costing $300 were used.

E15-7   (Associating debits and credits with account categories)

Each of the account categories listed in E15-1 is increased with either a debit or credit. Indicate which is used to record an increase in each type of account and identify the usual balance in that account category.

E15-8   (Using debits and credits)

William T. Fudd III acts as a rental agent for several large apartment houses. Fudd's income is determined by a commission on the number of apartments he rents. During the month of January, Fudd incurred the following transactions. Record the debits and credits, without explanations.

2004

January   2   Fudd placed $20,000 cash into a bank account to be used in the operation of his business, Apartment Locators.

	2	Fudd hired a secretary and agreed to pay her $700 per month.
	4	Fudd borrowed $10,000 from the Security Bank, signing a note for that amount.
	5	Fudd purchased, for cash, office equipment that cost $3,000.
	10	Fudd paid the rent for the month, $300.
	14	Fudd received a check from one apartment complex owner for $3,000. This amount was his commission for renting apartments during the first 2 weeks of January.
	17	Fudd paid his secretary half of the agreed-upon salary.
	30	Fudd earned an additional $3,000 of commissions. He has not received these amounts; therefore, he sent bills to the owners.
	31	Fudd collected $500 from one of the owners billed on January 30.
	31	Fudd made a payment on his loan. The total payment was $1,200, of which $200 was interest. The remainder was a reduction of the amount of the loan.

E15-9 (Recording transactions in a general journal)

Record the following transactions in general journal form for the Control Company, a private investigation service:

2004

January	2	Susan Bigger invested $10,000 in the business.
	2	Bigger paid the rent on office space for January, $500.
	4	Bigger purchased office supplies on credit for $200.
	5	Bigger billed customers for $5,000 for services performed.
	10	Bigger acquired an automobile for use in the business. The cost was $4,500. She paid $1,000 as a down payment and signed a note for the remainder.
	15	Customers paid Bigger $3,500 on their account.
	20	Bigger billed customers for $2,000.
	25	Bigger acquired the services of Answer Company, a telephone answering service. She paid $10 for their services for the remainder of the month.
	31	Depreciation of $100 was recorded on the automobile.
	31	Office supplies used during the month totaled $100.
	31	The utilities bills arrived in the mail; they totaled $800. She will pay them in February.
	31	The cost of gasoline and oil for the automobile for the month was $134. She paid the service station that amount.

E15-10 (Posting to a general ledger)

Post the transactions in E15-9 to general ledger accounts.

E15-11 (Recording transactions in a general journal)

Using the data in E15-8, record the transactions in general journal form.

E15-12 (Preparing a trial balance)

Using the following information, prepare a trial balance for the Forfeit Company at June 30, 2004.

Accumulated depreciation—equipment	$ 4,000
Taxes payable	200
Equipment	24,000
Cash	20,000
Utilities expense	1,000
Depreciation expense—equipment	600
Notes payable	24,000
Salaries expense	20,000
R. Key, Capital	15,800
Office supplies	2,000
Service revenue	32,000
Rent expense	8,600
Accounts payable	1,600
Office supplies expense	1,400

E15-13 (Preparing a trial balance)

Prepare a trial balance based upon the information in E15-10.

E15-14 (Computation of balance sheet amounts)

Based upon the following information, compute total assets, total liabilities, and total capital; in addition, determine whether all of the accounts are listed. (*Note:* This is the first month of operations of the business.)

Cash	$22,000
Accounts receivable	12,000
Accounts payable	15,000
Equipment	50,000
Rent expense	11,000
Service revenue	74,000
Notes payable	17,000
Accumulated depreciation	25,000
Depreciation expense	12,500
Office supplies	3,000
Office supplies expense	8,000
Salaries payable	4,000

E15-15 (Relating accounts and financial statements)

Identify the financial statement on which each of the following items would appear:

a. Bonds payable
b. Rent revenue
c. Owner's capital, beginning balance
d. Cash
e. Equipment
f. Supplies expense
g. Depreciation expense
h. Service revenue

i. Accounts receivable
j. Accounts payable
k. Owner's capital, ending balance
l. Rent expense
m. Accumulated depreciation
n. Net income
o. Salaries payable
p. Land
q. Supplies on hand

E15-16 (Fill in the blanks—definitions)
Match the items in the right column with those in the left column.

_____ 1. Statement of changes
    in owner's equity
_____ 2. Income statement
_____ 3. Net income
_____ 4. Additional investment
    by the owner
_____ 5. Ending balance in
    owner's capital
_____ 6. Balance sheet

a. A financial statement that
   presents the revenues and
   expenses of a business
b. A financial statement that
   presents a reconciliation of the
   beginning and ending owner's
   capital
c. An increase in owner's capital
d. A financial statement that presents the assets, liabilities, and
   owner's capital of a business
e. Can be found on a balance sheet
   and a statement of changes in
   owner's equity
f. An excess of revenues over
   expenses

E15-17 (Preparing closing entries and determining the ending balance in capital)
Prepare the appropriate closing entry based on the information in E15-12 and
determine the ending balance in R. Key, Capital.

E15-18 (Accounting for uncollectible accounts receivable)
South Salem Daycare Center is a not-for-profit organization that provides
daycare services. Prepare journal entries for the center to record the following
events. After making all the journal entries, calculate the net realizable value
of the Center's accounts receivable.
1. The Center billed its clients $120,000 for daycare services during the year.
2. The Center received $105,000 from its clients in payment of the bills.
3. The Center established an allowance for uncollectible accounts receivable
   in the amount of 10 percent of its outstanding receivables.
4. The Center could not locate three clients who owed a total of $800, and
   decided to write off their accounts as being uncollectible.

E15-19 (Accounting for the purchase and sale of merchandise)
Nomoto Cars is an automobile dealership. Prepare journal entries to record
these transactions:
1. Nomoto receives 10 automobiles from a manufacturer and puts them into
   its inventory for resale. Nomoto bought the autos on credit for $20,000 each.
2. During the following week, Nomoto sells four of the automobiles for
   $24,000 each. The customers pay in cash. (*Hint:* Prepare two journal entries,
   one to record the sale proceeds and one to record the expense of the sale.
   For the second entry, debit the account Cost of sales.)

PROBLEMS

P15-1 (Analyzing transactions on a work sheet)

Sally Golfo, a registered nurse, opens a new business called Sally's Elder-care. Golfo plans to care for the elderly herself in a facility that she will rent. The following transactions occurred during July 2004, her first month in business:

1. Ms. Golfo invested $5,000 of her own money to start the business.
1. She borrowed $20,000 from the local bank to provide her with additional cash. She agreed to repay the bank $1,000 on the last day of every month, starting July 31, with interest at the rate of 6 percent a year on the unpaid balance.
1. She rented the house next to hers for a 3-month period, paying a total of $6,000, to provide a facility to care for her patients.
1. She purchased furniture for the facility. She received an invoice for $4,800, payable in 10 days.
10. She paid the $4,800 invoice for the furniture.
18. She paid her assistant $800 for 2 weeks' work.
20. During the month, she billed her clients $12,000 for services rendered.
25. She received $9,000 cash from the clients who were previously billed.
30. At month-end, she received a bill for electric service in the amount of $300. She will pay the bill in August.
30. During the month, she paid $500 for food to provide lunch to her clients. (*Hint:* For this problem, consider the food as an expense when it is purchased.)
31. She paid the bank $1,100 on the borrowing. Of that amount, $1,000 was for the principal payment on the loan and $100 was for interest.

Required: Analyze these transactions on a work sheet similar to that illustrated in the text. You will need columns for Cash, Accounts receivable, Prepaid rent, Furniture, Notes payable, Accounts payable, and Sally Golfo, Capital.

P15-2 (Analyzing transactions on a work sheet)

Dr. Harlan Elliott opened a magnetic resonance imaging (MRI) facility, to be known as Harlan MRI. These transactions took place during his first month of operation:

1. Harlan invested $80,000 in the business.
2. He purchased MRI equipment from the manufacturer for $1.8 million. To pay for the equipment, Harlan gave the manufacturer a note. He was required to repay the note in five annual payments of $360,000 each, together with interest of 6 percent a year on the unpaid balance.
3. He purchased supplies for $25,000 on credit. The supplies were received and put in inventory.
4. At the beginning of the month, Harlan paid rent in the amount of $3,000.
5. He paid the bill for supplies in the amount of $25,000.

6. During the month, he incurred technician salaries of $12,000. Of this amount, he paid $11,000 in cash to employees. He withheld the other $1,000 from their salaries for taxes, which he will pay the government in August.
7. He billed his patients in the amount of $40,000 for MRI services.
8. On receiving the bills, the patients paid Harlan a total of $35,000.
9. During the month, he paid bills for utility services, amounting to $4,000.
10. Harlan took inventory of the supplies and found that he had consumed $2,000 of those supplies in the course of the month's activities.

Required: Analyze these transactions on a work sheet similar to that illustrated in the text. You will need columns for Cash, Accounts receivable, Supplies inventory, Prepaid rent, Equipment, Notes payable, Accounts payable, Withholding taxes payable, and H. Elliott, Capital.

P15-3 (Analyzing transactions on a work sheet)
Ted's Motor Pool provides taxi services. Ted, who went into business recently, keeps records on a work sheet similar to that illustrated in the text. At the start of the new year, his work sheet shows these balances: Cash—$30,000; Accounts receivable—$15,000; Fuel and parts inventory—$8,000; Vehicles—$192,000; Accounts payable—$12,000; Loans payable—$180,000; Ted Elias, Capital—$53,000. (You will also need columns for Investments, Prepaid rent, Prepaid insurance, and Withholding tax payable.) These transactions occurred in the first month of the new year:
1. Ted leased a garage to store his vehicles and to make minor repairs. He paid $6,000 for 2 months' rent.
2. Ted bought accident insurance for a 2-year period, paying $12,000.
3. He received $13,000 from charge-account customers he had billed last year.
4. During the month he purchased $10,000 of fuel and repair parts on credit.
5. He received $50,000 during the month from customers who paid in cash.
6. At month-end, he sent out bills for $14,000 to charge-account customers.
7. He paid $12,000 to suppliers from whom he had purchased on account.
8. Ted's drivers and other employees earned $30,000. He paid them $28,000 and withheld $2,000 in taxes, which he will pay the government next month.
9. On the 15th of the month, Ted invested some of his cash in a 6-month $20,000 Treasury note.
10. During the month, Ted used $6,000 in fuel and repair parts from inventory.
11. Ted paid utility bills amounting to $3,000. He also received a utility bill for $1,000 that he had not paid at month-end.

Required: Record the opening balances on a work sheet similar to that illustrated in the text, and then analyze these transactions on the work sheet.

P15-4 (Analyzing accrual transactions on a work sheet)
Analyze the following accrual-type events and add them to the work sheet you prepared for P15-1.

1. Adjust for the expiration of 1-month's rent.
2. Adjust for the "using up" of the furniture during the month. (Assume the furniture will have a useful life of 4 years.)
3. Accrue for $800 of salary earned by the assistant during the last 2 weeks of the month but not yet paid to her.

P15-5 (Analyzing accrual transactions on a work sheet)
Analyze the following accrual-type events and add them to the work sheet you prepared for P15-2.
1. Adjust for the "using up" of the MRI equipment during the month. (Assume the equipment will have a useful life of 10 years.)
2. Accrue for 1 month's interest owed on the note payable. (Add a column for Interest payable.)
3. Adjust for the expiration of the entire rent payment.

P15-6 (Analyzing accrual transactions on a work sheet)
Analyze the following accrual-type events and add them to the work sheet you prepared for P15-3.
1. Adjust for the expiration of 1 month's rent.
2. Adjust for the expiration of 1 month's accident insurance.
3. Adjust for the "using up" of the vehicles during the month. (Assume the vehicles have a useful life of 48 months from the beginning of the year.)
4. Accrue for 1 month's interest owed on the $180,000 loan. The interest rate on the borrowing is 8 percent a year. (Add a column for Interest payable.)

P15-7 (Recording transactions in journals and ledgers)
Using the information given in P15-1 and P15-4, record the transactions in general journal form. Then, post the journal entries to ledger T-accounts, like those shown in Table 15-11. (To help keep track of your postings, give each journal entry the same reference number or letter shown in the problems, and insert that number or letter to the left of the amount recorded in the T-accounts.)

P15-8 (Recording transactions in journals and ledgers)
Using the information given in P15-2 and P15-5, record the transactions in general journal form. Then, post the journal entries to ledger T-accounts, like those shown in Table 15-11. (To help keep track of your postings, give each journal entry the same reference number or letter shown in the problems, and insert that number or letter to the left of the amount recorded in the T-accounts.)

P15-9 (Recording transactions in journals and ledgers)
Using the information given in P15-3 and P15-6, record the transactions in general journal form. Then post the journal entries to ledger T-accounts, like those shown in Table 15-11. (To help keep track of your postings, give each journal entry the same reference number or letter shown in the problems, and insert that number or letter to the left of the amount recorded in the T-accounts.)

P15-10 (Matching accounts and financial statements)

Following are several financial statement classifications and accounts:

R	Revenue
E	Expense
A	Asset
L	Liability
C	Owner's capital (balance sheet)
SC	Statement of changes in owner's equity

Caution: Some items may appear in more than one statement classification.

Example: A Cash

_____ 1. Notes payable

_____ 2. Additional investment by owner

_____ 3. Automobile

_____ 4. Depreciation expense—automobile

_____ 5. Prepaid rent

_____ 6. Utilities expense

_____ 7. Consulting revenue

_____ 8. Accounts payable

_____ 9. Ending balance in owner's capital

_____ 10. Office supplies

_____ 11. Accumulated depreciation—automobile

_____ 12. Salaries payable

_____ 13. Office supplies expense

_____ 14. Service revenue

_____ 15. Interest expense

_____ 16. Accounts receivable

_____ 17. Loans made to other companies

_____ 18. Deposit made with utility company (This amount will be repaid to the company for which we are keeping the records in 5 years.)

_____ 19. Cash held in a separate bank account from that mentioned previously (This money will be used to buy a building in a few years.)

Required: Identify the proper financial statement classification for each account by placing the appropriate key letter in the space provided.

P15-11 (Preparing a trial balance and financial statements)

Required: 1. From the ledger accounts prepared for P15-7, prepare a trial balance.

2. Extend the trial balance into an eight-column work sheet like that shown in Table 15-16, and use the work sheet to prepare the following financial statements:

a. Income statement

b. Statement of changes in owner's equity

c. Balance sheet

P15-12 (Preparing a trial balance and financial statements)

Required: 1. From the ledger accounts prepared for P15-8, prepare a trial balance.
2. Extend the trial balance into an eight-column work sheet like that shown in Table 15-16, and use the work sheet to prepare the following financial statements:
  a. Income statement
  b. Statement of changes in owner's equity
  c. Balance sheet

P15-13 (Preparing a trial balance and financial statements)

Required: 1. From the ledger accounts prepared for P15-9, prepare a trial balance.
2. Extend the trial balance into an eight-column work sheet like that shown in Table 15-16, and use the work sheet to prepare the following financial statements:
  a. Income statement
  b. Statement of changes in owner's equity
  c. Balance sheet

P15-14 (Preparing a closing entry)

Required: Based on the answers you obtained in P15-11, prepare the closing entry.

P15-15 (Preparing a closing entry)

Required: Based on the answers you obtained in P15-12, prepare the closing entry.

P15-16 (Preparing a closing entry)

Required: Based on the answers you obtained in P15-13, prepare the closing entry.

P15-17 (Accounts receivable and sales transactions; comprehensive problem)
Camp Bryn Mawr, a summer camp, started the year with cash of $40,000, land costing $300,000, and buildings and equipment costing $250,000. Because the camp had no liabilities, the assets were offset by the equity account F. Jonas, Capital, in the amount of $590,000. The following transactions occurred during the year:
1. Jonas sent bills in the amount of $150,000 to the parents of 75 campers.
2. Jonas purchased 80 camper packages (consisting of uniforms and supplies) from a vendor on credit. He received the packages and put them in inventory. He also received a bill for $4,800 (80 packages costing $60 a package) from the vendor.
3. When they arrived at camp, each of the 75 campers received a camper package. Jonas sent bills in the amount of $6,750 to the parents, charging them $90 a package.

4. Jonas received cash in the amount of $148,750 from the parents based on the bills sent out in transactions (1) and (3).
5. During the summer, Jonas paid employee salaries in the amount of $100,000 and food expenses of $8,000. (Assume all the food was consumed.)
6. Jonas paid the invoice for $4,800 for transaction (2).
7. Anticipating that several parents might not pay their bills, Jonas set up an allowance for uncollectible receivables in the amount of $4,000.
8. One of the parents, who owed $2,000, declared bankruptcy. Jonas wrote off the account as uncollectible.
9. Jonas made a provision for depreciation for the year, assuming that the buildings and equipment had a useful life of 20 years.
10. Jonas promised the camp director a bonus of $5,000, based on the excellent work she did during the year. Jonas, therefore, accrued a liability for that amount.

Required: 1. Prepare journal entries to record the preceding transactions. (Among others, you will need accounts for Revenues—camper fees, Revenues—uniform sales, and Inventory—uniforms.)
2. Post the journal entries to ledger T-accounts.
3. From the ledger accounts, prepare a trial balance.
4. Using the trial balance, prepare an income statement, a statement of changes in owner's equity, and a balance sheet.

INDEX

Asset turnover, 611–612

Audit and Accounting Guide—Health Care Organizations (AICPA), 4n, 613, 553, 553n. 1, 560n. 5, 563n, 573, 574, 575, 576, 580n

Auditor's report, 401–405
  of a Comprehensive Annual Financial Report (CAFR), 371–372

Available
  defined, 21
  resources
    not available, 36
    for debt service, 31–32
    for spending, 26
  revenues, for use by General Fund, 28
  See also Measurable and available

B

Bad debts expense, 677–679

Balance sheet, 672
  defined, 671
  for General Fund, compared with business organization balance sheet, 26–28
  for Governmental Funds, 379–380, 381–383
  See also Financial statements; Health care organizations, accounting for

Basic financial statements, 372–373

Basic fund accounting system
  See Governmental fund accounting cycle

Basis of accounting, 18, 226
  Debt Service Funds, 228
  defined, 12
  fiduciary-type funds, 23
  financial statements for governmental funds, 379
  governmental-type funds, 21–22
  proprietary-type funds, 23
  See also Government-wide financial statements

Berne, Robert, 607n

Blanket order, 169

Blending, 369–370

Bonds
  between interest payment dates, issuance of, 247
  premium or discount, issuance of, 247

Budget
  defined, 64
  fixed, 273
  flexible, 273, 284
  in fund accounting, 117–119
  revisions, 166

Budgetary accounting
  See Governmental fund accounting cycle

Budgetary accounts, 120

Budgetary comparison schedules, 393–394, 395–396

Budgetary control report, 97–99

Budgetary cushion, 613, 630–631

Budgetary entries, defined, 119

Budgetary Fund Balance, 119–120

Budgetary fund balance reserved for encumbrances, 131

Budgetary interchanges, 135–136

Budgetary policy guidelines, 71–72

Budgetary process, federal
  See Federal government accounting and reporting

Budget authority, 466, 466n. 2

Budget calendar, 72, 73

Budget document, 94–95

Budget instructions, 72–73

Budget laws, 64–66

Budget message, 94

Budget process, 20–21, 62–63
  approaches to budgeting, 67
    object-of-expenditure approach, 68–69, 70
  budgetary information, using, 97–104
  budget laws, 64–66
  Governmental Budgeting in Practice (feature), 99–104
  preparing a budget, 69
    budgetary review, 89, 91–94
    budget document, 94–95
    calendar, 72, 73
    departmental expenditure requests, 81–88
    instructions, 72–73
    legislative consideration and adoption of the budget, 95–96
    nondepartmental expenditure and interfund transfer requests, 88–89, 90
    policy guidelines, 71–72
    property tax levy, 96–97
    revenue estimates, 73–81
    service efforts and accomplishments (SEA), 89
  types of budgets
    capital, 67
    cash forecasts, 67, 68
    operating, 66–67
  See also Departmental expenditure requests; Revenue estimates

Budget revisions, 166

Budget solvency, 612–614
  operating results indicators and budgetary cushion, 630–631
  operating margin, 629–630

Budget summary, 94

Budget-year revenue projections, 77–81

notes to financial statements regarding patient
revenue recognition, 559–560
uncollectible receivables, 558

S

Salary-vacancy factor (SVF), 82
Sales tax revenues, 432, 437
Security, other than trading, 560
Self-balancing accounts, defined, 11
Selling and buying merchandise, 679
Serial bonds, defined, 227
Service assessments, 341
Service efforts and accomplishments (SEA), 89
Services, contributed, 510–511
Servicing the debt, 227
Short-term borrowings, 134–135
Short-term investments, 610
Special assessments, 292–293
  control of and accounting for, 341–343
  description of project activities, 340–341
Special events, 78
Special Funds, 470
Special items, 38, 379
Special Revenue Funds, 30–31, 116
  year-end financial statements, 180
  See also Governmental fund accounting cycle
Special termination benefits, 179
Specific-Purpose Funds, 518, 566, 567–568
Spending, defined, 178
State government financial reporting, 9
  versus federal, 468–469
Statement of activities, 426, 503–506, 526–529, 530, 605–606
Statement of budgetary resources, 484, 485
Statement of cash flows, 389–392, 507, 508, 576, 579, 582, 672
Statement of changes in net assets, 575, 580–581
Statement of changes in net position, 483, 485
Statement of changes in owner's equity, 671
Statement of financial position, 501–503, 529–532
Statement of financing, 483, 485
Statement of functional expenses, 506–507
Statement of net assets, 604–605
  in fund financial statements, 387, 388–389
  government-wide financial statements, 423–425
Statement of net costs, 482, 484
Statement of operations, 574, 580–581
Statement of revenues, expenditures, and changes
  in fund balance, 28
  in fund financial statements, 380, 383–386
Statement of revenues, expenses, and changes in
  fund net assets
  in fund financial statements, 387, 389, 390

Statements of Federal Financial Accounting
  Standards (SFFAS)
  No. 3, "Inventory and Related Property," 471
  No. 6, "Property, plant, and equipment," 471–472
  No. 17, "Accounting for Social Insurance," 473
Statistical tables, preparing, 401, 402–403
"Stub period" interest on long-term debt, 434
Student Loan Funds, 567
Subscription income, 517
Subsidiary accounts, 126–130, 676
Supplementary information, 95, 606
Supporting schedules, 94
Surpluses, 74–77, 76–77

T

Tax Agency Fund, 42–43
Tax anticipation notes, 134–135
Tax collection rate, 628–629
Tax discounts, 162–163
Tax liens receivable, 164
Taxpayer-assessed revenues, 176
Tax refunds, 161
Tax revenues, accruing, 436–437
Temporarily restricted net assets, 503
Temporary accounts, 674
Term endowment funds, 566
Third-party payers, 555–556, 557, 558–559
Time-series analysis, 608
Total asset turnover, 612
Traditional approach to budgeting, 68
Transactions
  See Accounting fundamentals
Transfers, interfund, 174
Travel, as an expenditure, 84
Trial balance, 669, 670
Trust Fund, 470

U

Unallotted appropriations, 167
Uncollectible property taxes, 158–160
  adjustments to the allowance for, 160–161
Uncollectible receivables, 558
Unconditional promise to give, 509
Underassessments, 162
Unexpended appropriations, 469
Universities
  See Not-for-profit organizations, accounting for
Unreserved Fund Balance, 120
Unrestricted Current Fund, 11, 518, 520–523
Unrestricted net assets, 424, 503
Unrestricted Operating Fund, 518

V

Vacation pay, 179
Valuation, 515–516
Voluntary health and welfare organiza-
    tions (VHWOs)
    See Not-for-profit organizations, account-
        ing for
Vouchers, defined, 130–131
Vouchers payable, 130

W

Warrants, 169
Withdrawals by the owner, 675
Work sheet, 672–674

Y

Year-end financial statements, 180